GLADSTONE AND KRUGER
Liberal Government and Colonial 'Home Rule' 1880–85

STUDIES IN POLITICAL HISTORY

Editor: Michael Hurst

Fellow of St. John's College, Oxford

PRESIDENT KRUGER   MR. GLADSTONE

GLADSTONE

AND

KRUGER

Liberal Government and Colonial
'Home Rule' 1880–85

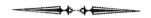

by
D. M. SCHREUDER
Kennedy Research Fellow
in New College, Oxford

LONDON: Routledge & Kegan Paul
TORONTO: University of Toronto Press
1969

First published 1969
by Routledge & Kegan Paul Ltd.
Broadway House, 68–74 Carter Lane
London, E.C.4
and in Canada and the United States by
Toronto University Press
Printed in Great Britain
by Richard Clay (The Chaucer Press) Ltd
Bungay, Suffolk
© D. M. Schreuder 1969
RKP SBN 7100 3157 2
UTP SBN 8020 1639 1

FOR
MY PARENTS

FOREWORD

IT is customary to ascribe the decline of Great Britain's Empire to events in this century. It is customary but incorrect. The Empire, in fact, died as it grew. First the North American colonies took their independence by 'U.D.I.' and war in the eighteenth century. Then the white colonies of settlement advanced to self-government and separate development in the next century; while Ireland had been trying to escape the imperial yoke since the early Victorian years. In this process, of revolution and evolution, India and Africa came last, and provided the dramatic finale to the twilight of the Empire.

Yet in their enthusiasm to describe and date the demise of British hegemony in Africa, historians and political scientists alike have ignored the original confrontation of British might and local nationalist revolt on the 'dark continent'.

This study is thus concerned with the first of the African nationalisms recognised by Great Britain: Afrikaner nationalism, in the form of the South African Dutch revolt and unrest in the early 1880s, centred about the Majuba campaign and the subsequent Pretoria and London Conventions.

From that decade onwards the Victorians anxiously faced this local challenge, both in time and manner, in company with that other Victorian enigma, Ireland. 'The question', Lord Derby could remark in 1884. 'is do you want to create another Ireland in South Africa?' Clearly they did not. But in their attempts to avoid this dread contingency, by adopting the techniques of 'Home Rule', the Gladstonians provided a fascinating portrait of the classic challenge presented by an evolving Empire: the extreme difficulty of conciliating local nationalist leaders, or of meeting the price of local collaborators, in the light of the metropolitan powers' needs, resources or prestige.

CONTENTS

CONTENTS

ILLUSTRATIONS

Frontispiece: President Kruger and *Mr. Gladstone*

MAPS

PREFACE

Gladstone and Kruger never met. Once, however, on a pleasure steamer off the British shores in 1877, they sat within glaring distance, and were pointed out to each other by their respective companions. When they did correspond it was on behalf of their governments. But there lies the interest of this narrative. By 1880 these two 'titans' both represented and symbolised diametrically opposed political creeds: nineteenth-century urban liberalism facing eighteenth-century Calvinistic conservatism. They were flung together by the exigencies of the British Empire in the late-Victorian age, and found themselves acting out an unequal relationship. Gladstone, leader of the mightiest of the European 'Great Powers', was to play the rôle of patrician in handling the nationalistic demands of Kruger, leader of the ramshackle, impoverished, but determined Boer state in rebellion.

In this context I have found it useful to employ 'Home Rule' as a modern term of convenience—a shorthand expression in current usage in many respects to imply the devolution of metropolitan power on to locally elected assemblies, with the retention of certain reserved powers to the central, or 'imperial' Parliament. But I am all too aware of the particular *dissimilarities* between the specific *Irish* Home Rule Bill of 1886 and the Transvaal Conventions of 1881–84. Ireland was an integral part of the United Kingdom in a manner that the South African Republic never was—Boer deputies, for example, had at no time sat at Westminster to represent their far-off African state—and this ultimately meant that Liberal policy towards Kruger's burghers could go far beyond the more limited nature of Irish Home Rule. The reserved powers in the Irish case were extensive, as befitted a province of the United Kingdom, whereas those in the Transvaal Treaty were few, so allowing greater self-government than in the more 'municipal'

xiii

character of the Irish gesture. (A comparison of the Irish Home Rule Bill with the Transvaal Conventions, as appended to this volume, amplifies this point.) Yet there is a sense in which Irish Home Rule shared common points with the earlier grant of power, and devolution of qualified self-government, to the Boers. The concurrent problems of conciliating rebellious, white and non-English populations in Her Majesty's dominions bore some sense of similarity. Interesting too was the contemporary use, in South Africa before 1886, of the phrase 'Home Rule' when local demands were being formulated or reported; and equally interesting was the English penchant, in both Official and Press circles, for seeing Paul Kruger, Jan Hofmeyr, and the Afrikaner *Bond* in terms of Parnell and Fenianism. I have not desired, however, to take this analogy beyond that suggested by the documents and journals of the time; and I have accordingly left open the question of the ultimate significance of this theme. It has been suggested to me that the legacy of these Anglo-Boer Conventions was influential in 1886 over Ireland. I would *not* claim that. At most I believe the Boer revolt, and subsequent Conventions, kept alive the meaning and value of conciliation and the devolution of power—'Home Rule'—in Liberal thinking; that it only formed part of Gladstone's existing imperial policy, of granting qualified degrees of local self-government to preserve the Empire. In this sense, as Gladstone himself stressed in his Irish Home Rule Address, the concept of Home Rule was long in the making in the imperial sphere and was relative to *all* Great Britain's 'colonial' relationships. Thus his involvement with Kruger and the Boers was merely the latter end of that tradition of thinking. At most it 'helped him on' towards the extension of Home Rule to the Irish as well. There the long-term significance of the Gladstone–Kruger involvement ended.

The fascination of this relationship was first brilliantly hinted at by Professor C. W. de Kiewiet, in his *Imperial Factor in South Africa* (1937). I have found it necessary to revise some of his conclusions, and I have considerably filled out his narrative for the years 1880–85. But I am all too conscious that his remarkable book will still be read when these pages are but of interest to the bibliographer. He modestly remarked that the story would be told again. I have tried to fulfil one of his hopes: to elucidate the nature of imperial policy as a product of the intricate workings of the British political system. I can but hope that in the very detail of the narrative there does emerge a cumulative portrait of a not wholly unimportant aspect of the later Victorian world-empire: the problem of adjusting, yet maintaining the imperial connection in the face of local nationalist challenge.

In examining this attempt of the Gladstonian Liberals to kill the problem of the Afrikaner with kindness I have incurred many debts. They vary from the assistance given me by the librarians at various institutions—notably the British Museum, the Public Record Office, and especially by Mr. Louis Frewer at Rhodes House—to the kindness afforded me by the owners of private MSS. collections—notably Mr. Jones, on behalf of Lord Derby of Knowsley Hall, where I was given access to the personal papers of the 15th Earl.

Numerous individuals gave me advice and answered queries. I hope they will not feel offended if I do not list them all. Some debts though must be recorded. If there is any precision in my use of such emotive terminology as 'imperialism', 'colonialism', 'jingoism', etc., I owe it to the watchful eye of Dr. A. F. Madden and if this study has grown well out of my Oxford doctoral dissertation I owe much of it to Professor Jeffrey Butler. Other debts are less obvious but equally important: Dr. Penry Williams and Dr. G. V. Bennett, both of New College, together with Dr. A. Sillery, Mr. D. K. Fieldhouse, and D. C. W. Newbury and members of the Oxford Commonwealth Seminar, have all done much to make Oxford seem like home to this 'colonial lad'. Michael Hurst of St. John's College greatly encouraged me to make a book of a dissertation; while my publisher, Mr. Colin Franklin, has been kindness itself in seeing this study to the press.

My debt to my first tutors at Rhodes University, Cape Province—Professor W. A. Maxwell and Mr. James Crompton —is, I am sure, evident in every page. *Utinam probent.*

Mrs. Margot Hole took endless trouble in typing the various drafts of this study; Miss Mary Potter produced the excellent maps; while Mr. Maurice Dixon kindly loaned me his volume of *Punch* cartoons from which the illustrations were taken. I am much indebted to them all.

I must also inscribe here the name of 'Bill' Williams, Warden of Rhodes House, Oxford. Only those who know him will understand his value as a friend. My debt to him extends far beyond his meticulous reading of the proofs.

Finally, three crucial obligations that I can never adequately express. To the Rhodes Trustees for awarding me a Rhodes Scholarship, so making my Oxford tenure possible; to Professor J. A. Gallagher—'*sweet Jack, kind Jack, true Jack, valiant Jack*'—without whom . . .; and to Paddy, who has made sure that I never forgot that life in the present ever comes before indulgence in the past.

New College, Oxford　　　　　　　　　　　　　　　　　D.M.S.
St. Mark's Day, 1969

ABBREVIATIONS

Addit. MSS.	Additional Manuscripts, British Museum. (Refers specifically to Gladstone Papers, Dilke Papers, Cabinet Papers, and Hamilton Diaries.)
P.R.O.	Public Record Office, Chancery Lane, London. (Granville Papers, Colonial Office, and Foreign Office Files.)
L.B. copy	Letterbook copy, Gladstone Papers.
C.O., W.O., F.O.	Colonial Office, War Office, and Foreign Office Files.
Afr. MSS.	African Manuscripts, at Rhodes House, Oxford. (Rhodes, Bower, and Merriman Papers.)
D.P. MSS.	Private Papers of the 15th Earl of Derby, at Knowsley Hall, Lancs.
H.P. MSS.	Private Papers of Lord Hartington, Duke of Devonshire, Chatsworth.
J.C. MSS.	Private Papers of Joseph Chamberlain, Birmingham University Library.
Letters of Queen Victoria	*Letters of Queen Victoria*, 2nd ser., vol. III, 1862–85. (Ed. by G. E. Buckle), (London, 1928).
Ramm	Agatha Ramm, *The Political Correspondence of Mr. Gladstone and Lord Granville, 1872–86*, 2 vols. (Oxford, 1962).

xvii

ABBREVIATIONS

De Kock   W. J. de Kock, 'Ekstra Territoriale Vraagstukke van die Kaapse Regering, 1872–1885', *Archives Year Book*, Part I (Pretoria, 1948).

Queen and Mr. Gladstone   Philip Guedalla, *The Queen and Mr. Gladstone*, 2 vols. (London, 1933).

Morley   John Morley, *Life of Gladstone*, 3 vols. (London, 1903).

I

BOER AND BRITON IN SOUTHERN AFRICA

Towards another Ireland?

As Disraeli left Downing Street for the last time in April 1880 a friend tried to comfort him by speaking disparagingly of Gladstone. Disraeli brushed this aside; but, as he closed the door to the house, he whispered with relish, 'Ireland!'

The crisis duly crashed upon the Gladstonian administration, in company with the autumn rains of that year, and the news that yet another imperial dominion was also about to collapse into disorder. In southern Africa, as in Ireland, there was soon to begin a revolt on the part of the Afrikaner people which threatened to be as bitter and costly as the Irish problem.

A pattern had been set. For the remainder of the life of this administration these two dilemmas were to run in harness, the one never present without the other. Though the parallel nature of the two 'revolts' was without significance—the one hardly sparked the other—it was of great import to the making of policy that both crises involved the same crucial principles of government: the decision whether to confront the 'rebels' with either a coercive or a conciliatory policy. Was it to be buckshot or soft words? Was it better to attempt to destroy the 'rebels', and suppress their organisations, with strong-arm measures— or to accept the justice behind many of the Boer (and Fenian) claims, and thus try to kill the problem through kindness?

That was the decision which Gladstone ultimately knew he

must take. That became the overriding significance of his momentous second administration. That is the concern of this study.

2

In calling upon the ghosts of 'colonial revolt' in Ireland, Disraeli it seems had evoked the most powerful of spirits. Faced with Fenian atrocities, Boer rebellion (and soon, too, Sudanese disaffection, in the form of the Mahdi), Gladstone was forced back on those very principles which he had just enunciated so forcibly, and righteously, in the attack on the last Disraeli administration, in his famed Midlothian campaign. Indeed, as the trouble-filled months passed, Gladstone was driven to reconsider the very bedrock of British colonial relations. The great intellectual and spiritual powers of the G.O.M. came increasingly to be focused almost exclusively on problems in the imperial sphere.

Gladstone's mind ever worked in mysterious ways. However, the final answer, as he saw it, had a logic that was easy to reject but hard to refute. The more Gladstone thought on the dilemma of maintaining the imperial bonds linking the Empire—and the longer the Boer and Fenian rebellions continued—the more he came to see a policy based exclusively on coercive measures as nothing but a temporary expedient; indeed an expedient which appeared to work against any final solution. By meeting violence with violence Gladstone felt that nothing but a lasting bitterness would be produced.

A conciliatory approach began to have new attractions for the Liberal leader. It promised to create bonds of loyalty rather than bonds of subservience; it promised to be kinder on the exchequer than costly military campaigns conducted over many years; and it promised to provide a long-term solution, not a temporary peace. To accomplish this settlement new doses of the old medicine were to be administered—*qualified* degrees of local self-government.

The concept of 'Home Rule' was in the making. The principle of applying conciliation in the face of local 'nationalist' challenges was soon to be established among the Gladstonian Liberals. In this process it is intriguing to reflect that Gladstone first came to grant 'Home Rule' to the Boers progressively between 1881 and 1884; and that his gestures to the Irish after 1886 were a later manifestation of a similar technique.

3

That is one major theme of this study: the fact of Gladstone's ultimate belief in the efficacy of a conciliatory policy. The corollary of this is an equally important concern: the very nature of the manifold factors which influenced the Gladstonian decision.

This study of Anglo-Boer relations, between the death of the confederation policies in 1880, and the Witwatersrand gold discoveries of 1886, is also an oblique commentary on the basic dilemma confronting the Victorians in the 1880s. How to maintain their foreign and imperial dominance in the face of a two-fold attack—local 'nationalist' challenges within the Empire and international challenges from other European powers outside the Empire.

Both these factors were at work in the case of southern Africa; both forces worked on the Gladstonian mind; and both brought him round to a belief in the ultimate wisdom of a conciliatory policy applied to the Afrikaner.

First to affect Gladstone's thinking was what may be termed 'the power of the Afrikaner'.[1] The Victorians, both ministers and permanent officials, came to believe that in the course of the Transvaal War of 1880–81 a new unity had been created among the Dutch-speaking population. They came to fear that ultimately they would not only be at war with the Transvaal Boers, but also with the Free State and the Cape Afrikaners. While they could afford to have a disaffected Transvaal, encircled in the interior of Africa, they could not afford to have a disloyal Cape controlling the vital coastline and naval stations of southern Africa. It was one thing to be at war with a body of some

[1] 'Afrikaner': modern form of a word spelt indiscriminately by the Victorians as 'Africander', etc. I use it only for 'Dutch-speaking' colonists and settlers, in both the Cape Colony *and* the Transvaal. Purists will argue that Afrikaans had not developed as a language by 1880 and thus there could be no 'Afrikaners'. But, in fact, the Afrikaans language was already becoming distinct from Dutch. Equally, Kruger could refer to his own people as 'Afrikaners', a term used also by the Victorians. I therefore use it as well, as a collective term of convenience.

6000 dissident farmers in the interior; it was quite another to have to go to war with the entire Afrikaner population of South Africa. It was a war which, no doubt, could militarily be won— but at what cost? and for how long? Would it not be necessary indefinitely to maintain thousands of troops in South Africa? In short, were the Victorians prepared to face the creation of 'another Ireland' in southern Africa?

That was the dilemma. That was the daunting prospect. Gladstone had never lacked for courage in making a decision; but dare he court political disaster by calling a halt to a war after Britain had sustained so inglorious a defeat as Majuba Hill? Gladstone wasted not a moment. It was to be immediate peace. The real battle now in fact followed, as the Liberal Premier, and his Colonial Secretary (Kimberley), attempted to bring the rest of the Cabinet round to their way of thinking.

They ultimately succeeded. Policy went into reverse over the Boers. A belief in the reality of the unity of 'Afrikanerdom' took hold in the 'official mind'. The Victorian approach to the South African problem was radically altered. The former belief had very largely contributed to the latter change. But this was not the whole story. A second major factor must be brought to bear. In evaluating their relations with the Afrikaner people the Victorians had been not inconsiderably influenced by the broader aspects of their world position. The second Gladstone administration coincided with a great period of flux abroad. The breakdown of order in Ireland was a major sympton of the troubles to come; the rise of Bismarckian Germany to a position of supremacy in Europe was a second and equally worrying portent.

Not that Britain's dilemmas ended there. Within a short space of time the Victorians were to face the Russian challenge in Afghanistan; the attempts on the part of the Mahdi to dominate the Sudan and upper reaches of the Nile; the general disorder in Egypt, and the Levant, consequent upon the collapse of the Turkish Empire; and the entry of Germany into the colonial field, at South-West Africa, so destroying the 'splendid isolation' of Britain's African colonies.

One complication tended to lead to another. The Egyptian crisis ultimately produced a severe Anglo-French rift—a rift which Bismarck felt able to encourage and exploit. The creation of a German colony, at Angra Pequena, materially affected

4

the already difficult South African situation, particularly as there was much talk, and many rumours, of a German–Boer alliance in the making.

The frontiers of the Victorian world were everywhere at risk. Some challenges Gladstone knew he could not ignore: the Egyptian situation was one, the Fenian activity was another. But equally there were certain challenges he was reticent to take on: the pursuit of the Mahdi was one, an unwelcome Anglo-Afrikaner war was another. The Victorian legions were without parallel in history; but even they could not be expected to pacify and secure all fronts simultaneously.

The vast extension in Victorian responsibilities and anxieties had the most practical effect on policy. It weakened the Victorian's resolve in facing local unrest; and it lured British statesmen to look to options which did not involve vast expenditure and expeditions.

Thus Kruger did not stand alone in defying Gladstone. Indeed, he stood in good company. By the mid-1880s his actions formed but a part of the world-wide threat to Victorian security as embodied in the figures of Parnell, Bismarck, the Mahdi and the Tsar. He may not have had the most powerful of armies to confront the Victorian military. But Kruger had something better still: the good fortune to stage his revolt when he did. In so doing he achieved victories out of all proportion to the size of the 'commandos' drawn from the distant farms on the highveld of the Transvaal.

4

Thus central to this study is a single working concept: the manner and timing of the decline of British influence—what Rhodes derisively termed the 'imperial factor'—in the politics of southern Africa; and the resultant rise to a position of new-found strength on the part of the Afrikaner leaders.

A re-examination of the sources provides surprisingly new, yet cogent answers, to the traditional if basic questions of 'how' and 'when' the Victorians lost their initiative to manipulate, at will, local events in southern Africa. The concern here is not so much with the endlessly debated 'motives for intervention' in Africa, but rather with the other side of that rather worn coin: the question of the nature and timing of what could be termed a 'failure of motive', or 'nerve', on the part of the British in their handling of the local southern African communities. The focus is thus essentially on the collapse of long-held beliefs; the attempt to grapple with new and disturbing forces, of local revolt in Africa, and elsewhere; the desire urgently to find new techniques of policy for retaining the old predominance.

Policy is a fragile concept: it owes as much to ignorance, and traditional habits of thoughts, as to the local reality fragmentarily reported by the administrators and journalists 'on the spot'. A fuller understanding of the motives that moved the policy-makers must proceed via their own criteria for judgment. The task of chronology, and of having a sensitive ear to contemporary opinion becomes crucial. The vagaries of official thinking at any moment must be our concern: and therefore such traces of their thinking as they have left us are invaluable. In an African idiom, we must 'follow their *spoor*', and interpret those tracks not obliterated by time.

More particularly, we need to isolate those significant moments when the attitudes and beliefs of the British policy-makers underwent more than a momentary change. A point of reference must be cited from which to pursue their evolving opinions. The year 1880 appears to be just such a useful starting-point. Not only did it witness the eclipse of Disraeli's political career, and the start of Gladstone's second and momentous administration but, most important for imperial policy, it saw the collapse of the decade of earnest attempts to federate the disparate colonies and republics of southern Africa.

It was more than just a temporary breakdown in policy. By June 1880—when the Cape Assembly declined even to call a conference to consider confederation—the policy-makers had run aground. They had boxed the whole compass of policy, from direct intervention to withdrawal, but had found all the alternatives wanting. The right course had rarely been charted: and now, in 1880, the British Colonial Office had played its trump card of confederation—and lost.

It was recognised at the time as a significant moment for the 'imperial factor' in South Africa. It forms one of those rare watersheds in the evolution of British imperial power at which the historian may take his stand. In this case to watch the Victorian colonial officials trying to orientate themselves to face the

6

new dilemma; to find a new bedrock for policy. As they attempted to fill the vacuum left by the untimely demise of confederation they revealed their process of thinking in an unusually frank manner. In Parliament and in the various ministries, they questioned themselves again on the traditional basis of their presence in southern Africa. In this litany of question and answer, they can be seen attempting, under Gladstone's tutelage, to underpin policy with principles and tactics more durable than had hitherto prevailed.

5

Just how the successive British ministers found themselves at the impasse is a fascinating polemic in the basic dilemmas facing the British Victorian Colonial Office in southern Africa: the impossibility of reconciling concepts of trusteeship with economy, or strategy, with independent 'self-rule'.

Two particular themes are pertinent in essaying the sequence of events which brought the Gladstone government to face this 'crisis year' of 1880—when the cumulative forces of the past tended to fuse with the new emergent forces of the present—and so pose the British with the most serious challenge to their supremacy in southern Africa since the days of the Kaffir wars and the *Trekker* exodus in the 1830s.

The first theme of significance and worthy of further illustration concerns the matter of 'strategy': why Britain had an Empire in southern Africa at all; were the same reasons which were applicable in Napoleonic times, when Britain first took the Cape, still relevant after the building of the Suez Canal?

Second, the question of imperial 'supremacy': taken that the Cape was a vital strategic British outpost, why had Britain allowed herself to be drawn ever deeper into the turbulent struggles of the interior of Africa, involving Boer and Bantu? and, indeed, did Britain really need to maintain a military, if not political control, over the vast area of 'darkest Africa' which stretched to the Limpopo?

STRATEGY

Africa, as a whole, was *terra incognita* to the early nineteenth-century British ministries, and even to the Victorian administrations. But it had a special place in their scheme of things temporal. It was important to them because of where it was, not what it was. Thus the two extremes of the continent, North and South Africa, were singled out as their immediate concerns; for these two areas held the key to the dual routes to India and the East.

In North Africa the Victorians were to keep more than a watchful eye on the freedom of passage through the Suez Canal, and also on the health of the 'sick man of Europe'. They dreaded a collapse in the political *status quo* of the Levantine area. Time, and the exigencies of trade, made the security of the British shipping route to India an unquestionable tenet of foreign and imperial policy.

By comparison, in South Africa,[1] the problem was somewhat different; and often rather more critical. The natural inclination of the Victorians was to abandon the troublesome dilemma of maintaining peace and authority in southern Africa. The fact that they could never bring themselves to do this had little or nothing to do with prestige, or to any blind-spot in their thinking. Such an option was never open to them: southern Africa, despite its multitude of internal problems, was too highly placed on the scale of imperial strategic needs to be jettisoned. Reluctantly the Victorians attempted to accept the necessity of maintaining an expensive, and not always successful, civil and military administration over a steadily widening area of rule.

Indeed, the only constant theme in official thinking about this problematic area of the Empire was its generally accepted value, its situation in the geometry of imperial defence. It had long been discounted as having any latent possibilities as 'another India'. As early as 1795 a director of the East India Company could write that the importance of the Cape 'consists more from the detriment which would result to us if it was in the hands of France, than from any advantage we can possibly derive from it as a colony'.[2] Its position made it an effective

___

[1] Though 'South Africa' did not exist until the Act of Union of 1910, the Victorians always wrote 'South Africa', meaning a geographic area. It is used in this latter sense throughout—to include the two British colonies and the multitude of Boer republics.

[2] Sir Francis Baring to Lord Dundas, 12 January 1795. Quoted in *C.H.B.E.*, VIII, 169.

guardian of the southern trade route, 'as Gibraltar doth the Mediterranean'.[1]

Nearly a century later the logic of this thinking remained. A confidential War Office memorandum of October 1884, emphatically called the Cape 'the most important of the imperial coaling stations'.[2] The opening of the Suez Canal, in 1869, left the strategic importance of the Cape route undiminished. Robert Herbert, twenty years permanent under-secretary at the Colonial Office,[3] saw it as the 'true centre of the Empire . . . clear of the Suez complications'.[4] His opinion was reinforced by the voice of Horse Guards, the Duke of Cambridge.[5] As Commander-in-Chief of the Army for nearly half a century,[6] the Duke never wavered in his belief that this stormy and troublesome Cape was a vital strategic necessity.[7]

The Cape, in fact, like the Duke of Cambridge, occupied a traditional place and function in the Victorian world. It was unofficially rated as the most important overseas base after the four strategic imperial fortresses.[8] This belief was reflected in the findings of the various Royal Commissions on imperial defence. The Milne Committee Report, of 1878,[9] recommended strengthening the Cape defences,[10] as did the Carnarvon Commission of 1879–81.

This Carnarvon Commission, the most important of Victorian defence enquiries, devoted nearly the whole of its first report[11]

[1] Idem.

[2] W.O. Confidential Files—W.O. 33/42, October 1884.

[3] Permanent under-secretary at the Colonial Office, 1871–93.

[4] C.O. 48/455. Minute by Herbert on Barkly to Kimberley, 31 May 1871.

[5] See Giles St. Aubyn, *The Royal George, The Life of H.R.H. Prince George, Duke of Cambridge 1819–1904* (London, 1963).

[6] Duke of Cambridge, 1819–1904: Field-Marshal 1862; C.-in-C. British Army, 1856–95.

[7] See W. Verner, *The Military Life of the Duke of Cambridge*, (London, 1905); and F. W. Wallace, *Wooden Ships and Iron Men* (London, 1925).

[8] Viz. Gibraltar, Malta, Bermuda, and Halifax. See D. M. Schurman, *Imperial Defence 1868–87*. Unpublished Cambridge Ph.D. Thesis (1955), Map, p. 295.

[9] P.R.O. 30/6-124. Report of Colonial Defence Committee on 'Temporary Defences of the Cape of Good Hope, Mauritius, Ceylon, Singapore and Hong Kong', 4 April 1878.

[10] Idem.

[11] The Commission issued three reports, the first on 18 September 1881; the second in May 1882; the third in July 1882. All in P.R.O. 30/6.

to the 'urgent matter' of the Cape defences. In pressing hard for immediate attention to the matter, the Commission left little doubt as to the value of the two Cape harbours to the Victorians.

On the strategic level it counted the bases as 'indispensable to Your Majesty's Navy', for it is 'essential to the retention by Great Britain of her possessions in India, Mauritius, Ceylon, Singapore, China and even Australia'. In short, that the 'integrity of this route must be maintained at all hazards and irrespective of cost'.[1]

On the commercial level the Commission evaluated the Cape as scarcely less important. More trade in 1878, went via the Cape (£91 million) than via Suez (£65 million).[2] Loss of the Cape might eventually mean losing the whole of this £156 million trade. As the Commission put it: '. . . the security of the route by the Suez Canal, might under certain contingencies, become precarious . . . in which case the long sea route would be the only one available.'[3]

Charles Dilke, in his famous *Problems of Greater Britain*, expressed the traditional thinking in a sentence: 'The Cape is our half-way house, the loss of which would be almost fatal to our Indian Empire and our China trade.'[4]

To Afrikaner propagandists this was more window dressing to conceal the real motive. 'History will show convincingly, Smuts could write in 1899, 'that the pleas of humanity, civilisation and equal rights, upon which the British Government bases its actions, are nothing else but the recrudescence of that spirit of annexation and plunder which has at all times characterised its dealings with our people.'[5] The charge is easy to make but

[1] C.O. 812/38 First Report, 18 September 1881, pp. 411–13.

[2] The figures break down as follows (in pounds sterling):

Trade to or from (in 1878)	Via Cape	Via Suez
India, China, and the East	59,033,000	54,416,000
Australasia	21,525,000	11,244,000
South Africa	10,794,000	
	£91,352,000	£65,660,000

Source: Robinson and Gallagher, *Africa and the Victorians* (1961), p. 59, footnote 3.

[3] C.O. 812/38. First Report, 18 September 1881, p. 411.

[4] Charles Dilke, *Problems of Greater Britain*, 2 vols. (London, 1890), I, 500. See also II, 168.

[5] J. C. Smuts, *Een Eeuw van Onrecht* (Bloemfontein, 1899), p. 3.

difficult to justify. History has tended to prove no such thing. Control of vast areas of the African continent was hardly advantageous to the economy-minded Victorians. There was little to 'plunder'; and, as a trading or investment area Africa, including southern Africa, was a decidedly unattractive part of the globe.[1] The most recent economic studies on imperial expansion speak with one voice on this matter. For example, British exports to all of Africa in 1880 were but 5·9 per cent of her total exports. By 1890 the figure had risen only to 6·7 per cent.[2] Imports from Africa were equally low—4·9 per cent of all British imports in 1880, a figure which actually *fell*, to read 4·7 per cent in 1890.[3] South America was more valuable as a trading area than troublesome British southern Africa.

Investment in Africa was also minute by international standards; and was almost entirely in the Cape Colony.[4] Even the

[1] W. Schlote, *Entwicklung und Strukturwandlungen des englischen Aussenhandels von 1700 bis sur Gegenwart* (Jena, 1938), pp. 160–63. Hereafter cited as *Schlote*. Published in English under the title *British Overseas Trade* (Oxford, 1952).

[2] United Kingdom Exports (per cent per continent):

Year	Europe	Africa	Asia	N. America	S. America	Australia
1880	35·9	5·9	23·4	17·9	9·4	7·5
1881	35·7	5·9	22·1	17·1	10·0	9·2
1882	35·5	5·7	20·1	17·7	10·5	10·5
1883	36·6	5·2	21·6	15·9	10·5	10·2
1884	37·4	5·0	21·6	14·6	11·1	10·3
1885	36·1	5·2	22·3	14·1	9·4	11·9
1890	34·8	6·7	21·8	15·7	12·2	8·8
1900	41·0	9·5	21·0	10·3	8·8	9·4

Source: *Schlote*, Table 19, pp. 158–9.

[3] United Kingdom Imports (per cent per continent):

Year	Europe	Africa	Asia	N. America	S. America	Australia
1880	39·1	4·9	14·1	29·5	6·1	6·3
1881	38·4	5·0	14·9	29·0	5·9	6·8
1882	42·1	4·7	16·5	24·0	6·6	6·1
1883	41·3	5·0	15·8	26·3	5·4	6·2
1884	42·4	5·3	15·9	25·1	5·2	7·3
1885	42·6	4·9	15·2	26·3	4·9	6·3
1890	44·4	4·7	13·3	26·2	4·4	7·0
1900	42·4	4·3	9·9	30·9	5·7	6·8

Source: *Schlote*, Table 18, pp. 156–7.

[4] Investment in South Africa in 1885 was roughly £34 million as compared with £300 million in the U.S.A., £150 million in South America, £270 million in India, and £240 million in Australasia. Source: *Africa and the Victorians*, p. 6, footnote 6.

opening of the Kimberley diamond fields, and later the Rand gold reef, did not completely alter the image of Africa in the mind of the European investor.[1] There were always safer and more profitable areas in which to invest. The three great South African speculative ventures, of the second half of the century, all had disappointing aspects. In the Kimberley diamond fields, 'speculative over expansion'[2] brought about a contraction of the industry in the later 1870s. The Witwatersrand gold was found to be highly expensive to mine, as a result of Kruger's 'dynamite policy', and the need for very deep-level shafts.[3] Lastly, Rhodesia was the greatest disappointment of all—the British South Africa Company did not pay a single dividend from its inception until 1923.[4]

In truth there was as little incentive to invest as to trade; and even less to emigrate.[5] In 1885 when 138,000 emigrants went to Australia a mere 3000 came to South Africa.[6] This figure was not to rise significantly until the early years of this century.[7]

The economic and social structure of South Africa reflected its classification in European thinking as a 'strategic backwater'. The white population of the whole of South Africa[8]—an area almost as large as Europe—was approximately 400,000 in 1880, mostly in the Cape. The Transvaal had at most 50,000 white settlers.[9] The entire annual revenue of the Cape Colony in the

[1] S. H. Frankel, *Capital Investment in Africa* (Oxford, 1938), Table 28.

[2] C. G. W. Schuman, *Structural Changes and Business Cycles in South Africa, 1886–1936* (London, 1938), p. 85. Hereafter cited as *Schuman*.

[3] G. Blainey, 'Lost causes of the Jameson Raid', in *Economic History Review*, 2nd ser., vol. XVIII, no. 2, August 1965, pp. 350–67: excellent description of Rand mining techniques and difficulties.

[4] Felix Gross, *Rhodes of Africa* (London, 1956), p. 253.

[5] Brinley Thomas, *Migration and Economics* (1954), pp. 266, 304.

[6] Idem.

[7] By 1911 the figure stood at 31,000 for the year, having averaged 3,000 per year for the decade after 1885. Ibid.

[8] There are no exact figures for 1880, but *Schuman*, the most reliable authority, gives the following data:

European population of South Africa:

Cape	1875	236,783	1891	376,987
Natal	1874	18,646	1885	36,701
O.F.S.	1880	61,000	1890	77,720
Transvaal	1875	40,000	1880	50,000

Source: *Schuman*, p. 38.

[9] Idem.

early 1880s would hardly have matched the municipal budget of an English city.[1] And the annual average revenue of the Transvaal, in the five years prior to the gold discoveries, was £188,400.[2]

Ironically at a period when Britain added vast areas of southern Africa to her Empire—in the form of Basutoland (1884) and Bechuanaland (1885)—trade and investment were falling dramatically. The depression of 1882–86 was, in the words of Professor Frankel, 'The most severe South Africa had to endure during the nineteenth century . . . imports declined by more than 50%, deposits by nearly the same percentage.'[3]

In sum, if the imperialists of the 1880s had a darker side to their motives than strategy, they concealed it exceedingly well. If that darker side was the hope of economic exploitation, as Smuts once hinted, and Lenin and Hobson were to declare, then the Victorians must be counted among the blindest optimists in history. In fact, as Sir Charles Dilke could write in 1890, the main problems facing British ministries in respect of South Africa was, 'the difficulty of inducing Parliament to sanction a continuous expenditure without direct return'.[4]

SUPREMACY

Jan Smuts styled it a 'Century of Wrong'.[5] With greater justification he might have termed British relations with the Afrikaner, prior to the Anglo-Boer War, a 'century of vacillation'. Around the touchstone of supremacy British policy swithered in search of an elusive panacea for dominance. Security had to be balanced against economy. In attempting to find this balance policy tended to be capricious, to move in fits and starts, as it reacted to the vagaries in the behaviour and movements of the Afrikaner people. The ultimate objective—strategic security at

---

[1] Annual average revenue of the Cape Colony in £000:

    1875–79:   1,648·4
    1884–85 to 1885–89: 3,355·7   Source: *Schuman*, p. 50.

[2] Ibid., p. 52.

[3] Ibid., p. 84. See also S. H. Frankel, *Capital Investment in Africa*, Table 5, p. 55.

[4] Charles Dilke, *Problems of Greater Britain*, I, 575.

[5] J. C. Smuts, *Een Eeuw van Onrecht* (Bloemfontein, 1899).

the Cape—was never in doubt. But the principles of conduct in securing political and military supremacy had never set firm.

As the nineteenth century advanced so the dilemma, and the Afrikaner, appeared to slip further and further from the grasp of the Colonial Office. This was partly because the Victorians could never reconcile the impulses that policy had to satisfy; and, more particularly, because the problem of restraining the activities of the restless Afrikaner frontiersman increased in dimension with each decade. In this search for a technique of successful control, the imperialists' proposals were invariably solutions for yesterday's problems. The time-lag, between Whitehall thinking and the local reality in the Boer states, was to bedevil policy and the policy-makers. The coming of the telegraph failed to close this gap.

If there is a pattern to this century of British endeavour in southern Africa it must be painted in mute if not negative colours. 'Reluctant Empire' is a just assessment.[1] Peace within a limited colonial frontier was the byword of that rule. Any territorial hunger in European dominance belongs rather to the colonists themselves, English and Dutch, than to the men of Downing Street. Again and again Britain had to extend the Cape 'pale' to secure her original objective. It was yet another example of the policy-makers applying their basic principle: extending the frontiers only 'when and where informal political means failed to provide the framework of security . . .[2]

The flag did not follow the trader, nor the missionary. Rather it followed the harassed frontier magistrate, and the imperial trooper, trying to bring some tranquillity and order within a delineated frontier-line. *The Times* of February 1853 caught the problems superbly: 'Once embarked on the fatal policy of establishing a frontier in South Africa and defending the frontier by force, there seems to be neither rest nor peace for us till we follow our flying enemies and plant the British standard on the walls of Timbuctoo.'[3]

Just as strategy kept the 'imperial factor' in South Africa,

[1] J. S. Galbraith, *Reluctant Empire—British Policy on the South African Frontier, 1834–54* (Los Angeles, 1963).
[2] J. Gallagher and R. Robinson, 'The Imperialism of Free Trade', in *Economic History Review*, 2nd ser., vol. VI, no. 1.
[3] *The Times*, 28 February 1853. Quoted in Galbraith, *Reluctant Empire*, p. 3.

so too it drove them to control the interior. A 'Strictly Confidential' Cabinet memorandum, drawn up by the War Office in 1884, makes plain the importance placed by the officials on securing paramountcy throughout southern Africa. 'It is impossible, for political reasons, to create a Gibraltar out of the Cape Town peninsula, and . . . [thus] the permanent retention of this peninsula . . . is dependent upon the maintenance of British ascendancy in all South African Colonies.'[1]

Lord Kimberley, twice Colonial Secretary,[2] was equally explicit when writing to his old Whig friend Selborne, late in 1881: 'It is an entire delusion to imagine that we could hold Cape Town, abandoning the rest. If we allow our supremacy in South Africa to be taken from us, we shall be ousted before long from that country altogether.'[3]

Axial to this question of supremacy were the Afrikaner republics. The predilections of their highly individualistic burghers, and in particular an insatiable hunger for arable land—played havoc with the Victorians' concept of the extent of imperial involvement in the interior. Thus ultimately the Victorians found the basis for their southern African policy being increasingly dictated, not by the stable and productive Cape Colony, but by the impoverished Boer republics to the north.

Dilke is unique among Victorians in pointing, at an early date, to the Dutch-speaking frontiersmen, or *trekboers*, as being central to Britain's vacillating policy. 'South Africa is a Dutch Colony', he wrote in *Problems of Greater Britain* 'which we have conquered in the Stadholder's name from his soldiers; then conquered a second time, and lastly bought; all three against the will of the Dutch population.'[4] Other observers were less sure. The complications of the Afrikaner's history were incomprehensible to the majority of Victorians. Vacillation in policy appeared to many as being as unavoidable as the wanderings of the *trekboer* themselves. Gladstone spoke for many when he referred to the dilemma of the Afrikaner as 'the one unsolved, perhaps

[1] W.O. 33/42. 'Strictly confidential Memorandum for Secretary of State for War', dated 1 October 1884. (See Appendix, printed in full.)

[2] Colonial Secretary: July 1870–February 1874; April 1880–December 1882.

[3] Kimberley to Selborne from C.O., 11 October 1881. Quoted in R. Selborne, *Memorials*, 4 vols. (London, 1896–98), II, 6.

[4] Charles Dilke, *Problems of Greater Britain*, I, 465.

unsolvable [*sic*] problem of our colonial system'.[1] Nor was there dissent when he wearily spoke of the vacillating policy as reflecting 'a history of difficulties continual and unthought of . . .'[2]

This despondency extended to a general malaise in official circles over the Afrikaner and his behaviour. The Colonial Office itself was acutely aware of the shortcomings of policy, and went through spasms of soul-searching. In 1885, Edward Fairfield, a promising young clerk in the Colonial Office, was asked to draw up a confidential memorandum on 'Vacillation in Policy in South Africa'.[3]

In blunt terms he revealed not only the instances of vacillation, but also the quandary in imperial thinking that existed. With unconscious humour he wrote: 'Colonel Stanley[4] has asked for some notes of instances in which there has been vacillation in policy of this country towards South Africa. To tell the story in full would be to rewrite the history of the country'. He cited Lord Glenelg as saying, as far back as 1836, that Britain's policy towards South Africa had 'assumed an appearance of caprice and confusion perfectly unintelligible to the natives'— not to mention the English and Dutch colonists. 'Similar remarks have frequently been made by later authorities during the intervening half century', but, as Fairfield drily put it, 'the evil does not appear to abate'.

Fairfield's analysis of the causes of the failure to control the ever-shifting frontiers is worth noting: 'There are two schools in South African frontier politics just as distinct as the two Indian schools. Sometimes the "forward school" . . . has prevailed in the councils of the Home Government, and sometimes the "school of inactivity". Add to this "blundering or masterfulness on the part of local agents",[5] and the impasse is reached,

[1] Gladstone in Commons, 25 June 1881. *Hansard*, 3rd ser., CCLXIII, col. 1857.

[2] Ibid., 16 March 1883. *Hansard*, 3rd ser., CCLXXVII, col. 720.

[3] C.O. 879/23. Confidential Prints, African No. 304: 'Vacillation in Policy in South Africa', by Edward Fairfield, 4 August 1885. (See Appendix, printed in full.)

[4] Col. Frederick Arthur Stanley, younger brother of Lord Derby. Colonial Secretary: 24 June 1885–6 February 1886.

[5] Surely a reference to Sir Bartle Frere, High Commissioner at the Cape, March 1877–September 1880, accepted as being responsible for the highly expensive, and not altogether successful, Zulu War of 1878–79.

in which "every course of policy which can be adopted in South Africa has its draw-backs".' Indeed, as he pointed out, it was not only Africa and the Afrikaner which bedevilled policy, but the British politicians as well. 'When we lean to the policy of controlling all sections of the population, and regulate their mutual relations, we find that a huge bill has been run up. Then the advocates of retirement and retrenchment have their day, until it is perceived that retirement and retrenchment have involved abandonment of some weak and friendly tribe.' The cry then becomes resumption of responsibility: 'Thus it comes about that not only do one set of ministers reverse the action of their predecessors, but that the same set of ministers, after a time reverse their own policy, and seem to go back on their own declarations'.[1]

These fluctuations in Anglo-Boer relations, so sharply observed by Fairfield in 1885, have more recently been characterised by Professor de Kiewiet as the 'failure of high motives and worthy ends'.[2] This is hard to credit, and barely accords with either the actions or the thinking of the imperialists. In all the federal schemes, for example, only that of Carnarvon[3] can be said to have been activated by anything but the 'miserable consideration' of economy. And even his policy had as its main concern and object imperial strategy, not colonial welfare.[4] Perhaps, as with that other troublesome 'colony', Ireland, there was no ultimate solution for regulating the frontiersmen which would be universally accepted. Clearly the Victorians never found it in either case.

At the lowest common denominator Britain's vacillation stemmed from the fact that her 'evangelical, economic and imperial inclinations were incompatible with one another'.[5] Or on a more tentative level, because there was a block in official thinking about this sphere of the Empire: the inability to reconcile the idea of South Africa as a colony of settlement, with

[1] C.O. 879/23. Memorandum by Fairfield.
[2] C. W. de Kiewiet, *The Imperial Factor in South Africa* (Cambridge, 1937), p. 5. Hereafter cited as De Kiewiet, *Imperial Factor.*
[3] Colonial Secretary: 6 July 1866–8 March 1867; 21 February 1874–22 January 1878.
[4] C. F. Goodfellow, *Great Britain and South African Confederation* (O.U.P., Cape Town, 1966).
[5] L. M. Thompson, *The Unification of South Africa*, (O.U.P., 1960) p. 1.

the basic concept of its function as a naval station—a strategic outpost guarding the southern sea route to India and the East.[1] It was intended as a Gibraltar and instead required the handling of an India. The whole history of relations between the economy conscious imperialists, and the multifarious races of South Africa, reveals the Victorians endeavouring to reconcile 'legitimate' expenditure—making the Cape secure—with 'unnecessary expenditure'—making the various races secure from one another.

British policy was, in fact, at the same moment both too fragile yet too rigid. It tended to shatter when it came up hard against the local situation—and in particular the wanderings of the *trekboer*. Not that the fault lay solely with the policymakers' appreciation of events. Because expenditure had to be stringently controlled it meant the range of initiatives open to them were limited, even before the difficulties created by the frontiersmen were taken into account; and also because the make-up of South Africa was exceptional by all standards. It was composed not only of a multitude of tribes but also of a politically dominant group of white colonists, the majority of whom were of Dutch origin.[2]

Despite the complexity of the problem, and the relative inexperience in handling such a combination of peoples, colonial policy in the early days of the British administration—from 1806 until that late 1830s—was remarkably firm and determined. Professor's Macmillan's classic study, *Bantu, Boer and Briton*,[3] has chronicled these courageous attempts of extending the new British liberalism of the Wilberforce era to the Cape. He has shown that this was perhaps the only period in which South Africa was ruled by principles which derived more from humanitarian than from racial considerations. In Professor Marais's *The Cape Coloured People*, we also see just how determined an attempt was made to make all men equal before the

[1] W.O. 33/42. Confidential memorandum—excellent analysis of basic Imperial attitudes to South Africa, 1 October 1884.

[2] Until the opening up of the Transvaal goldfields in the late 1880s the rough proportion of Dutch to English in South Africa was 3 to 2. See E. A. Walker, *A History of Southern Africa*, pp. 98–106, 310; and M. H. de Kock, *Selected Subjects in Economic History of South Africa* (Cape Town, 1924), pp. 55–108. Hereafter cited as De Kock, *Economic History*.

[3] W. M. Macmillan, *Bantu, Boer and Briton* (Oxford, 1929), 2nd edn. 1963.

law;[1] to abolish slavery; to make the master–servant relationship more humane; and to guarantee the tribes in the possession of their land.[2] Above all, to extend equal political and social rights to all men regardless of race, who had attained the necessary manifestations of civilisation as defined by the franchise.[3]

But even this policy had clearly defined limits. It was not solely a humanitarian experiment to be implemented without regard to cost or responsibility. The Colonial Office, though sympathetic to humanitarian ideals, rested its belief in the efficacy of such a policy on the attitude that, 'without justice there could be no peace on colonial frontiers, no security within them, no economy in defence growth of trade'.[4] Even James Stephen—who more than any man was the Colonial Office—could weary of casting the sweetness of his principles on the desert air of the South African frontiers.[5] As he wrote in 1841: 'I have no doubt that by far the least evil of it all, were it practicable, would be to abandon as worthless the whole of the Colony except the Seaport Towns and their immediate neighbourhood.'[6]

It is no surprise to find that it was the Boer frontiersmen who in the main began to throw this desire wildly off balance. By natural inclination he was unsympathetic to the very basis of British rule. Professor Marais's *Maynier and the First Boer Republic*,[7] leaves no doubt as to why the principles behind liberal multi-racial imperialism jarred against the Afrikaner's Old Testament beliefs. Both conservative and individualistic the frontier Afrikaner at heart disliked all government, and particularly that based on the new humanitarian spirit of the early nineteenth century, when his own beliefs dated back a century or more.

As a pastoralist, invariably with a large family, he required

[1] J. S. Marais, *The Cape Coloured People* (Johannesburg, 1957).
[2] Ibid., pp. 109–78.
[3] W. M. Macmillan, *Bantu, Boer and Briton*, pp. 95–172.
[4] *Africa and the Victorians*, p. 53.
[5] The best short study of Stephen is still the introduction to K. N. Bell and W. P. Morrell's *Select Constitutional Documents on the British Colonial System 1839–60* (Oxford 1928). See also P. Knaplund, *James Stephen and the British Colonial System* (Madison, 1953).
[6] C.O. 48/212. Minute by Stephen on Napier to Russell, 1 June 1841.
[7] J. S. Marais, *Maynier and the First Boer Republic* (Cape Town, 1944).

increasing areas of *veld* on which to graze his herds. P. J. van der Merwe's *Die Noordwaarste Beweging van die Boere voor die Groot Trek*,[1] in minute detail tells of the extent to which, long before the Great *Trek* itself, the Afrikaner in the form of the *trekboer*, had been drifting out of the Cape Colony and into the interior of the continent. This drift was an essential part of the structure of Afrikaner pastoral life. Each son had to have a farm of his own. Thus each generation moved further off into the interior, and in due course produced another generation of sons in need of land.

Professor Walker has rightly taken this 'roll' of the Afrikaner into the wilderness, as a central theme of what has become the standard *History* of southern Africa. 'White South Africa, like the United States of America expanded, as a rule, not by reason of newcomers passing through and beyond the existing settlements, but by sections of the resident population faring forth into the wilderness.'[2] Professor van der Merwe has devoted a lifetime's research to tracing these nomadic *treks* and wanderings in search of further pastures. He has left us in no doubt that the early *trekboers* went mainly on to what were later the plains of the Orange Free State, searching for new farms, new grazing lands for herds and flocks.[3] They went in peace, which perhaps explains the relatively tranquil behaviour of the Free State Republic—earning it the cognomen 'model republic', from a grateful Cape Governor.[4]

In contrast, those Afrikaners who left the Eastern Cape as *Trekkers*, in the exodus of 1835–38 were vastly different.[5] They went, as both Walker and van der Merwe agree, as irreconcilables, convinced that British rule was deliberately aimed at undermining their welfare, and safety, on a frontier in which life

[1] P. J. van der Merwe, *Die Noordwaarste Beweging van die Boere voor die Groot Trek* (The Hague, 1937).

[2] E. A. Walker, *The Frontier Tradition in South Africa* (Oxford, 1930), p. 3.

[3] 'When a boy was born his parents gave him a mare, a cow and some sheep. When he reached marriageable age he might have two hundred sheep, forty head of cattle and a dozen horses, enough to stock the new farm which was the height of his ambition.' De Kiewiet, *Imperial Factor*, p. 126.

[4] This rather unwise remark is generally attributed to Wodehouse, Governor of the Cape, 1862–70.

[5] See P. J. van der Merwe, *Trek* (Cape Town, 1945).

was already hazardous.[1] Their hopes of an independent Boer republic in the rich coastlands of Natal were cut short when, in 1843, the British flags followed them to this area. For strategic reasons Britain could not allow this vulnerable flank of her southern African Empire to fall into the hands of irreconcilable Dutch-speaking Calvinists. They might invite foreign intervention and so render useless the Simons Bay Naval Station.[2] Once again the *Trekkers* folded their tents and stole away into the night. This time to found the South African Republic, over the Vaal River. This second *Trek* left them more embittered than before. As to their relations with the 'imperial factor', they could only look back in anger. In this spirit the Transvaal was founded.

All the good intentions of the early policy seemed to have been negated. The only apparent fruit of the humanitarian approach was the existence of an Afrikaner state, albeit ramshackle, deep in the interior. It was a most unwelcome development; and an uncalled for challenge. It clearly could not be ignored, as had the slow *trekboer* drift—or could it? A new basis for imperial thinking was urgently needed in the face of the admitted failure of the humanitarian policy. From then on it became increasingly apparent that it was Africa, the Afrikaner and his relations with the native tribes, which determined the pattern of local developments, no matter how hard Downing Street attempted to set and regulate the pace of expansion.

British policy was forced to swing on its 'economic axis', away from positive humanitarian circles, to listen to the voices of the 'strategic consolidationists', who argued for limited, controlled frontiers. Practically this was expressed in the mid-century 'convention policy', as propagated by the influential Herman Merivale, architect of the policy of 'abandonment' in the Colonial Office.[3] This involved recognition of the independence of the two Afrikaner republics.[4]

[1] Ibid. See also P. J. van der Merwe, *Die Trekboer in die Geskiedenis van die Kaapkolonie* (Cape Town, 1938).

[2] *Hansard*, 3rd ser., LXIII, cols. 1169–70. Statement by Stanley.

[3] *Parl. Pap.*, 1861, XIII, C.423, pp. 228–9. Report of the Select Committee on Colonial Military Expenditure. Evidence by Merivale, 6 May 1861.

[4] C. W. de Kiewiet, *British Colonial Policy and the South African Republics* (1929), chaps. I–III.

The withdrawal from the Orange River Sovereignty (annexed in 1848), and recognition of the *Trekkers'* Transvaal, was part of this new approach. This was undertaken because Britain now believed she could accomplish her ends in South Africa by an 'informal paramountcy'. The Afrikaner republics were to be shut in the interior, thus making them dependent on the British-controlled ports, and preventing any outside aid.

The ablest of South African historians, Professor de Kiewiet, has cut to the heart of this policy, and placed the two conventions—the Bloemfontein Convention of 1854 with the Boers of trans-Orangia, and the Sand River Convention of 1852 with those across the Vaal[1]—in their proper perspective. The conventions were not intended as formal diplomatic acknowledgement of the existence of fellow nation-states. Rather they were designed merely as a method of 'casting to the winds' of a relatively few obdurate pastoralists. In time the natives, the wild animals, and the insects, or a combination of all three, might rid Britain of the problem altogether. Edward Fairfield, as the South African expert in the Colonial Office, had no doubts as to the aims of the Convention policy. 'It was not then supposed that any political importance would attach to *the small and isolated communities thus contemptuously abandoned in the interior . . .*'[2]

The Conventions are certainly dubious documents by the standards of international law. The Sand River Convention was not negotiated with elected representatives of the Transvaal, but with a self-appointed group of Boers. Nor was the Bloemfontein Convention sound. The abandonment of the Orange River Sovereignty was not actually legal. It was made by Order in Council and Proclamation without reference to Parliament, although it had been annexed 'with the knowledge to Parliament'.[3] But, the Conventions served the purpose required by the 'consolidationists': to delineate the British frontiers, and to contain the Boers in the interior.

The high hopes that launched the Convention policy—hopes

[1] For the texts of the later Conventions see Appendix.

[2] Minute by Fairfield, December 1875. Quoted in De Kiewiet, *Imperial Factor*, pp. 107–8.

[3] The complexities of the legal uncertainties of the Conventions are endless. De Kiewiet is the most succinct on this. De Kiewiet, *Imperial Factor*, pp. 281–2; and *British Colonial Policy and the South African Republics*, pp. 70–71.

22

of alleviating the Afrikaner problem by turning one's back and pretending it had gone away—were short-lived.[1] Removed from the restraint of colonial laws and moral suasion, the new republicans enjoyed their complete freedom to the full; they behaved as the mood dictated. In the 'model republic' this meant endless skirmishes on the Free State's eastern border, as the Boers relentlessly pushed the Basuto off the plains and into the mountains. In the Transvaal it was expressed in a relentless drive for 'Lebensraum': encroachment on to Swazi and Zulu lands in the east, Tswana lands in the west.

Britain's answer is most kindly described as 'watchful inactivity'.[2] When Sir George Grey in 1858, as High Commissioner at the Cape,[3] suggested that stability would come to South Africa only when it was federated under the British flag, he was censured by the Home Government—even though he had acquired Orange Free State support for the scheme.[4]

The policy-makers found themselves trapped in a web of their own creation. Additional expenditure, and extended responsibility, could alone bring the peace they desired. Yet they consciously rejected this course, and attempted to achieve their objective 'on the cheap'.[5] They clung to a policy of containing the chaos over colonial frontiers; and of neutralising the power of the republics, by frustrating Boer attempts either to unite— under President Pretorius of the Orange Free State in 1860— or to gain a seaboard access to the outside world—in 1860 and 1868 at Delagoa Bay and St. Lucia Bay in 1860 and 1866.[6]

At best, though, it was only a temporary solution: a method of feeding the crocodile. It was not a solution to the problem; and ironically in the end even inactivity was costly. Increasing

---

[1] For Transvaal western border 'expansion', see J. A. I. Agar-Hamilton, *The Road to the North* (London, 1937). For Transvaal eastern border activities, see C. J. Uys, *In the Era of Shepstone* (Lovedale, 1933).

[2] *Cambridge History of British Empire*, VIII, 2nd edn. (1963), pp. 400 ff.

[3] High Commissioner at the Cape: 5 December 1854–15 August 1861. See also, J. Rutherford, *Sir George Grey, K.C.B.* (London, 1961), pp. 406–43.

[4] The Orange Free State was pro-federation as they hoped for assistance in their latest 'war' with the Basuto. See A. J. H. van der Walt, *Die Geskiedenis van Suid-Afrika* (Cape Town, 1951).

[5] Agar-Hamilton, *The Road to the North*, chaps. II–III.

[6] *C.H.B.E.*, VIII (2nd edn.), pp. 424–38.

Boer encroachment made the plight of the Basuto impossible to ignore. The Colonial Office bowed to the inevitable humanitarian outcry, and annexed Basutoland in 1868, earning deep gratitude from the Basuto, but perpetually alienating the Orange Free State.[1] Nor did the Cape respond enthusiastically to liberal imperial overtures. Granted responsible government, in 1872, it was 'ungratefully' talking of the 'imperial factor' having acted in a high-handed manner, by annexing Basutoland and Griqualand West (1871), over the heads, and without the advice, of the colonial assembly.[2]

By 1872, some three-quarters of a century after the initial British occupation of the Cape, few sections of the South African 'community' had not been alienated in part, or wholly, from imperial rule. It was a poor record. Direct humanitarian Crown Colony government had produced two recalcitrant Boer states; later policy, a restive group of English-speaking Cape politicians. Abandonment of the Afrikaner republics, and liberal imperial gestures in the direction of self-rule in the Cape, had produced results no more fruitful. The republicans played havoc in the interior: the Cape colonists made the imperialists unsure of their strategic base.

Once again a radically new approach was called for. As the Victorian ministries groped for this new direction, the terms of the problem became even more difficult, with the discovery of diamonds at Kimberley, and the beginnings of investment, both English and foreign.[3] The possibility of a self-sufficient South Africa—and especially the Cape—slowly growing away from Britain was not lost on Downing Street. Lord Kimberley, who became Colonial Secretary in Gladstone's first administration,[4] approached the whole lingering dilemma, both past failures and present developments, with a cautious vigour characteristic of his nature. Sound Gladstonian principles were to be applied: devolution of responsibility on to loyal colonial

---

[1] De Kiewiet, *British Colonial Policy and the South African Republics*, pp. 208–42.

[2] E. A. Walker, *A History of Southern Africa*, pp. 327–86.

[3] De Kock, *Economic History*, Part II, pp. 108–34. Table, p. 325. In 1872 the Cape exported £1,618,000 worth of diamonds. By 1878 the figure had risen to £2,159,000. For rise of investments see S. H. Frankel, *Capital Investment in Africa* (Oxford, 1938), pp. 52 ff. and Table 28.

[4] Colonial Secretary: 6 July 1870–21 February 1874.

ministries to ensure maximum security at minimum cost.[1]

Kimberley turned to the classic imperial expedient of federation. This was to be the panacea for the intractable problem. Grey's scheme of the 1850s suddenly took on a new-found depth and understanding of the local situation. Hopefully the Victorians reminded themselves that Canada's apparently insoluble racial problems had been alleviated by the confederation of 1867.

The lesson seemed clear. 'Once united under the Union Jack and relieved of formal Downing Street control, surely the South African colonists' community of interest with Britain, in trade and freedom, if not in kinship and culture, would keep them loyal to the Empire.'[2] Unfortunately South Africa and the Victorians rarely saw a problem from the same angle. Kimberley's scheme soon came to naught, when the Cape ministry bolted at the prospect of being harnessed to carry the imperial burden in South Africa. There was little to be gained by the Cape in such a union. Federation would mean sharing her precious customs revenue with the impoverished and vulnerable Boer republics. Kimberley accepted the colonists' negative reply, as he was to do later in 1880, when his second federal plan also met with rejection from the Cape.

Lord Carnarvon though was made of sterner stuff. He became Disraeli's Colonial Secretary at a crucial moment in imperial relations with southern Africa. Kimberley's federal scheme had undoubtedly collapsed. The alternatives which presented themselves were singularly unpromising. He could hardly return to the Crown Colony technique of the 1830s; nor did the Convention's policy offer much. It had solved nothing, and done much harm. Carnarvon thus looked again at confederation. Perhaps Kimberley had failed, Carnarvon reasoned, because of his method in implementing the policy. Federation *was* possibly the answer: it merely needed a more determined advocate.

The new Colonial Secretary was known among his friends as 'Twitters'; but to the Afrikaners, and the Cape politicians,

---

[1] Kimberley's *Journal of Events During the Gladstone Ministry, 1868–74*. Published in Camden Miscellany, XXI (ed. E. Drus). Entry for 20 June 1872, p. 32.

[2] *New Cambridge Modern History*, XI, 634 (Cambridge, 1962).

Carnarvon became the 'compleat imperialist'.[1] Part of Carnarvon's spirited drive to achieve immediate federation stemmed from his belief that South Africa's native problem was again approaching the critical state it had been in prior to the Kaffir wars, of the early years of the century. Uniting the white colonists—English and Afrikaner—was thus to him 'a matter of immediate concern to Parliament and the United Kingdom'.[2] In keeping with this belief he was prepared to take the exceptional step of extending British authority and responsibility, even at great expense, to attain a firm and just settlement in South Africa.[3] It was a settlement he felt for both immediate problems, and more important still, a solution for the future. Carnarvon was convinced that only a radical step such as this would achieve peace once and for all. In this he was strongly supported by his nephew, Robert Herbert, conveniently permanent under-secretary at the Colonial Office, in succession to Merivale.

They approached the matter in almost sabre-rattling style. As has been ably demonstrated by Dr. C. F. Goodfellow, in his *Great Britain and South African Confederation*, Carnarvon refused to 'take no' as an acceptable answer from the colonists.[4] Initial Cape responses, in 1875, were negative. Afrikaner antipathy to the plan in the two Republics was clear by the end of the following year. Carnarvon pressed on. Events in South Africa seemed to favour Britain; or so Carnarvon claimed. The Transvaal was financially on its knees, anarchy and native invasion seemed imminent. Carnarvon did not flinch from adding this apparent millstone to the imperial burden of South Africa.

Sir Theophilus Shepstone was commissioned by Carnarvon to annex the Transvaal, *if* he found the majority of the inhabi-

[1] See Sir Arthur Hardinge, *Life of the 4th Earl of Carnarvon*, 2 vols. (Oxford, 1925).

[2] Quoted in De Kiewiet, *Imperial Factor*, p. 71.

[3] As Carnarvon put it to his Cabinet colleagues: '. . . the most immediately urgent reason for general union is the formidable character of the native question; and the importance of a uniform, wise and strong policy in dealing with it, [and] . . . by other considerations connected with the advance of civilization in Africa and the general interests of the Empire . . .' Ibid., p. 71.

[4] C. F. Goodfellow, *Great Britain and South African Confederation* (Oxford, 1966), is excellent on Carnarvon.

tants favourable. Shepstone was hardly in the Transvaal before he declared the Republic in favour of annexation.[1] He has been much maligned by historians, but perhaps Shepstone heard correctly: that the Transvalers did desire to come within the British Empire at that moment. The alternative to the *trekker* republic appeared to be destruction at the hands of the natives. In April 1877 the Union Jack once again fluttered above the rebellious men of the Eastern Cape. The prodigals had returned to the fold; or rather, the fold had moved on to recover them.

Carnarvon viewed his handiwork with satisfaction. It was the first step he believed towards federating and pacifying southern Africa. Annexation probably saved the Transvaal, but it also secured the worst of all ends for the imperial power. It angered the Cape Dutch, who began to express sympathy with their 'blood relations' in the Transvaal,[2] a feeling which had hitherto been dormant, and completely absent in the actions of the Cape Dutch; and, it began to rouse the Transvaal and Free State Boers.[3]

In 1878 Carnarvon left the Colonial Office, but so heavily had he committed Britain, by the annexation of the Transvaal, that his two successors behaved as if they were locked to an inevitable course of action. First Hicks Beach,[4] then Kimberley[5] again, attempted to pluck the flower of federation from its thorny background, to profit from Carnarvon's boldness— though privately questioning the wisdom of his policy of annexation.[6] In this they not only failed, but gave an added impetus to the awakening political consciousness of the Cape Dutch. And a political edge to the *Boere Beschermings Vereeniging*,[7] and the *Genootskap van Regte Afrikaners*.[8] These two associations

[1] C. J. Uys, *In the Era of Shepstone*, (Lovedale, 1933).

[2] *New Cambridge Modern History*, XI, 634–5.

[3] F. A. van Jaarsveld, *Die Ontwaking van Afrikaanse Nasionale Bewussyn* (Cape Town, 1959), is very good on this.

[4] Sir Michael Beach—'Black Michael'—Colonial Secretary, 4 February 1878–28 April 1880.

[5] Colonial Secretary: 28 April 1880–11 December 1882.

[6] *Africa and the Victorians*, pp. 63–75, for the finest short study of the confederation attempts.

[7] 'Farmers Association', organised by Jan Hofmeyr.

[8] 'Association of True Afrikaners', founded by S. J. du Toit.

were soon to become the nucleus of the Afrikaner *Bond* under
S. J. du Toit [1] and Jan Hofmeyr.[2]

The Victorians had hoped to find in federation the magical
formula for controlling South Africa. Instead they conjured up
the ghosts of the past, spirits which were to galvanize the desperate South African Dutch into a political movement which
must of its nature some day challenge British dominance in
South Africa. The legacy of the decade of attempts to pressure
the colonies and the republics into a confederation was vital: it
profoundly shook the foundation of imperial influence in southern Africa, by losing the whole-hearted co-operation of the self-
governing Cape; it changed the shape and tempo of Cape
politics, by bringing into the political arena the hitherto slum-
bering, numerically superior, Cape Dutch; and worst of all for
Britain, it appeared to reunite Cape Afrikaner and Transvaal
Voortrekker for the first time since the latter left the Cape some
forty years previously.[3] In short, it meant there was not only a
new element in the problem, but that the problem itself had
radically altered.[4]

The last two decades of the century were to see the working
out of this accentuated problem, and the factors elemental in
the ultimate collapse of imperial influence in southern Africa.
It was also to witness the gropings of the permanent officials to
find an approach that would fill the vacuum left by the bankruptcy in policy which followed the Transvaal War, or as
most Afrikaner historians would have it, *Die Eerste Vryheidsoorlog*—with its famous battle of Majuba, in February 1881.
In particular, the years which immediately followed the demise
of the confederation attempts witnessed British attempts to
implement a radically new approach: they were to try to kill
the problem of the Afrikaner with kindness. The Gladstonians
hoped to find in conciliation the merits of coercion. Policy was
to be based on the slenderest of pillars, informal control. The

---

[1] J. D. du Toit, *Dr. S. J. du Toit in Weg en Werk* (Paarl, 1917).

[2] T. R. Davenport, *The Afrikaner Bond* (O.U.P., Cape Town, 1966). I
am deeply indebted to Dr. Davenport for the loan of his study prior to publication, and for the correspondence we had on the Bond in the Transvaal.
See also J. H. Hofmeyr and F. W. Reitz, *The Life of Jan Hendrick Hofmeyr*.
Hereafter cited as *Life of Hofmeyr*.

[3] Kimberley in Lords, 31 March 1881. *Hansard*, 3rd ser., CCLX, col. 295 ff.

[4] Charles Dilke, *Problems of Greater Britain*, I, 529.

peace terms of 1902, at Vereeniging, have been given the cog-nomen 'magnanimous'; but the gestures of the second Glad-stone government have prior claim to the accolade.

6

These brief 'years of transition', from 1880–86, also promise much to the historian. It would appear to be both salutary and beneficial to move the weight of academic investigation away from those crowded years prior to the Anglo-Boer War, and examine this period before Rand gold clouded the issues; to review again those neglected years which spawned the majority of ideas, and 'habits of thought', which still prevailed in 1899.

Further, there is the overall interest of ideas and attitudes in flux. Men and minds were more flexible in 1880 than twenty years later. The options open to them are correspondingly wider; and their choice of a policy is more significant than in the emotive years after the Jameson Raid. A unique oppor-tunity is thus presented to the historian to study the major figures before they have struck the traditional poses of 1899.

It is certainly more than coincidental that nearly all the major players in the last act of the tragedy, the Boer War itself, first appear as participants in southern African dilemmas in the years just before 1886.[1] The two principals, Chamberlain and Kruger, had their first taste of responsible office. The effect on both was vital. Kruger, in his numerous negotiations on behalf of the Transvalers—first as Vice-President in 1880, then as President after 1883—acquired a unique understanding of the workings of the British 'official mind' as regards the Afri-kaner republics.[2]

Chamberlain also began his stormy rise to power in these years. From the unlikely post of Secretary to the Board of

[1] One significant figure is missing, Milner. But then the majority of his ideas had already formed at Oxford. See J. E. Wrench, *Life of Alfred Lord Milner, The Man of No Illusion 1854–1925* (London, 1958).

[2] Paul Kruger became President of the South African Republic, (then styled the 'Transvaal State', by Britain), for the first time on 9 May, 1883. Prior to this he had been the leading figure of a 'Triumvirate', as a Vice-President, since 1880. See D. W. Kruger, *Paul Kruger*, 2 vols. (in Afrikaans), (Johannesburg, 1963), I, 207–72, which has been of the greatest use.

Trade in Gladstone's second government, he became the South
African expert in that cabinet.[1] For the first time Chamberlain
came intimately into contact with the complexity of the problem of the Afrikaner.[2] His radical concepts on the Empire had
their first serious test under the rigors of office, significantly
on the 'test case' of the Transvaal Republic. As Colonial Secretary after 1895 he continually referred to his detailed knowledge of the imperial position in South Africa[3] most of it gained
in his days of 'apprenticeship' in the early 1880s.

These years were also of prime importance in the making of
Cecil Rhodes as the 'colonial imperialist'. He was shocked to
discover the vacillating character of British policy, especially
when any expense was involved. He resolved to give policy
some 'backbone', and began his personal mission as champion
of the imperial standard, in a turbulent collaboration with
Hofmeyr's *Bond*.[4]

In the Colonial Office, traditions of thought—and even
members of staff—lived long and died hard. When Chamberlain took over the Office in 1895 the faces that met him were
substantially the same as those whom he had dealt with in
1880.[5] And when Kruger finally declared the Transvaal 'unilaterally independent', in October 1899, he did so in defiance

[1] J.C. 9/1/1/4 (Chamberlain Papers). Kimberley to Chamberlain, 3 June
1881; Addit. MSS. 44544, f. 175 (L.B. copy). Gladstone to Kimberley, 3
June 1881; Addit. MSS. 44227, f. 106. Kimberley to Gladstone, 1 January
1882.

[2] A 'pro-Boer' group even began its existence in British politics: the
'*Transvaal Independence Committee*':
Founded 18 January 1881. Offices at 6 Draper's Garden, London.
Chairman: Capt. Edmund Verney, R.N.
Founding members included: J. A. Froude, G. B. Clarke, Auberon Herbert.
and three M.P.s. G. B. Clarke, in particular, wrote numerous pamphlets
arguing the Boer case.
Source: Rhodes House MSS. (Transvaal Pamphlets) for the only available
information on the committee.

[3] Chamberlain in Commons, 19 October 1899. *Hansard*, 4th ser., LXXVII,
col. 254.

[4] L. Michell, *The Life of Rt. Hon. Cecil John Rhodes 1853–1902* (London,
1910), 2 vols.—for Rhodes on the 'constant vacillation of the Home Government', and his consequent pact with Hofmeyr's 'Bond', I, 93–5.

[5] With the notable exceptions of Robert Herbert, who retired in 1893,
and Edward Fairfield, who died in 1897. See *Colonial Office Lists*, 1880–99.

of the London Convention of 1884, a treaty laboriously drawn up by the same colonial officials as he now challenged.[1]

The well-chronicled events of 1895–99 are in fact not a separate entity; rather they are the last phase of a sequence of events that date directly back to the early 1880s. If 1899 is the last scene in the dramatic decline of the 'imperial factor', then 1880 and the end of the federal attempts is more than a mere prologue.

On another plane, these transitional years reflected the immense influence of the hand of the past that existed on the making of policy. As personified by Whigs like Hartington and Kimberley, and Tories like Salisbury and Hicks Beach, these 'voices of conservatism' attempted to apply old solutions to new problems, to equate new fears with old familiar dilemmas. Ireland, in particular, would appear to have conditioned their thinking about the rebellious 'nationalism' of the Afrikaner.[2] Almost to a man, the later Unionists, with their belief in coercion and a strong imperial policy, are found to be the South African 'supremacists'; while the later Home Rulers, are seen to be the earlier advocates of devolution of authority, on to Afrikaner ministries throughout South Africa.

Towering above and beyond, on a separate level is the figure of Gladstone. This second ministry constituted the most important years of personal political involvement in his life[3] and thus the most traumatic years for the Liberal Party.[4] Gladstone flirted with, and finally embraced Irish 'Home Rule', so forcing his colleagues to take a definite stand.[5] The alliances for the 1886 rift in the party were now made; and, by bringing the Radicals within the cloak of respectability of office,

---

[1] It is an interesting sidelight that even the soldiers of the 1880s took a major part in 1899–1902. Warren, Wolseley and Roberts all came to know South Africa well between 1880 and 1885. See J. Lehman, *All Sir Garnet* (London, 1965); and W. Williams, *Life of General Sir Charles Warren* (Oxford, 1941), chap. XI for Warren Expedition of 1884–85.

[2] Derby in Lords, 13 March 1881. *Hansard*, 3rd ser., CCLXXVII, col. 339.

[3] Addit. MSS. 48630–48640 (Hamilton Diary).

[4] J. Morley, *Life of Gladstone*, 3 vols. (London, 1903), vol. III, book VIII; *C.H.B.E.*, III, 127–36; and P. Magnus, *Gladstone, a biography* (London, 1963), pp. 167–224.

[5] Hammond, *Gladstone and the Irish Nation*, Chap. 25.

Gladstone added a new and disturbing element into the higher councils of the Liberal Party.

Lastly, this was an unparalleled period of flux in British politics: a classic demonstration of the manner in which purely local colonial issues could become distorted once they reached the hub of the machinery of Empire. The Government, for example, in January 1881 was not only at 'war' with Irish Fenians and rebellious Afrikaners, but was also waging a war within itself.[1] Gladstone spoke of this period as being 'a wild romance of politics, with a continual succession of hairbreadth escapes and strange accidents pressing upon one another'.[2]

In no field did the 'escapes' and strange 'accidents' have greater effect than on imperial policy in Africa. Policy tended to pitch and yaw as it was tossed on the currents within the administration, with crucial and long-term results.

7

In examining, evaluating, and drawing on these diverse themes, two predominant irreverent ideas, or rather doubts, ultimately came to linger in the mind.

The first concerned the implicit faith placed by historians in the Witwatersrand gold discoveries as an explanation for the decline of imperial influence in southern Africa, and the consequent rise to power of Kruger's Republic. The research for this study has, however, indirectly cast serious doubt on that long-held concept. Indeed it would now appear that by the conclusion of the second Gladstone government, in mid-1885, and a year before the major gold discoveries on the reef, the Victorians had already lost the 'initiative' in South Africa to the

[1] On the wider front there was Chamberlain's urgent drive for electoral and social reform. On a narrower front, there was the personal duel between Gladstone and the Whig heart of the Cabinet, to come to grips with the newly recognised challenge from the Radical wing of the Liberal Party. Again and again the ministry nearly fell, not because of Irish obstruction in the Commons, or because of the sniping of Randolph Churchill's 'Fourth Party', but rather as a result of the deep divisions and tensions that gripped every action of the Cabinet. See Joseph Chamberlain, *A Political Memoir* (Ed. C. H. D. Howard), (London, 1953), pp. 85–108; Donald Southgate, *The Passing of the Whigs 1832–86* (London, 1962), p. 385; Morley, *Gladstone*, III, 72–143, 170–87; and Herbert Gladstone, *After Thirty Years* (London, 1928), pp. 180–84.

[2] Morley, *Gladstone*, III, 186.

Afrikaner. From the moment that the concept of a united pan-Afrikaner front took hold in the 'official mind', then the Victorians, by implication, abdicated from the major option of controlling Kruger by formal means, notably by a show or threat of force; and, instead, they accepted as a basic premise of policy, the fact that they could but exercise their influence in southern Africa via the suspect channel of Cape politicians, and the Hofmeyr-dominated colonial ministry. The price of supremacy was thus ultimately to be seen as nothing less than a full-scale war in 1899, something they had dreaded since 1881.

In short, it would appear that prior to 1886 the Victorians were already being hustled out of southern Africa; and that it was the Afrikaner who held the future in his hands. The gold discoveries merely confirmed this trend. They did not of themselves lift Kruger to power: the Gladstonians, by their reading of the situation, and by their conciliatory policy, had indirectly already done that.

The second doubt which has steadily grown, and which cannot be ignored, concerns the basic premise adopted by the Gladstonians: the concept of the unity of the Afrikaners as a people, consequent upon the Transvaal War of 1881. It is also a premise adopted by Afrikaner historians of note, such as Professor F. A. van Jaarsveld, for it fits well with their attempts to show how Afrikanerdom ousted the British by the very 'emotive unity' of the people. In addition it has been taken up as a concept, and made a major theme of the writings of modern Oxford and Cambridge historians, concerned with 'Africa and the Victorians'. It is certainly an attractive idea, and as this study will show, it does indeed provide a unified and comprehensive explanation for the decline of Victorian power in southern Africa. Indeed, it has been illustrated at great length below that the Victorians ultimately did come to believe in the reality of a united Afrikaner people.

But, were they right? did they read the signs correctly? It now appears doubtful. This is not to say that the Victorians did not base their policy on a belief in a pan-Afrikaner danger. However, these researches suggest that it is questionable whether that unity was anything but momentary.

The historian can now well ask: did the Victorians adopt a conciliatory and appeasing policy in the face of what was no more than the *chimera* of a nationalist revolt, nothing but the illusion of an Afrikaner unity?

In raising both these doubts—the importance of the gold discoveries, and the nature of the common bonds of the Afrikaners in the 1880s—numerous awkward questions present themselves, quite apart from the manner in which it discredits the neat pattern placed on Anglo-Afrikaner relations by those attempting to provide a unified and ordered theory for the decline of the 'Imperial factor' in southern Africa. But if these questions are disruptive to present theories, they are also necessary. For the alternative is to let sleeping dogmas lie.

PEACE & PROSPERITY | ...ITE'S EMPIRE

THE CHOICE OF HERCULES.

* * The dissolution of Parliament having been announced, it was felt that the coming campaign would be a pitched battle between the persons and policies of Lord Beaconsfield and his great rival, Mr. Gladstone.

II

GLADSTONE AND THE TRADITIONAL APPROACH

Principles and the Problem, 1880

1. Gladstonian Principles

GLADSTONE was jubilant. 'The downfall of Beaconsfieldism', he wrote to Argyll in April 1880,[1] 'is like the vanishing of some vast magnificent castle in an Italian romance.' Officially in retirement since 1875,[2] Gladstone had left his ecclesiastical writings at Hawarden, to awaken the conscience of the country to 'England's Mission' as a nation.[3] He had waged a political campaign in Midlothian that was in reality 'a crusade' against the policies and conduct of the last Disraeli administration. It was in keeping with Gladstone's character. Politics were to him a series of 'missions'; attempts to extend his deep belief in Christian principles and ethics into the practice of government. He often spoke of his 'earthly mission';[4] and in his Midlothian speeches[5] he called upon the electors to return a verdict of 'Guilty!' against Disraeli.[6] In embarking on these missions— either to free the Montenegrins, preserve the Zulus, rescind Disraeli's 'imperialistic' acquisitions, or 'to pacify Ireland'— Gladstone never doubted the source of his strength. 'It seemed',

[1] Gladstone to Argyll, 12 April 1880. Quoted in Morley, *Gladstone*, II, 629.

[2] Though ominously he did *not* resign his seat in the Commons.

[3] W. E. Gladstone, 'England's Mission', in *Nineteenth Century Review*, September 1878.

[4] Magnus, *Gladstone*, p. 378.   [5] Morley, *Gladstone*, II, 589.

[6] Magnus, *Gladstone*, p. 269.

he once remarked while tree chopping on Lord Rosebery's estates,[1] 'as if the arm of the Lord had bared itself for work that He has made His own.' Gladstone felt no unease in referring to the fall of Disraeli as 'a moral certainty', for he came to politics confirmed in the moral rectitude of his own attitudes and beliefs, or as his critics jibed, determined in his own omnipotence.[2]

Gladstone's approach was, to say the least, peculiarly his own. He claimed to differentiate in government between 'policies' —a word which smelt of morality—and 'principles'— which were the true charter of political action. The 'City of God' could be of this world: morality not expediency would realise this. Accordingly, he measured his contemporaries by his own particular and rigid standards. With notable fallibility he depicted them in unequivocal colours: Disraeli was 'evil' as he 'lacked morality';[3] Chamberlain and the new Radicals were suspect because they were 'all opportunism';[4] Bright, of course, was 'a splendid old man' for he had a 'grand moral tone'.[5] In return Gladstone provoked sharp reactions: Cobden put him in a class of his own, a politician with principles; Disraeli and Palmerston both thought him a righteous bore; while the Queen's attitude was hardly a secret.

Gladstone's highly personal approach was both his strength and his weakness: his rigid high moral tone was in fact brittle to criticism. Labouchere came uncomfortably near the truth when he remarked acidly, 'I do not mind Mr. Gladstone always having an ace up his sleeve, but I object to his always saying that Providence put it there.'[6] This view was given added impetus by Gladstone's manner: the lighter touch, the warmth of softening humour, were no ingredient to his style of politics. He could hardly be said to have had Peel's 'iceberg' effect on close associates: but, as one society hostess tartly remarked, if

[1] Ibid., p. 270.

[2] The finest brief approaches to Gladstone are: J. Vincent, *The Formation of the Liberal Party* (London, 1966); J. L. Hammond and M. R. D. Foot, *Gladstone and Liberalism* (London, 1952).

[3] Lord Kilbracken, *Reminiscences* (London, 1931), is excellent on Gladstone in the 1880s. He was his principal private secretary.

[4] Roy Jenkins, *Dilke, a Victorian Tragedy* (London, 1958), p. 157.

[5] Magnus, *Gladstone*, p. 290.

[6] A. L. Thorold, *Life of Labouchere* (London, 1913), p. xii.

he were squeezed dry 'not an ounce of fun would drop out'. Years of parliamentary debate, and the slings and arrows of public criticism, coupled with advancing age (Gladstone was 71 years old in 1880) toughened him to opposition, and blunted such receptivity to constructive criticism that he may once have had. He became impervious to sound counsel, even from close associates such as Granville. The image of the lone High Church figure, herding the remnants of a divided party along the corridors of Westminster, in the grim crusade for Irish 'Home Rule', replaced and obscured the image of the 'omniscient', almost elegant, utilitarian Premier of 1868–74.[1] The years of his second ministry, 1880–85, witnessed this change in process: they bore testimony to the fact that while the Gladstonian mind was still likely to produce volcanic objurgations of emotive rhetoric, on 'matters of general principle', the inner core of molten ideas and concepts had hardened. Even for Gladstone the years of growth, the moments of blinding revelation and understanding, were over.

Above all, of course, the Gladstone of the 1880s was the 'People's William'. His career mirrored the history of the party that was ever to stand in the shadow of his name. Gladstone's public career had broadened from decade to decade—from young Tory prig in the era of Peel, to the G.O.M. of 'the people'. So too with the Liberal Party: it had expanded and become less monolithic from the era of Melbourne, to the 'mass age' of Bright and Chamberlain. But, as with both Gladstone and the Liberal Party, much of the earlier 'baggage', in the form of traditional attitudes and habits of thought, had never been jettisoned. In the case of the Liberal Party, the time-honoured Whig concerns for the victories acquired during the Revolution —a concern for peace, for the prerogative of Parliament, for economy and civil rights—these still found expression in the heart of the Liberal creed; and still drew men to espouse their 'cause', rather than find company with the Tories. In the case of Gladstone the richness of past accumulations was so great, the 'barnacles' of experience so vast and so various, as to make

[1] For Gladstone's first and greatest ministry, see W. E. Williams, *The Life of Mr. Gladstone, 1859–68* (Cambridge, 1934); F. W. Hirst, *Gladstone as Financier and Economist*, (London, 1931); and J. Vincent, *Formation of the Liberal Party* (London, 1966), to which I am particularly indebted.

it almost impossible to fathom the core of his political strength. So that if the question were asked, 'where lay the source of his manifold appeal and success?', the answer might well be said to lie in the fact that he had come to mean all things to all people. He could at once ride comfortably in the gilded coaches of the aristocracy—and form aristocratic cabinets; he could walk unobserved amid gaitered High Churchmen—and deeply enjoy the dubious pleasures of making Church appointments as Premier; he could be a favourite of the cheap press and local radical movements—his fervent language and moral tone, in the name of reform, both social and political, led industrial constituencies to clamour for him as a parliamentary candidate; he could be popular in Dissenting circles—his views on religious toleration and respect for a man's beliefs went deep; and, he could be taken up as the spokesman for the rising commercial interests, who saw in this son of a wealthy Liverpool trader, their best hope for continued prosperity—without enquiring too deeply into his moralising approach to free-trade, and his passion against protective tariffs of any nature.

If that was his broad-based appeal, how had he acquired this unique position? Part of the answer lay in the suddenness with which Gladstone burst upon the Liberal camp, to steal the limelight from the Radical and Whiggish Wings of the Party. In 1858 Gladstone had left the political arena to become High Commissioner for the Ionian Islands. Disraeli took the common view in describing Gladstone's desire, to tread in the steps of Homer, as a major political blunder. Aberdeen had warned, though, that Gladstone 'was terrible on the rebound'. So it was to be. He returned, a flurry of activity, quite 'unmuzzled', and at last spiritually at ease, after years of suppressed growth amid his former Tory associates. He swept the ground from under Russell and Palmerston—by taking the fight to areas of public combat where they declined to follow—and he stole the support of Cobden, Mill, and Bright—by saying much the same thing and saying it a great deal better. In a intuitive manner he not only sounded notes familiar to the hearts of all Englishmen—reform, free-trade, economic growth and stability, and retrenchment abroad—but long after he had abandoned particular themes he was still identified with that particular clause. For example, he had so closely made the slogan of 'reform and retrenchment' his own, that his name was forever associated with it, though the conduct of his second ministry largely ignored his text for government. In the minds of the great 'classes' Gladstone had as many meanings as there were interests and impressions. In retrospect his critics have found in this unique appeal a hollow sense of cold calculation: in fact Gladstone simply pursued his enthusiasms. Men saw in him what they wished to see.

The nature of the Liberal Party also lent itself to this style of charismatic leadership. It was not a class-based organisation. Rather it was, as Dr. Vincent has brilliantly expressed it, 'a habit of co-operation and a community of sentiment'.[1] Gladstone could thus stand astride the Liberals. He favoured and mustered its aristocratic administrative leadership; he believed in the mystique of the governing classes governing. At the same time he held the more radical wing of the party fascinated with the sophistry of moral beneficence: the Liberals acquired the reputation for being philanthropic, the party of 'progress', more from Gladstone's soft words than from any concrete actions.

Gladstone's attitude to the world-at-large and to the Empire itself was, as might be expected, merely an extension of his Liberal creed, with its inherent beliefs in reform, *laissez-faire*, financial economy, Hellenism, and Christianity: a singularly strange yet practical gospel of power and trusteeship, as it turned out.

It has, indeed, been over Gladstone's exercise of power abroad that the greatest controversy has centred, both in his own time and more recently. The origin of this confusion, and of much of the criticism, has stemmed from a feature already noted above: his many-sided qualities in the eyes of his contemporaries. The occasional apostle of Bentham, the courtier at the Manchester School, the High Anglican apologist, the cartographer of Britain's tropical African Empire, were all said to be parts in his repertoire. He would have subscribed to some of those tags of convenience: certainly not to all of them. But, and this is more important, he more than occasionally gave the impression of espousing causes when in fact he was merely harnessing them for some quite different purpose. In 1877, for

[1] J. Vincent, *Formation of the Liberal Party*, pp. 227–335.

example, he duly appeared at the inaugural meeting of Chamberlain's National Liberal Federation, seemingly to place himself at the head of this new Radical drive for reform. In fact Gladstone was present for a far less 'suspect' reason: he wished the N.L.F. to swing its support round to his current moral-cum-political 'mission'—the eastern campaign against Turkey and the Bulgarian atrocities.[1]

The confusion over his motives was perhaps understandable: for in part it stemmed from his own convoluted personality. The qualifying clauses in his speeches were notorious, but indicative of his pattern of thought. His short statement on the decision on the Mahdi became a classic: it contained, as Goschen detected, 'a double negative and three hypotheses'.[2] Even those close to him often found him baffling. Lord Hartington, after ten years in two Gladstone administrations, could remark to Granville, 'I can never understand Mr. Gladstone in conversation, and I thought him unusually unintelligible yesterday.'[3] Gladstone alone, it seems, wandered through the prolixity of his own words claiming loyalty to old principles. His second ministry he explained to a friend, would act on the 'well tried and established lines', and 'will not derive its inspiration from me'.[4] In practice all his administrations were particularly personal: as with Lloyd George and Churchill, he was the Cabinet.

This gave Liberal foreign and imperial policy between 1868 and 1894 a totally individual, and Gladstonian, colour. His morality of power, and of the uses of power, had intricate roots. Though a partisan to the High Church cause, and to the 'landed interest', Gladstone had a political conscience that would have done justice to Peel. He shared the Manchester School aversion to the 'sabre rattling' tactics of Palmerston, and to the grand manner of Disraeli—can one imagine Gladstone approaching the old Queen with a block of Suez shares and proudly remarking, 'You have them ma'am'? Even the quali-

---

[1] See R. T. Shannon's superb account of *Gladstone and the Bulgarian Agitation 1876* (London, 1963).

[2] See February 1884, statement by Gladstone—'What we say is that we are not prepared, at the present moment to say that there is no obligation upon us to use, according to circumstances, efforts, if we go there, to leave behind us, an orderly government.' Quoted in Holland, *Devonshire*, II, 21.

[3] Ibid., II, 77. Hartington to Granville, 5 August 1885.

[4] Gladstone to Doyle, 10 May 1880. Quoted in Morley, *Gladstone*, II, 631.

fied attitude of Whigs, like Hartington and Kimberley, jarred against the subtlety of his own oblique approach. When Hartington finally broke with Gladstone in 1886 he explained the deep-seated rift between them thus: 'You see he was a Peelite, and I was a Palmerstonian.'[1]

This astute remark both clarifies yet confuses the nature of Gladstone's belief in the uses and morality of power.[2] There is the sense in which Hartington was right: Gladstone did have an 'isolationist' impulse, and did believe, like Cobden, in the moral good to be accrued from the extension of free-trade. This is the Gladstone who supported Cobden's 1860 French treaty; and the Gladstone who could ask:

> Is it in the nature of things, is it in the design of Providence, that besides the concerns of the vast Empire over which this little island rules, we should be meddling in the business of almost every portion of the globe?[3]

To which he gave as an answer a resounding 'No!' Yet this is by no means the complete story. There was the sense in which Hartington was wrong. It must never be forgotten that just as Gladstone had railed against Palmerston over Don Pacifico, and over the Opium War, it was in company with Palmerston that Gladstone found his most congenial stance, in facing the greater evil of Derby and Disraeli's pro-Austrian and pro-Turkish policy. It was, after all, over liberty in Europe in general, and the cause of nationalism in Italy in particular, that Gladstone had found common cause with Palmerston; and had crossed the floor to the Whig-Liberal side of the House. Cobden, and to a lesser degree John Bright, saw in free-trade a force for moral good that would allow all nations to live in 'perfect isolation'; 'foreign policy' would be rendered unnecessary. Gladstone, however, took a lesser view of the behaviour of nations and their governments: he favoured free-trade as a moral force, which would in his eyes bind together yet more tightly the 'virtuous nations' yet he could also *act* 'in concert' against nations, such as Turkey, who offended against the moral code

---

[1] Quoted in Holland, *Devonshire*, I, 30.

[2] Gladstone's foreign policy is thoroughly dissected in A. J. P. Taylor's *The Troublemakers*, p. 80 *passim*, to which I am greatly indebted, and on which these few pages are based.

[3] Idem.

of Europe. This was the Gladstone who initially supported the Crimean War, for he thought the cause just—the war was not one of aggrandisement, but represented rather 'a great combination of Powers acting against Russia, to vindicate and enforce against her the public law of Europe'.[1] This was the Gladstone who wished to get the powers to act together over the German seizure of Alsace-Lorraine;[2] this was the Gladstone who could write of the bombardment of Alexandria as 'an honest undertaking'.[3]

Yet again Gladstone made his stance on the exercise of power patently clear. He told a huge audience in Edinburgh, in March 1880, in words which deserve a full quotation:

> There is an allegation abroad that what is called the 'Manchester School' is to rule the destinies of this country if the Liberals come to power . . . what is called the Manchester School has never ruled the foreign policy of this country—never during a Conservative Government, and never especially during a Liberal Government. . . . Abhorring all selfishness of policy, friendly to freedom in every country of the earth, attached to the modes of reason and detesting the ways of force, this Manchester School has sprung prematurely to the conclusion that wars may be considered as having closed their melancholy and miserable history, and that the affairs of the world may hence forth be conducted by methods more adapted to the dignity of man. . . . But no Government of this country could ever accede to the management and control of affairs without finding that dream of Paradise upon earth was rudely dispelled by the shock of experience.[4]

This led Gladstone on to pronounce on the points at which necessity would dictate action, possibly diplomatic, probably military. It was here that he left Cobden and Bright isolated, like obsolete landmarks, in an age of 'real politik':

> However we may detest war . . . however deplorable wars may be, they are amongst the necessities of our condition; and *there are times when justice, when faith, when the welfare of mankind requires a man not to shrink from the responsibility of undertaking them.* And if you

[1] *Hansard's*, 3rd ser., CXXXVIII, col. 1071 (8 June 1855).

[2] See Addit. MSS. 44759, f. 203. Gladstone Memorandum on Alsace-Lorraine.

[3] Stead, *M.P. for Russia*, II, 130. Quoted Taylor: *Troublemakers* p. 89.

[4] W. E. Gladstone, *Political Speeches in Scotland, March and April 1880* (rev. edn., Edinburgh, 1880), I, 30.

undertake wars, so also you are often obliged to undertake the measures which may lead to war.[1]

In short, what we have is this: Gladstone had a moral concept of society and the power which derived from that nation's industry, religion and order. Likewise he saw the collective power of many nations as a force which could be collectively harnessed for good. At no time did he imply that this power, this force granted by providence, was to be kept locked away from the heart of political action. Just as his Christianity followed him into the Cabinet room, or out on to the streets at night when rescuing prostitutes, so too his ethics of government obliged him to accept the duty of exercising power wherever he saw the need. This does not justify his actions: it merely explains them. It is on the grounds for Gladstone's particular missions, his 'selective intervention' that he is justly most open to criticism. In the last resort of course, the decision whether to act or not, to invoke the 'resources of civilisation', and to set in motion his 'arm of morality', was a purely personal one; each case of Gladstonian action deserving special consideration. Gladstone's philosophy is unusual but intelligible.

How then does this philosophy find expression in relation to the formal Victorian Empire?

It has been most persuasively argued, by Professor Knaplund,[2] that the Gladstonian philosophy when brought to bear on the duties of imperial relations, on trusteeship and on the problems of colonial self-government, foreshadowed the formation of the 'Commonwealth of Nations'. Indeed he has depicted Gladstone in the noble rôle of 'creator' of this Commonwealth: a loose grouping of nation-states whose potential for good placed it in the category of a far-flung 'concert of states', acting in unison for the cause of liberty, democracy and progress.

On paper this argument has a forceful logic. Gladstone himself claimed late in his life that he had been moved by the same beliefs on colonial and foreign matters throughout the sixty years of his public career. The record apparently supports him.

[1] Idem. (My italics.)
[2] Paul Knaplund, *Gladstone and Britain's Imperial Policy* (1927) (new impression, London, 1966).

In May 1835, soon after he resigned as Parliamentary Secretary to the Colonies, he jotted down his own private thoughts on the future basis of ties of the Empire. 'The reins will be relaxed', he wrote, 'then removed, in the progress of years. They will launch into the world as free agents. . . .'[1] Eventual colonial self-rule was Gladstone's ideal. 'By vigour, and energy of character, our establishments have everywhere an expansive influence. Shall it be for the misery or happiness of mankind? for the glory of God, or in aid of the purposes of His adversaries?'[2] These thoughts were still prominent twenty years later when Gladstone spoke at length on 'Our Colonies', at Chester, in 1855: 'Experience has proved that if you want to strengthen the connection between the colonies of this country . . . never associate with them the hated name of force and coercion exercised by us, at a distance, over their rising fortunes.' He could be speaking of the Irish when he stated of the colonies, also at Chester—'Govern them upon a principle of freedom—let them not feel any yoke upon their necks—let them understand that the relations between you and them are relations of affection.' His remarks also foreshadowed his stand on Irish Home Rule: 'The affairs of the colonies are best transacted and provided for by the colonists themselves, as the affairs of England are best transacted by Englishmen.'[3]

Gladstone pulled these strands together in his first great Irish Home Rule speech of 1886; and which closely mirror his jottings of fifty years before:

> The principle that I am laying down I am not laying down exceptionally for Ireland. It is the very principle upon which . . . we have not only altered, but revolutionised our method of governing the colonies. . . . I had the honour to hold office in the Colonial Department . . . 51 years ago; England tried to pass good laws for the Colonies, at that period; but the Colonies said—'We do not want your good laws; we want our own'. We admitted the reasonableness of that principle and it is now coming home to us from across the seas. . . . I do not believe that local patriotism is evil.[4]

[1] W. E. Gladstone, 'Colonies and Colonisation'. Unpublished article, quoted in full in Knaplund, *Gladstone's Imperial Policy*, pp. 185–227.
[2] Idem.   [3] Idem.
[4] Speech in Commons, 8 April 1886. *Hansard*, 3rd ser., CCIV, col. 1082.

It was a noble vision; and ultimately a more reasonable one than suggested by any of his contemporaries. But by placing together these question of imperial and Irish relations, Gladstone did not so much provide a cogent exposition of his views, as partly blur the issues, and obscure what had been his actions in that regard, in earlier decades. Gladstone's conduct towards the Empire was, in fact, a supreme case of his political philosophy in action, *coupled* with his sense of pragmatism. His attitude to the 'second British Empire' gradually evolved: but it was broadly the same in 1880 as in 1835; and it was directly influenced by his understanding of the failure of the 'first British Empire'—the American colonies—and by his broadening liberalism.

Gladstone's rôle in relation to the Empire indeed was both more complex and more pragmatic than Professor Knaplund might allow. Gladstone started from the premise that the Empire was not to exist forever: the lesson of the Americas was ever before him. In essence he took a pessimistic view of the Empire —including the Indian Empire—and saw it as a temporary aberration in England's destiny. It made sense to treat the colonies with sensitivity for two good reasons: one, it would avoid another war of American independence, which Gladstone saw as quite needless; two, having acquired the Empire, it was clearly to be well governed—Gladstone's political morality would not allow otherwise.

But, it was *not* to be extended: he could conclude a long speech on foreign affairs at Leeds in 1881 with the apparently contradictory statement—'And so gentlemen I say that while we are opposed to imperialism, we are devoted to the empire'.[1] This distinction which Gladstone drew between existing 'Empire'—where he presumed the ethics of Christianity and liberty lay at the basis of colonial administration—and the spirit of 'imperialism'—the conquering of foreign peoples and the annexation of their lands—he took to be axial. He strongly objected to what he called the 'new form of jingoism', which seemed to him to imply a general scramble to annex any and every piece of land, the moment a foreign nation showed

---

[1] Speech at Leeds, 7 October 1881. Quoted in Magnus, *Gladstone*, p. 287. It is strange that Magnus misreads the significance of this significant remark, p. 286.

any interest in it—be it New Guinea, New Hebrides, or new Africa.

The ideal that Gladstone held up of Empire was the Greek not the Roman example. The idea of a closely organised and administered group of colonies—an extended 'Greater Britain' —left him cold. He rebelled against the 'Roman' concept. Instead he found in Homer an empire of which he could approve: self-governing, self-supporting, self-defending, democratic colonies, bound only by the tie of allegiance to the former mother-country. That was the ideal. Gladstone held it aloft as the example—then adapted it. The very fact that he continued to speak of 'colonies', rather than of 'nations' when expounding on the Empire, hints at his deeper, almost instinctive, and certainly pragmatic approach to relations with the peoples of Canada, South Africa, Australia, New Zealand, and India. Much could be written of his theory of colonies and colonisation, but it is here sufficient to note that Gladstone in essence failed to mould the Empire on the Hellenic pattern. His critics will see this as yet another sign of his subtle 'duplicity', his extravagant but fruitless use of words. The answer is rather more simple: while the Hellenic concept was the ideal to Gladstone the classical scholar, it was soon apparent to Gladstone, the disciple of Bentham, that it was too lofty and impractical an ideal. His attitude ultimately came to this: in an age when 'colonial separatism' was a live issue, Gladstone was quite prepared to see the colonies of white settlement take their independence in a sense of friendship; but if those same colonies desired to remain within the Empire they must contribute towards its continued existence. Their provision of 'closed' markets for British goods was, to Gladstone, a small matter in an age when Britain was playing from strength in the economic field. Until the 1880s the Victorians could out-produce and out-sell all their competitors in a free-trading market. Gladstone, with his family background of overseas trade, with his financial training under Peel, and his conversion to free-trade under the pressure of expediency at the Board of Trade, could see all this better than most men of his age. India aside, the formal empire of administration and colonisation held out no allure to him. Thus his response to the colonies was, not unexpectedly, one of 'firm benevolence'. He would not drive them from the imperial fold—

as was sometimes suspected of his close associate Granville—but he found few reasons overtly to try and hold that Empire together, if this implied a heavy drain on the treasury. In short, Gladstone placed Britain and British interests before local concerns and interests. Most recently Professor Ward has provided an excellent and lucid illustration of Gladstone's refusal to live up to the Hellenic ideal in relation to the colonies in the Pacific: 'Gladstone never understood Australia and had strangely defective notions concerning Britain's duty to her colonies.'[1] Much the same could be applied to the other colonies. For at root Gladstone was concerned not with Britain's duty to her colonies, but of the duties of those colonies to the Empire. He favoured self-government for the same reasons as he favoured the withdrawal of the garrisons: it would economize on administrative costs, while at the same time conciliating the desires of colonial ministers to be their own masters.

This policy ultimately had its limits; and it is intriguing to note that it was Gladstone who reacted most violently against it, when the policy came full circle, and when the colonies began to exercise that freedom of self-government that he had so proudly vaunted. The trouble arose over many small issues from Church matters to problems of native policy; but, it came to a head in that crucial and symbolic issue, tariffs. The colonies, notably Canada and later New South Wales, accepted their self-government at face value, and presumed that this meant that they could legislate for their own economic well-being. This, in practice, often meant rejecting free-trade, and erecting systems of protective tariffs, many of which would discriminate against British goods in favour of other suppliers. Gladstone was furious. He opposed the Canadian attempt; and fought the Australians to a standstill.[2] This was in line with his unspoken belief—as is extensively illustrated below in connection with the Boers—of implying *internal* self-government when he referred to 'responsible government'. At heart he still believed that the colonies were children: they could be given freedom, but it must be within the imperial framework. Their freedom lay *within* the Empire: they were not to deal with the

---

[1] John Ward, *Empire in the Antipodes—the British in Australia, 1840–60* (London, 1968), pp. 39–40.
[2] P. Knaplund, *Gladstone's Imperial Policy*, pp. 49–51, 103–21, 247–50.

outside world without reference to the mother-country and the imperial Parliament. Symbolically Gladstone pressed hard for a clear, if quite impractical definition in Anglo-colonial relations, between matters which were exclusively 'local' (i.e. pertaining to the colonial ministry), and those which he wished to reserve to the imperial metropolitan power. The alternative, in his eyes, was separation: either you were in the Empire, with all the implied obligations, or you were not. The concept of the modern Commonwealth—of free co-existing nation-states, including even republics, fixing their own tariffs, negotiating their own aid programmes, making foreign alliances, and meeting in Marlborough House to pontificate on the nature of Britain's rôle in the world—are all certainly alien to the Empire which Gladstone, in his less rhetorical moments, actually envisaged, and worked towards.

If Gladstone looks least successful, and appears most devious, in relation to the colonies and the Empire, it was in no small part due to the extended nature of his political career: he had known Wellington and he was to advise Lloyd George. The legacy of his pronouncements on the nature of liberty and on self-determination, began to catch up with him. It was all very well to talk idealistically of an Hellenic-like empire in an age when the colonies were so weak that it mattered little whether they were self-governing or not: the effect was the same. His career, though, witnessed a great economic growth, to an unimagined strength on the part of several colonies, notably Canada and South Africa—both of which, significantly for the future, contained a large element of non-British stock among the settlers. From the 1870s onwards the empire of colonisation demanded new techniques in handling the old imperial relations: Gladstone offered no more than continued doses of the old mixture, promises and talk of ultimate freedom, held in check by the practical demands which he placed on the backs of the colonial ministries. Guizot had once shocked Gladstone by remarking on the oppressive quality of English rule in Ireland at a time when Gladstone was filled with righteous indignation about 'oppression' in Europe. Now it was time to remind Gladstone of the same lesson in an imperial context: he could surely no longer deny to the Empire what he had been striving for in Europe.

THE COLOSSUS OF WORDS.

₊ Mr. Gladstone's first electoral campaign in Midlothian was a marvellous feat of physical energy and oratorical power, lasting upwards of a week, during which he delivered numberless speeches.

Or could he? The change was slow and painful, for Gladstone held no view lightly. In 1873 he was still fighting the Australian Customs Duties Bill; at the same time he was 'forcing' responsible government on the Cape. A decade later, in the Pretoria and London Conventions (with the Transvaal Boers), he was still finding methods of granting local self-government with one hand, and seeing that it was suitably circumscribed with the other. It appeared that his famous 'doctrine of nationality' was, like his theory of foreign intervention, and his concept of liberty, 'selective'. Many would be called but few would be chosen.

2. *Midlothian Promises*

In the 90,000 words of his great Midlothian speeches Gladstone not only launched a broadside on the Disraeli administration—'the worst and most immoral minister since Castlereagh'—he also presented the electors with a surprisingly cogent and lucid extraction of his traditional tenets of foreign and imperial policy conveniently reduced to six basic principles:

1 'The first thing is to foster the strength of the Empire by just legislation and economy at home, thereby producing two of the great elements of national power—namely, wealth, which is a physical element, and union and contentment, which are moral elements. . . .'

2 'My second principle of foreign policy is this: that its aim ought to be to preserve to the nations of the world . . . especially the Christian nations of the world, the blessings of peace. . . .'

3 'In my opinion the third sound principle is this: to strive to cultivate and maintain, ay, to the very uttermost, what is called the Concert of Europe. . . . Because by keeping all in union together you neutralise and fetter and bind up the selfish aims of each. . . .'

4 'My fourth principle is—that you should avoid needless and entangling engagements. . . . It comes to this, that you are increasing your engagements without increasing your strength.

5 'My fifth principle is this, gentlemen, to acknowledge the equal rights of all nations . . . if you claim for yourself a superiority over the whole of them, then I say you may talk about patriotism if you please, but you are a misjudging friend of your country. . . .'

6 'Let me give you a sixth, and then I have done . . . the foreign

policy of England should always be inspired by the love of freedom . . . a desire to give it scope, founded not upon visionary ideas,
but upon the long experience of many generations within the
shores of this happy isle. . . .'[1]

Moving from the general to the particular Gladstone was able
to indulge in his two favourite political predilections, pillory-
ing Disraeli for his policy of 'aggrandisement'; and plotting a
course of retrenchment abroad, and economy at home. *Punch*,
in a memorable cartoon,[2] portrayed Gladstone as the 'Colossus',
astride the harbour entrance, guiding in the 'ship of reform',
by the twin beacon lights of 'foreign policy' and 'finance'. Gladstone was at his searing best when castigating Disraeli's insensi-
tive imperialism—pursued for the sake of 'false phantoms of
glory'. That spirit had gloried in the annexation of Cyprus—'a
valueless encumbrance'. It had condoned the wanton invasion of
Afghanistan; it had involved Britain in a virtual protectorate,
with France, over Egypt—sheer 'financial profligacy'; it had
assumed the impossible task of heavy commitments in Turkey—
'a gross and manifest breach of the public law of Europe'; and
it had pursued a pointless war against the Zulu people—
'What was the crime of the Zulus? . . . no other offence than
their attempt to defend against your artillery with their naked
bodies, their hearth and homes, their wives and families. . . .'[3]

The campaign soon began to generate its own heat. Lady
Frederick Cavendish found Gladstone for the first time, 'a little
personally elated'. As the crowds increased in size and fervour,
Gladstone struck out even more wildly at Disraeli—now stigma-
tised as having endangered 'all the most fundamental interests
of Christian society'. Over twenty thousand people stood in the
chill of mid-winter awaiting him at one market town. 'All
Scotland is panting for a look at him,' his daughter wrote in her
journal.[4] Huge torchlight processions swirled through the winter
nights in Scottish towns fêting Gladstone. Disraeli, with cold

---

[1] W. E. Gladstone, *Political Speeches in Scotland, March and April 1880* (rev.
edn., Edinburgh, 1880), I, 115–17.

[2] *Punch*, 13 December 1879. (See p. 51.)

[3] All Midlothian quotations from Magnus, *Gladstone*, pp. 261–70, Morley,
Gladstone, II, book VII, chap. 6, pp. 592 ff. and 605; and W. E. Gladstone,
Speeches in Scotland, pp. 97, 98, 134–41, 334.

[4] Magnus, *Gladstone*, p. 264.

disdain, dubbed it 'a pilgrimage of passion'.[1] To Gladstone, however, it now became 'a festival of freedom'. He preached his creed of consolidation and reform, which alone would lead 'a free and high-minded people towards the blessed ends of prosperity and justice, of liberty and peace'.[2]

Like some great Old Testament prophet, Gladstone willingly took upon himself the rôle of interpreter of the 'Law' to the people. He raised the question of the status and future of the Transvaal Boers as one of those seminal issues of principle at stake. He saw in the annexation of the Afrikaner Republic, in 1877, the classic example of Disraeli's interfering, and morally unjustifiable imperialism, at work. It had all the hall-marks of Tory jingoism flowering into aggrandisement. As Gladstone explained, Britain had brought a free European Christian republic under the Crown, although 6500 of the 8000 male inhabitants had been against the act.[3] Gladstone's biographer has attempted to make light of his old master's promises to the Transvaal Boers,[4] so as to justify Gladstone's later inactivity. But it will not wash. Gladstone may not have categorically pledged himself to reverse the annexation, but his condemnation of the act was blistering and complete. The Transvaal, Gladstone stated explicitly, was a country 'where we have chosen most unwisely, I am tempted to say insanely, to place ourselves in the strange predicament of the free subjects of a monarchy going to coerce the free subjects of a republic, and to compel them to accept a citizenship which they decline and refuse. . . .'[5] Gladstone committed himself by this condemnation; and in these concluding plain words: 'If Cyprus and the Transvaal were as valuable as they are valueless, I would still repudiate them because they are obtained by means dishonourable to the character of the country.'[6]

Out on the *veld* Kruger was perhaps too optimistic in seeing the hand of providence at work—in the completion of tele-

[1] Idem.   [2] Ibid., pp. 264–5.

[3] Gladstone based his figures not on any referendum held at the time of annexation—Shepstone had conducted his opinion poll 'informally'—but rather on the first of the Transvaal petitions presented a year after the annexation in 1878. See De Kiewiet, *Imperial Factor*, pp. 210–11; and D. W. Kruger, *Paul Kruger*, I, 170 ff.

[4] Morley, *Gladstone*, III, 27.

[5] Gladstone, *Speeches in Scotland*, I, 63.   [6] Idem.

graphic communication from England in September 1879[1]—
which allowed the relay of Gladstone's words in a matter of
days to the farthest-flung Boer homestead. But he was not
unjustified in believing that he had found in Gladstone a British
statesman more than sympathetic to the demands of his people,
for the return of their political freedom, and their republican
status.[2] Just as Gladstone had once championed the cause of the
Montenegrins, so now it appeared to contemporaries that his
beneficence was about to be bestowed on another minority, the
Transvaal Boers, the *Trekkers* of old. In South Africa Gladstone's
words undoubtedly had an electric effect. The haughty Kruger
was moved to praise an Englishman.[3] He never lapsed again.

The complexities of the English parliamentary process were
beyond Kruger: he waited impatiently for Gladstone's return
to power, and the consequent retrocession of the Republic. His
impatience grew with the months. The elections of 1880 were
spread over a leisurely fortnight, and it was not until 7 April
that a Liberal victory was assured. 'The triumph grows and
grows,' noted Gladstone, 'to God be praise.'[4] Officially Gladstone had resigned the leadership of the Liberal Party in 1875,
and accordingly Disraeli advised Queen Victoria, on 18 April,
to send for Lord Hartington, Liberal leader in the Commons.
Kruger was puzzled by the political manoeuvres that now
occurred. He had assumed that Gladstone was the automatic
choice, having led the campaign, if unofficially. But on 22 April
the Queen sent for Hartington. The latter declined to take high
office without Gladstone as a member of the ministry. However,
Gladstone refused to accept subordinate office. 'At once his
accession to the highest became inevitable.'[5] On the evening of
23 April 1880 Gladstone became Premier by the will of the
people, but much against the will of the people's sovereign.[6]

[1] *Parl. Pap.*, 1880, LI, C.2584, pp. 209–11. Wolseley to Hicks Beach
enclosing Lanyon's speech opening Transvaal 'Legislative Assembly'.

[2] Professor D. W. Kruger, not unjustly expresses the Afrikaner view of the
annexation, as being a 'politieke flater deur 'n onderskikte omptenaar in die
naam van Haar Majesteit'. And the effects of the annexation as even more
disastrous: 'Die ou wonde wat byna genees was, is daardeur her open.' See
D. W. Kruger, *Paul Kruger*, I, 188.

[3] Ibid., p. 191.   [4] Magnus, *Gladstone*, p. 270.

[5] R. C. K. Ensor, *England 1870–1914* (new edn., 1960), p. 66.

[6] Ponsonby to Granville, 23 April 1880. P.R.O. 30/29/37.

Kruger had prayed for this moment. Victoria had dreaded it. 'The Queen', she wrote to Ponsonby, her secretary,[1] 'will sooner *abdicate* than have anything to do with that *half-mad firebrand* who will soon ruin everything and be a *Dictator*.'[2] But the inevitable had then taken place. The old 'spell-binder' was back in office. 'I am stunned,' remarked Gladstone, 'but God will provide.'

The fall of Disraeli was a joy to Kruger, a disaster to Victoria. She took cold comfort in writing to her favourite: 'Mr. Gladstone looks ill, very old and haggard, and his voice feeble.'[3] Gladstone's Journal would have dashed her hopes of his early retirement: 'I do believe the Almighty has employed me for His purposes, in a manner larger, or more special than before, and has strengthened me, and led me on accordingly.'[4]

In Africa the impatience of the Transvalers knew no bounds. As Gladstone went through the ritual of Cabinet making,[5] the temperature in South African politics rose. Hopes that had been kindled by the Midlothian speeches meant that his first actions were eagerly awaited. By 29 April, when Parliament met, Kimberley had become Colonial Secretary, Granville Foreign Secretary, with Childers at the War Office, Hartington in charge of Indian affairs, Harcourt at the Home Office, Chamberlain heading the lowly Board of Trade, and Gladstone both First Lord of the Treasury and Chancellor of the Exchequer.[6] The Cabinet soon settled into office, meeting for the first time on

---

[1] Ponsonby (after 1879) Sir Henry Frederick (1825–95): Major-General, 1868; Private Secretary to Queen Victoria, 1870–95.

[2] Queen Victoria to Sir Henry Ponsonby, 4 April 1880. See also Arthur Ponsonby, *Life and Letters of Sir Henry Ponsonby* (London, 1942), p. 184. Ponsonby to Queen Victoria, 15 April, p. 187.

[3] Queen Victoria to Disraeli. Quoted in Magnus, *Gladstone*, p. 273.

[4] Morley, *Gladstone*, III, 1.

[5] Addit. MSS. 48630, f. 1 (Hamilton Diaries). Entry for Saturday, 24 April. 'Cabinet meeting has been going on all day. . . .' On the Cabinet itself, see entry for Thursday, 29 April. 'A strong and representative Cabinet. . . .' f. 2. *Punch*, 8 May 1880, had a splendid cartoon of Gladstone as the 'old carpenter' busy 'cabinet-making'. The Queen is viewing his work and saying: 'I see most of it is well seasoned—let us hope the new wood will stand well.' As Chamberlain was the only major newcomer, it is a particularly barbed remark.

[6] See Biographical Notes at the back of this volume.

CABINET-MAKING.

HEAD CARPENTER.—"I HOPE YOUR MAJESTY LIKES THE NEW CABINET. IT'S BEEN HARD WORK—SUCH A QUANTITY OF MATERIAL!"

THE QUEEN.—"I SEE MOST OF IT IS WELL SEASONED—LET US HOPE THE NEW WOOD WILL STAND WELL!"

. Mr. Gladstone was called upon to form a Ministry. His Cabinet included Mr. Chamberlain, who was then the leading representative of Radicalism, and who was appointed President of the Board of Trade.

Monday, 3 May,[1] and five times again that month[2]—although the Gladstones did not move into Downing Street until Wednesday, 12 May.[3] But there was no word on the Transvaal. Kruger's patience ran out. On 10 May, in conjunction with Commandant Joubert, Kruger despatched a stiff letter to the Liberal Premier, from Cape Town, reminding him of his promises. The burghers of the Transvaal, Kruger wrote, had ever hoped,

> that one day or another, by the mercy of the Lord, the reins of the Imperial Government would be entrusted again to men, who look out for the honour and glory of England, not by acts of injustice and crushing force, but by the way of justice and good faith. And indeed this belief has [now] proven to be a good belief. . . .[4]

Accordingly, Kruger trusted that Gladstone would 'feel at liberty to rescind the Annexation of our poor country and to reinstate in its full vigour the Treaty of Sand River. . . .'[5]

Two days after this letter was written (12 May), the Liberal Cabinet decided to bury as embarrassing their leaders' Midlothian oratory, and to retain the Transvaal, in the hope of realising the long-standing dream of a united South African federation under the British flag.[6] Little wonder Gladstone passed Kruger's letter on to Kimberley when it arrived, with a pencilled note to the effect that he was at a loss as to how to answer it.[7]

The decision was publicly announced in the Queen's Speech on 20 May 1880.[8] But Gladstone did not reply to Kruger until late in June. A letter was finally sent on 8 June over his name, although it was written by the Colonial Office staff, having been

---

[1] Addit. MSS. 44642, f.2 (Cabinet Papers), 3 May 1881. See also Hamilton's Diary. Addit. MSS. 48630, f. 9. Entry for Tuesday, 4 May 1880.

[2] Cabinet meetings on 3, 5, 12, 14, 17, 22 and 29 May, (1881). Addit. MSS. 44642 (Cabinet Papers), ff. 2, 5, 8, 12, 18, 20 and 21.

[3] Addit. MSS. 48630, f. 13 (Hamilton Diary). Entry for Wednesday, 12 May 1880.

[4] Addit. MSS. 44644, f. 97. Kruger (and Joubert) to Gladstone, 10 May 1880 (Gladstone Papers). See also *Parl. Pap.*, 1880, LI, C.2675, p. 46 (a).

[5] Ibid.

[6] Addit. MSS. 44642, f. 8 (Cabinet Papers), Wednesday, 12 May 1880.

[7] Addit. MSS. 44644 f. 97. Minute by Gladstone on Kruger to Gladstone, 10 May 1880.

[8] *Hansard*, 3rd ser., CCLII, 20 May 1880.

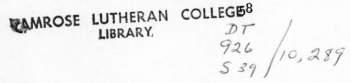

based largely on a confidential memorandum drawn up by Kimberley on 6 June.[1] Gladstone amended it mildly on 15 June, then signed it.[2] The letter is a polemic in political double-talk. In among the qualifying clauses, though, we find the two central issues. First the decision: '. . . . our judgement is that the Queen cannot be advised to relinquish her sovereignty over the Transvaal.' Then the logic behind the decision: 'We have to deal with a state of things which has existed for a considerable period, during which obligations have been contracted, especially though not exclusively, towards the native population which cannot be set aside.' Finally, imperial intentions: 'We desire that the white inhabitants of the Transvaal should, without prejudice to the rest of the population, enjoy the fullest liberty to manage their local affairs.'[3] This liberty 'can be most easily and promptly conceded to the Transvaal as a member of a South African confederation'.[4]

The decision took many observers by surprise—not only in the Boer camp, but in official circles as well. Wolseley, whose despatch of 13 December played a key rôle in the decision, had

[1] Addit. MSS. 44225, ff. 180–81. Memorandum by Kimberley, sent to Gladstone, 6 June 1880.

[2] Addit. MSS. 44464, f. 219. Gladstone to Kruger, 15 June 1880, enclosed in Gladstone to Frere, 24 June 1880.

[3] *Ibid.*, Gladstone to Kruger, 15 June 1880.

[4] Addit. MSS. 44225, ff. 180–81. Memorandum by Kimberley, 6 June 1880. It is interesting to compare the final letter with Kimberley's memorandum: '. . . whilst it is undoubtedly a matter for much regret that it should since the annexation have appeared that so large a number of the population of Dutch origin in the Transvaal are opposed to the annexation, it is impossible now to consider the question as if it were presented for the first time; that we have to deal with a state of things which has now existed for three years, a considerable time, during which obligations have been contracted especially towards the native population, which cannot be set aside; that looking to all circumstances both of the Transvaal and the rest of South Africa, to the serious sacrifice which this country has made in order to restore peace and order in and near the Transvaal and to the necessity of preventing a renewal of disorders, which might lead to disastrous consequences not only to the Transvaal, but to the whole of S. Africa, we had come to the conclusion that the Queen cannot be advised to relinquish her Sovereignty over the Transvaal; we desire that the white inhabitants of the Transvaal should enjoy fullest liberty to manage their own local affairs, and . . . this liberty may be promptly conceded to the Transvaal as a member of a South African Confederation.'

been personally sceptical of 'this triumph'. As he explained to his wife early in April: 'Gladstone and party would not . . . fight for the Isle of Wight if it were taken possession of by the enemy. They would find fifty reasons for concurring in the policy of masterly inactivity and some would . . . express great astonishment at it having been left so long in our possession.'[1] While Kruger's displeasure rose, the Queen was being increasingly mollified by the unexpected behaviour of her Liberal ministry; for on 12 May Gladstone had informed her, they would 'uphold the sovereignty of the British Crown in the Transvaal, but will be desirous to bestow upon it, at the earliest period, the gift of free institutions'. The qualifying factor for the grant of these 'free institutions' was the decisive instructions to Sir Bartle Frere, 'to promote Confederation and to avoid measures tending to advancement of the Frontiers'.[2]

Yet another Cabinet had found the attraction of federation too great to ignore. The prospect of cutting expenses, and responsibility, proved irresistible to Liberal and Conservative ministries alike. Gladstone now behaved as if there had not been a decade of failure in trying to impose an artificial unity on the centrifugal forces of South African politics. In looking to a federation, as the panacea for rule, he may have been returning to the traditional policy of the last decade, but he was also placing ill-founded faith in a concept long dead in the eyes of both colonists and republicans. It was to be a futile attempt to induce a corpse to march.

3. The Prophet in Action: Gladstone and Federation

Gladstone's private notes for the Cabinet of Wednesday, 12 May 1880, read simply: 'South Africa—to promote Confederation. Transvaal—retain sovereignty.'[3] From the moment this decision was taken, two results became inescapable. It was to be the *coup de grâce* for all federal proposals and hopes; and the immediate cause of the Transvaal rebellion that began in December

[1] Wolseley to wife, 11 April 1880. Quoted in Giles St. Aubyn, *The Royal George* . . ., p. 192.

[2] *Letters of Queen Victoria*, 2nd ser., III, 99. Gladstone to Queen, 12 May 1880.

[3] Addit. MSS. 44642, f. 8 (Cabinet Papers), 12 May 1880, 2 p.m.

1880. Only later was the irony to strike Gladstone that he hoped to avoid both these specific contingencies by embarking upon this policy.

Pragmatism rather than morality had guided the Cabinet in its thinking. The stress on 'obligations'—to the natives and to the loyalists in the Transvaal—was taken up after the Cabinet decision, as a useful justification which was ready to hand. Kimberley revealed the truth about the Cabinet's real intentions, when he remarked to Gladstone, that this policy would help Britain to 'escape from some of our embarrassments'.[1] Federation was to be the means to this end; a device to provide the smoke-screen necessary while the Liberal Government abandoned those very obligations set out so righteously in Parliament, and in the Gladstone–Kruger correspondence.

The immediate and obvious basis for the decision was an important confidential memorandum drawn up by the Colonial Office, and submitted to the Cabinet, specifically for its meeting of 12 May.[2] It was written by Edward Fairfield, but in fact mirrors not his opinion, but that of his departmental chief, Robert Herbert, the permanent under-secretary.[3] Herbert had been deeply involved in all the federal schemes, and was an energetic apostle of the 'confederation school' in colonial circles. He favoured holding the Transvaal, for the creation of a federation without the Boer republics would have been a hollow victory. Herbert was not propagating any philosophy of expansion.[4] Rather he too saw in federation an escape from South African burdens and responsibilities. The memorandum skilfully presented the most influential case possible—an apparently unbiased non-argumentative laying out of the facts. It was to prove irresistible to a Cabinet that was not altogether cognisant of the intricacies of Anglo-Boer relations in the Transvaal. In an

---

[1] Addit. MSS. 44225, f. 171. Kimberley to Gladstone. Undated, but very probably 24 or 25 May 1880.

[2] C.O. 879/17. Confidential Prints, African No. 217: 'Transvaal', by Edward Fairfield, 5 May 1880.

[3] Fairfield personally favoured retrocession. See his numerous minutes in C.O. 48/494–6.

[4] The *C.H.B.E.* fails to understand the 'consolidationist' beliefs of Herbert, and quite incorrectly labels him as the 'first expansionist under-secretary'. See *C.H.B.E.*, III, 744.

impartial tone Fairfield discussed these relations. He admitted that Transvaal dislike for annexation had been 'growing more and more intense', and that this opposition had expressed itself in two petitions to the Colonial Office since 1877, and in a deputation of Cape politicians to Sir Bartle Frere at the Cape in November 1879. But there was no urgency in its tone. He noted a 'certain amount' of discontent, which only existed 'up to a certain point'; while Kruger's various missions of protest to England were not even deemed worthy of discussion.[1] The memorandum ended with more questions than fears—and these questions are all answered in the documentary appendices to the memorandum; in particular, by Sir Garnet Wolseley's despatch of 13 November 1879 from the Transvaal, arguing forcibly and at great length for the retention of the Republic.[2]

This Wolseley despatch—received in the Colonial Office on 27 December 1879[3]—left a deep mark. Wolseley's flat military prose added the effect of cool astute reasoning to his grim warnings of the dangers of a British abandonment of the Transvaal. Wolseley dismissed the Afrikaner leaders, such as Kruger and Joubert, as mere 'designing men', intent on subverting British power by appealing to their fellow Boers' 'instinctive dislike of English rule and the English race generally'. Kruger had easily whipped up feeling against the annexation, for, Wolseley claimed, 'the Boers are essentially the most ignorant people [and] easily led . . .' The dangers of abandoning the semi-civilised farmers far outweighed those incipient in the maintenance of British authority. The position in the Transvaal gave promise of better things to come. Disorder had been put down; bankruptcy had been adverted by the regular collection of taxes; and public credit had even revived.[4] Further than that, gold and other minerals were known to exist and it required only one good gold discovery to bring a large English popula-

[1] C.O. 879/17. Confidential Prints, Africans No. 217, Memorandum by Fairfield, 5 May 1880.
[2] Addit. MSS. 44624, f. 85. Appendix, p. 11, to Memorandum by Fairfield.
[3] Ibid., Wolseley to Hicks Beach, 13 November 1879.
[4] Wolseley very largely based his opinions on the reports of Sir Owen Lanyon. See the latter's speech opening the Transvaal Legislative Assembly on Wednesday, 10 March 1880. *Parl. Pap.*, 1880, LI, C.2584, pp. 209–11. Lanyon to Wolseley, 11 March 1881.

tion there. 'The time must eventually arrive when the Boers will be in a small minority.' Against this Wolseley placed the obvious consequences of abandonment: as there 'can be little doubt in the minds of men who knew the Boers that they are in their present state utterly incapable of governing themselves', it became highly likely that the republic might collapse. This could 'reverse the relative positions occupied by the white man and the native generally throughout Africa, a result that might prove fatal to British interests by giving rise to further native wars.'[1] Add to this the positive factor of acquiring a degree of moral credit, for standing by Britain's 'obligations' to the native tribes, and Wolseley's argument became quite impossible for the economy-minded Cabinet to set aside.

Gladstone readily jettisoned his recently postulated policy as it seemed that if he now turned his back on federation, by abandoning the Transvaal to the Boers, he would be throwing away a golden opportunity to settle the 'unsolvable'. The documents placed before the Cabinet on 12 May were, however, not alone responsible for this change of heart. A belief had steadily been growing in official circles, since late 1879, that Transvaal hostility to the annexation was waning; and that with patience the sensitive Cape could be coaxed into accepting a federation. The Colonial Office files clearly show this trend of opinion in the process of formation.[2] It is easy now to find fault with this optimism, but with the data that were at their disposal, their attitude was not entirely unreasonable. The reports coming in from the Transvaal—penned by the administrator, Sir Owen Lanyon,[3] and the High Commissioner for South-East Africa, Sir

[1] Addit. MSS. 44624, f. 85. Wolseley to Hicks Beach, 13 November 1879, in Fairfield Memorandum, p. 11 (Appendix).

[2] C.O. 291/4–6. See despatches by Lanyon and Wolseley, and Minutes by Herbert, Mead, Bramston, and Hemming.

[3] LANYON, Sir Owen (1842–87)
born 1842   Ireland, son of civil engineer Sir Charles
      Lanyon—joined British Army—sent to West Indies.
1865   Active in suppressing Jamaica Rising.
4 March 1879   Administrator of Transvaal.
5 August 1881   Dismissed after Pretoria Convention.
1882 and 1883–85   Egyptian expeditions.
1887   Died in New York.
Excitable man, sickly, 'dark skinned', and unpopular with the Transvaal Boers.

Garnet Wolseley[1]—all spoke with a united voice: the Transvaal was being weaned from its old indolent ways. Taxation was seen as a good barometer of Boer feeling, and Lanyon was quick to point out that taxes were being paid in excess of expectations. Revenue for the previous year was already up 16 per cent and would be correspondingly higher in the next tax year. Even the amount collected by the native 'hut tax' was far greater than it had ever been under the Boer régime. Further than that, now that the Sekukuni war had ended, tranquillity reigned on the *veld*. The 'Legislative Assembly'—of Lanyon's nominated men—had not lacked volunteers for office. Government contracts were being rapidly accepted, and many of the older hostile Boers had even accepted employment in the British administration.

Tell-tale signs of a discontent were ignored, or explained away with strange logic. The local administration was not ill-informed of developments in the Transvaal—rather it completely misread the signs of rebellion that were plain for all to see. The most important single blunder was the misreporting of a mass gathering on the farm of M. W. Pretorius in the Wonderfontein district, from 8–11 March 1880. At this meeting a resolution was passed to send Kruger and Joubert to whip up support for the Transvaal cause among the Cape Dutch. Strong speeches were made against the annexation, and prayers were offered that Gladstone would be returned to power in England. The proceedings of this meeting were published in the *Volksstem* and reported to the Colonial Office:[2] but, with this bizarre commentary by Morcom, Her Majesty's Attorney-General in the Transvaal:

> The indolent life led by the Boers in this province lends a charm to the excitement of a public gathering . . . anything that can tend

[1] WOLSELEY, Sir Garnet (1833–1913)

1870 Red River Expedition.
1873 Ashanti War.
1879–81 High Commissioner for South-East Africa.
1882 Egypt.
1884–85 Gordon Relief Expedition.
1890–95 C.-in-C. Ireland.
1895–1900 C.-in-C. British Army.
1894 Field-Marshal.
1913 Died.

[2] *Parl. Pap.*, 1880, LI, C. 2676, p. 28.

to relieve the monotony of their life is eagerly seized by the farmers. *A large gathering has not the significance therefore which it might otherwise have.*[1]

As this report was received in Whitehall on 2 April, it could have been instrumental in producing a radically different policy from that which was followed. However, there was little reason to disbelieve Morcom's apparently detached analysis. It corresponded to Lanyon's optimism, and to Wolseley's cool reasoning. Or, perhaps, the decision reflected a logic no deeper than that suggested by Dilke—'as we were retiring from Kandahar we had better not also retire from Pretoria'.[2]

It should also be admitted that the Colonial Office were already disposed to accept this reasoning. Not merely because their predilections ran to a South African federation, but rather because they had a mistaken image of both the Boer character in general, and of the Boer leaders in particular. Kruger's visits to London, in 1877 and 1878, had done much to build up this false impression. He had arrived as a blustering indignant frontiersman, and left as a polite, and amenable subject of Her Majesty. Kruger's biographers have found his behaviour on these occasions bewildering;[3] his ardent admirers have found it distinctly embarrassing.[4] But it is not so difficult either to justify or to understand. Kruger gave the impression in the Colonial Office of being a 'sensible man', who listened to reason. But then his bargaining position was basically weak. So long as the Transvaal was threatened by a massive Zulu invasion, his fellow Boers found little to interest them in throwing off the British yoke—especially as the Redcoats were fighting the Zulu war for them. Nor could Kruger gain any support in Europe.[5] As he explained to friends at his farm, after the first deputation of 1877

---

[1] C.O. 291/5. Despatch received 2 April 1880. (My italics.)

[2] Addit. MSS. 43934, ff. 198–9 (Dilke Memoir). Monday 24 May 1880; and Gwynne and Tuckwell, *Dilke*, I, 319.

[3] See M. Nathan, *Paul Kruger: His Life and Times*, 4th edn., (Durban, 1944).

[4] D. W. Kruger; *Paul Kruger*, 2 vols. (Johannesburg, 1963).

[5] J. F. Van Oordt, *Paul Kruger en die Opkomst van der Zuid-Afrikaanse Republiek* (Amsterdam, 1935).

the European powers were all '*bang voor de Engelsche goewerment*'.[1] But, as the fate of the Transvaal became brighter with the Zulu defeats, so the pendulum of Boer opinion began to swing away from placid acceptance, to militant rebellion. Kruger returned distinctly forlorn to the Transvaal from his second mission to England and Europe in 1878; and was duly amazed at the change of heart that had come about in his fellow burghers. He had left the Colonial Office more or less resigned to British rule. A mere few months later he was the old fiery, ambitious, and plotting Kruger again.[2] The new spirit of defiance among the people had revived him. But the former image was the one which remained in Whitehall.

The Colonial Office began to believe in the mirage. And it is significant that the advocates of retrenchment—such as Joseph Chamberlain and Edward Fairfield[3]—could not gain the evidence to support their point of view, and had to rely on 'justice' as an argument for abandonment. In this instance 'morality' was not the most influential case that could be pitted against either the reports of the proconsular officials, or the promised charms of federation.

Events now also conspired to force the hands of the Victorians. At the Cape Sir Bartle Frere began to report a distinct restiveness among the Cape politicians, and the Cape Dutch generally.[4] In a long despatch he wrote of a Dutch 'republican movement', a small though 'influential class', which was helping to 'unite the malcontent Boer party in the Transvaal to the local opposition', at the Cape. The dangers from such a movement were not immediately worrying, for 'it is chiefly powerful only in opposition'. But Gladstone's Midlothian proclamations, followed by months of inactivity, were beginning to play havoc with the rising tempo of local politics.

Frere soon stopped writing and began telegraphing. On 3 May 1880 the Colonial Office received this telegram from a very

[1] i.e., 'frightened of the English Government'. D. W. Kruger, *Paul Kruger*, I, 188–94.

[2] Paul Kruger, *Memoirs* (London, 1902), 2 vols. See vol. I (1825–86).

[3] Joseph Chamberlain, *A Political Memoir* (Ed. C. H. D. Howard), (London, 1953), pp. 14–15.

[4] C.O. 48/493. Frere to Hicks Beach, 2 January 1880, Minuted C.O. 27 January 1880.

troubled Frere:[1] 'Uneasiness is caused here by a report of an intention to give up the Transvaal. *The result of abandonment fatal to confederation, and would possibly entail a Civil War in the Transvaal.*' His advice from Cape Town mirrored that of Wolseley, a thousand miles to the north in Pretoria. Unrest, Frere stated emphatically, could only be prevented in one way, '. . . . by an early assurance that the annexation is irrevocable'.[2]

All signs pointed in the same direction, and all authorities, both in Whitehall and out on the *veld*, interpreted these signs in a similar way: hold the Transvaal, treat the Cape generously, then press for federation once more. This overwhelming body of opinion was thrust upon the newly created Gladstone Cabinet by the permanent officials in a united front, before the Liberals had had an opportunity to find their way. They were clearly wavering in intent before the decision of 12 May. At the first Cabinet of 3 May,[3] it was decided to play for time. Frere was to stay at the Cape in a limited capacity—despite loud calls for his dismissal. To have removed him would have been to remove the immediate possibility of federation. He had a stay of execution, until early in August, when he was 'axed'. The longer the Cabinet took to decide, the better were the chances of the permanent officials' policy. Chamberlain alone in the Cabinet, at this very meeting, demanded Frere's recall, and the retrocession of the Transvaal.[4] It was to no avail—although it later gave Chamberlain a stock of political capital to use against the Whig section of the Cabinet, following the disaster of Majuba Hill.

In the Colonial Office, Robert Herbert and the 'confederation school' had found a ready ally in the newly appointed Colonial Secretary, Lord Kimberley. A man of distinct Whig tendencies,[5] he had already seen an earlier confederation attempt of his own flounder in South Africa.[6] Now he could neither resist the opportunity to press it again, nor fail to take advantage of Carnarvon's annexation. He could reap where he had not sown. In the five Cabinet meetings between 3 and 12

[1] C.O. 48/494 (Tel.) Frere to Kimberley, 3 May 1880.
[2] Idem.
[3] Addit. MSS. 44642, f. 2 (Cabinet Papers). 'Frere to continue at Cape. . .'
[4] Joseph Chamberlain, *A Political Memoir*, p. 4. 'I wanted to recall at once Sir Bartle Frere, to reconsider the annexation of the Transvaal. . . .'
[5] H. L. Hall, *The Colonial Office*, (London, 1937), p. 184.
[6] De Kiewiet, *Imperial Factor*, pp. 29 ff.

May Kimberley lobbied his fellow Cabinet ministers, and particularly Gladstone. Accordingly the vital Fairfield Memorandum—and its lengthy appendices—was in so many ways preaching to the converted.

Having taken the decision, the Gladstone government attempted to move with the air of surety. But it was soon having to weather heavy squalls. Liberal back-benchers accepted retention of the Transvaal, but could not see how this justified failure to recall Frere.[1] The issue of Frere's status bedevilled imperial politics for several months,[2] completely obscuring the growing problem in the Transvaal. It was the first severe test of the ministry, and it soon looked very serious. Dilke noted on 24 May in his Journal: 'I found that Courtney and my brother, with Dr. Cameron and Jesse Collings, were getting up an attempt to coerce the Colonial Office and Mr. Gladstone by preparing a list of between one and two hundred members who would vote with Wilfred Lawson for a censure on the Government for not recalling Frere.'[3] Dilke felt that Frere, 'while blameworthy for the Zulu War, was not responsible for the Transvaal business, which had been done by Shepstone and Lord Carnarvon before he went out . . . .'[4]

Gladstone, who began to feel that it was a little early in the ministry to be standing on the burning deck, was tempted to give way and part with Frere. He pondered on the uses of Frere, and wondered aloud if Sir Bartle could 'do more in regard to present and future changes, for us, than any other man?'[5] Kimberley answered his query, and stiffened Gladstone's resolve, with a long private letter.[6] Frere, he explained to Gladstone, 'who was sent out originally for the express purpose of

[1] Addit. MSS. 48630 f.16 (Hamilton Diary). Entry for 21 May 1880. 'Courtney violently attacked the Govt. for (apparently) so flagrant an act of inconsistency. . . .'

[2] Addit. MSS. 48630, f. 17 (Hamilton Diary). Entry for Saturday, 31 May 1880. 'Bradlaugh and Frere have been the main centre of interest during the last week.'

[3] Addit. MSS. 43934, ff. 198–9 (Dilke Memoir), Monday, 24 May 1880.

[4] Idem.

[5] Addit. MSS. 44544, f. 11 (L.B. copy). Gladstone to Kimberley, 24 May 1880.

[6] Addit. MSS. 44225, f. 170. Kimberley to Gladstone. Undated, but very probably 25 May 1880.

effecting Confederation has brought the matter to this point, that a proposal is about to be made for a Conference between the different colonies, and that his recall just at the moment when the Cape Parliament was about to consider this proposal might seriously endanger its success'. Worst of all, it could 'postpone the whole subject to some distant day'. And Gladstone was surely aware of the importance of federation: it would allow Britain to 'escape from some of our embarrassments by the establishment of a federal supreme Government under the Queen, which will manage native and frontier affairs, leaving the ordinary local administration to the provincial governments'. A postponement 'would be disastrous. We want to know whether Confederation is practical or not, and to know it soon, that if not we may consider in what way the affairs of South Africa are to be settled.'[1]

But, to the deep embarrassment of the Government—and Kimberley in particular—their sharpest critics were to be found within the fold of the Liberal Party. Leonard Courtney had already walked out on a 'Transvaal division' in the House. In June 1880 he began to muster discontented back-benchers.[2] The much abused Frere was chosen as their target; to Courtney he personified the Carnarvon policy.[3] Recall of Frere could lead to a collapse of the federal policy, which in turn could result in the reversal of the annexation. Courtney recruited Dilke and Chamberlain into his pressure group,[4] and the campaign against the unfortunate proconsul took on a new ferocity.[5] By 3 June they had collected over ninety signatures from Liberal M.P.s, in favour of a motion which stated that —'as there is a strong feeling throughout the country in favour of the recall of Sir Bartle Frere, it would greatly conduce to the unity of the party and relieve many members from the charge of breaking their pledges to their constituents if that step were taken.'[6] Within the Cabinet the matter was taken up by Chamberlain,

[1] Idem.

[2] G. P. Gooch, *Life of Courtney*, pp. 153–4.

[3] See Courtney in Commons, 31 August 1880. *Hansard*, 3rd ser., CCLVI, cols. 840–56.

[4] Addit. MSS. 43934, ff. 198–9 (Dilke Memoir), Monday, 24 May 1880.

[5] Gwynne and Tuckwell, *Dilke*, I, 319; and Garvin, *Chamberlain*, I, 439.

[6] Addit. MSS. 44624, f. 105. Memorial dated 4 June 1880.

and, if for different reasons, Harcourt[1] and Kimberley.[2] The Colonial Secretary disliked and distrusted Frere. 'It is inconceivable to me', Kimberley had written of Frere's activities in South Africa, 'that a Governor of Sir B. Frere's undoubted abilities could have lent his support to such blundering as he appears to have done.'[3] Harcourt's motives were purer. 'My opinion against the policy of annexation is as strong as ever,' he told Gladstone.[4] Chamberlain made out the best case against the policy for which Frere stood. 'I doubt the wisdom and the permanence of the annexation,' he informed the Premier on 9 June. 'Unless some unforeseen circumstances lead to a large immigration of Englishmen into the Transvaal, I believe the Boers will, sooner or later, worry this country into granting their independence.'[5]

The official reactions to these internal rumblings of discontent were neither noble nor satisfying. Frere was not immediately recalled, nor did Kimberley defend his servant. Instead Frere was informed that his salary was to be cut by a third: he was to lose his 'expenses supplement' of £2,500 p.a.[6] The reason given by Kimberley was that as Colley had been appointed High Commissioner for South-East Africa there was a diminution of Frere's duties, and thus the Government 'have come to the conclusion that they could not justify the continuance of your special allowance'.[7] The crudity of the explanation was matched only by Kimberley's later letter of recall. Frere was thus first financially ruined by the Colonial Office,[8] and

---

[1] Harcourt had been much against the annexation of the Transvaal from the start. He had coined the phrase 'prancing proconsuls' in March 1879, to characterise Frere's behaviour in South Africa. Gardiner, *Harcourt*, I, 350.

[2] Addit. MSS. 44225, f. 178. Kimberley to Gladstone, 29 May 1880.

[3] C.O. 48/495. Frere to Kimberley, 7 September 1880. Minute by Kimberley, 4 October 1880.

[4] Addit. MSS. 44196, f. 64. Harcourt to Gladstone, 8 June 1880.

[5] Addit. MSS. 44125, f. 30. Chamberlain to Gladstone, 9 June 1880. Printed in part in Garvin, *Chamberlain*, I, 439.

[6] Carnarvon had specially granted Frere this allowance, to supplement the Cape Governor's salary of £5,000 p.a., in order to get him to take the post He had also strongly hinted at a peerage. See Martineau, *Life of Frere*, II, 392–4.

[7] *Parl. Pap.*, 1880, LI, C. 2601, p. 7. Kimberley to Frere, 1 June.

[8] Frere had next to no private income and his expenses in South Africa— particularly when travelling—far outstripped his income, even when he had

then personally discredited. Kimberley supervised each stage of Frere's fall.[1] His behaviour was dictated as much from private reasons as from expediency. He did not approve of Frere as a consul, but Frere's removal would hamper his own federal proposals, then under consideration at the Cape. Thus Frere remained in Government House, under a stay of execution, his fate depending on the vote on confederation in the Cape Assembly. All Cape Town knew of his 'censure' by the Colonial Office, for the fact was revealed to the Press in London.[2] He lived like this until finally dismissed some two months later.

Kimberley's sole comment on the whole bizarre affair was to the effect that he was pleased that he was not a member of the Lower House, 'for say what we will, the question of Frere will be a very awkward one in the House of Commons'.[3] It was Gladstone who had to face a hostile Commons, on Tuesday 25 May, to justify Government policy. He gave a masterly performance, and confounded the critics. Drawing heavily from Kimberley's letter of 25 May,[4] he styled federation as 'all important' for South Africa. To him it was yet more urgent even than in Canada, for the imperial dilemma in Africa was far deeper. Confederation alone could find a 'remedy for a state of things so complicated and so unsatisfactory, so burdensome and so injurious to the interests of the people'. In one sweep of a sentence he expressed Government intentions and hopes: Federation 'is so important, it is so large, it eclipses and absorbs every other consideration in South African policy. . . .' In short, it will be the 'pole star of the present action of the government'.[5]

his special allowance. Its removal hit him hard; see Martineau, *Life of Frere*, II, 393.

[1] Gladstone saw, and approved, both the letter cutting Frere's salary, and that recalling him. He made no comment on either. Addit. MSS. 44225, f. 178. Kimberley to Gladstone, 29 May 1880.

[2] The only person who does not seem to have known was Colley, who stayed with the Freres in Cape Town for ten days before going up to Natal. The Capetonians took it to be a deliberate slight—but when Colley heard he was very embarrassed.

[3] Addit. MSS. 44225, f. 175. Kimberley to Gladstone. Undated, but very probably 25 May 1880.

[4] Idem.

[5] Speech in Commons, 25 May 1880. *Hansard*, 3rd ser., CCLIII, cols. 460–1.

As to Frere, Gladstone slipped in a brief reference to the controversial proconsul at the end of his speech. 'To have recalled
Frere at the moment when we were entering upon this phase
would have had the effect of completely deranging the course
of the measures which had been planned.' Nothing should be
done 'to incur any risk or failure of Confederation'.[1] The matter
of Frere was thus shelved for the moment.[2]

Outside Parliament Gladstone showed he was equally nimble-
footed in manipulating pressure groups. He advised Kimberley
on how to face a strong deputation from the Aborigines Protection Society, pleading for the abandonment of the federal
plans. Led by that eminent back-bencher Sir Wilfred Lawson,
the deputation visited the Colonial Office on 27 May, but received no more than tea and sympathy.[3] As to Leonard Courtney's anti-Frere Group, once again Gladstone was equal to
the challenge. He adroitly parried Courtney's initial attacks of
21 May, and successfully turned Radical against Humanitarian.[4] It was some while before the two groups of idealists
tumbled to the old spell-binder's tactics, of clouding issues with
multiple statements, followed by a flurry of qualifying clauses
to cover his retreat.[5]

In other aspects though the level of tensions steadily rose, and
not even Gladstone's conjuring hand could hide the fact that
the problems were gaining on the solutions. The issue of Bradlaugh and the Oath had ground parliamentary business to a
halt, and whipped up excited passions in the Commons. This
same unreasoning spirit was also at work in the Cabinet, where
Forster's proposed Irish policy was making the Cabinet a
debating society and not an executive council of government.
The Transvaal and Irish crises for the first time began to run in
harness, each exacerbating the other, and both rubbing Cabinet
divisions raw. Forster had sounded the clarion call for battle,
with the first of many restive letters to Gladstone, on 6 June
1880: 'I hope it will be understood that in giving the Boers "the

[1] Ibid., col. 461.
[2] Hicks Beach claimed the same reason for not dismissing Frere after the
Zulu War fiasco. See *Hansard*, 3rd ser., CCLVI, col. 865.
[3] See *The Times*, 28 May 1880.
[4] Addit. MSS. 48630 (Hamilton Diary). Entry for 22 May.
[5] See *Saturday Review*, 19 February 1881.

fullest liberties to manage their local affairs," it is understood that this does not give the 30 or 40,000 Dubliners full liberty to manage not only the English but also the 800,000 natives [in Ireland].'[1] The pointed recriminations, that were to distort this Cabinet's conduct, had begun. The problem of the far-off Boer Republic was soon inextricably entwined in the Irish issue.

The verbal battles in the Cabinet were not the only echoes of exchanges that reached Gladstone's ears in May and June 1880. Despatches from Frere at the Cape announced that another Cape frontier war had begun.[2] Gordon Sprigg's colonial ministry had decided to disarm the Basuto as a result of Chief Morosi's rebellion. The Basuto had, not unnaturally, refused to hand over their firearms—most of which had been bought with money earned at the Kimberley diamond fields, and which were an essential element in the Basuto struggle to retain their existing lands. The war which followed the Cape Disarmament Proclamation of 6 April 1880[3] placed the Liberal Government in a cleft stick. Both the Cape Colonists and the Basuto appealed to the imperial authorities for aid.[4] Kimberley, who was endeavouring to coax the Cape into a receptive frame of mind on federation, was not inclined to interfere. The dangers of intervention seemed far to outweigh the results of inactivity. Accordingly he made it plain to Frere that no imperial troops were to be involved on either side.[5] He broke the news to Gladstone with the sigh of a man already weary of Africa.[6] The price exacted by inactivity—so as not to endanger federation—was to be heavy. The plight of the Basuto was to grow so severe that Britain was forced to take them back from Cape 'trusteeship', in 1884. It is yet another example of the lengths to which the imperialists were prepared to go to find federation. Interesting

---

[1] Addit. MSS. 44157, f. 134, W. E. Forster to W. E. Gladstone, 6 June 1880.

[2] *Parl. Pap.*, 1880, LI, C.2569, p. 556. Frere to Hicks Beach, 2 March 1880.

[3] Cape Disarmament Proclamation, 6 April 1880, issued under 'Cape Peace Preservation Act of 1878'. *Parl. Pap.*, 1880, LI, C.2569. Frere to Hicks Beach, 2 March 1880. The war began in July, when the proclamation was enforced.

[4] Chief Letsie, senior Basuto Chief, petitioned Queen Victoria directly. The Cape Colonists appealed to Frere, who referred to Kimberley.

[5] *Parl. Pap.*, 1880, LI, C.2659, p. 596. Kimberley to Frere, 13 May 1880.

[6] Addit. MSS. 44225, f. 174. Kimberley to Gladstone, 24 May 1880.

too is the fact that Kimberley was also cautioned sharply by Herbert, in May 1880, against offending the Cape Government, when the question of the colonial debt of £252,000 claimed by the Treasury came up for review.[1] Kimberley was deliberately embarking on a policy of withholding the Letters Patent, granting Galekaland, Tembuland, and Bomvanaland to the Cape,[2] in the hope of persuading the Colonial ministry to pay the debt.[3] In the light of the sensitive relations with the Cape Colonists, he wisely dropped the matter.[4]

A sense of foreboding began to appear in the Colonial Office minutes,[5] as they awaited the Cape debate on the federal proposals scheduled for the end of June.[6] Herbert and his officials took very little comfort from Lanyon's news that the Transvaal's 'Legislative Assembly' had voted for the federal union,[7] for the despatches from Frere had a worrying undertone. Kruger's Transvaal deputation, he reported, was at work among the Cape politicians.[8] Thus Lanyon's claim—that 'no objections would be raised in the Transvaal against Confederation'[9]—was more than cancelled out by Frere's ominous phrase of 14 June, that events at the Cape had 'conspired to lessen the chance of such resolutions being carried by any considerable majority', in the Cape Assembly.[10]

[1] C.O. 48/494, D. 86. Kimberley to Frere, 13 May 1880. Minute by Herbert, 11 May. See also Frere to Hicks Beach, 12 April 1880, enclosing a Minute by Cape ministry of 10 April 1880.

[2] The matter had arisen under Hicks Beach, who had promised the Cape these areas, *if* the Colony paid for administration, and took full responsibility for peace and order. C.O. 48/494, D. 323. Frere to Hicks Beach, 29 January 1880; and Frere to Hicks Beach, 27 April 1880. *Parl. Pap.*, 1880, XLVII, C.3112, p. 141.

[3] C.O. 48/494. Kimberley to Frere (Tel.), 3 May 1880; and Frere to Kimberley, 4 May 1880.

[4] Addit. MSS. 44225, f. 165. Kimberley to Gladstone, 7 May 1880.

[5] C.O. 291/5-6. See Minutes, particularly by Herbert, Bramston, and Fairfield.

[6] *Parl. Pap.*, 1880, LI, C.2655. Frere to Kimberley, enclosing Frere's speech opening Cape Assembly. Debate on federal proposals had been set for 22 June 1880.

[7] C.O. 291/6, D. 91. Lanyon to Kimberley, 10 June 1880; and *Parl. Pap.*, 1880, LI, C.2676, pp. 48-9.

[8] C.O. 48/494. Frere to Kimberley (Tel.), 6 May 1880.

[9] C.O. 291/6. Lanyon to Kimberley, 2 June 1880.

[10] *Parl. Pap.*, 1880, LI, C. 2655. Frere to Kimberley, 14 June 1880.

Frere followed this up, on 22 June, with surely the most interesting despatch he ever sent from South Africa—a critical examination of Cape politics and politicians.[1] He was quick to point out that Britain's hopes of federation rested largely on the behaviour of the Cape Dutch leader, Jan Hofmeyr, 'member for Stellenbosch, editor of the *Zuid Africaan*, a young man and able wire puller'. Hofmeyr led a powerful body in the Cape Assembly, which was conservative, and normally supported the government of the day, 'when it does not excite opposition from the ministers of the Dutch Reform Church'. However, Hofmeyr's group 'are far from steady voters, and have been so much excited lately by the Transvaal delegates and their Republican friends, that *some of them are half connected to a sort of Home Rule strategy*, i.e. to refuse all support to the Government till the Transvaal is given back to the Republic'. In practical terms, this meant that on the question of Confederation the Cape Dutch 'would probably vote against the Government proposals avowedly to compel restitution of the Transvaal'.[2] Frere clearly had his ear close to the ground, for he included a report of a secret opposition caucus, when a member of the Transvaal deputation (probably Kruger) strongly urged their fellow Dutch to stand by them. 'This sentiment', Frere recorded, 'found great favour with the Dutch members', and Hofmeyr 'advocated speaking in the sense of immediate and entire restitution'.[3]

The all important Cape Assembly debate, on federation, began on the afternoon of the same day as Frere's despatch—Wednesday, 22 June—and continued until Saturday, 26 June 1880. Sprigg opened the debate with a long but well-reasoned speech, advocating a favourable consideration of the federal proposals.[4] He acknowledged that there were those in the Assembly 'who sympathised with the inhabitants of the Transvaal'

[1] C.O. 48/494. Frere to Kimberley, 22 June 1880, enclosed in private memorandum on state of Cape politics.

[2] Ibid., Memorandum by Frere, 22 June 1880.

[3] Saul Solomon was apparently the only objector to Hofmeyr's decision, for he said 'that whilst entirely sympathising with the advocate of Transvaal independence, he felt sure they must accept annexation as an accomplished fact'. Ibid.

[4] *Parl. Pap.*, 1880, LI, C.2655. Full report of Debate in Cape Assembly. Received in C.O., 21 July 1880.

and he himself admitted that the annexation 'was premature and a mistake'. But, it had been done, and South Africa must now make the best of it. He saw it as a splendid opportunity for 'South Africans' to govern themselves, particularly as the one great problem, of a native rising, had been destroyed by the imperial Government's crushing of Zulu power. He concluded with the persuasive argument that there was no need for the Transvaal to press for independence alone, when it would gain this very liberty within a self-governing 'South African federation'.

The mood of the Assembly, though, was not sympathetic to Sprigg's motion; and as the debate proceeded the tide of opinion receded, leaving him in an isolated position. Fuller, the senior member of the House,[1] received loud cheers when he 'doubted whether there was any urgency for confederation'; and cries of 'Hear! Hear!' when he suggested that 'the Cape ought to consider ... what would be the cost of carrying out confederation'. The Member for George felt that Britain was deliberately trying to escape from her South African responsibilities, by making the Cape bear the burden of federation. This opinion was supported by the influential John X. Merriman,[2] who stressed that the Cape generally was against federation; the only exceptions being the Grahamstown and Port Elizabeth regions, who hoped in this way to achieve their long-standing ambition of a separate 'Eastern Province'.[3] The prevailing mood of the Assembly was summed-up by a Dutch member when he said: 'The action of the imperial Government ... in the case of the Transvaal had greatly shaken the faith of people in this country.'[4]

[1] M.P. for Cape Town—intermediary between Rhodes and Robinson.

[2] MERRIMAN, John Xavier   (1841–1926)
born 1841   England
1849   Emigrated to South Africa.
1869   Entered Cape politics.
1896   Breaks with Rhodes.
1908–10   P.M. of Cape, 'The Gladstone of South Africa'.
1926   Died.
See P. Laurence, *Life of John Xavier Merriman* (London, 1930).

[3] *Parl. Pap.*, 1880, LI, C.2655, pp. 39 ff. Speech by Merriman, M.P. for Namaqualand.
See also speech by M.P. for Grahamstown, J. Ayliff.

[4] Te Water, ibid., pp. 45 ff.

In an almost electric atmosphere, on Friday, 25 June, Hofmeyr rose from his seat in the Cape Assembly, and in calm tones dissected Sprigg's motion. For a retiring man he had remarkable resources of political invective in debate; and, if the outcome of the debate were in any doubt, Hofmeyr swung the balance against Sprigg. 'Did any honourable member of the House propose to enter into a conference because, through confederation, the Colony itself would become stronger,' he jibed. 'At present we are capable of defending ourselves, but we should require imperial assistance to defend the Transvaal.' As colonists they surely knew that 'whenever the imperial Government spent money it had responsibilities; and it would undoubtedly and naturally want power'. The ultimate result was clear—the Cape Colonists 'would soon lose their Colonial independence'. Merriman was correct, there was no enthusiasm for union in South Africa—was Britain 'going to dragoon the Transvaal into confederation?'[1] Turning and pointing to the visitors' gallery of the Assembly, where sat Kruger and the Transvaal deputation, Hofmeyr put this rhetorical question to the Assembly: was this an 'opportune moment' for such a conference, 'when delegates from the Transvaal were in this very city, attending caucus meetings of members of Parliament, for the purpose of getting the House to vote against confederation'. The imperial Government was, in Hofmeyr's opinion, trying to drive the Cape down a road that 'would lead the way to war and bloodshed'.[2]

When Hofmeyr sat down he had not only destroyed the chances of Kimberley's scheme, he had scuttled Britain's fifth and final attempt to unite the ever-troublesome South African Colonies and Boer republics into a federal union.[3] Sprigg had no alternative but to withdraw the motion. Gladstone's hope of settling this particular colonial problem quickly had been snuffed out. Kruger was delighted. 'Yesterday', he wrote from

[1] Ibid., p. 45.
[2] Ibid., speech by Hofmeyr, pp. 80 ff. See also description of debate in *Cape Argus*, 26 June 1880.
[3] Viz: (1) 1873   Kimberley's first attempt.
     (2) 1873   Duke of Buckingham's plan.
     (3) 1875–77   Lord Carnarvon's attempts.
     (4) 1878–79   Hicks Beach's attempt.
     (5) 1880   Kimberley's second attempt.

Cape Town after the debate, 'the Imperial Policy of the last six years received its death blow.'[1]

The news was greeted in Whitehall with a certain stoicism.[2] Officialdom was conditioned to failure in South Africa. But Kimberley penned a letter of pique to the Premier:

> My dear Gladstone,
> As the Cape Parliament refuses to take even the preliminary step of a Conference, we must regard Confederation as adjourned *sine die*. In fact Carnarvon's policy has completely broken down.[3]

This radically altered the circumstances in regard to Frere— he 'was sent out for the express purpose of carrying through Confederation, and there is no longer any good reason for not recalling him'. Several members of the Cabinet were for his recall, and 'I am disposed to agree with them. If we delay it, we shall appear to have given way to pressure'. Gladstone was less easily moved on such matters.[4] His reticence in recalling Frere is probably attributable to the inevitable clash which he feared with the Queen, who was distinctly pro-Frere.[5]

At the Cabinet of 3 July it was Gladstone's opinion which prevailed. It was decided to await further particulars from Frere, as the Cabinet so far only had the single telegram with news of the failure.[6] The pressure on Gladstone, however, was very great, and two days later he admitted in the Commons— in answer to a question from Wilfred Lawson—that Frere's recall was a matter of time.[7] The issue hung fire for three weeks,

[1] G. P. Gooch, *Life of Courtney*, pp. 154–6. Kruger to Leonard Courtney, 26 June 1880. See also *Cape Argus* and *Zuid Africaan*, 3 July 1880.

[2] Addit. MSS. 44642, f. 42 (Cabinet Papers). Frere to Kimberley, forwarded to Gladstone.

[3] Addit. MSS. 44225, ff. 184–6. Kimberley to Gladstone, 29 June 1880.

[4] Addit. MSS. 48630, f. 35 (Hamilton Diary). Entry for Friday, 30 July 1880. 'The Queen strongly deprecates the recall of Sir B. Frere, on the ground that Colonial Governors ought not to have confidence withdrawn from them, because of a change of their political parties at home . . . it was partly owing to the well known wishes of the Sovereign that the Cabinet have shewn such long suffering.'

[5] (Devonshire Papers), 340, 980–81. Spencer to Hartington, 2 August 1880; and Duke of Cambridge to Hartington, 4 August 1880.

[6] Addit. MSS. 44642, f. 44 (Cabinet Papers), 3 July 1880. Point 3: 'Recall Frere—refuse to act on telegram.'

[7] Gladstone, statement in Commons, 5 July 1880. *Hansard*, 3rd ser., CCLIII, col. 1623.

while they awaited confirmation of events at the Cape with which to confront the Queen. At the Cabinet of 24 July it was decided that Frere was definitely to be recalled, though no date was fixed.[1]

Kimberley, with the Cabinet at his back, was now able to force the pace. As Hamilton noted in his Diary, on 27th: 'There at last seems to be a good prospect of the recall of Sir B. Frere.'[2] Kimberley took this matter into his own hands and drew up a telegram of recall, circulating it to Cabinet members, and gathering their comments: 'Every one except Argyll, Bright and Dodson (the two latter out of town) have seen the telegram to Frere. No one has made any remark. As time presses I presume I may proceed. . . .'[3] Gladstone concurred, and forwarded the telegram to the Queen.[4] Victoria attempted to stage a rearguard action to save Frere, in true 'Horse Guards' tradition'.[5] 'The Queen', she wrote from Osborne, 'has *always* considered it right to give her fullest support to her Governors abroad, especially in difficult & anxious moments, and must PROTEST against their removal *on* the change of *administration* or because a hostile feeling is supposed to exist among an *extreme* section of the House of Commons.' The Queen 'CANNOT approve of this step, but will not oppose it, *as soon* as she learns the name of the person who it is proposed sh[ou]ld succeed Sir B. Frere. . .'[6] Displaying great tact, Gladstone replied the next day, informing Her Majesty that Sir Hercules Robinson, 'the most eminent Colonial Governor', was to succeed Frere.[7] This apparently soothed Victoria, who acquiesced in the choice.[8]

The first intimation Frere had of these manoeuvres was a not very diplomatic telegram from the Colonial Office, on 1 August.[9]

[1] Addit. MSS. 44642, f. 57 (Cabinet Papers), Saturday, 24 July 1880. See point 9 on Minutes.

[2] Addit. MSS. 48630, f. 33 (Hamilton Diary). Entry for Tuesday, 27 July 1880.

[3] Addit. MSS. 44225, f. 208. Kimberley to Gladstone, 29 July 1880.

[4] Addit. MSS. 44225, f. 204 and f. 206; and Morley, *Gladstone*, III, 234.

[5] *Letters of Queen Victoria*, 2nd ser., III, 124.

[6] Guedalla, *Queen and Mr. Gladstone*, II, 108–9, no. 676. Queen to Gladstone, 30 July 1880.

[7] Ibid., II, 109, no. 677. Gladstone to Queen (Tel.), 31 July 1880.

[8] Idem.

[9] *Parl. Pap.*, 1880, LI, C.2655. Kimberley to Frere (Tel.), 1 August 1880, p. 99; and C.O. 806/167, no. 223.

In this telegram Kimberley explained the Cabinet decision on the grounds that Frere had been kept at the Cape only 'for the special reason that there was a prospect of your being able materially to forward the policy of confederation'; and, in Kimberley's crude phrase, 'This reason has now disappeared...'[1] The decision was made public by Hartington, in a short statement in the Commons on 2 August.[2] Frere was deeply hurt by his recall, and more particularly by the fact that he had been kept at the Cape—'weakened and discredited' —while the Cabinet tried to achieve a federation. He felt he was being made a scapegoat,[3] and protested vigorously, with lengthy petitions from hundreds of colonists who disliked his dismissal.[4] The official machine moved on regardless. Even before Frere's reply was received, telegrams had been sent to Sir Hercules Robinson in New Zealand. He accepted Frere's office on 5 August, with obvious delight.[5]

Frere left the Cape after a series of banquets and presentations late in September.[6] The significance of his departure was blurred by the passions which the conduct of this cultured and humane man had aroused.[7] Federation was now certainly a matter of mere academic interest. Frere had already written its obituary in his elegant style: 'It falls about us like a golden shower—vague, formless, intangible, but beautiful withal; only unlike the aureous downfall of the myth, it leaves no substantial result of its visit.' Maybe, he concluded 'some day we shall behold it in more compact form and clearer vision; but the time is not yet'.[8] South Africa—the 'graveyard of reputations'—had claimed another proconsul *and* another policy.

---

[1] Idem.

[2] *Hansard*, 3rd ser., CCLIV, col. 1961.

[3] *Parl, Pap.*, 1880, LI, C.2695. Frere to Kimberley, 3 August 1880, pp. 79–83.

[4] *Parl. Pap.*, 1880, LXVI, C.27040, enclosing numerous petitions.

[5] C.O. 48/494. Robinson to Kimberley (Tel.), 5 August 1880: 'After gratifying terms of your offer I can only make one answer, that I place my services at the disposal of Her Majesty's Government, and I shall leave for England.'

[6] E. A. Walker, *A History of Southern Africa*, p. 381.

[7] The most sensitive analysis of Frere is in Philip Woodruff, *The Men who ruled India* (1953), vol. II, chap. 1.

[8] C.O. 48/490, D. 204. Frere to Hicks Beach, 15 July 1879.

4. Kimberley's Masterly Inactivity: August—December 1880

The Irish crisis had crashed upon the Cabinet in the course of the autumn and winter of 1880. It soon became the all pervading theme of public concern, Cabinet behaviour, and parliamentary government. But, most important of all, it took Gladstone from behind.[1] He had not budgeted for it, and in his urgent desire to come to grips with the latest Irish outbreak, he dropped all other business and became obsessed with Fenianism.

In his Midlothian speeches he had dismissed Disraeli's warnings about Ireland as mere electioneering. Mounting disorder across the Irish Channel was a grim triumph for Disraeli's powers of foresight. Gladstone was profoundly shaken by the severity of the crisis. He scrapped the blueprints for his second administration, and relied on instinct in the coming months. As he admitted in the following year to Bright: 'I accepted my mission in April of last year as . . . special and temporary . . . I never hoped to get over it . . . sooner than in the autumn of the present year, and in most parts of it, e.g. India, the Eastern question, and perhaps finance, as much progress had been made as I anticipated or more.' But, in Gladstone's memorable phrase, 'Ireland, however, came upon us unawares, looming very large.'[2]

Ireland drew Gladstone away from the majority of problems facing the Government, and he increasingly expected ministers to run their departments without undue reference to the Cabinet. However, Ireland was an all-engrossing topic not only for the G.O.M. but for other members of the Government as well. It aroused intense passions, and raised inescapable sets of principles. Consequently Gladstone's delegation of authority to his ministers tended to be passed on to the permanent officials, for those very ministers were in turn far more engrossed in the Irish issue than by departmental details. This applied regardless of office. Kimberley's letters to Gladstone on the Irish issue in

[1] Donald Southgate, *The Passing of the Whigs, 1832–86* (London, 1962). 'That there should be an Irish problem was something of a shock to Gladstone.' (p. 373.)

[2] Addit. MSS. 44113, f. 158 (L.B. copy). Gladstone to Bright, 29 September 1881, from Hawarden.

1880–81 far outnumber those on the Transvaal,[1] although a war was being fought on the *veld*. It was not until Majuba that many fellow ministers took any interest in the Boer revolt at all.[2] Chamberlain, at the Board of Trade, Harcourt at the Home Office, and even old Selborne, the Lord Chancellor, became passionately involved in the Irish issue. The Gladstone Papers bulge with volume after volume of earnest letters on Ireland; and Gladstone is even said to have had a special cupboard where he collected all the ministerial resignations over Ireland—together with copies of soothing letters of reply.[3]

It has been written elsewhere that the scramble for Africa, in the 1880s, could be seen as one 'gigantic footnote' to the history of imperialism in India.[4] With equal justification British troubles with the Boer republics could be termed an intricate footnote to Anglo-Irish relations. Ministers were weaned away from their departments to take sides in the veritable 'cabinet battles' that now waged over Irish policy. In the Commons, Parnell led the superbly organised Irish party of parliamentary anarchists. Clôture was finally introduced in 1882, but before this the Irish members managed to twist parliamentary business to their own advantage. As Balfour said angrily to Randolph Churchill: 'The Irish have a talent for turning everything into an Irish debate.'[5]

In this concern over Ireland, that soon bordered on a mania with many politicians, there lies more than a partial explanation for the meandering Government policy in colonial and foreign matters; and also for the apparently inexplicable fears that began to grip the permanent officials in their handling of colonial 'nationalism', in Egypt and in South Africa. In the latter case it becomes more and more apparent that the Colonial

[1] For extent of Irish correspondence, see Addit. MSS. 44225, Kimberley to Gladstone; and Addit. MSS. 44544 (L.B. copy), Gladstone to Kimberley, for June–December 1880.

[2] Addit. MSS. 43924, ff. 39 ff. Dilke Diary for February–March 1881; Addit. MSS. 48630, ff. 132 ff. Hamilton Diary; Addit. MSS. 44642, ff. 147 ff. Cabinet Minutes for 21 March 1881.

[3] Lord Kilbracken, *Reminiscences* (London, 1931). Gladstone's secretary—best 'private portrait' of the G.O.M.

[4] The phrase is Robinson and Gallagher's.

[5] Robert Rhodes James, *Randolph Churchill*; particularly good on the Irish party in the Commons (pp. 93 ff.).

Office had begun to see the local discontent in terms of Fenianism.

The situation in the Afrikaner republics seemed to correspond to the Irish dilemma.[1] It was a short step to seeing Jan Hofmeyr, Paul Kruger, and the Afrikaner *Bond* in the image of Parnell.[2] This also worked the other way. The crisis in southern Africa developed faster and more drastically than discontent in Ireland and provided the Gladstone Cabinet with a unique 'test-run' on the vagaries of a policy of coercion, supplemented by sporadic conciliation. The merits of 'home-rule' for the Afrikaner republics, gradually implemented between 1882 and 1885, were not lost on Gladstone.

But, before that particular policy was embarked upon, the Gladstone government went through a painful year of blunders and self-revelation on the *veld*. The significance of the failure of confederation in South Africa was profound. The vacuum in policy was acutely felt. The editorial columns of the daily Press all proffered advice, that ranged from positive, if fanciful suggestions—to turn South Africa into 'another India,'[3]—to negative tirades against the behaviour of the Cape Assembly.[4] In Whitehall the range of opinions was equally wide. But nowhere in the Colonial Office minutes was there a suggestion as to the explosive legacy of federation. The failure was mourned by Kimberley and Herbert, but neither saw that their attempt could perhaps have markedly worsened a discontent that was already rife in the Transvaal. Policy slipped into a period of uneasy limbo, as the contending schools of opinion forced each other into a stalemate.

This sense of unreality existed from August until news of the Transvaal outbreak in December. The Boer discontent was not discussed at a single Cabinet from 24 July (dismissal of Frere), to 30 December (Robinson's 'Instructions').[5] The Cape–Basuto

---

[1] C.O. 48/503. Robinson to Kimberley, 15 May 1882. See lengthy Minutes by C.O. officials, 10 June 1882.

[2] *Life of Hofmeyr*, p. 211, footnote 1, quotes *Pall Mall Gazette* as describing Hofmeyr as 'the Parnell of South Africa'; see also p. 150 for further illustrations.

[3] See *Westminster Review*, 1 July 1880.

[4] *The Times*, 3 August 1880.

[5] Addit. MSS. 44642, ff. 57–125 (Cabinet Papers). The Cabinet met some twenty times, at roughly weekly intervals.

War was discussed twice—on 30 September,[1] and on 10 November,[2]—but it was an exception to what the *Standard* called the normal 'Irish concern' of the Cabinet.[3]

The despatches from the British administration in the Transvaal reinforced the Colonial Office's sense of unease, yet left policy becalmed for lack of correct information. On 25 September Kimberley received a long-awaited report from Lanyon on an extended tour of the outlying districts of the Transvaal. 'I am glad to be able to state,' Lanyon wrote, 'that all along the route the white population appeared more or less satisfied and content with the present régime, and that all the native chiefs . . . express their willingness to pay the taxes imposed, and abide by the laws of the country.'[4] Lanyon enclosed the memorials of welcome from each district. Kimberley replied, on 4 October, with the blithe comment: 'I have read your report with much satisfaction.'[5]

Lanyon followed this up with an application for leave. 'I feel very hopeful . . . that matters will be so far settled as to allow my leaving towards the close of the year.'[6] His assessment of the Transvaal situation becomes more dogmatic and less real with each despatch. 'There is a decided change for the better amongst the Boers, and the natives are paying up their taxes quietly.'[7] Three weeks later he learned that a Boer sub-committee had fixed 8 January 1881 for a mass meeting of protest. He enclosed the speeches by Kruger and Joubert with the casual statement, 'I do not contemplate that anything to disturb the peace will then occur.'[8] It was an artificial protest, Lanyon claimed, inspired by Kruger's 'foreigners'—his Dutch friends, Jorrissen and Bok. On the strength of these reports Kimberley telegraphed Lanyon on 27 October: 'You may take leave *if you are quite satisfied that the condition of affairs will permit it.*

[1] Addit. MSS. 44642, f. 71 (Cabinet Papers).
[2] Ibid., f. 73. The Cabinet interest over the Basuto War was in response to a Cape request for imperial troops. Cabinet decided against any aid.
[3] *Standard*, 13 November 1880, leading article.
[4] *Parl. Pap.*, 1881, LXVI, C.2740, p. 28. Lanyon to Kimberley, 19 August 1880. Received in C.O., 25 September 1880.
[5] Ibid., Kimberley to Lanyon, 4 October 1880, p. 29.
[6] C.O. 291/6. Lanyon to Kimberley, 3 September 1880.
[7] Idem.
[8] C.O. 291/6. Lanyon to Kimberley, 23 September 1880.

Colonel Bellairs will administer the Government.'[1] Lanyon *was* satisfied, and *did* take his leave.

Lanyon's interpretation of signs was becoming almost too confident, and the Colonial officials stirred most uneasily. Kimberley first expressed the growing doubts. 'I distrust the flourishing revenue', he minuted on Lanyon's despatch of 15 September,[2] —which had reported a surplus of nearly £20,000 in the Transvaal accounts. And, in answer to a War Office enquiry about reducing the size of the imperial army in the Transvaal, Kimberley noted: 'Not thought advisable.'[3] Clearly Kimberley—who was a cautious man—had an instinctive fear of Lanyon's assuredness. When Lanyon, in September, happily suggested a thorough Transvaal census, Kimberley was wary. 'Tell him not to press it if the opposition is serious,' he told Herbert.[4] The latter was also having qualms about Lanyon's abilities, 'It is possible', Herbert remarked on 25 November, 'that there is more disaffection and more danger . . . than Sir O. Lanyon perceives and reports. But I think if there were ground for serious apprehensions Sir G. Pomeroy Colley, an unbiased and shrewd observer, would be aware of it.'[5]

Colley had replaced Wolseley as High Commissioner for South-East Africa, and his reports in these months form a greater blunder than his tragic tactical error on Mount Majuba. Had he voiced the slightest doubts on the state of the colony, then the Transvaal War, in which he lost his life, might never have occurred. Kimberley, and the Colonial officials, already had suspicions about Lanyon's judgment, and would readily have grasped any substantial evidence contrary to Lanyon's optimistic ventures in prose. But they looked in vain; Colley was content to write that the Kruger–Joubert group 'does not . . .

---

[1] C.O. 291/7. Kimberley to Lanyon (Tel.), 27 October 1880, and confirmation in despatch of same date.

[2] C.O. 291/6. Lanyon to Kimberley, 15 September 1880. Lanyon reported revenue for 1879–80 at £123,458 17*s.* 1*d.*; and expenditure at £104,210 15*s.* 10*d.* with the overdraft at the Standard Bank down from £157,674 to £125,022 9*s.* 1*d.* Lanyon accordingly proposed to raise the salary of Transvaal Government officials.

[3] C.O. 291/3, no. 17283. Minute by Kimberley, 11 November 1880.

[4] C.O. 291/6, no. 15199. Minute by Kimberley, 5 October 1880.

[5] C.O. 291/9. Wolseley to Kimberley, Minute by Herbert, 25 November 1880.

appear to have had much effect in the country, and it is very doubtful if the disaffected party are prepared to take any decided action. *Garrison can be reduced with safety*'.[1]

On Christmas Eve, 1880, the Colonial Office received Lanyon's despatch of 19 November.[2] He told of a 'minor' revolt in one district where a man had refused to pay his taxes, and the authorities had seized his wagon. In the ensuing scuffle isolated shots had been fired. 'I do not think there is much, if any cause, for anxiety', Lanyon added.[3] 'I do not anticipate any serious trouble will arise out of the affair'.[4]

Kimberley was less sure. 'It is an unfortunate despatch', he minuted on 24 December, 'both on the amount of the mistaken estimate of the danger, and the general tone of the remarks on the state of feeling amongst the Boers.' Kimberley ever had an eye on the power of British opinion. 'Sir O. Lanyon, like many others who had lived long out of England, does not understand public opinion here. His observations will give offence, and cause some embarrassment, but this can't be helped.'[5] Why Kimberley did not send Lanyon a sharp telegram, demanding fuller details, is unclear. Perhaps his 'wait-and-see' approach to public affairs prevented this; more probably he shied away from revealing his anxiety to subordinates in the field, particularly as Colley had recently reported: 'Present agitation seems principally connected with annual tax notices.'[6] This was six days before the rebellion began on 19 December. Kimberley limited his fears to a single remark, in reply to Lanyon's despatch of 14 November,[7] informing him of the tax collecting incident: 'I trust that no consequences will ensue.'[8] By the time this message arrived in the Transvaal, Lanyon was besieged in Pretoria.

[1] C.O. 291/6. Colley to Kimberley, 24 August 1880.

[2] *Parl. Pap.*, 1881, LXVL, C.2740. Lanyon to Kimberley, 19 November 1880, pp. 115–20. Received in C.O., 24 December 1880.

[3] Ibid., Lanyon to Kimberley, 19 November 1880.

[4] Ibid., Lanyon to Kimberley, 14 November 1880.

[5] C.O. 291/7, no. 19856. Hemming to Bramston, 24 December 1880, with comments by Herbert and Kimberley.

[6] *Parl. Pap.*, 1881, LXVL, C.2783. Colley to Kimberley, 13 December 1880.

[7] *Parl. Pap.*, 1881, LXVL, C.2740. Lanyon to Kimberley, 14 November 1880, pp. 109–14.

[8] Ibid. Kimberley to Lanyon, 16 December 1880.

The gap between Whitehall fears and the local reality, continued right up to the outbreak, although from mid-December Kimberley's doubts were increasingly substantiated. President Brand of the Orange Free State warned the English Government of developments in the Transvaal. 'I read with very deep concern the account of the very serious aspect of affairs in the Transvaal', he telegraphed to Strahan, the acting High Commissioner at the Cape. 'The gravity of the situation will, I hope, be accepted by your Excellency . . .'[1] Strahan forwarded this information, but not by telegram; Brand's wise warnings did not arrive at the Colonial Office until 30 December.[2] Strahan is culpable on another charge as well. On 9 December he received a strong deputation of Cape politicians, representing a wide section of the Cape community, who presented him with three motions, passed on 7 December at a public meeting in Paarl.[3] The motions expressed sympathy with the Transvaal Boers—'a wronged community'; called for immediate restoration of Transvaal independence; and warned of the probable dangers if this were not done. Strahan was even more leisurely in handling this vital information, and did not despatch it for two weeks.[4] It arrived in London on 20 January 1881, full of details of Cape Dutch unrest,[5] just at the moment when the Cabinet was being torn between Kimberley's desire to crush the Transvaal rebellion, and Chamberlain's call for negotiations. Strahan departed to an undistinguished Governorship of Tasmania early in January 1881, blithely unaware of the effect in Whitehall of his slothfulness. It was to prove distinctly daunting to Gladstone's morale, for Strahan's report conjured up a picture of possible unrest throughout South Africa, in the manner of the Irish crisis.[6]

---

[1] *Parl. Pap.*, 1881, LXVL, C.2783. Strahan to Kimberley, 7 December 1880, enclosed in Brand to Strahan (Tel.) 6 December 1880.

[2] When questioned on this Strahan claimed that the telegraph wire was broken at the time. But this hardly explains why he did not telegraph when the wire was repaired. See Morley, *Gladstone*, III, 32.

[3] *Cape Argus*, Thursday, 9 December 1880.

[4] *Parl. Pap.*, 1881, LXVL, C.2783. Strahan to Kimberley, 22 December 1880. Received C.O., 20 January 1881, pp. 61–6.

[5] Ibid., pp. 66–7.

[6] Addit. MSS. 43935, f. 19 (Dilke Memoir). See also Gwynne and Tuckwell, *Dilke*, I, 366.

On the Transvaal *veld* the smouldering sense of injustice now flared into open rebellion. Kruger always claimed that the rebellion was provoked by the arrival of Gladstone's letter, explaining the retention of the Transvaal annexation. In Kruger's words,

> We were bitterly disappointed on receiving an answer from the Liberal statemen informing us that he was unable to annul the annexation or to advise Her Majesty to abandon her sovereignty over the Transvaal. . . . The general conviction was now arrived at that further meetings and friendly protests were useless.[1]

Kruger was saying no more than Joubert had said to Frere in June 1878, shortly after the annexation. 'Under the British flag you will have everything you desire', Frere had remarked, 'but that the [British] flag will continue to fly over the land.' To which Joubert replied: 'Over the land possibly; over the people —never.'[2]

The actual timing of the outbreak centred around the 'Bezuidenhout wagon affair',[3] which involved the classic issue of so many colonial rebellions—taxation. It was in the tradition of 'Slagters Nek'[4] (which had also involved a Bezuiden-hout); and Kruger claimed to see in it a root principle. 'You must admit this is open rebellion,' the officer commanding the Potchefstroom garrison had said to Kruger when the latter intervened on Bezuidenhout's behalf. 'I should agree with you', Kruger replied angrily, 'if we had acknowledged the annexation; but that is not the case. We do not look upon ourselves as British subjects, and the question of the tax is not a private question of Bezuidenhout's, but a question of principle which concerns the whole country.'[5]

The old Republican *Vierkleur* was hoisted over the heads of thousands of Boers massed at Paardekraal; and Cronje fired the first shot at Potchefstroom, on 16 December 1880, Dingaan's

---

[1] Kruger, *Memoirs*, I, 166.
[2] M. Nathan, *Paul Kruger, His Life and Times*, p. 131.
[3] Bezuidenhout owed £27 10s. od. in taxes. He claimed he owed only £14. This he finally proved, but refused to pay the £8 costs which the local land-drost demanded he pay. His wagon was seized, and put for auction. Several hundred Boers gathered, and led by Cronje, forcibly took the wagon from the landdrost. It was sufficient to spark off the rebellion.
[4] E. A. Walker, *A History of Southern Africa*, p. 153.
[5] Kruger, *Memoirs*, I, 170–71.

Day.[1] The first intimation the Colonial Office had of the outbreak was an alarming telegram from Colley, on 19 December: 'Boers about 5000 have occupied Heidelberg and established Government . . . I am sending up all available troops. . .'[2] A week later he despatched an even more worrying telegram. 'An uneasy feeling is general that *Boer disaffection extends through South Africa, and a large fire may be lit from the spark*. It appears to me most desirable to attempt to think quickly.'[3]

The Colonial Office were at first stunned.[4] 'These don't appear to us here like the clouds threatening an ordinary storm,' Herbert noted anxiously.[5] Kimberley's reaction was more positive. He was away at Kimberley House when the news arrived. He immediately wrote to Herbert, instructing him to arrange with the War Office for another regiment, 'to be sent to Natal at once', as all Colley's forces 'will be wanted to deal with the Boers'.[6] Kimberley broke the news to Gladstone, and he was hardly pleased,[7] as it came hard on reports of a further outbreak of violence in Ireland.[8] The Liberal Government was soon fighting a war on two fronts, with over 30,000 troops in Ireland, and a lesser number in South Africa.[9]

Kimberley's instinctive reaction was to defeat the Boers, but he had his fears. 'The rebellion in the Transvaal is a most untoward event', he wrote to Gladstone on 22 December.[10] 'I hope Sir G. P. Colley will be able to cope with the insurgents, but after consultation with Childers we have thought it prudent to send a regiment of infantry to reinforce him.'[11] Kimberley had been informed by Childers that Colley only had four regiments,

[1] E. A. Walker, *A History of Southern Africa*, p. 383, on significance of date.

[2] C.O. 291/9. Colley to Kimberley (Tel.), 19 December 1880.

[3] C.O. 179/135. Colley to Kimberley (Tel.), 25 December 1880.

[4] Ibid., Minute by C.O., 27 December 1880.

[5] Ibid., D. 247. Colley to Kimberley, 19 December 1880. Minute by Herbert.

[6] C.O. 291/7. Kimberley to Herbert (Private), 20 December 1880, from Kimberley House.

[7] Addit. MSS. 48630, ff. 107–19 (Hamilton Diary).

[8] Addit. MSS. 44642, ff. 75–125 (Cabinet Papers), particular Cabinets of 13, 14, and 16 December 1880.

[9] C.O. 291/9. W.O. to C.O., 22 December 1880.

[10] Addit. MSS. 44225, ff. 261–4. Kimberley to Gladstone, 22 December 1880, enclosing a copy of Robinson's Instructions'.

[11] Idem.

a total of 4734 men, 156 officers, and six guns.[1] 'In the present dangerous condition of South Africa', Kimberley remarked to Gladstone, 'it is important that the force should be sufficient to deal vigorously with the outbreak.'[2] Strahan's news of Cape Dutch restiveness had not yet arrived, and Kimberley's worries at first centred on the danger of a simultaneous Natal native rebellion. 'I live in dread that they may be moved by sympathy with the Basutos, with whom many are connected. But as they withstood all temptation to desert us during the Zulu War, I think it most probable that they will remain loyal.'[3]

Gladstone's reaction to the rebellion revealed him obeying instinct rather than reason. He wrote fully to Kimberley on 24 December: 'I cannot feel surprised that you and Childers should have deemed it necessary to send another regiment to South Africa, though I do not know that necessity lies on the surface of the case, but you are better judges.'[4] Kimberley replied immediately, impressing on Gladstone that the Transvaal crisis 'is so serious' that the extra troops were vital, the Boers having gained an initial victory. 'There is nothing disheartening in a military sense in a small body of troops being overpowered by numbers, but a first success is sure to give a great impetus to the rebellion. ... I do not think we could possibly take the responsibility of refusing the reinforcements which the general in command declares to be urgently needed.'[5] This was not the only grave letter Gladstone received. 'The Queen feels much anxiety about the Cape', Victoria wrote to the Premier on 26 December, 'and expects that the Government will take energetic measures to assert her authority in those parts of the Colony which have revolted. The Boers are a dangerous foe and we shall have to support Sir G. Colley strongly.'[6] The Duke of

[1] C.O. 291/9. W.O. to C.O. 22 December 1880 (C.O. Minute, 24 December 1880).

[2] Addit. MSS. 44225, ff. 261–4. Kimberley to Gladstone, 22 December 1880.

[3] Idem.

[4] Addit. MSS. 44544, f. 120 (L.B. copy). Gladstone to Kimberley, 24 December 1880.

[5] Addit. MSS. 44225, f. 265. Kimberley to Gladstone, 25 December 1880, from Kimberley House.

[6] Letters of Queen Victoria, 2nd ser., vol. III, 166–7. Queen to Gladstone, 26 December 1880, from Osborne.

Cambridge—'that grotesque shadow of the Duke of Wellington' —was soon complaining to Hartington that 'the news from the Transvaal is indeed most depressing'.[1] Gladstone wearily accepted the serious nature of the rebellion, and philosophically noted after the initial imperial defeat at Bronkhorstspruit: 'It may be that the poor fellows gallantly tried to make another Rorkes Drift of it.'[2] But he clearly had not yet been informed of a possible Cape–Transvaal Dutch line-up, for he wrote to the Queen on 28 December: 'Quite apart from opinions held and even retained on the policy of annexing the Transvaal, Lord Kimberley proposes to instruct Sir H. Robinson in unequivocal terms on the duty of maintaining the annexation.'[3]

Despite the criticism of Chamberlain, Bright, Courtney and Dilke,[4] Gladstone had committed the Government to repressing the rebellion, and in so doing deepened the crisis, for he was soon to have to travel back over this very road of coercion, admitting that it had been no solution for the Transvaal dilemma.

Historians have been quick to criticise Gladstone's actual handling of the rebellion; in fact his transgression was greater even than that. The Boer revolt did not take place simply because 'the British Government claimed to be paramount authority and trustee of south Africa, and the trek-Boers rejected the claims'.[5] Nor is Professor de Kiewiet's judgment any more balanced, in laying all the blame at the feet of that incompetent administrator, Owen Lanyon: 'The cardinal sins of strategy were all his. . . . Had he been either a good politician or a good soldier he might have prevented the outbreak or conquered it.'[6] This is to miss the basic point. The Boers revolted after a year's patient waiting for Gladstone to implement two sets of promises. First, the Midlothian gestures, and later his offer of 'liberal institutions'. Had Gladstone held to either, or both, of these affirmations, there might have been no revolt in December 1880.

[1] Devonshire Papers, 340, 1049. Duke of Cambridge to Hartington, 25 December 1880.

[2] Addit. MSS. 44544, f. 122 (L.B. copy). Gladstone to Kimberley, 29 December 1880, from Hawarden.

[3] Guedalla, *Queen and Mr. Gladstone*, II, 128, no. 717. Gladstone to Queen, 28 December 1880, from Hawarden.

[4] Addit. MSS. 43935, f. 19 (Dilke Memoir).

[5] *Africa and the Victorians*, p. 53.

[6] De Kiewiet, *Imperial Factor*, p. 274.

Lanyon's brash administration was not as detrimental as Gladstone's conduct. The G.O.M. had awoken Transvaal hopes, then dashed them. He had tried to impose a federation from without, then behaved as if he had had a fit of absence of mind. Kruger understood why he went to war. 'The [British] Government', he stated emphatically, 'has precipitated matters.'[1]

Gladstone however blamed all the Transvaal troubles on Carnarvon's policy,[2]—'The devil surely found something for his idle hands to do . . .'[3] But this is wishful thinking. Gladstone had every opportunity to retrocede the Transvaal, as was expected; or, to grant the Boers internal self-government, as he promised Kruger; or, to negotiate a settlement the moment Lanyon's mirage collapsed, as he later did after Majuba. To state, as Gladstone did to Kimberley, that ' I never . . . conveyed any encouragement to resistance or expectation respecting our withdrawal from the territory,' was to give way to complete self-deception.[4]

Chamberlain alone was realistic in assessing the causes of the rebellion.[5] He told his electors of Birmingham, 'Whatever the risk was . . . of civil war or anarchy if we had reversed the decision, it was not so great a danger as that which we actually incurred by maintaining the wrong doing of our predecessors.'[6] To this Gladstone haughtily replied that he was 'not prepared for himself, to concede that we made a mistake in not advising revocation of the annexation when we came in'.[7] In the midst of the strain of the war, though, Gladstone was to confide in Kimberley and admit the blunder. In a private note he wrote: 'Thoroughly disapproving of the annexation in principle and in policy, I had no means of forming a judgment that it could be revoked. Had I been prepared to work in that sense I should

[1] *Parl. Pap.*, 1881, LXVL, C.2783, pp. 25–6.

[2] P.R.O. 30/29/124. Gladstone to Granville, 7 May 1881. (Ramm, I, 273.)

[3] Addit. MSS. 44544, f. 122 (L.B. copy). Gladstone to Kimberley, 29 December 1880, from Hawarden.

[4] Addit. MSS. 44544, f. 137 (L.B. copy). Gladstone to Kimberley, 14 February 1881.

[5] C.O. 291/14. Minutes by C.O. officials, 8 June 1881.

[6] *The Times*, 8 June 1881. Full report of Chamberlain's speech at Birmingham of 7 June 1881.

[7] Garvin, *Chamberlain*, I, 441. Gladstone to Chamberlain, 8 June 1881.

have done it first in Parliament.'[1] Gladstone's confession is his finest defence: it rightly stresses the foolhardy reports notably of Lanyon, but also of Colley and Strahan, from South Africa. But, it is a sad admission of weakness that two such experienced ministers as Gladstone and Kimberley were blinded by the cocksure despatches of the local administrators. The truth is, they wanted to believe them; and they suppressed their own doubts.[2]

The unhappy year of 1880 ended with the Liberal Government pledged to suppressing the rebellion, confirmed in their belief in the efficacy of coercion as the right and proper response to the Boer defiance. Herbert expressed the official viewpoint when he minuted, on 29 December: 'Until they [the Boers] have submitted themselves to the Queen, and it has been ascertained how far it is possible to extend clemency to the ringleaders, H.M. Government can hardly proceed to consider terms of settlement.'[3]

This is also the tenor of the 'Instructions' drawn up for Sir Hercules Robinson, as the new High Commissioner for southern Africa, and Governor of the Cape. These 'Instructions' are in so many ways an exact record of the mind of the Cabinet and Colonial Office at that particular moment, in regard to South Africa.[4]

The 'Instructions' were drawn up over several weeks in the Colonial Office, with Robinson constantly in attendance for briefing discussion.[5] The first draft was circulated among all Cabinet ministers between 25 December and the Cabinet

[1] Addit. MSS. 44544, f. 137 (L.B. copy). Gladstone to Kimberley, 14 February 1881.

[2] The deeper causes of the rebellion were well put by Graham Bower, Robinson's secretary at the Cape: The Boers, 'fought for the right to live and govern the Transvaal according to the ideas of rough farmers and untrammelled by British ideas of progress or equality, or the rights of man, or of philanthropy or humanitarism. The Boers fought for freedom from the missionaries, the aborigines Protection Society, from the faddists and the notoriety hunters. . . .' Afr. MSS., S. 63, f. 5.

[3] C.O. 48/496. Minute by Herbert, 29 December, on Strahan to Kimberley (Tel.) 25 December 1880.

[4] *Parl. Pap.*, 1881, LXVL, C.2754. Kimberley to Robinson ('Instructions') 30 December 1880.

[5] He had gone straight from New Zealand to Britain, before setting out for South Africa, in January 1881.

meeting of 30 December.[1] 'Circulation seems hardly necessary', Gladstone remarked having read them, 'but I would I think invite perusal of the paper by Chamberlain or any other colleague who has taken a special interest in any great South African question of the present day.'[2] Chamberlain in fact objected sharply to several points in the 'Instructions', but was still in the minority in the Cabinet.[3] Chamberlain, it seems, objected in particular to the policy of military operations and sanctions, before beginning negotiations. He was as close to being a 'Little Englander' at this period as he ever came.[4] This is 'Radical Joe' in the tradition of Bright and Cobden. Three years later, in 1884, the first signs of 'Jingo Joe' begin to appear. But, in December 1880, Chamberlain looked to appeasement as a solution to the Transvaal dilemma. Not merely because he vaguely sympathised with the Boer cause, but rather as he could not see the value either of annexing the worthless republic, or of fighting a war to retain such troublesome subjects.

Gladstone and his Colonial Secretary were moved in more mysterious ways. Their aim in the Transvaal was clear enough. As Gladstone informed the Queen, 'Lord Kimberley proposes to instruct Sir. H. Robinson in unequivocal terms on the duty of maintaining the annexation.'[5] But honour was only part of the truth. A careful perusal of Robinson's 'Instructions' brings to light some intriguing sidelights on the workings of the official mind. Two apparent anomalies stand out.[6] First, federation was not completely discounted even at this date. Robinson was reminded that the South Africa Act of 1877 was still in existence, should he require it in calling a federation into being.[7] He was

---

[1] Addit. MSS. 44642, f. 118 (Cabinet Papers), 30 December 1880.

[2] Addit. MSS. 44544, f. 120 (L.B. copy), 24 December 1880.

[3] Addit. MSS. 44642, f. 118 (Cabinet Papers), 30 December 1880. Point 3: 'Chamberlain proposed a modification in the instructions to Sir H. Robinson . . .'

[4] W. L. Strauss, *Joseph Chamberlain and the Theory of Imperialism* (Washington, 1942), pp. 24 ff. 'The Transvaal was in 1881 rather unimportant and . . . [as] no other nation appeared interested in the Transvaal at this time; hence Chamberlain's penchant for favouring a strong policy to circumvent other nations could not exercise itself.'

[5] Guedalla, *Queen and Mr. Gladstone*, II, 128, no. 717. Gladstone to Queen, 28 December 1880.

[6] *Parl. Pap.*, 1881, LXVI, C.2754. Robinson's 'Instructions', pp. 1–8.

[7] Ibid., point 5.

also reminded that the validity of this Act would end in August 1882—with the obvious inference of getting a move on; or in the official language—'the time is therefore becoming short within which the confederation contemplated by that Act can be established'.[1] Thus 'any fresh movement for confederation or union' shown by the colonists, 'Her Majesty's Government will view with an earnest desire to be able to give their sanction'.[2] And, if a constitutional union were not opportune, 'it might be possible to bring about at once joint action in regard to customs dues, and such matters as postal and telegraphic communication, and above all to establish a well-considered and efficient system of mutual co-operation for the maintenance of peace and for defence against risings or attacks of natives, whether within or beyond the frontiers'.[3]

It is a clear indication that Gladstone went to war, in December 1880, as much to keep open the option for the grand vision of federation, as for honour, or supremacy. The lure of the panacea of a local self-governing, self-supporting South African union, was even strong enough to seduce Gladstone away from his Benthamite and Utilitarian principles of plain reasoning.

The second unusual feature of these Robinson 'Instructions' was the relative unconcern about the Transvaal. The main preoccupation was with the mounting Cape–Basuto War.[4] Gladstone and Kimberley tended to see the Transvaal rebellion as a temporary disturbance of the peace, soon to be put down. Their thinking is perhaps understandable. This was the first major clash with the Boers in arms, since the fracas at Boomplaats. They had no measure by which to gauge either Boer determination, or ability, on the field of battle. In contrast, the Basuto crisis came within the compass of their knowledge. They accordingly saw it as a possible full-scale war, which threatened to spread across the *veld*, and so involve the imperial troops in a conflagration as severe as the recent Zulu War. The dread of a 'general native rising', or of another Isandelwana, haunted the Victorians. It could mean intervention and expense on a scale hitherto only murmured in the darkest of moments at the

[1] Ibid., point 6, p. 3.
[2] Ibid., point 9, p. 4.
[3] Idem.
[4] Ibid., points 10 to 23.

Treasury. With the £1½ million cost of the Zulu War in mind Kimberley told Robinson emphatically: 'I must . . . strongly impress upon you the necessity of not extending the responsibilities of this country.'[1]

The third anomaly is that Gladstone had already decided to implement a 'generous peace' towards the Boers—but, only after 'the authority of the Crown has been vindicated'. Gladstone's desire to assure the Dutch of the Transvaal 'such full control of their local affairs as may be consistent with the general interests of Her Majesty's dominions in South Africa',[2] makes nonsense of the school of thought which attributes the liberal terms of the Pretoria Convention to the defeat of General Colley at Majuba. It also suggests anew the pointlessness of the war. By granting the concessions in December, instead of in March 1881, there would have been no Majuba, and no pan-Afrikaner danger.

On the *veld* the war of blunders had begun. It was pursued listlessly for some three months, with both sides ever looking for a way out, through negotiation: Gladstone fearing an 'escalation' of the unrest; Kruger dreading an all-out assault to which he could only succumb in the long run. The logic behind Kruger's declaration of independence, and the consequent rebellion, is easier to fathom than Gladstone's actions. Kruger wanted a protest not a war. Gladstone wanted voluntary federation, yet looked to war to achieve it. Ultimately the *casus belli* lay with Kruger. The Victorians had provoked him to rebel.[3] Gladstone by not honouring his word; Kimberley for becoming so concerned with Irish and Basuto unrest as almost to ignore the Transvaal; Lanyon, Colley, and Strahan for misreading the Boer protests; and Herbert, in the Colonial Office, for suppressing his suspicions and allowing the men on the spot to go unquestioned. In the last resort the war took place because, as President Brand told Lanyon, 'You cannot rule a people with

---

[1] Ibid., point 28, p. 8.

[2] Ibid., point 9, p. 4.

[3] Graham Bower put it thus: 'They [the Boers] wished to be free from the loud-voiced missionary and brazen faced women who form leagues and agitate for causes which are mischievous, by methods which are dishonest.' Afr. MSS., S. 63, f. 4 (Bower Papers).

bayonets.'¹ No man understood this better than Gladstone, who was already having qualms about Forster's tactics in Ireland. In the case of the Transvaal, Gladstone was to pursue the right course, but four months too late. His aim was impeccable. His timing was disastrous.

¹ F. A. van Jaarsveld, *The Awakening of Afrikaner Nationalism.* Brand to Lanyon, 27 November 1879, p. 179.

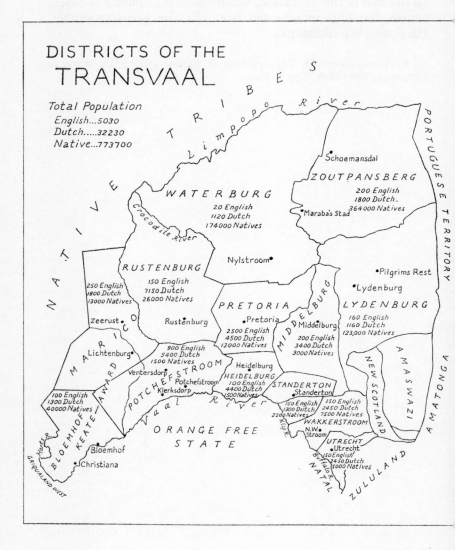

DISTRICTS OF THE
TRANSVAAL

Total Population
  English...5030
  Dutch.....32230
  Native...773700

NATIVE TRIBES

PORTUGUESE TERRITORY

Limpopo River

Schoemansdal

ZOUTPANSBERG
200 English
1800 Dutch
364000 Natives

Maraba's Stad

WATERBURG
20 English
1120 Dutch
174000 Natives

Crocodile River

Nylstroom

Pilgrims Rest

Lydenburg

RUSTENBURG
150 English
7150 Dutch
26000 Natives

PRETORIA

MIDDELBURG

LYDENBURG
160 English
1160 Dutch
123,000 Natives

250 English
1800 Dutch
13000 Natives

Zeerust

Rustenburg

Pretoria

2500 English
4500 Dutch
13000 Natives

Middelburg
200 English
3400 Dutch
3000 Natives

NEW SCOTLAND

AMASWAZI

AMATONGA

MARICO

Lichtenburg

900 English
5400 Dutch
1500 Natives

KEATE AWARD

POTCHEFSTROOM

Ventersdorp

Heidelburg

HEIDELBURG
100 English
4400 Dutch
1500 Natives

STANDERTON

Standerton

100 English
1300 Dutch
40000 Natives

Potchefstroom

Klerksdorp

Vaal River

Klip R.

150 English
2200 Natives

150 English
7500 Natives

WAKKERSTROOM

BLOEMHOF

Harts R.

**ORANGE FREE
STATE**

N.W.
Stroom

UTRECHT
Utrecht
150 English
2450 Dutch
5000 Natives

GRIQUALAND WEST

Bloemhof

Christiana

NATAL

Buffalo R.

ZULULAND

III
REVOLT IN THE TRANSVAAL:
POLICY IN FLUX

A 'loss of nerve' in official circles?

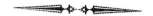

1. The way to Majuba: 16 December 1880—27 February 1881

'ANOTHER year past', Queen Victoria wrote in her Journal on 1 January 1881, 'and we begin one with heavy clouds. A poor Government, Ireland in a state of total lawlessness, and war at the Cape, of a very serious nature! I feel very anxious and we have no one to lean on.'[1] Gladstone was an even wearier traveller in the slough of despond; *he* numbered among his burdens the Queen as well. She had not been on speaking terms with him since August 1880.[2]

For a Premier who looked to his second administration as a temporary interlude[3]—a time for reform and retrenchment before retirement—the range of problems facing him were unique. Bradlaugh and the '4th Party' had disrupted his legislative programme.[4] The Irish party was cutting at Liberal Party morale in the Commons.[5] Within the Cabinet, Forster

[1] *Letters of Queen Victoria*, 2nd ser., III, 177. Journal of Queen Victoria. Entry for 1 January 1881, at Osborne.

[2] Magnus, *Gladstone*, p. 279. Gladstone had been at odds with the Queen since she deliberately failed to invite him to the Duke of Connaught's wedding in March 1879.

[3] Ibid., 291–4 and Addit. MSS. 48631, ff. 87–91 (Hamilton Diary.)

[4] The Bradlaugh incidents are admirably described in Henry Lucy's *Diary of Two Parliaments* (London, 1886), pp. 11, 35–9, 213; and W. L. Arnstein, *The Bradlaugh Case* (Oxford, 1965), pp. 102–312.

[5] Conor Cruise O'Brien, *Parnell and the Irish Party* (Oxford, 1957) is excellent on this.

was successfully dividing ministers on the issue of coercion for Ireland;[1] while Chamberlain and the Radicals were locked in personal combat with Hartington and the Whig faction.[2]

On the broader front Gladstone pondered on Ireland with the most severe problem of unrest since the Great Hunger of 1845–46.[3] Granville brought in news of possible chaos in Egypt, with the growing break-up of Turkish power in the Levant.[4] Kimberley spoke of two wars in South Africa: one involving the Basuto and Cape Colonists, another the rebellious Boers of the Transvaal. And, over and above this, Gladstone was valiantly attempting to frame his final budget as Chancellor of the Exchequer.[5] The load was to take its toll. In mid-January 1881 Gladstone was to be confined to bed, as much from the burden of office as from influenza. The conduct of government also suffered. Gladstone was drawn to the Irish crisis to the exclusion of other pressing business. His attention to foreign and colonial matters was spasmodic. Granville, who should have taken up the reins of foreign affairs into his own hands, was increasingly cast in the unlikely rôle of Cabinet 'jester', having to humour and reconcile the warring factions. He alone kept Hartington in the Cabinet at this time; and he alone persuaded Argyll to stay as long as he did. In the colonial field, Kimberley's mind was divided by his involvement in the coercion issue then at stake in the Cabinet.[6]

In the Transvaal the rebellion proceeded—unheralded by the

[1] P.R.O. 30/29/123. Gladstone to Granville, 10 December 1880; and Morley, *Gladstone*, III, p. 49 (Ramm, I, 228).

[2] Addit. MSS. 43924 f. 40 (Dilke Diary).

[3] P.R.O. 30/29/123. Gladstone to Granville, 10 December 1880 (Ramm, I, 228). And: 'During more than thirty-seven years since I first entered a cabinet, I have hardly known so difficult a question of administration, as that of the immediate duty of the Government in the present state of Ireland'. Gladstone, 25 November 1880. Quoted in Morley, *Gladstone*, III, 51.

[4] Addit. MSS. 44172, f. 337. Granville to Gladstone, 21 December 1880. (Ramm, I, 234–5.)

[5] Childers took over from Gladstone as Chancellor of the Exchequer in December 1882. See Spencer Childers, *Life and Correspondence of Hugh C. E. Childers 1827–1896*, 2 vols. (London, 1901).

[6] Addit. MSS. 44158 ff. 88, 95. Forster to Gladstone, 26 December 1880, and Gladstone's reply, 28 December 1880.

British Press and unnoticed by the British Parliament. The first question on the Transvaal War was not raised in the Commons until 22 January,[1] over a month after the news was received in England of the initial clash of arms. As Herbert Gladstone later said, 'The Opposition itself was as blind to the Transvaal danger as the Colonial Office and the Government.[2] Once the elemental decision had been taken to suppress the rising, the Transvaal War became a War Office matter, and lay beyond the realms of either debate or justification. Coercion was the dominant theme of the important Cabinet of 30 December, when the decision was taken to apply a heavy hand in Ireland and the Transvaal.[3]

Hamilton's Diary bristles with cheery cynicism on this period. He describes the meeting of 30 December as 'a happy Cabinet', with its move towards coercion, suspension of habeas corpus, and military operations. 'Her Majesty ought to be pleased.'[4] But there Cabinet involvement in the Transvaal War ended. The matter was not brought to ministerial level for over a month—until the meeting of Saturday 29 January.[5] While General Colley was going through a ritual of defeats in the mountains on the Transvaal–Natal border, the Liberal Government was totally immersed in Irish matters.[6] The existence of the Government was in fact at stake. Gladstone's secretary vividly recorded the tension at the time. He felt that only Gladstone's force, and Granville's infinite tact, could 'keep up a spirit of entire concord in the Cabinet. Any withdrawal . . . from resort to coercive measures would entail the resignation of the whole of the Whig element of the Cabinet'.[7] Gladstone saw his problem in biblical terms: 'The Christian religion requires a man smitten on one cheek to offer the other. This precept is fulfilled in me . . . today I am

[1] *Hansard*, 3rd ser., CCLVII, 22 January 1881.

[2] Herbert Gladstone, *After Thirty Years*, p. 212.

[3] Addit. MSS. 44642, f. 118 (Cabinet Papers), 30 December 1880.

[4] Addit. MSS. 48630, f. 113 (Hamilton Diary), Thursday, 30 December 1880.

[5] Addit. MSS. 44642, f. 136 (Cabinet Papers), Saturday, 29 January 1880.

[6] Addit. MSS. 44642, ff. 125–38 (Cabinet Papers). Cabinets of 31 December, 4, 15, and 29 January all concerned with Ireland, while Transvaal War was at its height.

[7] Addit. MSS. 48630, f. 110 (Hamilton Diary). Entry for Monday, 27 December 1880.

smitten to the right on coercion, tomorrow to the left on Land.'[1]

The drafting of the Queen's Speech of 6 January brought matters to a focal point. While Victoria accepted the provisions on Ireland and South Africa, she strongly objected to references on foreign matters. In particular, the announcement of withdrawal from Kandahar roused her anger, and she fought a full-scale rearguard action, deploying her supporters in a constant barrage of protests to Gladstone, Granville, and Hartington.[2] On the very day of the speech, Thursday, 6 January, the Queen sent her personal secretary, Ponsonby, to cajole the Premier. As Gladstone wrote anxiously to Granville, 'Ponsonby comes up at 3.15 charged I presume to renew the fight. . . .'[3] The speech was delivered unaltered in the Upper House by the Lord Chancellor, in Victoria's absence. It is a significant document. Apart from brief references to matters such as Kandahar, it was solely concerned with Ireland, and its problem of evictions. The forthcoming Parliament did indeed promise 'to be wholly Irish'.[4] The announcement of the vindication of authority in the Transvaal was no more than a public announcement of the Cabinet decision of a week before. The phrasing was drawn up by Kimberley, and agreed by Gladstone;[5] it takes no account of the private doubts that Kimberley was already entertaining about the trend of events in the Cape Colony and the two Boer republics.[6]

[1] P.R.O. 30/29/123. Gladstone to Granville (Private), 28 December 1880, from Hawarden. (Ramm, I, 238.) See also Addit. MSS. 48630, f. 111 (Hamilton Diary). Entry for 29 December 1880: 'The Great Man's birthday. . . . He holds a position of great responsibility. He has the whole weight of Ireland on his shoulders—and in the Cabinet stands between the two fires of the right and the left wing.'

[2] *Letters of Queen Victoria*, 2nd ser., III, 178–80. See also Gardiner, *Life of Harcourt*, I, 597–600. Guedalla, *Queen and Mr. Gladstone*, II, 133–5.

[3] P.R.O. 30/29/124. Gladstone to Granville (Private), 6 January 1881, from Downing Street. Addit. MSS. 48630, f. 114 (Hamilton Diary). Entry for Thursday, 6 January. 'We had a tremendous tussle with Her Majesty over the Queen's Speech. . . .' (See also Ramm, I, 239.)

[4] Addit. MSS. 48630, f. 114 (Hamilton Diary). Entry for Friday, 30 December 1880.

[5] Addit. MSS. 44544, f. 125 (L.B. copy). Gladstone to Kimberley, 4 January 1881, from Hawarden.

[6] C.O. 48/496. Minute by Kimberley, 31 December, on Strahan to Kimberley (Tel.) 30 December 1880.

The Irish and Transvaal crises were in fact now both pursued at two levels. There were the outward and visible signs of a Government dealing firmly with two sets of unrest in Her Majesty's domains. Then there were the inward conflicts, and increasingly bitter duels between the Whiggish faction of the Cabinet—Hartington, Kimberley, Argyll, Selborne, and also Forster—against the Gladstonians—Granville, Harcourt, Childers and the G.O.M.—who reacted by instinct against the principle of militant coercion. On the fringe, there stood Chamberlain at the head of an opportunist party, mainly radical, ready to throw in their weight at any moment to shatter Whig strength. The whole back-stage affair is excellently illustrated by the handling of the Transvaal rebellion. Initially the Whig faction triumphed, largely because the Gladstonians had little to support their objections, beyond voicing their instincts. Gladstone, in particular, was as reluctant a subscriber to Forster's coercion in Ireland, as to Kimberley's military measures in South Africa. But he accepted their traditional reaction and policy, as it seemed that a more durable solution would only be achieved once the unrest in both areas was quelled. In the case of Ireland his Land Act was to follow the initial coercion. In the Transvaal, local self-government was contemplated, consequent upon Colley's suppression of the rebellion. The Whigs saw it differently. They pressed coercion up to Majuba and beyond. But by then they had lost the open support of Kimberley and the reluctant support of the Gladstonians.

This regrouping of the Cabinet factions was more than a redefining of attitudes. It amounted to a complete change of heart. Gladstone found irrefutable facts to support his inclination to grant the Boers a modicum of independence. Kimberley was gradually converted to become a complete Gladstonian in regard to South Africa—if not on Ireland.[1] What caused this revolution in the Cabinet? It could be argued that it was merely the Gladstonians getting their way. Gladstone himself had been no more eager for the war than Chamberlain, but had accepted it as a necessary evil. He would yet snatch a self-governing confederation in South Africa from the midst of coercion and rebellion. But this leaves unexplained both Kimberley's conversion, and also the general acceptance of the new attitude to

[1] Addit. MSS. 44226, f. 145. Kimberley to Gladstone, 10 June 1881.

South Africa, by all but the die-hards in the Cabinet, and even they found their position increasingly untenable. Equally significant is the gradual *volte-face* that took place in the Colonial Office. The general bellicose mood of the permanent officials, that had resulted in the Boer declaration of independence, was to fade. They became the reluctant advocates of a policy of conciliation in South Africa.

The manner in which this Gladstone government swung away from the old traditional policy, to embrace an entirely new attitude to the Boers, is a fascinating exposé of policy-making. It was not caused by an isolated event. Rather it took place over some four weeks, as the reports of the local administrators and military now began to condition the officials to the fact that the war would solve nothing, and might even eliminate the imperial factor altogether in the long run. The accumulation of the local reports, in conjunction with the Irish disorder, gradually sapped the confidence of those advocates of coercion in the Transvaal. Kimberley had promised Gladstone a swift halting of the rebellion, but he found that he was possibly staring at the origins of another 'Irish situation' in embryo.

The first significant seed of doubt was planted by General Colley, in an alarming telegram on Christmas Day, 1880. He admitted that the full effect of the rebellion '. . . cannot be measured'; but that 'an uneasy feeling is general that Boer disaffection extends through South Africa'.[1] The official reaction was cautious; but clearly the telegram shook the Colonial Office. Herbert minuted: 'I fear this telegram indicates that the Dutch inhabitants of the Cape Colony are to say the least becoming restless in consequence of the collision between H.M. troops and the Boers. . . .' He found it particularly worrying that Chief Justice de Villiers, of the Cape, a most moderate man, was '. . . . in respect of the disaffection of the Transvaal Boers . . . fully committed as their supporter'.[2] Strahan, the acting High Commissioner of the Cape, gave substance to these fears with a long telegram on 30 December:

[1] C.O. 179/135. Colley to Kimberley (Tel.), 25 December 1880. See C.O. Minute dated 27 December 1880.
[2] C.O. 48/496. Minute by Herbert on Strahan to Kimberley (Tel.) 25 December 1880. Minute dated 29 December 1880.

Much sympathy for the Transvaal Republic has been excited in this Colony and in the Orange Free State, and it is necessary to face the probability of active assistance being rendered to the Transvaal Boers by a number at least of the inhabitants of the Free State.

And the Dutch were not his only concern. 'There is also undoubtedly a fear lest the natives in the Transvaal and elsewhere should be incited against British rule and join the disaffected.'[1] Kimberley viewed this new evidence uneasily and decided that he alone was not going to be responsible for a southern African conflagration. He willingly abdicated from the position of arbiter of policy. 'All important telegrams from S. Africa', he remarked to Herbert on 3 January 1881, 'should be circulated at once to the Cabinet as a matter of course, without asking me.'[2] To Sir Hercules Robinson, now on his way to the Cape, he wrote angrily that he had just received an earlier despatch from Strahan full of Cape unrest and Brand's warning telegrams about the Transvaal War. 'I regret that having regard to the grave importance of the question to which these telegrams relate, Sir. G. Strahan did not communicate them to me by telegraph instead of forwarding them in an ordinary despatch.'[3]

As Kimberley became more anxious, General Colley became more reckless. He had already written that, 'It appears to me most desirable to attempt to strike quickly', because of the general Dutch unrest.[4] Now, on 2 January, he began a long despatch by saying, 'It seems early yet to begin talking of the settlement of the Transvaal. But the breaking up of the Boer force is only a question of time—if I cannot do it with the force I have now in the country, I certainly can when I receive the reinforcements on their way. . . .'[5] Then followed a system for setting up a legislative assembly, and a method of making the

---

[1] C.O. 48/496. Strahan to Kimberley (Tel.), 30 December 1880. Minute dated 3 January 1881.

[2] C.O. 48/496. Minute by Kimberley to Herbert, 3 January 1886, attached to Strahan to Kimberley (Tel.), 30 December 1880.

[3] *Parl. Pap.*, 1881, LXVI, C.2783, p. 19. Kimberley to Robinson, 1 January 1881.

[4] C.O. 179/135. Colley to Kimberley (Tel.), 25 December 1880.

[5] Addit. MSS. 44226, ff. 17–19. Colley to Kimberley, 2 January, enclosed in Kimberley to Gladstone, 4 February 1881.

Boers pay for the war. Kimberley's reaction to all such schemes was very cool: 'We must first "catch our hare", at present we appear to be caught ourselves.'[1] This was in fact becoming increasingly true. The rebellion was not isolated to a particular area of the Transvaal;[2] nor were the Boers turning out to be the 'cowards' Lanyon predicted. 'Her Majesty's forces have been attacked at several points', Colley reported on 29 December, 'many killed and wounded. Peaceable citizens seized and taken prisoner, and threats and violence used against all loyal subjects.'[3]

The War Office provided the only light relief by earnestly asking to be informed as to how long the war would last. 'Is this intended as a somewhat elaborate joke on the part of the War Office?' Hemming asked in wonder. Kimberley suggested they inform the War Office that while they regretted the inconvenience they could not oblige, as the Secretary of State for the Colonies did not have the gift of prophecy.[4] Childers took this as a personal slight, and wrote unhappily to Gladstone that he could not budget correctly for the war as everything depended on the local situation, 'of which the War Office knows nothing'.[5] It was a bizarre admission by the Secretary of State for War in the midst of a war.

The mood on the *veld* was vastly different. The initial Boer success on 20 December—when they cut a British column to ribbons on the Bronkhorstspruit Road[6]—followed by the capture or besieging of major towns, lifted the Afrikaner spirits. As Colley informed Childers on 7 January: 'Boer forces at Langes [*sic*] Nek within Natal boundary augmented to 10,000 . . .'[7] Colley now set out on 8 January with inadequate troops to

[1] C.O. 291/9. Minute by Kimberley of 2 January on J. S. Christopher to C.O. of 28 December 1880.

[2] *Parl. Pap.*, 1881, LXVI, C.2740, pp. 122–5.

[3] C.O. 48/499. Colley to Strahan (Tel.), 29 December 1880, enclosed in Strahan to Kimberley, 4 January 1881.

[4] C.O. 291/13. W.O. to C.O. 1 January 1881; Minute dated 3 January 1881.

[5] Addit. MSS. 44129, ff. 1356. Childers to Gladstone, 8 January 1881.

[6] Full account of the so-called 'treachery act' in De Kiewiet, *Imperial Factor*, p. 276 *passim*.

[7] *Parl. Pap.* 1881, LXVI. C.2783, pp. 43 ff. Colley to Childers (Tel.), 7 January 1881. Ibid., (Tels.) 9–10 January 1881, referring to increasing Boer strength.

disperse the Boers at Laing's Nek.[1] Kimberley viewed his progress with the greatest concern. 'Let *all* papers relating to the Boer rebellion or Basuto war, be sent to me as soon as they arrive,' he told Herbert.[2] The next ten days were to be crucial to the conduct of the war and colonial policy. Kimberley's lingering fears were to be substantiated, and Colley's behaviour was to set the pattern for Majuba.

On 10 January, the Orange Free State Consul-General, P. J. Blyth, called at the Colonial Office, to present an urgent telegram, received from President Brand the day before.[3] 'Don't believe the malicious fabrications about the Dutch,' Brand stated, 'Free State only wishes peace and prosperity for whole of South Africa.'[4] However, Brand warned that feeling was growing among his fellow Boers to go and assist the Transvalers. Hence he 'fervently hopes that every effort will be made without least delay to prevent further bloodshed'; by calling a halt to the war, before it draws in the Free State burghers.[5] He followed up his initial message, with a veritable barrage of warnings and pleadings to Kimberley. On 12 January he wrote: 'I think not a moment should be lost, and someone, say Chief Justice de Villiers . . . should be sent to the Transvaal burghers by the Government with the view of stopping further collision, and with a clear and definite proposal for settlement. Moments are precious.'[6] Kimberley's reply to Brand, via Strahan—that Her Majesty's Government would agree to a 'satisfactory arrangement', if and when the Boers laid down their arms,[7]— provoked the strongest of Brand's telegrams urging that bloodshed on a large scale, with general Boer participation, could be prevented *only* if 'the British Government make a clear and distinct proposal to the Transvaal people without delay'.[8]

[1] C.O. 179/137. Colley to Kimberley, 8 January 1881.

[2] C.O. 48/496. Kimberley to Herbert, 8 January 1881, on Strahan to Kimberley, 18 December 1880.

[3] C.O. 291/14. Brand to Blyth, 9 January 1881.

[4] *Parl. Pap.*, 1881, LXVI, C.2783. Brand to Blyth on 9 January and 11 January 1881.

[5] Ibid., 11 January 1881.

[6] C.O. 291/14. Brand to Blyth, 12 January 1881.

[7] Ibid., Kimberley to Strahan, enclosed in Kimberley to Brand, 11 January 1881.

[8] *Parl. Pap.*, 1881, LXVI, C.2783. Brand to Kimberley via Blyth, 16 January 1881.

Brand's intervention was a significant moment for policy. Prior to this, as Gladstone admitted, the Government had 'nothing but telegraphic scraps as to the nature, breadth and solidity of the outbreak'.[1] Now an independent, most cautious and hitherto reliable Afrikaner, had been prompted to speak out in the strongest terms. It did not overnight change the basis of policy, as is evinced by Kimberley's reticent reply to Brand of 11 January—but it did underline the fears of Strahan and Colley; and it did show that Kimberley was not implacable in stance. He was prepared to accept a peace, without an obvious victory, so long as the Transvalers would disperse. Kimberley was in fact wavering. He was pulled between clinging to the traditional policy, already set in motion, and listening to the instinctive doubts that he felt as a result of the reports coming in from South Africa. As a cautious man, inclined to inertia, and wary of relying on the despatches of local men—particularly after Lanyon's blunders—he went through agonies of indecision. There was no inner consistency in his policy from now on. He increasingly probed the possibilities of peace; but, at the same time he was reluctant to shy away from the time-tested policy of coercion in the face of opposition. Chamberlain's insight allowed him to guess at Kimberley's dilemma, and this encouraged him to launch another embarrassing set of 'we were wrong' speeches. The aim was clear. Failing to drive Kimberley from the Cabinet over Ireland, Chamberlain hoped he might break the Colonial Secretary on the Transvaal issue. Gladstone rebuked him strongly.[2] It made little difference to Chamberlain, who stepped up the campaign, suspecting that he had Kimberley on the run. This view was confirmed, when, at the Cabinet of Saturday, 15 January,[3] Kimberley found himself alienated from his former Whig allies, as a result of his own sympathetic presentation of the Brand telegrams.[4] His Whig colleagues could not see why there had been a softening in attitude to the Boers. And they carried the Cabinet. It was to be the last Cabinet on the Transvaal at which Kimberley, and the Glad-

[1] Addit. MSS. 44544, f. 127. Gladstone to Childers, 10 January 1881.
[2] J.C. 5/34/5. Gladstone to Chamberlain, 8 January 1881.
[3] Addit. MSS. 44642, f. 130 (Cabinet Papers), 15 January 1881.
[4] Addit. MSS. 44226, ff. 5–10. Kimberley to Gladstone, 13 January 1881.

stonians, were to be in the minority. By the next Transvaal Cabinet, on 29 January,[1] the mass of evidence at Kimberley's disposal had built up sufficiently for him to make distinct peace overtures through Brand, and to present this action as a *fait accompli* to the Whigs—who were now his opponents on Transvaal policy, if not on Ireland.

Kimberley took the plunge, and abandoned the policy of coercion—between 21 January and 24 January. With Gladstone's full support his handling of the matter became firmer. When the government of Holland became restive, over British policy in the Transvaal, Kimberley minuted confidently: the Dutch 'no doubt remember that very slight action on our part would place them in inextricable difficulties in Sumatra, where they are waging a war of conquest. . . .'[2] Portugal received equally sharp treatment, when it protested over a rumour that Britain was to send troops through Lourenço Marques to fight the Boers. Kimberley instructed the Foreign Office to 'give the fullest assurances that we have no intention to claim any right or ask any leave to convey troops through Portuguese territory', for the simple reason that 'the prevalence of tsetse fly . . . makes it impossible for any horse or cattle to pass through the country. . . .'[3] Privately Kimberley remarked: 'Happy people who have nothing more serious to quarrel about!'[4]

Even more significant were Kimberley's secret communications with Brand. On 25 January the Free State President had sent his final urgent telegram,[5] suggesting an armistice now that Robinson had arrived at the Cape (on 22 January).[6] Kimberley replied on 26 January, offering peace negotiations if Brand could persuade the Transvalers to stop fighting.[7] However, two sets of people were kept ignorant of these negotiations—quite apart from the general public. First, the Whig faction of the Cabinet. Second, Colley and his staff in the Transvaal. As

[1] Addit. MSS. 44642, f. 136 (Cabinet Papers), Saturday, 29 January 1881.
[2] C.O. 291/3. Minute by Kimberley dated 23 January 1881.
[3] C.O. 291/13. Draft despatch by Kimberley, 13–29 January 1881.
[4] C.O. 291/13. C.O. to F.O., 29 January 1881.
[5] C.O. 291/14. Brand to Blyth (Tel.), 25 January 1881.
[6] C.O. 48/499. Robinson to Kimberley. First despatch, 22 January 1881.
[7] C.O. 291/14. Kimberley to Robinson (Tel.), enclosed in Kimberley to Brand, 26 January 1881.

Colley wrote to his wife on 21 January; 'I have not heard a word of any kind from either Colonial or War Secretaries, and am thus left entirely unfettered, and to my own discretion.'[1] This was not entirely by accident. Colley was kept in ignorance for a good reason. Should the negotiations come to nil, Kimberley would still have the best of both worlds, by playing two consecutive policies at the same time. Colley represented one: a swift military victory was still to Kimberley's liking. Brand represented the other: a peaceable dispersion of the Boers was even more attractive. Clearly Kimberley wished to see that neither avenue was closed, so reducing his options.

Gladstone played a key rôle in this policy by providing the parliamentary smoke-screen that was necessary. On 21 January, in answer to a motion of censure, by a back-bencher,[2] Gladstone made a masterly statement in the Commons on the Transvaal policy. It meant all things to all people. Was he in favour of the annexation? No—'I confess I thought it would involve us in unmixed mischief. . . .'[3] Why then had he not revoked the annexation?—by annexing the Transvaal, 'we contracted new obligations . . . I must look at the obligations'. To whom were these obligations?—'. . . towards the English and other settlers in the Transvaal . . . to the native races, an obligation which I may call an obligation of humanity and justice.' But, had not the Liberal Premier spoken out in Midlothian strongly against the annexation?—'I was not silent', he admitted but, 'the honourable member supposes that the word "repudiate" bears no sense except that of the intention to reverse a thing, although in fact, the word does not bear such sense at all . . . . To disapprove the annexation of a country is one thing; to abandon that annexation is another.'[4] The Government policy, Gladstone claimed, was quite clear. 'I can assure the House that we shall, with earnestness, with temper, . . . re-establish the authority of the Crown'; and having done so the Government shall make a 'full settlement of the question as will deserve and receive the approval of the House and the country.'[5] The speech had just the desired effect. Hamilton noted that 'Mr G. spoke; and his

[1] Colley to his wife, 21 January 1881, quoted in Herbert Gladstone, *After Thirty Years*, p. 222.

[2] *Hansard*, 3rd ser., CCLVII. Rylands was the back-bencher.

[3] Ibid., cols. 1140–41.   [4] Ibid., col. 1141.   [5] Ibid., col. 1147.

speech seems to have been well received.'[1] It gave Kimberley breathing-space to pursue his dual policy; and it rendered negative the radical pressure on Kimberley.

The radical challenge came and went. 'After dinner on the 21st,' Dilke notes in his Diary, 'I went down to the H. of C. and deliberately walked out on the Transvaal division, as did three other members of the Government—Bright, Chamberlain, and Courtney.'[2] It was to no avail. Kimberley's position was now beyond assault. The files of the Colonial Office show why.

Reports from the Cape began to beat an insistent theme: Cape Dutch restiveness of alarming proportions. 'Meetings being held in the Dutch districts of the Colony,' Strahan reported by telegram on 16 January, 'and petitions prepared expressive of sympathy with Transvaal Boers, and recommending mediation. . . .'[3] These petitions were duly presented to Strahan, by a deputation that included de Villiers.[4] He forwarded them, in conjunction with news of the Dutch activity in cuttings from *Het Volksblad*, and *Cape Argus*.[5] This deputation spoke strongly of the Transvaal Boers as a 'wronged community', and reminded Strahan of their blood-ties with the Transvalers.[6] The acting Governor was highly alarmed by the motions passed at the Dutch protest meetings. He sent them verbatim to the Colonial Office.[7] Speeches by the Dutch leaders were read with growing concern in official circles. 'Oppression will make even a wise man mad', the Rev. S. J. du Toit had stated at the Paarl meeting. 'We sympathise with the Boers. . . . I wish the Govern-

---

[1] Addit. MSS. 48630, f. 119 (Hamilton Diary). Entry for Saturday, 22 January 1881.

[2] Addit. MSS. 43935, f. 19 (Dilke Memoir). Entry for 21 January 1881.

[3] *Parl. Pap.*, 1881, LXVI, C.2783, p. 57. Strahan to Kimberley (Tel.), 16 January 1881.

[4] Ibid., pp. 61–6.

[5] Ibid., Strahan to Kimberley, 22 December 1881. Received in C.O., 20 January 1881.

[6] Idem.

[7] See *Cape Argus*, 9 December 1880, for the big Paarl meeting motion: 'This meeting regards a war between the Boers of the Transvaal and the British Government as in every way calamitous, not only to that country but also for the Colony and the whole of South Africa, since thereby the already existing and even increasing antipathy between the colonists of Dutch and English descent will be increased. . . .' Enclosed in Strahan to Kimberley, 9 December 1880; received in C.O. 20 January 1881.

ment to know that we and the Transvaal Boers are of the same flesh and blood. . . .'[1] Du Toit's *Genootskap van Regte Afrikaners*, and even Hofmeyr's *Boere Beschermings Vereeniging*, both began to have a political edge, and a new militancy.

On 25 January Kimberley was shown the latest despatch from Strahan, which included letters from Colley.[2] The General had telegraphed: 'There are ugly rumours in Natal of active sympathy with the Boers, throughout Orange Free State, and Cape of Good Hope. I understand people of Kimberley offered a volunteer corps to relieve Potchefstroom. This would be undesirable as it would raise the burghers.'[3] Strahan's reply to Colley had scant comfort. While he felt it unlikely that the Cape Dutch would also revolt, he had to admit that 'there is much sympathy between the people of Dutch descent in this colony and the Boers of the Transvaal. . . .' As to the Free State, 'I think that from what I can learn you will do well to provide for the contingency of a number of Boers rendering active assistance to those of the Transvaal.'[4] After consulting with Sprigg, the Cape Premier, Strahan requested the Colonial Office not to send any British troops to the Transvaal via the Cape, as had been proposed, for it would 'greatly add to the excitement which already exists among the Dutch population. . . .'[5] Herbert immediately informed the War Office, and the troops were diverted via Natal.[6] Colley had meanwhile telegraphed to Childers: 'In view of the effect which the success gained by the immigrant Boers is likely to have throughout the country . . . and the undoubted sympathy felt with the Transvaal rebels by the Boers generally, I have since asked that a battery of artillery may be added.'[7] Childers expressed the growing conviction among those immediately concerned with the war, when he wrote to Gladstone: '. . . the duration of the war largely de-

[1] Idem.

[2] *Parl. Pap.*, 1881, LXVI, C.2783, pp. 75 ff. Strahan to Kimberley, 4 January 1881, enclosed in Colley to Strahan and vice versa.

[3] Ibid., Colley to Strahan (Tel.), 27 January 1881.

[4] Ibid., Strahan to Colley (Tel.), 28 January 1881.

[5] Ibid., Strahan to Kimberley, 4 January 1881; received in C.O., 28 January 1881.

[6] Ibid., C.O. to W.O., 26 January 1881.

[7] C.O. 291/13, Colley to Childers, 29 December 1880. (Enclosed in W.O. to C.O., 27 January 1881.)

pends on our relations with the Orange Free State and the Boers generally. . . .'[1]

In the Colonial Office opinion was divided as to the value, and meaning, of the reports of Strahan and Colley. Herbert adopted a strange stance for so rational a man. He agreed that Cape Dutch restiveness was the danger to watch, but added that until the Transvaal Boers 'submitted themselves to the Queen, and it has been ascertained how far it is possible to extend clemency to the ring leaders, H.M. Govt. can hardly proceed to consider terms for settlement'.[2] Hemming was of like opinion: '. . . . until the rebellion is put down no compromise can of course be contemplated'. Fairfield disagreed, but was in the minority.[3] The news of Laing's Nek, of 28 January, cut at Herbert's confidence and made Kimberley even surer that the war must either be halted before it encouraged further Dutch unrest, and another Zulu rebellion—or successfully concluded immediately. The longer the war lasted the more likely it was to spread. The Basuto War was already being waged in the south; it would not need a great stretch of the imagination to see this war overspilling into the Transkei and to the eastern frontier.

This was basically Kimberley's position at the Cabinet of Saturday, 29 January, which discussed the significance of Colley's repulse at Laing's Nek. The peace overtures were revealed to the ministers; and, despite heated discussion, Kimberley was allowed to pursue this line of policy.[4] The Queen's Journal vividly records her feelings on Kimberley's methods: 'The news of Sir G. Colley's repulse are most distressing. Great Britain's star *is* NOT *in the ascendant since the last 6* or *7 months!*'[5] Childers was more philosophic He wired to Colley: 'Have heard of your check with much regret. Do you want reinforcements in addition to those already advised. . .?[6] The reply was emphatic: 'I think reinforcements on their way quite sufficient

---

[1] Addit. MSS. 44129, ff. 135–6. Childers to Gladstone, 8 January 1881.

[2] C.O. 48/496. Strahan to Kimberley (Tel.), 25 December 1880. Minutes by Herbert, 29 December 1880, and Hemming, 24 January 1881.

[3] Idem.

[4] Addit. MSS. 44642, f. 136 (Cabinet Papers), Saturday, 29 January 1881.

[5] *Letters of Queen Victoria*, 2nd ser., III, p. 186. Queen Victoria to Granville, 28 January 1881, at Osborne.

[6] *Parl. Pap.*, 1881, LXVII, C.2783, p. 3. Childers to Colley (Tel.), 29 January 1881.

... effects of check not serious. Men in excellent spirits, eager to attack again.'[1]

In the light of Colley's behaviour it is remarkable that Kimberley did not inform him at this stage of his peace problems. As it was, Colley achieved the worst of all ends: defeat before peace. On 23 January Colley had called on the Boers to disperse;[2] and then attacked them at Laing's Nek, on 28 January, before he received their reply.[3] Strange and tragic events were taking place in the mist and rain of the Transvaal–Natal border mountains. The 'undisciplined bands of yeomen'—as the *London Illustrated News*[4] called the Boers—were more than holding their own. Colley's conduct was becoming increasingly irrational. He turned a blind eye to all Boer overtures for peace, as he was determined on redeeming honour, as much for himself as for his country. A major reason why the Kimberley–Brand–Kruger line of policy came to nil, in these early days of the war, is directly attributable to Colley. Admittedly he did not know of Kimberley's desire for an early peace, but equally he did not desire peace himself. He put aside all the Boer offers of a truce, since he was determined on complete military victory. The Gladstone Papers suggests that his major blunder was not Majuba, but his behaviour in the weeks before the battle. Both the Premier, and the Colonial Secretary, more and more deplored his handling of the war. When Colley returned to the question of how to deal with the Boers after the war, Gladstone lost his patience. 'Colley with a vengeance counts his eggs before they are hatched', Gladstone remarked to Kimberley. 'His line is singularly wide of ours.'[5] A few days later—after Ingogo—he

[1] Ibid., Colley to Childers (Tel.), 30 January 1881.

[2] Addit. MSS. 44627, f. 105. Colley to Joubert, 23 January 1881.
This was in response to Kruger's letter of 17 December 1880, ibid., Colley: 'Still anxious to avoid unnecessary bloodshed I now call upon you and your followers to disperse to your homes, and submit to Her Majesty's Authority, which it is my duty to vindicate and maintain. The column which I am about to advance is only the advanced guard of the large forces which are now arriving from England and India ... [you] cannot but be aware how hopeless is the struggle you have embarked upon, and how little any accidental success gained can affect the ultimate result.'

[3] Ibid., ff. 107–8. Joubert to Colley, 5 February 1881.

[4] *London Illustrated News*, 29 January 1881.

[5] Addit. MSS. 44544, f. 134 (L.B. copy). Gladstone to Kimberley, 5 February 1881.

was even more emphatic. 'Colley's plan is all wrong', he told Kimberley.[1] But even Gladstone did not know that Colley's transgression was greater than that. Only later in the month did he learn of the great opportunity for settling the South African problem which Colley had allowed to slip through his hands.

'Ere long I hope Colley will find you are able to work . . . on safer lines than his,' Gladstone had written to Kimberley on 5 February.[2] The Colonial Secretary had agreed, and bemoaned the fact that the peace overture via Brand had proved sterile.[3] But so keen was Kimberley for stopping the war that he suggested they publish a statement to the effect that if the Boers dispersed, Her Majesty's Government promised the most liberal peace terms, with no reprisals for those who had taken up arms. As Kimberley explained to Gladstone: '. . . [It] might have a good effect, if not upon the most determined of our opponents, at all events on waverers of whom there are no doubt many'.[4] Colley was of a very different opinion; and while it was easy for Gladstone and Kimberley to by-pass Colonial Office opinion, it was impossible to circumvent Colley, the only man in direct contact with the Boer leaders. And it was Colley who now ditched any possibility of an early peace.

It would seem that in Joubert's reply of 5 February—to Colley's 'dispersal demand' letter of 23 January—the Boer commando leader spoke of a willingness on the part of the Republic to begin negotiations;[5] and even favourably to consider joining a South Africa confederation, if the Transvaal were granted full internal self-government in such a union. He claimed to enclose a proclamation by the triumvirate, laying out the detailed conditions demanded by the Transvaal before they accepted the confederation.

This unexpected suggestion was viewed with great scepticism by Colley, particularly as the 'proclamation' promised was not enclosed in the letter.[6] Colley interpreted Joubert's letter as no more than a clever ruse to gain time, while the Boer forces

[1] Ibid., f. 135 (L.B. copy). Gladstone to Kimberley, 9 February 1881.
[2] Ibid., f. 134. Gladstone to Kimberley, 5 February 1881.
[3] Addit. MSS. 44226, f. 23. Kimberley to Gladstone, 6 February 1881.
[4] Idem.
[5] Addit. MSS. 44627, ff. 107–8, Joubert to Colley, 5 February 1881 (in Gladstone Papers).
[6] Ibid., Colley to Joubert, 14 February 1881.

increased in numbers. Accordingly he ignored the offer, deeming it unworthy even of consideration; and did not forward it to London. Instead, he went ahead with his military schemes, and attacked the Boers three days later.[1] However, the Boer declaration was finally sent by Joubert to Colley on 15 February, with a covering note explaining that it had not been included in the letter of the 5th, as the Boers who had been sent to Potchefstroom, to have it printed, had met with armed resistance along the way.[2]

What is the historian to make of the Transvaal offer? Was it a calculated attempt to gain time? Colley may have been right, for the Boer forces did swell considerably after Laing's Nek. Or, was it less subtle than that? Neither Kruger nor Joubert ever thought they could achieve so complete a military victory over the might of the Imperial Army that they could dictate the peace terms.[3] Rather they were eminently practical men—Kruger in particular had no illusions as to Boer strength—and saw the rebellion as a great demonstration of their determination to regain their independence.[4] The timing of the offer is therefore suggestive. It came a week after the victory at Laing's Nek; and when Kruger and Joubert may have thought that as they were unlikely to gain another military triumph—in view of the large-scale reinforcements being sent to Colley through Natal—now was the time to negotiate, before they were defeated. It could

[1] He had also rejected Brand's advice. In a telegram to the Free State leader on 10 February 1881: 'I thank your Honour for your telegram and prompt action. I cannot however, allow any communications with Boers to affect my military operations. . . .' Ibid., f. 107.

[2] Ibid., Joubert to Colley, 15 February 1881. See also *Parl. Pap.*, 1881, LXVII, C.2794, p. 615. The Transvaal Proclamation, dated 27 January 1881, read: 'We repeat in the most emphatic manner that we are willing to co-operate in the desire of the Imperial Government for the confederation of South Africa, and in order to make this our offer as clear and unmistakable as possible . . . we declare that we shall be satisfied with the annulment of the Annexation; the restoration of the South African Republic, under the protection of the Queen; and that once a year the Dutch flag shall be hoisted. . . . The Proclamation is unsigned.

[3] This is well detailed in E. A. Walker's *Lord De Villiers and his Times* (London, 1925), pp. 144–66.

[4] As Professor D. W. Kruger has written: 'Op'n militere oorwinning kon hy [Kruger] nie hoop nie . . . Daarom het Paul Kruger die oorlog eerder gesien as 'n demonstrasie van die vasberadenheid van volk dan as 'n gewapende progmeting.' D. W. Kruger, *Paul Kruger*, I, 216.

possibly be argued that they made the offer believing that Britain would never accept it, bent as the imperial authority was on military suppression of the rising.[1] But this assumes that the Boers wanted to fight on—which they did not. It seems more likely that Kruger and Joubert were indeed 'taking their winnings' while events, or luck, still ran their way.

This is further suggested by their behaviour after their second victory, when Colley unexpectedly attacked them at Ingogo. Once again the Boers used the victory to sue immediately for peace.[2] Indeed the only complicating factor in all these events was Colley. It was he who was continually attacking, and continually being defeated; it was he who did not want peace after Laing's Nek, or after Ingogo; and it was he who not only ignored the Boer overtures, but even twisted Kimberley's peace probes to fit his own plans for a great military victory. As a bright young major-general he knew that his career could not stand a conciliatory peace, after a series of defeats. His biographer has pointed out that Kimberley kept him singularly ill-informed about the official desire for peace.[3] This is true, but only up to 8 February.[4] On that date Kimberley, fearing that Brand could achieve little—and greatly worried by Strahan's reports from the Cape—brought Colley into his own plans, and attempted to bring about an armistice via the major-general. Gladstone's fears, that Colley was irresponsible,[5] were soon borne out.

---

[1] If this were so, it was a miscalculation. Gladstone did not see confederation as dead, nor did Kimberley. Robinson's 'Instructions' clearly prove this. See Kimberley to Robinson, 31 December 1881, below.

[2] Addit. MSS. 44627, f. 109. Kruger to Colley, 12 February 1881. Kruger: '. . . [we] against our will are forced into a bloody strife. . . . The people has distinctly declared its will, that, on the cancelling of the deed of annexation to work together in all things with Her Majesty's Government that can be profitable to the whole of South Africa. We wish to seek no strife with the Imperial Government, but cannot do otherwise than give the last drop of blood for our good right. . . .'

[3] Butler, *Life of Colley*, pp. 357–9.

[4] It is interesting that after this telegram from Kimberley, Colley did forward the first of the Boer overtures, that of Kruger's of 12 February 1881. See Colley to Kimberley (Tel.) 13 February 1881 in Addit. MSS. 44627, f. 108.

[5] Addit. MSS. 44544, f. 135 (L.B. copy). Gladstone to Kimberley, 9 February 1881.

Kimberley revealed his hand to Colley in the carefully worded telegram of 8 February.[1] He suggested that the Cabinet were prepared to negotiate a peace if the Boers voluntarily laid down their arms. Much has been made of the fact that Kimberley did not emphatically instruct Colley to stop fighting. But surely this was implied in the fact that Kimberley expressed his desire to treat with the Boers; and equally it does not square with Colley's actions. He did not forward the offer for some days; instead he attacked the Boers once more—and was once more driven back, at Ingogo Heights, on the very same day as Kimberley's telegram, 8 February. The Colonial Secretary, despairing of Colley, telegraphed the same message to Robinson two days later.[2] Meanwhile Colley, having suffered his second defeat, forwarded Kimberley's message to the Boers, and received an almost immediate reply.[3] Kruger was happy to consider negotiations, and suggested that a Royal Commission would be acceptable to the Boers, if Britain annulled the annexation, as an act of good faith, before the discussions began. Colley acknowledged Kruger's letter;[4] and this time he *did* forward the offer to Kimberley at the Colonial Office.[5] It is interesting that Kruger's letter made no mention of the previous federal offer.[6] The Boers may have decided that their bargaining position was now infinitely better since Colley's latest repulse, or they may have concluded that it had met with no enthusiasm on the British side, in view of Colley's attack of 8 February, three days after the offer. Probably there is truth in both explanations. Kruger was possibly embarrassed by the earlier suggestion, when he unexpectedly found himself in a much better position—entirely as a result of Colley's military blunder—and so decided that as the general had not mentioned it, he would pretend it had never been made. The fact that the declaration was sent to Colley on 15 February,[7] was probably

---

[1] *Parl. Pap.*, 1881, LXVII, C.2837, p. 6. Kimberley to Colley (Tel.), 8 February 1881.

[2] C.O. 48/499. Kimberley to Robinson (Tel.), 10 February 1881.

[3] Addit. MSS. 44627, f. 108. Kruger to Colley, 12 February 1881.

[4] Ibid., f. 109. Colley to Kruger, 13 February 1881.

[5] Ibid., Colley to Kimberley, 14 February 1881.

[6] Ibid., f. 108. Kruger to Colley, 12 February 1881.

[7] Ibid., f. 107. Joubert to Colley, 15 February 1881; and *Parl. Pap.*, 1881, LXVI, C.2794, p. 615.

caused by lack of liaison between Kruger and Joubert at this time. Bad communications between them were to become even more important on the eve of Majuba, when it took several days to find Kruger in the Transvaal, although the Boer camp was a mere three miles from Colley.

These early days in February were an exceedingly trying time, not only both for the Boer triumvirate and Colley but also for the Liberal Government. Quite apart from Colley's failures, and the news of Cape discontent from Strahan, the Gladstone administration was making excessively heavy going of their legislative programme. Irish obstruction in the Commons was now at its height—and had been so since the night of 17 January.[1] Forster's 'coercion bill',[2] introduced on 24 January, had raised the temperature of the floor to a fever pitch. On 26 January the Commons sat for 22 hours; and from Wednesday, 2 February for $41\frac{1}{2}$ hours.[3] On Thursday, 3 February, Parnell and his Irish party walked out of the Commons, after being suspended by the Speaker. The debate on the bill ground on without them—until 25 February. The wearying Commons débâcle was played out with even greater ferocity in the Cabinet. Here the Gladstonians were at bay, in face of the Whig clamour for coercion. The G.O.M. was constantly in the minority in his own Cabinet.[4] Even nature seemed to challenge him. The January blizzards returned. The Thames even froze in places; and, on 23 February, Gladstone slipped on some soft snow, cutting his head open. He was confined to bed for nearly a week,[5] thus missing the crucial Transvaal Cabinets of early March.[6]

It was against this background that Kimberley conducted the

[1] It had begun over the Debate on the Address and proceeded thereafter with superb organisational skill. 'On Friday night the Parnell party played their first game of obstruction', (Hamilton Diary). Entry for 18 January 1881. (Tuesday, entry *not* Monday, as Hamilton writes.) See Addit. MSS. 48630, f. 116.

[2] i.e. 'Protection of Property in Ireland' Bill.

[3] Ibid., ff. 11–19, (Hamilton Diary). Entry for 'Friday', 4 February 1881. (Incorrectly dated by Hamilton.) See also Morley, *Gladstone*, III, 51 ff.

[4] Addit, MSS. 44642, ff. 108–38 (Cabinet Papers). Fully documented especially for Cabinet of Saturday, 12 February 1881, f. 138.

[5] Addit. MSS. 48630, f. 131 (Hamilton Diary). Entry for 25 February 1881.

[6] Addit. MSS. 44642, ff. 151–4 (Cabinet Papers). Granville took the Cabinets.

complex and tentative peace probes with the Boers. The Queen began to take a close interest in these events—a factor which complicated the situation. Without any great knowledge of the matter she took upon herself the duty of being Colley's champion. 'The Queen', she wrote in the first of many like letters on 14 February,[1] 'is vy. vy. anxious abt. her troops in South Africa and thinks Sir G. Colley's position very critical. . . .'

This was hardly news to Kimberley, who had far greater worries on his shoulder. Above all, both he and Gladstone feared their policy might be reversed if it fell into the hands of the extreme Whigs in the Cabinet. Hence the anxious tone of his letter of 14 February, to Gladstone:[2] 'The Chancellor [Selborne], Granville, Argyll and Spencer all think we ought to have a Cabinet tomorrow on the Transvaal telegram [from Colley].[3] They all more or less demur to so large a concession to the Boers at the moment, Argyll least'. Their objections were plain, observed Kimberley: 'They put strongly that after having said we would re-establish the Queen's authority we should be in a very awkward position if after our reverses we send such an answer as proposed to the Boers.'[4] Kimberley admitted that it was 'impossible to ignore the force of their arguments', but he felt confident in his own opinion about the South African Dutch, and decided that he must at some point argue the matter out with the Whigs: 'I have said enough I am sure to convince you that the matter cannot be settled without a Cabinet.'[5] Gladstone took the point, and called a special Transvaal Cabinet for 12.30 p.m. the next day,[6] though with reluctance. He rehearsed his defence, against the expected Whig attack, in a long letter to Kimberley on the eve of the vital Cabinet:[7] 'I never made any communication [to the Boer

---

[1] Guedalla, *Queen and Mr. Gladstone*, II, 139, no. 749. Guedalla incorrectly identifies Kruger on p. 140, footnote 2. Kruger was not 'President of the Transvaal Republic' until 1883.

[2] Addit. MSS. 44226, f. 26. Kimberley to Gladstone, 14 February 1881.

[3] Addit. MSS. 44627, f. 109. Colley to Kimberley, 14 February 1881.

[4] Addit. MSS. 44226, f. 26. Kimberley to Gladstone, 14 February 1881.

[5] Idem.

[6] Addit. MSS. 44642, ff. 144-6 (Cabinet Papers), Tuesday, 15 February 1881.

[7] Addit. MSS. 44544, f. 137 (L.B. copy). Gladstone to Kimberley, 14 February 1881.

leaders] . . . on the subject which conveyed any encouragement to resistance or expectation respecting our withdrawal from the territory.' As to the apparent contradiction between his statement in the Commons of 21 January, and the present policy, he now tried to resolve it thus:

> Thoroughly disapproving of the annexation in principle, and in policy, I had no means of forming a judgement that it could be revoked. Had I been prepared to work in that sense I should have done it first in Parliament.[1]

The Cabinet met shortly after noon on Tuesday, 15 February.[2] It marked a distinct triumph for Gladstone and Kimberley. It seems that the Premier, with great skill, put the case of a war that was likely to involve the burghers of the Orange Free State, and possibly the Cape Dutch;[3] and that Kimberley was indirectly to put the rebellion in familiar terms, by speaking to the Cabinet of the discontent that had swept Ireland.[4] The chance comparison was particularly appropriate at the time because since mid-December, the ministers had been discussing nothing but Ireland in the Cabinet. At the fourteen Cabinets, between 13 December and 5 March, Ireland and the problem of suppressing the unrest, had headed the agenda.[5] Thus at each of the major 'Transvaal Cabinets' (of 15, 29 January, and 15, 19 February) Parnell and Kruger were discussed within moments of each other. Certainly this was a major preoccupation in Kimberley's mind, and the reason he gave to Gladstone in private,[6]—and to the House in public,[7]—of his decision to halt the war, prior to any decisive military success.

The Gladstonians, with the unusual support of Chamberlain's faction, carried the day. It was a pleasant surprise for Gladstone to be in the majority in his own Cabinet again; and it was very

[1] Idem.

[2] Addit. MSS. 44642, f. 144 (Cabinet Papers), Tuesday, 15 February 1881.

[3] Addit. MSS. 43935, ff. 16–40 (Dilke Memoir).

[4] *Letters of Queen Victoria*, 2nd ser., III, 197. Gladstone to Queen, 15 February 1881.

[5] Addit. MSS. 44642, ff. 108–52 (Cabinet Papers).

[6] Addit. MSS. 44226, f. 32. Kimberley to Gladstone, 21 February 1881; and Addit. MSS. 44627, ff. 1–12. Kimberley to Gladstone, 29 April 1881.

[7] Kimberley in Lords, 21 February 1881. *Hansard*, 3rd ser., CCLVIII, col. 1372 ff.

much his success. As Dilke explained:[1] 'On Wednesday the 16th [February] I dined with Chamberlain who told me that there had been a special Cabinet that afternoon[2] to consider proposals from President Kruger of the Transvaal, which Mr. Gladstone was most anxious to accept'.[3] The Premier had in fact already telegraphed the Cabinet decision to the Queen; the Government were to instruct Colley to try and open negotiations, even though the initial Boer terms were not completely satisfactory. 'Conflict probably imminent, and much blood may, they hope, be avoided. . . .'[4] Gladstone enclosed a copy of the message to Colley, and asked the Queen to return it as soon as possible.

The important telegram to Colley went out the next day 16 February.[5] The Boers were to be told that Britain was quite prepared to appoint a Royal Commission, 'with extensive powers', if they would agree to a truce.[6] Colley's reply was extraordinary. He asked to be allowed to attack Laing's Nek once more; and then go to relieve Pretoria.[7] Kimberley, more than annoyed, cabled immediately: 'No'.[8] Colley's conduct was discussed at the Cabinet of 19 February,[9] at which it was agreed that Kimberley was to press on with the peace terms. 'Mr. Gladstone and Chamberlain were for a wonder in the majority,' Dilke wrote in his Diary, 'and it was decided to drop the [Irish] Arms Bill and to negotiate with the Boers. . . .'[10] The proviso that the Boers 'quit Natal' before discussions could begin, was

---

[1] Addit. MSS. 43935, f. 40 (Dilke Memoir).

[2] Dilke is incorrect. The date should be 15 February. There was no Cabinet on 16 February. The next meeting of the Cabinet was on the 19th. Addit. MSS. 44642, ff. 144–7 (Cabinet Papers).

[3] Addit. MSS. 43935, f. 40 (Dilke Memoir).

[4] *Letters of Queen Victoria*, 2nd ser., III, 140. Gladstone to Queen, 15 February 1881.

[5] *Parl. Pap.*, 1881. LXVII, C.2837, p. 10. Kimberley to Colley (Tel.) 16 February 1881.

[6] Idem.   [7] Ibid., p. 13. Colley to Kimberley (Tel.), 19 February 1881.

[8] Ibid., Kimberley to Colley, 19 February 1881.

[9] Addit. MSS. 44642, f. 147 (Cabinet Papers), 12 p.m., 19 February 1881. Point 3: 'Telegram from Colley' of 19 February. Points 1 and 2 were, as usual, Ireland.

[10] Addit. MSS. 43935, ff. 43–4 (Dilke Memoir). See also Dilke Diary, entry for Saturday, 19 February 1881. The close proximity of Irish and Boer discontent on the Cabinet agenda is once again instructive.

dropped.[1] The Cabinet was, more and more, coming round to the Gladstone–Kimberley point of view, at least on the Transvaal, if not on Ireland. The die-hards—Selborne, Argyll, and Spencer—stood their ground. But the moderates fell to Kimberley's logic—notably Childers, Harcourt, and Granville; and even Hartington acquiesced.[2]

The Colonial Office too was having its excitements: two distinct factions now fought around the issue of 'peace without honour'. The traditionalists, Herbert, Hemming, and Bramston—were in the majority. They bluntly suggested that Strahan at the Cape was over-anxious, that the Cape Dutch would not rise,[3] and that Colley must soon gain a victory. In either case, peace could not be concluded without the surrender of the 'rebels'.[4] Young Fairfield was of a different mind; and events increasingly supported his own view. 'I fancy it was always recognised that if they [the Boers] did brave death and destruction for the sake of independence, it would go far towards securing a political victory for the survivors.'[5] Even as regards the fighting ability of the Boers Fairfield was right. 'Our belief that the Boers could not fight', he minuted on 5 February, 'was not so much founded on reports from Colonel Lanyon that they were paying their taxes, as from a disbelief in their possessing the necessary heroism involved in risking death and defeat in the field. . . .'[6] To this Herbert was forced to reply: 'The Boers have no doubt been dubbed cowards on insufficient evidence. When a sufficiently strong cause stimulates their "Dutch courage" it is apparently equal to great deeds.'[7]

But the divergence of opinion did not end here; it soon extended to an open breach between Kimberley and his perma-

---

[1] Addit. MSS. 43924, f. 39 (Dilke Diary). Entry for 21 February 1881.

[2] Addit. MSS. 44226, f. 26. Note by Gladstone.

[3] C.O. 48/499. Hemming minuted on 4 February 1881: 'The Dutch in the Cape Colony are not likely to carry their sympathy with the Transvaal Boers, beyond meetings and resolutions.' Hemming on Strahan to Kimberley, 11 January 1881.

[4] C.O. 48/496. Minutes by Herbert, 29 December 1880, and Hemming, 24 January 1881, on Strahan to Kimberley (Tel.) 25 December and 27 December 1880.

[5] C.O. 48/499. Minute by Fairfield, 5 February 1881, on Strahan to Kimberley, 11 January 1881.

[6] Idem.   [7] Ibid., Minute by Herbert, 5 February 1881.

nent under-secretary, Herbert. They had already been sparring over the peace overtures, and now on 7 February they disagreed over the efficacy of the very basis of the traditional policy. 'If we had had a large force in the Transvaal', Herbert lamented,[1] 'the meetings would not have been held, or would have been dispersed before an irresistible popular feeling could roll up.' Kimberley's cold logical reply reveals just how far his attitude had changed from coercion to conciliation:[2] 'No doubt this country could maintain a force in the Transvaal sufficient to keep the Boers in subjection. But such a state of things would hardly be a proof of successful policy.'[3]

As Kimberley moved away from Herbert, he came closer to Gladstone. It was their combined front which overcame Whig objections, and Colonial Office reticence. Then there was always the Queen. She had a new worry about South Africa, apart from Colley. Her two sons were on an 'educational voyage', which involved a call at Cape Town. She feared for their safety, 'in a cruel *Civil War*',[4]—which was being fought over 1000 miles to the north. When queried about the 'Civil War' reference she replied tartly: 'So it is, the Boers being *my subjects*, and it being a rule that Princes of the Royal Family *ought not* to be mixed in it.'[5] She followed this letter up with protests about the proposed 'peace'. A typical letter is that of 20 February, from Windsor, dictated to Ponsonby.[6] The Queen, Kimberley was informed, also wanted peace, but 'if this is effected by any act which would appear to be a confession of weakness, such as an admission [that] we could not take Lang's Nek [*sic*], disastrous results would follow such a proceeding'.[7]

Kimberley stood his ground remarkably well; against the Queen, the Whigs, and the Colonial Office. Even when Gladstone was absent from the Cabinet, due to his accident, Kimberley successfully pressed his policy. For an indecisive, garrulous man, he was being singularly determined. The explanation is once again his reading of the Colonial files. The

[1] C.O. 48/499. Minute by Herbert, 9 February, on Strahan to Kimberley, 11 January 1881.

[2] Ibid., reply by Kimberley, 9 February 1881.   [3] Idem.

[4] *Letters of Queen Victoria*, 2nd ser. III, 197. Queen to Princess of Wales, 18 February from Windsor.

[5] Idem.   [6] Ibid., p. 198. Ponsonby to Kimberley, 20 February 1881.
[7] Idem.

Strahan despatches have already been mentioned; now the new Governor, Sir Hercules Robinson, began to speak in like voice. Throughout February Kimberley received a succession of petitions from the Cape Dutch—from areas all over the Cape colony—and also several starkly worded telegrams from Robinson. Kimberley was presented with the first of some fifty petitions of protest, on 10 February;[1] all confirming Strahan's earlier reports of Cape Dutch restiveness. The earliest Memoranda were from the colonists of the Graaff Reinet and Queenstown districts. They recorded the three resolutions passed at both meetings on 8 January. First they regretted the war, but claimed that it had been caused by the Transvalers 'having been deprived of their independence in a manner condemned in the strongest terms by the present First Lord of the Treasury, Mr. Gladstone. . . .' Second, they saw no reason why the Republic should not be given its independence, for the 'Transvaal republicans desire nothing which will in any way interfere with H.M. virtual supremacy over South Africa. . . .' Third, they felt it was the duty of all Cape Colonists to do 'all they can' to help the coming of peace. They would never cease to condemn 'enforcing H.M. rule at the point of a bayonet'.[2] Kimberley replied to both petitions, expressing concern about the war, and promising peace if the Transvaal Boers laid down arms.

These petitions were the first of a flood, all making the same point; although some added a fourth resolution, condemning the nature of British rule in the Transvaal after the annexation.[3] The longer the war lasted, the more petitions poured in. One despatch from Robinson contained thirty-four[4]; in all thousands of Cape Dutch signed, many of whom had journeyed many miles to add their names. Speakers at public meetings also took the same theme—'we are loyal, but Britain's action is straining that loyalty'—but in progressively angrier language. The veiled threats became steadily more vociferous. Dutch speakers referred to the Transvaal War as 'not improbably leading to serious complications . . . owing to the ties of blood and other relations existing between the Transvaal and this colony. . . .'

[1] Parl. Pap., 1881, LXVII, C.2866, pp. 44 ff.
[2] Idem.   [3] Ibid., p. 41, e.g. that from the Koeberg District.
[4] *Parl. Pap.*, LXVII, C.2950. pp. 29-54. Robinson to Kimberley 25 February 1881.

(Paarl, Monday, 10 January); '. . . of putting the country back for many years, and also alienating the affections of many of Her Majesty's loyal subjects. . . .' (Robertson, 7 January); '. . . on being calculated to arouse throughout the length and breadth of South Africa a feeling of hostility between the two largest elements which compose the population of this land. . . .' (George Town, 29 January).[1]

It seemed that this campaign against Britain's moves in the Transvaal took as its inspiration Kruger's public appeal to the Cape ministry of Sprigg.[2] 'We beg to request your government to assist as far as is possible in our noble struggle', it began. 'The colonists in your state are mostly our friends and brethren, and it is only a short time ago that their sympathy has shown itself in a most emphatic way.'[3] This message was enthusiastically endorsed by the mass meetings, to the embarrassment of the predominantly English Cape ministry; and Kruger soon provided an even more useful weapon for Dutch propagandists, a slogan—'Africa for the Africanders'.[4] Robinson who had only recently arrived from the relatively tranquil air of New Zealand, found himself trapped in the cross-fire of the two language groups. As Graham Bower reflected in later years: 'The problem that faced Sir Hercules Robinson when he landed . . . was how to conciliate the Dutch without alienating the English, or injury to the natives.'[5] The Cape Dutch came in several deputations to press him to influence the Gladstone ministry to stop the war.[6] To the most important—that led by the Chief Justice, de Villiers—he stated lamely: 'General Colley is in direct telegraphic communication with the Home Government and it would not therefore be right or proper for me to shove in my oar between them. . . .'[7]

[1] Idem.

[2] *Parl. Pap.*, LXVI, C.2794, pp. 3–4. Kruger to Sprigg, 11 January 1881, enclosed in Strahan to Kimberley. Received in C.O., 4 February 1881.

[3] Kruger surely refers to the Cape Assembly's refusal to call a conference to discuss federation, of late June 1880.

[4] *Parl. Pap.*, 1881, LXVII, C.2837. Quoted in Robinson to Kimberley (Tel.), 19 February 1881.

[5] Afr. MSS., S.63, f. 3 (Bower Papers).

[6] *Parl. Pap.*, 1881, LXVII, C.2950, pp. 29–54. Deputation to Robinson, on 21 February 1881 and 24 February 1881.

[7] E. A. Walker, *De Villiers*, p. 153.

In fact Robinson felt distinctly uncomfortable about the Cape Dutch. As an extremely shrewd man, with long experience in troublesome colonies, he was not easily moved to alarm. But equally, he was not prepared to be another Frere, and take upon himself the responsibility of formulating policy. He waited a month before he let up the kite of Cape Dutch unrest, and before he placed his own interpretation on the meetings and deputations. But in that month—between 22 January[1] and 19 February[2] —he came firmly round to the opinion that what he was seeing from Government House, was not an artificially stimulated campaign by agitators, nor a momentary protest movement. To 'cry wolf' too often could destroy a Governor's career; but clearly Robinson thought he was justified in sending his strongly worded telegram of 19 February.

It is probable that he was moved to act when he learnt that even the ultra-conservative Moderator of the Dutch Reform Church[3] was heard to be preparing a warning memorandum. This was duly presented, and forwarded immediately to Kimberley.[4] It is not hard to see why Robinson took this memorandum so seriously. After reminding Robinson that 'there are strong ties uniting the Dutch Churches in the Transvaal and our own', by reason 'of a common national descent, a common religion, and the continual influx of people into the Transvaal from the Dutch portion of the inhabitants of this colony', the Church leaders were emphatic on the meaning of these links.

> Since the annexation a deep sympathy with the Transvaal has been awakened among our people, and the present state of affairs has so intensified this feeling that unless a change of policy takes place there will henceforth be created a deplorable alienation between the Dutch and English races in South Africa, and the loyalty of thousands in this colony will be jeopardised. . . .[5]

As to the war: 'The success of British arms will only tend to intensify their aversion to British rule, and deepen the sympathy of the Dutch people in all South Africa with their grievances.'

[1] The date of his arrival at the Cape from England.
[2] The vital private telegram to Kimberley. See below.
[3] Rev. G. van der Walt.
[4] *Parl. Pap.*, 1881, LXVII, C.2867, pp. 163–9. Robinson to Kimberley, 23 February 1881.
[5] Idem.

Their final point must have rung chords in the minds of Gladstone and Kimberley. 'We fear that by persisting in the present line of policy to its bitter end you will preclude the possibility of a future union of South African colonies and republics into one harmonious whole.' If Robinson needed any encouragement to act, President Brand provided it, with a series of telegrams between 16 and 19 February, all framed in the most unequivocal language, and all desperately trying to get Britain to name precise peace terms to be taken to the Transvaal leaders.[1]

Robinson sent these telegrams to London on 19 February, together with his own careful analysis of the points. He included the recently published 'Petition of Rights', drawn up by Kruger, embodying the 'Africa for the Africanders' pledge.[2] The importance of this telegraphic despatch of 19 February 1881 therefore cannot be overstated. It steeled Kimberley's nerve to defy the Colonial Office and the Whigs; it convinced Gladstone that the war must be ended immediately; it was directly responsible for Kimberley's masterly speech in the Lords on 21 February; and it very probably was the evidence which determined Gladstone to make peace despite Majuba, and the calls for vindication, which followed Colley's death.[3]

'I hear', Robinson telegraphed.[4] 'from well-informed sources that a feeling of intense hatred between the two races is being revived over the whole of South Africa, and is rapidly spreading to an extent which if unallayed will assuredly give rise to grave trouble in future.' He had seen the Chief Justice de Villiers, who wholly agreed with this assessment; and de Villiers was sure that the Transvalers would die for their independence, or *trek* again. 'He believes that if we keep the country we can only hold it by subjection . . . by means of a large force; and he asked —"is it worth having on such terms?"'[5]

---

[1] Ibid., C.2837, pp. 12–13.

[2] Ibid., Robinson to Kimberley (Tel.), 19 February 1881, 11 p.m.

[3] See typed copy in Gladstone Papers. The original of the telegram is probably in Lord Kimberley's papers. The telegram was doubtless typed for Cabinet circulation. But there is no copy of even the typed version in the the C.O. files—nor any comment on it. Kimberley does indeed seem to have sent Herbert 'to Coventry'.

[4] Addit. MSS. 44476, f. 50 (Copy). Robinson to Kimberley (Tel.), 19 February 1881.

[5] Idem.

Kimberley wrote immediately to Gladstone.[1] 'You will observe in Robinson's telegram of the 19th that the Transvaal have made a violent address to the Free State Volksraad. *They evidently aim at raising the whole Dutch population of S. Africa against us.*' Kimberley thought that the peace was imperative; and that there was a good chance of achieving it. 'We are of course not pledged to any particular mode of settlement. If Commissioners are appointed they could have power to consider various plans....'[2]

The Colonial Secretary leaned even more heavily on Robinson's telegram, and its enclosures, when he rose to justify his peace policy in the House of Lords that same evening, 21 February 1881.[3] This speech is a synthesis of Kimberley's evolving attitude and beliefs about South Africa; it shows how far he had moved from his Whig outlook of six weeks before; and it is a clear indication of how deeply he had been affected by the telegrams of Brand, Colley, Strahan, and now Robinson. As to Ireland and Kimberley's thinking—the undertones of the comparative handling of that rebellion pervade his statement to the Lords.

After outlining the background to the annexation, and the three years of British administration of the Transvaal, Kimberley came to the central issue—the revolt, and the peace terms.[4] 'These emigrant farmers left our territory [in the Great Trek] because they did not acquiesce in our rule. We have not succeeded in conciliating them....' The annexation only increased this feeling '... unfortunately such was the antipathy which a considerable portion of the Boer population showed to our rule that it was evidently impossible to form a free Assembly to co-operate with us in the government of the country. There we touch on the root of the whole question ... their hostility has culminated in the insurrection now going on.' But the problem did not end there. 'It is well we should not forget that the difficulties we have had to contend with are not confined to the

---

[1] Addit. MSS. 44226, f. 32. Kimberley to Gladstone, 21 February 1881, enclosing Robinson's telegram of 19 February 1881. (My italics.)

[2] Idem.

[3] *Hansard*, 3rd ser., CCLVIII, col. 1369 ff. Statement by Kimberley, Monday, 21 February 1881.

[4] Ibid., col. 1371.

Transvaal. ... The ties of relationship and blood connected with their past history between the Orange Free State and the Transvaal Boers are so close ... that it is a matter of considerable difficulty for the President [Brand] to maintain the position which he has taken up.' But, most important of all, 'we must not forget ... that in the Cape Colony at least two-thirds of the colonists are of Dutch extraction. ... They watch what is going on with the deepest sympathy and anxiety; and there can be no doubt that *every blow we strike in the Transvaal is a blow felt by our own Dutch subjects in the Cape Colony*.'[1] Peace was thus 'of vital importance'; not only in the case of the Transvaal, 'but also to the peace and tranquillity of our own colonies. ...'[2]

Kimberley carried the House, and his own party, with him. It seemed he would be able to implement his beliefs within a short while. He had, however, counted without Colley. The general had not received Kimberley's peace telegrams kindly. In reply to Kimberley's instructions of 16 February Colley had telegraphed: '... am I to leave Laing's Nek in Natal territory in Boer occupation, and our garrisons isolated and short of provisions. ...?[3]' Kimberley had reacted sharply: '.... garrisons should be free to provision themselves ... but we do not mean that you should march to the relief of garrisons or occupy Laing's Nek. ... *Fix reasonable time within which answer must be sent by Boers*.'[4] This last sentence had been included at the insistence of Childers,[5] and agreed to by Kimberley; clearly they were both deeply suspicious of Colley's behaviour. Colley now confirmed their worst fears. He wrote the fatal letter to Kruger on 21 February:

> Sir, I have the honour ... to inform you that on the Boers now in arms against Her Majesty's authority ceasing armed opposition, Her Majesty's Government will be ready to appoint a Commission with large powers, who may develop the scheme referred to in Lord Kimberley's telegram of 8th instant, communicated to you through His Honour President Brand.

[1] Ibid., col. 1372. (My italics.)   [2] Idem.
[3] *Parl. Pap.*, 1881, LXVII, C.2837. Colley to Kimberley (Tel.).
[4] Ibid., Kimberley to Colley (Tel.), 19 February 1881. (My italics.)
[5] Addit. MSS. 44642 f. 144 (Cabinet Papers), Tuesday, 15 February 1881. See Point 2: 'Note from Childers to Colley.'

THE SCHOOL OF MUSKETRY.

BOER (*to* F.-M. H.R.H. THE COMMANDER-IN-CHIEF).—"I SAY, DOOK! YOU DON'T HAPPEN TO WANT A PRACTICAL 'MUSKETRY INSTRUCTOR,' DO YOU?"

_* The recent disastrous defeat of a detachment of British troops in South Africa, at Majuba Hill, called public attention very forcibly to the proved superiority of the Boers in marksmanship.

I am to add that upon this proposal being accepted within forty-eight hours, I have authority to agree to a suspension of hostilities on our part.[1]

Why Colley added the foolhardy '48 hour' stipulation is in little doubt. His biographer has suggested that this was a reasonable time. Maybe, in Western Europe; but Colley was on the *veld*. All communications to the Boer camp went by horse; and Colley did not know exactly where Kruger or Joubert were. It does not therefore seem unlikely, in the light of his previous conduct and telegrams, that he did not wish to receive a reply favourable to peace, as yet. His actions, after 21 February, betray his thinking. When the 48 hours expired, and it became obvious that Kruger could not be found,[2] Colley moved his forces forward, and made ready for battle. A day or two's wait for the reply would not have mattered either way; a negative reply, and he could have continued his campaign. But he would not wait,[3] *because* it was very likely Kruger would accept the offer, in the light of his own proposal of 12 February?

On the afternoon of Saturday, 26 February, Colley decided to take control of Mount Majuba, overlooking the Boer camp.[4] In London, the Cabinet decided to go back on one of its decisions of 19 February. Dilke explained why: 'At the Cabinet today—Mr. Gladstone being in bed with a sore head—the decision of last week was reversed, and it was decided to go on with the [Irish] Arms Bill.'[5] Only with great difficulty had Kim-

---

[1] Colley to Kruger, 21 February 1881. Quoted in Herbert Gladstone; *After Thirty Years*, p. 229.

[2] Bok, on 25 February—the day *before* Colley advanced on Majuba Hill—told the English General that Kruger had gone to Heidelberg. 'His Excellency was here for the purpose of inspecting camps, but had left. I did my best and forwarded the letters after him per express. *I do not expect an answer for four days from this date*, because it has to go to Heidelberg. . . .' Bok to Colley, 25 February 1881.

[3] Addit. MSS. 44627, f. 109. N.P. Smit—Commander at the Boer Camp – had on 26 February also informed Colley that Kruger was away. See Smit to Hamilton, f. 110. Smit: 'From this I fairly infer that through the President's absence some further slight delay may occur in the delivery of your letter.'

[4] T. F. Carter, *A Narrative of the Boer War* (of 1880) London, 2nd edn. (1896), pp. 244 ff. Carter was a journalist in Natal in the company of Colley, and was at the battle of Majuba. He luckily escaped with his life, though taken a prisoner of the Boers.

[5] Addit. MSS. 43924, f. 39 (Dilke Diary). Entry for Saturday, 26 February 1881.

berley prevented the Whigs from making it a dual triumph, and reversing the decision to press for peace in the Transvaal.[1] At almost the same hour, on the *veld*, Colley began to do the work of the Whigs and wreck Kimberley's policy. Without informing the War Office, or the Colonial Secretary, he moved forward to occupy Mount Majuba with a mere 554 men, and no artillery.[2] He left behind a pathetic letter to his wife, which almost suggests that he expected failure, or death:

> I am going out tonight to try and seize Majuba Hill, which commands the right of the Boer position, and leave this behind, in case I should not return. . . . Don't let all life be dark to you if I don't come back. . . . How I wish I could believe the stories of meeting again hereafter. . . . think lovingly and sadly, but not too sadly or hopelessly, of your affectionate husband. G.P.C.[3]

All night the troops toiled to climb the mountain; and it was not until 4 a.m. that they reached the saucer-shaped summit. Colley did not bother to dig the troops in, or to build defences. He regarded 'the Boer side' of the mountain as too flush to climb. At daybreak he heliographed to his own camp; 'We could stay here forever.'[4] In the valley below the lights of the Boer *laager* could be seen flickering; they were quite unaware of Colley's presence.[5] Joubert explained to Kruger what happened next: '. . . I was still sitting writing, and the sun had just risen, when it was reported to me that the troops were coming up the right-hand hill. Then it was "to saddle, to saddle", but to our astonishment we saw that the enemy had entire possession of the hill. . . . Apparently one would have thought that everything was lost to us; . . . but beyond all our expectations the Lord assisted us.'[6] The Boer attack on the mountain began shortly

---

[1] Idem.

[2] Only some 350 men actually ascended the summit – 200 were left to protect the supply and communication lines to the base camp.

[3] Colley to wife, 26 February 1881. Quoted in full in Butler, *Colley*, pp. 367–8.

[4] Sir Ian Hamilton, *Listen for the Drums* (London, 1944), p. 140, footnote 2. Hamilton was at Majuba.

[5] The best description of the 'battle' is the collection of first-hand accounts of the combatants in *Parl. Pap.*, 1881, LXVII, C.2950. The most recent account is Brian Bond, 'The Battle of Majuba Hill', in *History Today* (1965).

[6] Joubert to Kruger, 27 or 28 February 1881. Quoted in full in M. Nathan, *Paul Kruger, His Life and Times*, 4th edn. (Durban, 1944), p. 169.

after 7 a.m. By mid-morning they had climbed a considerable way up the 'impregnable' slope. Colley, though, signalled by flag, 'All very comfortable. Boers wasting ammunition.'[1] Using boulders for cover, the Boers reached the lip of the mountain at about 1 p.m. Colley was shot through the head as he stood, revolver in hand, organising the retreat of his men.[2] At last he had his moment of glory. His valiant death made him a popular hero.[3]

Majuba has often been seen as a major 'turning-point'; the 'Bunkers Hill' of imperial policy in South Africa. This is doubtful. Militarily it was a skirmish by Boer War standards;[4] and merely Colley's third consecutive defeat. It damaged British prestige, but not imperial supremacy. The importance of Majuba lay in the ready ammunition it supplied for the combatants in the real battle that was soon to be fought, in the Cabinet.[5] Colley's defeat and death re-opened the whole question of Kimberley's policy. No sooner had the news of the tragedy reached London,[6] than both Chamberlain and the Whig faction, began to plan their strategy to break Kimberley. It was clearly intended that there should be other prominent victims of Majuba, as well as 'Sir George Colley, stretched out exactly as the effigy of a Knight lies in a Cathedral, upon the flattened summit.'[7] Kimberley had to fight for his political life in the week which followed. Gladstone's 'generalship' alone saved him; but it did so with difficulty.

2. The Struggle for Peace: 28 February—22 March, 1881

The first report of Majuba reached the War Office too late on

[1] Colley to Stewart, 27 February 1881, 9.30 a.m. I. Hamilton, *Listen for the Drums*, p. 140.

[2] *Parl. Pap.*, 1881, LXVII, C.2837. Col. Bond, 58th Reg. to Childers (Tel.), 27 February 1881, 4.55 p.m. Full details of the battle.

[3] Joubert ironically commented to Kruger after the battle: 'I never thought that our men would charge in such a manner against the English forces.' Joubert to Kruger, 1 March 1881, in *Van Jaarsveld*, p. 172.

[4] 'These battles, more in reality small skirmishes in which the soldiers using barrack yard tactics were beaten by Boers using the tactics taught them by experience in the field.' Graham Bower. Afr. MSS. S. 63, f. 1.

[5] Addit. MSS. 43924, f. 40 (Dilke Diary), 2 March 1881.

[6] The first intimation of the battle was received in London at 11.45 p.m. on Sunday, 27 February 1881. *Parl. Pap.*, 1881, LXVII, C.2937.

[7] I. Hamilton, *Listen for the Drums*, p. 130.

the Sunday evening to be passed on to the ministers, or to the Queen. But it awaited them at breakfast on the Monday morning, 28 February. Gladstone slumped back in bed when told;[1] Queen Victoria took to her Journal: 'Dreadful news reached me when I got up. Another fearful defeat, and poor Sir G. Colley killed. . . . When I opened the telegram, I hoped it might be news of a victory. It is too dreadful. . . . We are indeed unlucky.'[2] Much the same thought came to Gladstone's secretary: 'Bad luck certainly dogs the steps of the present Govt.,' Hamilton noted in his Diary. He also sympathised with Colley, but with a more realistic understanding: '. . . he must have been actuated from a feeling (perhaps unconscious) of doing something off his own bat to re-establish his prestige as a general.'[3] But at least Colley was safe from his critics; Kimberley was not. The fury of the nation turned on the Colonial Secretary, who was somehow seen as being the architect of a policy of weakness, and directly responsible for the ignominy of Majuba.

Herbert Gladstone visited the Premier at Hawarden, and expressed the general feeling: 'Came back to dine alone with Father. Interesting talk about S. Africa. I doubted Kimberley's statesmanship.'[4] The national Press voiced more than doubt. Kimberley's policy had never been entirely acceptable to the men of the Press, and Majuba seemed to prove their argument that Kimberley was not acting in the best interests of Britain. *The Standard's* editorial spoke for most papers:[5] 'There can be no more talk now of terms or of conditions until a victorious British general at Pretoria publishes the terms which shall be granted to such of the defeated insurgents as shall come in and sue for pardon. The stigma of defeat must be wiped out. . . .' The *Daily Telegraph* recalled Isandelwana, and demanded vindication 'of the British arms'.[6] And the *Morning Post* openly spoke of revenge, and vindication 'at any cost'.[7] The only papers

---

[1] Addit. MSS. 48630, f. 132 (Hamilton Diary), 28 February 1881.

[2] *Letters of Queen Victoria*, 2nd ser., III, 198. Journal of Queen Victoria. Entry for 28 February 1881, at Windsor.

[3] Addit. MSS. 48630, f. 133 (Hamilton Diary), 28 February 1881.

[4] Herbert Gladstone (Diary), Monday, 28 February 1881. Quoted in *After Thirty Years*, p. 218.

[5] *Standard*, 28 February 1881.   [6] *Daily Telegraph*, 1 March 1881.

[7] *Morning Post*, 1 March 1881.

to reflect in a balanced way on the disaster were the *Pall Mall Gazette*[1] and *The Times*.[2] Both queried Colley's tactics and objective: but both questioned Kimberley's policy.

The pressure on Kimberley, to abandon his attempts at conciliation, steadily mounted during the week Monday, 28 February to Friday, 4 March 1881. The greatest pressure though came not from the Press, or from inflamed popular opinion which abhorred a military defeat, but from members of the Government. Ever since his 'conversion' to a policy of partial 'home rule' for the Boers, Kimberley's position had been precarious in the Cabinet. The inconsistency in his attitudes was mainly to blame. He was by instinct a Whig on Ireland—being in favour of Forster's coercion measures—but a sympathiser with the radical view on the Transvaal. Thus he was betwixt the devil-may-care-Radicals, and the deep-blue-Whigs. Not even Gladstone could justify holding such opposing positions at the same moment.

This was the background to the Cabinet manoeuvres which now followed. Both the Whig and Radical factions began to harass Kimberley. The Whigs fought to drive him from conciliation, to make him abandon his Transvaal policy, and to implement strong military measures to vindicate Britain's authority on the *veld*. The Radicals demanded the exact opposite—and wanted Kimberley's resignation if he did not pursue peace despite Majuba. It is significant that the Radicals thought they would drive the Colonial Secretary into the political wilderness. We do not know Kimberley's reflections on Majuba,[3] but the Gladstone, Chamberlain, and Dilke Papers would suggest that Kimberley was shattered in his purpose by the disaster; and by the volume of the public outcry for 'vindication'. It is not unlikely that he indeed momentarily gave way to a reaction to quell the victorious Boers, in accordance with his basic Whig approach to politics, and the world at large. Defending his Transvaal policy had already been a wearying matter, with

[1] *Pall Mall Gazette*, 2 March 1881.

[2] *The Times*, 1 March 1881.

[3] The Kimberley papers are unfortunately not available to the historian; and Kimberley does not seem to have written to any of his close associates on the matter. The C.O. files are barren on this vital point. It would seem Kimberley's private journals, and letterbooks, alone contain the answer.

other Whigs sniping at their part-time ally, and the Radicals approving his measures but withholding their full support for they disliked his Whig sympathies on other matters. Even the Gladstonians had been cool to him: his Irish beliefs alienated men such as Harcourt and Granville.

By Thursday, 3 March, Kimberley's future career and seat in the Cabinet was in serious doubt. *The Times*[1] had, on the Wednesday, brought out a major and trenchant article on Kimberley's policy; it was tantamount to a vote of censure in the House, for the paper used Kimberley's very own argument —of a pan-Afrikaner restiveness—to attack his wavering attitude. Vindication was vital, the article explained, not because of any 'burning desire to be avenged upon the Boers', but because 'the apparent admission of our incapacity to control them, would let loose the Africander [*sic*] spirit not alone in the Transvaal and the Orange Free State, but in Natal and in the western provinces of the Cape Colony'. And *The Times* added, this example 'would not be lost upon the native races. . . . who are watching the internecine struggles of the whites with the keenest interest'. Their advice was the broadly accepted opinion of the day: 'Unless we are prepared to retire from South Africa immediately and unconditionally, we must restore our authority where it has been defied, and [deal] only with those who submit to the representatives of the Queen.'[2] This public pressure reached its height on the Friday (4 March), when the *Liverpool Mercury* called for immediate military action on the grounds that, 'Joubert's sword is yet dripping with the blood of our best.'[3] The private pressure though was even greater. Dilke's Diary vividly records the backstage strategies, which he so enjoyed; particularly as the intended victim was a respectable Whig.

Dilke and Chamberlain met on Wednesday, 2 March, to hatch the plot. 'After a long interview between me and Chamberlain on the state of affairs', Dilke wrote, 'Chamberlain had [a talk] with Bright, and got him to write a strong letter to Gladstone about the Transvaal, which was put forward as our ground for proposed resignation, although of course the strength of the

[1] *The Times*, 2 March 1881.
[2] Idem.
[3] *Liverpool Mercury*, 4 March 1881.

137

coercion measures, the weakness of the land measures—and the predominance of the Whigs in the Cabinet are the real reasons.'[1] Dilke calculated the effect of this action thus: 'In the Transvaal matter we should not be two, but four, for Bright and Courtney must go out with us, and Lefevre might do so. On the other hand, we had reason to think that if the Whigs yielded to us on the Transvaal, Kimberley would go.'[2] Bright duly fell in with these plans; and wrote the necessary letter to Gladstone the same day.[3] 'I wish much to have some talk with you on the Transvaal business,' he informed the Premier. 'I am grieved to ask to take up any of your time but the question is serious, and is very pressing.'[4] Gladstone saw Bright the next day, Wednesday, 3 March,[5] and learnt for the first time of the obvious plot to rob him of his Colonial Secretary; or to break-up the Government altogether, with the departure of Chamberlain, and the other Radicals.

Gladstone's attitude to the ultimatum was crucial. Had he fallen into the trap, of choosing between Kimberley and the Radicals, disastrous consequences might have ensued for his administration. But Gladstone was too wily a politician to be lured into such implacable alternatives. Instead of meeting the Radical challenge full on, he merely turned it aside. He listened to Bright's statement, then explained that as they did not have the full details of the Transvaal matter, nothing could be done; that Chamberlain and Dilke must be patient; and that the matter would receive his close attention in Saturday's Cabinet.[6] Gladstone's tactics gave him three vital days of grace, until the Cabinet of 5 March. He used the days to 'work on' Kimberley— to bring him round to the correct policy; to acquire all the necessary information from the Transvaal—to discover what had happened to the Colley peace offer; and to publicise the Boer acceptance—once it was known.

The first step which Gladstone took was to bring Kimberley into unison with his approach. They met for lunch, on Friday,

[1] Addit. MSS. 43924, f. 40 (Dilke Diary). Entry for Wednesday, 2 March 1881.
[2] Addit. MSS. 43935, ff. 50–51 (Dilke Memoir).
[3] Addit. MSS. 44113, f. 147. Bright to Gladstone, 2 March 1881.
[4] Idem.
[5] Addit. MSS. 43924, f. 40. (Dilke Diary). Entry of 3 March 1881.
[6] Idem.

4 March, and reviewed the whole position.[1] Kimberley outlined not only his attitude to the Boers, in the light of Majuba, but also his own actions since receiving the news. His initial move had been to stop any possible Boer 'victory campaign'. Wood had been appointed to succeed Colley temporarily;[2] and Childers had been instructed to send reinforcements at once, '. . . consisting of 85th from India, six companies 102nd from Ceylon, and the 99th from Bermuda.'[3] Kimberley had also tried to ascertain the fate of his own peace overtures of 21 February, forwarded to Kruger by Colley. Three days after the battle he still did not know, for on 1 March he telegraphed Wood: 'Inform me, if you know, when Sir G. Colley made communication to Kruger . . . what time he fixed within which answer must be given, and whether any . . . communications have since passed between him and Boer leaders.'[4] Wood could not find Kruger's reply; it had not yet arrived. Kruger had only received Colley's letter on 28 February;[5] he replied immediately, but Colley was already dead, and this reply took four days to reach Wood. As the latter did not answer Kimberley's telegram of 1 March—he was trying to ascertain if Kruger had replied—Kimberley grew anxious and telegraphed again, on 3 March.[6] 'My telegram March 1st. If you find that Sir G. Colley made communication to Kruger, but no answer has been received, inquire of Boer leaders whether an answer will be sent to you.'[7] Wood now revealed to Kimberley the chaos on the *veld*, and particularly in the British camp. 'Am told by Hamilton, A.D.C. he believes 24 hours given',[8] he informed Kimberley on 4 March, 'and on expiration there was no result, and Colley

---

[1] Addit. MSS. 44226, f. 38. Kimberley to Gladstone, 4 March 1881—with notes on the letter by Gladstone, giving details of the discussions.

[2] *Parl. Pap.*, 1881, LXVII, C.2837. Childers to Colley (Tel.), 28 February 1881.

[3] Ibid., Kimberley to Governor of Ceylon, 1 March 1881.

[4] C.O. 291/14. Kimberley to Wood (Tel.), 1 March 1881. See also *Parl. Pap.*, 1881, LXVII, C.2837, pp. 19–21.

[5] Addit. MSS. 44627, f. 109 (Gladstone Papers), Kruger to Colley, 28 February 1881.

[6] C.O. 291/14. Kimberley to Wood (Tel.), 3 March 1881.

[7] Idem.

[8] This suggests that Colley discussed the matter with no one; nor showed the letter, with the forty-eight hour ultimatum, even to his aide-de-camp.

moved.'[1] The news that Colley had possibly set a mere 24 hours was worrying enough; but even more serious was Wood's telegram of 2 March: 'Bok's answer to Colley arrived here yesterday, explaining he could not answer for 4 days as Kruger was in Heidelberg.'[2]

This was the main imponderable that weighed heavily with Gladstone at his important private meeting with Kimberley on that Friday, 4 March. 'Suppose for argument's sake,' Gladstone remarked to Kimberley,[3] 'that at the moment when Colley made the unhappy attack on the Majuba Hill there shall turn out to have been decided on, and possibly even on its way, a satisfactory or friendly reply from the Boer Government to your telegram?' To Gladstone this was the fact which must decide their policy. For as he carefully explained to his perplexed Colonial Secretary: 'I fear the chances may be against this [Boer acceptance], but if it prove to be the case, we could not because we had failed on Sunday last [at Majuba] insist on shedding more blood.'[4] Kimberley took the point. Once again Gladstone, with his political shrewdness, had seen the possible pitfalls of a hasty policy;[5] and also the weakness of the Chamberlain–Dilke approach—which was indeed 'all opportunism'— being concerned solely with political strategy, rather than the realities which contributed to policy.

Gladstone settled Kimberley's wavering—by making up his mind for him. As Dilke himself admitted, Gladstone's innate caution, and refusal to be hustled into an unwary declaration, had scuttled the Radical plan: '. . . So the difficulty was over before the Cabinet was able to meet.'[6] Bright found that Gladstone basically agreed with him on the Transvaal; and Kim-

---

[1] *Parl. Pap.*, 1881, LXVII, C.2837. Wood to Kimberley (Tel.), 4 March 1881.

[2] C.O. 291/14. Wood to Kimberley (Tel.), 2 March 1881.

[3] Addit. MSS. 44226, f. 37 (copy). Gladstone to Kimberley, 2 March 1881.

[4] Idem.

[5] It was fortunate for Kimberley that Gladstone's head wound had recovered sufficiently for him to deal with the Radical challenge, and to guide colonial policy in this difficult stage. See Addit. MSS. 48630, ff., 131 ff. (Hamilton Diary) for Gladstone's health at this time.

[6] Addit. MSS. 43924, f. 40. (Dilke Diary).

berley simply 'gave in, and telegraphed what he was told'.[1] The special Transvaal Cabinet, which met at 2 p.m. on Saturday, 5 March,[2] found Kimberley in an infinitely stronger position than he had been in a mere two days previously. It was in fact another Gladstonian triumph—although the Transvaal difficulties were by no means over.

The Cabinet of 5 March centred round the central issue at stake; had Kruger replied to Colley, and if so, had he accepted the proposal? The ministers, under Gladstone's guidance, rightly decided that the entire future policy turned on this matter;[3] and that vindication was out of the question if the Boers had accepted the peace overture in Colley's '48 hour' letter.

The intitiative, for the moment, therefore lay with the Boers. Fortunately, Sir Evelyn Wood was no Colley,[4] and conducted relations with the Boers in a firm but fair manner.[5] Kimberley was later to admit that they owed Wood a great debt in bringing peace about.[6] Certainly they relied very heavily on Wood's tact and judgment in the next two weeks. The fifty telegrams which were exchanged between Wood and Kimberley—from 5 to 22 March—give a fascinating picture of the diplomatic struggle for peace, and of how nearly it came to a renewal of war. But what the telegrams cannot show is the evolving attitudes and atmosphere in the Gladstone government.

March 1881 was another of the crucial months in the tortuous life of this administration. It is one of the ironies of this period that all the serious crises, which struck the government, did so in unison; overlapping in time and intensity, so that

[1] Addit. MSS. 43935, f. 51 (Dilke Memoir).

[2] Addit. MSS. 44642, ff. 152–3 (Cabinet Papers).

[3] Ibid., f. 153. Point 5: 'Colley wrote 21 February to Joubert offering suspension if answer came within 48 hours.'

[4] Wood's finest testimonial is the Parl. Pap., 1881, LXVII, C.2837, containing all his telegrams to the C.O., with full details of his negotiations.

[5] It should be noted that Wood did not have much alternative but to embark upon peace talks, for Joubert had written on 4 March: '. . . It is expected that Your Excellency will view everything in its true light, and that you will so advise your Queen that there shall come a speedy end to this slaughter of former friends, and shedding of innocent blood. To co-operate to this end everyone in the Republic will be ready. . . .' See Joubert to Wood, 4 March 1881. Addit. MSS. 44627, f. 112.

[6] C.O. 291/10. Kimberley to Wood (Tel.), 23 March 1881.

Gladstone was never able to dispose of a particular issue for long enough to allow him to give his undivided attention to the latest crisis. Certain problems were with him always: Ireland was one, the composition of his own party and Cabinet was another. But in March of that year he was not only struggling with the principle of a Land Act for Ireland,[1] or with the Kimberley–Transvaal dilemma, he was also attempting to come to grips with the serious situation developing in the eastern Mediterranean. Granville reported a steady breakdown of order in Egypt; and also broached the smouldering subject of Greek claims to Thessaly.[2] Not that this was all. Gladstone was concurrently waging an intense personal duel with the Queen, on three fronts: the issue of vindication in the Transvaal;[3] the Wolseley peerage affair;[4] and the problem of his own reporting of Cabinet decisions to the Queen—she demanded to know exactly who had been for or against each measure; Gladstone declined to give more than the final decision.[5] The weight of these problems began to crush Gladstone. As he wearily explained to Ponsonby: 'My day is drawing to a close and when a man gets worn out he gets gloomy.'[6] The Queen's attitude really worried him: 'Formerly I saw no reason why Monarchy should not go on here for hundreds of years, but I confess the way Monarchy has been brought to the front by the late Government in political and foreign affairs has shaken my confidence. . . .'[7] The most serious assault on that confidence though

[1] P.R.O. 30/29/124 (Granville Papers). Gladstone to Granville, 22 February and 24 February 1881. See also Addit. MSS. 44173, f. 2. (Gladstone Papers). Granville to Gladstone, 26 February 1881. (See Ramm, I, 243.)

[2] P.R.O. 30/29/124 (Granville Papers). Gladstone to Granville, 28 March 1881. See also Addit. MSS. 44173, f. 22. Granville to Gladstone, 29 March 1881. (Ramm, I, 249.)

[3] Letters of Queen Victoria, 2nd ser. III, 200. Queen to Kimberley, 9 March 1881.

[4] Guedalla, Queen and Mr. Gladstone, II, 144. Queen to Gladstone, 4 March 1881. See also Addit. MSS. 44173, f. 4 (copy). Gladstone to Granville, 5 March 1881. (Ramm, I, 244.)

[5] P.R.O. 30/29/124 (Granville Papers). Gladstone to Granville, 17 March 1881. See also P.R.O. 30/29/38. Ponsonby to Granville, 18 March 1881; and P.R.O. 30/29/124. Gladstone to Granville, 19 March 1881. (Ramm, I, 247.)

[6] Confidential talk with Ponsonby in March 1881. Quoted in Magnus, Gladstone, p. 298.

[7] Idem.

was in his own Cabinet. Due to the sudden Irish crisis, of the previous November, there had been no autumn planning Cabinets, with the result that in March 1881 the Government were without any blue-print for combined action. This allowed the ministerial rifts to widen, as the opposing factions pulled the ministry this way, then that. The first important casualty, and loss to the Cabinet, was Argyll. He finally left the Cabinet on 31 March,[1] having threatened resignation for some time.[2] His departure was a personal blow to Gladstone, who counted him a close friend.[3] Argyll's later letter on the affair, well illustrates the Cabinet position in March: 'You think you have the Cabinet behind you,' he jibed at Gladstone, 'I wish you had heard the talk when you went off to see the Queen and left us mice without the cat. . . .'[4]

This complicated backdrop of events and animosities did not critically damage Kimberley's handling of the Transvaal peace struggle; but it did create the tension within which he had to work and it did lose him the attention of Gladstone at vital moments. Kimberley found the ground underfoot exceedingly difficult to negotiate, particularly in view of the uncertainty of the actual events on the *veld*. Kimberley walked 'blind' for several days, while Wood tried to ascertain the fate of the earlier peace offer. 'River impassable, one swimmer drowned, hence delayed in receiving yours of yesterday,' Wood informed the Colonial Secretary on 5 March, 'Colley wrote Kruger on 21st [Feb.] addressing to Langes Nek [*sic*]. Bok[5] opened letter and writing at Heidelberg 25th, says Kruger is away, and cannot answer for four days. . . .'[6] Kimberley's determination for peace was not to be undermined by the doubts expressed over Kruger's possible reaction. He had already been thinking of possible

---

[1] P.R.O. 30/29/124 (Granville Papers). Gladstone to Granville, 31 March 1881. Argyll left over the principle of the Irish Land Bill. See Addit. MSS. 44105, f. 19, and Ramm, I, 250.
[2] P.R.O. 30/29/124 (Granville Papers). Granville to Gladstone, 31 March 1881. 'A great blow indeed . . . I do not think I have a chance of success with Argyll—but I will try . . .' (Ramm, I, 250.)
[3] P.R.O. 30/29/124, D.24. Gladstone to Argyll, 31 March 1881.
[4] Argyll to Gladstone, 13 April 1881. Quoted in Magnus, *Gladstone*, p. 298.
[5] W. E. Bok (1846–1904): Secretary to the Boer triumvirate, 1880–83; Transvaal State Secretary, 1884–88.
[6] C.O. 291/10. Wood to Kimberley (Tel.), 5 March 1881.

members of the Royal Commission on the Peace. 'I would inquire of Sir H. Robinson,' he wrote to Gladstone on 6 March,[1] 'whether he would act, and whether he would recommend that Chief Justice de Villiers should be associated with him. . . . President Brand could be asked to join the Conference as representing a friendly state deeply interested in the issue.' The only question still open in Kimberley's mind was whether peace overtures 'should now be given to Sir E. Wood, or whether we should wait for the answer to Colley's communication to Kruger'.[2] Even the issue of ammunition for the Orange Free State did not cut at Kimberley's determination. Gladstone had written to him on 6 March: 'It is plain . . . that the Free State Govt. must on a former date have requisitioned for ammunition not intended for its own use.'[3] To which Kimberley replied: 'I think the more prudent course will be to allow the ammunition to go on. . . .'[4] Brand was not to be angered; nothing was to be done to disturb the possibility of peace.

The Cabinet of Tuesday, 8 March[5] found Kimberley a decidedly happier man. Gladstone's Cabinet notes reveal why: 'Answer to Wood's tel. of 7th March conveying Kruger's ans. dated Heidelberg Feb. 28, considered and agreed on.'[6] Two factors contributed to this state of affairs. First, Gladstone and Kimberley had managed to devise peace terms flexible enough to answer the basic dilemma, as set out by Hamilton: '. . . it will be difficult to find terms which they will accept, and to which we can honourably accede.'[7] Second, Wood had been a dutiful servant in the Transvaal. 'Have signed agreement with Joubert for suspension of hostilities till midnight, 14th March, for the purpose of receiving Kruger's reply and any further communication,' he had telegraphed on 6 March.[8] He had

[1] Addit. MSS. 44226, f. 41. Kimberley to Gladstone, 6 March 1881.
[2] Ibid., f. 42.
[3] Addit. MSS. 44226, f. 45. Gladstone to Kimberley, 6 March 1881.
[4] Ibid., Kimberley to Gladstone, 6 March 1881. Over 200,000 rounds of ammunition were involved.
[5] Addit. MSS. 44642, f. 154 (Cabinet Papers), Tuesday, 8 March 1881.
[6] Ibid., Points 1 to 3 all on Transvaal, including telegram to Robinson *re* Royal Commission.
[7] Addit. MSS. 48630, f. 134 (Hamilton Diary). Entry for 8 March 1881.
[8] C.O. 291/10. Wood to Kimberley (Tel.), 6 March 1881.

followed this up with the details of the armistice;[1] and showing the realism of which Kimberley much approved. 'Want of food prevents advance for about ten days,' Wood wired on 7 March,[2] 'I have therefore lost nothing in suspending hostilities, and gained eight days' food for garrison. . . .'[3] Kimberley readily agreed to the terms of the armistice, praising Wood's success.[4] Kimberley must have been even more grateful for Gladstone's counsel when he learnt, on 7 March, of Kruger's reply to Colley.[5] It was dated Heidelberg, 28 February; and Kruger was plainly in favour of peace:

> . . . It appears to us that, for the first time since unlucky annexation, there is chance of coming of peaceful settlement. Our hearts bleed over necessity of shedding more blood. . . . In our opinion, a meeting of representatives from both sides will probably lead speedily to satisfactory result. . . .[6]

These were the telegrams laid before the Cabinet of 8 March. Gladstone and Kimberley had had their policy entirely vindicated. Had they pressed on, and avenged Colley's defeat, and then received Kruger's agreeable reply, the Government would have achieved perhaps even greater unpopularity than they already enjoyed. The whole Cabinet agreed on the telegram to Wood, instructing him to probe for firm peace terms;[7] even the Whigs acquiesced in the face of the evidence. As Northbrook ruefully admitted: 'Negotiations for an honourable settlement had been begun by the Boers, and accepted by us. These negotiations were jeopardised by our General exceeding his instructions. The only right course . . . was to recognise the error of the

[1] Ibid., Wood to Kimberley (Tel.), 7 March 1881.

[2] Ibid., Wood to Kimberley (Tel.), 6 March 1881, received in C.O., 7 March 1881.

[3] Peace, Wood felt, was almost a certainty in view of '. . . the very unfavourable weather and their [the Boers'] admitted certainty of eventual suppression.' Addit. MSS. 44627, f. 112. Wood to Kimberley, 5 March 1881, 12 p.m.

[4] Ibid., Kimberley to Wood (Tels.), 7 and 8 March 1881.

[5] Addit. MSS. 44627, f. 110. Kruger to Colley from Heidelberg, 28 February, enclosed in Wood to Kimberley (Tel.), 7 March 1881. Kruger: 'Your letter of 21st February 1881, reached me on the 28th February, when I returned from an inspection in Heidelberg.'

[6] Ibid., f. 114. Enclosed in Wood to Kimberley (Tel.), 7 March 1881, 2 p.m.

[7] C.O. 291/10. Kimberley to Wood (Tel.), 8 March 1881.

General and to continue the negotiation as if that error had not been committed.'[1] Colley had indeed died in vain. Hartington said the kindest thing of Colley, when he remarked to Gladstone, 'We never directed our Commander.'[2] Majuba was not a defeat; merely an embarrassment.

By 12 March Kimberley could at last feel he had the crisis under control; and that he had a fair grasp of the situation. The armistice gave him room to probe for peace via Wood, and also to have an 'insurance' policy—major reinforcements were organised, just in case the negotiations broke down, and also to prevent another Majuba.[3] Kimberley's most serious opposition came from the Queen, and from a section of the Press. 'I do not like peace before we have retrieved our honour,'[4] Queen Victoria had already written privately. Now she took a stronger line. 'I find an impression prevails,' she telegraphed on 9 March, 'that we are about to make peace with the Boers on their own terms. . . .'[5] Kimberley replied courteously, but curtly, that this was not so.[6] Queen Victoria's sole comfort took the form of a letter from Chief Cetewayo of the Zulus. 'Let the Queen cheer up,' he informed her, 'the Boers will soon flee before the British soldiers. . . .'[7]

Press reaction, to the possibility of peace, was divided. The *Manchester Guardian* led the attack: 'If the Boers are to have their independence after all, it is the severest possible reflection upon the policy of the Government, which on this showing has been wasting lives to no purpose. . . .'[8] This was supported by the *Daily Telegraph*[9]—which felt Great Britain had been 'vanquished by a band of farmers',—and by the *Scotsman*[10] and *Standard*.[11]

[1] Quoted in G.P. Gooch, *Life of Courtney*, p. 164.

[2] Addit. MSS. 44642, f. 156 (Cabinet Papers). Note by Hartington, 8 March 1881.

[3] C.O. 291/10. Childers to Wood (Tel.), 8 March 1881. '. . . we are sending Horse Artillery Battery . . . also a Mountain Battery. . . . 1000 mules for transport purposes. . . . Two additional transport companies will also be sent. . . . The three Infantry Regiments from Mediterranean will be ordered to Cape Town to wait orders . . .'

[4] *Letters of Queen Victoria*, 2nd ser., III, 199, 6 March 1881.

[5] Ibid., p. 200, 9 March 1881.   [6] Ibid., pp. 202–3, 17 March 1881.

[7] *Parl. Pap.*, 1881, LXVII, C.2838, p. 185. Cetewayo to Robinson, 1 March 1881.

[8] *Manchester Guardian*, 8 March 1881.   [9] *Daily Telegraph*, 8 March 1881.

[10] *The Scotsman*, 8 March 1881.   [11] *Standard*, 9 March 1881.

But perhaps *The Times* was more representative of opinion, when its leader column noted '. . . There is in this country so strong a desire to see this unhappy business brought to a close,' that no one can object.[1] The *Pall Mall Gazette*[2] and *Daily News*[3] went even further, and were enthusiastic about peace. 'There is a very general wish,' the *Daily News* claimed, 'to give them back the liberty for which they have struck such vigorous blows.'[4]

To Kimberley's surprise the local South African reaction to peace was even more divided. The Cape Dutch were openly delighted; and Jan Hofmeyr immediately telegraphed Joubert '. . . Pleased to hear of Armistice—make it easy for Great Britain to give you your terms by behaving in a conciliatory way.'[5] But the predominantly English ministry was alarmed at the news. Sprigg, the Cape Premier, immediately contacted his Agent-General in London. Accordingly, Mills made representation to the Colonial Office. 'Capt. Mills has been here today,' Kimberley informed Gladstone on 9 March,[6] 'and brought me a telegram from Mr. Sprigg. He too fears "disastrous consequences"[7] to the colony if we now make peace. Capt. Mills thinks Mr. Sprigg means that the Cape Dutch will declare their independence. There is no doubt a revolutionary element in the colony which might stir up a movement for a Dutch Republic. The Germans in the colony, a rather important body, sympathise, it is said, with the Dutch.' It was a difficult warning to assess. Had it come ten days earlier it might have affected Kimberley's thinking after Majuba; but by 9 March he had determined his course, and so classed the message, together with Queen Victoria's warnings of doom, as an 'alarmist telegram'.[8] In fact he waved it aside, and proceeded with his selection of the

[1] *The Times*, 8 March 1881. [2] *Pall Mall Gazette*, 7 March 1881.
[3] *Daily News*, 8 March 1881. [4] Idem.
[5] *Parl. Pap.*, 1881, LXVII, C.2837, p. 24. Hofmeyr to Joubert (Tel.), 8 March 1881.
[6] Addit., MSS. 44226, f. 48. Kimberley to Gladstone, 9 March 1881, enclosed in Sprigg to Mills, 8 March 1881, and Queen Victoria to Kimberley, 9 March 1881.
[7] The phrase is Queen Victoria's, and forms part of a telegram she sent to Kimberley on 20 February, and also enclosed in this same letter to Gladstone. See *Letters of Queen Victoria*, 2nd ser. III, 197.
[8] Addit. MSS. 44226, f. 48. Kimberley to Gladstone, 9 March 1881.

Commissioners.[1] Robinson had already agreed to head the peace negotiations;[2] and all that remained was to draft the broadest possible basis for a settlement, and also see that the armistice was extended as needed. Gladstone and Kimberley met at 2.30 p.m. on Friday, 11 March,[3] to discuss these factors in readiness for the Saturday Cabinet.[4] They were hoping to present another *fait accompli*, thus avoiding the possibility of allowing the issue to fall back into the hands of the warring factions.

The names of Robinson, Wood, and de Villiers were accordingly presented at the Cabinet of 12 March,[5] together with letters of instructions already drafted. No objections were raised; and telegrams were despatched the same afternoon to the three wise men of South Africa.[6] But over the exact peace terms there was much discussion. The thorny question of 'suzerainty' and 'sovereignty'—which was to bedevil constitutional lawyers and imperial relations with the South African Republic[7]—was introduced for the first time. Gladstone was searching for a useful word that would imply a British 'overlordship' over the Transvaal, yet allow the Transvalers to talk of self-rule. Gladstone did not know whether to substitute 'protectorate' or 'suzerainty' for annexation in the coming treaty.[8] Granville favoured 'suzerainty'. Gladstone was still not sure. 'Will the word suzerainty be of any use in South Africa?' he asked Granville. 'Yes', the Foreign Secretary replied, 'But I am afraid in the other direction—of how a stipendary officer is to provide efficiently for land and native questions.'[9] Granville's fears over the usefulness of the Resident were to be well founded in the light of later events. If we owe the word 'suzerainty' in Transvaal–Imperial relations to Granville, it

---

[1] Addit. MSS. 44226, f. 50. Kimberley to Gladstone, 11 March 1881.

[2] C.O. 291/10. Robinson to Kimberley (Tel.), 11 March 1881.

[3] Addit. MSS. 44226, f. 50. Kimberley to Gladstone, 11 March 1881.

[4] Addit. 44642, f. 158 (Cabinet Papers), Saturday, 12 March 1881.

[5] Idem.

[6] *Parl. Pap.*, 1881, LXVII, C.2837, pp. 24 ff., 8 March 1881.

[7] See G. H. Le May, *British Supremacy in South Africa*, 1899–1907 (O.U.P., 1965) chap. I, pp. 1–3.

[8] Addit. MSS. 44642, f. 159 (Cabinet Papers), 12 March 1881. See Points 3 to 5.

[9] Idem.

seems we owe the optimism over the Resident to Gladstone.[1] Kimberley's telegram of 8 p.m. that evening (12 March) to Wood, conveyed the complete Cabinet mind on the Transvaal:[2]

> ... Commission would be authorised to consider following points—complete self-government under British suzerainty, with British Resident at Pretoria, and provisions for protection of Native interests and as to frontier matters. Control of foreign powers to be reserved ... also to consider scheme for severance of territory eastward to divide Transvaal from Zulus and Swazi. ... You may consent to prolongation of armistice till 18th. ... [Such a Commission could begin once] the Boers will undertake to desist from armed opposition and disperse to their homes. ...[3]

This telegram was to inaugurate ten days of anxious negotiation; and to provoke serious objections, from the Queen[4]— who had not seen it before it was sent—and from the Boers— who disliked the terms offered.[5] The difficulties of finding a peaceful solution must soon have seemed more complicated than waging the war. Not only were the Boers unhappy about the basis suggested, but in Parliament awkward questions were asked as to who had initiated the recent armistice—had Britain sued for relief from the war? *The Times* now took up the campaign, and began to speak of Britain 'surrendering'; of her supremacy in South Africa being 'fatally jeopardised, alike among the English Dutch, and natives. ...' For, *The Times* claimed, 'In the Cape Colony the loyalty of the Dutch inhabitants is being sorely strained, and *the Boer dream of a free South African Republic seems in the Boer mind hastening towards realisation.'*[6] Wood helped Kimberley considerably, by suggesting that Brand had started the train of moves towards the armistice.[7] But even he could not temper the Boers' demands.[8] Kimberley

---

[1] *Letters of Queen Victoria*, 2nd ser., III, 201, Gladstone to Queen, 12 March 1881, reporting on Cabinet.

[2] C.O. 291/10. Kimberley to Wood (Tel.), 12 March 1881, 8 p.m.

[3] Ibid., see also *Parl. Pap.*, 1881, LXVII, C.2837, pp. 24–5.

[4] *Letters of Queen Victoria*, 2nd ser., III, 202. Ponsonby to Kimberley (Tel.), 12 March 1881.

[5] Addit. MSS. 44226, f. 53. Kimberley to Gladstone, 17 March 1881; and C.O. 291/10. Wood to Kimberley (Tel.), 13 March 1881.

[6] *The Times*, 12 March 1881. (My italics.)

[7] C.O. 291/10. Wood to Kimberley (Tel.), 14 March 1881, 7.15 a.m.

[8] Ibid., Wood to Kimberley (Tel.), 12 March 1881, 10.30 p.m.

decided to stand firm and Gladstone agreed with him.[1] The issue at stake was the proviso that the Boers disperse before negotiations began. 'What is essential', Kimberley telegraphed Wood, 'is that it should be a real dispersion of armed force. If Boers retire, it is not intended that you should follow them with troops, and you may give engagement to that effect. . . .'[2] Kruger had by now arrived at the battlefront,[3] and was pleased to learn of Kimberley's guarantee; but he still raised several objections.[4]

Kimberley laid out the Boer terms, and his own attitude, in a detailed letter to Gladstone.[5] (His objections are in italics.)

The points raised . . . seem to be as follows—two Boers to be on commission (*we cannot treat on the terms which would be implied by a joint commission, which would be recognition of them as independent power*); withdrawal immediately of our troops from Transvaal (*this I think wholly out of the question*); Transvaal to be 'what we annexed and have since held' (*This implies rejection of all schemes of division*); Gov[ernment] to deal with interior native affairs (*This would render control of native affairs illusory*); Boers fear loyal English and cannot entirely disperse (*My opinion is that we must insist on dispersion*); Boers accept sovereignty.

The only agreement was on Boer acceptance of British 'sovereignty'. 'I write this hurriedly,' Kimberley added, 'and my views might be modified by discussion and further consideration, but nos. 2 [withdrawal of British troops] and 6 [Boer dispersal] are I think very serious points. Ought we not to have [a] Cabinet this morning?'[6] Gladstone called the Cabinet for 2 p.m.[7]—but sorted out a workable basis for peace with Kimberley, before the ministers assembled.

Gladstone once again played a key part; for it was he, and not Kimberley, who found ways round the Boer objections.[8] He

[1] Addit. MSS. 44226, f. 51. Kimberley to Gladstone, 15 March 1881.

[2] *Parl. Pap.*, 1881, LXVII, C.2537, p. 26. Kimberley to Wood (Tel.), 16 March 1881, 10.45 a.m.

[3] Ibid., Wood to Kimberley (Tel.), 15 March 1881.

[4] Ibid., Wood to Kimberley (Tel.), 16 March 1881.

[5] Addit. MSS. 44226, f. 53. Kimberley to Gladstone, 17 March 1881. (Order of letter rearranged).

[6] Idem.

[7] Addit. MSS. 44642, f. 163 (Cabinet Papers), Thursday, 17 March 1881.

[8] Addit. MSS. 44226, f. 55 (copy). Gladstone to Kimberley, 17 March 1881.

was quick to point out that while difficulties did exist, 'the concession made by the Boers in agreeing to the principle and main business of dispersion is enormous—and it will be a sad pity if after this we cannot work things out—with the agreement to disperse I join the *acceptance of the (Sovereignty)*[1] *Suzerainty*, and I think that out of the two we ought to be able to extract and adjust materials of a peace'.[2] Gladstone did not think they need answer the Boer claims as yet for,

> The Commission is not a tribunal of arbitration, but is intended to advise, with great moral authority, the British Government. Its proceedings will be open—let the Boers appoint their agents who shall have cognisance of everything, and if the Boer agents differ, we shall wish to be let known.[3]

As to Britain's forces in the Transvaal: 'Our troops must remain, with the function of a friendly police force, and it will be an essential part of their duty to prevent loyal English from using the situation to the prejudice of [the] Boers.' Gladstone was adamant about the powers of the Resident—'I should incline to stiffen on this'—but he took heart from the fact that the Boers would accept British suzerainty—'Concession to us most important.' In short, as he told Kimberley, 'My first views are a little more rosy than yours, but not I think in conflct with them.'[4]

Into the midst of these complications came yet another protest from the Queen: 'Am sorry your telegram of the 15th was sent to Sir E. Wood before it was submitted to me. Cannot understand any surrender to Boer demands which this implies.'[5] Gladstone was weary of such protests, and got Kimberley to write a very firm explanatory letter.[6] Victoria was informed that '. . . Lord Kimberley trusts that a peaceful settlement may follow on terms honourable to this country and as advantageous as the difficult nature of the questions to be dealt with will permit.' And that, 'It is very satisfactory that the Boers accepted at

---

[1] In the letter, the word 'Sovereignty' is crossed out, and 'Suzerainty' written above it.

[2] The italics are Gladstone's.

[3] Ibid., ff. 55–6.   [4] Idem.

[5] Guedalla, *Queen and Mr. Gladstone*, II, 148, no. 765. Queen to Gladstone (Tel.), 17 March 1881.

[6] *Letters of Queen Victoria*, 2nd ser., III, 202–3.

once the Suzerainty of the British Crown. . .'[1] The Queen's intervention was, as usual, particularly untimely, both for Gladstone and Kimberley, in the light of the uncertainties of the peace negotiations, and in view of the obvious dissension that was going to be voiced at the Cabinet of that very day, Thursday, 17 March.[2] The Whigs did not like the idea of bargaining with the Boers; many felt, as Hartington did, that either the Boers must sign on Britain's terms, or the war must go on.[3] Kimberley achieved a token victory at this Cabinet, and at the next, two days later (Saturday, 19 March),[4] in that it was agreed to await news from Wood before calling the Boers' bluff, and proceeding with the war.

Kimberley's most anxious period now followed. Between Saturday, 19 March and Tuesday, 22 March the Boers made up their minds about the peace terms while Wood and Brand endeavoured to bring them round to acceptance.[5] Interest was added to the affair when the *New York Tribune*[6] reported that 500 'wild Irishmen', well armed, and with 4 gattling guns, had sailed from New York in a barque, 'secretly heading for Delogoa Bay'[7]—presumably to aid the Boers. It came to naught,[8] but it whipped up the public's excitement while Britain awaited Kruger's reply. The anxious days were unexpectedly extended when Kruger and Pretorius both fell 'ill' on the same day, 18 March.[9] Their malady could be called 'second thoughts'. Since the original overtures much had taken place. Majuba, in particular, affected the attitude of the Boer leaders. It obviously encouraged them to demand peace on their own terms; and it also made them deeply suspicious of the already questionable British tactics. Colley's behaviour they took as being

---

[1] Idem.

[2] Addit. MSS. 44642, f. 163 (Cabinet Papers), 17 March 1881, 2 p.m.

[3] Idem.

[4] Ibid., f. 164. Saturday, 19 March 1881, 2 p.m.

[5] Brand, in particular, put great pressure on the Boer leaders. See telegrams Brand to Joubert, in Addit. MSS. 44627, f. 112.

[6] *New York Tribune*, 6 March 1881.

[7] C.O. 291/13, with cutting from the *New York Tribune* and C.O. comment.

[8] Ibid., C.O. to F.O., 20 April and 6 May 1881. No one knew what happened to the Irish.

[9] *Parl. Pap.*, 1881, LXVII, C.2837, p. 28. Wood to Kimberley (Tel.), 18 March 1881, 4 p.m.

directed from Downing Street.[1] As Kruger explained to Brand:

... [Colley] writes on the 23rd January a letter, waited not for an answer, and attacked on the 28th. The English Government thereupon takes your Honour by the hand to correspond with us, and although Colley is immediately informed that the Vice-President [Kruger] was away, and that eight or ten days must expire before an answer could be given. ... Colley attacks again and thereby puts an end to all.[2]

Thus Kruger was indeed justified in asking, 'Have we not the right to say now, England does not wish for peace but a false dishonourable one?'[3]

Boer misgivings did not end there. The initial peace terms, as suggested by Kimberley, had been deliberately broad, almost vague, so as to provide an extensive common denominator from which to work. Now that Kimberley began to narrow the terms, to make it look more like a hard bargain, and less like an open-handed restoration of the old republican status, the Boers became restive. Two points, in particular, angered the triumvirate.[4] The first was the composition of the Royal Commission. The Boers had expected it to include their own representatives, and instead they learnt they were only to be called as witnesses.[5] Second, Kruger suspected that 'the British Government wished to keep back for themselves a portion of the Republic, namely, the Utrecht and Wakkerstroom Districts'.[6] This *was* in fact being contemplated—both to protect the extensive tribal populations in the two districts, and also to provide a 'buffer state' between the Transvaal Boers and Zulus and Swazi.

The Boer leaders considered the situation in the tent of General Smit. Wood waited patiently in the English camp some miles off. On the night of Saturday, 19 March, as the rain fell heavily outside the tent, Kruger and the other members of the

[1] Addit. MSS. 44627, f. 112. Joubert to Brand, 4 March 1881: 'It is alone in the power of the English Ministry to prevent [the War continuing] against whose attacks we defend ourselves.'

[2] Ibid., ff. 110–11. Kruger to Brand, 3 March 1881.

[3] Idem.

[4] Paul Kruger, *Memoirs* (London, 1902), I, 179–80.

[5] Addit. MSS. 44627, f. 119. Wood to Kimberley (Tel.), 20 March 1881, 3 p.m.: 'Brand says Boers want Chief Justice Reitz, on Royal Commission.'

[6] Kruger, *Memoirs*, I, 179–80.

triumvirate decided to renew the war.[1] They drew up a challenging 'Proclamation' addressed to all the Dutch in South Africa. It gave a history of the war and the peace overtures, pointed out the apparent British intransigence, and appealed for aid, ending with these emotive words: '*Dit is vir u om te sê wie Afrika sal regeer; die Afrikaner of 'n paar dwingelande in Downingstraat.*'[2]

The rain had now stopped, and the mist was clearing, when Brand rode into the Boer camp on the Sunday morning, 20 March. Discussions went on all day, and they were still arguing when night fell. Brand strongly advocated peace, and called on Kruger to reconsider. Finally Kruger, Joubert, and Pretorius revealed their *pièce de résistance*, the Proclamation. Jorissen read it out, 'in a deep but soft voice', and with obvious pride—he probably wrote it. Brand listened in silence. He finally said simply, '*Mag God ons daarvoor bewaar.*'[3] Later he told Kruger he could not publish it. Brand begged and cajoled. Kruger began to weaken, and spent a sleepless night, partly walking the *veld* with Jorissen, and partly praying. Brand at last persuaded him at least to discuss the terms with Wood.[4] Accordingly, on Monday, 21 March, the two sides met. The results were explosive. Kruger picked up his hat and walked out when Wood spoke of detaching Utrecht and Wakkerstroom; and General Smit kept saying 'Let the sword decide.'[5] Even when a rough basis was beaten out it nearly came to grief for Wood despatched a rider, with the news that the armistice had been prolonged, before the agreement had been signed.[6] Kruger enquired where the man was going; and when told suddenly shouted, in English, 'Stop that man.' As he later remembered:

I then went into the tent and said to General Wood that I asked him, as an honest man, first to sign the agreement containing the points discussed by us. The document lay on the table, but Sir

[1] The period 19 March to 21 March is graphically described by Professor D. W. Kruger in his *Paul Kruger*, I, 241–5, to which I am indebted.

[2] Ibid., quoted p. 242. Translation: 'It is for you to say who will rule Africa; the Afrikaner or a few fools in Downing Street.' It is traditionally known as the '3rd Proclamation', although it was never published.

[3] Ibid., quoted p. 243. Literally: 'God forbid!'

[4] Kruger, *Memoirs*, I, 181.   [5] Ibid., I, 180.

[6] Sir Evelyn Wood, *From Midshipman to Field Marshal*, pp. 119 ff. for his side of the peace negotiations.

Evelyn refused to sign. It was not until I cried, 'Burghers, saddle!' that Wood . . . gave in and signed.[1]

In London, Kimberley, unaware of the great tension on the *veld*, grew despondent. 'We rely on you,' he telegraphed Wood on Sunday, 20 March, 'to give us time to consider points on which you may be unable to come to agreement with Boer leaders.'[2] But, on Monday, 21 March, there came the first encouraging news from the Transvaal for many months. 'Conferring since 8 a.m. not certain yet, but anticipate peaceful solution,' Wood reported.[3] Then in the early hours of Tuesday, 22 March came news of the Boer acceptance of the modified peace terms. 'After sitting $12\frac{1}{2}$ hours without intermission,' a bargain had been struck. 'I urge your approval,' Wood advised, 'and, if you can, to shorten the interval to four months;[4] authorise me to ratify proceedings, when Boers will disperse.'[5] The Transvalers had agreed to accept British suzerainty, so long as the promised self-government was instituted 'within six months'. They also accepted the presence of the British Resident, 'with such functions as the British Government may decide on the recommendation of the Royal Commission'. The control of foreign relations were 'reserved' to Britain; but the Commission was to 'consider the provisions for the protection of the native interests. . . .' Finally, it was guaranteed that 'no civil action [was to] be entertained in respect of proceedings taken during or in reference to the war, and equally no action shall be taken in respect of taxation until the self-government is accorded'.[6]

The news was immediately conveyed to Gladstone; and his

[1] Kruger, *Memoirs*, I, 181.

[2] *Parl. Pap.*, 1881, LXVII, C.2837, p. 29. Kimberley to Wood (Tel.), Sunday, 20 March 1881, 11 p.m.

[3] Ibid., Wood to Kimberley (Tel.), 21 March 1881, 3 p.m.

[4] i.e., the period in which 'self-government' was to be granted to the Boers.

[5] Ibid., Wood to Kimberley (Tel.), 21 March 1881, 9.25 p.m. Received C.O., 22 March 1881, 4 a.m.

[6] Idem. The most trenchant comment on the terms come from the *Pall Mall Gazette* of 18 March 1881: 'A good many people believe that it would be far better in the long run to come out of the Transvaal, bag and baggage, without nominal hoisting of the flag, nominal protectorate, Resident, or other apparatus for involving us in future complications with the troublesome gentry.'

reaction well illustrates the pressure under which he and Kimberley had been working. He wrote to his Colonial Secretary the moment he had scanned the telegram:

My dear K.
Thank God.
I have read with a critical eye as well as I could the long telegram, and I do not detect any reason for hesitation.
If I am right in this, we two agreeing, it is of utmost importance to proceed without losing an hour. . .
In my view the Telegram is, as a whole, rather better than we had any right to expect. . . .
If we approve, Wood ought to receive emphatic praise. And query whether we can hereafter do anything complimentary for Brand.
In haste ever yours,
W. E. Gladstone.[1]

If Kimberley was relieved, the G.O.M. was clearly delighted—particularly as it meant the matter had been cleared up in time for his budget. The very same day—22 March—he sent a memorandum to Childers and Northbrook:[2] 'The Transvaal war being now happily settled, I presume you will both review the estimates of war expenditure for 1881–2. As the budget stands fixed for April 4, it would be well that anything to be done in this matter should be done at once.'

The Gladstonians were well-pleased with themselves; they celebrated accordingly. 'At dinner this evening', Hamilton recorded in his Diary.[3] 'Mr. G. was in great spirits at the news from the Transvaal. . . . The Radical party have certainly behaved extremely well under trying circumstances.' Gladstone's cup positively ran over. 'Apropos of their behaviour, Mr. G. remarked tonight that he never remembered the Liberal party —certainly for the last 30 years—as a whole, in a more satisfactory state.'[4] The Downing Street celebrations did not extend

[1] Addit. MSS. 44226, f. 57 (copy). Gladstone to Kimberley, 22 March 1881.

[2] Addit. MSS. 44266, f. 93. Memorandum by Gladstone to Childers and Northbrook, 22 March 1881.

[3] Addit. MSS. 48631, ff. 5, 7 (Hamilton Diary). Entries for 21 March, and Tuesday, 22 March 1881.

[4] Argyll was already contemplating resignation; he left the Cabinet a few weeks later.

156

to Windsor. The Queen was informed of the Wood telegram soon after Gladstone received it[1]—and that acceptance of the terms had *already* been wired to the Transvaal.[2] Ponsonby was instructed to inform Kimberley that the Queen objected to his method of immediate telegrams, without consulting her; that the Queen felt 'the Boers have obtained all they fought for, viz., independence within their borders'; and that while Her Majesty did not wish to see more bloodshed, she only 'reluctantly gives you permission to support the actions of Sir Evelyn Wood. . .'[3] Kimberley's reply was the model of tact; and the answer of a man unconcerned by her criticism. 'The terms secure all the points of real importance to this country,' she was informed,[4] and 'Lord Kimberley does not think better terms could have been made after a successful war.' It was to no avail. Two weeks later, when presented with the formal instructions for the Royal Commission, the Queen was still furious. 'I sanction these instructions, but I cannot refrain from repeating how deeply I deplore giving up a territory which the Government [had] declared they would maintain, and especially after defeats, and the abandonment of Candahar. . .' It was all, 'very damaging to the prestige of this Empire'.[5]

The Queen was not alone in this opinion. The *Daily Telegraph*[6] styled it 'a most remarkable capitulation'; the *Manchester Guardian* observed that such terms could have been secured without a war;[7] and the *Morning Post* felt it set 'a dangerous precedent'.[8] The *Daily News*, *The Times*, and the *Daily Chronicle* were more stoical, and accepted it as a necessity. But the most intuitive comment came from the *Pall Mall Gazette*:[9]

There is one lesson which South African history teaches more plainly than any other—that wherever native claims have been

[1] *Letters of Queen Victoria*, 2nd ser., III, 203–4.
[2] *Parl. Pap.*, 1881, LXVII, C.2837, p. 30. Kimberley to Wood (Tel.), 22 March 1881, 7 p.m.
[3] *Letters of Queen Victoria*, 2nd ser., III, 203–4. Ponsonby to Kimberley, 22 March 1881, from Windsor.
[4] Ibid., pp. 204–5. Kimberley to Queen, 22 March 1881.
[5] Ibid., p. 206. Queen to Kimberley (Tel.), 31 March 1881.
[6] *Daily Telegraph*, 23 March 1881.
[7] *Manchester Guardian*, 23 March 1881.
[8] *Morning Post*, 23 March 1881.
[9] *Pall Mall Gazette*, 23 March 1881.

supported from England in just opposition to the claims and even the prejudices of the European population, the native has always been the sufferer in the end.

The proposed powers of the Resident, to safeguard native interests, really fooled no one—least of all the Boers.[1] Even within the Gladstonian circle, after the initial relief, the real significance of the peace began to be grasped. Hamilton—surely Gladstone's most loyal apostle—spoke of 'bringing a most unsatisfactory business to a somewhat unsatisfactory close . . . ';[2] and that, 'it is difficult to give any plausible answer to the very natural question why, if the Govt. concede now that for which the Boers rose in rebellion, we did not at the outset grant their demands. . . .'[3] His analysis of the failure in policy is perhaps a fair representation of the 'average' thinking man at the time:

> Of course the real mistake committed was not to have given the Boers self-government or independence many months ago. . . . Nothing, however, will ever justify the annexation and the grossly bad way in which the Colonial authorities allowed themselves to be misinformed as to the real feeling of the Boers.[4]

Kimberley implemented the decision; and also cleared-up loose points. Wood was immediately instructed to accept the Boer demands[5] —a decision taken by Gladstone and Kimberley, without reference to the Cabinet.[6] Lanyon was recalled, on 'leave', in complete disgrace—'. . . it will be better that you should at once take leave applied for last year and return to this

[1] The *Standard* was most realistic: 'If we are to continue to govern South Africa, our supremacy must be recognised both by the native races and by the colonists, whether English, Dutch, German or French.' *Standard*, 21 March 1881.

[2] Addit. MSS. 48631, f. 7 (Hamilton Diary). Entry for Saturday, 26 March 1881.

[3] Ibid., f. 8.

[4] 'We have just had enough fighting to wound the Peace Party, and just stopped short, momentarily, to kindle up all the Jingo feelings afresh. We have, in short, fallen between two stools; and to this circumstance coupled with the Irish difficulties is probably attributable the loss of the seat at Coventry.' Ibid., ff. 1–2.

[5] *Parl. Pap.*, 1881, LXVII, C.2837, p. 30. Kimberley to Wood (Tel.), 22 March 1881, 7 p.m.

[6] Addit. MSS. 44642, ff. 164–7 (Cabinet Papers). The Cabinet did not meet until 26 March, though the decision was taken on 22 March.

country.'[1] Sir Frederick Roberts, who had just arrived in Cape Town, on the way to take over the post temporarily held by Wood, was instructed that he was no longer needed in the interior, and could return.[2] The Instructions for the conduct of the Royal Commission was drawn up in the Colonial Office.[3] An attempt to exclude the Boer leaders from the general amnesty was blocked by Kimberley—'Joubert commanded in the affair and to exclude him from the amnesty would be to renew the war.'[4] He was equally firm when the question of ammunition supplies to the Free State came up yet again[5]—'My fear is that if we refuse permission we shall make Brand's position untenable, and lose his friendly aid.'[6] His last act, in preparing the way for peace, was to see that the troop reinforcements were sent to Natal just in case the negotiations collapsed.[7] Beyond this Kimberley could do no more.

At the Cabinet of Saturday, 26 March the ministers were told of the Gladstone and Kimberley actions since 22 March.[8] They were accepted as a necessary *fait accompli;* but hardly with any enthusiasm.[9] It was cold comfort to know that Lord Acton had declared that Burke would have made the peace with 'the Africanders'—'which is the noblest work of the Ministry'.

But Spencer, who had recently dined at Windsor, gave an account of how bitterly Queen Victoria still spoke of the

---

[1] C.O. 291/10. Kimberley to Lanyon (Tel.), 23 March 1881. See also Kimberley's comments on Lanyon's long despatch of 23 January 1881; 'Lanyon most misleading . . .'

[2] *Parl. Pap.*, 1881, LXVII, C.2858, p. 1. Kimberley to Roberts (Tel.), 23 March 1881, 7 p.m.

[3] C.O. 291/14. 'Instructions to the Royal Commission for the settlement of the Affairs of the Transvaal.' Printed in *Parl. Pap.*, 1881, LXVII, C.2892, pp. 1–11.

[4] Addit. MSS. 44226, f. 60. Kimberley to Gladstone, 25 March 1881.

[5] C.O. 291/14. Robinson to Kimberley (Tel.), requesting instructions on this question (28 March 1881, 8 p.m.).

[6] Addit. MSS. 44226, f. 62. Kimberley to Gladstone, 29 March 1881. It is interesting that Childers entirely disagreed. See f. 64.

[7] C.O. 291/13. W.O. to C.O., 24 March 1881. This referred particularly to the 7th Hussars and the 85th Regiment.

[8] Addit. MSS. 44642, f. 167 (Cabinet Papers), 26 March 1881, 2 p.m.

[9] Addit. MSS. 43924, f. 45 (Dilke Diary). Entry for Saturday, 26 March 1881.

'prompt vindication' phrase in the Queen's speech of 6 January:

> *Queen Victoria:* 'I cannot see how my authority has been vindicated in the Transvaal.'
> *Spencer:* 'There was nothing else to be done, Ma'am.'
> *Queen Victoria:* 'I quite understand that—but I still do not see how my authority has been vindicated.'[1]

The Cabinet was hugely amused.[2] But perhaps only Kimberley grasped, or admitted, the nature of the situation. Privately he stated, more in anxiety than in optimism: 'The Commission will have to make the best terms they can for us.'[3]

3. Resumé: Kimberley's abandonment of the traditional approach

Policy had swung on its axis; it had moved from coercion to conciliation. Gladstone and Kimberley had supervised the change. But they had not so much dismantled the traditional approach, as watched it totter and collapse under the stress of local events. They clearly grasped the significance of the breakdown, even if modern historians have ignored it; and they helped to shift the emphasis in policy, from formal to informal control over the Afrikaner Republic. As Kimberley bluntly explained: '. . . the fact is the policy in the Transvaal has been a failure, and everyone connected with it (in which I include myself since I have been in office) will have to bear a share of blame in the opinion of the public.'[4] He acutely felt the vacuum in policy; and, equally surely, determined that the new basis for policy must not only take due cognisance of the changing behaviour of the Afrikaner and English colonists, but must also attempt to heal the wounds left by the old approach. 'What we have to do now,' Kimberley explained to his Colonial officials, 'is to avoid all recriminations as to the past, and endeavour to effect as tolerable a settlement as we can considering all the circumstances.'[5]

---

[1] Addit. MSS. 43935, ff. 60–61 (Dilke Memoir); and Dilke Diary, Addit. MSS. 43924, f. 45.
[2] Ibid., see also Gwynne and Tuckwell, *Dilke*, I, 369.
[3] C.O. 291/14. Minute by Kimberley, 24 March 1881.
[4] Idem.   [5] Idem.

In his personal stock-taking of the resources and the intentions of the imperial factor, Kimberley both publicly[1] and privately,[2] justified the new approach in terms of the evolving southern African dilemma. One factor had led to another. To break the chain-reaction of events had been impossible. 'I confess,' he admitted, 'that I had not sufficient insight to see behind all the information I received.'[3] This was the reason why he had not relinquished the Transvaal on taking office: 'The official evidence . . . was to the effect that the political aspect of affairs in the Transvaal was decidedly improving.'[4] Both Colley and Lanyon 'informed me up to the last moment before the rebellion broke out that things were quietening down, and that all our difficulties would disappear'.[5] There were also positive reasons against reversing the annexation: 'It has been said, and I believe with great justice, that nothing has done more harm in South Africa than the want of continuity in British policy, in consequence of which neither colonists nor natives have any confidence that we shall long pursue any course of action.'[6] Thus, 'we thought it our duty to endeavour to carry on the government of the Transvaal, and to see whether we could not bring the people of that country to such a state of contentment that they might acquiesce in our rule and be willing to enjoy the blessings of self-government under the sovereignty of the Queen'.[7] Further than this Britain was 'bound also to take into consideration the probable consequences of our retirement, to English settlers, to loyal Boers, and to the natives . . .'[8] In sum: 'Could we have justified the abandonment of the territory without stronger evidence than we then possessed that we could not govern it peaceably? . . .'[9] The effects could have been disastrous: 'By retiring we should have run the risk of leaving the province in a state of confusion, if not of civil war. . . .'[10]

[1] Kimberley in Lords, Thursday, 31 March 1881. *Hansard*, 3rd ser., CCLX, col. 279 ff.

[2] Addit. MSS. 44627, ff. 1–21. Memorandum by Kimberley on Transvaal policy, 29 April 1881.

[3] Kimberley in Lords, 31 March 1881. *Hansard*, 3rd ser., CCLX, col. 280.

[4] Addit. MSS. 44627, ff. 1–3. Memorandum by Kimberley, 29 April 1881.

[5] *Hansard*, 3rd ser., CCLX, col. 280.

[6] Addit. MSS. 44627, ff. 1–3.   [7] *Hansard*, 3rd ser., CCLX, col. 280.

[8] Addit. MSS. 44627, ff. 1–3.   [9] Idem.   [10] Idem.

This initial decision—taken on all the available information —led to the second stage of the dilemma. Self-government for the Transvaal had been withheld prior to the outbreak as the 'question of federation was about to be brought before the Cape Parliament, and Sir Bartle Frere told us that there was no good prospect of the resolution for the assembly of a conference being carried, but that the abandonment of the Transvaal would be fatal to the prospects of confederation'.[1] After the outbreak had begun 'was that the moment . . . to announce that we were to leave the Transvaal . . . and simply say that, an insurrection having broken out, we would withdraw our garrison, and leave the Boers [to] their independence?'[2] As to the awkward time-lag between the Cape rejection of federation in July and the rebellion in late December, Kimberley had an explanation for that as well: 'My answer is that, the time was most inopportune for attempting such a change. Sir Bartle Frere left Cape Town on the 15th of September, [and] . . . the confederation scheme, though suspended, was not given up—and until Sir H. Robinson arrived . . . we could not tell precisely in what direction it might be advisable to make the next move.'[3] Great Britain was thus trapped into an unwelcome and unexpected war by the Boer challenge. 'Is it not practically certain that the Boers would have refused at that time to listen to any reasonable terms. . .?'[4] Kimberley was equally emphatic on why he made peace after Majuba: 'Now, could we, because we had been unfortunate in that engagement, draw back from the undertaking we had previously entered into with Mr. Kruger?'[5]

The vital issue at stake, in the formation of his policy, is thus the question: why did he embark on any peace negotiations at all while the rebellion was still at its height? What happened to change his mind between 19 December—when he spoke so strongly of 'vindication'—and 24 January, when he began to advocate an immediate negotiated peace? It has already been suggested that, in examining Kimberley's handling of the rebellion, a gradual 'loss of nerve' took place as he began to fear that the war could breed even more unrest among the Afrikaners, than it would settle. His own reflections, on this crucial

[1] Ibid., ff. 2–3.   [2] *Hansard*, CCLX, col. 281.
[3] Addit. MSS. 44627, ff. 2–3.   [4] Idem.
[5] *Hansard*, CCLX, col. 283.

period, support this interpretation of his behaviour. As he explained to the Queen:[1] 'Considering the great ferment of opinion in South Africa, and the imminent dangers which threaten our whole position in this country, Lord Kimberley cannot but feel a sense of great relief that the war is brought to a close.'[2] The 'great ferment of opinion' in the colonies and republics had been the deciding factor in Kimberley's change of approach. President Brand, of the Free State, had first suggested the impending storm's strength. It deeply affected Kimberley's thinking.

> We knew that the action of the Free State trembled in the balance, [Kimberley told the Lords after the armistice had been signed][3] that at any moment it might enrol itself among the number of our enemies; and considering the comparative weakness of our forces in the field, an attack upon their flank by the Free State might have proved disastrous. It was my duty to intimate to President Brand that we were not prepared to push matters to extremities if an honourable settlement of the difficulty could be arrived at.[4]

Kimberley's initial doubts had broadened into major fears when he asked himself the question, 'Who are those rebels of the Transvaal? With whom are they connected?'[5] His answer closely reflected his thinking:

> They are men of Dutch origin. They are connected by the closest ties with the inhabitants of the Orange Free State, and with the subjects of the Queen at the Cape. . . . [So intimate was this connection] by marriage and every possible tie, that a war carried on in South Africa brings into play forces and rouses passions which might well make a bold man hesitate before he rejected any mode of preserving peace which would be likely to succeed. . . . There is not a shot fired throughout South Africa in anger which does not re-echo throughout every portion of that dominion. . . .[6]

The files of the Colonial Office had hardened his attitude, and provided him with the proof to back his fears. About Brand's Republic he felt there could be no debate: 'The connection between the Orange Free State and the Transvaal is such that it is scarcely possible, had the war continued long, that the former

[1] *Letters of Queen Victoria*, 2nd ser., III, 204–5. Kimberley to Queen, 22 March 1881.
[2] Idem.   [3] Kimberley in Lords, 31 March 1881.
[4] *Hansard*, CCLX, col. 283.   [5] Ibid., col. 286.   [6] Ibid., cols. 285–6.

would have been able to refrain from joining our enemies.'[1] On the Cape he was less pontifical; but the signs deeply worried him. 'The state of feeling throughout the Colony was also becoming of a very alarming character. The sympathy felt by the Dutch population with the people of the Transvaal was such as could not be overlooked by the Government.[2] Graham Bower—twenty years in the Governor's office at the Cape—heartily agreed: 'To have continued the War would have been to humiliate the Cape Dutch—to strain their loyalty, to sacrifice their confidence in our Honour and Justice, and to weaken our hold on South Africa.'[3]

Kimberley pulled together all his basic attitudes in a long private memorandum,[4] in which he traced the logic behind his decision to abandon the old approach, and to move towards conciliation. The most significant paragraph reads:

> Then [in 1880] we had fair ground for the expectation that all these evils might be avoided by patience and wise government. Now bitter experience has proved that the great majority of the Boers will resist our rule to the uttermost. We know that if we conquer the country we can only hold it by the sword, and we have every reason to believe that the continuance of the war would have involved us in a contest with the Free State, as well as the Transvaal Boers, if it did not cause a rebellion in the Cape Colony itself. . . .[5]

It does seem that Kimberley's 'loss of nerve' had little to do with incompetence, or his excitable nature; but rather had been a reaction to apparently well founded fears, and was an attempt to come to grips with the local situation. Kimberley liked to quote Wood's telegram of 24 March as substantial proof of his policy.

> You ought to know, in justification of your measures, that Brand asserted another check to our arms would bring into field all young Dutchmen of South Africa. . . . I can endorse his opinion only as regards the Free State men, of whom I saw today some 300 on Laing's Nek position.[6]

[1] Idem.   [2] Idem.   [3] Afr. MSS. S.63, f. 1 (Bower Papers).
[4] Addit. MSS. 44627, ff. 1–21. Memorandum by Kimberley, 29 April 1881. (Printed in Gladstone Papers.)
[5] Ibid., ff. 1–2.
[6] Ibid., f. 122. Wood to Kimberley (Tel.), 24 March 1881.

In placing policy on an entirely different footing Gladstone and Kimberley were thus making a calculated move; a decision based not only on the ignominious failure of the traditional approach to southern Africa, but on the inescapable truth of the existence of the disruptive spirits of the Afrikaner's past—conjured into reality by the old techniques of policy. The mood and beliefs of the *Trek* had been revived; the old fires of militant anti-English feeling had been re-kindled; the voices of Retief and Pretorius were heard again.[1] Thus the unthinkable had taken place: the loyalty of the Cape Dutch was in serious doubt. In Bower's assessment: 'It may seem a paradox but a successful war in which we should have beaten down the opposition of the farmers by force of numbers would have damaged our prestige with the Dutch more than peace did.'[2] This awkward factor could not be ignored. The imperial presence in southern Africa ultimately turned on control of the Cape, not on the challenge from the Republican north. From the moment that this spectre of a pan-Afrikaner front came before the eyes of the policy-makers—and was accepted as more than an alarmist portrayal of a momentary protest—imperial initiative was seriously narrowed. Constant sensitivity to the mood of local Afrikaner opinion was forced on the Colonial officials as the touchstone for the future imperial actions and attitudes in South Africa.

The Pretoria Convention[3] was to enshrine the new approach to the Afrikaner of the republics. 'The task before us,' as Bower explained, 'was to conciliate the Dutch without alienating the English.' The new Convention was to be the first attempt to solve that problem—the first step in a policy which was pursued for fifteen years'.[4] With its faith in conciliation, and informal control, it sought a more durable basis for policy than had hitherto prevailed.

It is tempting to see in the new approach a return to the mid-century convention policy—as is suggested by Professor de Kiewiet, and more recently by Dr. Robinson and Professor

---

[1] F. A. van Jaarsveld, *The Awakening of Afrikaaner Nationalism*, is excellent on this, especially. chap. IX.

[2] Afr. MSS. S.63, f. 2, (Bower Papers).

[3] See Appendix I in this volume; see also Eybers, *Select Documents* (London, 1917), pp. 455 ff. 3 August 1881.

[4] Afr. MSS. S.63, f. 3 (Bower Papers).

Gallagher.[1] It is tempting, but misleading. The later Victorians were not hoping to emulate their predecessors in office; indeed, they were busy blaming their tribulations of the 1880s on that earlier policy.[2] We credit them with less understanding than they had, by suggesting that there were only two cards to play— intervention and abandonment.

The Gladstonian approach to the problem was, in essence, more oblique, and certainly more subtle than that. Both Gladstone and Kimberley grasped what later observers have missed: that the whole complex of the position of the imperial factor in southern Africa had been changed by the 'desultory warfare'— Kimberley's phrase[3]—waged by Colley's redcoats. It was no longer possible to grant the Transvaal complete independence, and to abandon the Afrikaner in the interior—as had been done in the Sand River Convention of 1852.[4] If Gladstone contemplated this option, then the facts at his disposal forced him to reject it. It was not a viable alternative; and his stress on the value of the suzerainty clause of the Pretoria Convention shows that he was well aware of the fact.[5] Much as he personally deplored the emotional concern among a certain sector of the British electorate, over the imperial responsibilities to the native tribes in and around the Republic, he could not ignore it; and Gladstone went so far as to see the fate of the Convention in the House as turning on the acceptability of the native provisions of the treaty. Whereas in 1850 the Afrikaner could be 'contemptuously abandoned'—Fairfield's phrase[6]—now in 1880 informal suasion, via a British Resident, was a necessity. Kimberley privately expressed great hopes over the usefulness of such a Resident:

[1] *Africa and the Victorians*, pp. 72–3 and 202–3.

[2] Addit. MSS. 44545, f. 30. Gladstone to Kimberley, 29 September 1881. P.R.O. 30/29/124. Gladstone to Granville, 7 May 1881, (Ramm, I, 273). See also *Hansard*, 3rd ser., CCLI, cols. 136–52.

[3] C.O. 48/499. Minute by Kimberley, 9 February 1881, on Strahan to Kimberley, 18 January 1881.

[4] Eybers, *Select Documents*, pp. 357–9, 16 January 1852.

[5] Addit. MSS. 44544, f. 180 (L.B. copy). Gladstone to Kimberley, 12 June 1881: 'It is upon the question of protection for the natives that we shall justly be subjected to the sharpest scrutiny . . .'

[6] Minute by Fairfield, December 1875. Quoted in De Kiewiet, *Imperial Factor*, pp. 105–7.

I see no reason why he should not exercise a salutary influence, and at all events we shall be in a better position than if we had no regular means of knowing what was going on, and no opportunity of making representations at the early stages of frontier differences when a timely interference might prevent serious consequences.[1]

In the case of external relations the position in the Republic had radically altered since the 1850s. The new convention was forced to take these relations into account. As Kimberley explained:

It has been supposed that they mean simply relations with native tribes. This is an entire mistake. The South African Republic had relations with various foreign powers. Besides two treaties with Portugal, whose colonial possessions adjoin the Transvaal, it had concluded treaties with Holland and Belgium, and its independence and international status had been recognised by Germany, France and the United States.[2]

Thus Kimberley saw no hope of returning to the mid-century policy. He made his logic clear:

It can scarcely be denied that it is important for the maintenance of British supremacy in South Africa, and to the prospects of future union between the white communities, that the foreign relations of the white settlements should be in British hands. Nothing could be more injurious to the permanent interests of the South African colonies than they should become the theatre of contention between rival European influences....[3]

Kimberley's initial 'loss of nerve' was thus more than momentary in effect. The degree of change was beyond doubt. Queen Victoria epitomised the old approach. She still spoke of an 'humiliating peace', which would 'ruin our position in South Africa';[4] and of retrieving honour through 'vindication'.[5] Gladstone and Kimberley stood for the new attitude. To them it was a 'just and timely' peace; conciliation not vindication was to be their pole star.

In changing policies in mid-war Kimberley had accomplished a genuine revolution in the official attitude to the Afrikaner republics. Whether it was a permanent revolution was yet

[1] Addit. MSS. 44627, f. 9–10. Memorandum by Kimberley, 29 April 1881.
[2] Idem.   [3] Idem.
[4] *Letters of Queen Victoria*, 2nd ser., III, 202.
[5] Ibid., p. 199.

to be seen. Certainly the margin of options open to policy had, by his own admission, been drastically reduced. Kimberley defined the basis of the new approach when he warned the Colonial officials: 'It will require great tact and patience to restore a healthy feeling in South Africa.'[1]

[1] C.O. 291/14. Minute by Kimberley, 24 March 1881.

IV
THE PRETORIA CONVENTION

Boers and Fenians 1881: attempts at conciliation

1. The Royal Commission, April 1881

MAJUBA dominated and twisted the proceedings of the Royal Commission. As the mountain itself had towered above the armistice negotiations on O'Neill's farm, so now the battle provided the emotive backdrop for the sittings of the Commission in Rider Haggard's house, at Newcastle, in Natal.[1] Several weeks after the last shots had been fired on the 'hill of the wild pigeons' the Royal Commissioners, advisers, witnesses and observers, all behaved as if they were continuing the battle. Wood clearly desired to achieve the victory at the conference table denied to Colley on the *veld*: Kruger determined to press his advantage, and behaved as if the British had been routed and were fleeing before him.

Both the battle and the Commission were desultory affairs. If the former lacked glory, the latter ignored common sense. But, both shared the dubious honour of providing the basis for much of future discord. This legacy, in the core of the convention, stemmed as much from the wrangles in the Commission, as from the actual clauses in the final document. These verbal skirmishes, between April and August 1881, forever cast the convention for the Boers in an unfavourable light. The

[1] C.O. 291/18. The Commission first sat at Newcastle, in a house rented from Rider Haggard, from 29 April to 1 June 1881. They then moved to Pretoria. Haggard remarked on '. . . the strange fate which decreed that the retrocession of the Transvaal, over which I had myself hoisted the British flag should be practically accomplished under my roof.' See Edgar Holt, *The Boer War* (London, 1958), p. 39.

discrepancy between Kimberley's original broad peace offer and the final Instructions for the Commission was already wide enough; but the conduct of the Commissioners themselves, and Wood in particular, tended to confirm Kruger's suspicions of 'double dealing' in the Colonial Office approach to the Boers. Kruger was heard to remark that he had learnt one thing from the whole business—'*Wees getrou, maar vertrou niemand*'.[1]

The seeds of discord were to be found in the terms of reference for the Commissioners. In drawing up these Instructions[2] Kimberley took scant cognisance of the protests already voiced by the Boer leaders in the Kruger–Wood armistice discussions. In particular he rode roughshod over the Boers' desire to have a Transvaal or Free State leader on the Commission; and what was more serious he ignored the virulent Boer feeling against even the possibility of partitioning the Transvaal. For a cautious and wary man Kimberley managed at once to achieve the worst of all worlds. By including Chief Justice de Villiers of the Cape he neither satisfied the Transvalers nor the 'Empire loyalists'.[3] By throwing into doubt the unity of the Transvaal he roused the Boers' deepest animosities, yet failed to provide a workable scheme as to how it could be done. By demanding that the Boers accept a British Resident in Pretoria he revealed the weakness of his position: the powers of the Resident were to be extensive, but the strength needed to enforce those powers was missing.

Not that the Instructions themselves lacked purpose. The Commissioners were to use as their basis of negotiations Kimberley's telegrams to Wood of 17 and 21 March, 1881.[4] Certain points were already reserved as being outside the scope of the Commission's enquiry. The 'Transvaal State' was to be granted 'complete self-government under the suzerainty of the Queen: the control of its relations with foreign powers being reserved to the British Government'.[5] There was to be a British Resident, 'at the capital of the Transvaal State'. The provision

[1] Kruger, *Kruger*, I, 251 viz: 'Be trustworthy, but trust no one.'

[2] *Parl. Pap.*, 1881, LXVII, C.2892, pp. 1–6. 'Instructions to the Royal Commission for the Settlement of the Transvaal.' Dated 31 March 1881.

[3] A vociferous 'English party' had grown up in the Cape to counter the Dutch *Bond* influence. They met under the banner of the 'Empire League'.

[4] *Parl. Pap.*, 1881, LXVII, C.2837, pp. 28–9.

[5] Ibid., C.2892, p. 3. Kimberley to Robinson, 31 March 1881, Instructions to Commission.

in the Sand River Convention against slavery 'must of course be reaffirmed'. But there the closed articles ended, and the points of dissent began. It all basically stemmed from a single sentence in the Instructions: 'The Commission is to consider provisions for the protection of native interests.'[1] Here was the difficulty. In asking the Commission to admit the Transvaal to self-government with one hand, yet take away their control of the native people with the other hand, Kimberley was proposing the impossible. He partly understood this anomaly; but saw a way round it, by suggesting that the Commission should consider severing from the Transvaal certain districts which had large native populations. As to the natives thus left inside the Boer lands, the Resident was to be their protector, 'with such functions as Her Majesty's Government may determine on the recommendation of the Commission'.[2] For full measure, Kimberley desired also to put an end to the continual frontier disputes on the eastern and western Transvaal borders. The Keate Award line of 1871, on the west, he considered out of date, and the cause of much of the unrest in that region. It was to be revised, on the basis of Colley's original findings in the area, with the assistance of Colonel Moysey, the Special Commissioner in the Keate Award district. 'It will be for you to consider what line should be adopted,' Kimberley informed Robinson, 'I will only add that this border has been so long in an unsettled condition that it is urgently necessary that the frontier line should be definitely fixed with as little delay as is possible'.[3]

As to the Zulu–Swazi frontiers of the Transvaal, here the separation of the eastern districts of the Boer territory would serve a dual purpose. It would do more than protect the natives within the Wakkerstroom and Utrecht Districts, 'inasmuch as they would separate the Transvaal State from Zululand, and prevent the occurrence of those dangerous border disputes between Boers and Zulus, which were in large measure the cause of the Zulu War'.[4] If the Transvalers objected very strongly— particularly over the Wakkerstroom area—then 'so much only might be retained as would be necessary to maintain the communications between Natal and the British territory further northward. . .'.[5] Much the same applied in the case of the Lydenberg, New Scotland areas, on the Swazi frontier. They

[1] Idem.   [2] Idem.   [3] Ibid., p. 6.   [4] Ibid., p. 4.   [5] Ibid., p. 5.

171

too could be part of this buffer-zone to halt Boer encroachment. The fact that all the grand visions of protection for the natives came to nought—and at the same time angered the Boer leaders—is not really surprising, for Kimberley's Instructions contained within them the basis for their own destruction. After outlining all the schemes Kimberley added, almost as a foot-note, that the Commission should not forget while reshaping the fortunes of the Transvaal and the natives, that 'Her Majesty's Government are averse, on the grounds of policy, to the exten-sion of British territory in South Africa.' In other words, while admitting the desirability of protected native areas, Kimberley was in the same voice refusing to pay for their protection or ad-ministration. As he admitted, such a buffer-zone 'could scarcely be annexed to Natal and as a separate British province it would form an inconvenient narrow strip of territory, which would probably for some time to come not pay its own expenses'.[1] The fact that these remarks are placed alongside his own schemes is a sad commentary on his concern for the Transvaal natives.

His whole approach to the question of the future status, power and stability of the Transvaal in fact bordered on the schizophrenic. The Boers were to be self-governing, yet the Resident was to have extensive powers. The annexation was to be withdrawn, yet the Transvaal could not conduct its own foreign relations. The natives were to be protected, but Kim-berley would not pay for it. The Keate line was to be redrawn, but there was to be no more means of halting Transvaal en-croachment than before. The Transvaal was to be forced to pay its 'public debt', yet Kimberley dreaded a non-viable state which might collapse and lead to more unrest. The Transvaal demand for independence was to be recognised, but it was to be denied the right to return to its old name, the 'South African Republic.'[2] Districts were to be lopped off as he might see fit,

[1] Idem.
[2] It was to be called the 'Transvaal State'. Kimberley's reason for this eccentricity was: 'I am disposed to think that instead of reviving the name "South African Republic" (which never was appropriate, having regard to the fact that there were two Republics in South Africa) it would be prefer-able to adopt the name "Transvaal State". Before the annexation, the country was commonly spoken of as the Transvaal, and it would be con-venient, as in the case of the Orange Free State, to describe it by the river which forms its southern boundary'. Ibid., p. 6.

and yet what had the Boers gone to war for, other than to regain their former republican status, and their republic, as they had founded it?

This strange dichotomy in Kimberley's approach is reflected in his choice of Commissioners. He rejected out of hand a suggestion that a British team should be sent out from England to form the Commission. 'I believe', he explained to Gladstone, 'a Commission sent out from home would only add fresh cause of confusion to the many which now exist.'[1] And yet whom did he choose?—Sir Hercules Robinson, the new High Commissioner at the Cape, an extremely able and experienced colonial servant, but who had only just arrived from New Zealand, and who had no prior experience in South Africa;[2] and Sir Evelyn Wood who was doubtless included as he was not only on the spot, but had concluded the armistice with Kruger. He has been described as the 'realist' on the Commission: the only member who stood up to the Boers, and who had a 'no-nonsense' approach to Kruger and his tactics.[3] This is indeed one way of looking at it. In reality, Wood gave much offence throughout the sittings. The Boers came to hate him, and his fits of temper achieved nothing. He continually wanted to resign—to Kimberley's embarrassment[4] and Robinson's annoyance.[5] His minority report of dissent[6] hardly helped to bring about an air of cordiality in which to work the Pretoria Convention. Far from being a cool, reassuring man, Sir Evelyn Wood was a strange complex figure. A hypochondriac who, despite his physical valour, was a victim of deep periods of depression and continual

[1] Addit. MSS. 44469, f. 56. Kimberley to Gladstone, 20 April 1881. (See also T. R. Statham to Gladstone, 8 April 1881, f. 47.) Kimberley's letter is incorrectly filed in the general correspondence, not in the 'Kimberley Volumes'.

[2] He proved in fact to be an exceedingly patient and moderate chairman, but Kimberley appointed him more from hope than knowledge. There is no *Life* of Robinson.

[3] See Agar-Hamilton, *The Road to the North*, pp. 164–5.

[4] Addit. MSS. 44544, ff. 171–9. Gladstone–Kimberley correspondence, 25 May–9 June 1881, *re* Wood, and Addit. MSS. 44226, ff. 166–9. Kimberley to Gladstone, 6 July 1881.

[5] E. A. Walker, *De Villiers*, pp. 158–9.

[6] C.O. 291/18–21. Full Report and Dissent. See also *Parl. Pap.*, 1882, XXVIII, C.3114, pp. 34 ff. and Wood's own account of the Commission in *From Midshipman to Field-Marshal*, pp. 131–3.

psychosomatic illnesses. Kruger drove him to the edge of despair.

The third and last member, was Chief Justice de Villiers of the Cape Colony.[1] He was included as a sop to the Transvalers' feelings; but he was in fact nobody's Dutchman. With few constructive ideas of his own, he stood estranged from *both* Kruger and Wood. He too attempted to resign during the course of the Commission.[2] A thorough conservative, de Villiers sat on the bench—and the fence—for most of his life. He stuck as close as he could to the Instructions, but when in doubt tended to accept Robinson's moderating counsel and advice. Brand or Kotze might have been a wiser choice; and either would certainly have been a more representative member of the South African Dutch of the Republics. As it was, Kruger was able to speak of having 'no representation at all' on the Commission.[3]

With these inauspicious beginnings the Royal Commission started to take evidence at Newcastle on 29 April 1881.[4] Robinson was absent from the early sittings, being detained by the political and Basuto crises at the Cape.[5] Wood headed the Commission until 8 May, when Robinson at last arrived. From the earliest sittings a pattern of conduct developed. Wood was determined to have his pound of flesh. Kruger was equally determined to extract the last possible concession from Britain. Robinson struggled to keep the Commission together; Brand to tone down the Boer demands. Pretorius, Jorissen, and Joubert all tended to follow Kruger's line. The results of these divergent pressures was rarely constructive. Facts tended to be lost amid repetitive arguments; the Commissioners squabbled among themselves; question-and-answer sittings turned into verbal duels between Boer witnesses and Wood. Kruger personally contributed greatly to the Commission's difficulties. He was determined to grant them little, to admit nothing unless he was absolutely forced to—in short, to throw the Commission into confusion. He soon adopted the tactic of demanding proof for everything the Commissioners said; or, of complaining that he

[1] E. A. Walker, *De Villiers*, pp. 155–65.
[2] Ibid., p. 158.
[3] D. W. Kruger, *Paul Kruger*, I, 240–49.
[4] C.O. 291/18. Report of Royal Commission, 3 August 1881.
[5] Sprigg resigned as Cape Premier on 8 May 1881. Scanlen then took office; resigned 12 May 1884.

lacked the necessary documents to prove his own case, the documents being in Pretoria.

The Commission met officially 22 times; 12 times at Newcastle, and 10 times at Pretoria. They sat for over three months, and nearly half that time was spent in fruitless arguments. Kruger had quickly set the precedent at an early sitting. The Commission was trying to discuss the south-eastern frontier of the Transvaal. 'Does the boundary go back to 1845?' Wood asked. 'Yes,' replied Kruger. Wood then reminded him of Pretorius' proclamation of 1852, telling the Boers to stay north of the Drakensburg.

> *Kruger:* 'I should wish to see the document referred to, so that I can write a reply and we have the truth.'
> *Wood:* 'Do I understand Mr. Kruger to say that he has never heard of this proclamation . . .?'
> *Kruger:* 'I did not say I did not know about the proclamation—I said I wanted the proclamation and documents connected with it in order to avoid mistakes in replying.'[1]

It was a taste of things to come.

Over the Keate Award area Kruger opted for another tactic: 'We have not got all the documents here as to the Keate award, and I should therefore request that this matter may be postponed.'[2] He extended this technique to destroy the normal functions of the Commission. Wood tried to pin Kruger down with a map of the western boundary—'I cannot well understand this map. I should rather have the documents here. . .'[3] Robinson tried to press him on the Bechuana chiefs. It was to no avail—'The documents will show that everything is pointed out in the documents. The Commission will see it in the documents which are at Pretoria.'[4] When pushed to present 'the documents' Kruger was exceedingly '*slim*'. 'Have you got those papers?' de Villiers asked. 'I believe they are in the hands of Dr. Jorissen,' Kruger replied. To which Jorissen added, 'They were in my hands, and I wrote for them at once, but they have not arrived. . . .'[5] Wood's patience finally ran out. He demanded the documents: 'I have spoken again and again about this subject

[1] C.O. 291/18. Report of Royal Commission, p. 18.
[2] Ibid., p. 29. [3] Ibid., p. 38.
[4] Ibid., p. 41. [5] Ibid., p. 52.

since the 8th of April, till I have been absolutely ashamed of mentioning it. . . .'¹ The mysterious 'documents' remained elusive to the end, although the Commissioners moved from Newcastle to Pretoria, on 17 June, in an attempt to come closer to Kruger's archives. It made little difference: the documents which Kruger did eventually present were rarely pertinent to the case. Wood plainly said so. But Kruger was equal to the occasion: 'It has grieved us very deeply', he replied,² 'to think that blame has been cast upon us for delays, for which we are not responsible.'

The Gilbertian atmosphere was never far away. Wood, short, lumpy and excitable, became steadily more exasperated by Kruger; the Boer leader became more and more evasive; Joubert's falsetto laugh, and wry sense of humour, more prominent;³ de Villiers increasingly at loggerheads with Wood; and Robinson steadily more weary and disillusioned with the whole proceedings. That a 'bargain' was finally struck at all owed little to any weakening on the part of the Boer leaders: it was rather the result of a compromise overture initiated by Robinson, and approved by Kimberley. It was a purposeful act of conciliation, and Wood's minority report of dissent testified to the extent of the appeasement. If Joubert's frontal attack had been triumphant at Majuba, Kruger's more complex tactics at the conference were even more successful. Ultimately both British generals, Colley and Wood, tasted the bitterness of defeat.

2. Inter-locking dilemmas; April to August 1881

Gladstone and Kimberley played a far greater part in bringing the Pretoria Convention about than has hitherto been supposed. 'I am so pressed by South African business,' Kimberley informed a colonial governor in April⁴, 'that I have only just time to acknowledge and thank you for your two letters.' Gladstone

---

¹ Ibid., p. 45.   ² Ibid., p. 67.

³ Ibid., p. 20. The talk was of the eastern Transvaal. Robinson: 'Are there any Englishmen there at all?' Joubert: 'No real Englishmen, only Scotchmen.'

⁴ Kimberley to Pope Hennessey (Governor of Mauritius), 22 April 1881. Uncatalogued 'Secretary of State' letter file.

could have said much the same, with the added postscript, 'not forgetting Ireland'.

The Gladstone Papers—volumes and letterbooks—are filled with the correspondence between the Premier and his Colonial Secretary on the Transvaal peace negotiations.[1] The Colonial Office files also bear witness to the constant, almost incessant, stream of telegrams and despatches from Robinson,[2] most of which Kimberley minuted personally, and sent on to Gladstone. Further, the matter was constantly at Cabinet level,[3] and second only to Ireland in importance at this time. Interest in the negotiations extended beyond the formal Cabinet meetings, as the Granville,[4] Chamberlain,[5] and Dilke Papers[6] testify. This swept the issue of the Boers from the minor desks of the Colonial Office into the mainstream of political debate. It continued, and reinforced, a tradition already more than formative in this Liberal Cabinet, of seeing in the Irish and Transvaal disorders a similar set of principles at stake; and it also perpetuated the growing tactic, used increasingly by the Radical and Whig wings of the Government, of exploiting the minor Transvaal issue to undermine their opponents' position on the major concern, Ireland.

Quite apart from these political strategies, the indirect effect of 'boycotting' and Fenianism on the handling of the Boers in 1881 was very great. The two dilemmas were not only handled at the same Cabinets,[7] but they seemed to be marching in unison. The Gladstonians, including Kimberley, had been advocating conciliation in southern Africa since late January. They had also taken the same approach to Ireland. In both cases Gladstone had agreed to initial coercive measures, to put the rebellions down, but only on the condition that Ireland be

[1] Addit. MSS. 44226, 44627, 44470, 44544 (L.B. copy) and 44642 (Cabinet Papers).

[2] C.O. 291/18–21. See numerous Minutes by Kimberley, together with a major memorandum on the Transvaal of 29 April 1881. Printed copy in Addit. MSS. 44627, ff. 1–21.

[3] Addit. MSS. 44642, ff. 152–220 (Cabinet Papers).

[4] P.R.O. 30/29/153 (Granville Papers).

[5] J.C. 9/1/1/4 (Chamberlain Papers).

[6] Addit. MSS. 43924, f. 48 (Dilke Diary).

[7] Addit. MSS. 44642, ff. 152, 154, 158, 163, 164, 174, 176, 181, 182, 189, 203, 217, 220 (Cabinet Papers) for Cabinets of 5, 8, 12, 17, 19 March; 8, 29 April; 20, 28 May; 15 June; 23 July; 12 October; and 10 November 1881.

conciliated with a Land Act,[1] and the Transvaal be conciliated with internal self-government.[2] This dual approach was Gladstone's touchstone for policy throughout the winter of 1880, and into the spring 1881. But it began to falter in mid-summer, and by autumn the Premier was thinking of arresting Parnell,[3] and of renewing the war against Kruger.[4] At the basis of this transformation in attitude lay the behaviour of the Irish and the Boers. In Ireland, Gladstone looked to his proposed Land Commission to relieve the worst cases of suffering, and so to undermine the Fenians' support.[5] In the Transvaal, he expected the Pretoria Convention to do much the same—to blunt the edge of the demands of the more militant Boers.[6] In neither case, of course, was he bestowing full 'Home Rule': he genuinely believed that both the Irish and the Boers had grievances, which sensible reform could alleviate. He was no more abdicating from the Transvaal than from Ireland. But he was implementing a more conciliatory policy, at the expense of Forster, in Ireland,[7] Hartington and Argyll on the Transvaal.[8] It was a triumph for the 'centre' of the Cabinet—Gladstone, Granville, Harcourt and Childers.

But it was a tenuous triumph. It depended on the 'good behaviour' of the Irish and the Boers, on their response to liberal overtures. This was the crux of the Gladstonian approach. It is significant that it broke down in Ireland, and so very nearly collapsed in the Transvaal, for the same reason. And even more significant for policy, that the crises for this approach in Ireland and Africa occurred at the same moment in time—August and

---

[1] Morley, *Gladstone*, III, 57; and J. L. Hammond, *Gladstone and the Irish Nation*, p. 175.

[2] Addit. MSS. 44113, f. 158 (L.B. copy). Gladstone to Bright, 29 September 1881.

[3] Addit. MSS. 44173, f. 186. Granville to Gladstone, 7 October 1881, on Gladstone's 'Resources of Civilisation Speech'. (See also *The Times*, 8 October 1881; Magnus, *Gladstone*, p. 299; and Ramm, I, 301–2.)

[4] Addit. MSS. 44545, f. 30 (L.B. copy). Gladstone to Kimberley, 29 September 1881, from Hawarden.

[5] Morley, *Gladstone*, III, 47–56.

[6] Addit. MSS. 44642, f. 203 (Cabinet Papers). Cabinet memorandum on Terms of Transvaal Peace and Convention, 23 July 1881.

[7] Addit. MSS. 44158, ff. 167, 172. Forster to Gladstone, 29 May 1881. See also Reid, *Life of Forster*, pp. 321–2.

[8] *C.H.B.E.*, III, 131, 136.

September 1881. From late summer Gladstone began to suspect that Parnell,[1] and Kruger,[2] were working to wreck his policy in their respective countries: Parnell by bringing 'impossible' cases before the Land Commission, Kruger by haggling over the Convention, and then attacking it once he had signed it. The effect on Gladstone—and Kimberley—was dramatic. The G.O.M. began to speak of 'boycotting Parnell',[3] and of returning to a coercive policy;[4] Kruger and his fellows again became rebels in Gladstone's eyes,[5] and plans to invade the Transvaal anew were mooted.[6] In the case of Kimberley his natural desire for coercion in Ireland became almost vituperative, and he looked on the policy of the Pretoria Convention rather uneasily. By early winter the springs of his passions had been released. He called on Gladstone to bring terrible coercive measures against the Irish;[7] and to be ready for war against the Boers[8] if the Volksraad refused to ratify the Convention. This lack of inner consistency in Kimberley's approach is puzzling to the modern observer; but Kimberley, in fact, saw no contradiction in his attitude. He reasoned thus: Ireland was an essential and indivisible part of the United Kingdom; a British Government should no more tolerate unrest in that region than in say Wales, Scotland, or even Cornwall. The Transvaal was a different matter. It had no intrinsic value to the Empire, except in a negative sense: it could, by its weakness, and by the restless

[1] P.R.O. 30/29/124. Gladstone to Granville, 27 September 1881; and Addit. MSS. 44159, ff. 24, 27. Forster to Gladstone, 25 September, and Gladstone to Forster, 27 September 1881. (Ramm, I, 295.)

[2] Addit. MSS. 44545, f. 28 (L.B. copy). Gladstone to Kimberley, 25 September 1881.

[3] 'You must shun him at the fair and market place and even in the house of worship by leaving him severely alone, by sending him to a moral Coventry, by isolating him from the rest of his kind as if he was a leper of old. . . .' Gladstone at Glasgow quoting Parnell's own words—25 January 1881. Quoted in J. L. Hammond, *Gladstone and the Irish Nation*, p. 215.

[4] Morley, *Gladstone*, III, p. 61. Gladstone at Leeds, 8 October 1881.

[5] Addit. MSS. 44545, f. 38. Gladstone to Kimberley 19 October 1881; and P.R.O. 30/29/124. Gladstone to Granville, 21 October 1881. (Ramm, I, 305.)

[6] Addit. MSS. 44545, f. 30 (L.B. copy). Gladstone to Kimberley, 29 September 1881.

[7] Addit. MSS. 44226, ff. 145 ff. Kimberley–Gladstone correspondence, 10 June 1881, onwards.

[8] Addit. MSS. 44226, f. 269. Kimberley to Gladstone, 30 September 1881.

nature of its Afrikaner peoples, cause much unease in the rest of southern Africa. It needed to be controlled, though not necessarily governed, from within. The situation had now been complicated by the talk of sympathy for the Transvalers by the Afrikaners in the Orange Free State, and the Cape Colony. This had radically altered the basis for policy, but not the intentions of policy. It narrowed the options within which he could work, but it did not revolutionise his ultimate objective. To Kimberley, the real difficulty of 1881 was not trying to reconcile his approach on Ireland and the Transvaal, but to conduct and to contribute to a successful policy in both areas, given the vociferous behaviour of the local inhabitants.

His dilemma in southern Africa took a recognisable form: how to coerce a particular province without alienating all the surrounding regions. The policy of conciliation seemed to offer a reasonable answer. The Transvaal was to be granted internal self-government, with Britain retaining the external powers, and also the right to bring internal suasion, via the Resident, on all matters dealing with the natives. It was to be independence within locked doors.

The merits of 'conciliation' were obvious: the Transvalers would be under control; the Afrikaners of the Free State and Cape would be pacified; the Humanitarians could not object, for the Resident was there to save their interests; 'Imperialist' and 'Horse Guards' opinions was not entirely satisfied, but even they had to admit that Britain retained a 'suzerainty' over the Boers; and lastly, this approach had that great attraction to Victorian statesmen, economy. Policy could count on that rare thing, official Treasury support.

Thus the scheme lay on paper. But, how did it measure up to the stress of events? and what was the impression made by those events on the policy? As suggested above, the pattern which evolved in Anglo-Irish and Anglo-Boer relations, throughout the summer and autumn of 1881, was strikingly similar. The consequences of parallel Irish and Boer unrest was not isolated to the respective ministries: as the problems were continually at Cabinet level, policy in both areas tended to reflect a common basis of opinion about two sets of local 'nationalist' challenge. The weakening of Gladstone's approach on Ireland soon extended to undermine Kimberley's tactic in southern Africa.

Equally, the steady eroding of the conciliatory policy by Kruger at Kimberley's expense, strengthened the hands of the Whigs in the administration, who used the occasion to draw parallels for Ireland, making the Gladstonian policy look decidedly untenable in both spheres.

The story of 1881 is thus the complex narrative of inter-related attempts by Gladstone and Kimberley to place the two most intractable dilemmas in the Empire on a way to tolerable solution, through the balm of conciliation. The crucial test that faced both Gladstone and Kimberley was the question: was conciliation enough? It was an ill omen that it had already failed in Ireland before it had to face the first serious challenge in southern Africa;[1] and that Gladstone was forced back on to the old strong-arm technique for controlling Ireland. Glad-stone's failure in Ireland, and consequent disillusionment with Parnell, has often been chronicled;[2] Kimberley's attempts in Africa with the Boers have been passed over.

Too often the Pretoria Convention, and the tortuous nego-tiations which led up to that ill-fated Treaty, have been held up for ridicule, the results of a weak policy consequent upon Majuba.[3] The Gladstonians would have disagreed. Nor will this argument square with the facts as found in the Colonial Office files and the private papers of the Gladstonians. The import-ance of the Gladstone–Kimberley policy for southern Africa has been vastly underrated. Admittedly they made mistakes— the selection of the Commission, the lack of purpose in enforcing the Convention, the choice of Hudson as Resident, the vacil-lation over frontiers—but over and above this, the direction and basis for policy was far sounder than that pursued by Disraeli and Carnarvon; and, one which came within an ace of success. The advent of Rhodes, the German intervention, the discovery of gold on the Rand, and the Jameson Raid, were all events which could hardly be prognosticated. To trace the ills of the close of the century to the Pretoria Convention is to

---

[1] Morley, *Gladstone*, III, 47–56.

[2] J. L. Hammond, *Gladstone and the Irish Nation*, pp. 175 ff. Magnus, *Gladstone*, pp. 282–99.

[3] *C.H.B.E.*, VIII, 518–32; G. H. Le May, *British Supremacy in South Africa, 1899–1907*, chap. I, pp. 1–3; E. A. Walker, *A History of Southern Africa*, pp. 378–89.

misread both the trend of events and the achievement of Gladstone's policy. It deserves better. As Graham Bower wrote of this period: 'The task before us ... was to conciliate the Dutch without alienating the English or injuring the natives. ... The Pretoria Convention was the first attempt to solve that problem —the first step in a policy which was pursued for fifteen years with such success that it placed the British Government in a stronger position than it had ever been before ...'.[1] The working relationship of Gladstone and Kimberley, throughout 1881 reveals them attempting to lay the foundations for that new approach.

Not that they did not live perilously. Wood supplied Kimberley with much discouraging news from the Transvaal.[2] 'Kruger', Wood wrote, 'was without culture, untutored, impulsive and ready on the least occasion to lose his temper.' The Boer leaders 'had no confidence in Her Majesty's Government [and] ... put the worst construction on even those proposals which were formed with a view to their own advantage'. And, more than this, Wood feared that the Boers might 'at any future time make their voices heard in the event of the Royal Commission giving any decision which may be unpalatable to them, or which may fall short of what they may expect'. In short, 'the horizon is by no means clear of clouds, which, under certain conditions, may gather into a storm and cause shipwreck to our present peaceful arrangements'. Thus he strongly advised Kimberley to keep 'a large force' at Newcastle, 'until the termination of the labours of the Royal Commission'.[3] News from other sources was equally depressing. Robinson telegraphed from the Cape repeating the rumour that the young Transvaal Boers had not accepted the Peace and were marauding the countryside, burning farms and cutting the telegraph line between Newcastle and Standerton. Wood had apparently written privately to Robinson doubting 'whether he should be able to advise Commission going into Transvaal unless excitement subsided. . .'. Robinson's assessment of the situation was plain: 'I greatly fear that unreasonable spirit reported may endanger observance of any settlement Commission may recommend.'[4]

---

[1] Afr. MSS., S.63, ff. 3–6 (Bower Memoir).
[2] C.O. 291/10. Wood to Kimberley, 28 March 1881.   [3] Idem.
[4] Addit. MSS. 44226, f. 92 (Tel.), Robinson to Kimberley, 15 April 1881 (Private). Copy enclosed in Wood to Robinson, 11, 13, and 14 April.

Kimberley's concerns did not end here. He learnt from Granville that the Portuguese were reported to be selling large quantities of arms to the Boers—and possibly the Zulus—at Delagoa Bay.[1] Kimberley called on Granville to make diplomatic protests to Portugal.[2] To Gladstone he wrote despondently:[3] 'The state of the Transvaal is most unsatisfactory and we may easily drift into fighting again. I have thought it as well to tell Wood[4] to point out to the Boer leaders the grave dangers which will again arise if peaceful intercourse is interrupted and plunder of English farms goes on. . . .'. The 'unreasonable' behaviour of the young fighting Boers in fact continued; and Kimberley soon faced a most unpleasant matter. The garrison at Potchefstroom, which had been besieged throughout the war, had at last surrendered—but, after the war had ended. The Boer general concerned had failed to inform the British troops of this salient fact, and had gone on besieging the garrison.[5] The British Press reaction was to talk of 'uncivilised' methods of war.[6] The old cry of 'vindication' was heard again. At the Cabinet of Friday, 8 April 1881, Kimberley was questioned on the matter;[7] and at the meeting of 29 April he faced severe criticism from his fellow Whigs for doing little to seek some compensation.[8]

This was unfair. Kimberley was deeply concerned with the matter, as his correspondence with the Premier reveals. He saw

[1] Idem.

[2] P.R.O. 30/29/135, f. 37 (Granville Papers). Copy enclosed in Wood to Kimberley (Tel.), 13 April 1881, and Kimberley to Granville, 14 April 1881.

[3] Addit. MSS. 44226, ff. 66–8. Kimberley to Gladstone, 13 April 1881.

[4] Ibid., f. 70. Kimberley to Wood (Tel. in cypher), 13 April 1881. 'You should consult Robinson after arrival upon all matters. . . . Interruption of peaceful intercourse with Transvaal or continued plunder of English farms or inhabitants will seriously endanger settlement.'

[5] Addit. MSS. 44129, f. 209. Childers to Gladstone, 22 April 1881. Full details of the affair. Cronje was the Boer general concerned, Col. Winsloe the English commander.

[6] P.R.O. 30/29/124. Gladstone to Granville, 28 April 1881. (Ramm, I, 269.) See also The Times, 22–4 March 1881.

[7] Addit. MSS. 44642, f. 174 (Cabinet Papers), Friday, 8 April 1881, 12 p.m. Point 4: 'Lord Kimberley stated the difficulties which might arise in the Potchefstroom case . . . was the surrender done in bad faith, was it a valid transaction.'

[8] Ibid., f. 176. Friday, 29 April 1881, 3 p.m.

four courses open:[1] to 'replace the garrison'; to 'send it back without escort'; to 'send it back with escort'; and to 'accept reparation'. He strongly favoured the last course: 'As long as we simply insist on replacement we are within our undoubted rights, and the responsibility for resistance ... will rest exclusively on the Boers. The moment we quit this position we get on slippery ground.'[2] Kimberley's dilemma was, though, deeper even than this. On the one hand, he believed Britain needed to stand firm once the conciliatory peace terms had been offered; for as he explained, 'unless we show plainly that we will not allow the terms made with us to be set aside by [the] Boers ... we shall have no reasonable expectation that the terms of the final settlement will be observed'. Kimberley's thinking was logic itself: 'When they see we are not to be trifled with, they will probably be glad to offer us a suitable alternative.'[3]

But Kimberley could not afford to be too firm. He had gained the confidence of the South African Afrikaners with his liberal peace terms, and his disregarding of Majuba.[4] Renewal of the war could change all that. His handling of the Potchefstroom garrison débâcle shows how aware he was of his delicate position. At all costs he wished to avoid a return to hostilities. Thus his decision on the Potchefstroom matter: 'We propose to give secret orders for the removal of the garrison after occupation of Potchefstroom, as it would obviously be imprudent to leave a small force there at the mercy of an unruly and hostile population.'[5] The decision to hold the Commission at Newcastle was significant: it is in this tradition of cautious diplomacy that Kimberley was determined to pursue. As he explained to Gladstone: 'In the present state of excitement in the Transvaal, the Commission should remain in Natal and invite Brand and the Boer leaders to meet it there.'[6]

In this approach Kimberley had Gladstone's full support,[7] though he had to weather two difficult meetings at the War

[1] Addit. MSS. 44226, ff. 84–90. Kimberley to Gladstone, 16 April 1881.
[2] Idem.   [3] Idem.
[4] *Parl. Pap.*, LXVII, C.2959, pp. 3–5, Cape Dutch addresses of approval, forwarded by Deputy Governor at Cape, Smyth to Kimberley, 22 April 1881.
[5] Addit. MSS. 44226, ff. 84–90. Kimberley to Gladstone, 16 April 1881.
[6] Ibid., f. 90.
[7] P.R.O. 30/29/124. Gladstone to Granville, 28 April 1881. (Ramm, I, 269.) See also Addit. MSS. 44226, f. 102. Gladstone to Kimberley, 23 April 1881.

Office with the Duke of Cambridge, on 16 and 22 April.[1] It was no secret that the Duke had only recently visited Osborne. Kimberley agreed to send a force to help the returning garrison move through the Transvaal without attracting attack. But, once the operation was complete this force was to retire completely from the Laing's Nek area.[2] Kimberley's reading of the position in the Transvaal was more intuitive than informed: 'Joubert and Kruger seem to be working for peace against their followers, and it is both fair and politic to give them the opportunity to propose an alternative, [re the Potchefstroom garrison].' Kimberley was quite clearly prepared to put up with much bellicosity from the younger Boers for the sake of peace. Wood's desire to go to the aid of the garrison met with a cold response from Kimberley:[3] 'Wood's scruples as to Lang's [sic] Nek are based on a misconception. Our position is perfectly clear. His engagement was not to occupy the Nek or "follow up" the Boers. The entrance of an escort into the Transvaal is forbidden by this equally with the occupation of the Nek.'[4]

Gladstone knew it to be a critical moment. 'Till the question is settled whether the older Boers can controul [sic] the younger,' he remarked to Granville,[5] 'we must I fear consider the South African peace as provisional—H[er] M[ajesty] writes about it[6] as you might expect.' Kimberley was even more concerned, and considered he was failing at the Colonial Office. 'I wish I could congratulate myself on anything connected with my affairs,' he wrote to Gladstone on 15 April, 'I really congratulate you on the way in which the Land Bill has been received.'[7] Kimberley's optimism on this point was misplaced. The Land Bill may have been well received in the House, but hardly so in the Cabinet.

[1] Ibid., f. 84. Kimberley to Gladstone, 16 April 1881. Ibid., f. 97. Kimberley to Gladstone, 22 April 1881. See also Addit. MSS. 44129, f. 209. Childers to Gladstone, 22 April 1881: '. . . the garrison should be replaced if only for 24 hours. Our insisting on this will have a good effect on the work of the Commission, which the younger Boers appear disposed to obstruct.'
[2] Addit. MSS. 44226, ff. 97–9. Kimberley to Gladstone, 22 April 1881.
[3] Ibid., f. 100. Kimberley to Wood (Tel.), 22 April 1881 (Copy).
[4] Ibid., ff. 97–9. Kimberley to Gladstone, 22 April 1881.
[5] P.R.O. 30/29/124. Gladstone to Granville, 18 April 1881. (Ramm, I, 260.)
[6] See Queen Victoria to Gladstone, 16 April 1881, in Guedalla, *Queen and Mr. Gladstone*, II, 152.
[7] Addit. MSS. 44226, ff. 79–81. Kimberley to Gladstone, 15 April 1881.

Argyll had resigned on 8 April, over Gladstone's Irish policy:[1] and, at the Cabinet of 29 April,[2] the ministers divided equally 6–6 over the proposal to arrest the Irish leader Dillon.[3] Gladstone held the casting vote, with Granville and Spencer absent. This same Cabinet found the ministers almost as equally divided over the trend in the Transvaal peace negotiations. It was fortunate for Kimberley though that the Irish issue was coming to the boil at that moment,[4] for it did indeed deflect the interest and zeal of Forster, Hartington, Spencer and Selborne away from the matter of being firmer with the Boers. As it was, Gladstone took the brunt of the attack from the 'Forster faction',[5] who incessantly demanded greater coercion in Ireland.[6] Once this group had got their way over Ireland—as they did in September and October—would they turn on Kimberley? and if they did could his policy prevail?

It was all a matter of timing; and of diplomacy. Kimberley needed to complete the Transvaal negotiations as quickly as possible: yet, he must not attempt to coerce the Boers into a settlement. He needed to maintain a very fine balance between a necessary determination and an unnecessary and destructive forcefulness. His position was rendered even more precarious by the other affairs of state. Gladstone's budget—on 4 April[7]— had been well received, but it was an isolated triumph. The Liberal administration was maintaining its tradition of living dangerously. The matter of coercion in Ireland was cutting deeply into Cabinet conduct.[8] Hartington had wanted to re-

[1] Addit. MSS. 44642, f. 174 (Cabinet Papers), 8 April 1881.

[2] Ibid., f. 176. 29 April 1881.

[3] Idem. Gladstone cast his vote for the arrest of Dillon, a significant move away from his previous attitude.

[4] Addit. MSS. 44470, f. 43. Cowper to Gladstone, 2 June 1881. See also J. L. Hammond, *Gladstone and the Irish Nation*, pp. 180 ff.; Magnus, *Gladstone*, pp. 297 ff.; Morley, *Gladstone*, III, 53 ff.

[5] Addit. MSS. 44173, f. 118. Gladstone to Granville, 2 June 1881, with enclosures. (Ramm, I, 277.) See also P.R.O. 30/29/124. Gladstone to Granville, 4 June 1881. (Ramm, I, 278.)

[6] Addit. MSS. 44158, ff. 167, 172. Forster to Gladstone, 1 June 1881. For Forster's attitude at this time see T. Wemyss Reid, *Life of Rt. Hon. W. E. Forster*, 2 vols. (London, 1888), II, 321–2.

[7] Magnus, *Gladstone*, p. 292.

[8] Addit. MSS. 48631, ff. 13–52 (Hamilton Diary) for numerous examples of the tensions within the Government.

sign with Argyll;[1] he was only restrained from doing so by Granville's persuasive powers.[2] Selborne felt much the same though he, like Spencer, tended to take his call from Hartington.[3] For slightly different reasons the Radicals also began to 'play up',[4] hoping no doubt to drive Hartington out, so that the Cabinet could be reformed without the Whigs.[5] Gladstone's response was to put Granville on to Hartington; and to avoid Cabinets, unless absolutely necessary. After Argyll's departure he avoided a full Cabinet for three weeks.[6] Harcourt characterised the less than rational, and more than emotional atmosphere of the spring Cabinets on Ireland, when he blandly remarked that 'coercion was like caviare: unpleasant at first to palate, it becomes agreeable with use'.[7]

If only Gladstone's problems had ended here. But, the dilemmas were many. The rough Cabinet agenda,[8] noted by Gladstone, show just how diverse were his problems. The matter of Ireland, for instance, went deeper than being an issue of principle in Cabinet. While the Commons had responded favourably to Gladstone's Land Act, the Lords had looked on it with great animosity. In Hammond's neat phrase, Gladstone's dilemma was this: 'the House of Lords would not let him satisfy the minimum demands of the Land League, and the Land League would not let him satisfy the minimum demands of the House of Lords'.[9] Gladstone understood this, and prepared for unequal combat with the Upper House. There was also another lingering parliamentary dilemma: Bradlaugh and

[1] J. L. Hammond, *Gladstone and the Irish Nation*, p. 216.
[2] Ramm, *The Political Correspondence of Mr. Gladstone and Lord Granville 1876–1886* (Oxford, 1962), pp. xxiv ff.
[3] Earl of Selborne, *Memorials*, 4 vols, (London, 1895), Part II.
[4] Chamberlain, *A Political Memoir* (Ed. C. H. D. Howard), (London, 1953), pp. 14–17. See also Addit. MSS. 43924, f. 48 (Dilke Diary), and Gwynne and Tuckwell, *Dilke*, I, 370.
[5] This no doubt would have meant eliminating Kimberley as well. See Kimberley's views on Ireland. Addit. MSS. 44226, f. 145. Kimberley to Gladstone, 10 June 1881.
[6] Addit. MSS. 44642, ff. 174–6 (Cabinet Papers). No Cabinet from Friday 8 April, to Friday, 29 April 1881.
[7] Gardiner, *Life of Harcourt*, I, 426.
[8] Addit. MSS. 44642, ff. 170–78 (Cabinet Papers), 2–29 April 1881.
[9] J. L. Hammond, *Gladstone and the Irish Nation*, p. 205. See also p. 193.

the Oath.[1] The Speaker had stumbled in his handling of Bradlaugh when the matter had come up a year before, in April
1880: and Gladstone had found no acceptable 'middle of the
way' solution in the months that passed. Accordingly the problem was still with him in April 1881. On Tuesday, 26 April,
amid an almost riotous scene in the Commons, Bradlaugh presented himself again—to no avail. He was turned away by his
fellow M.P.s. It was no solution. Bradlaugh took to presenting
his case at public meetings throughout England, culminating in
an enormous Trafalgar Square rally on 2 August. Gladstone
may have appreciated Bradlaugh's stand—admitting his constitutional rights—but his handling of the matter was indecisive
and deterimental to the Government. Much the same could be
said in regard to Gladstone and the death of Disraeli. The old
Tory leader had been ill for some time;[2] Gladstone had promised
to pray for him. He died on 19 April, aged 76. Gladstone had
been worrying over his expected speech of tribute to Disraeli
for some time.[3] In the event Gladstone's oration was ill received,[4] for he had revealed his true feelings by refusing to
attend Disraeli's funeral at Hughenden—on the grounds of
'pressure of work'. He even jibed at Disraeli's desire to be buried
at Hughenden and not in Westminster Abbey. 'As he lived',
Gladstone said to his secretary, 'so he died—all display, without reality or genuineness.'[5] Gladstone's hand in all this was
remarkably unsure for so experienced a politician and parliamentarian. He was to behave in much the same way over the
death of Gordon—and again be genuinely surprised at the
anger he aroused.[6]

Then there was the Queen. It is easy to characterise the
Queen's involvement in politics in the terms of ridicule. The
Gladstonian Cabinet did not see her in this light. They always

[1] Addit. MSS. 44642, f. 179 (Cabinet Papers), Friday, 13 May 1881.

[2] P.R.O. 30/29/124. Gladstone to Granville, Good Friday, 15 April 1881.
(Ramm, I, 257.) See also Addit. MSS. 44173, f. 42. Granville to Gladstone,
11 April 1881. (Ramm, I, 255.)

[3] Gladstone is said to have had diarrhoea for several days before his
statement in the House; he was wracked with indecision. Magnus, *Gladstone*,
pp. 280–81.

[4] Speech in Commons, 9 May 1881.

[5] Addit. MSS. 48631, ff. 21–30 (Hamilton Diary).

[6] Magnus, *Gladstone*, pp. 320–27.

took her into account when contemplating a particular policy.[1] Her negative influence was very great: she was a great strain on the Premier. In April 1881 they were at odds over several issues. The question of a peerage for Wolseley dragged on;[2] as did the question of the Queen approving all Colonial Office telegrams of any importance.[3] A new issue though was added by the death of Disraeli. Gladstone had long wished to grant any vacant K.G. to Lord Derby:[4] Granville had warned of the very great opposition she would have to this—'it would be a bitter pill for the Queen to have to give him Beaconsfield's'.[5] But it was on the Transvaal that the Queen was most virulent in attack. 'The news from the Transvaal are very unsatisfactory,' she telegraphed Gladstone on 20 April. 'The Queen trusts Mr. Gladstone will urge on Lord Kimberley to be v[er]y firm and *not* to let the Peace be carried out *unless* EVERY condition is firmly adhered to by the Boers.'[6] The Queen's anger stemmed from the fact that she not only felt that Gladstone was ignoring her 'sound advice', but that he was impairing the honour and prestige of Britain. 'The Peace itself is felt so generally to be so painful and humiliating in many ways', Victoria claimed, 'that we must not go a step farther and let ourselves be deceived. Already what Sir. E. Wood . . . told the Queen seems likely to come true, viz: "that he was certain if we gave it [the Transvaal] up now we sh[ou]ld have to reoccupy in a few years". '[7] Queen Victoria rarely changed her views: and the Transvaal was no exception. She was persistently to wear away at Gladstone's patience, and Kimberley's determination, throughout 1881.

It was from this highly unstable base—of Cabinet disorder,

[1] See Addit. MSS. 48639, f. 47 (Hamilton Dairy). Entry for Wednesday, 11 February 1885.

[2] P.R.O. 30/29/124. Gladstone to Granville, 26 April 1881. Wolseley, in fact, did not receive the much debated peerage until 25 November 1882, after the Egyptian Campaign. (Ramm, I, 266.) See also Addit. MSS. 44173, f. 110. Granville to Gladstone, 20 May 1881; and f. 141, Granville to Gladstone, 8 September 1881. (Ramm, I, 289–90.)

[3] *Letters of Queen Victoria*, 2nd ser., III, 214–15.

[4] P.R.O. 30/29/123. Gladstone to Granville, 28 August 1881. (Ramm, I, 287).

[5] Addit. MSS. 44173, f. 92. Granville to Gladstone, 27 April 1881. See also f. 46, Granville to Gladstone, 13 April 1881. (Ramm, I, 257, 268).

[6] Guedalla, *Queen and Mr. Gladstone*, II, 152, no. 772, 16 April 1881.

[7] Idem.

parliamentary difficulties, Irish unrest, and public discontent with the Government—that Kimberley now had to work. He took the position to be so serious that he never once left London —for Kimberley House—from Christmas 1880 until early June 1881.[1] Kimberley's preoccupations were four: the possible behaviour of the young Boers; the difficulty of avoiding a parliamentary debate while the delicate negotiations were in progress; the problem of diplomatically handling the Queen's incessant protests; and, most serious of all, the inescapable dilemma of finding a viable method in the Convention for protecting native interests in and around the Transvaal. Kimberley had no immediate answer for any of these questions. Some were to get worse before they got better. There was no answer to the matter of the young Boers—beyond hoping that an early settlement would calm them. Parliament was almost as difficult to influence; Kimberley and Gladstone were forced to a debate—after much prevarication—on 25 July 1881,[2] when Hicks Beach proposed a motion of censure. Questions in the House were yet more difficult to fend off. Demands by back-benchers for full details in regard to the 'Potchefstroom Treachery'[3] placed Kimberley in an awkward position. As he wrote to Gladstone, advising him on how to reply: 'We are in communication with Boer leaders as to reparation for Potchefstroom treachery and . . . it would not be for [the] advantage of public service to enter into further particulars.'[4] Such an answer was hardly likely to satisfy disgruntled back-benchers, and Gladstone was continually under fire in the Commons right until the end of the session, on 27 August. Equally much the same might be said of ministerial relations with the Queen over these peace negotiations. Nothing but resumption of the war, or Boer capitulation, would

---

[1] Addit. MSS. 44226, f. 137. Kimberley to Gladstone, 6 June 1881. Gladstone was also mainly in London, and rarely at his beloved Hawarden—though his concern was, largely, Ireland. See Addit. MSS. 48631, ff. 13–43 (Hamilton Diary).

[2] *Hansard*, 3rd ser., CCLXIII. Debate in Commons, eds. 1763–1867. See earlier attempts by Hicks Beach to force a debate—15 July: 'I gave that Notice more than 3 months ago. . . .' (Col. 1008); 20 July: 'Before the Easter Vacation, I gave notice of the Motion. . . .I again appealed to the Prime Minister after Easter. . . .' (Cols. 1368–9).

[3] See question by Gibson in Commons, 28 April 1881.

[4] Addit. MSS. 44226, f. 103. Kimberley to Gladstone, 27 April 1881.

satisfy Victoria. There was little Kimberley could do to mollify her in view of his own policy, which was aimed in the opposite direction—towards retrenchment and conciliation. Victoria became hypersensitive over Kimberley's every move. She let loose a barrage of telegrams to the Colonial Office when Kimberley despatched another telegram of instructions to Wood, on 24 April, without consulting her.[1] Kimberley's explanation— that it was a Saturday afternoon, that it was very urgent, and that it was 'in accordance with the course already approved by your Majesty',[2]—made little difference to her opinion of her Colonial Secretary.

The Cabinet of Friday, 29 April,[3] the first for three weeks, was told by Kimberley that Wood had opened the Royal Commission at Newcastle, Robinson being detained at the Cape. Kimberley also suggested that the 'Instructions to the Commission' should be laid before Parliament. Further than that he had no news.[4] But, privately, he spoke to Gladstone of '*the present critical* state of Transvaal affairs'.[5] In anticipation of a possible Commons or Lords debate, or merely to clear his mind and make his position absolutely clear to fellow ministers, Kimberley now drew up his lengthy memorandum, of 29 April,[6] outlining the history of the recent Transvaal difficulties. It is a consummate justification of his own policy. He had made peace fearing a pan-Afrikaner rising;[7] he had not granted self-government earlier as the Transvaal appeared to be settling down and accepting British rule; he had waged war so as to stop the unrest before granting the liberal institutions promised.[8] There is little in the memorandum that he had not already stated in correspondence to Gladstone, or in the Lords on 31 March 1881[9]—except for one point. Kimberley felt that events had all

[1] *Letters of Queen Victoria*, 2nd ser., III, 214–16.
[2] Ibid., Kimberley to Queen, 25 April 1881.
[3] Addit. MSS. 44642, f. 176 (Cabinet Papers), Friday, 29 April 1881, 3 p.m.
[4] P.R.O. 30/29/124. Gladstone to Granville, 28 April 1881. '. . . Perhaps Kimberley may also report on Potchefstroom: but nothing to my knowledge stands for decision.' (Ramm, I, 269.)
[5] Addit. MSS. 44226, f. 103. Kimberley to Gladstone, 27 April 1881.
[6] Addit. MSS. 44627, ff. 1–21. Memorandum by Kimberley, dated C.O., 29 April 1881. (Printed copy.)
[7] Ibid., ff. 1–3.   [8] Ibid., ff. 6–7.
[9] *Hansard*, CCLX. Debate in Lords, 31 March 1881.

turned on a single detail, a matter strangely ignored by modern scholars. 'The one thing indispensable to conciliate the Boers, I was constantly assured,' Kimberley wrote,[1] 'was to secure the construction of a railway from Lorenzo Marques [*sic*] to the Transvaal. Accordingly every effort was made to get the Portuguese Government to ratify the Treaty which was made on this subject by the late Government.' The matter had fallen through. 'We made certain concessions to Portugal, and I hoped that I should be able soon to announce to the Boers that we were making a survey with a view to proceeding at an early date with the project.'[2] The record supports Kimberley. The Morier negotiations with Portugal had yielded a treaty[3]—but too late. It had been agreed, by 1879,[4] that there was to be free navigation of the Zambesi, free access for troops at the Portuguese port, and that a rail-line could be built to the Transvaal border, together with a telegraph line, if a commission (to be appointed) thought it a financially viable idea. Finally, both countries were to suppress slavery on the east coast of Africa. The Treaty was to be ratified in London or Lisbon—and here was the difficulty. It was not ratified until 8 March 1881,[5] by which time the Transvaal war had not only begun, but was over. Kimberley had had great hopes for the scheme. He had told Granville that once the Treaty was ratified he would go ahead with plans to organise a rail-line from the Transvaal to the sea.[6] Before the rebellion even broke out Kimberley had shrewdly seen the value of such a rail-line.[7] As he remarked to Granville, 'The treaty is important as a means of reconciling the Boers, and to secure free transit through Delagoa Bay.'[8] Kimberley understood the need for haste, for it was not going to be easy to float a railway company for the Transvaal, bearing in mind the possible unrest

[1] Addit. MSS. 44627, ff. 2–3. Memorandum by Kimberley, 29 April 1881.

[2] Idem.

[3] C.O. 291/13. F.O. to C.O., 26 January 1881, enclosing full details.

[4] Ibid., signed by Morier on 13 May 1879.

[5] Ibid., see Morier to F.O., 8 March 1881, enclosed in F.O. to C.O., 9 March 1881.

[6] C.O. 291/6, no. 16254. Antrobus to Meade, 26 October 1889 with comments by Kimberley, 31 October 1880.

[7] Ibid., Kimberley to Granville, 12 November 1880 (Draft copy).

[8] P.R.O. 30/29/135, f. 1. Kimberley to Granville, December 1880.

in that province. Colley had already made the possible difficulties absolutely clear: 'The reiterated assertions of agitation
that sooner or later the country will be restored to Dutch Republican rule, and the avowed sympathy of many members of
the English Legislative with these aspirations, all tend to in-
juriously affect the credit of the Province and increase the difficulty of raising a loan.'[1] The war had done just that, and more.
The Portuguese were very slow to ratify the Treaty: Kimberley
thought he knew why. 'I am told', he remarked to Granville,
'that the Slave Trade clauses are the chief obstacle as wounding
Portuguese pride.'[2] Even when the Treaty was ratified, matters
did not run smoothly. A new ministry took office in Portugal
and demanded changes. Kimberley took the news with resignation—though he was annoyed when Morier attempted to
press for a treaty on the Congo. 'It would not be desirable to
open any negotiations at the present time', Kimberley minuted.[3]
He wanted the east coast treaty completed first. 'Lord Melbourne's saying "Can't you let it alone?" should be telegraphed
to Mr. Morier.'[4] Kimberley came more and more to blame
Morier[5] for the collapse of Anglo-Portuguese relations over the
Transvaal question. He accepted that the recent war with the
Boers had disturbed the atmosphere, and felt that only time
could heal the breach. 'It will be charity also to give these
wretched Portuguese time to recover their self-possession',
Kimberley grumbled, 'which under Mr. Morier's vigorous
treatment they have completely lost.'[6] Morier saw it differently:
he blamed colonial policy for wrecking the treaty.[7] Kimberley's

[1] C.O. 291/7. Colley to Kimberley, 6 November 1880.

[2] P.R.O. 30/29/135, f. 1. Kimberley to Granville, December 1880.

[3] C.O. 291/13. F.O. to C.O., 20 April 1881; Minute by Kimberley, 22
April 1881.

[4] Ibid., Minute by Kimberley, 27 April 1881.

[5] MORIER (after 1882 Sir) Robert, B. D. (1826–93).

1866–70   Secretary at British legation at Frankfurt.

1870–72   Chargé d'affaires, Stuttgart.

1872–76   Chargé d'affaires, Munich.

1876–81   Minister at Madrid.

1881–85   Minister at Lisbon.

1885–93   Ambassador at St. Petersburg.

[6] C.O. 291/13. Minute by Kimberley, 14 May 1881.

[7] Ibid., see Morier to Granville, 21 May 1881, enclosed in F.O. to C.O.,
9 June 1881.

response was acid: 'For Morier's sake I hope the Foreign Office will freely "edit" the papers [before publication].'[1] Kimberley could indeed wistfully remark in private, 'I still think that if we could have announced that the Treaty had been ratified, and have taken practical steps to start the project in the Transvaal, it would have had a considerable effect on the mind of the people.'[2]

Such was the stuff of dreams: the reality was vastly different. The war was over, but the peace negotiations had only just begun. From the very moment of Robinson's arrival at Newcastle[3] the Commission began to consider the most difficult problem which they faced—the native people's protection, which involved the explosive issue of boundaries, both to the east and west. The session of Monday, 10 May, revealed the theme of the Commission—the impossibility of reconciling Kimberley's instructions to secure the rights of the native tribes in and around the Transvaal, while at the same time extending self-government to the Boers. The meetings of 10, 12, 16 and 21 May (Keate Award boundary) were very stormy;[4] those of 28 May and 13, 15, 19 July[5] (Swazi and south-western border) even more so. Kimberley's reporting to the Cabinet on 20 and 28 May, 15 June, and 23 July[6] can hardly have lifted ministerial spirits, especially Gladstone's. The Transvaal issue, and the manner in which it lingered on month after month, was something of a 'last straw' to the already burdened Premier. The strain began to tell. 'Mr. Gladstone has been seedy the last few days,' his secretary noted,[7] 'He had had one of his old diarrhoea [sic] attacks, brought on I believe by excessive mental worry, of

[1] Ibid., Minute by Kimberley, 9 June 1881.

[2] Addit. MSS. 44627, ff. 4–5. Memorandum by Kimberley, 29 April 1881.

[3] On Sunday, 8 May 1881. See Parl. Pap., 1882, XXVIII, C.3114, pp. 11–34.

[4] C.O. 291/18–21. Report of Royal Commission (with maps) dated 4 August 1881.

[5] The Commission did not sit between 25 May and 17 June (1881) as it was in the process of moving from Natal to Pretoria.

[6] Addit. MSS. 44642, ff. 181, 182, 189, and 203 (Cabinet Papers). There is no mention in Gladstone's agenda of the Transvaal between 15 June and 23 July.

[7] Addit. MSS. 48631, f. 30. (Hamilton Diary). Entry for Sunday, 8 May 1881.

which he has plenty.' Gladstone began to lose patience with his critics—notably a former Colonial Secretary. 'Carnarvon,' Gladstone complained to Granville,[1] 'has and had had a *cacoethes* of action, or stir in him, which has been at the *root*, I am sorry to say, of all these mischiefs in South Africa. I do not wish to say this if I can help it but it is my conviction.'[2]

A crisis point in the peace negotiations was reached very early on. The Boer leaders refused to consider any break-up, or separation of territory, from the Transvaal. They took it as a point of dogmatic principle: they would rather have returned to the battlefield than concede a square yard of territory. Their implacable front presented the Commissioners with a harsh choice: recognise the Boer point or abandon the negotiations. General Wood was for standing firm, even if it meant war. Robinson and de Villiers felt that a divided Transvaal would only lead to even more unrest. Kimberley was advised not to divide the Transvaal in any way, but rather to safeguard the native tribes in some other manner.[3] Kimberley reported immediately to Gladstone;[4] and, three days later, to a special Transvaal Cabinet, on Saturday, 28 May.[5]

It was a pivotal point in the negotiations. After consulting a wide group of their companions—and particularly Granville as Foreign Secretary, and Childers, Secretary of War—it was decided to 'agree with the military council in siding with Robinson and De Villiers [*sic*] against Wood'.[6] To compensate for any loss of influence in the future settlement Gladstone spoke of 'taking strong powers for the Resident . . .'.[7] The vital decision was communicated to the Queen—before the Cabinet had met.[8] Gladstone was determined that this issue was not going to

---

[1] P.R.O. 30/29/124. Gladstone to Granville, 7 May 1881. (Ramm, I, 273.)

[2] Ibid., see Carnarvon's observations in the Lords, Kimberley's reply, and Argyll's attack, 10 May 1881. *Hansard*, 3rd ser., CCLXI, cols. 136–52.

[3] C.O. 291/10. Robinson to Kimberley (Tels.), 24 and 25 May 1881.

[4] Addit. MSS. 44544, ff. 171–2 (L.B. copy). Gladstone to Kimberley, 25 May 1881.

[5] Addit. MSS. 44642, f. 182. (Cabinet Papers), Saturday, 28 May 1881, 2 p.m.

[6] Addit. MSS. 44544, ff. 171–2. (L.B. copy). Gladstone to Kimberley, 25 May 1881.

[7] Idem.

[8] *Letters of Queen Victoria*, 2nd ser., III, 220. Kimberley to Queen (Tel. in cypher), 25 May 1881.

go the way of Irish dilemma in the Cabinet.[1] It might be kept out of the hands of the Whigs, but the Queen could not be by-passed. 'Robinson and De Villiers [sic] recommend that no part of the Transvaal should be retained as British territory', Kimberley telegraphed Victoria, on 25 May,[2] 'on the ground that we shall have half the rebel population in the parts retained and dissatisfied Transvaal alongside, and that by giving up the whole we shall increase the chance of settlement of other questions. . . . Wood dissents.' Kimberley pressed for an early answer. 'If your Majesty approves, Lord Kimberley would hope to be informed by telegraph as Sir H. Robinson presses for an early decision.' The Queen's reply arrived the next day, Thursday, 26 May: 'I cannot understand the necessity for such haste in deciding a question which demands calm deliberation.'[3] Victoria wished to be informed why the Gladstone administration wished to 'sacrifice the interests of our loyal friends and natives who in any case must suffer considerably by our cession of the Transvaal? . . . Should we desert our friends for the sake of a few discontented Boers within our borders, which must ever be the case as long as we hold any territory in South Africa?' Queen Victoria obviously understood Kimberley (and Gladstone's) motive in pressing for such a hasty reply, for she added at the close of her telegram: 'Can so grave a question be settled without the consent of the Cabinet?'[4]

Gladstone was thus more or less forced to hold a Cabinet on the issue. To Kimberley's relief it agreed with his decision[5] and approved of the telegram which he had already drawn up to Robinson—and which had been included in the message to the Queen on 25 May.[6] Victoria had been out-manoeuvred by

[1] Addit. MSS. 44544, f. 172 (L.B. copy). Gladstone to Kimberley, 25 May: 'We [Gladstone and Childers] mentioned it to Granville, and he agreed with us it need not go to the Cabinet, particularly as Forster . . . is in Dublin.'

[2] *Letters of Queen Victoria*, 2nd ser., III, 220. Kimberley to Queen (Tel. in cypher), 25 May 1881.

[3] Ibid., Queen to Kimberley (Tel. in cypher), 26 May 1881.   [4] Idem.

[5] Addit. MSS. 44642, f. 182 (Cabinet Papers) 28 May 1881.

[6] *Letters of Queen Victoria*, 2nd ser., III, p. 220. Kimberley to Queen (Tel.), 25 May 1881, enclosed in Kimberley to Robinson (draft telegram). According to Hamilton, the decision by the Cabinet was taken 'in deference to the majority of the Transvaal Commission'. See also Addit. MSS. 48631, ff. 33–8 (Hamilton Diary).

Gladstone and Kimberley; and she knew it. 'After considering my remonstrance', she wrote in her Journal, 'they still determined to disregard my opinion. Feel very indignant . . . utterly disgusted and disheartened.'[1] Gladstone's secretary superbly captured the moment: 'The Queen has written a frantic letter to Lord Granville. . . . She maintains that the policy of the Cabinet is nothing but surrender, after surrender, and all to satisfy the Radicals . . . and what with India,[2] South Africa, and Ireland, she contends that the Government have been at any rate "eminently unsuccessful". . . .'[3] It was extremely cold comfort for Victoria to be told that Kruger, Pretorius, and Joubert had, via Robinson, extended their 'most "hearty" congratulations' to the Queen for her birthday, on 24 May.[4]

Gladstone and Kimberley had no sooner despatched this problem, with telegrams of Instruction to Robinson,[5] than another appeared from the same horizon. A petition was received from the 'loyalists' in the Transvaal, begging the Gladstone government not to 'abandon' them to Boer rule.[6] It was an extremely skilful petition, and designed to cause Gladstone the maximum of embarrassment. It pointed out that 'the towns are almost exclusively inhabited by loyal settlers, and English farmers and traders are scattered all over the country'; that 'in Pretoria alone . . . 700 volunteers out of a population of 4,000 men, women and children, took arms for the honour of England; all endured privations, and some laid down their lives for their country, in full trust that she would never desert her children'; and that by a revocation of the annexation 'the growing prosperity of the country must be stopped and its civilisation retarded . . . the banks are leaving, capitalists are endeavouring to withdraw, and all enterprise, including the railway scheme, is paralysed'.[7]

It is not surprising that Gladstone took the petition so

[1] Ibid., p. 221. Journal entry, dated Sunday, 29 May 1881.
[2] A reference to the withdrawal from Kandahar.
[3] Addit. MSS. 48631, ff. 33–8 (Hamilton Diary).
[4] *Parl. Pap.*, 1881, LXVII, C.2961. Triumvirate to Queen Victoria, 24 May 1881, enclosed in Robinson to Kimberley, 24 May 1881. Queen Victoria 'acknowledged' the message on 7 July 1881.
[5] C.O. 291/10. Kimberley to Robinson (Tels.), 28–30 May 1881.
[6] *Parl. Pap.*, LXVII, C.2950, pp. 152 ff. Dated 11 April 1881.
[7] Idem.

seriously. It was suggesting in a most cogent form that the very basis for British policy—abandonment in view of Boer feeling—was ill conceived. It was the sort of information Opposition members in the House had been looking for; and it was more than grist for the Press. Kimberley personally drafted the reply,[1] and sent it on to Gladstone for comment.[2] They had, in fact, wrestled over the exact wording for several days.[3] Kimberley suggested they state that 'Her Majesty's Government had always [had] in view the importance of giving the white settlers the fullest liberty to manage their own local affairs, and had hoped that this might be effected through a South African Confederation.' But, in view of the 'disinclination' of the Cape Parliament to do so 'this hope was frustrated', and the revolt in the Transvaal 'proved in the most unmistakable manner that the great majority of the white settlers were strongly opposed to British rule ...'. Hence, the belief that the Transvalers were willing to be British subjects—'the original ground upon which the Transvaal was annexed'—had been proved to be 'entirely devoid of foundation'. The war had been ended as it threatened 'the most disastrous consequences not only to the Transvaal but to the whole of South Africa ...'. And that while Her Majesty's Government 'willingly acknowledge the loyal co-operation' which they received 'at Pretoria and elsewhere' the petitioners should not forget 'that so great was the preponderance of the Boers who rose in arms against the Queen that the whole country... fell at once practically into their hands'. Thus, 'it would be obviously impossible to maintain the Government against the will of so large a majority'.[4]

Gladstone was not altogether happy with this reply. He queried the basis for the loyalists' claims; he thought Kimberley might go more deeply into the history of their own policy.[5] Kimberley's reply reveals his own dry humour at its best.

I quite agree with your draft generally, but I suggest an alteration ... because there have been strong declarations as to not

[1] Addit. MSS. 44226, f. 119. Kimberley to Gladstone, 29 May 1881.
[2] Ibid., f. 122. Gladstone's comments are written on the back of the letter.
[3] Ibid., f. 126. They were still arguing over the wording minutes before it was despatched, on 1 June 1881.
[4] Idem.
[5] Ibid., f. 122. Gladstone note to Kimberley, 29 May 1881.

giving back the Transvaal, especially by Wolseley, who said the sun would cease to set and the rivers would run back to their sources, (or something of that kind), before it happened. Carnarvon, Frere and Hicks Beach all made strong declarations. Your draft seems to me rather to invite the memorialists to prove their statement by citations. I suggest to pass over the point.[1]

Gladstone finally agreed:[2] and the 'loyalists' were answered in the sense of Kimberley's draft.[3] There the matter rested for the moment. The next time Gladstone heard of the 'loyalists' they were publicly burying a Union Jack in Pretoria—to protest against the Pretoria Convention.[4]

Gladstone's concern over the Transvaal went further than the loyalists allowed. 'I am told', he wrote to Kimberley on 3 June,[5] 'that the constant inflammatory telegrams and speeches, with our silences, are working mischief in the Constituencies.' His remedy was to suggest that selected ministers include the Transvaal in their public statements. Chamberlain was about to make a speech to his constituents: Gladstone took it to be an excellent opportunity. 'Would it not be well to ask him to speak fully on the Transvaal?' he enquired of Kimberley. The Colonial Secretary took the hint, and wrote to Chamberlain the same day.[6] It is a significant letter, in that it shows even at this early date, that Chamberlain was taking a deep interest in the Boers. 'Mr. Gladstone tells me you are about to address your constituents', Kimberley wrote on 3 June,[7] 'and suggests that you should speak fully on the Transvaal. I certainly agree. My memorandum[8] which you have says all I have to suggest on the subject. Your own knowledge of the subject will doubtless suggest many other points.'

---

[1] Ibid., ff. 126–8. Kimberley to Gladstone, 1 June 1881.

[2] Addit. MSS. 44544, f. 174 (L.B. copy). Gladstone to Kimberley, 1 June 1881.

[3] Parl. Pap., 1881, LXVII, C.2950, pp. 171–2. Gladstone to C. K. White (Secretary), 1 June 1881.

[4] Ibid., C.3098, p. 79. Wood to Robinson, 17 August 1881.

[5] Addit. MSS. 44544, f. 175 (L.B. copy). Gladstone to Kimberley, 3 June 1881.

[6] J.C. 9/1/1/4. Kimberley to Chamberlain (from C.O.), 3 June 1881.

[7] Idem.

[8] Addit. MSS. 44627, ff. 1–21. Memorandum on Transvaal by Kimberley, dated 29 April 1881—and printed for Cabinet and C.O. circulation.

Kimberley received no reply from Chamberlain, but he was not unduly concerned by this. 'I conclude silence implies consent,' he noted in his letter to Gladstone of 6 June.[1] But what did worry him was the matter of a Commons debate. 'I think we ought not to defer much longer the discussion in the House of Commons,' he had written to the Premier on 3 June.[2] Not that Kimberley saw the matter as cut-and-dried. 'The question of the debate is difficult. Prolonged silence emboldens the carriers of false news, and the agitators in the Transvaal. On the other hand the settlement has scarcely begun to assume a shape.'[3] It was an awkward moment, for the Commission was not even sitting. 'I have telegraphed Robinson[4] to obtain from him the latest information for the Cabinet when we meet again.[5] But he is now at or on his way to Pretoria, from which communications are not immediate.'[6] Gladstone was sympathetic; but he felt that he could not sanction a Commons debate until 'the general substance of the arrangements with the Boers [are] beyond all serious risk of being broken up and frustrated'.[7] Kimberley was not to worry; there would be a debate, and a defence of his policy, when it was judicious to do so. For the moment Chamberlain's impending speech would suffice. Kimberley took Gladstone at his word, and retired for a few days rest in the country, at Kimberley House—'enjoying some fresh air which I sorely need, not having left London since the end of December'.[8]

Chamberlain dropped his bombshell on Tuesday, 7 June. Speaking to a packed hall in Birmingham he stated emphatically that Britain should have given the Transvaal its independence in April 1880, when the present Liberal Government came to power.

I frankly admit we made a mistake . . . whatever the risk was—and I believe it was a great one—of civil war or anarchy in the

[1] Addit. MSS. 44226, f. 137. Kimberley to Gladstone, 6 June 1881.
[2] Ibid., f. 135. Kimberley to Gladstone, 3 June 1881.
[3] Ibid., f. 137. Kimberley to Gladstone, 6 June 1881.
[4] See C.O. 291/11 (Tels.), Kimberley to Robinson, 3–6 June 1881.
[5] The Cabinet in fact did not discuss the Transvaal until ten days later, on Wednesday, 15 June 1881. Addit. MSS. 44642, f. 189 (Cabinet Papers).
[6] Addit. MSS. 44226, f. 137. Kimberley to Gladstone, 6 June 1881.
[7] Addit. MSS. 44544, f. 177 (L.B. copy). Gladstone to Kimberley, 4 June 1881.
[8] Addit. MSS. 44226, f. 137. Kimberley to Gladstone, 6 June 1881.

Transvaal if we had reversed the decision, it was not so great a danger as that which we actually incurred by maintaining the wrong doing of our predecessors.[1]

He saw no harm in admitting a mistake if measures were being taken to redeem it. 'We are a great and powerful nation. What is the use of being great and powerful if we are afraid to admit an error when we are conscious of it. Shame is not in the confession of a mistake. Shame lies only in persistency in wilful wrong doing...'[2]

This was not what Gladstone wanted or expected. His censure of Chamberlain was biting in its brevity: '[I] am not prepared, for myself, to concede that we made a mistake in not advising a revocation of the annexation when we came in.'[3] The Opposition used the speech in just the manner dreaded by Gladstone.[4] It was on the Whitsun week-end, and politicians throughout the country were casting about for texts for their mid-summer statements to constituents.[5] Chamberlain provided that text. Hicks Beach's speech at Cheltenham is typical:

> These men came into office and having, as Mr. Chamberlain said considered the subject in all its bearings, they decided, and for reasons that might have been copied from my own despatches, that it was necessary that the Queen's sovereignty should be maintained. . . . [But having had to fight to do so,] they thought about injustice, which they did not dream of last summer. . . . No more disgraceful surrender has ever been made by a British Government.[6]

Lord Carnarvon, at Burton-on-Trent, thought the Transvaal had been fortunate to be annexed: 'Their exchequer contained 12/6d (laughter). . . . Our advent was welcomed.' But once the

[1] Speech fully reported in *The Times*, 8 June 1881. Quoted, in part, in Garvin, *Chamberlain*, I, 441.

[2] Idem.

[3] Gladstone to Chamberlain, 8 June 1881. Quoted in Garvin, *Chamberlain*, I, 441.

[4] Addit. MSS. 44470, f. 207. Gladstone carefully collected copies of the hostile speeches.

[5] Addit. MSS. 48631, f. 38 (Hamilton Diary). 'Political speeches have been the order of the day during the short Whitsun recess, mostly from the opposition— . . . Hicks Beach Boer wild.'

[6] Speech by Hicks Beach at Cheltenham, 8 June 1881. Quoted in full, *The Times*, 9 June 1881.

Boers were on their feet, they 'rose in insurrection', and committed 'a foul and cold-blooded massacre (hear! hear!).'[1] The Colonial Office officials fulminated at the fact that they could not reply to these attacks.[2] Neither Kimberley nor Gladstone would be drawn: a counter-attack could only hamper the peace negotiations. Both of them still looked to the Transvaal debate in the Commons to state and vindicate their policy.

In Natal the first phase of the Commission was over: and the second stage at Pretoria was about to begin. The state of play was still undecided.[3] One major decision had been taken: the Transvaal was to remain intact in the final solution.[4] Several matters were also nearing an agreement: the Keate Award boundary was to be altered in favour of the Transvaal;[5] and the questions of taxation,[6] and the payment of civil servants,[7] were largely concluded. But, many key issues lay undecided: the question of the Transvaal's 'debt' had only been touched on (16 May), and so had the thorny matter of the 'Potchefstroom Treachery' (26 May). At the ten meetings in Pretoria the Commission tackled these matters,[8] and also the two outstanding dilemmas—the powers of the Resident, and the protection of the native tribes over the Transvaal frontiers (4, 5, 6, 15, 19 and 30 July). In all this Kimberley and Gladstone took a leading hand: the actual rôle of the Commissioners lessened with each meeting. They may have conducted the negotiations, but the decisions were not theirs.

A great deal has been written of these final sessions of the Commission: perhaps too much. One historian has found in the question of the debt the central issue;[9] another has looked deeply into the Keate Award discussions in search of the significant.[10]

---

[1] Speech by Carnarvon at Burton-upon-Trent, 7 June 1881. Quoted in the Standard, 5 June 1881.

[2] C.O. 291/14. Minutes by Fairfield, Hemming, and Bramston, 8–10 June 1881.

[3] C.O. 291/18–21. Verbatim evidence of proceedings at Commission.

[4] Agar-Hamilton, The Road to the North, pp. 164–82.

[5] Sessions of 12, 16, and 21 May 1881.

[6] Session of 4 May.   [7] Session of 3 May.

[8] Potchefstroom 'Treachery', 20 June 1881; Transvaal Debt, 8 July; Keate Award Area, 13 July.

[9] De Kiewiet, Imperial Factor, pp. 283–6.

[10] Agar-Hamilton, The Road to the North, pp. 168–82.

But this is to stand too close to the Commission: it is to examine the peripheral topics and miss the main objective. The Pretoria Convention was designed in Whitehall to fulfil a particular function: to provide a smoke-screen to cover revocation of the annexation, and to conciliate the South African Afrikaners by this apparent act of magnanimity. It has been supposed that Britain insisted on the retention of the 'suzerainty' for the sake of prestige, and because of an inborn reluctance to part with portions of the Empire. This is not so. Gladstone, who knew his parliamentary system and his electorate, gave the true reason when he remarked to Kimberley: 'It is upon the question of protection for the natives that we shall justly be subjected to the sharpest scrutiny.'[1]

This is what the Convention was about. It was an illusionist's trick: the Boers were to be independent, yet this independence was not to interfere with imperial protection of the tribes. Gladstone was laying claim to the impossible—and he knew it. When the native chiefs within the Transvaal appealed to the Liberal leader not to place them under Boer rule, Gladstone was sympathetic, but he was aware of the fact that he was abdicating from the Transvaal and accordingly could do little. 'I have read the reports of the representations from [the] native chiefs', Gladstone told Kimberley, 'I cannot but think something joint would be more satisfactory . . . than the mere statement from us, who are in one sense about to leave the country.'[2] Thus the rôle of the Resident was crucial.[3] The extent of his powers, even if only on paper, would be the final defence against Tory and Humanitarian attacks. Reservation of the powers of the future Boer government to conclude treaties with native chiefs over the frontiers, would do the same for the Gladstone government in connection with the Bechuana, Swazi, and Zulu tribes.[4]

This, however, was not Gladstone's most immediate or abiding fear, in June and July 1881: he had more explosive

[1] Addit. MSS. 44544, f. 180 (L.B. copy). Gladstone to Kimberley, 12 June 1881.

[2] Addit. MSS. 44544, f. 177 (L.B. copy). Gladstone to Kimberley, 4 June 1881.

[3] Addit. MSS. 44642, ff. 203-5 (Cabinet Papers). Memorandum by Gladstone, 23 July 1881.

[4] Addit. MSS. 44226, f. 157. Kimberley to Gladstone, 23 June 1881—on controlling the Transvaal's foreign relations.

problems. With the Irish crisis beginning to reach new and unexpected heights,[1] he wished the Transvaal matter to be concluded as soon as possible[2] How he was to enforce the Convention he would worry about later. Beyond securing certain basic points Gladstone cared little for the exact details, or the minor clauses, of which there were all too many. For example, when Wood tried to revive the matter of a 'buffer-strip' on the eastern border, to protect the Swazi and Zulu tribes,[3] he was castigated by Gladstone,[4] and officially censured by Kimberley.[5] Failing to get his way Wood attempted to resign from the Commission —'to devote all my time to Natal, the army and the Zulu settlement'.[6] Kimberley was not to be fooled. 'Wood's attempt to reopen the boundary question is ingenious,' he remarked to Gladstone, 'but should be firmly resisted.'[7] Gladstone's initial reaction was one of indifference: 'He has certainly, I think, committed a venial error.'[8] Kimberley was more anxious, and even more concerned over the affect of the act. 'We must persuade him to remain in the Commission,' Kimberley wrote to the Premier, 'His leaving it would greatly encourage all those, both whites and natives, who wish to disturb the settlement.'[9] Kimberley's anxieties did not end there. 'I think it would be well to mention it at the Cabinet,[10] as the Queen throws so much obstruction in the way of everything I do, and she may take it into her head that Wood ought to be allowed to get quit of a discreditable business.'[11] Gladstone completely agreed—'apart

---

[1] Addit. MSS. 48631, ff. 38–41 (Hamilton Diary). 'Accounts don't improve from Ireland. It is clear that the crisis is very severe.' See also Addit. MSS. 44158, ff. 167, 172. Forster to Gladstone, 27 May and 1 June 1881.

[2] Addit. MSS. 44544, f. 183 (L.B. copy). Gladstone to Kimberley, 18 June 1881.

[3] Addit. MSS. 44226, f. 130. Kimberley to Gladstone, 2 June 1881.

[4] Addit. MSS. 44544, f. 179 (L.B. copy). Gladstone to Kimberley, 9 June 1881.

[5] Addit. MSS. 44226, f. 168. Kimberley to Gladstone, 6 July 1881.

[6] Ibid., f. 141 (Tel.), Wood to Kimberley, 6 June 1881.

[7] Ibid., f. 168. Kimberley to Gladstone, 6 July 1881.

[8] Addit. MSS. 44544, f. 179 (L.B. copy). Gladstone to Kimberley, 10 June 1881.

[9] Addit. MSS. 44226, f. 139. Kimberley to Gladstone, 7 June 1881.

[10] This was done at the Cabinet of Wednesday, 15 June 1881. Addit. MSS. 44642, f. 189 (Cabinet Papers).

[11] Addit. MSS. 44226, f. 139. Kimberley to Gladstone, 7 June 1881.

from the embarrassment it would produce, [it] would be so far as I know without precedent, and very damaging to him as well as us'.[1] Gladstone's attack on Wood displays his whole approach to the conclusion of a settlement: 'He accepted the Commission under the terms of March 17, and how can he have title to retire upon a decision which lies evidently and strictly *within* the options given by them.' This was not strictly true, as a clause in the Instructions had specifically allowed the Commission to consider the creation of just such a buffer-zone.[2] But Gladstone had conveniently forgotten this fact. His desire for an early conclusion to the matter was all-pervading. 'It occurs to me to suggest . . . a hint to Robinson or Wood on this subject,' he urged on Kimberley.[3]

Gladstone took much the same approach to the other outstanding Transvaal problems. He swept aside the 'Potchefstroom Treachery' as a futile bone of contention, which was only holding up the settlement. As Kimberley explained: '. . . the Boer leaders are quite free from any imputation of unfair conduct in this matter, and we have never charged them with it.'[4] In like manner, Gladstone and Kimberley refused to support Wood in haggling over the amount of debt for which the Transvaal was to be assessed. When the Boer leaders flatly refused to pay the cost of the Sekukuni campaign of 1878—some £385,000[5]—the two British statesmen immediately gave way. 'I always thought we should have to forgo demanding repayment of the cost of the expedition against Sikukuni [*sic*] . . .' Kimberley remarked; and Gladstone agreed.[6] The final debt

[1] Addit. MSS. 44544, f. 179 (L.B. copy). Gladstone to Kimberley, 9 June 1881.

[2] Kimberley knew this—hence his own embarrassment over the matter. See his letter to Gladstone, 2 June 1881—in Addit. MSS. 44226, f. 131.

[3] Addit. MSS. 44544, f. 183 (L.B. copy). Gladstone to Kimberley, 18 June 1881.

[4] Addit. MSS. 44226, f. 189. Memorandum by Kimberley, 13 July 1881. (Printed for Cabinet circulation.) 'General Cronje was . . . solely responsible . . . Cronje therefore violated the armistice in not notifying to Colonel Winsloe, on the 10th, that an armistice was concluded, that provisions were on the way, and that after their arrival hostilities would be suspended for eight days. The conclusion of the whole matter is, I think, that Cronje cannot be acquitted of dishonourable conduct.'

[5] Ibid., f. 169 (Tel.), Robinson to Kimberley, 5 July 1881.

[6] Ibid., f. 166. Kimberley to Gladstone, 6 July 1881.

was assessed at £562,793.[1] But, even here neither Gladstone nor Kimberley pressed for immediate settlement; indeed, they advanced the Transvaal £136,900 to help them on to their feet.[2] As a Colonial Office official noted with relish, 'Pleasant reading for the Treasury.'[3]

This sense of urgency, in the closing weeks of the Commission, stemmed from a particular factor. 'In view of a Transvaal debate a fortnight or 3 weeks hence,' the Premier wrote to his Colonial Secretary on 18 June,[4] 'it is very desirable that when it comes it should find *main* points already settled in South Africa and [be] beyond the risk of disturbance.' Gladstone worked towards this end with singular determination and to some effect. When it was rumoured that a misunderstanding was growing over how the Transvaal was to conduct its external relations,[5] Gladstone had Kimberley and Granville sort it out within days.[6] It was decided that Transvaal citizens abroad were to be under British protection; and that the Boers were to appoint no diplomatic consuls: all foreign business was to be conducted via British consuls.[7] By 23 June that matter was closed, and Kimberley could report to Gladstone: 'I think the question should be placed beyond doubt, as it would be very embarrassing to have misunderstandings hereafter on such a point. . . . I have consulted Granville and he agrees with me . . . that the interests of the Transvalers abroad should be under the care of our Ministers and Consuls.'[8] Gladstone could view the matter with satisfaction. 'The Transvaal Commission have nearly completed their labours,' his secretary recorded on Sunday, 24 July,[9] 'and a very tolerable settlement of a most difficult and complicated question, seems in prospect.'

[1] C.O. 291/12. Minutes in 'Treasury' section. See De Kiewiet, *Imperial Factor*, pp. 283–6, analysis, at length, of the debt.
[2] Idem., see also C.O. 291/18. Wood to Kimberley, 30 May 1881, enclosing Lanyon on the question of indebtedness.
[3] C.O. 291/10, no. 11723, by Bramston, 4 July 1881.
[4] Addit. MSS. 44544, f. 183 (L.B. copy). Gladstone to Kimberley, 18 June 1881.
[5] Addit. MSS. 44226, f. 157. Kimberley to Gladstone, 23 June 1881.
[6] P.R.O. 30/29/135, f. 43. Kimberley to Gladstone, 18 June 1881.
[7] Ibid., f. 46. Granville to Kimberley, 18 June 1881 (Copy).
[8] Addit. MSS. 44226, f. 157. Kimberley to Gladstone, 23 June 1881.
[9] Addit. MSS. 48631, f. 52 (Hamilton Diary). Entry for 24 July 1881.

Against severe odds, and in spite of several other concurrent problems, the G.O.M. had yet again apparently confounded his critics, and his Queen. He had not only survived the stigma of 'Majubanimity'—a word coined in derision by his 'jingo' critics[1]—but he had made political capital of it. The month of July 1881 was indeed to be an isolated high-water mark for this Gladstone government. Since the departure of Argyll there had been relative tranquillity in the Cabinet— broken only by the slowly widening rift between Granville and Hartington,[2] over Egyptian policy.[3] But that was not an important problem, as yet. The Land Act had been a considerable success in the Lower House;[4] while Gladstone's swift move against Dillon had softened the demands of the Forster faction.[5] Then there was the Transvaal. The coming settlement appeared to be extricating Britain from an awkward position not altogether unsuccessfully. The 'suzerainty clauses,' and the Resident, would maintain the old powers of influence over the Boers —but without the heavy drain on the Treasury. In all this Gladstone stood supreme. It was indeed his energies that had steered the Land Act through; that had guided Kimberley's hand in the Transvaal; and had reconciled the warring factions in the Cabinet. 'The ministry themselves,' *The Times* intuitively noted,[6] 'have disappeared behind one central figure, and it is only at Trinity House banquets that we are reminded that the Cabinet includes other statesmen besides Mr. Gladstone.' A sharp observer would have noted tell-tale signs of the storm to come—the Granville–Hartington split was to increase as the Egyptian crisis deepened;[7] Parnell was already talking of the limitations of the Land Act;[8] Forster was preparing a new

[1] E. B. Iwan-Muller, *Lord Milner and South Africa* (London, 1902), pp. 191–327, chap. V.
[2] E. Fitzmaurice, *Life of Granville*, II, 198–238, chap. VI.
[3] Addit. MSS. 43924, f. 58 (Dilke Diary). 'Lord Granville and Hartington fell out rather more than usual . . .'
[4] Ibid., f. 48. Diary entry for 3 May 1881.
[5] J. L. Hammond, *Gladstone and the Irish Nation*, p. 219 *passim*.
[6] *The Times*, 22 July 1881.
[7] Addit. MSS. 44173, f. 139. Granville to Gladstone, 30 August 1881; P.R.O. 30/29/124. Granville to Gladstone, 31 August 1881; Ibid., Gladstone to Granville, 13 September 1881. (Ramm, I, 288–91.)
[8] J. L. Hammond, *Gladstone and the Irish Nation*, p. 221 *passim*.

campaign for stiffer coercion;[1] and Kruger was known to be dissatisfied with the trend of the Commission at Pretoria.[2] But, for the moment, all was sweetness and light. The Gladstonian team for the Transvaal debate was presenting a united front: even Joseph Chamberlain, having said his piece was toeing the party line, and had been marked down as a major Government speaker for the impending Transvaal debates.[3]

The timing of the Commons debate was thus propitious for Gladstone. It came just after several storms had abated and before other storms blew up; and it allowed him to justify his actions in a more tranquil air than that which had prevailed only a week before in parliamentary circles. The immediate background to this Transvaal debate in the Commons is also important. In the days before the debate Gladstone shrewdly briefed all the ministers most carefully on the exact details of the Commission, its progress and the probable terms of the final settlement. In this way he not only rehearsed the probable objections that would be raised in the Commons, but he brought the whole Cabinet behind him, by bringing even hostile ministers into his confidence. Kimberley was instrumental in securing this. At the important Cabinet of 23 July[4] the only subject discussed was the Transvaal settlement.[5] Gladstone recorded the final decisions of the Cabinet on every point in the draft settlement which Robinson had forwarded from Pretoria.[6] This memorandum reveals the settlement in a surprisingly advanced stage, and very close to the Convention as announced on 3 August. The only matter still in flux was the matter, or rather the definition, of the suzerainty clause.[7] The Transvaal were still standing by certain objections—more in hope than in determination. The Boer leaders, in a last fling of obstruction, at-

[1] Addit. MSS. 44158, ff. 167, 172. Forster to Gladstone, 1 June 1881.

[2] D. W. Kruger, *Paul Kruger*, I, 253 *passim*.

[3] W. L. Strauss, *Joseph Chamberlain and the Theory of Imperialism* (Washington, 1942), p. 25 ff.

[4] Addit. MSS. 44642, f. 203 (Cabinet Papers), Saturday, 23 July 1881.

[5] P.R.O. 30/29/124. Gladstone to Granville, 23 July 1881. 'The Transvaal Debate is really our main subject'. Granville was the only minister absent. (Ramm, I, 286.)

[6] Addit. MSS. 44642, f. 203 (Cabinet Papers). Memorandum by Gladstone, 23 July 1881.

[7] Ibid., f. 205. Cabinet Committee appointed for this purpose.

tempted to wrest a final concession from Britain before facing their own *Volksraad*, and asking their fellow burghers to ratify the settlement.[1] Gladstone's memorandum, written at the Cabinet of Saturday, 23 July, is therefore all the more interesting. It not only displays what the Liberal Government regarded as essential in any treaty with the Boers, but equally what the Boers saw as essentially corrosive in the coming settlement.

Gladstone enumerated nine basic points of dissension and importance—together with the Cabinet decision:[2]

(1) Control of foreign affairs—'*Hold our ground.*'[3]

(2) Compensation for property taken by Boers for war purposes—*Do.*

(3) Payment of gratuities to officers unwilling toserve—'*Agree with Boers.*'

(4) Transvaal want control of natives—'*We see great objections.*'[4]

(5) Native locations Commission—'*Hold our ground.*'

(6) Pensions for Burgers and Hamilton—'*Disposed of.*'

(7) Payment of Resident—'*We undertake it.*'

(8) Suzerainty—'*Committee of Cabinet appointed.*'[5]

(9) British Resident—'*Hudson*'[6] (selected; one of two candidates).

The only issue on which Gladstone still felt there was room for further discussion was on the suzerainty. A Cabinet Committee was appointed, to be headed by Kimberley, and to include Selborne, Harcourt, Chamberlain, and Childers.[7] But even this Committee was not intended as a decision-making body; it was

---

[1] Addit. MSS. 44226, ff. 219, 222. Kimberley to Gladstone, 26 July 1881.

[2] Addit. MSS. 44642, f. 203 (Cabinet Papers), 23 July 1881. (Note rearranged.)

[3] The Boer leaders were particularly critical of this clause, as it included relations with tribes on the Transvaal frontiers. Significantly it was the first clause to be ignored. But Gladstone and Kimberley determined to be tough on this point. See Addit. MSS. 44226, f. 157. Kimberley to Gladstone, 23 July 1881.

[4] Gladstone saw this as probably *the* most important clause for the British. See Addit. MSS. 44544, f. 180. Gladstone to Kimberley, 12 June 1881: 'It is upon the question of protection for the natives that we shall justly be subjected to the sharpest scrutiny.'

[5] Addit. MSS. 44642, f. 205 (Cabinet Papers). This Cabinet Committee met that Saturday afternoon, 23 July 1881.

[6] Hudson, British Resident in Transvaal, 1881–83. The post was abolished in the London Convention of 27 February 1884. Hudson was involved in a land 'scandal', and left the post in disgrace.

[7] See Addit. MSS. 44642, f. 205.

created to frame the wording of the suzerainty clause, and to examine the final draft of the Convention as telegraphed by Robinson.[1]

The Transvaal debate which began the following Tuesday—26 July 1881—found the Gladstonians happy in the knowledge that the Transvaal treaty was, to all intents and purposes, completed and beyond criticism. It is not surprising that the long-awaited debate, with its much vaunted vote of censure, was to sound rather 'hollow'.

> The Transvaal debate on Monday[2] fell rather flat [Hamilton wrote in his journal.[3]] Several spoke well, notably [Hicks] Beach, Rathbone and Chamberlain; but there prevailed on both sides a certain hollowness: the fact being that it was difficult for the annexers of the Transvaal to condemn it, and it was not wholly easy for the Government to defend. . . .'

But, it was a lively debate. It was the first opportunity the Opposition had had to criticise the Gladstone–Kimberley handling of the Transvaal since the short debate of 21 January 1881.[4] It was equally a one-sided debate. The Opposition had been starved of information: they could only guess at the final terms of the settlement. Their criticisms were thus, in essence, merely arrows shot into the dark: that none landed on target is hardly surprising. Hicks Beach, who moved the vote of censure, could do no more than charge the Gladstone administration in the vaguest terms. The Government, he claimed, had announced a firm policy in the Speech from the Throne, on 6 January,[5] but had only 'carried it on for a certain time, and then they abandoned it'.[6] They had halted the war after three defeats, so that not only had British blood 'been shed to no purpose', but a most unfavourable time had been chosen to negotiate. 'By making peace at the time and in the manner in which

[1] Addit. MSS. 44226, f. 223. Kimberley to Gladstone, 28 July 1881.

[2] Hamilton's memory was incorrect. The debate began on the afternoon of Tuesday, 25 July 1881. See *Hansard*, CCLXIII, col. 1763 *passim*.

[3] Addit. MSS. 48631, ff. 52–5 (Hamilton Diary). Entry for 27 July 1881.

[4] See *Hansard*, CCLVII, 21 January 1881. There had, of course, been a debate in the Lords on 31 March 1881 and a statement by Kimberley on 21 February 1881.

[5] Ibid., CCLVII. Speech from the Throne, 6 January 1881.

[6] Ibid., CCLXIII, col. 1763 *passim*. Hicks Beach in Commons, 25 July 1881.

they made it,' they had not only created 'the precursor of infinitely worse trouble', but they had aided that very wild spirit,
among the South African Dutch, which they had wished to
allay. 'They have encouraged a spirit which is not merely confined to a small body of farmers in the Transvaal who desire
local self-government, but which is expressed in the words
"Africa for the Africanders," [sic] from the Zambesi to Simons
Bay. . .'.[1]

Hicks Beach was best supported not by the official Leader of
the Opposition, Sir Stafford Northcote,[2]—who made a ram-
bling speech,[3]—but by John Gorst[4] and Baron Henry de
Worms.[5] Gorst called on Gladstone to explain the vacillation in
policy between late December and mid-March,[6] and to state
whether he really believed that a Resident would be sufficient
to protect the tribes in the Transvaal. Gladstone's peace moves,
he suggested, were a disgrace: 'On the same principle we need
not have put down the Indian Mutiny, but should have ceded
India; and we need not have resisted Fenians and Land
Leaguers, but should have given up Ireland.'[7]

Chamberlain led the Government reply with a superb debating speech.[8] He tossed aside the Opposition's charges, and
claimed that they argued from a false premise: a belief that the
Transvaal could be kept in the Empire. This could not be
done, Chamberlain stated, other than by Britain pursuing 'a

[1] Ibid., col. 1777.
[2] NORTHCOTE, Sir Stafford (1818–87)
1885   1st Earl of Iddesleigh.
1842–45   Private Secretary to Gladstone.
1855–85   Conservative M.P.
1880–85   Leader of Opposition in House of Commons.
[3] Ibid., cols. 1866–8.
[4] GORST, John Eldon (1835–1916)
1866–68   Conservative M.P.
1868–75   Organiser of Conservative Party.
1875–1906 Conservative M.P.
1880–84   Member of '4th Party'.
1885   Knighted.
[5] WORMS, Henry (1840–1903) Baron de, of Austrian Empire: Conservative M.P. for Greenwich, 1880–85; Liverpool, 1885–95.
[6] Hansard, CCLXIII, cols. 1834–6.
[7] Ibid., col. 1781.
[8] Ibid., cols. 1817–31.

practically despotic' rule over the Boers, and by maintaining 'a large force constantly in South Africa'. Were the Opposition prepared to keep thousands of troops in southern Africa indefinitely? 'Here is the plain issue for the House.' In framing an answer he reminded the Conservatives that they should remember that they 'would have to face, probably, the opposition of the Free State; and the ... agitation among the Dutch Colonists of the Cape'.[1] Far from pursuing a weak policy the Government had carefully avoided 'the greatest danger—bad relations between the different white races in the Transvaal'. The peace was not 'dishonourable'. If a brave man committed an injustice unwittingly, but had the courage to admit his wrong, he gained not lost in public estimation. 'I can see no distinction', Chamberlain claimed, 'between private and public morality.'[2]

Mr. Gladstone's long-awaited speech was not among his great orations. Even his devoted secretary admitted: 'Mr. Gladstone was not up to his mark. He was overstrained, feeling as he said, like a sucked-out orange; and after 32 days of [Irish] Land Bill Committee no wonder.'[3] But, it was an exhaustive *tour de force* of statistics, details, and motives for policy.[4] Gladstone attempted to touch on every facet of the Transvaal dilemma: and not even the 'unmannerly interruptions which emanated from the rowdy Tories',[5] could move him from his course. At the root of all the evils, Gladstone felt, was Carnarvon's policy. 'In 1852 we solemnly covenanted ... to respect the independence of the Transvaal. ... What right had we to infringe that Treaty?'[6] And what of the people that the annexation of 1877 violated: who are the Boers? 'They are the descendants of the Calvinists of the United Provinces, who defied the power of Spain ... and of the French Huguenots, who maintained such a contest against the dominant party in France. ... We are dealing with persons of extraordinary vigour and tenacity of character.'[7]

If Gladstone blamed Carnarvon for the war, he credited the peace to his own administration. 'If we had not accepted it we

[1] Ibid., col. 1817. [2] Ibid., col. 1830.
[3] Addit. MSS. 48631, ff. 53–5 (Hamilton Diary), 27 July 1881.
[4] *Hansard*, CCLXIII, cols. 1848–67.
[5] Addit. MSS. 48631, ff. 53–5 (Hamilton Diary), 27 July 1881.
[6] *Hansard*, CCLXIII, col. 1851. [7] Ibid., col. 1854.

should have incurred a heavy responsibility, and deserved the censure which is now sought to be cast upon us.'[1] The Liberal Government had spent its time rectifying the mistakes and extravagances of the Tory period. Not that they could simply put policy into reverse. 'I do not think that with the view we take of our obligations in this matter it would have been possible for us to recognise the Transvaal State simply as a foreign power, even to the extent to which it was recognised by the Sand River Convention.'[2] Equally, 'I cast aside the plan of governing the people of the Transvaal by the officialism of Downing Street as visionary and impracticable.' Carnarvon had left Gladstone with but two alternatives. Either, 'that of giving a Colonial Constitution ... with real and responsible government;' or, 'some plan fixed and agreed upon between us, so that they should know what obligations they were under to us, and that we should have no powers except such as were well understood by them'.[3] As to responsible government, 'I do not believe it would have been acceptable.' This left the second choice—a contractual agreement. 'That is the plan which we have actually adopted.'

The Convention, according to Gladstone, would safeguard all Britain's interests and obligations. In particular, the rights of the native people had been carefully safeguarded. 'The whole of the interests of the natives beyond the frontier of the Transvaal will be retained in the hands of the British Government by the retention of the suzerainty. As to the interests of the natives in the Transvaal, I can only say that we have decided on and embodied in the fixed terms of the instructions by which the veto of the Crown will be reserved over any law enacted in the Transvaal concerning the natives.' As to other interests, this Convention would give Britain 'a great deal more power than we should have had if we could have established that kind of Colonial Parliamentary Government with responsible ministers'. In short, it was even more than a just or workable settlement—it was an expedient settlement. The Opposition should never forget that had Britain continued the struggle it would have been a war not only on the Transvaal, 'but too probably, in the end upon a very large portion—nay, on the whole of the

[1] Ibid., col. 1854.
[2] Ibid., col. 1858.   [3] Ibid., col. 1859.

Dutch population of South Africa, which numbers two to one of the English'.[1]

The debate was over. Northcote's attempt at a reply fell flat.[2] The vote of censure was defeated 314–205, a Liberal majority of 109. The Transvaal peace was now a matter for the Cabinet Committee alone. The matter was not discussed at a full Cabinet again. Indeed, the Transvaal was not on a single Cabinet agenda until Thursday, 12 October,[3] when Kimberley reported that the Convention had been ratified by the Transvaal *Volksraad*. Nor did the Commons ever debate the final terms of the settlement, even after it was made public. The next major 'Boer debate' in the Lower House was in March 1883,[4] on the situation in Bechuanaland. Gladstone had succeeded in both steering the delicate matter away from the Cabinet factions, and also around Parliament. He had thus allowed Kimberley the maximum secrecy and privacy in which to conduct the negotiations. By throwing a dark cloak over the whole proceedings, and taking the responsibility on his own shoulders, Gladstone displayed a predilection that was steadily to grow throughout this Government: a technique of centralising all business in his own hands at the expense of the Cabinet. By working closely with individual ministers—Granville on foreign affairs, Kimberley and Derby[5] on colonial matters, Chamberlain and Dilke on reform, Hartington on India, Childers on the budgets—Gladstone achieved a semblance of efficient government in spite of his factious Cabinet, and the unsettled Commons. It was in so many ways a negation of Cabinet government, yet it appeared as the only viable choice in the face of the diverse stresses at work in his own ill-assorted ministerial team.

The Transvaal Cabinet Committee was just such a device. Headed by Kimberley it included two lawyers, (Selborne and Harcourt), a Gladstonian, (Childers,) plus Chamberlain.[6] Hartington, Forster, and Spencer were carefully avoided. The only

[1] Ibid., col. 1862.   [2] Ibid., cols. 1866–7.

[3] Addit. MSS. 44642, f. 217 (Cabinet Papers), 12 October 1881.

[4] *Hansard*, CCLXXVIII. Debate in Commons, 13–16 March 1883.

[5] Derby entered the Cabinet in December 1882, and replaced Kimberley who moved to the India Office.

[6] Addit. MSS. 44226, f. 209. Kimberley to Gladstone, 23 July 1881, giving details of the working of the Committee.

member of the Committee who might cause Kimberley any trouble would be Chamberlain, but he had largely been brought round to the Gladstonian approach, and diplomatically 'muzzled'—by being promoted to be the southern African spokesman for the Government in the Commons. The final stages of the treaty with the Transvaal therefore went smoothly, safe from the Whigs, the Humanitarians and the Queen. Kimberley had Selborne, as Lord Chancellor, carefully scrutinise the suzerainty clauses;[1] and then had the complete Convention, in its final draft stage, studied by the full Committee on 28 July.[2] In Kimberley's phrase, they looked for 'some unguarded expression' in the draft, which might later 'get us into difficulties'.[3]

But all went smoothly. Robinson was able to telegraph that the Boers were willing to sign the Convention[4] as stipulated at the Cabinet of 23 July.[5] The Boer leaders had, in fact, realised that there were limits beyond which even this Gladstone government would not, or could not go. The signing of the Convention was publicly announced by Robinson in full proconsular dress, plumed helmet and sword, from a hastily made platform of planks and straw-bales in Church Square, Pretoria, on Wednesday, 3 August 1881.[6] The Union Jack was lowered—and promptly buried in a ceremony of even greater pomp by the 'Transvaal Empire Loyalists'.[7] The following Monday, 8 August, Kruger, Joubert, and Pretorius, together with several thousand armed Boer horsemen, cheered the raising of the old republican *Vierkleur*.[8]

---

[1] Ibid., ff. 219, 221. Kimberley to Gladstone, 26 July 1881.
[2] Ibid., f. 223. Kimberley to Gladstone 28 July 1881. See Robinson to Kimberley (Tel.), 28 July 1881, enclosed in Draft of Convention.
[3] Idem.
[4] C.O. 291/10. Robinson to Kimberley (Tel.), 28 July 1881; and C.O. 29/20. Proceedings of Commission.
[5] Addit. MSS. 44642, f. 203 (Cabinet Papers), Saturday, 23 July 1881, 12 p.m.
[6] *Parl. Pap.*, 1882, XXVIII, 37–44. Robinson to Kimberley, 4 August 1881.
[7] *Times History of the War* (London, 1900), vol. I. See also *Parl. Pap.*, 1882, XLVII C.3098, p. 79, Wood to Robinson, 17 August 1881.
[8] D. W. Kruger, *Paul Kruger*, I, 249–51. It was signed on 3 August, and the transfer of power took place on 8 August. See Preamble to Convention (in Appendix).

The matter, however, was far from over. The Convention still had to be ratified by the *Volksraad* within three months;[1] and few Transvaal burghers understood the implications of the Convention. Most Boers took it to be a simple restoration of their republican status. It seemed a natural corollary to Majuba. Kruger knew this was not so; and also that he was going to have some difficulty in convincing his countrymen that the triumvirate had made the most of their military victory. It is significant that Kruger left his beloved farm, 'Bokenhoutfontein', for the first time, and moved into a house in Kerkstraat, Pretoria.[2] Having fought the British he was now preparing to fight his fellow Boers. His own political aspirations turned on the *Volksraad's* acceptance of the Convention. He would have to assert his dominance in the Boer triumvirate. Failure to secure ratification of the Convention could result in a renewal of hostilities,[3] an idea not unfavourable to the younger Boers. The whole peace settlement turned on Kruger's rise or fall. He could no longer afford to play Cincinnatus. Gladstone's hopes, and Kruger's ambitions, ironically now ran in harness.

3. A Matter of Suzerainty: August 1881

The Commission broke up on Friday, 5 August. Robinson wrote a very full report on the proceedings;[4] and Wood submitted a minority report of dissent.[5] The three Commissioners then quit the 'Transvaal State', as it was now styled. They had not only left the Boer leaders with a circumscribed independence, that would rankle in the *Volksraad*, but also a country with a barren treasury, and a heavy overdraft with the Standard Bank.[6] The price of independence was indeed high. Wood was of the opinion that the Transvaal did not have the resources to maintain

[1] Pretoria Convention, Clause 33. See Appendix I, and Eybers, *Select Documents*, pp. 455–62.

[2] D. W. Kruger, *Paul Kruger*, I, 253–4.

[3] The Convention had to be ratified by 3 November 1881. See Addit. MSS. 44544, f. 31 *passim*. Gladstone to Kimberley, 2 October 1881, on possibility of renewing the war.

[4] C.O. 291/13. Robinson Report, dated 4 August 1881.

[5] *Parl. Pap.*, 1881, XXVIII, C.3114, p. 34. Wood's dissent.

[6] Ibid., Robinson to Kimberley, 4 August 1881, pp. 248–9, appendix no. 15 (a)–(c).

its independence. 'Within a few years', he wrote to his wife,[1] 'we shall have to take over the country.' Sir Hercules Robinson equally viewed his own handiwork without enthusiasm. Before the Convention had even been tested, under the strains of Anglo-Transvaal relations, Robinson had committed it to oblivion. 'My dear Wood,' he had remarked in private, 'it will all end in smoke.'[2]

The Queen and the *Volksraad* both immediately declared against the Convention, if for different reasons. 'Mr. Gladstone *promised* the Queen when he took office', Victoria protested on 7 August,[3] 'that there should be no reversal of *facts*; but the precedent of the Transvaal is a most unfortunate one, and naturally makes the Queen apprehensive of further attempts of this nature. . . .' The language of the *Volksraad* was even more forceful. In a rather strange metaphor, the Boer elders characterised the Pretoria Convention, and its 33 clauses, as 'a glass of milk with 33 dead flies in it'.[4] The British Press generally took the stoical line of *The Times*,[5]—'The Empire is big enough without the Transvaal'—with a fringe supporting the *Daily Telegraph*,[6] in denouncing it as a 'surrender'. Perhaps the most permanent and wide-felt comment came from a Balliol College undergraduate, who defaced a college wall by carving a caricature of Mr. Gladstone, and the ill-spelt words 'No more Jajubas. [Majubas]' His protest is still there.[7]

As Gladstone had predicted, the most closely examined and widely debated clauses dealt with the protection of the native tribes in and around the Transvaal.[8] Robinson's report, that the native chiefs had immediately protested on hearing of the terms of the Convention, gave an added edge to the criticisms of the extent of British power retained in the Transvaal. This, Victoria wrote,[9]

[1] Quoted in Walker, *De Villiers*, pp. 164–5.
[2] Quoted in Wood, *From Midshipman to Field-Marshal*, p. 71.
[3] *Letters of Queen Victoria*, 2nd ser., III, pp. 228–30. Queen to Gladstone, 7 August 1881, from Osborne.
[4] D. W. Kruger, *Paul Kruger*, I, 256–7.   [5] *The Times*, 21 July 1881.
[6] *Daily Telegraph*, 4–7 August 1881.
[7] Between staircases 13 and 14, in the garden quad.
[8] Addit. MSS. 44544, f. 180 (L.B. copy). Gladstone to Kimberley, 12 June 1881.
[9] *Letters of Queen Victoria*, 2nd ser., III, pp. 228–30. Queen to Gladstone, 7 August 1881.

is another subject which causes the Queen *great anxiety*, for she thinks we shall be guilty of *great injustice* and *cruelty* if we do not assist and support them. . . . It *was* on *this very account* . . . that Lord Carnarvon felt the Government was *forced* to annex the Transvaal; and the Queen *must* ask that . . . we shall not abandon them to the tender mercies of a most merciless and cruel neighbour, and in fact oppressor.

Gladstone's reply was full of reassurance to the Queen,[1] but he stood by the clauses of the Convention. Privately he and Kimberley had discussed the matter in a series of pencil notes hastily written from their respective seats in the Lords and Commons.[2] The notes run like a conversation, and are an excellent insight into Gladstone and Kimberley's attitude to the natives. Britain would give them such protection as they could, but this protection was not going to interfere with a determination to conciliate and pacify the Transvaal Boers:

> *Kimberley:* 'I had a telegram this morning from Robinson, saying Chiefs [had] assembled much discontented with terms.'
>
> *Gladstone:* 'Ought we not to hold friendly communications and try and reassure them?'
>
> *Kimberley:* 'Certainly—when I go to the office *I will try to concoct some telegraph*, but I apprehend that Sir H. Robinson has been doing very much this.'[3]

This question of the native tribes raised the central issue that has forever been associated with the Pretoria Convention—the question of the implications of the word 'suzerainty' in the preamble. The whole Convention turned on this word; and, all the other clauses which referred to foreign relations, or internal rule, took their power from this suzerainty 'reserved to the Crown'. The rest of the Convention—the retention of the western boundary, compensation for war losses, the trial of persons accused of uncivilised methods of war, even the matter of the debt—all these clauses counted for nil in comparison with those which were hinged on the suzerainty. The entire question of the powers of the Resident, control of frontier behaviour, treaties with native chiefs, native legislation, and foreign relations pivoted on

[1] Ibid., p. 231. Gladstone to Queen, 8 August 1881.
[2] Addit. MSS. 44226, f. 230. Gladstone to Kimberley, and vice versa, 3 August 1881. The notes are in pencil on a single sheet of House of Commons notepaper. There are no signatures, but the handwritings are unmistakable.
[3] Idem.

the definition of the suzerainty. As Gladstone explained to Victoria:

> It is hoped your Majesty will find the provisions on the part of the indigenous population to be judiciously framed; and as they form part of the Convention, which substitutes Suzerainty for Sovereignty ... upon their violation the Convention would fall to the ground.[1]

In the years which immediately followed, suzerainty came to mean many things to many people. It is as well to avoid that circular debate and explore the meaning placed on it by its architect, Gladstone. The exact phrase reads: 'Her Majesty's Commissioners ... do hereby undertake and guarantee, on behalf of Her Majesty, that from and after the 8th day of August 1881, complete self-government, subject to the suzerainty of Her Majesty, her heirs and successors, will be accorded to the inhabitants of the Transvaal territory ...'[2] In Gladstone's somewhat obscure style this power could be defined as 'a portion of sovereignty expressly reserved by us ... at the time when the suzerainty is constituted'.[3] This is hardly enlightening. However, the Gladstone–Kimberley correspondence, over the question 'Will the Boers be British subjects,' clearly reveals the intention behind the word. 'It seems to me', Kimberley wrote to Gladstone,[4] 'that we shall get into great difficulties if we treat citizens of the Transvaal State as "British subjects", because they are under the suzerainty of the Queen ... There are numerous Indian Princes under the suzerainty of the Queen or Empress of India, whose people have never, I apprehend, been considered "British subjects"...' Kimberley amplified this thinking in a later letter to Gladstone. 'My view is that the Transvalers will be in a sense British subjects,' he wrote on 8 July,[5] 'insomuch as they will be subject to British suzerainty, but that in the technical sense they will not be "British subjects" in which term is implied subjection to sovereignty.' The

---

[1] *Letters of Queen Victoria*, 2nd ser., III, pp. 230–31. Gladstone to Queen, 8 August 1881.

[2] See Appendix I—Preamble to Pretoria Convention.

[3] Addit. MSS. 44544, f. 185 (L.B. copy). Gladstone to Kimberley, 24 June 1881.

[4] Addit. MSS. 44226, ff. 172–4. Kimberley to Gladstone, 6 July 1881.

[5] Ibid., ff. 178–81. Kimberley to Gladstone, 8 July 1881.

selection of the word suzerainty was therefore a very deliberate and careful choice. As Kimberley explained, 'The Boers may if we do not make a clear distinction between them and British subjects, think we have some hidden design to bring them practically under British Sovereignty. . . .'[1]

The complex problem facing Gladstone and Kimberley was thus how to reconcile 'complete self-government' with an unspecified British overlordship over the Boers. Suzerainty was their answer. Their choice of so debatable a word, in constitutional language, was deliberate. Its very indefinite nature was its merit. It was needed to imply power without defining it. 'Our difficulty is,' as Kimberley admitted[2], 'that as the Transvaal will retain a certain dependence on the Crown, Transvaal citizens will in a sense remain British subjects. . . . In the American case we acknowledged the independence of our former colonies without any reservation.' It was vital in Kimberley's opinion, 'to avoid asserting categorically in any of our documents that the Transvaal citizens are British subjects . . .'.[3] The ambiguity in the status of the Transvaal Boers was acknowledged. Within the Transvaal State they were self-governing burghers. But, when they left the country, then 'they will retain the position and rights . . . of British subjects'.[4] The difficulties of trying to explain this to the Boer leaders was quickly solved: they were not told, nor was the suzerainty ever fully explained to them. In Kimberley's phrase 'As in the case of the Orange River Sovereignty there is no need to say anything on this point in the Convention.'[5]

A cynic might have defined this suzerainty as sovereignty at a cheaper price. It retained in Gladstone's mind the powers of sovereignty but not the obligations. There was overlordship without direct rule. There was control without administration. Suzerainty thus perfectly fitted Gladstone's requirements of defining the Transvaal's independence as freedom within locked doors. It was to give Britain the suasion needed to contain the Boers, and to curb their acts, while avoiding the pitfalls and burdens of Crown Colony government.

Gladstone once, in an unguarded moment, came near to explaining the bounds of suzerainty in words and phrases

[1] Idem.   [2] Ibid., f. 211. Kimberley to Gladstone, 16 July 1881.
[3] Idem.   [4] Idem.   [5] Idem.

which are intelligible. The term, he explained, 'is intended to signify that certain portions of sovereignty are reserved ... but that all that is not reserved is given up'.[1] The two particular 'portions of sovereignty' retained were—'those which relate to the relations between the Transvaal community and foreign countries ...', and, 'sufficient power to make provision for the interests of the natives'.[2] Lord Selborne, Gladstone's Lord Chancellor, went even further and stated that 'Suzerainty means nothing if it does not mean that the Suzerain is lord paramount of the people who are subject to it.'[3] As to the difference between suzerainty and sovereignty Selborne was equally clear: 'It has been said the [suzerainty] does not mean sovereignty. ... It involves, however, the ultimate principles of sovereignty. My noble friend [Kimberley] has happily expressed it, as an "Over-lordship".'[4] In the same debate Lord Northbrook placed suzerainty in a familiar context. In India, he claimed, 'the word had a very well-known meaning'[5]—the subordinate state could not enter into foreign relations except through the Suzerain or Paramount Power. 'This is precisely the position which the State of the Transvaal would occupy with respect to the British Empire.'[6]

Lord Salisbury was neither so sure nor so optimistic.[7] His criticisms have the ring of reality about them; and he alone, in either House, saw Gladstone's scheme for what it was, a method to cloak a calculated retreat. 'A suzerainty over a Republic is merely a diplomatic invention', Salisbury remarked,[8] 'The suzerainty contains no atom of sovereignty whatever.' He was deeply suspicious of Northbrook's explanation. 'The noble Earl the late Viceroy of India [Northbrook] compared it to the suzerainty of the Queen in India: but nobody knows better than he that suzerainty does not preclude interference with internal affairs. The peculiarity of this suzerainty in the Transvaal is that interference is absolutely excluded.' The only comparison which Salisbury thought valid was the unusual case of the Turkish Empire, 'in which suzerainty had sometimes been employed to

[1] *Hansard*, CCLXIII, col. 1859. Gladstone in Commons, 25 July 1881.
[2] Idem.
[3] *Hansard*, CCLX, col. 309. Selborne in Lords, 31 March 1881.
[4] Idem.   [5] Ibid., col. 301.   [6] Idem.
[7] Ibid., cols. 317 *passim*.   [8] Idem.

cover the loss of power by the Sultan'.[1] Indeed, Salisbury not only deplored the Government's intentions, he suspected he knew what Gladstone was attempting. 'The truth is that this is merely a device to cover surrender.'[2] And, more than this, he astutely pointed to the basic weakness in the settlement—it 'will not be enforced by any force of troops whatever'. Again and again in the coming months his words of warning became almost prophetic, a capacity normally reserved to Gladstone.

To pull these threads together: the wording and the definition of the Convention may be complex, but the objective was simplicity itself. The Pretoria Convention was not a contractual agreement between two peoples. It was, in Salisbury's term, 'a device'; a method of leaving the Transvaal without trailing the imperial cloak too obviously. Its parentage betrays its intentions. It was not a negotiated treaty. It was a document imposed on the Boers, closely based on previous 'Instructions', and drawn up by three Commissioners, who had tested the winds of opposition before implementing each particular point.

The Queen could indeed speak of the 'Old Spell-binder' up to his tricks again. It was a superb piece of Gladstonian conjuring. The Transvaal had its independence, but it did not. The natives were protected, but they were not. Only Gladstone could surely have achieved so wide an acceptance for so ambivalent a document.

The Pretoria Convention turned on a nicety: the behaviour and response of the South African Dutch. The Convention was meant to reassure them; it made no provision for land-hungry frontier Boers who might ignore the stipulated frontiers. It was designed to conciliate not coerce. Any viable settlement would probably have had to straddle both techniques. It needed to conciliate the Cape and Free State Dutch, and yet be firm with the Transvaal Boers. This is not the impossibility it might have appeared to be. The Convention went a long way to performing the first task. The Cape and Free State Dutch reacted most favourably to the settlement.[3] A firm defence of this settlement,

[1] Ibid., cols. 317–18.   [2] Ibid.

[3] *Parl. Pap.*, 1882, XLVII, C.3098, pp. 121–2. Wood to Kimberley, 5 November 1881. See also 1881, LXVII, C.2959, pp. 3–5. Robinson to Kimberley, 30 April 1881.

which they took to be most liberal, was unlikely to provoke further anti-British feeling; and, it was bound to be an excellent and timely initial warning to the Transvaal Boers.

Here was the rub. Kimberley was not prepared to take the chance. He feared to undo the settlement, and rouse the Cape and Free State Afrikaners anew, if he physically remonstrated, by military means, against the Transvaal. He was now deeply distrustful of the loyalty of Hofmeyr's Cape Dutch, and in no doubt as to where the sympathies of Brand's burghers lay.[1] Kimberley often quoted a despatch by Wood on this matter: '. . . many of the younger and more impetuous Boers, both in the Free State, and Natal, sympathise strongly with their brethren in the Transvaal, and from love of adventure may join in any war which breaks out.'[2]

The extent of Kimberley's suspicions and fears were sharply outlined in two letters passed between Gladstone and Childers in July 1881. The Premier had noted, to his surprise, that in the Army Estimates there were two full regiments of troops at the Cape. He wanted to know why they were there[3] and not in the Transvaal. Childers, as Secretary of State for War, explained:

> I should not have added to the Cape Garrison. But *Kimberley was urgent for a 2nd Regiment in consequence of the anti-English feeling in the Cape, which a Second Regiment might keep under control.*[4]

In the light of these facts there can be little doubt as to the extent and intensity of Kimberley's fears about the Cape Dutch. Thus in the last resort he was a prisoner of his own doubts and suspicions. Having come, as he believed, so close to an Anglo-Boer War, throughout South Africa, he did not wish to repeat the exercise. The possibility of a pan-Afrikaner rising haunted him, especially as it might be the signal for a general

[1] C.O. 291/13. W.O. to C.O., 30 June 1881, enclosed in Wood to Childers, 8 May 1881. Kimberley minuted (4 July): 'The observations as to the Free State show what we had to expect if the war had gone on.'

[2] C.O. 291/10. Wood to Kimberley, 11 May 1881.

[3] Addit. MSS. 44545, f. 2 (L.B. copy). Gladstone to Childers, 27 July 1881. Gladstone found it difficult to understand why 'any considerable garrison should be necessary at [the] Cape'.

[4] Addit. MSS. 44129, f. 227. Childers to Gladstone, 27 July 1881. (My italics.)

native revolt—long a contingency in the minds of the permanent officials. It made him a bad defender of his own Convention.

Kimberley's early concern over the obvious possibility of a united Afrikaner front challenging the 'Imperial Factor' had grown, and become a deep-seated belief, as the Transvaal War proceeded, and as the Afrikaners of the Cape and Orange Free State became more restive. The possibility of creating another Ireland was very real to him, and it was a fear which was transferred to the policy of his successor Lord Derby.

Indeed, it does not seem fanciful to suggest that from Kimberley's reading of the Afrikaner discontent there slowly emerged a new foundation for imperial policy towards southern Africa. By suggesting that British security was threatened not only by the Boer Republics, but by all the Dutch-speaking colonists, Kimberley had revolutionised the official approach. His growing disquiet had become a dominant factor in policy-making; his initial 'loss of nerve', it seems, had become a permanent fear.

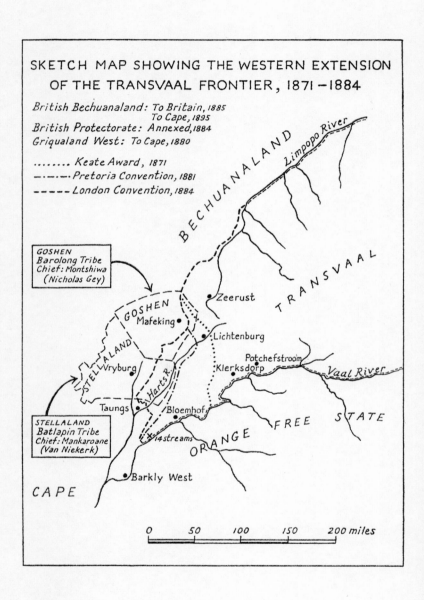

SKETCH MAP SHOWING THE WESTERN EXTENSION
OF THE TRANSVAAL FRONTIER, 1871–1884

British Bechuanaland: To Britain, *1885*
To Cape, *1895*
British Protectorate: Annexed, *1884*
Griqualand West: To Cape, *1880*

.... *Keate Award, 1871*
—·—·—· *Pretoria Convention, 1881*
— — — — *London Convention, 1884*

GOSHEN
Barolong Tribe
Chief: Montshiwa
(Nicholas Gey)

BECHUANALAND

Limpopo River

TRANSVAAL

GOSHEN
•Zeerust
Mafeking •
STELLALAND
•Lichtenburg
Vryburg •
Potchefstroom
Klerksdorp•
Harts R.
Vaal River

STELLALAND
Batlapin Tribe
Chief: Mankaroane
(Van Niekerk)

Taungs •
•Bloemhof
×14 streams

ORANGE   FREE   STATE

•Barkly West

CAPE

0   50   100   150   200 miles

V

TREK WITHOUT END:
POLICY ON A TURBULENT
FRONTIER

Boers and Fenians 1882: attractions of coercion

T HE Pretoria Convention had valiantly aimed at finding a
method of bringing peace to the *veld* without endangering
the basic Victorian concern for British supremacy in southern
Africa. The Afrikaners of the interior did not share this aspira-
tion. They were not to rest until the old name and status of the
'South African Republic' had been restored. The Convention
and the frontiers which it delineated became their special target
for attack. This assault on the recently signed treaty was largely
acted out along the south-western border of the new 'Transvaal
State'. This region soon became the most hotly contested of all
southern African frontiers. More than a geographic line was at
stake though. The total collapse of this border, and the extension of the Boer lands westwards, would by implication have
been a vital and symbolic erosion, or violation, of the Pretoria
agreement. It would also have been a most practical blow struck
against the basic intention behind that agreement: the up-
holding of British paramountcy in southern Africa. For as both
Cecil Rhodes and the Rev. John Mackenzie could shrewdly see
in May 1883, the scramble for the lands of the Tswana across
the Transvaal border meant the struggle for both control of the
interior, and for the ultimate supremacy in southern Africa.
The next two chapters of this study, concerned with the short
life-span of the Pretoria Convention, are therefore also largely

concerned with the turbulent affairs of that particular frontier, and of the fate of the Tswana chiefs beyond it. Defending the chiefs and defending the Pretoria Convention was soon to mean much the same thing.

1. Renewed local Afrikaner defiance: 'rousing the British lion'?

It was to be an awkward autumn. Even the weather seemed to conspire against the Government.[1] When the summer parliamentary session had ended on 27 August 1881, Gladstone could feel that many of the most severe problems which faced him in the spring were now well behind him. In South Africa a Convention had brought the Transvaal War to a tolerable end; in Ireland his Land Act was calculated soon to take effect; in the eastern Mediterranean there was no apparent storm to be seen; in Parliament the Irish party's tactics had been curtailed by the *clôture* measure; and in the Cabinet there did not even appear to be a forthcoming resignation.

The calm was deceptive. Just as the brief summer gave way to a biting cold northern wind, so too in the political sphere Gladstone faced unexpected squalls. First Parnell, then Kruger, rejected Gladstone's conciliatory gestures. Both thought they detected weakness in kindness. Parnell brushed aside the Irish Land Act and demanded further concessions; he condoned the rising spate of criticism to secure that end.[2] Kruger's *Volksraad* thought in a like manner;[3] they hedged over ratifying the Pretoria Convention, and wished to throw out several of the crucial clauses in the Convention.

Gladstone had keenly looked forward to the parliamentary recess, as a time to recover his energies, and to review his difficulties in the seclusion of home at Hawarden Castle. Instead, he was forced to work at an even greater pressure than during the summer. 'The indications in Ireland, and in South Africa, [are] as may develop into a very disagreeable state of things', he wrote to Bright,[4] 'and secure for us as uneasy a recess as that

---

[1] Addit. MSS. 48631, f. 59 (Hamilton Diary), 1 September 1881.

[2] P.R.O. 30/29/124. Gladstone to Granville, 27 September 1881. (Ramm, I, 295.)

[3] D. W. Kruger, *Paul Kruger*, I, 256–7.

[4] Addit. MSS. 44113, f. 158. Gladstone to Bright, 29 September 1881.

which we passed last year. On all accounts we shall unite in saying God forbid.'

Just as the Irish and Boer troubles had run a parallel course since the autumn of 1880, so now another major 'nationalistic' challenge joined the two earlier problems as a constant companion. In Egypt rumours of unrest gave way to actual violence.[1] Colonel Arabi[2] led a popular rising in certain regions aimed directly at the European population.

Gladstone was forced into grappling not only with three concurrent major threats to imperial supremacy in three widely distant parts of the Empire, but equally to reviewing the wisdom of his policy of conciliation and moderation. He knew the next Cabinet would provide a 'field day' for those ministers who had constantly advocated coercion and strength in face of resistance and unrest. Forster could justifiably call for 'more buckshot' in Ireland: Hartington could press for greater determination in handling the Suez area; and Kimberley could regain his doubts about the efficacy of attempting to conciliate Kruger. Gladstone also knew that the Cabinet rifts would once again widen. Egypt, in particular, with its challenge for either an 'advance or withdraw' policy, was bound to throw Hartington against Granville, Harcourt against Bright.[3] The ministerial battles of the autumn of 1880—which had finally claimed Argyll as its major victim—were about to be repeated with depressing similarity.

The first and most immediate result of these cumulative difficulties was Gladstone's almost total avoidance of all Cabinets. He did not once call his ministers together between 20 August and 12 October,[4]—this at a time when the three parallel crises were taking on a furious urgency. In these nine weeks the total responsibility thus fell on the weary Premier.[5]

---

[1] Addit. MSS. 44173, f. 144. Granville to Gladstone, 9 September 1881; P.R.O. 30/29/124. Gladstone to Granville, 12 September 1881; (Ramm, I, 290.); F.O. 27/2486. Minutes on the revolt.

[2] Ahmed Arabi el Hussein (1839–1911): Pasha, Colonel in Egyptian Army; Minister of War, 1882; defeated at Tel-el-Kebir and exiled to Ceylon, until 1904.

[3] *C.H.B.E.*, III, 131–3.

[4] Addit. MSS. 44642, f. 211 (Cabinet Papers). Meeting of 20 August; and f. 217 for meeting of 12 October 1881.

[5] Addit. MSS. 48631, ff. 61–89 (Hamilton Diary).

He was simply afraid to call his ministers together. Instead he tended to grapple with the concurrent problems by consulting long-standing associates: Granville on Egypt, Kimberley on the Transvaal, Spencer and Granville on Ireland.

For two crucial months, from mid-August to mid-October, Gladstone was more than ever the Government; and at a time when he was extremely weary, both in body and mind. The cumulative effect of his nine week 'personal rule' was fourfold. He retreated back to a coercive policy in Ireland;[1] he vacillated over North Africa/Egypt and allowed Bismarck virtually to split the Anglo-French *entente* over Egypt;[2] he was tempted either to renew the Transvaal War, or to let the Boers play havoc with the Convention;[3] and, above all, he yet again laid no blueprint for government. When Parliament reassembled in the new year it had no clear legislative programme to follow; nor was the Government front-bench able to speak with a united voice.

This total lack of the traditional 'autumn planning Cabinets' was to be vital. Much of the rudderless drifting of the administration in 1882 can be directly attributed to this basic omission in the normal process of government. It was yet another sign of an existing trend: this Gladstone government was steadily losing the initiative in almost every field. It was no longer able to dictate the course of events, and came to be increasingly at the mercy of unexpected developments.

The immediate dilemma was the fact that Gladstone soon achieved the worst of all ends: he accentuated the divergent force in the ministry by allowing them to play out their opposing opinions in the public arena, and not within the debating atmosphere of Cabinet. More than this, he himself stood at bay from his own ministers, and tended to take a more dogmatic approach to the cumulative crises. It was a sign of weakness not of certainty.

The repercussions were vast. In Egypt, policy vacillated between the extreme factions of the Cabinet, and finally resulted

---

[1] Parnell was arrested on 12 October 1881. See Addit. MSS. 44642, f. 217 (Cabinet Papers).

[2] *Africa and the Victorians*, pp. 76–119, 132–55.

[3] Addit. MSS. 44545, ff. 29–30 (L.B. copy). Gladstone to Kimberley, 28 and 29 September 1881, from Hawarden.

in the tragic Gordon affair—which reflected more on Government indecision than on that strange, irrational man's behaviour. Equally, in South Africa, the Afrikaners began to think that they could violate the Convention at will, for there appeared to be no discernible British policy. Within eighteen months they had established three further Boer republics, all at the expense of the native peoples of Bechuanaland and Zululand. The Warren expedition of 1884—like the Wolseley expedition to Egypt at the same times—should never have been required. Neither of these expensive imperial gestures achieved anything of worth, nor did they visibly improve imperial influence in Africa. Both reflected on Gladstone's steadily diminishing control over his own Cabinet, and ultimately over events: both betrayed the Government drifting on the tides of the moment.

It is no surprise that Gladstone wearied of it all, and wished to return to his retirement. This thought became almost an obsession with him in the winter of 1881–82. Almost daily he shared this hope with his private secretary Hamilton,[1] and with close associates. Granville grew so anxious that he secretly consulted Gladstone's doctor, Sir Andrew Clark, as to the G.O.M.'s health;[2] and Hartington was openly canvassed as the next Liberal Premier.

Gladstone's frequent suggestion that April 1882 would be a splendid moment to retire,[3]—thought to be the 50th anniversary of his entry into public affairs—can hardly have helped to stabilise an already divided Cabinet. The Radicals talked of the reform of the ministry under Hartington's leadership, but without Granville, Spencer, Selborne, or Kimberley.[4]

The uncertainties and private divisions within the Government were soon translated to the country at large. Several by-elections revealed a distinct swing to the Tories: the Liberals lost six seats.[5] The same trend was discernible in the annual municipal elections held in November.[6]

[1] Addit. MSS. 48631, ff. 72–6, 87, 90 (Hamilton Diary).
[2] Magnus, *Gladstone*, p. 293.
[3] Addit. MSS. 48631, f. 75 (Hamilton Diary). Entry for 16 October 1881.
[4] Gwynne and Tuckwell, *Dilke*, I, 439 ff.
[5] Addit. MSS. 48631, f. 61 (Hamilton Diary). Entry for 2 and 5 September 1881.
[6] Ibid., f. 79. Entry for 2 November 1881.

Gladstone blamed most things on Parnell. 'I accepted my mission in April of last year as special and temporary,' he told Bright,[1] 'I never hoped to get over it . . . sooner than in the autumn of the present year, and in most parts of it, e.g. India, Eastern Question, and perhaps finance, as much progress has been made as I anticipated or more. . . .' But, Parnell and the Fenians 'came upon us unawares'. Hence his autumn dilemma: 'This question and the question of the Transvaal still hang in the balance. From neither of them can I run away.'[2]

Although he did not wish to 'run away', he did not foresee himself as leader of the party much longer: nor did he yet have any long-term plan for Ireland or the Transvaal. 'I must, health and strength continuing, remain chained to the oar until each of them has reached what, in our way of speech, we call a settlement.'[3] He still had hopes that this would be soon: '. . . when it pleases God that that point is arrived at, then I think it will be . . . time for me to retire.'[4]

If Gladstone was an unwilling captive of events as the autumn crises dragged into winter, he was also a determined participant: he took a distinct attitude to the three crises hoping for an early settlement. Although Granville had informed him that as regards the eastern Mediterranean 'the plot thickens',[5] he would not be drawn away from his belief that it was no more than a routine Levantine disturbance.[6] Granville was left to do as best he could with foreign policy. Gladstone also took much the same attitude to Kimberley's anxious remarks about the Transvaal and the Convention. Gladstone was plainly irritated that a matter which he felt should have been settled was dragging on. He was soon to come near to uncharitable thoughts about Kruger's government, and refer to 'those dirty Boers'.[7]

Ireland, though, was a different matter. This held his atten-

---

[1] Addit. MSS. 44113 f. 158. (L.B. copy). Gladstone to Bright, 29 September 1881.

[2] Idem.   [3] Idem.   [4] Idem.

[5] P.R.O. 30/29/124. Granville to Gladstone, 31 August 1881. (Ramm, I, 289.)

[6] See Gladstone to Granville, 13 and 16 September 1881, Ibid., (Ramm, 291–3.)

[7] Addit. MSS. 44545, f. 38 (L.B. copy). Gladstone to Kimberley, 19 October 1881.

tion to the exclusion of all else. This was his obsession; this is what most held him from retirement. He could perhaps forgive the Afrikaner, Kruger, for behaving as he did; he was only a frontier Boer. Parnell was different: here was an articulate, educated and subtle parliamentarian adopting the methods of a Boer, seemingly encouraging the resort to arms, the disruption of the peace, the disregard of civil and military laws. And all this despite the Land Act which he, Gladstone, had so heroically pushed through, against stiff opposition, in the Lower House. The old Liberal undoubtedly felt he had been betrayed. He thought he could no longer trust Parnell and became exceedingly bitter about the Irish leader.[1]

This anger—and consequent sense of failure—had wide repercussions on Government policy. Coercion came to have a new attraction for Gladstone. He had deplored it, constantly and vehemently, but at what cost?—Irish revolution and Transvaal rebellion. He came seriously to consider courses of action which a mere six months previously he would have dismissed as foolhardy: the imprisonment of Parnell, and the renewal of hostilities in the Transvaal.

Gladstone came to think in terms of short, sharp doses of coercion, to settle both problems. For he saw them as two manifestations of the same evil: a skilful local leader deliberately fanning the fires of local patriotism, and directing it in such a manner as to destroy imperial security. Gladstone felt that he had already offered both cheeks and yet neither 'nationalist' leader was satisfied. 'The resources of civilisation' were about to be called upon; Gladstone's 'arm of morality' was ever there to strike at those whom he considered as the 'ungodly.'

Thus, on 12 October 1881, after nine weeks of individual activity, the ministers found themselves reassembled in the Cabinet room at Downing Street.[2] Abandoning caution, and his fears of further ministerial rifts, Gladstone had recalled the Cabinet,[3]

[1] P.R.O. 30/29/124. Gladstone to Granville, 27 September 1881. (Ramm, I, 295.) See also Magnus, *Gladstone*, p. 299; J. L. Hammond, *Gladstone and the Irish Nation*, pp. 218 ff.; Morley, *Gladstone*, III, p. 57.

[2] Addit. MSS. 44642, f. 217 (Cabinet Papers). Meeting of 12 October 1881, 2 p.m.

[3] The Cabinet was actually called to discuss the critical state of affairs in the Transvaal. See Addit. MSS. 44545, f. 32 (L.B. copy). Gladstone to Kimberley, 6 October 1881.

and took the opportunity of crushing the Irish leader. During his months of personal rule, from the seclusion of Hawarden Castle, he had brooded over Parnell's behaviour until he could accept the latter's jibes and criticisms no longer.

The fact that Gladstone did not also press for further military and coercive measures in the Transvaal, at this crucial Cabinet, turned on a technicality. The Transvaal *Volksraad* had not officially rejected the Convention, though they had torn its clauses apart in a series of violent and angry debates.[1]

Gladstone was in fact just as bitter with the Boer leader as with Parnell; and just as anxious to crush any possible Transvaal 'fenianism'. He dare not move against the Boers for fear of being accused of unnecessary aggression. He would have to wait for the formal rejection of the Convention by the *Volksraad*.

He was, however, sorely tempted to strike down both Parnell and Kruger in one broad blow. His private correspondence reveals how closely he came to doing just that.

Gladstone's concerned interest in Ireland and the Transvaal had turned to anxiety at almost the same moment. From early September the Press reported the steadily increasing violence in Ireland;[2] at the same time they guardedly published rumours that the *Volksraad* was intending to throw out the Convention.[3] By 16 September Gladstone had accepted the fact that he had another major Irish crisis on his hands;[4] by 25 September he knew that his Transvaal settlement might also fail, even before it was tried or implemented.[5]

The fears which Gladstone entertained about the Boers were brought to a head with the publication of a long denunciatory speech by Joubert, reported in the *Standard* of 24 September.[6] Gladstone immediately wrote to Kimberley enclosing the article. He wanted to know what basis there was for the *Standard's* claims. 'I hope to hear from you tomorrow, as you can by this

[1] D. W. Kruger, *Paul Kruger*, I, 255–8.
[2] *The Times*, 5 and 16 September 1881.
[3] The *Standard*, in particular, gave prominence to the Transvaal rumours. See *Standard*, 3 and 26 September 1881.
[4] P.R.O. 30/29/124. Gladstone to Granville, 16 September 1881, from Hawarden. (Ramm, I, 293.)
[5] Addit. MSS. 44544, f. 28 (L.B. copy). Gladstone to Kimberley, 25 September 1881.
[6] *Standard*, 24 and 25 September 1881.

time hardly be without official news.'[1] Gladstone took the matter so seriously that he was prepared to recall the Cabinet for this single item: 'We must have no scruple in calling a hasty Cabinet if need be, though it might not be attended by all our colleagues.'[2] Clearly Gladstone's mind was already working in the direction of the possibility of renewed hostilities, for his letter ended with this statement: 'I hope Sir E. Wood is in the way, for military questions may turn up [at the Cabinet]. The speech of Joubert reads ill, but this may turn on niceties in the translation.'[3]

He was soon to discover that there were no 'niceties' involved, either in South Africa or in Ireland.[4] 'The news from Ireland is certainly not satisfactory,' Granville wrote anxiously to Gladstone the following day.[5] 'And bad news from South Africa'.[6] Nor was Kimberley's attempt to reassure Gladstone filled with any more positive information.[7] He hastened to point out to Gladstone that the *Volksraad* had not as yet 'refused to ratify'; but he had to admit that the 'disposition of the *Volksraad* is averse'.[8] Kimberley's real opinion of the situation was betrayed in the concluding sentence of this letter. 'I have therefore telegraphed to Childers, who is in Scotland, that I think no troops should in present circumstances be withdrawn from Transvaal or Natal.'[9]

Gladstone, not unnaturally, became very alarmed. He confided in his close associate, Granville.

I am very sore and uneasy about the South African news. It means at least and at once the *detention* of the force, if there is anything

[1] Addit. MSS. 44544, f. 28 (L.B. copy). Gladstone to Kimberley, 25 September 1881.

[2] Idem.   [3] Idem.

[4] See *Letters of Queen Victoria*, 2nd ser., III, p. 240. Journal of Queen Victoria. Entry for 21 September 1881: 'Saw Lord Hartington. . . . The State of Ireland was one of the subjects touched on. . . . He feared it was very bad. The news from the Transvaal is also rather threatening.'

[5] Addit. MSS. 44173, f. 160. Granville to Gladstone, 26 September 1881, from Walmer Castle. (Ramm, I, 295.)

[6] Idem.

[7] Addit. MSS. 44226, ff. 265–8. Kimberley to Gladstone, 27 September 1881.

[8] Idem.

[9] Ibid., f. 268.

beyond an appeal to us as [a] matter of reason and justice for alterations; and may mean more.[1]

Very soon alarm gave way to anger. The more Gladstone studied this new development of an old problem, the more he became convinced that the Boers 'may be seeking to intimidate' Great Britain.[2] 'This is a very hazardous game for them.' Such a 'game' Gladstone felt could have serious repercussions.

It *will* in truth be an outrageous course. A people in revolt declining to be bound by, or rather to satisfy, the engagements contracted by those to whom were entrusted their whole civil and military destinies, strains violently the principles of good faith.[3]

The dangers of concluding a peace after a defeat at last came home to him. Gladstone thought the Boers should be reminded that Britain 'could not have carried our Transvaal policy under the circumstances existing in South Africa, unless we had a strong Government, and we spent some, if not much, of our strength in carrying it . . .'.[4] Indeed, he was so concerned that the Boers saw weakness in magnanimity that he pondered whether Wood ought not to be given special instructions on how to handle the Boer leaders. 'He ought I think to found himself on these ideas: . . . it was the . . . strength of our Administration which enabled us, rather to the surprise of the world, to spare them the suffering of a war.'[5]

Both the Transvaal and the Irish crises now simultaneously began to increase in their severity. Gladstone wrote a plaintive letter to Bright, on 29 September,[6] complaining of the problems which faced him, and of the fact that he was 'chained to the oar' until each reached some solution. He also wrote a less than

[1] P.R.O. 30/29/124. Gladstone to Granville, 27 September 1881, from Hawarden. Marked 'private'. (Gladstone's italics), (Ramm, I, 295.)
[2] Addit. MSS. 44545, f. 29 (L.B. copy). Gladstone to Kimberley, 28 September 1881 (Private).
[3] Gladstone even entertained the nightmare that the mass of the Transvaal Boers might still reject the Convention even if the *Volksraad* ratified it: 'A little extension of the strain, and we might have the constituency declining to accept the judgement of the *Volksraad*, which is only acting, as the Triumvirate were, on a commission received from the mass.' Ibid.
[4] Idem.   [5] Idem.
[6] Addit. MSS. 44113, f. 158 (L.B. copy). Gladstone to Bright, 29 September 1881, from Hawarden.

constructive letter to Kimberley the same day,[1] which is an excellent example of the many letters which he hastily despatched to his Colonial Secretary during the following week. 'The successive telegrams as they come in are not very reassuring,' he wrote. Indeed, Gladstone had come to the opinion that the Colonial Office should ascertain 'the exact military position, with reference to command of practicable ways of access to the Transvaal country'. Gladstone understood that Wood had suggested a new 'invasion route' into the Transvaal, which avoided Laing's Nek and Majuba. He considered that this could be vital: '. . . it is evidently an important point in the case that we should be sure of this access whether by Laing's Nek or otherwise; and it *may* very speedily become a question for consideration whether we ought not if need be to give ourselves this command.'[2]

Kimberley received several such 'warlike' letters from Gladstone before he finally penned a comprehensive reply,[3] in which he analysed the evolving situation and suggested the options open for action. He took as his working hypothesis the belief that the Boers were 'always ungovernable, excessively ignorant, and now elated beyond measure by their success, [and that] they probably fancy they ought to dictate their own terms. Their leaders know better, but they are very difficult to lead'.[4] His own reading of the situation in the Transvaal he suggested was rather better founded. 'I do not give up the hope that they may ratify. It is not improbable they may ask for further concessions. If they are trifling . . . we may perhaps be able to indulge them.' But, Kimberley feared it was more than this; and would thus be more difficult to settle. 'If serious it may be more hazardous to yield than to insist.'[5]

Coercion, or the threat of coercion, was the central issue at stake once again; and Kimberley knew it. He worried as to whether the Boers could be intimidated into ratification; or whether it would be 'a mistake and probably stimulate the opposition to the Convention'. His advice to the Premier was

[1] Addit. MSS. 44545, f. 30 (L.B. copy). Gladstone to Kimberley, 29 September 1881, from Hawarden.

[2] Idem.

[3] Addit. MSS. 44226, f. 269. Kimberley to Gladstone, 30 September 1881, from Kimberley House (Private).

[4] Idem.   [5] Idem.

positively Gladstonian: 'I do not see that we can do better than wait.' By holding back their coercive measures Kimberley saw the possibility of putting Britain into a strong position, if force were needed. There was to be no second Majuba.

> We might telegraph instructions to Wood to quietly prepare,[1] in such a manner as not to excite attention, for an advance, and to carefully watch whether the Boers are making military preparations and report at once any indication that they are doing so.[2]

The most remarkable feature of this illuminating Kimberley letter, which reads more like a departmental memorandum, is its note of caution, and of restraint. There is no hasty desire to reopen the war, or to avenge Colley's death. Clearly Kimberley entertained the possibility of renewed hostilities, as he suspected the Boers would launch an attack once the Convention was thrown out. But his 'wait-and-see' policy contrasts strongly with his attitude of December 1880, when he was happy to sanction coercive measures against Kruger's followers. The lesson of the Transvaal War—of a possible pan-Afrikaner front —appears to have run deep, and Kimberley now refused to be cajoled by Gladstone's anger with the Boers into taking on all Afrikanerdom.[3] It was a complete reversal of the relationship which he and Gladstone had played out during the early months of the war.

Kimberley had not only abandoned the old technique of imperial swagger in southern Africa, he now deliberately ignored his own Whig instincts, and listened to the harsh reality of experience. The Transvaal War had taught him three elemental facts: *one*, that to coerce the Transvaal Boers meant ultimately facing the Orange Free State Boers, and angering the Cape Dutch: *two*, that the Boers were excellent fighters: a colonial war on their own territory would be as difficult to wage, and win, as the struggle in Ireland—if not more so; *three*, that work-

[1] This telegram was finally drawn up by Kimberley on 1 October 1881, and circulated to Gladstone and Childers, before being secretly despatched to Wood. See Addit. MSS. 44227 f. 1. Kimberley to Gladstone, 1 October 1881, enclosing draft of secret telegram.

[2] Addit. MSS. 44226 f. 269. Kimberley to Gladstone, 30 September 1881, from Kimberley House (Private).

[3] See Addit. MSS. 44227, f. 11. Kimberley to Gladstone, 4 October 1881 (Private); and ff. 20–22. Kimberley to Gladstone, 6 October 1881.

ing through intermediaries on the *veld* had dangers all of its own. Colley had ultimately done more harm than good; Kimberley now also distrusted Wood, not so much for what he had done, but for what he might do. This unexpected judgment of the later Field-Marshal, was passed on to the already nervous Gladstone on 30 September,[1]—in response to the Premier's suggestion that Wood might give Kruger 'a hint' that Britain would not stand for Boer rejection of the Convention.[2] Kimberley rejected this out of hand: 'I have *between ourselves* by no means absolute confidence in his [Wood's] discretion.' Kimberley suggested that Wood 'half regrets the part he had played; he is very amenable to Court influence to which he looks for advancement, and though he will most honourably obey orders, he is very likely to unwittingly give a colour to his language which we do not intend. In short, he is a soldier, not a diplomatist.'[3]

Gladstone thus moved into October 1881—one of the most dramatic months in his life—in the knowledge that he had largely failed in Ireland, and that his Colonial Secretary was not quite in step with him over the Transvaal. Gladstone wanted an immediate threat of action to be made to the Boer leader: Kimberley, who was coming to know the Boer mentality rather better, preferred to wait. 'The Boers are proverbially slow in their deliberation and resolve,' he wrote to Gladstone on 1 October.[4] The pupil was instructing the master in his own principles.

The secret telegram to Wood of early October, was to bring Gladstone and Kimberley closer together. It was a happy compromise. There were to be no provocative threats to the *Volksraad*, but Britain was to take up the best possible military position just in case the Boers did revolt again. Kimberley, and not Gladstone, in fact, drafted the telegram.[5] It admirably captures Kimberley's whole approach at the crucial moment:

[1] Addit. MSS. 44226, f. 269. Kimberley to Gladstone, 30 September 1881. (Private).

[2] See Addit. MSS. 44545, f. 29 (L.B. copy), Gladstone to Kimberley, 28 September 1881.

[3] Addit. MSS. 44226, f. 269. Kimberley to Gladstone, 30 September 1881 (Kimberley's italics).

[4] Addit. MSS. 44227, f. 1. Kimberley to Gladstone, 1 October 1881.

[5] The telegram is in Kimberley's hand. It was written at Kimberley House. The C.O. did not see it until it was despatched. Ibid.

I

Secret. Are you in a position in case of need to seize the passes into Transvaal? Make preparations quietly for possible advance, and report to me at once any indication that the Boers are preparing for armed resistance.[1]

Kimberley ignored both the Cabinet and the Colonial Office in drawing up the telegram. He did not, however, ignore the War Office—perhaps remembering Childers' earlier complaints of being left in the dark. 'If you agree,' Kimberley wrote to Gladstone, 'I will telegraph to Childers for his concurrence. The telegram I think should go from him as Secretary for War.'[2]

The matter lay fallow for three days—until the vital telegram from the Transvaal later on 4 October. Kimberley was unmoved by exhortations from the Queen: 'The news from South Africa are serious. The Queen *relies confidently* on the firmness of the Gov[ernmen]t and on their *not* yielding farther to these . . . Boers. We have gone as far as we could already, but *yielding more* w[ou]ld only be weakness and injure us seriously. . .'.[3] Nor was he ruffled by anxious notes from Gladstone, such as that of 2 October: 'It will be a deplorable predicament, if the Boers attempt any broad reopening of the negotiations. I am glad to find from London that our military position is so good.'[4] Kimberley's reply was straight to the point and can hardly have comforted Gladstone. 'My expectation is that the *Raad* will ask for modifications and on this we shall have to assemble a Cabinet —probably the beginning of next week.'[5] Until the receipt of the Transvaal news—'supposing the news of the *Raad's* decision to arrive this week'[6]—he advocated the 'present policy', of diplomacy through Robinson, and secret military preparations through Wood.

The bad news arrived at 4.30 p.m. on Tuesday, 4 October, 1881. Hudson, the British Resident at Pretoria, telegraphed that 'The Triumvirate is instructed by *Volksraad* to apprize you that

[1] Idem.   [2] Idem.

[3] Guedalla: *Queen and Mr. Gladstone*, II, 168–9. See also *Letters of Queen Victoria*, 2nd ser., III, p. 241.

[4] Addit. MSS. 44545, f. 31 (L.B. copy). Gladstone to Kimberley, 2 October 1881, from Hawarden.

[5] Addit. MSS. 44227, f. 11. Kimberley to Gladstone, 4 October 1881.

[6] Idem.

in their opinion, the Convention is contrary to the Treaty of Sand River of 1852.'[1] Further telegrams revealed that the *Volksraad's* objections centred round clauses 2, 3, 8, 13, 15, 16, 18, 20, 26 and 27.[2]

Kimberley was staggered by the scope of their demands and rejections: nothing less than another Royal Commission would be acceptable, Robinson now wired.[3] Kimberley's immediate action—a telegram to Gladstone—leaves no doubt as to his despondency. 'Robinson's telegram of today. Message to you seems almost as bad as rejection. When will you have Cabinet?'[4]

Gladstone was also in no doubt about the implications of the Transvaal news. 'The telegrams received today are very grave', he replied to Kimberley,[5] 'the worst that could have been expected.' However, the course of action was by no means clear. It would hardly be diplomatic immediately to invade the Transvaal; nor even to threaten action by moving Wood's army to the Transvaal's borders. Immediate military action was thus ruled out.[6] The initiative in fact lay with the Boers. 'I shall be ready to call the Cabinet', Gladstone wrote to Kimberley,[7] 'as soon as you may think the intelligence sufficiently developed . . .'

What would Kimberley advocate at this proposed Cabinet? Dare he still advance moderation as a viable policy in the face of the Boer demands? Hartington's Whig faction within the Cabinet was bound to renew its demands for a stronger policy, if not to vindicate Majuba, at least to demonstrate that the peace had been made from a position of strength. Selborne, who represented this viewpoint in the Cabinet, spoke for the Whigs

[1] C.O. 291/11. Hudson to Kimberley (Tel.), 4 October 1881—Received 4.30 p.m., October 1881.

[2] Ibid., telegram correspondence printed in full in *Parl. Pap.*, 1882, XLVII, C.3098, pp. 87–9.

[3] Addit. MSS. 44227, f. 17. Robinson to Kimberley, 5 October 1881, enclosed in Kimberley to Gladstone, 5 October 1881.

[4] Ibid., Kimberley to Gladstone (Tel. in cypher), 5 October 1881, 10.30 p.m.

[5] Addit. MSS. 44545, f. 32 (L.B. copy). Gladstone to Kimberley, 6 October 1881, from Hawarden.

[6] Addit. MSS. 44227, ff. 20–22. Kimberley to Gladstone, 6 October 1881.

[7] Addit. MSS. 44545, f. 32 (L.B. copy). Gladstone to Kimberley, 6 October 1881.

when he remarked, on hearing the news: 'I see no alternative but that the *Volksraad* must yield, or war be renewed.'[1]

Kimberley refused to see it in these stark terms. Despite Gladstone's anxieties, and the Whig pressure, he stood his ground. Part of the explanation for his determined defence of his own approach is to be found in the telegrams from Robinson at the Cape.[2] For the first—but not the last time—this influential colonial governor had more than a hand in shaping events and policy. Kimberley now rested heavily on Robinson's despatches. The High Commissioner, being closer to the local situation, did not accept the alarmists' opinions. Indeed, Robinson strongly supported Kimberley's diplomatic approach; he advised the Colonial Secretary to be firm with the Boers over the Convention, but not to threaten them. To use diplomatic pressure, but no military sabre-rattling.

Kimberley's debt to Robinson's counsel at this crucial moments is beyond doubt. 'You will have seen Robinson's telegrams', he wrote to Gladstone in a remarkable letter on 6 October.[3] 'My present opinion is that we shall do well to follow his advice.' Kimberley's analysis of the Boer case is virtually that of Robinson's several telegrams:

> The Boers have not a leg to stand on in argument. They asked for a Royal Commission. Our instructions to the Commissioners were published. The Boer leaders who were authorised by the Boers to meet the Commissioners could have objected to any of the stipulations . . . have refused to sign, or have signed under protest. They deliberately assented, and now the *Volksraad* practically repudiate the work of the Commission. They in fact demand nothing short of independence.[4]

The most interesting portion of the letter though is Kimberley's balanced analysis of the options open for policy. He admitted that simply to give way would be disastrous: 'We should so weaken our position in South Africa that it would soon

[1] Earl of Selborne, *Memorials*, II, 4–5.
[2] Addit. MSS. 44227, f. 17. Robinson to Kimberley, 5 October 1881, enclosed in Kimberley to Gladstone, 5 October 1881.
[3] Addit. MSS. 44227, ff. 20–22. Kimberley to Gladstone, 6 October 1881.
[4] Idem.

become untenable.' Equally, he faced the fact that the Boers might force war on Britain: 'Lamentable as a renewal of hostilities would be, I see no alternative if the Boers refuse to yield but to fight it out.' However, in the last resort, Kimberley clearly believed that diplomatic pressure would do the job required: 'We may reasonably hope that if we make a firm stand now, as Robinson advises, wiser counsels may prevail.'[1]

Had Robinson's telegrams not intervened when they did Kimberley might well have given way to the 'coercive school' of opinion. Lord Selborne, a close friend of Kimberley, vigorously advised the Colonial Secretary: 'Let the *Volksraad* do what they may, *we shall stand our ground*, and not abandon, under Boer dictation, anything of importance in the terms of the Convention.'[2] This prompted Kimberley to voice his private fears to his friend.

> The situation of the Transvaal affair is very serious. The Boers are so ignorant, self-willed, and triumphant at their victories that I am not so sanguine as Robinson and Wood are that they will yield. Still Robinson and Wood ought to be much better judges than I can be of their real temper.[3]

The storm-centre of the two crises, concerning Boers and Fenians, had now been reached. Both Parnell's party, and Kruger's *Volksraad*, had thrown down their respective challenges to the Gladstonian technique of conciliating local 'colonial' governments or peoples. The Premier's patience with Parnell and Kruger ran out at almost the same moment. At Leeds, on 7 October, Gladstone warned Parnell that 'the resources of civilisation against its enemies are not yet exhausted'.[4] Parnell was quick to reply with icy invective. Gladstone, he said, was in fact a man 'prepared to carry fire and sword into your homesteads unless you humbly abase yourselves before him and before the landlords of your country'.[5]

[1] Idem.

[2] Earl of Selborne, *Memorials*, II, 4–5. Selborne to Kimberley, 10 October 1881. (Selborne's italics.)

[3] Ibid., p. 6. Kimberley to Selborne, 11 October 1881.

[4] See *The Times*, 8 October 1881; and Addit. MSS. 44173, f. 182. Granville to Gladstone, 7 October 1881. (Ramm, I, 302.)

[5] Magnus, *Gladstone*, p. 299.

Parnell had become, in the words of Gladstone's secretary, 'an utter irreconcilable'.[1] Parnell's reply steeled Gladstone's resolve to cut the Irish leader down. Clearly Gladstone had decided, by 10 October to arrest Parnell. He said almost as much, in a guarded comment, in a letter to Granville.[2]

It has often been stated that the crucial Cabinet of 12 October was called together specifically to arrest Parnell. This is not so. The Cabinet meeting had already been arranged, between Gladstone and Kimberley, to discuss 'the grave matter'— Gladstone's phrase—of the Transvaal.[3] Kimberley had wanted it immediately after he heard the rejection news from Pretoria; but Gladstone was already committed to his major speech at Leeds, fixed for Friday, 7 October.[4] Thus the Cabinet was put off to the following week, giving Kimberley time to gather further South African news from Robinson, Wood, and Hudson; and giving Gladstone time to decide to strike at Parnell.

The events between 7 October—Gladstone's Leeds speech— and 12 October—the Cabinet decision itself—came to have a critical influence on Government policy, both in Ireland and South Africa. Parnell's jibes at Gladstone had a distinct effect on the G.O.M. Equally Robinson's advice from Cape Town had a determining effect on Kimberley. Thus the proposed 'Transvaal Cabinet' became in fact an 'Irish Cabinet'. This change of agenda was a natural progression from the Gladstone and Kimberley thinking—Gladstone wanted Parnell removed from the political arena; and Kimberley wanted no more than 'watchful inactivity' in South Africa. In this sense the object of the 12 October Cabinet was completely revised. Originally envisaged as a policy-making discussion on Transvaal policy, as a result of the *Volksraad's* action, it was instead used to register and confirm two carefully predetermined policies. As Gladstone admitted to Granville, 'Although the subjects of Ireland and Transvaal are very grave, yet I think and hope

[1] Addit. MSS. 48631, f. 66 (Hamilton Diary). Entry for Friday, 16 September 1881.

[2] P.R.O. 30/29/124. Gladstone to Granville, 10 October 1881, from Hoar Cross. (Ramm, I, 303.)

[3] Addit. MSS. 44227, f. 17. Kimberley to Gladstone, 5 October 1881; and f. 18, Bickersteth to Hamilton, 6 October 1881.

[4] Addit. MSS. 44545, f. 32. Gladstone to Kimberley, 6 October 1881.

they will not call for prolonged discussion, the right course being in each case pretty clear.'[1]

Kimberley's own approach stemmed from a very clear conception of the place which southern Africa held in the broader context of imperial security and British overseas trade. On the eve of their Cabinet, of 12 October, he laid out his beliefs in a remarkably cogent and frank letter. It was in answer to a demand by Selborne—who could not attend the Cabinet owing to a cold—that a firm stand be taken in face of the Boers.

> . . . I entirely agree with you that we ought to maintain a firm attitude. But there is a disposition in so many members of our party to imagine that an Empire can be and ought to be maintained without ever resorting to force, that I foresee difficulties when it comes to the real pinch. We have, as you justly say, to consider our position not only in South Africa, but all over the world. South Africa itself is treated with far too much indifference by many of our politicians. Everyone who has considered the question knows that the route to India via the Suez Canal and Egypt cannot be relied on in case of a great war. The Cape route will then be of enormous importance to us, and it is an entire delusion to imagine that we could hold Cape Town, abandoning the rest. If we allow our supremacy in South Africa to be taken from us, we shall be ousted before long from that country altogether.[2]

What this letter does not touch on is how Kimberley proposed to maintain that supremacy. The Pretoria Convention, with its stress on informal control, and restriction of the Transvaal in the interior, was clearly the answer. Thus it was that Kimberley went to such lengths to get it ratified. He considered it a far more useful instrument to achieve his ends of supremacy than another risky war,[3] and another costly annexation of the Transvaal.

Holding such determined, and informed views, it is not

[1] P.R.O. 30/29/124. Gladstone to Granville, 10 October 1881. (Ramm, I, 303.)

[2] Earl of Selborne, *Memorials*, II, 6. Kimberley to Selborne, 11 October 1881. Written from C.O., Kimberley was obviously already in London for the Cabinet of the following day.

[3] Kimberley was haunted by the practical difficulties of waging a war on such difficult terrain as the Transvaal–Natal mountain *veld*. See Addit. MSS. 44227, f. 1. Kimberley to Gladstone, 1 October 1881: 'The difficulty of course will be transport . . .'

surprising that Kimberley had his way at the Cabinet of 12 October.[1] Gladstone recorded what an easy 'triumph' it had been for Kimberley. The Cabinet decided, 'after a short conversation, which hardly amounted to a discussion, not to entertain any question of change in the Convention by instituting a new negotiation, but to await its ratification until the 3rd of November, when the time allowed for it expires. . .'.[2] Gladstone's own Cabinet notes are even more to the point: 'Transvaal. Lord Kimberley stated the case . . . i.e. no change before ratification.'[3]

The Transvaal was in fact the second item on the Cabinet agenda. The first was Ireland; and the Cabinet had no hesitation in accepting Gladstone's decision to arrest Parnell.[4] Forster, after all, had been pressing for this since June 1881,[5] and most vociferously since early October.[6] The other two items were Egypt—where Granville revealed a lull in the crisis;[7] and the Channel tunnel[8]—that nebulous scheme which has ever fascinated the English people.

That same evening Gladstone announced the Cabinet decisions, in a dramatic speech in London's Guildhall.[9] During the

[1] Addit. MSS. 44642, f. 217 (Cabinet Papers). Meeting of Wednesday, 12 October 1881, at 2 p.m.

[2] *Letters of Queen Victoria*, 2nd ser., III, pp. 241–3. Gladstone to Queen, 12 October 1881, from Hawarden.

[3] Addit. MSS. 44642, f. 217 (Cabinet Papers).

[4] Addit. MSS. 48631, f. 72 (Hamilton Diary). Entry for 16 October 1881; and Addit. MSS. 44642, f. 217 (Cabinet Papers). Point 1.

[5] Addit. MSS. 44158, ff. 167, 172. Forster to Gladstone, 29 May and 1 June 1881. See also P.R.O. 30/29/124. Gladstone to Granville, 1 June 1881. (Ramm, I, 277.)

[6] Addit. MSS. 44545, f. 31. Gladstone to Granville, 3 October 1881, enclosed in Forster to Gladstone, 2 October 1881. (Ramm, I, 297–8.) See also Gladstone's reply in Addit. MSS. 44159, ff. 29, 39. Gladstone to Forster, 3 October 1881.

[7] See Addit. MSS. 44173, f. 182. Granville to Gladstone, 7 October 1881: P.R.O. 30/29/124. Granville to Gladstone, 3 November 1881, re the Anglo-French approach on trade. See also Addit. MSS. 44173, f. 165. Granville to Gladstone, 1 October 1881; P.R.O. 30/29/124. Gladstone to Granville, 2 October 1881; Addit. MSS. 44173, f. 175. Granville to Gladstone, 4 October 1881; P.R.O. 30/29/124. Gladstone to Granville, 5 October 1881. (Ramm, I, 301–9.)

[8] Addit. MSS. 44642, f. 217 (Cabinet Papers). Point 4, Cabinet of 12 October 1881.

[9] Magnus, *Gladstone*, p. 300, and Morley, *Gladstone*, III, 61 ff.

course of his long oration news arrived that Parnell had already been arrested: so Gladstone included this in his speech, to the enormous satisfaction of the audience. It was the climactic moment of months of concern over Ireland; and it left Gladstone exhausted.[1] Perhaps too, he privately had second thoughts as to the wisdom of the act. Would Parnell prove a greater inspiration to the Fenians when in jail than when openly attacking him?

The news of Parnell's imprisonment was the talk of Britain: the 'grave matter' of the Transvaal was now banished from the headlines. Kimberley moved in comparative quiet and freedom. Though Gladstone himself was still 'somewhat oppressed by the Transvaal news',[2] and made it the first item of his letter to Queen Victoria reporting his Guildhall speech,[3] it was hardly a matter of public concern any more. Most observers considered that it was not the Boers who were destroying the normal process of legislative government, or threatening to wreck imperial security, but rather the Irish parliamentarians and Irish Fenians.[4]

Thus it was that there came about the supreme irony of British interest in the Transvaal actually fading just as the South African crisis moved closer and closer to an explosive end—the renewal of the war. The Press tended to say what Queen Victoria had already telegraphed to Gladstone: 'Much pleased that you are acting with vigour in Ireland, and that you are firm about the Transvaal. Parnell's arrest a great thing.'[5]

As 3 November approached (the day the Convention *had* to be ratified), the omens for a peaceful solution to the South African dilemma were hardly encouraging. The native chief Montshiwa reported that the Boers on the western Transvaal frontier were raiding cattle and stealing corn, while others were encroaching on to his tribal lands. 'The treaty you made with

---

[1] P.R.O. 30/29/124. Gladstone to Granville, 21 October 1881, from Hawarden. (Ramm, I, 304–6.)

[2] Addit. MSS. 48631, f. 72 (Hamilton Diary).

[3] *Letters of Queen Victoria*, 2nd ser., III, 244. Gladstone to Queen, 13 October 1881, from Downing Street.

[4] Addit. MSS. 44173, f. 191. Granville to Gladstone, 21 October 1881. (Ramm, I, 305–6). See also *The Times*, 14 October 1881.

[5] *Letters of Queen Victoria*, 2nd ser., III, p. 244. Queen to Gladstone (Tel. in cypher), 13 October 1881.

the Boers is no peace, *they break it every day,*' he complained to Wood.[1]

Just as it seemed that a renewal of hostilities was inevitable, and Britain's position in South Africa 'hangs in the balance,'[2] Kimberley's firm diplomacy paid dividends. The Boers reduced their objections to the financial clauses of the Convention.[3] Kimberley took heart from this news. He wrote to Gladstone, who was then ill in bed: 'I think it augurs well for the ratification that their demands are now confined to a debtor and creditor account.'[4] The Premier's reaction was characteristic of Gladstone, who had lost all faith in Kruger's nation: 'I had already learned[5] that the Boers (a dirty lot!) had now taken their stand on £.s.d., and I think, with Robinson, we need only hold our ground . . .'.[6]

The Premier and his Colonial Secretary were now completely united in their approach to the Boers. 'I am very glad we are so entirely agreed,' Kimberley wrote to Gladstone on 21 October.[7] 'If hereafter it should be found that the burden on the Transvaal finances is really more than can reasonably be borne, an application for a remission of part of our charge might properly be made and considered . . .'.[8] However, Kimberley too found the Transvaal demands more than audacious: 'It is preposterous to make a demand for a "debtor and creditor" account[9] as a ground for not ratifying the Convention, where the

[1] C.O. 291/10. Montshiwa to Wood, enclosed in Wood to Kimberley. 19 October 1881. See Minute No.: Transvaal 9014, Just to Bramston. (Montshiwa's italics.)

[2] Addit. MSS. 48631, f. 74 (Hamilton Diary). Entry for 16 October 1881.

[3] *Parl. Pap.*, 1882, XLVII, C.3098, pp. 98 ff. Wood to Kimberley, 19 October 1881, and Robinson to Kimberley, 19 October 1881.

[4] Addit. MSS. 44227, f. 27. Kimberley to Gladstone, 19 October 1881.

[5] Presumably a copy of Robinson's telegram of 19 October (to Kimberley) had been sent immediately from the C.O. to Gladstone. It is not though in Gladstone Papers. See C.O. 291/10. Robinson to Kimberley (Tel.), 19 October 1881.

[6] Addit. MSS. 44545, f. 38. Gladstone to Kimberley, 19 October 1881, from Hawarden.

[7] Addit. MSS. 44227, f. 29. Kimberley to Gladstone, 21 October 1881.

[8] Idem.

[9] The Transvaal objections centred around clauses X, XI (financial matters) in the Convention. These clauses 'provided that the Transvaal should take over the debts for which the South African Republic was liable up to

whole matter has been fully laid before the representatives of the Boers, and the charge accepted by them ...'.[1]

Gladstone summarised the position as it stood on 21 October, in a brief note to Granville. 'No new point of doubt has arisen in the Transvaal and the Boers rather dirtily haggling about LSD—We simply hold our ground.'[2]

Four days later, on 25 October, Kimberley was able to send Gladstone some very welcome information: 'The news just received[3] of the ratification of the Transvaal Convention is a great relief.'[4] However, it was a premature triumph. On 27 October Robinson cabled the details of the actual terms of the *Volksraad's* ratification.[5] It appeared that while the Boers had accepted the terms of the negotiated Convention, they had added a preamble of their own creation. It makes strange reading.[6] They agreed to the existing Treaty, but immediately went on to say they were 'not satisfied with this Convention [it being] an unsatisfactory State document;' and that the *Volksraad* ratified it only for 'fear of renewed bloodshed between people who are bound mutually to forbear and respect each other', and to halt 'a new dissension between the white races in South Africa which would ... undermine the welfare of every state and Colony of South Africa'. In short, the *Volksraad* 'finds itself *compelled* to ratify it by the same motives which led the Triumvirate to sign'.[7]

It was hardly a gracious start to the new Anglo-Boer relationship. Kimberley did not quite know how to take the 'preamble'. Did it in any way lessen the effectiveness of the Convention? Gladstone, who must by then have been thoroughly weary and wary of the Boers, was of the firm opinion that 'ratification is a simple and formal *Aye* to the Treaty, and that the

the annexation, and the expenditure, £265,000, incurred by Britain on its behalf since the annexation.' (Ramm, I, 305, note 5.)

[1] Idem.

[2] P.R.O. 30/29/124. Gladstone to Granville, 21 October 1881. (Ramm, I, 305-6.)

[3] C.O. 291/10–11. Robinson to Kimberley (Tel.), 25 October 1881.

[4] Addit. MSS. 44227, f. 31. Kimberley to Gladstone, 25 October 1881.

[5] C.O. 291/11. Robinson to Kimberley (Tel.), 27 October 1881.

[6] It is printed in full in *Parl. Pap.*, 1882, XLVII, C.3098, pp. 94-9. Hudson to Robinson (Tel.), 27 October 1881.

[7] Idem.

sense of it cannot be affected, nor the force of it impaired, by any preamble'.[1] His advice to Kimberley on future policy was equally clear-minded:

> We, I suppose, shall take the explanations in the best sense of which they are susceptible, but shall maintain the full force of the Treaty which is not in any sense provisional though open to change like all other instruments by mutual consent.[2]

The matter, however, did not end here.[3] The 'dirty Boers' had yet another card up their sleeve. They asked to be allowed to announce the ratification, via their own representatives, 'to illustrious Governments'. This was an awkward request, as the Transvaal were by the terms of the Convention prevented from maintaining foreign embassies, or conducting their own foreign relations.

In the Colonial Office opinion was divided on how to react to the request. Both Courtney, the parliamentary under-secretary, and Herbert, the permanent under-secretary, felt Britain should say no:[4] they saw it as a breach of the Convention. Kimberley decided to overrule them. 'Such a communication would not be a violation of the Convention', he explained.[5] 'The fact of the Boers making the communication independently makes it more apparent to all the world that they have freely accepted the conditions under which they are henceforth to be governed.'[6]

Gladstone was of like mind. 'I agree with you very decidedly

[1] Addit. MSS. 44545, f. 44 (L.B. copy). Gladstone to Kimberley, 30 October 1881.

[2] Idem.

[3] Britain's acceptance of the Boer ratification took some time as Kimberley demanded to see the full text of the *Volksraad's* discussions, and the exact wording of the ratification and the contentious 'preamble'. He suspected the Boers might even add further provisos to the ratification, if left to their own devices. See Addit. MSS. 44227, f. 48. Kimberley to Robinson (Tel.), no date, but probably 1 November 1881. See also Kimberley to Gladstone, 1 November 1881, f. 44, enclosed in Kimberley to Robinson (Tel.), in draft.

[4] C.O. 291/11. Minutes by Leonard Courtney and Robert Herbert, 1 November 1881.

[5] Addit. MSS. 44227, f. 44. Kimberley to Gladstone, 1 November 1881.

[6] Idem.

that the *Volksraad* should not be hindered from making the proper communications to foreign powers.'[1] He had been thinking the whole matter over, and had come to the opinion that the recent Boer preamble and request could have 'no more effect on the ratification than any rigmarole which you or I might prefix to a cheque giving a man a £100'.[2]

When the details of this arrangement were sent to the Foreign Office[3] Granville was most unhappy.[4] He completely disagreed with Kimberley and Gladstone; but, finally gave way under protest.[5] The Queen was also far from sanguine when she learnt of this development. She too protested strongly—equally to no avail.[6]

Kimberley was determined not to allow any complication to unsettle the fact of the ratification, nor to obscure the apparent triumph which his policy had secured. Indeed, he was prepared to go to great lengths to see that the new Anglo-Boer Treaty was not disturbed. If it meant turning the other cheek for the moment he was ready to do that as well. In Gladstone's words, 'it is for us to minimise this rather tricky and ineffectual manifestation', of Boer reluctance to admit the loss of their independence in the Convention.[7] In agreeing with Gladstone Kimberley revealed the thinking behind his 'kid glove' handling of the Boers: 'At all events I think this view would afford us a way out of the difficulty which would be caused by a wrangle with the Transvaal Government on this point.'[8]

The lengths to which Kimberley went to be conciliatory, to avoid 'a wrangle' at this difficult period, were to be the cause of much controversy in the years which immediately followed. A growing body of critics were to point to his reluctance to

[1] Addit. MSS. 44545, f. 47 (L.B. copy). Gladstone to Kimberley, 3 November 1881, from Hawarden.

[2] Idem.

[3] C.O. 291/11. C.O. to F.O., 7 November 1881.

[4] P.R.O. 30/29/135, f. 76. Kimberley to Granville, 9 November 1881.

[5] Ibid., f. 78. Draft reply to Kimberley. No date.

[6] Addit. MSS. 44227, f. 51. Kimberley to Gladstone, 8 November 1881, enclosed in Ponsonby to Kimberley, 8 November 1881.

[7] Addit. MSS. 44545, f. 46 (L.B. copy). Gladstone to Kimberley, 2 November 1881, from Hawarden.

[8] Addit. MSS. 44227, f. 44. Kimberley to Gladstone, 1 November 1881.

challenge the Transvaal's behaviour in late 1881 as leading to Boer expansion over frontiers, and to disregard for the Convention in general. Dilke, in particular, regarded Kimberley's policy as too conciliatory.[1]

The controversy was to centre around four aspects of Kimberley's conduct of policy in autumn 1881. There were, first, those like Granville, who felt that the Boers should not have been allowed to communicate the Convention to foreign powers.[2] They claimed that this weakened those clauses in the Convention which expressly reserved to Britain all the Transvaal's external relations.[3]

A second, and more serious charge, was that Kimberley refused to object to the 'preamble' which the Transvalers had attached to the Convention when ratifying it, as his policy was 'too weak'. It may have been a questionable act, but it was not unintentional. Indeed, it was at the core of his new approach. As he explained to Gladstone, when submitting the draft of his reply to the *Volksraad*, he was ignoring the preamble 'to avoid controversy on the objections of the *Volksraad*. Otherwise it would be easy to show that they have no foundations.'[4] Gladstone's reply is equally interesting: 'I wish to keep a little further than you do from any admission that the carping preamble can have any ... effect on the ratification.'[5] Gladstone thus more than shares the responsibility for not rebutting the preamble immediately.

The third major criticism concerned a matter not resolved

[1] Addit. MSS. 44149, f. 51. Dilke to Granville, 14 December 1881, from Toulon.

[2] P.R.O. 30/29/135, f. 76. Kimberley to Granville, 9 November 1881.

[3] In fairness to Kimberley it should be noted that while he acceded to this request, he made it plain to the Boers that this did not affect the binding clauses in the Convention. In particular, he had Robinson remind them that all Transvaal diplomatic conduct in regard to the proposed rail-line to Lourenço Marques must go via the Foreign Office to Lisbon. See C.O. 291/11. Kimberley to Robinson, 16 January 1882, and *Parl. Pap.*, 1882, XLVII, C.3098, pp. 122–4.

[4] Addit. MSS. 44227, f. 85. Kimberley to Gladstone, 6 December 1881, from Kimberley House. See also Addit. MSS. 44545, f. 44 (L.B. copy). Gladstone to Kimberley, 30 October 1881: 'Such one-handed interpretations are contrary to the nature and law of treaties.'

[5] Addit. MSS. 44545, f. 69 (L.B. copy). Gladstone to Kimberley, 10 December 1881, from Hawarden.

until the Anglo-Boer War of 1899. This was the title of the Boer state. In the Pretoria Convention the old republic was named as the 'Transvaal State'. It was chosen as a compromise name to imply internal self-rule, but also to make it clear that full independent republican status had *not* been restored. The Boer leaders ignored this point, both in the discussions which lead to the Convention, and in the ratification itself.[1] They spoke only of the 'South African Republic', and refused to talk of the 'Transvaal State'.[2] Once again Kimberley declined to press them on the matter, though he privately expressed his annoyance at their action. 'An asserture on the part of the Boers cannot give the State any legal name but that which the Convention gives it, as the legal existence of their state rests on that document only.'[3] When the Colonial officials taxed him on the matter he bluntly replied that the British Government 'can't make a serious quarrel about it . . .'.[4]

Lastly, Kimberley's critics pointed to the fact that in his haste to see the Convention ratified, he turned a blind eye to Boer behaviour on the Transvaal borders. In the light of what did happen, it is impossible either to ignore or discount this charge. While Kimberley had worked hard to bring the Convention about, he made no attempt to defend it. And, it is at least arguable, that had he protested more strongly, and more frequently, over Boer behaviour on the western frontier, in the autumn and winter of 1881–82, the Convention might well have survived beyond 1884, and the Bechuana tribes have been saved from the 'freebooters'. As it was, Kimberley did little to dispel the Boers' impression that they could do as they liked on their western frontier.[5] Robinson kept Kimberley well informed of their

[1] *Parl. Pap.*, 1882, XLVII, C.3098, pp. 46–85. Robinson to Kimberley (Tel.), 14 August 1881. Full details and Robinson's angry comments.
[2] C.O. 291/10. Minute by Herbert, 10 August 1881, commenting on *The Times*' article of 9 August: 'The Boer Government has issued a proclamation to the people announcing the establishment of the South African Republic.' Kimberley's comment: 'I *do not* think it would be advisable to raise the question at all events till we hear further.'
[3] C.O. 291/11. Minute by Kimberley, 2 November 1881. (Transvaal Minute No. 19036.)
[4] Idem.
[5] *Parl. Pap.*, 1882, XLVII, C.3381, p. 46. See Transvaal Proclamation of 21 October 1881.

activities,[1] and called on the Colonial Secretary to act more sharply with Kruger.[2] But, Kimberley refused to be moved; and Robinson ultimately gave up trying. The pattern for 1882–83 had been set.

Kimberley moved as a deaf man through the growing criticism, and at the last Cabinet of 1881—on 10 November[3]—he went a step further, and advocated the recall of those regiments sent to South Africa to fight the Boers. With Gladstone's aid the measure was carried; and the troops on the *veld* were reduced to 4,700.[4] Policy had indeed come full circle. Not only had Kimberley abandoned that policy which had led to the Transvaal War, but he was determined to take the new approach to the Boers, despite the difficulty of resting supremacy on the slender pillars of informal paramountcy and conciliation.[5]

Gladstone was as eager as Kimberley to make the new policy work: if for slightly different reasons. Throughout 1881 Gladstone regarded the South African dilemma as an annoying, recurrent aggravation; and, in late 1881, he wanted it out of the way, as swiftly as was compatible with security, so as to face the Irish crisis. Equally the thought of an early retirement was still with him, and had become almost an obsession. 'There is no doubt that the bent of Mr. Gladstone's mind is on resignation in the course of next year,' Hamilton wrote in his Journal on 16 October 1881.[6] A month later he wrote of the same desire: 'Mr. Gladstone's mind continues to work on the question of disentangling himself from office.' Gladstone confided in Hamilton that Ireland, and the Transvaal, alone kept him from doing so. Once he had ridden out both these storms he would definitely

[1] *Parl. Pap.*, 1882, XLVII, C.3098, pp. 139–45. Hudson to Robinson, 5 December 1881, is particularly valuable. It includes several reports from men on the spot.

[2] C.O. 291/15. Robinson to Kimberley, 5 December 1881, enclosed in Hudson to Robinson.

[3] Addit. MSS. 44642, f. 220 (Cabinet Papers), Thursday, 10 November 1881.

[4] Ibid., the troops were not reduced any further, as 'Lord Kimberley stated that affairs in Zululand had not yet attained a settled aspect'.

[5] Queen Victoria was quick to read the signs, and protested vehemently over the reduction of the troops. See Guedalla, *Queen and Mr. Gladstone*, II, 172, no. 820, Ponsonby to Gladstone, 4 November 1881.

[6] Addit. MSS. 48631, ff. 74–87. Entries for 16 October 1881 and 23 November 1881.

retire completely to Hawarden, 'making the reform of Parliament procedure his final political stroke'. At the very latest Gladstone put this at mid-1882.

His haste in trying to settle the Boers, and their demands, thus becomes all the more understandable. Gladstone had voluntarily cast himself in the rôle of 'caretaker', openly recognising Hartington as the man who should lead the Liberal party on into the later 1880s and '90s. It is possible to read too much into his frequent talk of retirement; but, it does not seem fanciful to suggest that a major reason why he yet again failed to call the vital November planning Cabinets[1] was not merely fear of Cabinet rifts—a very real danger—but also because he had lost interest in the broader aspects of Government policy, being concerned only to dispense with the two outstanding crises, in Ireland and the Transvaal. This becomes all the more plausible when it is shown that Gladstone deliberately ignored criticism, both publicly and privately, over his conduct as leader of the Government.[2] 'The Tory Press are commenting on the "indecency" of the absence of Cabinet meetings in the present state of things in Ireland', Hamilton wrote on 3 December, 'I confess I somewhat share the feelings.'[3] In fact Gladstone only called one more Cabinet that year—on 10 November—to nominate a Cabinet committee on Ireland.[4] Thus between 20 August 1881, and 6 January 1882, there were only two Cabinets.[5] A casual observer of this fact alone might well be tempted to think that the Liberal Government had nothing to worry about and nothing to talk about. Unfortunately, quite the opposite was true.

A strange optimism began to cloud Gladstone's understanding of events. He saw the imprisonment of Parnell as more of an answer to the Irish troubles than it really was; and equally he thought, or hoped, that in the Pretoria Convention there lay

[1] The Cabinet did meet once, on 10 November 1881, but the agenda was: Transvaal, Ireland, Zululand. See Addit. MSS. 44642, f. 220 (Cabinet Papers).

[2] Addit. MSS. 48631, f. 106 (Hamilton Diary), Christmas Day, 1881.

[3] Ibid., f. 93 (Hamilton Diary), 3 December 1881. See also entry for 8 December 1881, f. 95.

[4] Addit. MSS. 44642, f. 220 (Cabinet Papers), Thursday, 10 November 1881.

[5] Ibid., ff. 217 and 220. Meetings of 12 October and 10 November 1881. The first Cabinet in 1882 was on 6 January. See also Addit. MSS. 44643, f.2.

the complete solution to the Boer dilemma. Accordingly, in November, he celebrated his release from these crises with many afternoons of tree chopping,[1] a sure indicator of Gladstonian morale. Christmas Day 1881 found Gladstone in excellent spirits.[2]

It required Queen Victoria's deep pessimism to come closer to the true state of affairs. 'The Queen wishes Mr. and Mrs. Gladstone a happy new year, though the clouds which overhang the political horizon are not very encouraging, and darken the opening of '82.'[3] Victoria's pessimism stemmed more from instinct than from detailed knowledge. But in fact she was unwittingly close to the truth. The omens for the future were not encouraging. The imprisonment of Parnell did not halt the violence in Ireland, and it hardly helped the working of the Land Act. In the eastern Mediterranean the Egyptian crisis was not over: it was merely going through a momentary lull. Equally in Europe, Bismarck was coming to see the possibilities for diplomatic mischief in the Anglo-French *entente* over Egypt.

Nor were prospects any better within the Government. The lack of Cabinets, Gladstone's autocratic isolation at Hawarden, the 'stop-go' policy on Ireland, the retreat before Boer demands, Radical dissatisfaction with the Whigs and the Whigs' dissatisfaction with Gladstone—all these factors cut at Cabinet solidarity and at the normal processes of government by the executive.

Local events in the Cape Colony were also taking on an aspect that could only lead to future discord. On the broader front, Kimberley was forced to give up his plans for transferring further native areas to Cape rule;[4] and he was even forced to consider taking Basutoland away from the Cape. In Zululand the defeat and removal of Cetewayo had solved nothing;[5] and

[1] Addit. MSS. 48631, f. 89 (Hamilton Diary). Entry for Wednesday, 23 November 1881. See also f. 90, entry for Friday (?), 20 November 1881, for a fascinating account of life at Hawarden at this time.

[2] Ibid., f. 106.

[3] *Letters of Queen Victoria*, 2nd ser., III, p. 250. Queen to Gladstone, 31 December 1881.

[4] Annexation of the Transkei territories was postponed, on setting up of a Cape Commission to consider Native policy generally. *Parl. Pap.*, 1882, XLVII, C.3112, p. 178.

[5] C.O. 48/501, D. 38. Minutes by Herbert.

in Damaraland open hostilities had broken out.[1] While in Natal hopes of granting the colonists self-government, and of letting them 'pay their way', came to naught.[2]

Major problems elsewhere in southern Africa were also in an embryonic stage. In Berlin a merchant, by the name of von Weber, was beginning a campaign in the German Press calling for a German settlement in South-West Africa; and British misreading of the campaign was also beginning. Lord Odo Russell assured Granville that such a scheme had no chance of being taken up by Bismarck. This information was passed on to the Colonial Office.[3] Kimberley duly informed a worried Robinson at the Cape that all was well, and that Bismarck had no designs on the area to the north.

But even this major diplomatic blunder did not hold the latent dangers which were present in the trend of events in the interior of Africa, in the Transvaal itself. The Boers saw what they wanted to see in the Convention. The majority took the agreement to be a straight return to full republican status; and they behaved accordingly. Their leaders did little to dispel their reading of the Convention. Within days of the ratification the continual 'roll' of the Afrikaner herdsmen further out across the *veld* had intensified.

They moved largely in two directions. A great many Boers began to infiltrate the new land granted by the Convention on the western boundary. Within a short while many were crossing not only the original Keate boundary line of 1871, but also the new Convention boundary into Bechuana territory.[4] A lesser number went to the east, into Swazi grazing areas, and on to the land of the old Zulu kingdom, in Natal.[5]

The era of *trekking* had reappeared; and not only in respect of land hunger. There was a conscious revival of the spirit of the 1830s, when the Triumvirate organised a 'festival of thanks-

[1] *Parl. Pap.*, 1881, LXVII, C.2950, p. 376. Kimberley to Robinson, 12 April 1881.

[2] Natal was not self-governing until 1893. See C.O. 179/138. Wood to Kimberley (Tel.), 22 October 1881. See also Addit. MSS. 44227, ff. 35 ff. Kimberley to Gladstone, 29 October and 21 November 1881.

[3] C.O. 48/498 F.O. to C.O., 22 September 1880, enclosed in Russell to Granville, 18 September 1881.

[4] Agar-Hamilton, *The Road to the North*, pp. 183–216.

[5] De Kiewiet, *Imperial Factor*, p. 309 ff.

giving' for the return of their independence—to be held at Paardekraal, from 13 to 16 December 1881.[1] The *trek* had never been forgotten, but it had also never been so consciously recalled. Speaker after speaker referred to that early epic journey in their lives. Kruger, who had walked the *trek* as a boy of ten, reminded his listeners of their early struggles, and of how each time the Creator had guided them onward. The ceremonies culminated on 16 December, with a call by Kruger to all true Afrikaners throughout South Africa to be bound together in a patriotic unity.[2] Just as 16 December 1838 had been a turning point in the life of the *trekkers*, so now 16 December 1881 was, in Kruger's words, a beginning 'of still greater salvation'.[3]

The significance of the occasion was not lost on the Colonial Office. Hemming noted the reference to 16 December—Dingaan's Day—and explained the Afrikaner's pride in that victory.[4] He noted that it hardly augured well for the future, particularly as greetings were read out from branches of the Afrikaner *Bond* in other parts of South Africa, and that the audience included delegates from the Orange Free State.

The celebration was in fact more important than historians have hitherto allowed. The strength of the Transvaal clearly did not lie in the diminutive extent of its man-power reserves; nor in its ramshackle financial or administration resources. Its strength lay rather in its symbolic independence in the midst of an area of British imperial paramountcy; of itself it had little strategic value. Thus any emotive patriotic movement within the Transvaal was bound to be of vast importance.

The Paardekraal Festival, with its deliberate cultivation of what has become the '*trekker* tradition' in South African politics—recourse to Slagter's Nek, the annexation of Natal and the Transvaal, as examples of imperial tyranny—gave the republicans a new courage for independence. They were made to feel that the *trek* was yet in progress. And when it is remembered

[1] C.O. 291/11. (Transvaal Minute No. 19121.) Wood to Kimberley, 5 November 1881.

[2] *Parl. Pap.*, 1882, XLVII, C.3098, p. 101. Robinson to Kimberley, 31 December 1881.

[3] D. W. Kruger, *Paul Kruger*, I, 264. Kruger: 'Die Here het ons tot hier toe gelei. . . .'

[4] C.O. 291/11. Minute by Hemming, No. 19121.

that all three members of the Triumvirate were of *trekker* stock, this became all the more acceptable to the Transvaal burghers.

Indeed, though it was still two years before Kruger became the sole President, and though the Transvaal was still economically weak,[1] with the vague British suzerainty still in existence, the state did not lack either for leadership or for emotive strength. Its future was not assured, nor its ultimate independence inevitable. But with 'Oom Paul' at the helm it had more than a fighting chance. The rise of Kruger's republic had in fact begun.

2. The drive for 'Lebensraum': Boer frontier expansion August 1881–July 1882

No sooner had Kruger pushed the Convention through the *Volksraad* than he began to work to undo the Treaty. He described Britain's attitude to Transvaal independence in characteristic terms: ' "First you put your head quietly in the halter, so that I can hang you up; then you may kick your legs about as much as you please." *That is what they call self-government.*'[2]

Kruger's behaviour—which so annoyed Gladstone and perplexed Kimberley—revealed how subtle was his approach to the question of Anglo-Boer relations. He had signed the peace and Convention to retain the advantages gained at Majuba; and he had pushed the Convention to ratification to avoid a renewal of the war. Now that he had carried out his side of the 'bargain'—in getting his fellow burghers to agree to the Convention—he felt free to point out its shortcomings, and to talk of being forced under duress to accept what the Royal Commission had proposed. He allowed the *Volksraad* to affix the strange 'Preamble' to the Convention as a mean of expressing his, and the Transvalers', sense of injustice at not having regained their complete republican status.

A similar manifestation of this attitude was Kruger's deliberate reluctance to control the Transvaal's frontier Boers. It was a studied case of diplomatic 'brinkmanship'. Kruger gave his burghers free rein to behave as they wished on the Transvaal

---

[1] In Professor Kruger's phrase, the finances were in "'n swak toestand'. D. W. Kruger, *Paul Kruger*, I, 254.

[2] M. Nathan, *Paul Kruger, His Life and Times*, p. 145. (My italics.)

frontiers, to test the resolve behind the newly signed Treaty, and newly defined borders. Meeting no challenge, apart from verbal admonishing, he became ever bolder, and finally threw a quasi-official Transvaal protection over the 'freebooters' who soon set up Boer states in the Tswana lands.

These manifold moves to undermine the very basis of the Convention began early. A mere ten days after the Triumvirate had signed the Treaty, Robinson reported that the Transvaal Boers were already disregarding many clauses of the agreement. And by October 1881, three months later, one of the Tswana[1] chiefs, Montshiwa, was under constant Boer attack.[2] This attack increased in tempo and ferocity with the weeks, so that Hudson, as the new British Resident in Pretoria, could report on 5 December 1881 that 'altogether there seems to be a desperate muddle down there, and how the Boer Government are going to deal with it, or can deal with it, is a serious question'.[3]

It was on the matter of the attitude of the Boer Government that so much depended. Kruger's apologists have suggested that he had not the power to control the frontier Boers even if he had wanted to do so. In fact such orders as he did issue on the matter hardly put an end to the frontier encroachment. The 'Procla-mation' of 21 October 1881 is a good example. It was addressed to the 'commandants and officers on the western borders in the districts within the line prescribed by the Convention', and it called on the Boers in the area to 'take no part in the blood-thirsty conflicts of wild barbarians . . .' (i.e. the Tswana tribes) on 'pain of prosecution according to the law'.[4]

As the 'law' was shown to be implicated in the local quest for land, Kruger's proclamations were hardly of the most effective kind. Nor were they intended to be. Within months Kruger revealed his true hand when he despatched Joubert to the area 'to report' on the disturbances; and it then transpired that the

[1] *Parl. Pap.*, 1882, XLVII, C.3098, p. 46. Robinson to Kimberley (Tel.), 14 August 1881.

[2] C.O. 291/15. Robinson to Kimberley, 5 December 1881, enclosed in Hudson to Robinson, 29 November 1881. See also Report by R. Rutherford, Secretary to British Resident, on position in Bechuanaland, printed in *Parl. Pap.*, 1882, XLVII, C.3098, pp. 139–45.

[3] *Parl. Pap.*, 1882, XLVII, C.3381, p. 46. Dated 21 October 1881 at Pretoria.

[4] Idem.

Transvaal was supplying certain of the Tswana chiefs with ammunition in return for land concessions.

If the origins of these Bechuana struggles lie buried in the morass of claims and counter claims of the participants, the ultimate objective of the white men involved is beyond doubt. They bartered their services for land, and then threw over the chiefs who had granted them the land, in order to set up a Boer dominated area.

The immediate explanation for their involvement was the long-standing internal quarrel, over land and water-holes, among the Tswana people themselves. The Transvalers had become intimately involved in these struggles during the recent Transvaal War, when certain of the chiefs had indulged in a policy of 'real-politik' and sided with the Transvaal. By this strange alliance the chiefs gained white volunteers to help them in their struggles. The chiefs in question were Moswete and Mosweu, all of whose lands bordered most closely on the Boer state. Their 'volunteers' were to prove highly effective against the chiefs further south, Montshiwa of Tshidi Rolong, and Mankurwane of the Molopo area. Payment for services were ingenious in manner: the volunteers were granted farms in the lands of the conquered tribes, together with such cattle as were captured. Ultimately it could be no more than feeding the crocodile: when the volunteers had acquired the best land and water-holes in the conquered lands, they must inevitably look to the lands of the tribes who employed them.

The first of the new-style raids took place in January 1882, when Moswete and his white volunteers raided Montshiwa's lands, and drove off 5,000 cattle and some 300 horses. The matter was immediately taken up by Hudson, at Pretoria, at the request of Montshiwa, and of Mankurwane—who feared a similar fate.[1] The protest was presented on 14 January, and Bok (the Transvaal Secretary) replied the same day. Hudson was informed that Joubert was personally going to the troubled area to investigate.[2]

What Joubert actually did, once he got to the frontier, is still a dark secret. Perhaps he did the most advantageous thing for

[1] *Parl. Pap.*, 1882, XLVII, C.3381, pp. 15–16. Hudson to Kruger, 14 January 1882.

[2] Ibid., State Secretary Bok to Hudson, 14 January 1882.

the Transvaal, i.e. nothing, for from early February reports of the fighting in the area began to take on a new urgency. Captain Nourse, the British representative in the area, informed Robinson by telegram: 'Hostilities spreading rapidly, was unable to arrange amicable understanding between hostile chiefs.'[1] Once again diplomatic representation was made to the Transvaal, this time on Kimberley's instructions.[2]

Just how effective were these verbal censures on the Transvaal Triumvirate, and how determined was Joubert's attempt to halt the stream of volunteers to Moswete, can be gauged from Nourse's important report of 16 February 1882.[3] He had toured the area concerned, and written down exactly what he saw. It had very much the ring of truth about it, and there is no reason to reject his statements. He was grinding no axe: he was not a missionary, nor a marked humanitarian. It is a soldier's report, and it leaves no doubt as to Transvaal involvement in the unrest.

Nourse noted that the Triumvirate had issued a proclamation to their Boers to be neutral, but 'there is no doubt that the proclamation has in no way been adhered to'.[4] The primary reason for this was that the Transvaal's local representatives—the Field Cornets—had failed to do their duty. Nourse saw some classic examples of deliberate negligence on the part of these frontier officials. He cited names, dates, and places—which he could hardly have fabricated, as the later Transvaal claimed.[5] Certain Transvaal officials were even drawing double pay, as they worked for both their own government and that of the Tswana chiefs. 'The number of Boers assisting Moshette [sic] will shortly be considerably increased as their Commandant

[1] *Parl. Pap.*, 1882, XLVII, C.3381, pp. 4–5. Nourse to Robinson, 9 February 1882.

[2] Ibid., Kimberley to Robinson (Tel.), 11 February 1882, pp. 5–6.

[3] C.O. 291/15. Nourse to Robinson, 16 February 1882, enclosed in Robinson to Kimberley, 22 February 1882.

[4] Idem.

[5] See his report of events of 26 January 1882. 'On morning of 26th I was accompanied as far as the line by some of the border guard. On the way passed a Boer driving 12 oxen, and again, two Boers driving 4 donkeys. They had just come across the line, but were taken no notice of by the men of the guard, and were allowed to pass on. I questioned them why they did not stop such men; they informed me, their orders were only to stop armed men . . .' Ibid.

Hendrick Weebers was, on my arrival, recruiting in the Transvaal.'[1] Mosweu was also up to much the same tricks: '. . . the chief then had more than one agent recruiting in the Transvaal. These agents' instructions are, to raise 300 Boers, their pay to be half the booty and a farm each in Mankaroane's [sic] territory, should they succeed in driving him out.'[2]

Nourse was in no doubt as to what would be the ultimate result of this situation. 'Unless Montsioa [sic] obtains assistance very shortly he must either be routed or surrender . . .'. And, when that happens then Moswete's forces will join in common cause with Mosweu 'which in my opinion will end in the defeat [of] Mankaroane [sic]'.[3]

Nourse's words were to be prophetic: in June 1882 Mankurwane admitted defeat; and in October Montshiwa signed a most unfavourable treaty with Moswete. Two factors alone contributed to this sad train of events: Boer aid to Moswete and Mosweu, and the lack of British aid to Montshiwa and Mankurwane. This turned on a basic issue—the supply of ammunition. Moswete and Mosweu had a plentiful supply: and all bought in the Transvaal. They even had several ship's cannon, whose ammunition also came through the Transvaal.[4] In contrast, Montshiwa and Mankurwane were constantly short of arms and ammunition,[5] as Britain not only refused to supply them, but also put an end to the Cape sale of ammunition to these 'loyal chiefs'. The official attitude was captured by Herbert when he minuted, 'We must practise what we preach.'[6] But this was hardly comforting to those chiefs who professed allegiance to Britain; nor was it particularly realistic, as the Transvaal was not stopped by Britain from supplying her own allies.

The Colonial Office and the Colonial Secretary retained this position despite all the information which flowed in from the area—some of it very moving in the story which it told. Montshiwa's friend, Christopher Bethel, told of how the chief was being constantly raided by Boers who took shelter over the

[1] Idem.   [2] Idem.   [3] Idem.
[4] *Parl. Pap.*, 1882, XLVII, C.3381. Robinson to Kimberley (Tel.), 9 February 1882. The Landdrosts were selling up to 500 rounds to all Boers who applied for it.
[5] Ibid., Nourse to Robinson (Tel.), 9 February 1882.
[6] C.O. 291/15. Minute by Herbert, 8 June 1882, on Robinson to Kimberley, 9 May 1882.

Transvaal boundary.[1] Further telegrams from Nourse and Hudson painted much the same picture.[2]

Britain's action was restricted to reminding the Transvaal Government of the Convention, and of Article 19 in particular, and of calling on them to enforce their proclamation of 21 October 1881.[3] The official explanation of the Boer behaviour revealed an understanding of the Triumvirate which is singularly wide of the mark. 'Uncle Paul is a very illiterate Boer,' Herbert wrote on 7 March,[4] 'and probably remembers little of the contents of the Convention.'

This was hardly true. In fact, Kruger knew the Convention all too well—as the Colonial Office were very soon to discover. On 11 March Kruger led a deputation to Hudson, in Pretoria, and asked that the western border of the Transvaal be changed.[5] He stated that unless this was done Great Britain would find that the frontier troubles could not be controlled. Once the disturbed area and the warring tribes were in the Transvaal, then Kruger would soon have the matter ended, with law and order once again supreme. Hudson replied that this was not possible, as it would mean destroying the frontier lines, as drawn up in the recently negotiated Convention.

Robinson saw Kruger's request for what it really was: an attempt to annex very large tribal lands. 'Convention boundary should be maintained . . . quarrels between tribes outside [boundary] afford no sufficient grounds for annexation.'[6] His assessment of the Boer attitude to the Tswana lands was indeed memorable: 'There always will be liability [of] native troubles outside any line that stops short of the Atlantic.'[7]

Robinson's advice was equally down to earth. Britain must stand by the Convention: and, more important still, must get

[1] *Parl. Pap.*, 1882, XLVII, C.3381, pp. 62–3. Enclosed in Robinson to Kimberley, 15 March 1882.

[2] C.O. 291/15. Robinson to Kimberley (Tels.), 11, 12, 14 and 16 March, enclosed in Nourse and Hudson to Robinson, reports and telegrams.

[3] See *Parl. Pap.*, 1882, XLVII, C.3381. Proclamation of 21 October 1881 (translation by Nourse).

[4] C.O. 291/22. Minute, Herbert to Ashley, 7 March 1882.

[5] C.O. 291/15. Robinson to Kimberley, 19 March 1882, enclosed in Hudson to Robinson, 13 March 1882.

[6] Idem.   [7] Idem.

the Transvaal administrations to control their own citizens.[1] It was sound advice, but it was never put into practice. Kimberley declined to be drawn into military action in the western Transvaal, having only recently conducted a war in the eastern Transvaal. Robinson's calls for action were pigeon-holed;[2] as were Mankurwane's pleas for help—'I have no ammunition, I have no assistance, I think you my friends are throwing me away....'[3]

Finding that the British response to these incursions into Bechuanaland was not to be more than verbal censure, the Transvaal Government stepped up their campaign to have the border altered. Bok sent Hudson a long letter on 10 March 1882, pointing out that in their opinion the Bechuana unrest has 'no other origin than the border line as now fixed by the Convention'.[4] This has split the tribes 'contrary to their expressed desire'. The Transvaal demanded that Britain must act in the area and restore law and order, or consent to the Transvaal going in and doing so for Britain—it would give us very little trouble indeed, and thus further bloodshed will be prevented'.[5]

It was a shrewd attempt to drive Britain into an awkward impasse. The Boers now knew that it was highly unlikely that Kimberley would despatch a force to the area, and that therefore their offer must either be accepted, or Britain must allow the peace-time invasion to continue. Kruger indeed hoped to win no matter what answer Kimberley gave. Just how confident the Transvaal was can be seen from the nature of Joubert's report on the area, which reached Robinson on 4 April 1882.[6] It read like comic opera. There had been *no* violation of the

[1] *Parl. Pap.*,, 1882, XLVII, C.3381, pp. 53–4. Robinson to Kimberley, 19 March 1881.

[2] C.O. 291/15. Minute by Kimberley, 31 May, on Robinson to Kimberley, 5 May 1882.

[3] *Parl. Pap.*, 1882, XLVII, C.3381, pp. 72–3. Enclosed in Robinson to Kimberley, 1 April 1882.

[4] Ibid., p. 66. Bok to Hudson, 10 March 1882. Enclosed in Robinson to Kimberley, 25 March 1882.

[5] Idem.

[6] Ibid., Report by Joubert, dated February 1882, forwarded by Hudson, 18 March 1882, and enclosed in Robinson to Kimberley, 4 April 1882, pp. 74–80.

frontier which he could find; the Transvaal border guards *were* doing their duty splendidly; and he had only seen *two* white men involved in all the fights. The report was received in the Colonial Office with wry humour.[1]

Kimberley's official reply—that Her Majesty's Government 'are not prepared to entertain any proposals for any alteration of the terms of the Convention'[2]—did little to dampen Transvaal dreams of expansion. Indeed, the Boer leaders began to talk in terms of devising a frontier which would 'give satisfaction to all the natives concerned', and which would follow 'that made by President Burgers'.[3] In fact this meant Transvaal 'empire building', for such a border would have included not only the lands of their 'allies' Moswete and Mosweu, but also those of Montshiwa and Mankurwane. A strong protest was delivered by Hudson, to the effect that the Transvaal should not interfere in matters beyond its borders.[4]

The Boer reply was immediate; and dramatic. Taking Hudson at his word, Kruger withdrew all the border guards—on the grounds of 'Lord Kimberley's latest instructions not to interfere at all in outside native quarrels'.[5] The Colonial officials at last woke up to Kruger's tactics. 'Under the pretence of non-interference they withdrew their guards', Hemming noted, 'so that people may cross the boundary for warlike purposes with complete care and impunity. This is sheer impudence, if nothing worse.'[6]

Impudence was certainly involved. On 22 May Robinson reported a rumour to the effect that a Boer Republic was to be set up in the Batlapin territory, under the general protection of the Transvaal.[7] Kimberley was also told, in the same despatch,

[1] C.O. 291/15. Minutes by Hemming and Herbert, 16 May 1882.

[2] *Parl. Pap.*, 1882. XLVII, C.3381, pp. 80–81. Kimberley to Hudson, enclosed in Kimberley to Robinson, 4 May 1882.

[3] Ibid., Bok to Hudson, 15 March 1882, enclosed in Robinson to Kimberley, 4 April 1882. For detailed description of President Burgers' claims in Bechuanaland, see Agar-Hamilton *The Road to the North*, p. 194.

[4] C.O. 291/15. Hudson to Robinson, 21 April 1882.

[5] *Parl. Pap.*, 1882, XLVII, C. 3381, p. 85. Robinson to Kimberley, 21 April 1882.

[6] C.O. 291/15. Hemming to Bramston, 16 May 1882.

[7] *Parl. Pap.*, 1882, XLVII, C.3381, pp. 85–9. Robinson to Kimberley, 22 May 1882.

that the Transvaal Boers in the Bechuana territory 'have been largely reinforced by men from the Free State'.[1]

Whitehall-thinking at last began to catch up with the reality of the local situation. A series of Minutes of 20 April aptly captured the 'official mind' immediately prior to the creation of the Goshen and Stellaland Republics.[2] 'They claim the remainder of the Keate Award territory', Bramston wrote. 'The incident resembles what happens near the Danube—protection followed by annexation is what they wish.'[3] Herbert agreed: 'The Boers clearly intend to use steadily all opportunities for extending the boundaries of the Transvaal State to the old claimed, but not recognised, frontiers of the South African Republic.'[4] His opinion on what British policy should be was significant: 'We can only with similar obstinacy repeat our own pressures. It would not be prudent to consent this early to entertain any proposals for altering the Convention.' Kimberley's remarks are also to the point: 'I agree—we must decline firmly.'[5]

But what did 'firmly' mean? It certainly did not mean a military expedition, nor did it include a police force on the spot to patrol the frontier. In fact, it meant nothing more than renewed protests via the already overworked Hudson. The latter did his duty, but it was to little avail. In that month—May 1882—Hudson made a tour of the troubled frontier. His report confirmed, and amplified, what Nourse had already written.[6] The heart of the report is contained in two sentences. 'There can be no doubt of the fact that a really considerable number of Boers have been and are still participating . . . in the conflicts between Montsioa [sic] and Moshette [sic], and between Mankaroane [sic] and Massauw [sic], and also that many Free State Boers are associated with them . . .'. Nor did he doubt the ultimate outcome of the struggles. The pro-Boer chiefs Moswete and Mosweu must win, as the 'support given by the British

[1] Idem.

[2] C.O. 291/15. Minutes of 24–8 April 1882, by Bramston, Herbert, and Kimberley.

[3] Idem.   [4] Idem.

[5] Idem.

[6] *Parl. Pap.*, 1882, XLVII, C.3381, pp. 122–45. His report is in Robinson to Kimberley, 6 June 1882. The Report is dated 12 May 1882.

Government to Montsioa [*sic*] and Mankaroane [*sic*] has hitherto been limited to such "moral support" as could be afforded by
my earnest representations . . .'.[1]

Clearly this was not enough. Kruger opened a new session of
the *Volksraad*, on 19 May, with a sharp speech denouncing the
existing border as 'imposed' by the Convention. His 'friend',
Joubert, had succeeded in 'maintaining peace within our South
Western Borders and in punishing the guilty'; but, to Kruger,
beyond the border all was chaos, 'which can be attributed to no
other cause than the very impracticable way in which the boundaries had been defined'.[2]

Kruger had unfurled his standard: he was to use this argument over and over again in the months to come. It was a useful
piece of sophistry: it was broad enough to include any and every
disturbance across the frontier lines. And no amount of protests from Kimberley to the contrary would change Kruger's
tactic.

The atmosphere at Pretoria indeed took on a farcical air.
Hudson would call Kruger in to warn him that he must control
his own Boers; and Kruger would receive the protest with the
traditional reply that he had already called on his burghers
to observe neutrality in the Tswana disputes,[3] and that the
disputes would go on until the 'Convention frontiers' were
altered.[4] These discussions were apparently conducted with
great civility, and great frequency—but to no effect whatso-
ever.

By late May 1882 the first stage of the Tswana struggles were
drawing to a close. Mankurwane was besieged at Taungs by
Mosweu and his Boer volunteers. The old Tswana chief sent a
unique letter to Hudson:[5] 'I have the honour to inform you that
there is a Commando of Free State and Transvaal subjects besieging my town of Taungs . . . I am told that those who form

[1] Idem.

[2] Ibid., pp. 103–5. Kruger's speech, enclosed in Robinson to Kimberley,
19 May 1882.

[3] Kruger referred to the Proclamation, of 21 October 1881, already cited
above.

[4] C.O. 291/15. Robinson to Kimberley, 6 June 1882, enclosed in Hudson
to Robinson, 22 May 1882.

[5] *Parl. Pap.*, 1882, XLVII, C.3381, pp. 145–6. Mankurwane to Hudson,
24 May 1882, enclosed in Robinson to Kimberley, 23 June 1882.

this Commando wish to take my country to form an independent Republic.'[1] This was written on 24 May, and by the time it had reached Robinson in Cape Town—23 June—the siege was over, and the Boers had won. Mankurwane gave in, and watched as his lands were divided up into farms, of 6,000 acres each, for Mosweu's volunteers. His defeat did not end here. He was forced to sign a treaty in which he agreed to refer all future disputes to the Transvaal authorities and not to the British representative.

Having disposed of Mankurwane as an effective challenge, the volunteers and their tribal allies now turned on the remaining pro-British chief—Montshiwa.[2] He lasted three months, during which time neither the Colonial officials, nor the Colonial Secretary, lifted a hand to save him—though the question of a pension for the near-landless chief was discussed in the following year. The furthest Kimberley would go to aid the retreating Montshiwa was to suggest, to Robinson, that if it was really true that the chief was in dire straits then perhaps 'it will deserve your consideration . . . [whether] under such circumstances [Montshiwa should] be precluded from obtaining arms and ammunition from the Cape Colony for his defence against the white marauders'.[3] But beyond this Kimberley would not go.

With this fact in mind the Transvaal leaders began to challange the Convention in new ways. Apart from their involvement in the Bechuana territory they had already claimed the right to use the old title 'South African Republic';[4] and, they had also begun openly to question the matter of the debt as set out in the Convention.[5] Now they took a new and radical step. They declared 'war' on a native chief within the Transvaal. They claimed that he had failed to pay his taxes, and thus the

[1] Idem.

[2] Ibid., pp. 139–40. Report by Major Lowe, enclosed in letter from H. Jarvis: 'The natives are ready to fly before them; the Boers have put the fear of God into their hearts.' 24 May 1882.

[3] Ibid., p. 107. Kimberley to Robinson, 15 June 1882.

[4] C.O. 291/15. Robinson to Kimberley, 4 March 1882 (enclosed in Bok to Hudson); and Robinson to Kimberley, 3 May 1882 (enclosed in Hudson to Robinson, 20 April 1882).

[5] Ibid., Robinson to Kimberley, 19 May 1882 (enclosing speech by Kruger opening Volksraad).

Government felt itself 'compelled to take action against Mampoer'.[1]

Hudson immediately protested that this was contrary to the clauses in the Convention, which clearly stated that all matters concerning the native people of the Transvaal must come before the Native Locations Commission. Kruger's reply was typical of his whole approach: it was useless attempting to deal through the Commission while affairs beyond the south-western border remained unchecked by Britain. When they were settled, to his satisfaction, then he might consider working through the Commission.[2] Thus in a matter of months, and with the help of vast amounts of dynamite, Mampoer was quite literally blasted into submission, with Hudson protesting all the way.

By August 1882—the first anniversary of the Convention—it was generally agreed in official circles that the Boers were behaving as the mood dictated, and without the slightest concern for the treaty.[3] Not content with expanding into Bechuanaland they had begun to drift over the eastern frontiers. Bulwer, the Governor of Natal, reported that Boer pastoralists were grazing their cattle well in the Zulu Reserve;[4] and that they were also encroaching into Swaziland in search of land.[5] Joubert's claim, that the Boers and Swazi on the frontier 'live together in perfect peace',[6] could not hide the fact that many Boer frontiersmen were intent on doing in Swaziland what had already happened in Bechuanaland.

A profound sense of disillusion and of helplessness enveloped the Colonial Office when these latest intelligences arrived in London.[7] It had taken the permanent officials a year finally to grasp the fact that the Boers were still continuing their war

[1] *Parl. Pap.*, 1882, XLVII, C.3381, pp. 140–43. Robinson to Kimberley, 10 June 1882 (enclosed in Hudson to Robinson, 27 May 1882).

[2] Idem.

[3] C.O. 291/15. Minute by Hamilton to Bramston, 1 July 1882; and C.O. 291/16. Minutes by Fairfield and Wingfield, 3 August 1882.

[4] *Parl. Pap.*, 1883, XLIX, C.3466, p. 163. Bulwer to Robinson, 30 August 1882.

[5] *Parl. Pap.*, 1882, XLVII, C.3419, pp. 31–2. Bulwer to Robinson, 30 June 1882. See also Robinson to Kimberley, 9 August 1882.

[6] *Parl. Pap.*, 1883, XLIX, C.3466, p. 11. Joubert to Hudson, 24 August 1882; and Robinson to Kimberley, 4 November 1882.

[7] C.O. 291/16. Minutes by Fairfield and Wingfield, 3 August 1882.

against Britain, albeit under the guise of the peace treaty and the Convention; and, that they were succeeding on the *veld* where they had failed at the conference table.[1] Indeed, the Transvaal burghers were succeeding in a way that was beyond Kruger's wildest dreams. They had virtually occupied and annexed that portion of Bechuanaland denied to them by the Royal Commission; they were conducting their own native frontier policy again, irrespective of the British Resident and his paper protests; they were implementing their own particular internal native policy, without the slightest regard for the humanitarian rights proclaimed in the Convention, or for the Native Locations Commission: and they were even stealing on to the long-coveted, lush pastoral lands of the Swazi and Zulu tribes, so long denied them.

Kimberley's refusal to go beyond verbal protests increased the sense of anger which the officials felt towards Kruger and his followers. There was no doubt where the initiative lay; though it was difficult for the officials to accept this reality. Hamilton, a rising young clerk, wrote angrily: 'Whatever the Transvaal Government may say, it seems pretty clear that they have not *really* exerted themselves to prevent their subjects from taking part in these disturbances.'[2] Many of the officials appeared not only annoyed at Kruger's behaviour, but even surprised: clearly he was not a gentleman; nor clearly were his people to be trusted. Edward Wingfield spoke for many when he minuted, on a despatch containing the latest Boer infringements of the Convention. 'They are a slippery people.'[3]

3. Strange allies: Robinson and Mackenzie campaign for action, July–December 1882

The critical state of affairs on the Transvaal frontiers produced four main reactions. Kimberley, as Colonial Secretary, watched Boer behaviour with a patient resignation; his Whitehall officials attacked the Boers but would not propose any practical plan, such as a military expedition, to halt the frontier expansion; the Humanitarians, led by the Rev. John Mackenzie,

[1] Addit. MSS. 44227, ff. 206–10 (Tels.), Robinson to Kimberley, 8–9 July 1882—forwarded to Gladstone. Fully discussed below, p. 273.
[2] C.O. 291/15. Hamilton to Bramston, 1 July 1882.
[3] C.O. 291/16. Minute by Wingfield, dated 3 August 1882.

called for a British Protectorate over Bechuanaland; and the senior British representative in southern Africa, Sir Hercules Robinson, the High Commissioner at the Cape, searched for a scheme which would bring order to the troubled areas without involving war with the Boers, for the sake of the Convention.

It is Robinson's plans which are the most interesting and important. As the head of the Royal Commission he had seen Kruger in action at close quarters. Equally he had gained some clear understanding of the Boer people in the negotiations, and during his tour of southern Africa after the Commission was over. As Governor of the Cape, and High Commissioner, he was well placed to assess Afrikaner opinion, both in the Colony and in the Republics. He was a cautious man, of vast experience, and his proposals deserve the closest scrutiny. They show just how sure a grasp he had of the divergent forces and emotive local patriotisms involved in southern African politics.

His scheme grew directly out of his belief that events in Bechuanaland were reaching such a stage that the Boers might be tempted to repeat them on the eastern frontiers. His despatches from the Cape became more frequent, and more anxious, from early July 1882.[1] His long despatch of 6 July is a model of factual reporting and calm analysis. After describing the whole series of tribal battles, and the rôle of the white volunteers in Bechuanaland, Robinson wrote: 'The meaning of this is simply that the services of the Dutch marauders . . . are to be paid for if they should be successful, by farms selected from the lands of their neighbours, Mankerwane [sic] and Mathlabari [sic]. . . .'[2] His final conclusion was even more to the point: 'If the Transvaal Government were really in earnest in putting an end to these discreditable proceedings they could do so by calling in their subjects, or confiscating their property.'[3] However, this had not even been contemplated, with the result that in the case of one chief 'a clean sweep has been made of everything in his country larger than a domestic fowl'.[4]

On 8 July, Robinson despatched the first of four telegrams

[1] *Parl. Pap.*, 1882, XLVII, C.3419, pp. 19 ff. Robinson to Kimberley, 6 July 1882, and very frequently thereafter.

[2] Ibid., pp. 19–21. Robinson to Kimberley, 6 July 1882. Received in London, 2 August 1882.

[3] Idem.   [4] Idem.

which might be said to constitute the 'Robinson Plan' for Bechuanaland.[1] They have not hitherto been known to historians of Empire, as they were sent privately to Kimberley, and thus do not appear in the official Colonial Office files. The timing of the first of these four telegrams came as a result of Hudson's reports to Robinson.[2] Mankurwane had surrendered and Montshiwa was in a desperate state. The Transvaal leaders held to their opinion that Boers were not responsible, and that all they could do was offer the chiefs 'protection', as an integral part of the Transvaal. Robinson thought this would be a 'fatal precedent, which would bear fruit on the Zulu and Swazi borders, once let it appear that burghers, by stirring up strife between the natives and organising marauding expeditions, may possibly achieve the annexation of the disturbed territory, the Convention boundary line upon the east as well as the west will no longer be maintainable'.[3]

Robinson's idea was 'to suggest to you a middle course'[4]— presumably between present inactivity, and the humanitarian call for a protectorate. He laid out the basis of this 'middle course' in his telegram of 9 July,[5] which he sent in cypher. He first pointed out the difficulty of getting the Transvaal, or Free State, or Cape, to go in unilaterally and remove their own subjects, who were involved in the frontier raids. Thus he came to the logical conclusion that a joint-force of local men would be the most practical solution to the matter:

> I suggest that I invite Transvaal, Free State and Cape Governments to unite [with] Imperial Government in sending a small force of mounted police to scour Keate Award territory and arrest

[1] Addit. MSS. 44227, ff. 206–10. Robinson to Kimberley, 8–10 July 1882. They are all in the Gladstone Papers, as Kimberley forwarded the four telegrams to the Premier on the 11 July. See Kimberley to Gladstone, 11 July 1882, f. 202.

[2] C.O. 291/16. Hudson to Robinson, 8 July 1882, enclosed in Robinson to Kimberley, 10 July 1882.

[3] Ibid., Robinson to Kimberley, 10 July 1882. He amplified his fears: 'Mosette [sic] and Massouw's [sic] territories would at once be given out in farms and natives subject to taxation.' Thus the absorption of Montshiwa and Mankurwane would soon follow. This despatch was forwarded to Gladstone. See the note on the back, in pencil.

[4] Idem.

[5] Addit. MSS. 44227, f. 209. Robinson to Kimberley (Tel. in cypher), 11 July 1882.

all deserters and violaters of the various neutrality proclamations, removing them for trial within their respective jurisdictions.[1]

As to the practical problems of men and costs, he was equally clear:

> About fifty mounted police each or a total of two hundred men would probably suffice, the cost would be trifling.[2]

The very announcement of such a force would, Robinson felt, lead to many of the 'volunteers' fleeing; and it would also act as a warning to those contemplating further border violations that 'such a remedy was always available'. It would thus 'prevent a recurrence of such proceedings'. Imperial involvement he saw as essential to allay local 'jealousies', and to provide a lead. 'No time should be lost.'[3]

He backed up his scheme with a final telegram outlining the urgency of putting his plan into action.[4] Robinson reminded Kimberley that every recent action of the Transvaal indicated an 'intention to escape if possible from the agreements in [the] Convention respecting the debt and boundary. I think you should know this when dealing with my telegrams. . . .' Indeed if they are allowed to go on pulling the 'Convention to pieces all that is valuable in it will soon be lost'.

The four telegrams made a deep impression. Kimberley forwarded them to Gladstone with this note: 'I think Sir Hercules Robinson's advice should be followed.'[5] Kimberley saw the plan as a sensible way of avoiding 'a general conflagration', or 'the establishment of a new Republic on the frontier, composed of the worst elements', and which could only 'lead to the most serious consequences in South Africa'.

There is no record of Gladstone's reaction, but he must have agreed, for the next day—12 July—Kimberley instructed Robinson to proceed with his scheme as outlined in the telegram of 9 July.[6] Kimberley, though, added two provisos. First, Robinson

---

[1] Idem.   [2] Idem.   [3] Idem.

[4] Ibid., 4th telegram (in cypher), 11 July 1882. Received London, 11 July 1882, 11.30 a.m.

[5] Ibid., f. 202. Kimberley to Gladstone, 11 July 1882 (enclosing Robinsons's four telegrams of 8–10 July).

[6] C.O. 291/16. Kimberley to Robinson (Tel.), 12 July 1882. The despatch which confirmed this telegram is printed. See *Parl. Pap.*, 1882, XLVII, C.3381, pp. 144–5. Kimberley to Robinson, 13 July 1882.

'should give as little prominence as may be possible to the imperial part of the intended action'; and second, Robinson should make it clear that imperial assistance was given as this was an exceptional situation, and 'in order to facilitate united action on the part of the local governments'. The British Government could not permanently undertake to do the 'duty of preserving tranquillity on the border, which properly belongs to the governments of the adjoining territories'.[1]

In London Kimberley awaited Robinson's news of the formation of the police force; in Cape Town Robinson found that it was impossible to get the various South African governments to work together. The Transvaal and Free State were unenthusiastic if not hostile to the idea. It is not surprising; their frontier Boers were succeeding all too well, and their respective governments had no intention of making war on them. But the cruellest stab was the attitude of the Cape. Although the actions of the white volunteers had been deplored by the Cape Assembly, the Colony's government, led by Scanlen, was determined that the Cape was going to stay neutral, in what they considered to be an Anglo-Transvaal problem.[2] If it flared up into renewed warfare they did not want to be caught fighting Britain's wars for her, especially with so large a Dutch proportion of Cape electors now taking an active part in colonial politics. Thus Robinson was told that the Scanlen government, 'after due consideration', did not 'feel warranted in altering their determination to preserve an attitude of strict neutrality between the parties engaged in conflict on the frontiers of Bechuanaland'.[3]

The Boers took the opportunity provided by Robinson's suggestion to renew their attack on the Convention itself. They had already had the nerve to cable him—on 3 July—that it was 'high-time that steps should be taken to put an end to the present intolerable state of affairs'.[4] Now, on 31 July, Kruger

[1] Idem.

[2] *Parl. Pap.*, 1882, XLVII, C.3419, pp. 51 ff. Robinson to Kimberley, 1 August 1882. Robinson was informed that the Cape ministry 'do not wish Major Lowe to cross the border'.

[3] Ibid., The Cape would only act if the Transvaal Government did so. And they knew this was highly unlikely. See Robinson to Kimberley, 18 July 1882.

[4] Ibid., pp. 27-8. Robinson to Kimberley, 15 July 1882 (enclosed in Hudson to Robinson, 3 July 1882).

telegraphed that he was 'surprised' at Robinson's suggestion of a united police force, and that he felt 'the proposed remedy is worse than the disease, seeing that it touches only accidental consequences and leaves the root of the evil unremoved'.[1] And Kruger had no doubt as to the 'root of the evil'; he wanted the Convention boundaries altered. 'No measure will avail so long as this is not remedied.'[2]

Robinson's assessment of this blunt refusal was moderate: 'It is, I think, difficult to resist the conclusion that the action of the freebooters has not been really viewed with much disfavour by the Transvaal Government.'[3] As to Kruger's suggestion about the frontier Robinson merely repeated his long-held opinion that 'any concession as regards the existing boundary line would establish a precedent which would before long bear fruit on the eastern as well as upon the western borders'.[4]

The Colonial Office reaction was rather more sharp. 'It's all very awkward,' Fairfield minuted.[5] Kimberley's approach was rather more sanguine. He was prepared to believe anything about the Boers.[6] When the Transvaal failed to pay the first instalment of the debt, in August, Kimberley minuted: 'I shall be agreeably surprised if we get a farthing out of them.'[7] He took much the same attitude, of weary resignation, to the matter of the Transvaal's determination to call itself the 'South African Republic'. Hudson had appealed to Robinson to make the Transvaal hold to the title 'Transvaal State', as defined in the Convention.[8] When it came before Kimberley he merely remarked: 'Let the matter drop.'[9]

[1] C.O. 291/16. Robinson to Kimberley (Tel.), 4 August 1882 (enclosed in Kruger to Robinson, 31 July 1882). See also *Parl. Pap.*, 1882, XLVII, C.3419, pp. 23 ff., for Hudson's visit to Cape Town early in August, and discussion with Robinson.

[2] Idem.

[3] *Parl. Pap.*, 1882, XLVII, C.3419, Robinson to Kimberley, 7 August 1882.

[4] Idem.

[5] C.O. 291/16. Minute by Fairfield to Bramston, 4 August 1882.

[6] *Parl. Pap.*, 1882, XLVII, C.3419, pp. 43–4. Kimberley to Robinson, 16 August 1882.

[7] C.O. 291/16. Minute by Kimberley, 4 August 1882.

[8] *Parl. Pap.*, 1882, XLVII, C.3419. Robinson to Kimberley, 6 July 1882 (enclosed in Hudson to Robinson, 24 June 1882).

[9] C.O. 291/16. Minute by Kimberley, dated 4 August, on Robinson to Kimberley, 6 July 1882.

Robinson's initiative having come to naught, there was no attempt either on the part of Whitehall or the colonial government to advance an alternative approach. Accordingly it was the Boers who prevailed in Bechuanaland. Mankurwane had collapsed in June:[1] Montshiwa suffered a like fate in October.[2] He had to surrender over 70 per cent of his land to what Robinson called 'the freebooter population' of Bechuanaland. The volunteers took all of his land south of the Molopo River; and he was forced to acknowledge allegiance to the Transvaal. Mankurwane spoke for both chiefs when he analysed his defeat as follows: 'Seeing therefore that I had been deserted by the British Government . . . I have done that which I ought to have done long ago, namely made my peace with the Boers . . . and have had to give up a considerable portion of my country.'[3]

The direct result of these events was the establishment of two further Boer republics. Mankurwane's territory provided the land for the Stellaland Republic,[4] centred at Vryberg near Taungs; and Montshiwa's domain became the other 'robber republic'[5] of Goshen, with its capital at Rooi-Grond near Mafeking.

The fact of the existence of these make-shift Boer states did not shake Kimberley in his attitude: he continued his policy of studied neglect. This was not as a result of an ignorance of local conditions, or lack of accurate information from the *veld*. On 6 August Robinson telegraphed the terms of Mankurwane's defeat;[6] and Kimberley even placed a non-committal note on the despatch, to the effect that all British subjects involved—army deserters—should possibly be arrested.[7] Shortly after this he was warned of the probable fate awaiting Montshiwa if he was not helped;[8] and Kimberley was informed of the early

[1] C.O. 291/16. Robinson to Kimberley (Tel.), 6 August 1882. *Parl. Pap.*, 1882, XLVII, C.3419, pp. 76–77. Robinson to Kimberley, 18 August 1882 (enclosed in Mankurwane to Robinson, 7 August 1882).

[2] Idem.

[3] *Parl. Pap.*, 1882, XLVII, C.3419, pp. 76–7. Robinson to Kimberley, 18 August 1882 (enclosed in Mankurwane to Robinson, 7 August 1882).

[4] Idem.   [5] Robinson's phrase to characterise the 'freebooter' states.

[6] C.O. 291/16. Robinson to Kimberley (Tel.), 6 August 1882.

[7] Ibid., Minute by Kimberley, dated 7 September 1882.

[8] *Parl. Pap.*, 1882, XLVII, C.3419, pp. 57–60. Robinson to Kimberley, 7 August 1882. (Received in London, 30 August 1882.)

rumours of the probable creation of the two new Boer republics.[1] Hudson made an extensive tour of the troubled area between 17 July and 31 August,[2] and then had lengthy conversations with Robinson at Cape Town. All this information was forwarded to London.[3]

Despite this mass of evidence at his disposal—all of it pointing to violation of the Convention by the Boers—Kimberley refused to be moved from his position of detached observation. His letters to Robinson are a masterpiece of non-committal official language. His reply to Robinson's urgent warnings, that Montshiwa was about to be destroyed, is a typical Kimberley despatch of this period. Robinson was to inform Kruger that Her Majesty's Government 'observe with extreme surprise' the behaviour of Kruger's burghers.[4]

With the protests limited to 'extreme surprise' it is hardly surprising that Kruger began to test the extent of Kimberley's conciliatory attitude. On 8 August 1882 Robinson wrote: 'The Transvaal Government request me again to bring to your notice the lamentable condition of affairs in Zululand, which they state is causing them great difficulty upon their Eastern border. . . .'[5] Kimberley's reply was once again non-committal;[6] but he privately minuted: 'I do not, I am sorry to say, rely on them at all to keep peace on their own border.'[7]

Thus encouraged the Transvaal Government looked round for other means to 'cheek' the imperialists. They succeeded eminently well; and created what must to this day stand as a classic hoax, bluff, or joke. It took the form of a financial claim against Britain. By the assessment of the Royal Commission the Transvaal was liable for a debt of £265,000, of which £100,000 was due on 8 August 1882, and the rest payable over 25 years.[8]

[1] Ibid., p. 89. Robinson to Kimberley, 5 September 1882.

[2] Ibid., pp. 101–3. Robinson to Kimberley, 2 October 1882 (enclosed in Hudson to Robinson, 10 September 1882), 2,300 miles in forty-five days in horse-drawn coaches.

[3] Ibid., pp. 23–4. Robinson to Kimberley (Tel.), 4 August 1882.

[4] C.O. 291/16. Kimberley to Robinson, 16 August 1882.

[5] *Parl. Pap.*, 1883, XLIX, C.3466, p. 78. Robinson to Kimberley, 8 August 1882.

[6] Ibid., p. 129. Kimberley to Robinson, 11 September 1882.

[7] Ibid., 291/16. Minute by Kimberley, 3 September 1882.

[8] See Pretoria Convention, clause 11.

As 8 August approached, and it became clear in the Boer capital that the initial £100,000 could not be paid, they were hovering on bankruptcy, the Transvalers decided to put in a counter-claim so as to throw the question of the debt into doubt.[1]

It was most skilfully done; and must have been accompanied by great mirth in Pretoria. To take the two largest amounts only—£51,850 loss in 'War Tax', and £45,000 loss in 'Kaffir Tax'. The 'War Tax' had been imposed by the South African Republic in 1876 to fight Sekukuni (21 September 1876). This tax was remitted by Sir Theophilus Shepstone, after he had annexed the Transvaal, and when Britain fought the war for the Transvaal. The Boers now claimed the money back again.

As to the 'Kaffir Tax', it shows an even more inventive mind at work. In 1876 the Transvaal claimed to have collected £4,380 from the natives, while the British administration of the Transvaal had ignored this form of taxation and collected nothing in 1877, a mere £473 in 1878, and £596 in 1879. Thus Kruger now claimed that £15,000 *ought* to have been collected between 1877 and 1879; and since it was now three tax years since then, and the war had prevented the Triumvirate from collecting the amount, he claimed a further £30,000 bringing the total to £45,000 on this item alone.[2]

So the claim goes on, being largely concerned with amounts

---

[1] The Transvaal Government claimed that £176,755 10s. 10d. should be deducted from the total debt of £265,000. This claim can broadly be broken down as follows:

	£	s.	d.
(1) Loss in War Tax	51,850	0	0
(2) Loss in 'Kaffir Tax'	45,000	0	0
(3) Difference in expenditure for Colonial Defence	28,175	17	10
(4) Estates alienated by grants	5,045	0	0
(5) Loss in Railway funds	34,061	8	6
(6) Salaries owing and now paid by Transvaal Government	623	4	6
(7) 2,000 cattle remitted to Sekukuni	12,000	0	0
	£176,755	10	10

See Hudson to Robinson, 24 June 1882, in *Parl. Pap.*, 1882, XLVII, C.3419, pp. 15–19.

[2] The phrase in the claim reads: '. . . ought to have been got in under proper administration'. Idem.

that 'ought' to have been acquired, and amounts lost in trade
due to the unsettled condition of the Transvaal. Robinson took
one look at these claims and wrote:

> I only regret the Transvaal Government has not frankly stated its
> inability to pay this instalment of the debt agreed upon. . . . This
> would I think have been a more straightforward and creditable
> course than the concoction of this counter account, which can
> only be described as a *trumped-up claim*.[1]

When the claim was forwarded to the Treasury their reply
was immediate, and not unexpected. The Treasury 'cannot
recognise any claim for a reduction of the debt . . . on account
of non-collection of taxes during British administration, still
less are they able to entertain the claim prefixed on account of
the fine which the South African Republic wished to levy upon
Sikukuni.'[2]

Much to the surprise of all the officials concerned Kimberley
decided to overrule the Treasury. In his desire not to become
involved in a wrangle with the Transvaal Boers he was even
prepared to go some way to meeting their 'trumped-up claim'.
His reply to Kruger[3]—on 14 August 1882—is a strange letter
from the Colonial Secretary of a great imperial nation. Kruger
was informed that while the British Government 'received
with much surprise the extraordinary counter-claim put forward by the Transvaal Government, the greater part of which is
altogether inadmissible', Britain did however 'desire to meet
any reasonable request on the part of that Government'. Accordingly the Colonial Office having 'carefully considered
whether there are any items on which any remissions from the
total debt due,' had recommended a reduction in the debt
'amounting in the whole to about £10,000'.[4]

To Kimberley it was a trifling amount, a means of blunting
the Boer claim without remitting the bulk of the debt. Kruger
looked at it rather differently. To him the amount mattered

[1] Ibid., Robinson to Kimberley, 6 July 1882, enclosing details of the
claim. (My italics.)
[2] C.O. 291/16. Treasury to the C.O. 10 August 1882.
[3] *Parl. Pap.*, 1882, XLVII, C.3419, pp. 15–19. Kimberley to Kruger,
enclosed in Kimberley to Robinson, 14 August 1882.
[4] Idem.

little: the important thing was the principle involved. By reducing the debt, even so slightly, Britain had admitted that the Convention could be modified. He now saw it as his task to make sure that the campaign to have the Convention revoked was continued—even stepped up in its determination.

Another onlooker, and participant, who learnt much from the matter, was the High Commissioner at the Cape. Robinson began to alter his whole approach to the question of Boer duplicity on the Transvaal borders. He had pressed hard for action, and had found that the Cape would not move against Transvaal citizens; and he saw that unilateral imperial action was ruled out, due to the cost involved. Now, in the matter of the debt, he finally grasped the central issue at stake in Kimberley's policy: the Colonial Secretary was not going to move to save two impoverished Tswana chiefs who occupied barren lands in the heart of Africa. As an experienced colonial official Robinson knew the hazards of 'crying wolf' too often. He had no desire to sacrifice his own career—and his dreams of being Viceroy of India—for the sake of the chiefs. Robinson thus accepted the inevitable and directed his attention to other matters. His despatches on the Bechuana situation noticeably decline after this date, and are in fact limited to forwarding Hudson's reports. He made no comment on the events reported, and completely opted-out of the Anglo-Boer wrangle over the Convention frontier. He did not take a decisive rôle again until called upon by Lord Derby at the London Convention discussions, by which time he had secured Cape support for his views.

Robinson's behaviour was an object-lesson for aspiring colonial governors. It is perhaps the secret of his large success: the ability not only to advise when called upon, but the knowledge of when to say nothing, particularly when that advice might lead to a head-on confrontation with the Colonial Secretary or permanent officials.

The campaign to 'save the chiefs' thus shifted its centre: as Robinson bowed out of his unequal and tentative struggle with the Cape and British Government, so now it was the Rev. John Mackenzie who took up the cause. With nothing to lose, and everything to gain, Mackenzie began a six-month all-out bid to rouse public opinion in England over Bechuanaland. His first campaign began in autumn 1882, and lasted until summer 1883.

It was followed by a similar effort in the winter of 1883–84, when the Transvaal delegation was in London.

Mackenzie's remarkable efforts[1] took particular forms: a spate of public meetings throughout the country, but mainly centred in the populous midlands towns and cities; a series of critical articles in the Press—W. T. Stead had opened the columns of the *Pall Mall Gazette* to him; the lobbying of parliamentarians and ministers—he had a direct line to Chamberlain through Dr. Dale, the famous Birmingham preacher; attempts to pressure the permanent officials—he was a constant if unwelcome visitor at the Colonial Office; and, finally, the spreading of informed opinion on British policy in Africa via the creation of the 'South Africa Committee'—whose members included W. E. Forster, Chamberlain, Fowell Buxton, Sir Henry Barkly (a former governor of the Cape), and Lord Grey (former Colonial Secretary). Combined, these various aspects of his labours made for a uniquely active campaign: rarely can a single 'humanitarian' have brought together so many talents and have organised so efficiently for his cause.

All that Mackenzie's campaign lacked was success. It is easy to write of his rousing campaign—his lively speeches, his numerous informed pamphlets, his letters to M.P.s, his meeting with Chamberlain and his dogged 'besieging' of the permanent officials; but it is even more to the point to enquire as to the effect of all these sincere words. At very best it can be argued that Mackenzie's efforts created the atmosphere for the debate in Parliament, in March 1883, on the Tswana chiefs. But even that debate failed to change the 'Kimberley policy' in the slightest. A realistic appraisal of his efforts must not confuse activity with effect. Too often historians of Empire are attracted to humanitarian campaigns in search of the significant. It is one of the myths of 'imperial history' that the 'humanitarian school of politicians' merely had to voice their discontent and the conscience of the nation was roused to pressure the Government's policy. The fallacy in that thinking is twofold: it assumes that the 'working man' is at all interested in African miseries

[1] The best existing description of this campaign is W. D. Mackenzie, *Life of Mackenzie* (London, 1902), pp. 257–311. See also Agar-Hamilton, *The Road to the North* and Dr. A. Sillery's forthcoming *Life of Mackenzie*, which he has kindly allowed me to read.

when his own social conditions are poor; and it presumes a direct causal relationship between a momentary public concern and the changing of official policy. Both these beliefs are dubious in the extreme; and the Mackenzie campaign shows why. He failed to swing policy in a more humanitarian direction not because of any lack of effort on his part, but because the very methods which he used are very rarely successful on matters dealing with African tribes, and the expenditure of large amounts of British money abroad.

On paper the campaign should have succeeded. Mackenzie *did* reach a wide audience in an age without mass communications; he *did* have his views considered in the Colonial Office; he *did* have the matter discussed in a full debate in Parliament; and he even, via Chamberlain, *did* reach the Cabinet agenda. It was to no avail: Robinson had already tried much the same thing from the inside—as one of the policy-makers—and he had failed. In the last resort men of power, like Chamberlain, were not prepared to make a stand on the Tswana chiefs' fate when larger issues—such as plans for a new Reform Bill, and the further extension of the franchise—really held their attention, and would require all their political ingenuity and influence. In like manner, other members of Cabinet found Egypt more worrying than Bechuanaland, Parnell more distracting than Montshiwa, Bismarck's activities more destructive than Boer expansion.

Two letters from Mackenzie to his sons show to what degree his energetic efforts were merely exercises in shadow-boxing: he was never able to land a blow for the cause in which he so passionately believed, nor to corner Kimberley and so force a change in policy.

To take Mackenzie's letter of 30 November 1882 first:[1] he writes of an interview with Evelyn Ashley, parliamentary under-secretary to the Colonial Office.[2] 'He was very dry indeed when I went in,' Mackenzie reported, 'Did not say sit down.' Nor was Ashley's first question very encouraging: 'Well, Sir, anything fresh—more than we know?' Mackenzie was finally asked to sit down and Ashley pulled no punches about

[1] W. D. Mackenzie, *Life of Mackenzie*, pp. 268–9. John Mackenzie to his son, Jonnie, 30 November 1882.

[2] The interview was on 29 November 1882 at the C.O.

the campaign then in full swing: 'What I do say heartily and earnestly is, Mr. Mackenzie, that I wish all your meetings and resolutions etc., would go further and tell us what we are to do. I would forbid the right of criticism, for my part, except when accompanied by practical suggestion.'[1]

Mackenzie protested that he had made just such practical suggestions. '[I] . . . suggest that Her Majesty's Government and the Cape Colony should combine to establish order there.' Ashley could not then tell Mackenzie that this had been the Robinson plan; and that it had no chance of success until the Transvaal gave the Cape the 'go ahead'. But his reply as it stands suggested that the official policy saw no *via media* available to them. Ashley: '. . . You mean that we should march an army through the Transvaal for the purpose . . .?'[2]

Equally revealing was Mackenzie's record of his meeting with Leonard Courtney, until that point Kimberley's associate at the Colonial Office. Mackenzie wrote to his son, Willie, on 26 November 1882:[3] '. . . Courtney made "no bones" about admitting right off, that those who think with him want to "clear out" from South Africa entirely'. '. . . He expressed an opinion that this entire "letting alone", would soon be announced publicly.'

Courtney also gave Mackenzie a clear, if crude outline on the official thinking about this area of the Empire. 'We never could govern South Africa in the past. We have as fine men trying as any we are likely to have now or in the future. *The lowering of the suffrage in this country has rendered all government more difficult.* . . . We can't do it—it's impossible [i.e. to control South Africa] and by and by the suffrage will be still more widened.'[4]

Officialdom presented a united front to the earnest missionary —not only because this was the traditional tactic, but because people thought alike about the troubles of South Africa. It was the attitude of 'letting alone' which so shocked Mackenzie: 'This is exactly what Lord Kimberley said. . . .'[5]

The Times had already captured the general thinking behind the official policy. The native question in South Africa was

1 Idem.
2 Idem.
3 Ibid., p. 266. Mackenzie to his son, 26 November 1882.
4 Idem. (My italics.)
5 Idem.

'slowly, if somewhat sadly, settling itself'.[1] It is significant that in that final settlement Britain was playing no part; and that the settlement was being dictated by a Boer government.

4. Strange Logic: Kimberley Justifies Inactivity

Kimberley's abdication from responsibility, in the case of Boer expansion, has generally been attributed either to sheer sloth, or the exigencies of Gladstonian economy. In either case—and as a result of the fate of the Tswana chiefs—he has been an easy target for the critical historian. But as with so many snap-judgments about this garrulous, yet hard-thinking man, the truth is somewhat more complex.

The factors which made up the stock of information, the reservoir of fact and opinion on which he based his policy, is diffuse and varied; but, combined, the various factors all point to one conclusion—external matters, quite as much as internal Boer behaviour, determined the pattern and scope of Kimberley's approach. To see the relationship of the Colonial Secretary with a particular colony as an exclusive and insular channel for policy, quite removed from other problems and policies, has ever been a dubious approach to imperial matters; and it is particularly so in this instance. Foreign events, European diplomatic pressures, tensions within the Gladstone Cabinets, local British party political wrangles, and concurrent problems in Africa, all crowded in to bias Kimberley's approach to the Boer Government. The first and most immediate factor to take into account was the manner in which the Bechuanaland dilemma coincided in time and intensity with other vital and far-reaching imperial crises. In particular the secret discussions with the imprisoned Parnell; and the beginnings of Gladstone's bondage in Egypt.

The period February–June 1882 was crucial to Mankurwane in his struggle to retain his independence. But it was also the period of Chamberlain's negotiations with Parnell, which led to the Kilmainham Treaty;[2] and the time of the open clash

[1] *The Times,* 21 September 1882.
[2] From 17 February to 9 March. The Land Law was finally passed in the Commons by 303 to 255.

between the two Houses over the issue of the Land Law.[1] On 9 March the Government majority in the Commons fell to 39; and Cowper resigned (28 April) as Lord Lieutenant of Ireland, on hearing of the secret negotiations. Less than a week later, on 2 May, Forster also resigned from the Government to protest at the terms agreed on with the Parnell.[2]

This was still not the peak of the crisis. On 4 May Parnell was released from prison;[3] on 5 May Lord Frederick Cavendish, Cowper's replacement in Ireland, was hacked to death in Phoenix Park, Dublin, by men armed with long surgical knives. The effect of his death, and its circumstances, was immediate and far-reaching.[4] On 16 May Gladstone faced a Commons which howled for revenge. Balfour mercilessly attacked Gladstone in the lower House; and Salisbury did so with even greater effect in the Lords. As Gladstone's secretary recorded: 'We have been living at the mouth of volcanoes again this week. Crisis on Egypt. Crisis on Ireland.'[5] Indeed, tensions became so extreme that at one Cabinet meeting Gladstone actually hissed through his teeth in fury at Harcourt, to the hushed amazement of the rest of the Cabinet.[6]

It is not surprising that the meeting of 9 July 1882 was taken by many ministers present to be possibly the last of this Liberal

[1] J. L. Hammond, *Gladstone and the Irish Nation*, p. 290, *passim*.

[2] The resignation of Forster at the Cabinet of 2 May led to the strange Selborne 'attempted resignation'. Granville left the Cabinet room to go and inform the Queen of Forster's action. After he had gone Selborne suddenly said: 'But I agree with him, and must resign also.' Harcourt, who sat next to him remarked: 'It is too late, it would not now be respectful to the Queen as Granville has started.' So Selborne stayed in the Government! See Addit. MSS. 44643, f. 85 (Cabinet Papers), 2 May 1882. See also Gwynne and Tuckwell, *Dilke*, I, 439–40.

[3] Addit. MSS. 48632, f. 19 (Hamilton Diary). 'Ireland seems to be in a worse state than ever. It is going through by far the most terrible social revolution . . . that has ever disturbed that wretched island'.

[4] Ibid., f. 39. Entry for 5 May and 8 May 1882. See also *Letters of Queen Victoria*, 2nd ser., III, pp. 282–3: 'How could Mr. Gladstone and his violent Radical advisers proceed with such a policy. . . . Surely his eyes must be opened now'. Journal of Queen Victoria. Entry for 6 May 1882.

[5] Ibid., f. 80. Entry for Friday, 7 July 1882.

[6] Addit. MSS. 43924, f. 74 (Dilke Diary). Refers to Cabinet of 22 February 1882. See also Addit. MSS. 44643, f. 54 (Cabinet Papers), for Wednesday, 22 February 1882.

Government. This was not to be; but a new coercive law was agreed upon. On 12 July the 'Crimes Bill' was accordingly rushed through the House. Parnell took it as a betrayal of the Kilmainham pact; and launched a fresh attack, via parliamentary obstruction, on the weary Gladstone. The Arrears Act, of 10 August, hardly changed the Irish leader's opinion of the G.O.M.; and by 30 October the Commons was in a constant state of unrest, with the Irish members wrecking the very process of legislative government.

If this had been the only prevailing crisis Kimberley might not have been drawn too seriously away from the Transvaal–Tswana troubles. But this was unfortunately not so. From early May—the murder of Cavendish and the beginning of major raids on Mankurwane—Britain became ever more deeply involved in the crumbling stability of the Levant.[1] Colonel Arabi's rebellion has already been noted above. Now, in May 1882, he was in control of large areas of Egypt. France and Britain felt reluctantly drawn to intervene so as to secure their original interests.[2] By 15 May a joint fleet was on the way to the area; on 25 May the Khedive attempted to dismiss the Arabist ministers; and, on 11 June, 50 Europeans were massacred, and over 10,000 fled Egypt.[3] The Constantinople Conference of late June, called to discuss the crisis, produced nothing of worth. At the moment when Mankurwane was facing extinction at the hands of the freebooters, Kimberley was participating in the ultimatum which was sent to Arabi (10 July); and applauding the bombardment of Alexandria by the British fleet (11 July).[4] Or as Fairfield put it: 'In 1879 when we had difficulties with the Boers the Ruler of Egypt became restive: now that we have trouble with the Egyptians, the Rulers of the Boers become restive.'[5]

Gladstone's attention was, not unnaturally, now divided

[1] P.R.O. 30/29/126. Gladstone to Granville, 9 July 1882. (Ramm, I, 387–8).

[2] Addit. MSS. 48632, f. 57 (Hamilton Diary). 'Egypt is again in the acute state. . . .' Entry for 22 May 1882.

[3] Ibid., f. 68. Entry for Sunday, 11 June 1882.

[4] Harcourt's remark on the action is worthy of record: 'At last we have done a popular thing: we have bombarded Alexandria.' Quoted in G. P. Gooch, *Life of Courtney*, p. 174.

[5] C. O. 291/16. Minute by Fairfield, 3 August 1882.

A DIFFICULT PART.

W. E. G. (as *Hamlet*).—" THE TIME IS OUT OF JOINT ;—O CURSÈD SPITE,
  THAT EVER I WAS BORN TO SET IT RIGHT!"—*Act I., Sc.* 5.

. The problems which confronted Mr. Gladstone at this time, both at home and abroad, were many and perplexing.

exclusively between Egypt and Ireland.[1] On 9 July he struggled to survive the Irish crisis in his Cabinet;[2] on 22 July he battled to swing the Commons behind him in case there should be need for a full-scale military campaign.[3] In Hamilton's words, 'We are in for it—and are practically embarked on an Egyptian War.'[4] A few days later Gladstone announced that he would suspend his principle, of 'economy and retrenchment', in calling for a *rise* in the income tax—to 8*d*. in the pound—to pay for the costs of the Egyptian campaign which soon followed. The G.O.M. remarked with a sigh to Rosebery that as for his great theme of economy in government he felt he was becoming 'an old mouldy landmark on a deserted shore'.[5]

These two major crises leap-frogged over each other in time. Late in July Gladstone turned his attention back to the matter

[1] A third, and time consuming 'crisis', was the behaviour of the Queen at this time. Although she had recently recovered from an assassination attempt (2 March) she saw even greater danger in the behaviour of Gladstone's Government. On 27 May she wrote a letter to the Prince of Wales which must surely stand as her ultimate vituperative outburst against Gladstone: 'Dearest Bertie,—The state of affairs, this dreadfully Radical Government which contains many thinly-veiled *Republicans* . . . weigh on my health and spirits. You as my eldest son, and so intimate as you are with Lord Hartington *might* and *should* I think speak strongly to him, *reminding* him *how* HE *asked you to tell me in* '80 *that if I took Mr. Gladstone I should certainly* NOT *have to take these violent and dangerous Radicals*, instead of which *two* days after I had *most unwillingly* taken this most dangerous man; *all* the *worst men* who had no respect for Kings and Princes or any of the *landmarks* of the Constitution *were put into the Government in spite of me*. The mischief Mr. Gladstone does is *incalculable*; instead of *stemming* the current and downward course of Radicalism, which he could do *perfectly*, he leads and *encourages it* and alienates all the true Whigs and moderate Liberals from him. Patriotism is nowhere in their ranks.' (*Letters of Queen Victoria*, pp. 298–9.) And, there was also the brief but explosive resurgence of the matter of Bradlaugh and the oath, which obsessed several generations of Victorians. See Addit. MSS. 48631, f. 122 (Hamilton Diary)—'The session opened badly this afternoon, the Bradlaugh business came on early'. Entry for 7 February 1882.
[2] Addit. MSS. 48632, f. 78. Entry for 30 June 1882, 'Hideous news again from Ireland.'
[3] Ibid., f. 77. Entry for 28 June 1882: 'Egypt continues to be the object of greatest public interest for the moment.'
[4] Ibid., f. 95. Entry for 25 July 1882.
[5] Ibid., f. 29. Entry for Thursday, 20 April 1882.

of an Arrears Act; early in August he intently watched the progress of the Constantinople Conference; on 10 August he secured the passage of the Arrears Act; and between 18 August and 13 September he anxiously followed Wolseley's campaign against Arabi, ending at the great victory of Tel-el-Kebir.[1] By 15 September Wolseley had control of Cairo, and the Egyptian crisis went into a limbo state for a few months.[2] But, at almost the same moment, Parnell launched the first of his new attacks in Parliament when it returned from the summer recess, on 24 October.[3] These obstructionist tactics, and the increase in Fenianism in outlying areas, coincided in time with the second stage of the Bechuanaland dilemma; the surrender of Montshiwa in October to his white attackers, led by Moswete.

Thus in the scale of things Bechuanaland rated rather low. As much as Egypt was vital to British routes to India, so the vast desert territory of Bechuanaland seemed relatively unimportant; and as much as Parnell was a crucial figure in Gladstone's struggle to hold the Liberal Government together, so two obscure Tswana chiefs hardly seemed to tip the balance either way, no matter what their fate. And no ministers—least of all Kimberley—thought of resigning over Bechuanaland; yet Gladstone lost three important ministers in four months over Ireland and Egypt[4] while several others hovered on the edge of resignation.[5]

It is Gladstone's personal Cabinet papers which best tell the story. From the first Cabinet of the year (6 January 1882)[6] through to the last (4 December),[7] it is Irish unrest and Egyptian responsibilities which grip the attention of this Govern-

[1] Hamilton reacted like many Liberals of the time—'I feel quite Jingoish for the moment.' Ibid., f. 112. Entry for 25 August 1882.

[2] Victoria, as usual, held the extreme views: 'The Queen is keen for the hanging of Arabi.' Ibid., f. 135.

[3] The House had been in recess since 18 August 1882.

[4] The resignations were; 28 April, Cowper (Ireland); 2 May, Forster (Ireland); 15 July, Bright (bombardment of Alexandria).

[5] It was also feared that Chamberlain might go with Bright. See Addit. MSS. 48632, f. 75. Entry for 25 June 1882. And even Selborne began to rumble with discontent. See also Gwynne and Tuckwell; Dilke, I, pp. 439-40.

[6] Addit. MSS. 44643, f. 2 (Cabinet Papers).

[7] Ibid., f. 195.

ment; and which most severely divided the administration.[1] The divisions over Ireland continued, with the Whigs, including Kimberley, pressing for a stiffer Crimes Act; and the Gladstonians, including Granville and Harcourt, trying for a 'middle-of-the-way' policy, with their faith in new land and rent acts.[1] Over Egypt the divisions became even sharper, if that were possible, and even more difficult to define.[2] By-and-large the Cabinet split three ways: Granville led the Gladstonians in calling for limited military action in concert with France; Hartington led a rather more 'forward party', and pressed for more decisive action regardless of France and Bismarck; while on the wings stood the Radicals, thoroughly divided among themselves[3]: Bright was shocked and disquieted at the bombardment of Alexandria—'simply damnable, worse than anything ever perpetrated by Dizzy'—while Chamberlain and Dilke tended to feel it was a necessary evil.

These two topics—Parnell's Ireland and Wolseley's Egypt— soon obsessed the ministers.[4] It would have required a crisis of

[1] Hamilton felt that it was Gladstone alone who kept the Government together. He was probably right—'He is not only the sole man who can hold together the many sections of the Liberal party. He is the cohesive and modifying power. He impels the sluggard Whig, and holds in check the impulsive Radical'. See Addit. MSS. 48633, f. 9 (Hamilton Diary). Entry for Sunday, 27 October 1882.

[2] Gwynne and Tuckwell, *Dilke*, I, 459.

[3] These Cabinet wrangles over Egypt and Ireland in early 1882 were to have important long-reaching effects. For example Gladstone had intended the February Cabinets to be 'planning Cabinets', preparing the legislative programme for the session. This he had already failed to do in the previous November. Now in February 1882 it was Ireland and Egypt which turned the Cabinets into sharp clashes on foreign policy—the meeting of 1 February lasted seven hours. (Addit. MSS. 44643, f. 26)—and no planning was done at all (Ibid., ff. 26–61). The effect was disastrous on the parliamentary session when nothing of worth was achieved; or in Hamilton's words, 'The failure of the Govt. as regards legislative work'. Addit. MSS. 48633, f. 26 (Hamilton Diary).

[4] Addit. MSS. 48633, f. 4 (Hamilton Diary). Entry for 22 October 1882. Egypt also obsessed Queen Victoria. She was terrified lest Gladstone reduce British forces in the Nile area and so allowed another Majuba. Queen Victoria to Gladstone, 30 September 1882: 'She cannot forget the unfortunate result of the haste with which our troops were brought back from Zululand and South Africa, and the consequent humiliation and loss of prestige which ensued in the Transvaal: this should be a warning to us in the present instance.' (*Letters of Queen Victoria*, pp. 343–4).

enormous latent dangers to draw their attention away from the challenge of Fenianism, or the problem of how to get out of Egypt without allowing unrest to return.[1] Bechuanaland and the Boer quest for land was hardly such a crisis. The really serious divisions within the Government were played out around Hartington and Granville on Egypt, Gladstone and the Whigs on Ireland.[2] There was no division over what to do in South Africa. The reason for this was simple: it was not discussed at a single Cabinet in 1882, nor was it ever lifted to more general attention of ministers. There were 54 full Cabinets in 1882, and 4 quasi-Cabinets.[3] The nearest the ministers came to discussing southern Africa was the question of Basutoland (on 4 March);[4] the restoration of Cetewayo (on 3 and 12 August, and 27 November);[5] and the Congo (on 24 October).[6] The Tswana chiefs are totally absent from the agenda, as are the Boers—in contrast to the frequent references in the previous year. Indeed, the matter of the Convention, and its enforcement or violation, was not discussed at Cabinet level between 10 November 1881[7] and 10 March 1883.[8]

The contents of the Gladstone–Kimberley correspondence is also significant for 1882. They corresponded frequently, but very largely on Ireland, *not* on South Africa.[9] In fact after the Robinson telegrams—suggesting the police, which Kimberley did discuss with Gladstone[10]—there is no further reference to Kruger. It is as if the destruction of the Tswana chiefs was not known to Kimberley, which, of course, was not true.

It is one of the harsh facts of 'imperial history' that humanitarian matters were coldly received in official circles. In this

[1] It all pressed heavily on Gladstone: 'Mr. G. has been rather *low* lately, owing to his seeing great difficulties about escaping from office.' Ibid., f. 22 (Hamilton Diary). Entry for 21 November 1882. See also f. 24: 'Mr. G. went and had a long talk with Lord G.—the main topic of the conversation must have been Mr. G's personal position.'

[2] Addit. MSS. 44643, ff. 2–195 (Cabinet Papers).

[3] i.e. an informal meeting of certain Cabinet ministers called by Gladstone at his rooms in the Commons. The four meetings in question were: 22 January, 22 April, 10 and 20 June 1882 (ff. 54, 75, 129, 132).

[4] Ibid., f. 66.   [5] Ibid., ff. 166, 171, 191.   [6] Ibid., f. 180.

[7] Addit. MSS. 44642, f. 220.   [8] Addit. MSS. 44644, f. 7.

[9] Addit. MSS. 44227, ff. 201 ff. Kimberley to Gladstone, 10 July 1882 on.

[10] Ibid., ff. 206–10. Robinson to Kimberley (Tels.), 8–9 July 1882, in Gladstone Papers.

case the Colonial Secretary was deeply involved in two of the most important dilemmas which faced the Victorians; and he was also sufficiently a Gladstonian on the question of the extent of expense abroad. Before the question of sending an expedition to clear the white 'freebooters' out of Bechuanaland was raised, the Wolseley campaign in Egypt, together with the account for the Afghan War, had already provided a touchstone on which to test the priorities of further expense. Wolseley's campaign meant high income-tax; the Treasury estimate of the cost of the Afghan War was revealed, on 16 March 1882, as £5 million.[1] And if these were not cautionary enough tales for Kimberley, his memory could go back to the cost of the Transvaal rebellion, the Zulu War, and the campaign against Sekukuni.[2] The cumulative effect of these 'extravagancies', which hit hard at Gladstone's intuitive quest for economy, was to prove an extremely powerful if negative force in deterring Kimberley's actions.

This is hardly surprising. None of these measures in expediency had yet wrought any positive gains to Britain. And the most successful—Wolseley's campaign—looked like being the most worrying, for it could draw the Victorians permanently into North Africa as they had been lured deeper into South Africa. It was on this question of long-term commitments that a forward policy turned. Kimberley did not take exception to financing immediate action which could halt a deteriorating situation. As he wrote to Gladstone, when Robinson suggested a police force for controlling the Bechuanaland border area, 'You will observe that it will involve some small expenditure, [but] ... I think Sir Hercules Robinson's advice should be followed.'[3] Thus Kimberley was prepared to advance these emergency amounts; but where he baulked was on committing Britain to a long-term financial responsibility, such as was involved in annexing Bechuanaland and ruling it as a Crown Colony. Kimberley had already considered this course of action,

[1] *Parl. Pap.*, 1882, XXXVIII, C.125, p. 481. Treasury estimates 16 March 1882. Annual cost of the border disturbances was £½ million; while the Indian Government had been loaned £2 million for a similar purpose.
[2] De Kiewiet, *Imperial Factor*, pp. 180, 237–8. Sekukuni campaign: £55,000; Zulu War: nearly £1 million.
[3] Addit. MSS. 44227, f. 202. Kimberley to Gladstone, 11 July 1882.

and abandoned it: 'There is no real remedy for this', he minuted on a despatch from Robinson concerned with the Tswana chiefs' defeats,[1] 'but the annexation of the country, a remedy which in my opinion would be worse than the disease.'

Quite apart from these important factors—the question of the overlapping of other vital crises, and the matter of economy—there were several other interests which bore heavily on Kimberley's thinking. It is often forgotten by writers on Bechuanaland that the early 1880s also witnessed important development in other parts of southern Africa. By 1882 for example, when Mackenzie was calling for imperial expenditure in Bechuanaland[2], Kimberley was having to accept the fact that Basutoland might well return to the imperial fold in the very near future. The Cape government, who had administered the Basutos since 1868, had hardly proved to be the best trustees of the native interests. The outbreak of the Cape–Basuto 'war of disarmament', in 1880–81, had been the culmination of many years of friction. Attempts to reconcile the parties had failed; and when 'Chinese' Gordon was sent to the scene, from Mauritius in 1882, he lived up to his controversial name[3] by bluntly putting the dilemma in its true perspective: 'I like the Boers. They are a fine people, but ask them outright which they like best—farms or Basutos.'[4]

This remark did not endear him to the Cape Colonists. 'His conduct has been that of a man whose mind is unhinged', a

[1] C.O. 291/16. Minute by Kimberley, 31 August 1882.

[2] It should also be borne in mind that until Mackenzie's campaign, which began in autumn 1882, there was little or no interest in Bechuanaland and its problems, either in the Press or in the Commons. The C.O. even remarked on this—no doubt with a sense of relief. (C.O. 291/17. Minutes for 23–6 April 1882.) The first question in the House on Tswana chiefs was not asked until it was too late (5 June 1882). And even then the questioner—Gorst —was easily fobbed off with a non-committal reply. See also *The Times*, 6 June 1882, enclosed in Kimberley to Robinson, 7 June 1882, in *Parl. Pap.*, 1882, XLVII, C.3381, p. 96.

[3] Why Kimberley allowed him to go to the Cape is difficult to understand. On 3 November he minuted—after Gordon had stirred up Cape feeling— 'The Cape Govt. should never have employed him unless they meant to put the affairs really in his hands. There is nothing new in his eccentricities. Everyone who knows about his career (which apparently the Cape people have never studied) is well aware of them.' C.O. 48/504. Robinson to Kimberley, 10 October 1882. Minutes by Kimberley, 3 November 1882.

[4] De Kiewiet, *Imperial Factor*, p. 290.

Colonial minister wrote.[1] Gordon then departed to die at the other end of the continent, having exacerbated Cape–Basuto relations; and failed to get Cecil Rhodes to come with him to Egypt.[2] Thus Kimberley found himself facing the unwelcome reality of administering Basutoland again just at the time when the Tswana chiefs also needed imperial protection.

Much the same could be said for the state of affairs in Zululand.[3] Wolseley's settlement—an attempt to devolve Zulu power on to thirteen nominated chiefs—was collapsing. The question of restoring Cetewayo became more than an academic topic.[4] It was thought by many observers that a 'reformed' and controlled Cetewayo held out better prospects than the attempt to hold thirteen aspiring chiefs in line[5] This plan was also operated in August 1882, when Cetewayo visited the Colonial Office—dressed in a morning suit, top hat but shoeless[6]—to agree to the British terms for his restoration: 'Let Lord Kimberley . . . grasp him by the arm, and let the Queen take him by the waist, for then they will hold him fast.'[7]

Kimberley's policy had therefore to take into account not only the international and home position of the Government, but also the local developments in Africa. The extension of imperial responsibility in Basutoland was moving from the possible to the probable; and the Zulu situation seemed to point in the same direction. Why then did he place the Zulu and Basuto-

[1] Idem.

[2] The thought of Rhodes *and* Gordon at Khartoum is a fascinating one. When Rhodes heard of his death in 1885 he said immediately; 'I wish I had been with him.' Others wished this as well.

[3] De Kiewiet, *Imperial Factor*, for Wolseley's settlement, pp. 246–7.

[4] Addit. MSS. 48632, ff. 70–77 (Hamilton Diary). Entry for Monday, 26 June 1882. See also, Addit. MSS. 44227, f. 168. Kimberley to Gladstone, 27 May 1882: 'Our security for the future would be that if restored—by an act of the Queen, he would consider himself hereafter her servant and creature, and be amenable to the advice and guidance of the Resident. . . . But can we [do] it without the Queen's approval. She is sure to object to Cetewayo's restoration.' In fact she did object, see f. 173, Ponsonby to Kimberley, 10 June 1882.

[5] C.O. 48/501. Minute by Herbert, on Robinson to Kimberley, 26 October (Tel.), Minute dated 27 October 1882.

[6] Lucy, *Diary of Two Parliaments*, p. 289.

[7] C.O. 879/19, nos. 247, 248. Cetewayo at C.O., Monday, 7 August, Tuesday, 15 August, and Thursday, 17 August, Shepstone was present, and Dunn acted as interpreter.

land people on a higher scale of priorities than the Tswana tribes? First, because they promised to involved Britain in even greater troubles if left unchecked: Kimberley could afford to allow the Tswana to fall under the Boer control without much concern for the consequences; he could not allow the Zulus or the Basuto to break-out in a full-scale rising. Second, Basutoland and Zululand were more pertinent to the question of imperial strategy. Both areas were situated on the vulnerable eastern flank of British South Africa. Loss of control in these territories could be serious. This could hardly be said for Bechuanaland.

The effect of the local situation on Kimberley's thinking went even further than this. Perhaps the single most important issue which Kimberley took into account was not Cetewayo, the Basutos, or the Tswana chiefs, but the attitude of the Cape, and the Cape Dutch in particular. His concern over not endangering Anglo-Cape relations was very great. It is significant that at this crucial period for British policy that a private report was produced by Sir Thomas Brassey evaluating the importance of the Cape route to India.[1] As the report stated: 'Recent events have attracted attention to the relative advantages of communication with India by the Cape and the Suez Canal respectively.' The report then went on to give some surprising statistics. The distance from Portsmouth to Calcutta, via the Cape, was 3,000 miles longer than via Suez—and the difference in sailing time, at 14 knots, was 6 days 21 hours,[2]—but take into account 'the great heat experienced during a considerable part of the year, and the increased liability to interruptions from the attacks of an enemy' and the longer Cape route took on a unique value. It 'would seem to turn the scale decidedly in favour of the Cape as the best military route to India'.[3] In evaluating the allocations for the defence of coaling stations the memorandum was

---

[1] Addit. MSS. 44628, f. 118. Memorandum by Sir Thomas Brassey, dated 5 July 1882.

[2] Ibid., the actual figures are:

	Via Suez	Via Cape
Portsmouth to Bombay:	6,120 miles (18 days, 18 hours)	10,530 miles (27 days, 10 hours)
Portsmouth to Calcutta:	7,760 miles	11,763 miles

[3] Idem.

equally explicit: the Cape was placed second only to Aden in importance.[1]

Both Gladstone and Kimberley studied this memorandum, though it does not appear to have gone to the Cabinet. The effect on Kimberley can only be gauged from his official correspondence, but this hardly leaves any doubt that he agreed fully with Brassey's findings. The implications of the memorandum were obvious: supremacy at the Cape was as vital as it had ever been. This factor tied in with the Bechuanaland matter in a uniquely 'colonial' manner. Kimberley would have liked the Cape to have exerted influence in Bechuanaland to counteract the activities of the Transvaal burghers—but this was soon clearly an impossibility. As Robinson wrote on 24 June: 'Public feeling in this colony at present is strongly opposed to any extension of its borders or to the assumption of any responsibilities beyond them. . . .'[2] But what even Robinson had not grasped was the reasoning behind the Cape reluctance on this particular territory. It was not merely a refusal to take on 'another Basutoland'; rather it involved feelings among the Cape Dutch about the Transvaal Boers. Robinson tumbled to this fact when he attempted to assemble his united police force in August. The Cape said they would participate only if the Transvaal also took part;[3] if not, they would hold to 'an attitude of strict neutrality'.[4] When the Transvaal did turn the idea down—it was hardly to their interests—the Cape ministry refused to move in concert with the imperial power alone.

The lesson was not lost on Kimberley, especially as it reinforced his already jaundiced view of the loyalty of the Cape Dutch. Robinson's attempts to reassure him that the Pretoria Convention had 'done much to allay the race animosities which were revived by the annexation of the Transvaal . . . and inflamed by the unhappy events of last year',[5] hardly dispelled Kimberley's fears. Nor were the permanent officials sanguine about the news contained in Robinson's despatches from the

[1] Ibid., see also Addit. MSS. 44629, f. 81.
[2] *Parl. Pap.*, 1882, XLVII, C.3381, pp. 147–8. Robinson to Kimberley, 24 June 1882.
[3] Ibid., C.3419, p. 23. Robinson to Kimberley (Tel.), 4 August 1882.
[4] Ibid., p. 5. Robinson to Kimberley, 1 August 1882.
[5] C.O. 48/503. Robinson to Kimberley, 15 May 1882.

Cape. Early in June the Colonial Office received Robinson's lengthy analysis of the new political party in the Colony—the Afrikaner *Bond*—which had just held its first congress at Graaff Reinet.[1] Robinson's preliminary conclusions about the *Bond* make intriguing reading in the light of later developments. 'The character of the Association varies in different districts of the Colony. . . . It is to be feared . . . that as the members of the Afrikaner *Bond* became absorbed in the more vigorous and wealthy Farmers Protection Association some of the local branches of the latter may become for a time at all events more anti-English in their character.'[2] He predicted that the future would see the *Bond* continuing 'to exercise great political influence in the colony. The farmers have now been awakened by its operation to a sense of their political power, and have begun to realise that if they are united they can, under the existing form of government, control the legislation and administration of the country.'[3]

It was this sort of conclusion which so worried the Colonial officials in Whitehall. Robinson did not take such an alarmist view: 'The Dutch as a rule are slow, cautious, parsimonious and unprogressive.' He saw no danger in a Cape Dutch ministry: 'If they were in power, their tendency would be strongly conservative whilst [the English], who would then be united in opposition, would by their superior intelligence, energy, enterprise and capacity for Parliamentary government, always be able to frustrate any policy that was not fairly liberal and progressive.' Indeed he saw a Dutch ministry as essential within a few years, otherwise they would have 'about half the members declining the responsibility of office, and devoting themselves . . . to the furtherance of a . . . class, without any regard to the effect which such action may have upon the state of parliamentary parties'.[4]

It is in fact a remarkable despatch. Long-trained in handling the affairs of white colonies enjoying responsible government, Robinson held an extremely 'modern' conception of the rôle of colonial ministries. He never talked down to his ministers which

[1] Davenport, *Afrikaner Bond* (O.U.P., 1966) Congress of 1–2 March 1882. (p. 54 *passim*.)

[2] C.O. 48/503. Robinson to Kimberley, 15 May 1882. See also Minutes of 10 June 1882.

[3] Idem.   [4] Idem.

perhaps explains his success as a governor in the treacherous waters of colonial politics—in New South Wales. Thus at the Cape he saw in the *Bond* a movement of moderates, through which the opinions of the predominant Cape Dutch could be channelled, and even controlled. Hofmeyr, in his opinion, was no Parnell.

It all looked very different from England. While Kimberley agreed that the actual discussions at the various *Bond* congresses were indeed 'very harmless proceedings,'[1] the aims of the *Bond*, and its ties with the Transvaal, gave it a sinister character. Robinson's assurances about the Cape Dutch fell on deaf ears in the Colonial Office: perhaps, they were too close to Parnell to think otherwise. One official minuted on this very despatch: the *Bond* 'would appear to be decidedly mischievous and revolutionary in its tendencies, though happily not sufficiently organised to do much harm at present . . .'.[2] Another found the slogan of the *Bond* distinctly worrying: 'It is worthy of notice that "Africa for the Africanders" means apparently the entire exclusion of the natives from any share in the Government. They are to be, according to the universal Dutch practice—expressly exhibited in the African Republics of the Transvaal and the Orange Free State—mere "hewers of wood and drawers of water".'[3] And as Evelyn Ashley, the parliamentary under-secretary was soon to remark, 'The Cape is daily getting more Dutch.'[4]

Robinson's despatches thus had just the opposite effect to that which he intended. Kimberley became even more anxious about the state of Cape colonial opinion, and its ties with the Transvaal Boers. In many ways his fears were reasonable. The Cape refused to act against the Boers in Bechuanaland without Transvaal agreement; and, it soon transpired, that the *Bond* was now established in the Transvaal, with Joubert as its patron. It had first been talked of, by Joubert, at Heidelberg in April 1881; it had opened its first branch at Rustenburg

[1] C.O. 48/504. Minute by Kimberley, 25 October 1882, on Robinson to Kimberley, 25 September 1882, enclosing proceedings of Cradock Congress.
[2] Ibid., Minute by Hamilton, 10 June 1882.
[3] C.O. 48/503. Robinson to Kimberley, 15 May 1882. Minute by Hemming, 11 June 1882.
[4] C.O. 179/141. Minute by Ashley, 22 October 1882, on Bulwer to Kimberley, 14 September 1882.

(Kruger's home) in August 1881; and the first meeting of the *Bond's* Transvaal *Bestuur* (roughly, 'national council') was held on 12 January 1882. Therefore it is not surprising that the Cape tended to see deeper links than there were between Hofmeyr's Dutch and Kruger's Boers. Thus Kimberley considered a direct imperial military action against the white volunteers in Bechuanaland would not only risk a probable renewal of the war with the Transvaal, but could well rouse the Cape Dutch once more —this time to open rebellion, not merely to protest meetings.[1]

Graham Bower's unpublished 'Memoir'[2] gives a clear picture of the broad aims of the Kimberley policy towards the South African Dutch: 'We had to win the loyalty of the Cape Dutch not their hatred,' but the 'English jingoism [after Majuba] was an anxiety and unfortunately the Boers on their side gave ample provocation. In 1882–3 they invaded Bechuanaland . . .'. Because of the feeling among the Cape Dutch, Britain was made 'to begin by negotiations', and not by acting with an armed force; and in those negotiations with the Transvaal Government it was desirable to show a sweet reasonableness. 'The aim of our attitude of moderation . . . was to convince the Cape Dutch of our moderation and our pacific disposition.' If this failed, 'we could not take stronger measures without weakening our hold on the Cape Dutch'.[3]

Kimberley's desire to keep his options open became his prime objective; but he also began to think that those options were being reduced at an alarming rate, certainly faster than they really were. When the question of the sale of arms to the Tswana chiefs was raised once more in November 1882—the Colonial Office wished to see the chiefs getting arms via the Cape, but the Colonial government declined to allow this, even though they freely sold arms to the Transvaal—Kimberley refused to become involved in any disagreement with the Cape. The fact that the Tswana chiefs were desperate for the arms made no difference. Kimberley minuted: 'An attempt to press the matter

[1] Kimberley also laboured for some time under the misapprehension that the Transvaal could be treated like any other European nation state. As late as 4 September Kimberley was still writing in this unreal view to Robinson: 'The Transvaal must be sensible of the discredit which will attach to it if a satisfactory answer cannot be given to these accusations.' See also *Parl. Pap.*, 1882, XLVII, C.3419, p. 71. Kimberley to Robinson, 4 September 1882.
[2] Afr. MSS., S.63, ff. 7–9, (Bower Memoir).   [3] Idem.

on them [the Cape Ministry] will only produce irritation in the Colony, and not do the Bechuana chiefs the slightest good.'

The official Government thinking is best illustrated in a letter by Chamberlain, who brought together these various fears in a reply to Dr. Dale.[1]

> My dear Dale,
> I am in receipt of the resolution of the public meeting . . . [called by a missionary society] and will give its contents careful consideration. . . . If the strict execution of the Convention is pressed home, we must not conceal from ourselves the probability that we may be engaged in a Boer War, the most costly and unsatisfactory, and difficult of all the little wars which we can possibly undertake.[2]

Chamberlain, like the Colonial Secretary, found the greatest concern in the attitude of the South African Dutch:

> In the event of a new conflict they [the Transvaal] would probably secure the assistance of the Orange Free State and the sympathy of the Dutch, and possibly Germany. . . .[3]

The situation in Africa, Chamberlain suggested, was far more explosive than Dale and his missionary colleagues realised.

> The circumstances attending the surrender of the Transvaal have no doubt given the Boers an excessive opinion of their power . . . and I should be reluctant to press matters to the utmost unless it became imperatively necessary; and even then I should feel the gravest anxiety as to the result.[4]

Speaking from greater knowledge of the Colonial Office files Kimberley's fears in fact extended further than Chamberlain's; and further than the question of the South African Dutch. From Natal Bulwer reported—in what Kimberley referred to as a 'verboso et grandis epistola' of 377 pages[5]—that the colonists were

---

[1] Garvin, *Chamberlain*, I, pp. 489–90. Chamberlain to Dale, 14 September 1882.

[2] Ibid., It is rather a pity that this letter, together with the rest of this Dale–Chamberlain correspondence, is 'absent' from the Chamberlain Papers.

[3] Idem.   [4] Idem.

[5] Addit. MSS. 44227, ff. 225–32. Kimberley to Gladstone, 25 August and 29 September 1882, on position in Zululand, based on Bulwer's reports. See also Addit. MSS. 44228, ff. 6, 25. Kimberley to Gladstone, 17 October and 23 November 1882.

moving steadily into the Transvaal orbit of influence, as much from economic reasons of trade, as from antipathy to the Cape, for which Natal had ever felt the reservations of jealousy. To Kimberley this was indeed the last straw.[1] He minuted angrily —'The Natalians may be very British but they are not very loyal, and I think their desire (however natural) to draw closer to the Transvaal and Free State, where there are scarcely any English, rather than the Cape . . . does not show any particular love for closer union with England.'[2]

The cumulative effect of these various fears and contingencies was to result in Kimberley's policy of watchful inactivity. Thus the Colonial Office notes on the question of the fate of the Tswana chiefs took on a resigned air. Herbert summed up the position admirably, in a minute of 31 May 1882:

> The Cape Govt. and Legislature will not interfere, and we cannot establish an Imperial Protectorate in this district; *so the Boers will probably get possession of the country*.[3]

It is a highly unusual admission; had the humanitarians seen it they would really have had explosive material for their campaign. As it is the minute does reveal, if brutally, the official attitude to the Tswana people.[4] The possibility of a further Boer

[1] Kimberley had already tired of the Governor (25 August 1882): 'I do all I can to stir up Bulwer but he is as slow as a tortoise. . . .'; (29 September): 'I have received and send you a *verboso et grandis* from Bulwer, being his report on Zululand in 377 pages!'; (17 October): 'I am getting much disquieted about Bulwer. He seems to be frittering away his time, unable to make up his mind to take any step.' Idem.

[2] C.O. 179/141. Minute by Kimberley, 22 October 1882, on Bulwer to Kimberley, 14 September 1882.

[3] C.O. 291/15. Minute by Herbert, 31 May 1882. Robinson to Kimberley, 5 May 1882. (My italics.)

[4] There is also the unique logic contained in a letter from the C.O. to the Aborigines Protection Society. The letter had pointed out that Great Britain was not stopping this supply of arms to the Transvaal via the Cape, yet they *had* stopped supplies reaching the loyal Tswana chiefs. John Bramston replied for Kimberley: 'Representations have been made to the Transvaal Government. . . . This however could not have been done with equal force if British subjects had at any time been permitted to take part in the conflict or to supply arms and ammunition to either of the contending native chiefs.' *Parl. Pap.*, 1882, XLVII, C.3381, pp. 101–3. C.O. to Aborigines Protection Society, 14 June 1882.

The Cape attitude is also revealing. When Robinson greatly protested at

republic in the area was also accepted. Herbert again:

This could be a mischievious nuisance. *The absorption of the territory in the Transvaal would be preferable, although we have said that the Convention boundary must be maintained!*[1]

Fairfield wrote much the same in regard to the Transvaal expansion on to Zulu lands. 'It's all very awkward. I think it would be best for the peace of the district to let the Boers extend themselves.'[2]

There is no clearer state of the condition of the 'official mind' at a particular moment than these bizarre minutes. One fact is abundantly clear: Kimberley, and the permanent officials, neither cared about the fate of the Tswana,[3] nor wished to risk

their gun-trade with the Transvaal, the Cape ministry replied that it was part of the normal trade with the interior, and, if it were stopped, the Transvaal would merely turn to the 'unlimited supply', which could be obtained 'from the Portuguese settlement of Delagoa Bay'. (Scanlen to Robinson, 29 November 1882 in Robinson to Derby, 16 April 1882. *Parl. Pap.*, 1883, XLIX, C.3486, p. 27.) In fact this was hardly true: the guns referred to wer e not the 'usual trade', but consisted of 3″ × 6″ howitzers and 3″ × 8″ mortar s with 300 rounds each.

[1] Idem. (My italics.)

[2] C.O. 291/16. Fairfield to Bramston, 4 August 1882. This was in fact the origin of the New Republic.

[3] It is important to note that Kimberley was not sympathetic to the fate of the chiefs, as he thought that they had brought their troubles on themselves. Robinson was partly to blame for this. He had written to Kimberley on 1 April 1882: 'I think that Mankaroane [*sic*] is himself alone to blame for his present troubles. He was living in peace and security at Taungs until he interposed unnecessarily in the quarrel between Moshette [*sic*] and Massouw.' [*sic*] (*Parl. Pap.*, 1882, XLVIII, C.3381, pp. 72–3. Robinson to Kimberley, 1 April 1882.) Hence, Kimberley's attitude that the Tswana affair was a 'local matter' which should be handled by the Governments concerned— the Transvaal and Cape. As he wrote to Robinson on 13 July: 'Her Majesty's Government cannot undertake the duty of preserving tranquillity on the border which properly belongs to the governments of the adjoining territories.' (Ibid., pp. 144–5. Kimberley to Robinson, 13 July 1882.) And when it was thought advisable for the boundary line between Mankurwane and Mosweu be redrawn Kimberley wrote: 'The cost would probably be small, and would, of course, have to be defrayed by the two chiefs!' (Ibid., p. 54. Kimberley to Robinson, 23 March 1882.) General Warren, who tried to point out this bias in the Robinson–Kimberley approach, wrote to the Colonial Secretary with great justice: 'I know that many of them [the Tswana] prefer peace to war, but they would prefer fighting to losing their land.' (C.O. 291/17. Warren to Kimberley, 17 March 1882.)

a war with the South African Dutch, over the matter of the behaviour of the Boers on the Convention's frontiers. Whether
Montshiwa and Mankurwane survived, whether Moswete and
Mosweu finally fell victims to their own white volunteers,
whether the Transvaal crushed Mapoch,[1] and whether the
Transvaal admitted the existence of the Convention clauses,
were all questions of mere academic interest in Whitehall.

Indeed what actually happened deep in the interior of Africa
counted for little—so long as it did not send ripples of reaction
to disturb those areas vital to the British presence in South
Africa. Thus it was that the behaviour of the Cape Dutch mattered,[2] and that of the Transvaal Boers in Bechuanaland hopefully, did not;[3] that the fate of the Basuto and Zulu tribes was
vital, while that of the Tswana tribe was less so; that the expansion of the Boers over their border into Zululand and Swaziland
towards St. Lucia Bay was crucial, while the existence of Boer
republics in Bechuanaland was apparently not.

The intentions of the Victorians centred on retaining that
supremacy which was vital to the Cape sea route to the East:
their concern was with the continued existence of an informal
paramountcy, it was not in extending British administration
and government. The Victorians worried about those forces
which might upset the delicate balance of power in southern
Africa. They cared little for systems of rule which implied direct

[1] For full details of this tragic affair, see C.O. 291/16. Minute by Kim-
berley, 2 November 1882, and *Parl. Pap.*, 1882, XLVII, C.3419 (Tel.),
Robinson to Kimberley, October–November 1882, and *Parl. Pap.*, 1883,
XLIX, C.3486, pp. 24 ff. Robinson to Kimberley (Tels.), November–
December 1882.

[2] But, both Kimberley and the C.O. officials refused to see the significance
of Robinson's reports that the Cape Dutch were moving away from sympathy with the Transvaal Government. The conservative Cape Dutch considered the Boer actions a flagrant attack on the Convention. Even the
Dutch newspaper *Het Volksblad*, on 22 August 1882, came out with a leader
critical of Kruger and Joubert's behaviour. (See *Parl. Pap.*, 1882, XLVII,
C.3419, pp. 83–5. Robinson to Kimberley, 28 August 1882. Received at
C.O., 19 September 1882, and enclosing translations of *Het Volksblad*.)

[3] Kimberley was quite prepared to see the Transvaal sign a trade agree-
ment with Portugal. He feared nothing from such a treaty; nor did he see
any advantage in attempting to monopolise Transvaal exports or imports.
See C.O. 291/17, enclosed in F.O. to C.O., 24 October 1882, with a copy of
S.A.R.–Portuguese Treaty of 11 December 1875; and *Parl. Pap.*, 1882,
XLVII, C.3381, p. 5. Kimberley to Robinson, (Tel.), 15 February 1882.

imperial control as a method of retaining the balance. Kimberley was quite prepared to accept the *status quo*—even if it meant a 'Balkanised' South Africa. When the editor of the *Natal Witness* suggested that another attempt should be made at federation in late 1882 Kimberley replied coldly: 'To make another attempt now at federation after the recent failure would be simply folly.'[1]

In the ultimate test, when the cards were really down, all that mattered was the maintenance of British paramountcy and influence at the Cape, together with coastal dominance along the flanks of southern Africa. Policy began and ended with this premise. The difficulty was now that British policy could not be pursued without reference to Kruger and his republican burghers. Because of the Victorian concern for Kruger's influence at the Cape, imperial policy had now been twisted and warped, so that the fulcrum of local politics was no longer Cape Town but Pretoria.

[1] C.O. 48/504. Robinson to Kimberley, 10 October 1882. Minute by Kimberley, 5 November 1882.

VI

ENTER LORD DERBY:
INACTIVITY AS A PRINCIPLE
OF POLICY

Conciliation in retreat

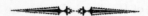

1. The 15th Earl of Derby at the Colonial Office, December 1882

O N 13 December 1882 Gladstone celebrated a private jubi-
lee: it was 50 years since he had first entered public life—
as Member of Parliament for Newark. The same month was also
important in another direction: Gladstone, now a weary 73
years of age, decided to reshuffle his Cabinet in such a way as to
ease the burden on his own shoulders. He gave up trying to be
both First Lord of the Treasury and also his own Chancellor.
Childers was moved from the War Office to take this weighty
office from Gladstone; and two new members were brought into
the Cabinet—Lord Derby, who went to the Colonial Office,
and Charles Dilke, who took over the Local Government Board
from Dodson.[1]

It was more than ministerial musical chairs. Gladstone really
believed he was greatly strengthening the Cabinet, and the

---

[1] The full reshuffle was as follows: Childers became Chancellor of the
Exchequer; Hartington took over Childers' old post at the War Office;
Kimberley became Secretary to India, in succession to Hartington; Lord
Derby moved into the Colonial Office; Dodson was eased into the Duchy of
Lancaster; and Dilke thus took his place at the Local Government Board.
Rosebery still remained outside the Cabinet, and did not enter until March
1885.

working of the administration, by the changes. He considered that Childers would make as good a Chancellor; that Kimberley naturally belonged in control of Indian affairs;[1] that Hartington was happier at the War Office; that Dilke was a young minister of great promise, and particularly useful as the new Anglo-French Commercial Treaty was yet to be negotiated; and, above all, that the Government now had an additional major pillar of support with the entrance of Lord Derby into the Cabinet.

Lord Derby has been harshly treated by the historians—the man who raised indolence and sloth to the level of an art. This is not worth debating; it is more to the point to place Derby in his Victorian context. Quite apart from his extensive political connections in Lancashire—as head of the Stanley family, with its bastion of Lancashire society at Knowsley Hall, near Liverpool—Derby was seen as a great 'catch' for the Gladstone government because of his vast administrative experience. A figure of fun, if not of ridicule for modern observers, Derby was taken seriously by the majority of his Victorian contemporaries as being a man of sound if cautious thinking, with a clear reasoning mind, and an extremely popular personality. Dilke, no lover of the aristocracy, wrote of him: 'Lord Derby could sum up a discussion better probably than anyone has ever done, unless it was Sir Edward Grey.'[2] Derby's supposed failure as Colonial Secretary from 1882 to 1885 has blurred the image he presented when he joined the Gladstone government. Dilke again: 'During his tenure of Secretary of State for the Colonies . . . he lost his credit with the Liberals . . . and his influence reached a point of decline which makes it difficult even to remember the enormous weight he had possessed in the earliest part of his career.'[3]

Derby, in fact, had an extremely varied career. He was 'removed' from Eton to Rugby; took a first in classics at Trinity, Cambridge; entered political life in March 1848, and had his maiden speech praised by Peel. He was a member of the Commons for 21 years, and a member of the Lords for 24 years. He was twice Colonial Secretary—once in his father's Cabinet and

---

[1] Gladstone had wanted Kimberley to be Viceroy in 1880.
[2] Addit. MSS. 43937, f. 163 (Dilke Memoir).
[3] Gwynne and Tuckwell, *Dilke*, I, 537–8.

once under Gladstone; and twice Foreign Secretary—to his father, and to Disraeli. He was considered as a serious candidate for the leadership of the Tory Party, until he went over to the Liberals in 1882. After 1886 he became an influential Unionist. In 1862, it had even been rumoured that he was to be offered the throne of Greece—prompting 'Dizzy' to remark, 'It is a dazzling adventure for the House of Stanley, but they are not an imaginative race, and I fancy they will prefer Knowsley to the Parthenon, and Lancashire to the Attic Plains. . . .'[1]

Derby's personality is also more interesting than historians will allow. His portraits show him as a pug-faced man, balding, with a severe demeanour. But his contemporaries knew him as an easy-going cheerful man, who told very good political anecdotes.[2] He was a country lover and a competent mountaineer. His private life was unusual. He had married Lord Salisbury's step-mother; and it was she who had to control Derby's one major shortcoming—kleptomania. It was a weakness he never conquered. Sent down from Eton for this, gossips said he was still 'stealing' silver at dinner parties in the 1880s.

Lecky wrote of his political philosophy: 'Lord Derby, when a Conservative always represented the Liberal, and when a Liberal the Conservative, wing of his party.'[3] But his mind had much of the Whig character. Even this analysis though leaves much unsaid. Perhaps because of his Lancashire background, Derby was classed as a 'Radical' on matters concerning the well-being of the working classes; and on religious toleration he was also something of an apostle of the future—for example, he was a strong advocate of divorce. John Stuart Mill's *Liberty* he considered 'one of the wisest books of our time'. But here his independent views ended. He had been an uneasy Tory but he found himself to be a happy Gladstonian—even on religious matters.

Gladstone indeed looked upon him as a natural ally and colleague. In particular, they approached foreign and colonial

[1] Lecky (Ed.), *Derby's Collected Speeches* (1894), see Preface.

[2] Addit. MSS. 43934, f. 66 (Dilke Memoir). 'My low opinion of Lord Derby as a politician does not prevent my thinking that in private life he is a most agreeable man.'

[3] Lecky (Ed.), *Derby's Collected Speeches*, see Preface.

matters with the same basic beliefs and bias. Like the G.O.M. he looked to the 'Concert of Europe' as the panacea for international affairs; and to the consolidation of British possessions abroad as the soundest basis for the maintenance of imperial supremacy. If he was a Whig on Ireland he was a Gladstonian on everything else. His attitude to the expansionist theories of Empire was clear: 'I have no love for annexations.'[1]

The Queen thought his views would have a corrosive effect on British influence abroad.[2] On 15 December 1882 she wrote to her secretary, Ponsonby: 'Would Sir Henry tell Mr. Gladstone *how* unpleasant it is for her to have Lord Derby as a minister for *she utterly despises him* . . . in the colonies he may also do grt. harm—by letting everything go.'[3] The Queen's influence was decisive on one matter: Gladstone's original idea of placing Derby at the India Office had to be abandoned as she protested so vigorously.[4] Derby accepted this change, and the post of Colonial Secretary with grace: 'The transfer to the Colonial Office though at first a surprise, is so far from being disagreeable that it is of all, the office I should have preferred. . . .'[5]

In the Colonial Office his appointment was received with resignation rather than enthusiasm. While he was known in official circles as a sound administrator, he was also noted for his great caution and lack of original thought. The charge of indolence is vastly exaggerated, but the absence of constructive suggestions in his minutes was to be crucial. Henry Warr, the secretary to a Royal Commission chaired by Derby,[6] wrote of him: 'Nature has not endowed him with much imagination, but he has a great fund of information, good sense, and has most remarkable industry.'[7] A *Times* leader captured him

---

[1] Addit. MSS. 44141, f. 68. Derby to Gladstone, 23 April 1883.

[2] Addit. MSS. 48633, f. 38 (Hamilton Diary). 'Sir H. Ponsonby tells me that as regards Lord Derby Her Majesty's objections to him were deep-rooted. She thinks he is ready to sacrifice his country at any moment.'

[3] *Ponsonby*, pp. 192–3, Victoria to Ponsonby, 15 December 1882.

[4] Addit. MSS. 48633, f. 27 (Hamilton Diary). Friday, 1 December 1882: 'Lord Derby has consented to join the Government. . . . He is to go to the India Office.' And also ff. 31–8. Entry for Sunday, 17 December 1882. Derby to C.O. 'as it will be less painful for the Queen'.

[5] Addit. MSS. 44141, f. 63. Derby to Gladstone, 25 December 1882.

[6] i.e., Royal Commission on City companies.

[7] Addit. MSS. 43934, f. 313 (Dilke Memoir).

best in a single phrase: Lord Derby was a 'cold water engine'.[1]

In 1882 he was also a well-worn 'engine'; though only 54 years old, he was beyond his prime. Perhaps, under his father's mentorship, he had been too much of a prodigy, and had burnt himself out. Certainly he was no Pitt to his father's Chatham.

Derby succeeded Kimberley in more than name alone. He not only accepted and continued Kimberley's policy towards southern Africa and the Afrikaner Republics, he found new reasons for supporting the 'old' policy. If Kimberley had seen in conciliation the most viable of alternative policies, Derby saw conciliation as the only policy. He gave an added emphasis to Kimberley's approach, and turned his back on all the Whig alternatives which embodied degrees of coercion.

It was not a blind choice. Indeed, if the range of options open to a Colonial Secretary is taken as the prime basis for policy, then Derby can initially be said to have made a more conscious choice than Kimberley; perhaps even a more significant choice. Whereas Kimberley's move towards a conciliatory approach had been forged in the heat of a multitude of concurrent crises—not least of them being a possible pan-Afrikaner rebellion in South Africa, and a full-scale Fenian rebellion in Ireland—Derby was less pressed. Indeed Derby moved through calmer seas in many ways. By early 1883 the heat had gone out of the Irish and Indian (Afghanistan) dilemmas; and the problems in Egypt and the Sudan had not yet arisen. The spring and summer of 1883 was not so much a period of calm before the storm as rather a lull between storms; and it was then—particularly in February, March, and April of 1883—that Derby formulated the basis for his particular policy towards South Africa and its multifarious problems. By the time the Egyptian dilemma arose in September, with Hicks Pasha's advance and defeat against the Mahdi, luring the Gladstone government even nearer to becoming an Egyptian administration, Derby had settled on his 'line' of approach.

Nor was this policy influenced very greatly by happenings within the Gladstone government. Such strains as existed in the ministry, Chamberlain vs the Whigs over the terms of the coming Reform Bill, Gladstone vs Harcourt over the London Government Bill, Granville vs Hartington on Egypt, did not initially

[1] Quoted in Nathan, *Paul Kruger, His Life and Times*, p. 202.

bias Derby's decisions on the Transvaal–Bechuanaland crisis. This was partly because once again the tensions grew from May, after he had taken his decision on the Convention; and mainly because those issues at stake did not call up the same principles as had been involved over the question of coercion or conciliation in Ireland. Whereas the Cabinets of 1880–82 could find common principles in dealing with Irish and Afrikaner local 'nationalist' rebellion, and the Radicals could try to 'dish the Whigs', by playing the Transvaal card on Irish issues, it was vastly different in 1883. Ireland appeared to be comparatively calm: acts of violence had fallen from 4439 in 1881, to 870 in 1883,[1] and Parnell momentarily appeared to be 'reformed' by the Kilmainham agreement.

There was also the important factor that Derby's personal position in the Cabinet was vastly different from that of his predecessors. Not only was he more acceptable to the Radicals, because of political philosophy, but he was not trying to maintain the almost impossible position which Kimberley had taken on Ireland and South Africa. To be 'pro-Kruger' but 'anti-Parnell' was unique even for this Gladstone government: but this is crudely how Kimberley stood, or balanced, throughout 1881–82. Derby did not try for the impossible. He early made it plain that he would secure and protect Great Britain's interests in South Africa, but only so far as they really were endangered: and he did not see the unofficial Boer expansion on Tswana and Zulu lands as a great danger. In a word, he gave the appearance of basing his approach on studied indifference.

This becomes even more apparent when the position in South Africa is taken into account. Kimberley had felt bound to change horses in mid-battle: to throw policy into reverse while committed to suppressing a rebellion. He had accomplished it with a certain skill, even at the price of the charge of inconsistency. In contrast Derby took over the reins of office at a time when Robinson at the Cape was talking of Cape Dutch criticism of the Transvaal Boers for their defiance of the Convention boundaries; and when the possibility of another Anglo-Boer War was becoming more remote.

Clearly this is the way he wished to keep it: and all his actions were a means to this end. Derby did not see in the Pretoria

[1] Magnus, *Gladstone*, p. 304; Morley, *Gladstone*, III, 110–15.

Convention a final solution to the problem of the Boer frontiersman, which had plagued British administrators since 1835; but
equally he believed implicitly in the basis of the policy which
that Convention represented: a stress on moral and diplomatic
suasion as against military coercion; and a faith in informal
supremacy as against crown colonies or protectorates, and their
consequent burden of direct imperial administration.

The local situation in Africa had also changed; but whether
Derby actually appreciated the extent of the change in the local
situation—particularly at the Cape—is an extremely moot
point. Despite Robinson's excellent reports from the Cape,
Derby continued in his belief that the Cape Dutch were un-
trustworthy; and in this way made his options narrower than they
actually were. Derby's stance became in many ways a strange
one. He accepted the fact of Transvaal expansion over the
frontiers, for he claimed to find it without significance; and yet
on the same matter he justified inactivity by pointing to Cape
Dutch opinion. Thus alternately he was doubly wrong: the
Cape Dutch were moving *away* from the Transvaal, while in
Bechuanaland the Transvaal Boers *were* moving closer to Germany. This duality in Derby's thinking and approach is easier
to define than explain. The most charitable view is surely that
he was never entirely clear in his own mind, at any one time,
as to what the situation actually was, nor what the consequences
of his attitude of abstention might be. His policy was occasionally
not so much pragmatic as enigmatic.

Not that he lacked either clear information or precise advice.
In addition to the normal despatches from the Cape, he conducted an extensive private correspondence with Robinson;
and he did not have to select between the conflicting opinions
of the military men and administrators—as Kimberley had had
to do during the troubled months of 1881.

He also had the advice of Kimberley to hand. The latter continued to take a deep interest in southern African affairs; and,
on one occasion, was to 'save' Derby in a debate in the Lords.
The hand-over to Derby was accordingly smooth. Derby went
to the Colonial Office late in December to read all the recent
correspondence. Then he wrote to Kimberley: 'I do not see that
immediate action is possible on it. We do not know who may
be minister, or what may be the policy, at the Cape, in a few

weeks.'¹ Kimberley replied almost immediately: 'Mr. Herbert has seen the correspondence. I agree with you that no action is required at present.'²

On 4 January (1883) Kimberley received the latest of his private reports from Robinson who, when he wrote the letter, did not know that Lord Derby had taken over the Colonial Office. This letter, an extensive end-of-year survey of local developments, was forwarded to Derby, and formed the basis of his evolving understanding of the South African scene.³ This important letter dealt at length with two main topics: the restoration of Cetewayo, and the question of Bechuanaland. On the first Robinson was emphatic: the 'more I look into this settlement the less I like it'.⁴ Cetewayo was to be restored with too many of his old powers stripped from him; he would be too weak to survive in Zululand 'with plotting enemies on either side of him', and thus 'it appears to me wanting in all the elements of permanency'.

On the question of Transvaal expansion, Robinson was equally emphatic, if not more so. This he saw as the real problem facing Britain in South Africa. 'It is clear that neither the Transvaal nor the Free State Government will do anything to restrain their marauding subjects. Nothing but the annexation of the Keate Award territory by either this Colony or the Imperial Government can now save Montsioa [sic] and Mankaroane [sic] from extinction.' Robinson knew that the Gladstone government had 'no love of annexations', thus he had looked to the Cape ministry for a solution: 'I have spoken to Mr. Scanlen but he says whatever claim these chiefs may have on the Imperial Government they will have none on the Colony, and he will not entertain for a moment the idea of accepting any fresh native responsibilities.'⁵

There the matter stood, with Robinson working hard on the Colonial ministry: 'ministers are at this moment sitting in Cabinet discussing the propriety of summoning Parlt. for a short

¹ Derby Papers, Trunk X. 24. Derby to Kimberley, 28 December 1882 (on Knowsley Paper).
² Ibid., Kimberley to Derby, 31 December 1881.
³ Derby Papers, Trunk X. 23. Robinson to Kimberley, 12 December 1882 (received 4 January 1883) and forwarded to Derby. This is the original letter.
⁴ Idem.   ⁵ Idem.

special session next month. I have strongly urged this course upon Mr. Scanlen ... but naturally Mr. Sauer would like to put off the evil day.'[1] But, the moment Robinson learnt that Kimberley had moved to the India Office, he changed his tactic; and went back to his old plan of a police force, this time mainly imperial-supported. Clearly he hoped to succeed with Derby where he had failed with Kimberley, or he would not have taken up a once-rejected scheme that had evoked no great enthusiasm either in London, Cape Town, or Pretoria.

On 22 January Robinson let off his first salvo: a long despatch aimed at exposing Transvaal duplicity on the Convention frontiers.[2] 'It appears to me difficult to resist the conclusion that the Transvaal Government are morally responsible for these proceedings,' and are accordingly 'fairly open to the imputations of having connived at these discreditable proceedings.' Robinson saw only four available options: 'intervention by a large imperial force to drive out the freebooters; division of the disturbed area between Cape and Transvaal Governments; annexation of the whole area and the tribes to the Transvaal; or adhering to the present Convention line and refusing to acquiesce on any expansion'. A time to stop Transvaal 'drift' over the frontiers must come, and the sooner it was faced the better. 'So long as there were native cattle to be stolen and native lands worth appropriating, the absorbing process would be repeated. Tribe after tribe would be pushed back and back upon other tribes, or would perish in the process, until an uninhabitable desert, or sea, were reached or the ultimate boundary of the State.'[3]

Robinson reinforced this determined despatch with the first of his private letters to Derby,[4] within the next day, 23 January. This letter is even more frank and forceful than the 22 January despatch. 'The present mail takes home a deplorable account of the state of the Keate Award territory in consequence of the doings of the freebooters.' As to the so-called 'courses of action'

[1] Idem.
[2] *Parl. Pap.*, 1883, XLIX, C.3486, pp. 50–52. Robinson to Derby, 22 January 1883 (received 13 February 1883).
[3] Idem.
[4] Derby Papers, Trunk X.24. Robinson to Derby, 23 January 1883: 'I am much obliged for your telegram inviting me to write to you freely and confidentially as I have been in the habit of doing to Lord Kimberley.'

Robinson was a great deal more doubtful than in the official despatches, which he knew would ultimately be published in the parliamentary papers. 'What ought or can be done to put a stop to such disgraceful proceedings is a most embarrassing question. I do not think H.M. Government should consent to the Transvaal State absorbing territory outside the boundaries laid down by the Royal Commission—most certainly not by the process they have resorted to in the present case.'[1]

Robinson's central point was that a neutral attitude by Britain would be equally disastrous: '. . . the Suzerain would be put in the position of becoming a party to the scandalous transactions of the marauders. Besides, it would effect no permanent good; but would on the contrary act as an incentive to further similar proceedings on all sides—East as well as West—where native territories abut on the Transvaal.' His conclusion was not far from that which he tried to force on Kimberley in the previous July.[2] 'After looking at the question all round I fear that unless the Suzerain power is prepared to step in, and put a stop by force to these infamous proceedings, there is nothing to be done but sit still and look on.'[3]

Without realising it Robinson also came close to pin-pointing the negative thoughts that must have been going through Derby's mind: 'Before long I think H.M. Government will have to decide the larger question whether they intend to enforce the fundamental conditions of the late Convention, or to allow them to become a dead letter.'[4] This is in fact what Derby was already considering,[5] despite Robinson's clear logic: 'I feel certain the Transvaal Government intend to get rid of the Convention, if they can. Indeed, Kruger stated in his election address lately that he meant to try to get back to the lines of the Sand River Convention.'[6]

[1] Idem.

[2] See Addit. MSS. 44227, ff. 206–10. Robinson to Kimberley (Tels.), (Private), 8–9 July 1882.

[3] Derby Papers, Trunk X. 24. Robinson to Derby (Private), 23 January 1883.

[4] Idem.

[5] C.O. 879/20. Derby to Robinson (Tel.), 21 February 1883; and C.O. 291/22. Minute by Derby, 23 February 1883.

[6] Derby Papers, Trunk X. 24. Robinson to Derby (Private), 23 January 1883.

Ultimately Robinson was thrown back on his long-standing belief that the Boers would go on advancing and ignoring treaties until one was enforced; and that firm action would not jeopardise the imperial position, but rather strengthen it. His conclusions are worth quoting in full as they contain all the elements of the later problems and decisions at the London negotiations of December 1883–January 1884, in the Colonial Office:

> It appears to me that if you mean to stand by the Convention of Pretoria, and say so firmly, there will be no further trouble in the matter. The Transvaal do not mean fighting, but at the same time they do not mean to observe the last Convention unless they see that you mean to enforce it. If you do not mean to insist, if necessary by force, upon the fulfilment of the fundamental conditions of the compact as regards the natives, it is worth considering whether it would not be better to give up at once the whole Convention with a good grace instead of waiting till the concession will have the appearance of yielding to . . . the Transvaal Government.[1]

Robinson never wrote stronger words than these; and yet it was his negative last suggestion which Lord Derby began to play with. The idea of modifying the Convention 'with a good grace' grew with the months. Initially, though, while Derby was taking an implacable 'wait-and-see' attitude, their correspondence centred on two matters: the cost of a possible 'police' expedition, and the deeper question of what to do with the area when it had been cleared. The first proposal ran into immediate difficulties when Derby was informed by Robinson that such an expedition would cost a minimum of £100,000;[2] the second collapsed when the Cape ministry, in no uncertain terms, repudiated the idea of taking on a further native protectorate, even when the imperial authorities took Basutoland off their hands.[3]

Derby was thus thrown back on the extreme alternative of

[1] Idem.

[2] C.O. 879/20. Derby to Robinson (Tel.), 21 February 1883, and Robinson's reply (Tel.), 22 February 1883. He calculated that at least 500 police would be needed.

[3] *Parl. Pap.*, 1883, XLIX, C.3686, p. 24. Scanlen to Robinson, 22 February 1883, enclosed in Robinson to Derby, 26 February 1883. The Cape ministry suggested that Britain 'assume full responsibility of maintaining a protectorate in Bechuanaland'.

unilateral action in Bechuanaland with a regular police force; and he felt no enthusiasm for such a course. 'Keeping a force permanently in Bechuanaland is disguised annexation, or at least a protectorate.'[1] His under-secretary, Ashley, saw it differently: 'The main object of our proposal is to clear ourselves of responsibility—and show people at home that we are doing all we can. It might not do appreciable good to the Bechuanas but it would do much to strengthen our position.'[2]

Derby declined to see the logic in that mercenary view; and indeed began to enunciate the line to which he was going to cling in the months to come: a large imperial force might be effective at first but it would be very costly, and what would happen when it was withdrawn? Thus on 27 February 1883 he killed the idea of a police force with an emphatic telegram to Robinson: 'As you think only effectual course would be clearing country with large force and afterwards occupying it, I fear no present action possible.'[3] The reason he gave to Robinson is mere window dressing: 'Her Majesty's Government cannot undertake large military operations and protection of territory where only 1/10 marauders British.'[4] Far closer to the truth was the letter John Bramston despatched to the Aborigines Protection Society, which had, like Robinson, been pressing for some imperial action on the *veld*. Her Majesty's Government could not intervene as it would ultimately mean 'a permanent *occupation* and end protection of the territory'.[5]

Robinson received the news with little grace: indeed he decided to make one last appeal to Derby.

I clearly see all the serious risks entailed by armed intervention, and I therefore hesitate to press such a course on Her Majesty's Government, but I am anxious that they should have fully before them both sides of the case, and realise that, if our native allies are abandoned, the [Pretoria Convention] may as well be dropped.[6]

[1] C.O. 291/22. Minutes by Derby and Ashley, 23 February 1883.
[2] Idem.
[3] C.O. 879/20. Derby to Robinson (Tel.), 27 February 1883. This telegram is *not* printed in *Parl. Pap.*
[4] Idem.
[5] *Parl. Pap.*, 1883, XLIX, C.3686, p. 13. Bramston to Aborigines Protection Society, 25 February 1883.
[6] C.O. 879/20. Robinson to Derby (Tel.), 1 March 1883. This telegram, not surprisingly, was also kept out of the *Parl. Pap.*

Derby's reaction was unusual, to say the least. He was looking for a way out and so he picked on the phrase 'native allies', and began to question whether they were allies at all. When Robinson referred to obligations already entered into with the Tswana chiefs,[1] Derby minuted churlishly: 'It may be as well to know exactly what was promised—a good deal turns on the exact amount of liability to which we have pledged ourselves.'[2] The inference was clear: the fewer the obligations the better, and such obligations as exist must be minimised.

A policy was slowly emerging, even if a negative one. Early in March Derby allowed the number of British troops in South Africa to be dropped to an all-time low of 2,100 men,[3] as compared with 4,700 a year before, and twice that number during the Transvaal War. When Gladstone returned from his holiday in Cannes, on 2 March, Derby wrote to him immediately. The letter leaves no shadow of doubt as to his attitude:

> All well and quiet in this department, except that the irrepressible Boer is over-running Bechuanaland in spite of all [the] conventions and promises, and *nothing will stop him short of a British occupation of the country, which I presume is no more your wish than it is mine.*[4]

A short while later Derby was to write to Gladstone, on the Australians' call for New Guinea, that he had 'no love for annexations'.[5]

The Boers were indeed being 'irrepressible'. On 11 January they protested that Britain was not keeping to the Convention: '. . . we have the honour to fix the attention of the British Authorities on the Convention, and, particularly, on the 20th Article thereof.'[6] On 8 February they carried their unusual protests a stage further, and actually stated that the situation on the borders was becoming 'worse by the day, and that action of

---

[1] *Parl. Pap.*, 1883, XLIX, C.3686, p. 31. Robinson to Derby, 1 March 1883.

[2] C.O. 291/22. Minute by Derby, 6 March 1883.

[3] See C.O. 48/510. W.O. to C.O., 6 March 1883, for full details of cavalry (400) and infantry (1,700).

[4] Addit. MSS. 44141, f. 65. Derby to Gladstone, 3 March 1883, 2.45 p.m. (My italics.)

[5] Ibid., f. 68. Derby to Gladstone, 23 April 1883.

[6] *Parl. Pap.*, 1883, XLIX, C.3686, p. 12. Bok to Hudson, 11 January 1883, enclosed in Robinson to Derby, 29 January 1883.

some kind cannot longer be delayed'.[1] If Britain did not act, they would. The reaction in Whitehall was one of incredulity.[2] Hemming derided their 'virtuous indignation'; Bramston thought it denoted 'the first steps towards undisguised intervention by the Transvaal Government'; but it was Ashley who best caught the moment, 'It's all part of the farce.'[3]

The matter first came before the Cabinet on 10 March, and once again the Kimberley–Derby approach prevailed.[4] This is hardly surprising. No minister was likely to press for an expensive military operation and a permanent administration at a time when Hicks Pasha was busy campaigning in the Sudan;[5] and many Cabinet members were beginning to ponder on the latest problems and complications in North Africa. They were decidedly cool at becoming even more deeply involved in South Africa. As Gladstone so neatly put it in his Cabinet notes— there was no reason for imperial interference.[6] It was strange logic when a negotiated Convention was being openly flaunted, but it was inexpensive logic. If it meant condoning chaos, it was at least contained chaos. And direct military intervention without annexation seemed equally pointless. Gladstone again: 'Place the border where you will, [the Boers] will always arise with another border.'[7]

It was easy for Gladstone and Derby to take this attitude. Bechuanaland itself not only seemed extremely unimportant, it also seemed extremely distant. Robinson, though, watched the situation crumbling before his eyes, and yet could do nothing. On 13 March he wrote privately to Derby: 'I am anxiously looking for instructions from you.'[8] He had heard, via a Reuters' telegram, that there had been 'a Cabinet Council held on Sunday

[1] Ibid., p. 33. Bok to Hudson, 18 February 1883, enclosed in Robinson to Derby, 5 March 1883 (received 29 March 1883).

[2] C.O. 291/22. Minutes by Hemming, Bramston and Ashley, 29 March 1883. There is no comment by Derby.

[3] Idem.

[4] Addit. MSS. 44644, f. 9 (Cabinet Papers), Saturday, 10 March 1883, 2 p.m.

[5] The 'time-table' was as follows: January 1883: Hicks Pasha sent by Khedive (with 10,000 men) to conquer Sudan. May 1883: Victory; Tewfik decides to reconquer.

[6] Addit. MSS. 44644, f. 9 (Cabinet Papers), 10 March 1883.   [7] Idem.

[8] Derby Papers, Trunk X. 24. Robinson to Derby (Private), 13 March 1883.

last', but Derby had not bothered to inform him of the negative decision. The rumour was, Robinson said, that the Cabinet had decided in *favour* of intervention. 'The result . . . will too probably be that having saved the chiefs and their tribes from annihilation, they will in a few years, when they wax fat, trick us again, and, like the Basutos, prove ungrateful and disobedient. Nevertheless I do not see how we can without dishonour allow these chiefs to be now exterminated. It would be a disgrace to the name and good faith of England if we were to abandon them when they are suffering in consequence of their loyalty to us.'[1]

Robinson's delight at the rumoured news knew no bounds. Immediate intervention would have far-reaching effects.

> I think we shall have less trouble hereafter about the Convention. I do not believe the people of the Transvaal generally object to the Convention. The Hollanders . . . are trying for their own reason to set the Burghers against it: but when once it becomes apparent that we mean to enforce the fundamental conditions of the compact, as ratified by the *Volksraad*, I think we shall have no further serious trouble about the matter.[2]

Derby was shocked when he received this letter: he forwarded it to Gladstone with this comment:

> I am afraid his views as to native affairs are not exactly in accordance with those of the Cabinet. . . . [But] I find his letter written before the receipt of my telegram of March 13, which explained the decisions arrived at here.[3]

Robinson's hopes of a swift military 'clean up' of Bechuanaland were indeed dashed by the telegram Derby referred to;[4] and later in the same month he received a letter from Derby, written on 8 March, amplifying the telegraphic message.[5] This particular letter is not the most important Derby wrote privately to Robinson, but it does give a rare insight into the Earl's approach to politics and colonial questions. Derby admitted that the Boers

[1] Idem.   [2] Idem.
[3] Ibid., comments on back of letter. Gladstone saw it on 4 April, Derby having received it on 3 April 1883.
[4] C.O. 291/22. Derby to Robinson (Tel.), 13 March 1883, conveying Cabinet decision of 10 March 1883.
[5] Derby Papers, Trunk X.24. Derby to Robinson (Private), 8 March 1883 (Copy).

presented 'the most perplexing and troublesome, or rather set of questions, that I have ever had to deal with'. And, that the Boers do indeed 'seem bent on forcing us to revise the Convention by ostentatiously displaying their disregard of it'. But, significantly, what Derby feared was not the extinction of the Tswana chiefs but rather that the Boers might arouse English public opinion—their 'policy is simple and ingenious in its way. but it may be carried too far: for the English mind is liable to fits of excitement—sometimes springing up very suddenly, and it is quite possible that the news of a massacre by Boers, or a studied insult to England, might create a feeling so strong as to override all the obvious and forcible considerations that make against a renewed occupation, or an enforcement of the Convention by military means'. In fact, such a thing had already begun, with the Transvaal–Bechuana troubles 'engaging the serious attention of the Government', together with the possibility of it being debated in Parliament, 'where the non-observance of the Convention will be made a charge against the ministry'.[1]

In spite of all this, Derby's cautious mind remained quite unaltered. He regarded the pressures of Press and parliamentary opinion as a nuisance and not a guide. He could not be moved from the determination that direct military intervention would be both pointless, hazardous and expensive. 'If by clearing Bechuanaland of marauders once [and] for all we could prevent their return I should not hesitate; but how long will the effect last? Will they not return like flies that have been driven off, again and again?'[2]

Derby had made his stand, and further appeals from Robinson,[3] together with further affronts from the Transvaal Government, who now vehemently claimed that they had 'not departed *one inch breadth* from the Convention',[4] left him unmoved. If anything Derby's attitude hardened further. The more he pursued his 'wait-and-see' approach the more he became convinced of

[1] Idem.   [2] Idem.

[3] They were numerous and extensive. A typical example is that of 1 March 1883: 'If our native allies were now abandoned the Convention might as well be dropped.' *Parl. Pap.*, 1883, XLIX, C.3686, p. 31. Robinson to Derby, 1 March 1883.

[4] *Parl. Pap.*, 1883, XLIX, C.3686, p. 36 (Tel.), Hudson to Robinson, 10 March 1883. (Hudson's italics.)

the value of non-intervention. It was to critics Nelson's blind eye methods with both eyes closed.

The more extraordinary factor though was that Derby stated as much in his private letters to Robinson. Two letters in particular show more than clearly the extent to which he would go to avoid becoming involved on the *veld* with the Transvaal Boers. On 14 February he admitted to Robinson, after the latter had pointed out a flagrant violation of the Convention:

> We are not disposed here to look minutely into the fulfilment of the provisions of the Convention; and *I would readily shut my eyes to many evasions of it.* But if the Boers do what they seem inclined to do—tear it up before our faces—they may raise a feeling of irritation here that will make non-interference difficult . . .'[1]

When Robinson expressed surprise at these sentiments Derby reiterated his point, in a letter of 8 March, in much the same words, with this added lament:

> I wish they could be made to understand that though we are patient, and ignore small offences on [the] system, we are not inclined to tolerate affronts, and that they may produce exactly the contrary effect to that which is intended.[2]

Derby was, in fact, granting the Transvaal Boers a licence for marauding and plunder, with the proviso that they do it quietly:

> The English nation, and the Government, will bear a good deal before they go into another Transvaal War; but it is fully on the part of the Boers to try [and see] how far patience can be stretched . . . surely they must have sense enough to see this?[3]

The collective effect of such reasoning on Robinson was sharp and dramatic. He suddenly decided he needed a 'holiday'; and that his return to London was imperative, so as to see Lord Derby personally. 'I am much obliged for your telegram,' he wrote to the Colonial Secretary on 13 March,[4] 'saying you approve of my leaving when I think I can do so without public inconvenience.' Derby took the news with grace. 'I am glad you

[1] Derby Papers, Trunk X.24. Derby to Robinson (Private), 14 February 1883 (Copy).
[2] Ibid., Derby to Robinson (Private), 8 March 1883 (Copy).
[3] Ibid., Derby to Robinson (Private), 8 February 1883 (Copy).
[4] Ibid., Robinson to Derby (Private), 13 March 1883.

are coming home, for South Africa is my great difficulty, and I shall be glad to have the advantage of your experience.'[1] Whether this was Derby's real feeling on the matter is questionable: certainly they both knew why Robinson was coming, to try and put some backbone into the policy. In Robinson's eyes conciliation was one thing, and could work wonders: retreat was very different, and could provoke as much trouble as it attempted to avoid. Clearly he thought Lord Derby was confusing the two concepts.

2. Liberal Policy Under Fire: The Parliamentary Debates of March and April 1883

Between Robinson's decision to return to London, in March, and his actual arrival, in May, the question of Boers and the Convention underwent a new development. In the Cabinet a small 'forward party' emerged, arguing for some firm action in Bechuanaland; and in Parliament, Derby's policy was scrutinised by the Opposition in two sharp debates, in both the Lords and the Commons.

The activities of a more forward party, Chamberlain, Dilke, and Hartington were more worrying to Gladstone than Gorst's motion of censure. Gladstone had reluctantly returned from his holiday at Cannes—'He feels like a boy going back to school'[2]— only to find two new Cabinet rifts emerging. Harcourt was determined to be difficult about the clauses of his proposed London Government Bill, not least because he was still smarting at Childers being preferred by Gladstone for the post as Chancellor. Secondly, there was the worsening position in Egypt, which increased the gulf between the 'Granville approach' to foreign affairs, and the Hartington Whiggish 'school of thought'.

Into this delicate situation—weekly Cabinets were suspended in May because of internal animosities[3]—there was now thrust,

[1] Ibid., Derby to Robinson (Private), 8 March 1883 (Copy).
[2] Addit. MSS. 48633, f. 66 (Hamilton Diary). Entry for 1 March 1883. Gladstone arrived in London on 2 March, having been away since 17 January 1883.
[3] Addit. MSS. 44644, ff. 53–8 (Cabinet Papers). The Cabinet had been meeting regularly once a week since 5 March; but on 7 May it was suspended until 26 May, mainly due to Harcourt's attitude to the London

again, the question of the future of the Convention. Gladstone approached the whole matter with grave misgivings. A preliminary skirmish took place in the Lower House, on 8 March, which further deepened Gladstone's pessimism. He told his secretary, Hamilton, that the speeches had 'only touched on the fringe of the great controversy which has perplexed us for half a century—the one side holding that the British military power should "controul"[1] [sic] the relations between the settlers and the natives—the other that such "controul" [sic] has done more harm than good. This South African question is a really difficult problem ahead.'[2]

Gladstone's immediate concern though was with Chamberlain's three-man 'Cabal'. The Cabinet of 10 March brought an open clash between the 'forward' group, on one side, and the Gladstone–Derby–Kimberley alliance, on the other. Dilke has left an admirable description of the attempt to force a more positive, and imperialist policy, on the Cabinet: 'A Transvaal debate was coming up on Thursday the 15th, and in view of this Chamberlain asked for support of his opinion that an expedition should be sent out to save Montsioa [sic]. He was supported only by Hartington and myself.'[3] The Gladstonians were clearly in the majority, so the Chamberlain group changed their demands 'He passed a paper to me when we found we could not win at the Cabinet: "How far would the difficulty be met by supplying arms to Mankarone [sic] and (query) to Montsioa, [sic] and permitting volunteers to go to their assistance?" I replied, "I don't think it would stand House of Commons discussion".'[4]

Though Gladstone had prevailed at the Cabinet he did not let the matter rest there. He was determined to take as strong a

Government Bill. The same was to occur in August, when Egyptian divisions grew so sharp that Gladstone once again suspended the Cabinets—between 8 August (f. 95) and 21 August (f. 100). And in September there were no Cabinets at all. In fact none from 22 August (f. 103) until 25 October (f. 108)—at a critical time in Egypt.

[1] Gladstone's spelling of the word? The inverted commas are Hamilton's.

[2] Addit. MSS. 48633, f. 68 (Hamilton Diary). Entry for Thursday, 8 March 1883.

[3] Addit. MSS. 43937, f. 78 (Dilke Memoir).

[4] Idem., see also Addit. MSS. 43925, f. 51 (Dilke Diary). Entry for 10 March 1883.

team as possible into the coming debate. He had been in political life too long not to know how to break cliques of junior ministers. Hartington presumably was beyond persuasion, but Dilke and Chamberlain were different. Thus, on 16 March, Gladstone attempted to divide the forward group, by asking Dilke to speak in the Commons for the Government on the Transvaal. Dilke refused to be 'bought' with so tempting an offer, 'as I do not agree in the policy pursued'.[1] Chamberlain had fewer scruples, and greater ambitions. When Gladstone turned to him after Dilke, he abandoned his friends, and agreed to defend Derby's policy. Dilke wrote somewhat churlishly in his Diary: 'Chm. will speak in my place. He sided with me in the Cabt.—but in reality his opinion is with Mr. G's.'[2]

Gladstone thus faced the coming debate with few qualms; particularly as *The Times* and the *Pall Mall Gazette* had both come out with very strong calls for inactivity. The *Pall Mall Gazette's* leader title read: 'Not another War?',[3] while *The Times* was equally emphatic and clear-thinking.[4]

> In spite of the lessons of the past, we are once again invited to undertake an armed interference with the affairs of South Africa. It is certain that the Government and the House will not accept Mr. Gorst's motion. The country, they are well aware, has no wish to be involved any further than it can help in the concerns of South Africa. Our connection with that entire country has been most disastrous to ourselves.[5]

As for the Tswana chiefs *The Times* article was to be a precursor of so much that was to be said in Parliament: 'The native chiefs for whom we are asked to reverse our determination have no claim upon us direct or indirect. . . . They are not British subjects: we have promised them nothing; we owe them nothing. . . .'[6]

---

[1] Addit. MSS. 43937, ff. 83–4 (Dilke Memoir).
[2] Addit. MSS. 43925, f. 52 (Dilke Diary). Entry for 16 March 1883. Chamberlain's account of the matter suggests that Bechuanaland was not important enough an issue on which to take a stand; and that the key question to him in early 1883 was to commence a 'campaign of constructive Radicalism. . . .' Joseph Chamberlain, *A Political Memoir*, pp. 85–7. See also Garvin, *Chamberlain*, I, 490–91.
[3] *Pall Mall Gazette*, 12 March 1883.   [4] *The Times*, 12 March 1883.
[5] Idem.   [6] Idem.

The actual parliamentary debates began on the afternoon of 13 March 1883. In the Upper House, Lord Salisbury had put down a question for Derby,[1] asking what was to be done about the Tswana chiefs in the present 'calamitous condition' of Bechuanaland. The key speeches were those of Derby, Cairns, Kimberley and Salisbury. The honours ultimately rested with the Liberals, despite a fighting speech from Salisbury.

Derby hardly reached the heights of oratory, but his cautious logic, with fact carefully built upon fact, undoubtedly had a great effect. He argued in favour of a 'wait and abstain' policy on four main grounds. First, he reminded the House that it was not only the Transvaal Boers who were involved, for the freebooters had 'the very general support of the Dutch population ... not only in the Transvaal but throughout South Africa, where we know that a considerable majority of the white population are of Dutch descent, the sympathies of that population are, I am afraid, all in one direction'.[2]

Second, as the Transvaal Government itself was quite incapable of controlling their own frontiersmen, 'the only force it could possibly bring into the field, would be a force consisting of volunteers ... the majority of whom would join the adventurers beyond the frontier', it became crucial as to whether Britain should intervene. In view of the feeling among the South African Dutch[3] it would have to be a very large force. 'It would be madness ... to send a small force upon such an errand.'[4] And a large force would mean large cost. 'I dare say your Lordships will reflect that we did something of the sort in the case of the Abyssinian War. We thought it would be enough to spend £2,000,000 or £3,000,000 upon that Expedition; but it cost us nearly £10,000,000.' Even if the cost were not prohibitive, would an expedition achieve anything? Derby had grave doubts: 'What good should we do by sending out an army

[1] *Hansard*, CCLXXVII, col. 316 (Lords, 13 March 1883).

[2] Ibid., cols. 325–6.

[3] 'It is not the 500 or 600 who are actually on the spot with whom you have to deal. I am afraid you will find that a very large proportion of the Transvaal population and the people of the Orange Free State would be ready to help them.' Idem.

[4] Ibid., col. 326: 'We have had some lessons in that respect already, and we cannot afford to receive another check such as those we have received once or twice in South Africa before.'

merely to clear the country of the filibusters? They would return again directly the very moment our backs were turned. . . .'[1]

Thus Derby came to his third, and crucial point: the only final solution was 'occupying the country, and holding it with a British garrison'. Derby now spoke of the dreaded word 'annexation'. He felt sure that neither their Lordships, nor the nation itself, 'would contemplate with pleasure the creation and maintenance of a fresh British Province in the interior of South Africa—a Province which would be absolutely useless for the purposes of emigration, for it is not a place where European settlers are likely to go'. Indeed, there were few areas of Africa as unattractive as Bechuanaland. 'It is absolutely unproductive for the purposes of trade; and, in fact, there is no countervailing advantage to be gained by the occupation.' In short, 'Bechuanaland is of no value to us for any English or any Imperial purposes.'[2]

Lastly, what was then to happen to the chiefs? All the Government could do was to compensate them 'in some measure for their losses'. This might itself be quite expensive, but 'that difficulty is as nothing compared with the only other practical alternative we have to face'. And, in the last resort, that alternative, of military coercion, was not really viable: '. . . we have compelled the Boers to trek from one part of the country to another. . . . We cannot continue the process forever.' At best it would be expensive and basically impractical. At worst it could create as many dangers as it was attempting to avoid: '*We do not want another Ireland in South Africa.*'[3]

Derby's conclusion neatly pulled his ideas together:

> . . . whatever may be urged against *the policy of retrocession*, which is really the question involved in the debate . . . I think it is preferable to retaining a Province which added nothing while we held it to the strength and security of the Empire, and which would have been a source of endless bitterness and trouble.[4]

Earl Cairns, who followed Derby, claimed to find his reasoning inadequate. 'The question is, what are we morally bound to do?'[5] This provided the cue for Kimberley to enter the debate; and he was soon drawing heavily on the lessons learnt during

---

[1] Ibid., cols. 327–8. [2] Ibid., col. 328. [3] Ibid., col. 330.
[4] Idem. (My italics.) [5] Ibid., col. 336.

his own tenure at the Colonial Office. He quickly dismissed Lord Cairns' concern: Britain was 'under certain obligations', to the chiefs, but this obligation should not be placed 'too high'. They had 'never been subjects of the Queen', nor could they 'even be correctly described as our allies'. They had not participated in the Transvaal War. 'They maintained a friendly attitude, but they took no part in the disturbances.'[1]

Having disposed of that point, Kimberley moved straight on to what he had for several years considered as the crux of the matter, the question of the loyalty of the white colonists. No imperial gesture, however mighty, would bring the right results if the loyalty of the majority of the colonists were lost: and as a majority of the colonists were of Dutch descent this gave the problem a particularly awkward shape. Surely their Lordships had not forgotten the position immediately after the battle of Majuba?—'that open revolt had the sympathy of the great majority of the Dutch in South Africa'.[2]

The position in South Africa, Kimberley said, had not altered since those fateful months in mid-1881. Either Britain 'must hold South Africa strongly by force', and face the possibility of an Anglo-Dutch war in southern Africa, *'or else we must acquiesce in a great many things being done in these Colonies which the majority of the people in this country do not approve'.*[3]

Lord Salisbury, as usual, made the best speech of the debate, by asking the most pointed questions. What had caused the present trouble?—'this Convention, which, two years ago, we were assured was to be so brilliant a success of extricating ourselves from all difficulties in the Transvaal . . .'. Why had the Convention been a failure?—because it did not recognise the basis of the Boer way of life:

As Sir Hercules Robinson says, encroachment has been their very life. They have been engaged in a perpetual career of filibusting . . . and if the Government imagined that by simply signing a Treaty, that by simply expressing a wish, they could induce the Boer to give up this habit . . . they might reasonably have hope to . . . persuade the wolves, in some woodland impossible of access, to abandon the habit of feeding upon sheep.[4]

[1] Ibid., col. 338.   [2] Ibid., col. 339.   [3] Idem (My italics).
[4] Ibid., cols. 344–5.

As to the suzerainty, Salisbury saved his sharpest jibes for this section of the Convention: 'It served its purpose at the moment in hoodwinking the public opinion of England. It covered a retreat which otherwise would have been too disgraceful even for the tolerant public opinion of England. . . .'

There the debate ended. Though Salisbury had scored heavily off his Liberal counterparts, few observers agreed that Derby's had been a 'pathetic and melancholy speech'.[1] Indeed, the Press were delighted that Derby had refused to be pushed into a costly military venture. He was almost eulogised in *The Times* and the *Pall Mall Gazette*; while the *Daily Telegraph* praised his wisdom for not involving Britain in 'this miserable squabble' in Bechuanaland. Only the *Standard* and *Daily News* dissented.

The omens looked good for the debate in the Lower House; and so it proved. The Commons debate was to take place on three days, 13 and 16 March, and 13 April.[2] Gladstone, ever sensitive to the mood of the House, was happy to let the debate run on in this manner, and even arranged for the special morning sitting of the Commons on 13 April,[3] to allow Chamberlain to speak at length, for he knew which way the tide was running. With the Egyptian situation worsening, he must have been both anxious and pleased to bring the Transvaal issue to a full debate, and so dispose of it for some time. It was indeed a successful tactic. The next major debate on the Afrikaners, and the Convention, was not held until 29 October of the following year (1884), some nineteen months later. Gladstone may have been losing his grip on the Cabinet, but he never lost his understanding of the manipulation of the machinery of government, which is open to a Prime Minister.

The first phase of the debate on the evening of 13 March provided merely the preliminary rounds of the real clash to come. Gorst moved his motion[4] with 'moderation and ability'—

[1] Ibid., col. 344.
[2] *Hansard*, CCLXXVII:
Tuesday, 13 March (1883), col. 413.
Friday, 16 March, cols. 706 ff.
Friday, 13 April, in CCLXXVIII, cols. 207 ff.
[3] Addit. MSS. 48633, ff. 85–6 (Hamilton Diary). Entry for Saturday, 14 April 1883.
[4] *Hansard*, CCLXXVII, cols. 413–22.

Gladstone's opinion[1]—and John Morley made his maiden speech,[2] with a slightly irrational and strangely ill-aimed attack on the Tswana chiefs, blaming them for all Britain's troubles over the Convention. Gladstone was *not* impressed.[3] But the principal Government speaker of that evening, Evelyn Ashley, did somewhat better. He prepared the ground for Gladstone's major speech to come, though he hardly set the House alight with his style of speech.[4] His arguments were largely those of Derby and Kimberley: neither the chiefs nor the Boers were blameless for what had happened;[5] an expedition would be costly and might achieve little;[6] and the Imperial Government was not bound to help the chiefs concerned, for the latter had only declared for Britain in 1881 'because they thought our alliance more likely to profit them than that of the Boers'.[7] What *is* new in Ashley's speech though, is his stress on the failure to bring together a colonial police force to patrol the area. Ashley told the House of Robinson's attempts to create a joint Anglo-Cape Transvaal force; of how the Cape had agreed, but only if the Transvaal and Free State also came into the scheme; and of how it had thus collapsed.[8] Why had the Cape behaved in this way? '. . . the Dutch element at the Cape, which was two thirds of the whole, would not give Her Majesty's Government any assistance in carrying out any repressive moves.'[9] Further attempts to create this united police force, in February 1883, had also met with failure when the Cape refused to move against fellow Dutchmen. An all-British force was a possibility, but a bad risk. Sir Hercules Robinson had long warned of the dangers of starting a full-scale Anglo-Dutch war. Ashley felt sure that in such circumstances 'the Dutch at the Cape and in the Orange Free State should join those . . . who had sprung from the same race and spoke the same tongue'.[10]

---

[1] Addit. MSS. 48633, ff. 71–2 (Hamilton Diary). 'Gorst had moved his resolution in a speech which much commended itself to Mr. G. for its moderation and ability. Beach had been angered at having been cut out by Gorst (this is the third occasion this session on which the Fourth Party has been first in the field) and at Mr. G.'s refusing him (Beach) a separate day.'

[2] *Hansard*, CCLXXVII, cols. 423–5.

[3] Addit. MSS. 48633, f. 72 (Hamilton Diary). Entry for 18 March 1883.

[4] *Hansard*, CCLXXVII, cols. 434–45.

[5] Ibid., col. 434.   [6] Ibid., col. 439.   [7] Ibid., col. 435.

[8] Ibid., cols. 436–41.   [9] Ibid., col. 438.   [10] Ibid., col. 439.

The debate was adjourned until 16 March, when W. E. Forster made a spirited defence of the chiefs, and in the first of the 'humanitarian' speeches,[1] called on Britain to take over Bechuanaland in the same manner as they were resuming their responsibilities in Basutoland. He admitted that he relied heavily on the 'truthful description of these people by the Rev. Mr. Mackenzie, tutor of the educational institution which has been set up in this so-called savage country, in its capital town'; but he felt the House should know that Bechuanaland was not as valueless as Lord Derby had suggested. The next portion of his speech could well have been written by John Mackenzie; certainly it was what Mackenzie had been saying in his public meetings. Bechuanaland's annual trade was worth a $£\frac{1}{4}$ million p.a.; there were 'fountains'; shops sold European commodities; money had replaced the old barter system; schools were "well attended"; there were village churches; 'potatoes, wheat and other crops are grown, and cattle are exported in considerable numbers into the neighbouring country'; in short, because of the 'enterprise and progress of these people', they had 'got their lands into cultivation, and have made them so valuable that they are a great temptation to the marauders and fili-busters.'[2] The real sting was in the tail of his speech: 'I ask, are we entitled to repudiate their claims to be treated as Allies be-cause they are Black men?'[3] There were only two possible courses of action: '. . . either to fulfil our duty, or to de[c]lare with honesty and due humility that we will not and cannot.'[4]

Gladstone now decided to intervene in the debate. What followed is probably his major speech on South Africa, cer-tainly he never again spoke at such length, or with such force on the question of the Afrikaner republics. The theme of his speech was close to Kimberley's heart: the extreme delicacy of the balance of power in South Africa; that the slightest disturbance in one area might set the whole vast region ablaze. In particu-lar, Gladstone stressed the fact that no problem, in say Bechu-analand, could be isolated from the rest of South Africa. To confront the Boers on that border meant facing the Dutch on all borders; and of rousing pan-Afrikaner feeling, only now being allayed by the policy of conciliation.

[1] Ibid., col. 703.   [2] Ibid., cols. 704–6.
[3] Ibid., col. 706.   [4] Ibid., col. 715.

Thus Forster provided an easy target and a good start for Gladstone's speech.

> Considering that the right hon. Gentleman has had experience at the Colonial Office, he ought to have known better (No! No!— 'Order!') I will take no notice of that. I think he ought to have formed a more adequate estimate of the magnitude and complication of the question with which we have to deal.

Gladstone now really warmed to his subject. Britain's relations with the Afrikaner 'were a history of difficulties, continual and unthought of'; it was not a new problem—'it has been the one standing difficulty of our Colonial policy, which we have never been able to settle'. And Gladstone's memory, of course, was longer than most parliamentarians.

> It was my lot, Sir, in the latter part of the Administration of Sir Robert Peel, to be Secretary of State for the Colonies; and on the breaking up of that Administration. . . . I distinctly told Lord Grey that the case of South Africa presented problems of which I, for one, could not see the solution. And so, Sir, it has continued from that day to this.[1]

Gladstone then went into attack. The motion, if it were put into effect, could lead to an Anglo-Afrikaner war—'Are you not aware that a strong feeling of sympathy passes from one end of the South African settlement to the other, among the entire Dutch population?'[2] This fact, Gladstone claimed, changed the whole complexion of the dilemma.

> It is not a question between Bechuanaland and some other country . . . it is a question between one portion of the people of Bechuanaland and another portion, which other portion is backed unquestionably both by sympathy and co-operation . . . in alliance with the Boers of the Transvaal.[3]

Gladstone's speech was thus in reality an 'attack' on the loyalty of the Cape Dutch. Clearly he saw them as the crucial figures in the débâcle; if they were totally reliable then Britain could move against the Boers without any qualms. As it was, the price of rescuing two obscure Bechuana tribes could be the loss of Britain's strategic base at the Cape, or at least a war for the Cape itself. 'Sir, we are not without experience of war in South

[1] Idem.   [2] Ibid., cols. 721–2.   [3] Ibid., col. 726.

Africa. It is a melancholy history. We have not had a Colony in South Africa for a century, but we [have] had wars in 1811, in 1819, in 1834, in 1846, in 1850, in 1877, in 1879 and in 1880–81.' The cost had been daunting: Zulu War £4,890,000; Transvaal War £2,720,000; 'Kaffir Wars' at least £3,000,000. 'And what are the causes of these wars; indeed of all of them? . . . It has always been the defence of a frontier that has been in question. A fighting frontier has been incessantly the cause and object of war. . . .'[1] Annexing the territory will not remove the danger of such a frontier war—'. . . whatever country you occupy you will have the same difficulties to contend with . . . that your emigrants will go out beyond your frontier wherever they find farms convenient to be taken.'[2]

A war in Bechuanaland might even be worse than previous colonial frontier wars: it was over 1,000 miles from the nearest sea base; there was no railway and the roads were 'miserable'; and the cost would be exorbitant, for so many men would be needed to avoid the possibility of another Majuba. And this brought him directly back to the importance of the Afrikaner, not only in the republics but at the Cape.[3]

This was the very essence of the Gladstone–Kimberley–Derby approach to South Africa: the question of how to create firm Anglo-Afrikaner bonds for the future, recognising that unless by some miracle the English section of the population completely swamped the Dutch, it was with the Dutch that the Imperial Government would have to deal. The steady growth of the Afrikaner *Bond* at the Cape, and indeed all over South Africa, was a sure indication of the growing political consciousness of the Dutch-speaking population. Sir Hercules Robinson had already written of the time when the Cape would have its first Afrikaner ministry with, presumably, Jan Hofmeyr as the first Dutch-speaking Cape Premier. This would mean Dutch ministries in charge of affairs from Cape Town to the Limpopo.

This was the calculation on which policy had to be based. To ignore this obvious development would be to ignore the realities of the local situation. Equally, the implications of the Afrikaner ruling South Africa could not be dismissed, or Britain would suddenly, in the very near future, wake up to find

[1] Ibid., col. 727.   [2] Ibid., col. 728.   [3] Ibid., col. 729.

imperial overlordship at the southern end of Africa in such a perilous position that a full-scale war would be required to re-conquer, garrison, and militarily hold South Africa. It would be Ireland and India rolled into one frightful nightmare.

Gladstone's answer to this dilemma was superbly expressed in one section of his speech; and it is indeed the heart of the Liberal approach to South Africa while he was at the helm of the party:

> If it were the fact that there was an outlying handful of those people [the Boers] severed from the rest, and isolated from the rest in sympathy and feeling, that would be one thing, but it is not so. . . . *The Dutch population is, in the main, one in sentiment throughout South Africa.*[1]

In the present circumstances this meant one thing—'we decline to . . . undertake a military expedition for the purpose of rectifying disorders in a country which has always been dis-orderly . . .'. Everything pointed against a military expedition or solution; Gladstone refused to ignore common sense: 'I believe the enormous efforts, risks and uncertainties of the ex-pedition . . . are entirely out of proportion to the objects that are in view or to the ends that you can possibly achieve.'[2]

Hicks Beach rose after Gladstone; but it was rather like trying to speak after an Old Testament prophet had just explained the Law to the people. In effect Hicks Beach's whole lengthy speech consisted of one allegation: 'I thought it had been admitted that the Bechuana chiefs were persons to whom we are under special obligations.' He was followed by Lord Randolph Churchill, who amused the House, rather than informed it. He shot barbed remarks into the air, mainly in Gladstone's direction, but he cared little where they really landed, so long as they produced some sharp reaction. His short, pointed speech also revealed the near American connection of his famous family. A police force would work in Bechuanaland, he said, 'if such a force were to treat the Boer marauders as the Texas Rangers treated the pirates and half-breeds who infested and plundered the prairie settlers . . .'.[3] He was not taken very seriously; and in fact, the whole debate fell flat after Gladstone's long oration.

The reaction of the Press to the debate was almost unanimous:

[1] Ibid., cols. 729–30. (My italics.)
[2] Ibid., col. 730.   [3] Ibid., col. 750.

a Liberal, or rather Gladstonian triumph, had taken place.[1] The shrewdest comments came from the *Pall Mall Gazette*, who devoted their whole front page to a leader on 'Philanthropy and Imperialism'. The issue of the Tswana chiefs, they said, raised a much broader principle in southern Africa: '*The question is whether we want to take the burden of another India,* because it is to this that Mr. Forster's policy will inevitably lead.' On the dilemma of the loyalty of the white colonists of the Cape the article was equally clear thinking:

> The influence of the Dutch race, as Mr. Gladstone says, has not diminished but is still the dominant influence in South Africa. English statesmen will be slow to commit themselves to a policy that will bring us into sharper and sharper antagonism with this race, without doing any more good than we have done for the Basutos and the Zulus.[2]

The Cabinet of the same day, 17 March,[3] in a mood of high optimism about the outcome of the debate, got down to the question of drafting a major amendment to the motion already proposed by the Tories on the Transvaal. The draft is in Gladstone's hand and is a good insight into the limited overture that he was prepared to make to the Humanitarian feeling on Bechuanaland:

> That in view of the inability of the Transvaal Government to restrain those agencies which have been productive of crime and outrage in Bechuanaland and have aggravated its disorders, this House trusts that Her Majesty's Government will make an adequate provision for the interests of Chiefs who may have claims upon them.[4]

The idea of sending an expedition to defend the Convention and frontier was clearly dead, both in ministerial and parliamentary circles, before Chamberlain stood up, on 13 April, to make the concluding speech for the Liberals, in the third and last phase of the debate.[5] He did not say much that was new, but what he did say he said extremely well. Dilke must have

[1] See also *The Times, Daily Telegraph, Daily News, Pall Mall Gazette*—all of Saturday, 17 March 1883.

[2] *Pall Mall Gazette*, Saturday, 17 March 1883. (My italics.)

[3] Addit. MSS. 44644, f. 12 (Cabinet Papers). Meeting of Saturday, 17 March 1883, at 2 p.m.

[4] Ibid., f. 13.

[5] *Hansard*, CCLXXVIII, cols. 232–47. (Commons, 13 April 1883.)

regretted turning the opportunity down. Chamberlain immediately got to the heart of the matter. He admitted that Britain
did indeed have 'what is called a *casus belli*' for intervention,
but 'before we go to war we should ask whether the result of the
war will be at all adequate to sacrifices we are called upon to
make . . .'. Here, Chamberlain felt, was the rub. 'There are no
Imperial interests at stake in those miserable squabbles, and I
do not believe even the Natives . . . can benefit by our interference. Whoever gains they always suffer, like the dwarf in his
alliance with the giant.'[1]

The major portion of Chamberlain's speech, though, was
devoted to the matter of the South African Dutch. Peace despite
Majuba had avoided a pan-Afrikaner rising; armed intervention now could again rouse that feeling. 'A near relative of a
Member of the Cape Government told me the other day that
*at the time of the retrocession we were within a few weeks of a general
uprising of the Dutch population*. That would have been a more
serious and a greater disaster than any we are now considering.'[2]
The position in 1881 had not been altered by the passage of two
years. The dangers were still as great, and signs of anti-English
feeling among the Cape Dutch even clearer for everyone to
read: '. . . when the English Government appealed to the
Orange Free State and the Cape colonists to join with them and
the Transvaal to send a police force to clear the country, *it was
not the Transvaal only that refused, but the Orange Free State and our
own Colony.*'[3]

This was the crucial factor to Chamberlain; a factor which
just could not be ignored in dealing with any South African
problem from now on. He put his concerns and beliefs in a sentence:

> There is no use blinking the fact that the opinion of the Dutch popu-
> lation, which constitutes the majority of the Cape, is altogether
> opposed to what they consider the sentimental and humanitarian
> views of this House and Her Majesty's Government.[4]

On this note the debates of 1883 ended. The message seemed
clear: the Victorians declined to adopt the technique of 'formal
empire' either to save the Tswana chiefs, or to preserve the

[1] Ibid., col. 242.   [2] Ibid., col. 234. (My italics.)
[3] Ibid., cols. 239–40.   [4] Ibid., col. 240.

niceties of the Pretoria Convention. Their new-found faith in informal paramountcy, to maintain their overlordship in southern Africa, and their belief in conciliation to retain and nurture the loyalty of the Cape Dutch, if not of the republican Boers, had been greatly strained, but not abandoned. For at the heart of this Gladstonian approach was the pragmatic understanding that the defiant Afrikaner could not be ignored. He had either to be challenged or conciliated. In enjoying the option of even so limited a choice the Gladstone administration was in doubt in preferring that policy which would avoid a renewed war on the *veld*.

3. Undermining the Convention: a new Anglo-Boer Treaty? April–July 1883

The immediate result of these debates though was to allow Derby to work more easily; they almost disposed of the topic in the eyes of public and parliamentarians alike. Derby now had time not only to decide what to do about the Convention, but equally he had room for manoeuvre which allowed him to do nothing: to watch and see how the Boers would behave now that they knew that there was to be no imperial military gesture. Derby counted it as a possibility that if they expanded 'quietly', and did not overtly flaunt imperial overlordship, as implied in the suzerainty clauses, then he would not be called upon to do anything. There would be no need to count annexation as one of the options; no need to fear committing Britain to further heavy expenditure abroad; and no need to worry unduly about the sympathy and loyalty of the Cape Dutch.

With this in mind Derby had already proposed that Britain opt out of the difficult situation, leaving the Cape ministry to supply an area of land on which the broken tribes could live. Robinson, who had been detained at the Cape by the Basuto crisis, reacted most unfavourably to this latest attempt by Derby to slip out from under any burden of responsibility, though he phrased it tactfully: 'I do not wonder at your casting about for some means of avoiding so expensive and hazardous a course as armed intervention, but I am afraid the half measures you propose in the shape of removal and allowances are impracticable.'

His reasoning though was blunt: 'This Colony is already over-laden with native troubles, and would certainly decline to assume fresh responsibilities of that character by undertaking the government of Montsioa [*sic*] and Mankaroane [*sic*] with their sections of the Baralong and Batlaping Tribes.'[1]

Robinson's rejection of the Derby 're-distribution plan' was complete. He could not see how moving the Tswana tribes would be of any use, nor where they could go.

> I do not know any uninhabited part of this Colony in which these tribes could be located and live. There is a large unoccupied tract of country on the northern border, south of the Orange River; but it is waterless and no better than the Kalaharis [*sic*] desert which joins Bechuanaland. ... Natal is full to overflowing of natives; and besides the Cape and Natal, there is no other British territory in South Africa.[2]

Robinson took much the same jaundiced views of Derby's other proposal: giving the chiefs monetary compensation for their losses.[3]

> As to allowances whilst Montsioa [*sic*] and Mankaroane [*sic*] remain in the small corners left to them by the freebooters, I see great difficulty in doing them any real good by helping them in this way. Money allowances would be spent upon arms and ammunition which would but prolong their misery, whilst supplies of food or cattle would be captured by the freebooters.[4]

His advice to Derby was very much to the point, and shows the extent of his disillusionment with the Colonial Secretary:

> Looking at the matter from every point of view, there appears to me only the choice between clearing the territories of these two Chiefs by force, or abandoning them altogether, leaving them to be exterminated by the freebooters. I can see no middle course: and if we abandon them I think we had better make up our minds

[1] Derby Papers, Trunk X.24. Robinson to Derby (Private), 20 March 1883.

[2] Idem.

[3] C.O. 291/22. The proposal actually came from Robert Herbert and was taken up by Derby. See Herbert to Derby, 21 March 1883. See also *Parl. Pap.*, 1883, XLIX, C.3686, p. 41. Robinson to Hudson, 27 March 1883, enclosed in Derby to Robinson (Tel.), 22 March 1883.

[4] Derby Papers, Trunk X.24. Robinson to Derby (Private), 20 March 1883.

... to drop the Convention also as quickly and as quietly as we can. It will otherwise be little more than an expensive and mischievous sham—deluding the natives with false hopes, and exposing ourselves to constant altercations and humiliations. . . .'[1]

Derby was loth to accept such thinking: his whole policy was aimed at finding that 'middle course' which Robinson declared to be an impossibility. He was not prepared to protect the chiefs, but equally he did not wish to see them exterminated, for that would only awaken the public conscience again, and perhaps force another debate. He refused to accept Robinson's rigid interpretation. He was determined to find more than two options, i.e. involvement or withdrawal. His *modus vivendi* proved to be a reliance on the system of compensation. His approach is captured in a telegram to Robinson after the debates: 'Tell Montsioa [*sic*] Her Majesty's Government cannot intervene by force for his protection, but will consider, in the event of either he or Mankaroane [*sic*] being driven out of their country, what assistance can be given them.'[2] The chiefs found this extremely cold comfort.[3]

Derby was totally unmoved by their plight, particularly as the matter of Basutoland now overlapped both in time and similarity with the case of the Tswanas. Cape administration of the Basuto people had collapsed; a frontier war had been fought; and if the Basutos had not been defeated the Cape had not won. Both parties now called for a reparation, and both looked to Britain to resume her previous responsibilities. Robinson's private letters told a sorry story. He wrote here in his capacity as Governor of the Cape:

> The Basutos have beaten us, and they know it. They are completely inflated with the idea of their own importance, and their own invincibility. Natives cannot be governed on these terms. Indeed there is at present but little attempt on the part of the Colony

---

[1] Idem.

[2] C.O. 291/22. Derby to Robinson (Tel.) 27 March 1883. The draft of the telegram is in Herbert's hand.

[3] Mankurwane wrote (12 April): '. . . if Her Majesty's Government delays its assistance until such time as Montsioa [*sic*] and I are driven out of our countries, our people will by such time have been almost exterminated, and the survivors enslaved by the Boers. . . .' See *Parl. Pap.*, 1883, XLIX, C.3686, p. 68. Mankurwane to Hudson, 12 April 1883.

to govern them. They are rather governing the Colony, and make it pay £100,000 a year for the connection.[1]

This was the crux of the matter. Cape disillusionment with the Basuto was complete. Hopes of ruling a peaceable and trading tribe had been dashed. Robinson reported that the Free State President (Brand) had told Scanlen that 'unless the Colony was prepared if need be to enforce its authority, it would be better not to assert it'.[2] This was in fact the attitude that Scanlen's ministry now took; they also grasped every opportunity to point out to Robinson and Derby that the Basuto tribe itself wanted to return to the imperial fold.[3] As Scanlen told Robinson early in April, 'the bulk of the Basutos desire to remain British subjects. They would prefer Imperial to Colonial rule.'[4]

This was a responsibility that Derby could not put aside or pigeon-hole. For, as Robinson explained, in an urgent letter: 'The Basutos are evidently so elated by their successful opposition to the Colony as to be quite out of hand. The Colony is certainly not prepared to employ force to bring them under authority, and so the passing of a dis-annexation Act by the Cape Parliament in the next session would seem to be inevitable.'[5] The implications of this would be equally 'inevitable'. It 'would of course throw on the Imperial Government the responsibility of deciding how Basutoland is to be dealt with; as the Basutos will remain British subjects, whether annexed to the Cape or not, until some action is taken on your part'.[6]

This threw Derby into a 'panic'; and he appealed to his Cabinet colleagues. Robinson's letter[7] was circulated 'at Mr. Gladstone's suggestion'.[8] The clearest advice came from Kim-

[1] Derby Papers, Trunk X.24. Robinson to Derby (Private), 20 March 1883.
[2] Idem.
[3] *Parl. Pap.*, 1883, XLIX, C.3717, pp. 55-73.
[4] Derby Papers, Trunk X.24. Robinson to Derby (Private), 10 April 1883, enclosed in Scanlen to Robinson (Tel.), 5 April 1883.
[5] Ibid., Robinson to Derby (Private), 27 March 1883, enclosing copy telegram, Scanlen to Merriman, 26 March 1883.
[6] Idem.
[7] Ibid., Robinson to Derby, 3 April 1883, on Basutoland. See below.
[8] Minute by Derby, dated 25 April 1883, on back of letter. It also went to the Queen on 28 April 1883.

berley and Chamberlain. The former Colonial Secretary was quick to put his finger on the basic weakness of Derby's position; 'The difficulty in this case is that all parties want to force the Imperial Govt. to take the responsibility of governing Basutoland.' On the one hand the colonists wanted to escape further responsibility, and 'very naturally, want to be relieved of the expense and risk of managing their unsettled frontiers. . . . Past experience shows that this means a Caffre War [sic] from time to time at Imperial expense.' On the other side there was the Humanitarian pressure group. 'The missionaries want the Basutos, who are their special pets, to be under the Imperial Government because they hope that we shall keep the colonists out of the country [and] preserve Basutoland exclusively for the Basutos.' Of the two attitudes Kimberley feared the latter most: 'This has a very tempting look, but I have no belief in the permanence of any system which closes the country to white colonisation.' Kimberley's suspicion of the cause of the unrest is manifestly unfair but it is not untypical of contemporary belief: 'The strong feeling which now exists among the Basutos against being under Colonial Govt., has been sedulously fostered by the missionaries.'[1]

Chamberlain's remarks are even more interesting. Though he had been a cautious advocate of 'saving the Tswana chiefs', at the Cabinet of 10 March,[2] he had had second thoughts about further African responsibilities. Perhaps the position in Egypt altered his approach to southern Africa. On 26 April he minuted, after Kimberley's comments: 'I incline to the opinion that the ultimate return of this business must be the abandonment of the Basutos by both the Imperial and Colonial Govt.'[3] It was indeed the Derby attitude to Bechuanaland transferred to Basutoland. His reasoning was not unlike that of Derby's over the Tswana chiefs: 'I agree with Lord Kimberley as to the probable result of Imperial rule viz.—a Caffer War [sic] periodically forced upon us. It is worth noting that even if [Chief] Letsie is sincere in desiring British rule, he cannot answer for

[1] Ibid., Memorandum by Kimberley, dated 24 April 1883—attached to Robinson to Derby, 3 April 1883.
[2] Addit. MSS. 44644, f. 9 (Cabinet Papers), 10 March 1883.
[3] Derby Papers, Trunk X.24. Memorandum by Chamberlain, dated 26 April 1883.

Masupha, and our first business on resuming authority in Basutoland would be an armed intervention against this Chief.' He felt there was a 'chance that the Cape Colony and Letsie may come to terms'.[1]

If such a chance even existed, which is doubtful, it was rudely destroyed on 4 May, when the Cape Assembly decided to repeal the Basutoland Annexation Act (No. 12 of 1871), 'in order that steps may be taken for relieving the Colony from all further responsibility connected therewith ... '. Derby realised what was happening: he was being hustled into a decision against his will. He sent a belated telegram to the Cape ministry four days later; 'Her Majesty's Government cannot hold out any expectation that steps will be taken by them to relieve the Colony from its responsibilities in Basutoland.'[2]

In fact Derby was caught in the web of his, or at least British, creation. Once the Cape had taken this stand it was difficult, if not impossible, for Derby to 'opt out'. Not only had Basutoland been under British and Cape administration since 1868, which technically made the Basutos British subjects in the eyes of most observers, but it was strategically placed along the vulnerable eastern flank of British southern Africa. Together these factors have rightly been seen as the traditional reasoning behind the decision of the Cabinet, on Saturday, 26 May 1883,[3] when it was decided to resume responsibility for the Basutos.[4] However two further motives emerge from the correspondence of the period, and both need to be stressed. First, there was the logic which pointed out that if Britain took Basutoland back it was quite possible that they could persuade the Cape to exercise some administrative control in southern Bechuanaland, below the Molopo River, at the least. In other words it could be a safe 'exchange'[5]; Derby feared Basutoland less than Bechu-

---

[1] Ibid., Memorandum by Chamberlain, dated 26 April, below Kimberley's on same paper. Gladstone's comments do not appear, nor do the Queen's.

[2] Ibid., p. 73. Derby to Robinson, 6 May 1883.

[3] Addit. MSS. 44644, f. 58 (Cabinet Papers), Saturday, 26 May 1883.

[4] See Addit. MSS. 43937, f. 78 (Dilke Memoir); and Addit. MSS. 43925, ff. 52–3 (Dilke Diary).

[5] Addit. MSS. 43937, f. 134 (Dilke Memoir). Entry dated 'June 13th'— 'As to South Africa, the Colonial Office told us that *they hoped to induce the Cape to take Bechuanaland.*'

analand, and with good reason. In Basutoland he would only have the natives to deal with; in Bechuanaland he was in fact facing the Transvaal and Kruger.

There was also the second point, that Derby was most anxious to cultivate good and amicable relations with the Cape; an earnest desire to regain Cape loyalty and to ensure Cape support for imperial supremacy even if a Cape Dutch *Bond* ministry came to power. Thus the acceptance of the Cape wish to abandon Basutoland to the imperial administration was good politics. Whether it was expensive politics was another question; but then the query became, could Britain afford to snub the Cape ministry? The answer to that was the Cabinet decision of 26 May.[1] Britain took Basutoland reluctantly, but significantly she accepted the province at a time when imperial involvement in Egypt was growing; and at a time when the Cabinet refused to sanction a Bechuanaland protectorate, or accept Australian calls for the annexation of New Guinea. It seemed that when real priorities were at stake the Victorians were prepared to go to the extreme of burdening themselves with further responsibilities 'to keep what they had', and to assure crucial political alliances, such as those with the Cape Dutch.

The whole Basutoland affair highlights rather sadly the place of Bechuanaland in Derby's scheme of imperial security and stability. It rated extremely low; Mackenzie alone campaigned for the Tswana chiefs,[2] and even he began to recognise defeat by spring 1883.[3] Derby saw every reason as to why Britain should not again become involved in the heart of Africa, though late in March 1883 even he began to have qualms of conscience about the plight of the Tswana. When the Cape happily sold the Transvaal large 'siege guns'[4] he refused to stop the transaction,[5] but privately he admitted the injustice of the arms

---

[1] Addit. MSS. 44644, f. 58 (Cabinet Papers), 26 May 1883.

[2] In May 1883 he had his last 'fling'—against the decision not to send an expedition—with a long article in the *Nineteenth Century Review* entitled 'England and South Africa'. He argued his now familiar line—imperial and Cape action to clear the area of freebooters; a 'Governor-General' for native areas; and possible imperial annexation at a later date.

[3] W. D. Mackenzie, *Life of Mackenzie*, pp. 274–6.

[4] *Parl. Pap.*, 1883, XLIX, C.3686, p. 24. Robinson to Derby, 15 March 1883.

[5] Ibid., Derby to Robinson (Tel.), 15 March 1883.

situation.[1] The Bechuanas were starved of guns and ammunition while the Transvaal freely supplied the freebooters. 'There seems nothing to be done', Bramston minuted; but which prompted one of Derby's rare Colonial Office comments: 'I am afraid not. But it is unfair. White men can get ammunition, as it seems, easily enough.'[2] But this was as far as Derby's philanthropy went; it extended to sympathy alone.

The matter took on a new tempo in April when the Transvaal, to Derby's disgust, began to take the offensive. This took two particular forms: a personal deputation to the Colonial Office by Dr. Jorissen, one of Kruger's close Hollander advisers;[3] and, a series of increasingly impertinent telegrams from Kruger,[4] who became President of the 'Transvaal State' on 16 April 1883.[5] It would have been amusing except that the repercussions were likely to be serious.

Jorissen had two 'unofficial' meetings with Derby at the Colonial Office, on 6 and 18 April. The verbatim transcripts of the conversations[6] show how sure the Transvalers felt their position to be. Jorissen's tone was positively hectoring. 'The South African natives cannot . . . be civilised or Christianised. . . . Every South African war has been directly or indirectly caused by the ill-considered action of the Aborigines' Protection Society and other English philanthropists.' Thus he went on, for pages, in the same carping tone. In fact he said only five things: the Transvaal 'objected to the tone of the recent despatches from Her Majesty's Government'; he denied the existence of

---

[1] C.O. 291/22. Herbert to Ashley, 13 March 1883. See also Minute by Derby, 8 March 1883.

[2] Ibid., Minutes by Bramston and Derby, 30 March 1883.

[3] JORISSEN, Edward, Johann Pieter (1829–1912).

　　Born, Holland. Ordained minister.

1868　Became journalist.

1875　Accompanied President Burgess to Holland.

1878　State-Attorney to S.A.R.

1881　Took part in Peace Negotiations with Wood.

1888–1900　Judge in S.A.R.

[4] *Parl. Pap.*, 1883, XLIX, C.3686, pp. 74–5.

[5] Ibid., p. 49. Hudson to Robinson, 20 April 1883 (Tel.), enclosed in Robinson to Derby (Tel.), 23 April 1883.

[6] See C.O. 879/20 (Confidential Files), nos. 258 and 260. Reports of meetings of Lord Derby and Dr. Jorissen, 6 and 18 April 1883.

'Bechuanaland'—it was a 'no-man's land' of squabbling tribes; not all the freebooters were from the Transvaal; Montshiwa had caused most of the trouble; and, above all, the unrest would *only* be stopped when Britain acknowledged that the Convention boundaries needed modification.

The Jorissen interviews produced sharp reactions from certain Cabinet ministers. Gladstone found the second discussion even 'less pleasant than the first';[1] and Chamberlain was so roused by Jorissen's accusations that he wrote to Derby: 'If you see Dr. Jorissen again soon, would it not be worth while to ask him for his observations on the complaints made against the Transvaal Govt. in reference to their dealings with the Natives?' Chamberlain referred to three main charges against the Transvaal Boers:

1. The murder of Natives within the Transvaal by another native force and almost within sight of the Boer Commando—who I think handed over their prisons to their native enemies.
2. The treatment of the Native Chief [Mapoch], also *within* the Transvaal, and mentioned by Sir H. Robinson. He was heavily fined by Joubert and stripped of his cattle and possessions, as Robinson says, solely on account of his fidelity to the English.
3. The conduct of the Transvaal in relation to the Chiefs Montsioa [*sic*] and Mankaroane [*sic*].[2]

Chamberlain felt that it was time Britain protested more vigorously. 'The Transvaal Govt. undertook by the Convention to do all in their power to prevent their subjects from attacking the Natives beyond the boundary. What *have* they done in this case? What are they willing to do? What excuse do they put forward for doing nothing or so little?'[3] Though Chamberlain admitted that Britain 'can guess beforehand what sort of reply he [Jorissen] will make', he felt that such a statement would be useful to have in countering Transvaal claims.

The indirect result of this strong letter was that Gladstone asked Derby to produce a memorandum on the Transvaal. As Derby wrote to the Premier on 8 May: 'I am pressing on [with] the preparation of the case against the Boers, as you

[1] Addit. MSS. 44546, f. 104 (L.B. copy). Gladstone to Derby, 25 April 1883.
[2] Derby Papers, Trunk X.24. Chamberlain to Derby, 24 April 1883.
[3] Idem.

wish.'[1] This memorandum, 'The Transvaal Government and
the Convention'[2] was complete ten days later. It was intended
as a brief for less informed members of the Cabinet; and
as a useful piece of collective information to counteract the
extravagant demands being put forward by the Transvaal
Government.

Meanwhile, Kruger, in his inaugural speech as President, had
told the *Volksraad* that the time had come to press strongly for
modification of the Pretoria Convention.[3] The State Secretary,
Bok, took this a stage further and wrote to the British Resident
in Pretoria, that 'it is becoming high time'[4] that Britain agreed
to look again at the Convention, because—in Kruger's words—
'it has been proved that some of its articles have not been able
to bear a practical test and are unworkable'.[5] And, more than
this, Britain should admit failure in Bechuanaland, and allow
the area to be 'brought under the Government of the Republic
so that order there, and within this state, may be enforced'.[6]

The cumulative effect of these pressures and protests on
Derby was to be highly significant. As early as 14 February
1883 he had toyed with the idea of modifying the Convention
in such a way as to remove the majority of the Transvaal's grievances, yet presumably not to the extent of giving way completely. He had written to Robinson: 'Do you know what are
the changes in the Convention that would satisfy them—or the
more reasonable part of them?'[7] Robinson's reply[8]—that such
a thing was unthinkable, and would only encourage Transvaal
expansion—had momentarily frozen this idea. But as the weeks
passed it returned to Derby again and again. It might well be
the 'middle course' he had been searching for between annexation and complete abandonment; a method of conciliating the

[1] Addit. MSS. 44141 f. 78. Note by Derby to Gladstone, 8 May 1883.
[2] See C.O. 291/24. African Memorandum No. 262, 'Printed for Cabinet'.
[3] *Parl. Pap.*, 1883, XLIX, C.3686, p. 49.
[4] Ibid., pp. 74–5. Bok to Hudson, 1 May 1883.
[5] Ibid., Smyth (acting High Commissioner) to Derby, 21 May 1881,
enclosing Kruger's speech (8 May) to *Volksraad*.
[6] Ibid., Bok to Hudson, 7 April 1883 (p. 62), enclosed in Smyth to Derby,
30 April 1883.
[7] Derby Papers, Trunk X.24. Derby to Robinson (Private), 14 February
1883.
[8] Ibid., Robinson to Derby, 13 March 1883.

Transvaal without unduly rousing the Humanitarians, the Opposition, or the Queen.

Derby must have mentioned the idea to Gladstone for, on 25 April, the Premier wrote that the coming Colonial Office memorandum, on the case against the Boers, would help the Cabinet in 'coming to a judgement' about the Convention.[1] He also, in the same letter, referred to the Treaty as 'the best, perhaps only feasible, expedient in a critical situation'. Gone was the Gladstonian confidence that the Pretoria Convention was the panacea for all Anglo-Boer differences. Thus when Montshiwa wrote on 31 March, 'I must ask you, Sir, to tell me whether it is now done away with,'[2] he was asking a very real question.

The matter hung fire for a few weeks while Derby awaited Robinson's arrival from the Cape. He arrived in mid-May, and Gladstone, for one, was delighted to have him in London. 'I am glad to see Sir H. Robinson is arrived, and I hope this may enable you to despatch your list of exceptions to the conduct of the Transvaal Govt.'[3] Derby was probably less happy, for he had gradually come round to the opinion that a modification of the Convention was a useful way of deflecting the Transvaal's demands; he would thus avoid having to meet them 'head-on'[4]. Derby indeed expected Robinson to put up a stiff resistance against such a 'middle course' of action. He had already sounded Robinson out on this question,[5] and received an extremely firm and well-reasoned reply from the worried proconsul:

> As to a modification of the Convention, to which you refer, I do not myself see any good to be gained by moving in that direction. Nothing but a complete return to the 'status quo ante' annexation, as defined by the Sand River Convention, will satisfy [the Boers]

[1] Addit. MSS. 44546, f. 104. Gladstone to Derby (L.B. copy), 25 April 1883.

[2] *Parl. Pap.*, 1883, XLIX, C.3686, p. 64. Montshiwa to Hudson, 31 March 1883, enclosed in Smyth to Derby, 30 April 1881.

[3] Addit. MSS. 44546, ff. 113–14 (L.B. copy). Gladstone to Derby, 15 May 1883.

[4] Addit. MSS. 44141, f. 84. Derby to Gladstone, 26 May 1883, 7 p.m.; and f. 93, Derby to Gladstone, 28 May 1883.

[5] Derby Papers, Trunk X.24. Derby to Robinson (Private), 16 February 1883.

... and I believe that if we once begin to tamper with the present agreement it will soon have to be abandoned altogether.[1]

Robinson's advice was once again a repetition of his 'hard line' thinking on the Convention, i.e. enforce or abandon: 'Unless we are prepared to restore complete independence to the Transvaal we must maintain the provisions of the Convention which define boundaries—secure justice and fair treatment for the natives within and upon the borders of the state—and provide for the non-molestation of loyals.'[2] There were only two points on which Robinson considered a concession might safely be made: 'We might perhaps, if there were anything to be gained by yielding, give up some of the debt, as well as the conduct of diplomatic intercourse with foreign powers.'

The first meeting of Derby and Robinson at the Colonial Office was therefore expected to be crucial; and this is indeed how it proved to be. The first, and most important discussion took place on Wednesday, 16 May 1883.[3] Robinson had clearly thought out his approach; and it can be detected from this very first meeting. Having failed to persuade the Colonial Office and Colonial Secretary to embrace his policy of a limited imperial police force, he had decided that the best he could hope for was to get an early decision on the Convention either way. Britain must support it, or admit that it was being dismantled. To this end Robinson worked steadily, seeing his best tactic as a clear and forceful presentation of the facts of the situation in southern Africa. His views were at all times frank; his words and reasoning plain. He immediately discounted Jorissen's opinions: 'Dr. Jorissen is not to be relied upon, and cannot be safely dealt with.' On the more serious question, of the aims of the Transvaal Government under the presidency of Kruger, Robinson was also determined to demolish any misconceptions which Derby might hold:

> The object of the Boers is, of course, to break down and get rid of the Convention. They want to shake off the suzerainty and the

[1] Ibid., Robinson to Derby (Private), 13 March 1883.
[2] Idem.
[3] C.O. 879/20, no. 263—'Strictly Confidential'. Report on discussion of Sir Hercules Robinson and Lord Derby, held at C.O., Wednesday, 16 May 1883.

debt, to be free from all restrictions as to interfering with the Natives, within or without the State, and to conduct their foreign relations as they choose; to be fully inscribed on the roll of nations as they pompously say.[1]

Their recent behaviour towards the Convention, Robinson argued, was not in the least unexpected to him:

They have never intended, and do not intend to obey the Convention in the absence of any clear determination to enforce it. Under all circumstances it was perhaps a mistake to make the Convention, but it *would be certainly foolish to adhere to it if it is not proposed to enforce it strictly.*[2]

This was the heart of the Robinson approach: a determined push for a clear decision. As to the balance of the argument, for and against the Convention, he refused to take a stand. Indeed, he was prepared to present the case either way.

Robinson saw three things against maintaining the Convention ineffectually: it deluded the Tswana people into thinking that Britain would protect them; it harmed British prestige in South Africa if the Boers could defy the imperial power so blatantly; and, it could very soon 'impair the good feeling between Dutch and English throughout South Africa'. On the other hand, enforcing the Convention would act as a salutary warning to the Boers not to encroach elsewhere; and it would reassert British paramountcy in South Africa, at a low point since Majuba, and continually being eroded by the existence of the two 'Robber Republics'—Robinson's phrase—in Bechuanaland.

The Boers know that we shall never fight to enforce the Convention. As England has not recognised the obligation to protect the Bechuanas, they are satisfied she will not interfere on behalf of any other natives who have not the same special claims upon her. The Boers will do what they choose, and may both do so without any Convention than with one.[3]

Where Derby was encouraged was in finding that Robinson had shifted his ground in regard to armed intervention. Robinson was no longer taking the dogmatic attitude of his letter of 13 March. Even in regard to his 'pet-scheme', of 500 police, his

[1] Idem.   [2] Idem.   [3] Idem.

line had softened; and to Derby's delight, he heard Robinson say:

> No doubt there would have been considerable risk, and, as a disaster would have been the beginning of great troubles throughout South Africa, he cannot say there would have been advantage commensurate with the risk, and was on that account relieved when Her Majesty's Government decided that they were not bound to interfere.

This must have been the thaw in attitude which Derby looked for. Robinson was not saying that he was in favour of a modification—that might come later—but he was coming round to see Derby's point of view in regard to the refusal to act unilaterally in Bechuanaland.

Derby, on the other hand, was happy to accept Robinson's definition of the course to be charted: 'If the Convention is abandoned, the Bechuanaland question will be disposed of; the Boers will be free to do what they please there or elsewhere. If it is not abandoned the Transvaal should not be allowed to amend its boundaries.'[1]

Derby forwarded the text of this meeting to the Premier: and Gladstone read it with 'great interest'.[2] He was in agreement on most points, but he added a significant footnote to Robinson's ideas—everything depended on whether 'we give up the Convention'.[3] Clearly Gladstone and his Colonial Secretary were thinking along far more radical lines, for solving the problem of the Boers, their frontiers and the Convention, than was Robinson, the creator of that Convention.

It also now transpired that the memorandum which Gladstone asked for—listing Britain's complaints against Boer behaviour—was not merely intended as a protest document. Gladstone had already hinted at his intention in a letter to Derby, of 8 May: 'I hope you will soon be able to send off your "case" to the Transvaal Resident, as a step towards clearing up the subject of the Convention.'[4] Hemming, in the Colonial

---

[1] Idem.
[2] Addit. MSS. 44546, f. 117 (L.B. copy). Gladstone to Derby, 23 May 1883.
[3] Idem.
[4] Addit. MSS. 44546, f. 110. Gladstone to Derby, 8 May 1883.

Office, rightly remarked in connection with this memorandum: 'It is no use, I imagine, making any more protests against the behaviour of the Transvaal Government.'[1] But, in fact, he had not been briefed on the object of the memorandum. Nor had its architect, Edward Fairfield. When it was complete, and presented a most damning and conclusive set of facts against the Transvaal Government, Derby expressed his concern over the tone of the memorandum. He wrote in the margin: 'I think Mr. Gladstone wanted something written in the way of a protest, but this does not harmonise with *the idea of inviting or accepting a revision of the Convention.* . . .'[2]

The game was up. Gladstone and Derby intended to use the document as the basis for the 'British case' when it came to discussing the Convention with the Boers—with a view to modifying it in such a way as to dampen Boer demands, even if this meant giving ground to the Transvaal, both literally and figuratively. This is presumably why the document was printed for the Cabinet,[3] and marked 'Most confidential'. If a decision was taken to embark on negotiations with the Transvaal the whole Cabinet would need to be consulted. It could not be settled between Gladstone, Derby, and Robinson.

But at this stage, 26 May, the decision, and the plan to modify the Convention, was still a secret between the Premier and Colonial Secretary. Robinson had been invited, by Derby, to write out his own consideration of the alternatives available to Britain. This he did, on 26 May.[4] He outlined four possible options: Britain could use force and 'clear the freebooters', but the Government had already decided against this course; Britain could 'cancel the Convention of Pretoria reverting to the provisions of the Sand River Convention'; Britain could 'adhere to the present Convention line', and refuse to recognise the Transvaal advances into Bechuanaland; or, Britain could 'amend the

[1] C.O. 291/22. Minute by Hemming, 22 May 1883. See also Addit. MSS. 44141, f. 96. Derby to Gladstone, 29 May 1883.

[2] C.O. 291/24. Minute by Derby (18 May 1883) on the draft of Fairfield's Memorandum. It was ultimately printed for the Cabinet. (My italics.)

[3] C.O. 879/20, no. 262 (Confidential Prints) for the final Cabinet version of the document.

[4] C.O. 291/22. Robinson (in London) to Derby, 26 May 1883. This letter was later printed, in part. See also *Parl. Pap.*, 1883, XLIX, C.3686, pp. 70–71.

Convention line', and just hand over the area to the Transvaal. Of the four 'I think the last the most undesirable'.[1]

Clearly Robinson was being deliberately kept in the dark, for the idea of amending the Convention was still anathema to him. He wanted it defended or abandoned. The alternative middle course he termed 'most undesirable'. Yet, this is the very course that Derby was privately not only contemplating, but preparing. Derby forwarded this letter, to Gladstone on 26 May, with these comments: 'I have a letter from Sir H. Robinson. . . . He thinks we ought not to delay a decision as to the Convention. I am rather inclined to agree. Once let negotiations for its modification or abolition begin, and we are safe from questioning for this year, or at least have an answer ready.'[2]

When it was rumoured in London that the British Resident in Pretoria, Hudson, was financially involved in land schemes in the Transvaal,[3] Derby was even more explicit to Gladstone on his intentions over the Convention. 'It is only within the last few weeks that we have heard of Hudson being mixed up in the Transvaal speculations to an extent which is undesirable in his position, and lessens his influence. If we go [on] with a Resident it may be better to remove him: *but possibly we shall not want one.*'[4] The more Derby thought of the policy of negotiations, the more enthusiastic he became for the idea. 'If once we open negotiations formally with the Transvaal authorities, there is an end of questioning for this session, as they are not likely to be ended by August or September.'[5]

The matter was side-tracked for a few days, as a result of the 'Hudson affair'.[6] Gladstone had suggested that if the Convention was to be amended the British Resident in the Transvaal

---

[1] Idem.

[2] Addit. MSS. 44141, f. 84. Derby to Gladstone, 26 May 1883, 7 p.m.

[3] C.O. 291/22. Minutes by Bramston, Herbert, Ashley, and Derby (14 April 1883) on Hudson, based on despatches from acting High Commissioner at Cape (Smyth). See also *Parl. Pap.*, 1884, LVII, C.3841, pp. 1–4.

[4] Addit. MSS. 44141, f. 93. Derby to Gladstone (Private), 28 May 1883.

[5] Idem.

[6] Herbert's Minute succinctly gave the case against Hudson: 'I entirely distrust Mr. Hudson's statements, and feel no doubt that he used his official information to secure a property for which he ought to have been competing with others; and which when he applied for it as a farm he knew it to be of great mineral value.' See C.O. 291/22. Minute by Herbert, 14 April 1883.

should be asked for his suggestions. Derby wrote to Herbert in this vein, with the added proviso, 'If possible we want it in early July.'[1] Herbert's reply is extremely interesting.[2] Not only did it reveal his grave doubts about Hudson—'Mr. Hudson, the Resident could not give an opinion of any value on this question. His loyalty to this country and his personal honesty are freely questioned'[3]—but Herbert also revealed that this was the first he had heard of the Convention being modified. While he agreed that the Convention 'has done no good whatever, and checked no evil whatever', he was equally sure that the answer was not to amend that Treaty, but rather to enforce it. In Herbert's mind 'the balance of experienced opinion' suggested that, 'if we intervene [in Bechuanaland] permanent good results would follow. Mankaroane [*sic*] and Montsioa [*sic*] would apparently not need our protection against other natives if . . . freebooters were put down.'[4]

Derby, like Kimberley before him, decided to ignore Herbert's advice, and to press on without his permanent under-secretary. Herbert made a last bid to influence Derby against amending the Convention in favour of the Transvaal. Taking Robinson's letter of 26 May as a basis, he suggested a fifth alternative for Britain—'that Bechuanaland should be neutralised under a Commission representing the Colony and the Dutch States which would help keep the road open and regulate settlement in Bechuanaland'.[5] Derby did not even bother to comment on this idea for a joint-protectorate. Instead, on the same day (29 May), he wrote this vitally important letter to Gladstone:

> Is it not time to tell the Transvaal government that we are prepared to listen to what they have to say officially as to the Convention. At present we know as a fact that they wish it done away; but we do not know this in such a manner as to be able to make any use of the knowledge. . . .[6]

Derby wondered whether it could be done without consulting

[1] Addit. MSS. 44141, f. 86. Memorandum by Derby to Herbert, 26 May 1883.
[2] Ibid., f. 87. Herbert to Derby, 26 May 1883.
[3] Idem.   [4] Idem.
[5] C.O. 291/25 (R). Minute by Herbert, 29 May 1883.
[6] Addit. MSS. 44141, f. 96. Derby to Gladstone, 29 May 1881.

other ministers; and if not, he suggested 'breaking the news' to them, at the coming Saturday Cabinet, 2 June.[1]

Derby's attitude was hardening to the exclusion of all other proposals. He refused to be influenced by Robinson's idea of a police force; or by Herbert's plan of a joint-protectorate. He even declined to be bound by his own remarks in the Lords debate about 'compensating' the Tswana chiefs. Hicks Beach had put down a question in the Commons, for 29 May, asking whether any money had been paid; and if not, when was it going to be paid to the destitute chiefs. As Gladstone had to answer the question he asked Derby to draft a rough reply[2]. Derby wrote back on the same piece of paper: 'Has the case arisen? They are not exiles, they continue to live in their own country, though they have lost some of their lands. I hardly see what ground there would be for offering them relief under present circumstances.' Gladstone was somewhat taken aback at this, and queried whether he give such an answer to Hicks Beach. 'My impression is that we came under a sort of obligation . . . more fully than we knew it.'[3] This did not perturb Derby, who now had Herbert draw up a memorandum showing that Britain had no obligations to the chiefs,[4] and who added this bizarre remark: 'Sir H. Robinson has not, I think furnished any answer on this point. It may be well to ask him whether he thinks the time and occasion for giving assistance to any chiefs have arrived. But as there is no fighting at present any money sent to the chiefs would be understood, I presume, to be a subsidy to purchase ammunition with.'[5]

Gladstone gave the answer as suggested by Derby. It was not very well received by the House, and it may well have acted as the spur to him to speed up Derby's plans to settle the matter once and for all, by amending the Convention. The following day—30 May—he wrote fully to Derby, laying out what he considered to be the basis for future action and policy.[6] He

[1] Addit. MSS. 44644, f. 62 (Cabinet Papers), Saturday, 2 June 1883, 2 p.m.

[2] Addit. MSS. 44141, f. 102. Memorandum note, Gladstone to Derby (29 May) and reply.

[3] Idem.   [4] Ibid., f. 103. Herbert to Derby, 29 May 1883.

[5] Idem.

[6] Addit. MSS. 44546, ff. 119–20 (L.B. copy). Gladstone to Derby, 30 May 1883.

accepted the fact that 'by the end of June or early in July we may have to arrange a discussion', with the Transvaal. Thus: 'We ought to prepare ourselves. . . .' by considering—

1. What is our attitude with respect to the Convention.
2. Whether we think there is any case for rendering aid to any Bechuana chief.
3. What is our information about the troubles in Zululand and [the] conduct of Cetewayo.
4. What course we shall take as to the Cape and Basuto question. I therefore think you may be quite right in asking the Transvaal Government to state their case on the Convention: but probably as it is a distinct *measure* it would be well to name it in Cabinet.[1]

Before the matter could be discussed at the full Cabinet a new and most unwelcome factor entered the dilemma. With that unfailing sense of being able to interfere at the crucial moment, Queen Victoria began to ruffle her feathers over the Convention. She had not yet been informed of Derby's intentions, but she rather 'sensed' them. On 31 May she instructed Ponsonby to inform Gladstone that, she had 'always objected to the Convention . . . though of course sanctioned it on the advice of the Government';[2] and she had always doubted that advice. 'Her Majesty thinks you will agree with her that the present state of affairs in South Africa is not pleasant—and she hopes we shall not now abandon our allies and our rights to satisfy the demands of a few agitators.'[3]

If this letter was intended as a warning shot across Derby's bows it clearly failed, for on 2 June the Cabinet met to discuss the plans for modifying the Convention.[4] The records of this Cabinet are very full, and the discussion can be reconstructed in fascinating detail. Derby had planned his proposals most carefully. His idea was to select a Commissioner who would go to South Africa, visit the troubled frontiers, talk to the Cape ministers, and ascertain the Transvaal case. He had even selected a Commissioner in advance. As Gladstone's Cabinet minutes recorded: 'Point 2. *South Africa*, Transvaal: Ld. D.

[1] Idem.
[2] Guedalla, *Queen and Mr. Gladstone*, II, 235, no. 970. Queen to Gladstone, 31 May 1883.
[3] Idem.
[4] Addit. MSS. 44644, ff. 62–5 (Cabinet Papers). Meeting of Saturday, 2 June 1883, 2 p.m.

asked authority to initiate motion of a Commr. started (Lord Reay possibly).'[1]

To Derby's relief he found the Cabinet ready to follow his policy; they accepted the idea of modifying the Convention without much discussion. In fact the only debate concerned whether Lord Reay[2] was the right man for the job. Dilke and Chamberlain passed a note, on Downing Street paper, between each other on the idea:

> *Chamberlain:* 'To send Reay out is not really a bad one.'
> *Dilke:* 'Not at all. He wants it very much. It wd. have to be done through Mr. G. who likes him,—not through the Cabinet as a whole I think.'
> *Chamberlain:* 'Harcourt has just whispered to Hartington—probably he guesses that you mean Reay.'
> *Dilke:* 'Harcourt suggests Rosebery. I don't think he wd. go.'
> *Chamberlain:* 'In my opinion Reay would do the job much better. Rosebery has no qualifications for this special work.'[3]

The reference to Harcourt was important, for it was he who put up the objections to Reay, and prolonged the Cabinet discussion unnecessarily. Dilke, who had the sharpest ear for the slightest whisper of gossip, thought he knew why 'the virulent opposition came from Harcourt'—'I wonder if the fact that L[ad]y Reay refused Harcourt, a few years before she accepted Reay, has anything to do with it?'[4] But it was Granville who provided the most memorable comment on the matter. 'We all agree that Reay is a bore, but I have never been able to make up my mind whether that is a drawback or a qualification as far as public service is concerned.'[5]

There the Cabinet left the final decision on a Commissioner until the next meeting, on 13 June,[6] ten days later. Perhaps if

[1] Idem.
[2] REAY, Donald James (1839–1921) 11th Baron, 1st Baron U.K. Dutch: naturalised British, 1877.
1885–90 Governor of Bombay.
1894–95 Under-Secretary for India.
Close friend of Childers and Gladstone.
[3] Addit. MSS. 43886, ff. 50–51 (Dilke Papers). Note, dated 2 June 1883, on 'No. 10 Downing Street' paper.
[4] Addit. MSS. 43925, f. 64 (Dilke Diary), 2 June 1883.
[5] Ibid., and Addit. MSS. 43937, f. 129 (Dilke Memoir).
[6] Addit. MSS. 44644, f. 69 (Cabinet Papers), Wednesday, 13 June 1883.

Harcourt's advice had been followed, and Rosebery had been persuaded to undertake the mission, then he might not have resigned from the Government two days later, on 4 June.[1] But Gladstone still considered Rosebery too young, and too inexperienced, for full Cabinet membership.

The ten days which elapsed between these vital Cabinets, 2 and 13 June, were to witness important developments. In the Cape the Colonial ministry began to stir: the position on the north-west frontier of the Cape was so severe that it could not be ignored. It was rumoured that many of the freebooters in the area south of the Molopo were of Cape origin. Accordingly the Cape Assembly agreed to a suggestion that a three-man commission should go to the area 'to investigate and report upon the northern boundaries of Griqualand West'.[2] The members of the commission were to be Samuel Melville, a surveyor, William Palgrave, a magistrate, and as Chairman, an unknown young man, the member for Barkly West, Cecil John Rhodes. In the Colonial Office his name, as yet, meant nothing, and it passed unnoticed; so that a year later an official could write, 'Who is Mr. Rhodes?' But in the Cape Rhodes' connection with the Bechuanaland area was already noted. He had made several speeches in the House on the value of the 'Road to the Interior', as he termed the area. He and John X. Merriman were still friends in 1883, and the future of the Cape trade through this area into the interior of Africa, was the subject of a long correspondence. The most interesting letter was that from Rhodes to Merriman, of 8 April.[3] Merriman had first suggested the idea of a chartered company to take over the region as the Colony would not do so. Rhodes' initial reaction is ironic when one remembers how he struggled to get a charter for the B.S.A. Co. five years later:

I do not agree with you as to your plan of a chartered company for this district. It is a poor country and no company would cope with the intrigues of the Transvaal. It must either remain under

[1] Addit. MSS. 48633, f. 121 (Hamilton Diary). Entry for Monday, 4 June 1883.
[2] Parl. Pap., 1883, XLIX, C.3686, pp. 94–6. Smyth to Derby, 4 June 1883.
[3] Rhodes Papers (Rhodes House), Afr. MSS. T.5, f. 40. Rhodes to Merriman, 8 April 1883.

the Imperial protectorate or else be annexed to the Cape Colony. Any other plan will simply hand the interior over to the Transvaal.[1]

Rhodes was, as yet, not worried over the fate of this area, the 'Suez Canal to the interior', for he believed that while 'England may be determined not to continue a heavy expenditure in Bechuanaland, . . . at the same time I do not see how she is going to retire from it and practically hand Mankaroane [sic] and Montshiwa [sic] back to their despoilers. . . .'[2]

Rhodes was soon to learn that this was not the impossibility that he assumed. In London the plans to send a Commissioner to South Africa advanced apace. Derby determined to send Reay. 'Turning the whole matter over, I can find no man better fitted than Lord Reay to negotiate with the Boers; and if you don't object, I would at once proceed to sound him.'[3] To Kimberley he was even more explicit in explaining the reasoning behind his choice of Reay:

I think the choice would be a success here *and would please the Africanders*: how he would do the work is less easy to judge. What do you say to him?[4]

Kimberley replied immediately. 'I remain of opinion that you will not find a better man than Reay.'[5] At the Colonial Office Evelyn Ashley minuted that the despatch of a Commissioner might provide an excellent opportunity to make an advantageous deal with the Cape ministers: 'We should strike while the iron is hot—and make it a condition of our relieving them of Basutoland (and Transkei) that they should take over part of Bechuanaland.'[6]

The Cabinet of Wednesday afternoon, 13 June, was devoted entirely to colonial matters, the Boers, Basutoland, and New Guinea.[7] The crucial decisions, definitely to amend the Con-

[1] Idem.   [2] Idem.
[3] Addit. MSS. 44141, f. 106. Derby to Gladstone, 6 June 1883, from C.O.
[4] Derby Papers, Trunk X.24 (Private), Derby to Kimberley, 7 June 1883. (My italics.)
[5] Ibid., Kimberley to Derby, 7 June 1883—on back of Derby's letter.
[6] C.O. 291/22. Minute by Ashley, 8 June 1883.
[7] Addit. MSS. 44644, f. 69 (Cabinet Papers), Wednesday, 13 June 1883, 2 p.m.

vention, and to despatch a Commissioner to assess those changes needed, were now taken.[1] Gladstone personally recorded the decision of the Cabinet:

> Commr. to be sent for revision of the Convention, which would of necessity involve his examining the questions connected with the state of Bechuanaland in conjunction with the High Commr.[2]

The wording of the announcement to Parliament and the Press was also agreed upon.[3]

Then Gladstone wrote to the Queen. He made no great attempt at phrasing it tactfully: 'The Cabinet adhere to the opinion that a Commissioner should be despatched to South Africa to enquire into our relations with the Transvaal Government, and into the working of the Convention as it has now been tested by experience.'[4] He also included the name of the new commissioner: 'It is probable that Lord Derby will very shortly submit to your Majesty the name of Lord Reay for this office. The office would give to the Commissioner a concern in settling questions which have arisen in Bechuanaland.'[5]

But these two Gladstonian statements partially hid the truth, and it was his secretary, Hamilton, who best captured the Government's intentions: 'Cabinet this afternoon. It was decided that a Comm. should be sent out to S. Africa to arrange with the Transvaal Govt. some *modus vivendi* (*Lord Derby evidently for giving up altogether the Convention*) . . .'[6]

All that apparently remained to be done was to communicate this information to the Transvaal and Cape Governments. By a rare coincidence on 17 June the Transvaal *Volksraad* had resolved to ask Britain whether they were 'prepared to receive [a] deputation from the Transvaal, of which President or Vice-President will be one, either in London, or before Imperial

---

[1] Addit. MSS. 43925, f. 65 (Dilke Diary). Entry for 13 June 1883.

[2] Addit. MSS. 44644, f. 69 (Cabinet Minute). 'Point 1'; in Gladstone's own hand.

[3] Ibid., f. 72. Also in Gladstone's hand.

[4] *Letters of Queen Victoria*, III, 428–9. Gladstone to Queen (from Downing Street), 13 June 1883—'Cabinet Report'.

[5] Idem.

[6] Addit. MSS. 48633, f. 130 (Hamilton Diary). Entry for Wednesday, 13 June 1883. (My italics.)

Commission in Cape Town'.[1] Thus, to their complete surprise, Derby was now able to cable back immediately: 'Yours 17th. Inform Transvaal Government Her Majesty's Government consent to inquire into working of Convention.'[2] A Commissioner would be despatched in due course.

But here Derby's well-laid plans ran into unexpected trouble. The Transvaal Boers demanded to be able to send a full deputation to London.[3] They reasoned that it was far more likely that they could secure real concessions from Derby, at the Colonial Office, than to rely on a commissioner who would not have the same powers to negotiate. He would merely report; and the Boers wished to put the maximum pressure on Derby—not merely to amend the Convention, but to abolish it.

The Cape also began to 'play-up'. Their hypersensitivity had once again been roused. Urged on by the Rhodes group in the Assembly, they hinted that Derby was about to make a secret agreement with the Boers, giving away their trade route to the interior. They demanded to be consulted on any decision taken over the western border of the Transvaal. If need be the Cape Prime Minister would go to London with the Boer deputation.[4]

Gladstone took the news badly. He was very much against the idea of allowing the Boers to send a deputation to England. As he argued to Derby:

> I am rather averse to working the subject here.
> 1. I do not see how we can deal with the Bechuana question here, as the High Commissioner and the Cape are concerned.
> 2. . . . if men come here from the Transvaal they will come closely tied up with instructions leaving them little or no elbow room, so that they would continually refer and make very slow work indeed.
> 3. It is awkward in this matter which has become so polemical again to shift our ground.[5]

---

[1] C.O. 291/22. Smyth to Derby, 17 June 1883, enclosing Resolution of Transvaal *Volksraad*.

[2] *Parl. Pap.*, 1883, XLIX, C.3659. Derby to Smyth (Tel.), 23 June 1883.

[3] Ibid., Smyth to Derby, 17 June 1883.

[4] C.O. 291/22. Minute by Herbert on the situation, 18 June 1883.

[5] Addit. MSS. 44546, f. 127 (L.B. copy). Gladstone to Derby, 20 June 1883.

Gladstone's reasoning was sound. It was to the Liberal Government's advantage to negotiate, at arm's length, with the Boers in South Africa. Not only would it arouse less parliamentary opinion, but it was easier to handle the Boers' demands, with the delays in communication, than if they sat on Derby's doorstep at the Colonial Office, which was clearly their intention.

This new development was reported to the Cabinet of Saturday, 23 June.[1] The crucial factor was, as Gladstone noted in his Cabinet minutes, the 'views of Cape upon Bechuanaland'.[2] Once again the Liberal Government hesitated before it angered or displeased the Cape ministry, with its Dutch backing from Hofmeyr. Thus the Cabinet gave way, not to the Transvaal but to the Cape.[3] The entry in Hamilton's Diary for 23 June recorded the decision:[4] in the Cabinet it was 'settled that the idea of sending a Commissioner (Reay) to the Transvaal should be abandoned, and that the inquiry into the working of the Convention should be conducted here by means of agents from the Transvaal.'[5]

On 11 July Derby communicated the information to the Transvaal Government; by 25 July the Transvaal had named Kruger, N. J. Smit, and S. J. du Toit as their three 'ambassadors'; and on 27 July Derby suggested that the Boer deputation should come to London in October, *after* the parliamentary session was over.[6]

Anglo-Boer relations moved towards a new phase, and a phase in which it was most unlikely that Britain would gain in any way. The Transvaal immediately claimed it as a victory. The very fact that Britain was prepared to reconsider the Convention, with the possibility of modification was, in their reasoning, a triumph for their campaign to wreck the Convention; a step towards its complete abolition. Equally, the fact that Britain

[1] Addit. MSS. 44644, f. 77 (Cabinet Papers), Saturday, 23 June 1883, 12 p.m.

[2] Ibid., point 2: 'Offer of Transvaal to send . . . a person with full powers subject to *Volksraad*.'

[3] Addit. MSS. 43925, f. 66 (Dilke Dairy). Entry for 23 June 1883.

[4] Addit. MSS. 48634, f. 6. (Hamilton Diary). Entry for Saturday, 23 June 1883.

[5] Idem.

[6] *Parl. Pap.*, 1884, LVII, C.3947, pp. 1–10 (Tels.), Derby to Smyth and vice versa, 17 June–27 July 1883.

had acceded to their demand to send a deputation to London and had abandoned the original plan to send a commissioner to South Africa, was taken as a signal token of British weakness. In the language of the *veld*, Kruger was considered to have Derby 'on the run'.

The Colonial Secretary declined to see it in this way. On 29 May Derby had written to Gladstone: 'We do not pledge ourselves to accept their solution or indeed any change they may propose, by the mere fact of inviting them to speak out.'[1] But, in the Colonial Office, Hemming had come far closer to the reality of the situation when he minuted: 'This is another nail in the coffin of the Pretoria Convention.'[2]

[1] Addit. MSS. 44141, f. 96. Derby to Gladstone, 29 May 1883.
[2] C.O. 291/22. Minute by Hemming, 22 May 1883.

362

VII

THE LONDON CONVENTION

'Home Rule' for the Transvaal, 1884

1. British Imperial Policy and Cape Party Politics: the Search for Collaborators (July to November 1883)

A crucial phase was now fast approaching. The period July 1883 to February 1884 was to be vital not only for the demise of the Pretoria Convention, and the further involvement of imperial rule in Africa, but also for the whole future of the British presence in South Africa. The Derby settlement of early 1884—termed the London Convention—created the framework of politics and policies which ultimately resulted in the Anglo-Boer War. Indeed, at the lowest common denominator, the London Convention was what the Boer War was about: Britain's attempt to assert her supremacy in southern Africa, and in particular the controversial 'suzerainty' over the Transvaal republic. Kruger challenged the first, and denied the second. Thus in 1899 Chamberlain was at last facing head-on the basic problems left unresolved by the London Convention, problems which Lord Derby had preferred to circumvent.

Chamberlain admitted as much.[1] As a member of the second Gladstone government, and already regarded as the Liberals' South African specialist in the Commons, he had followed each stage of the Kruger–Derby negotiation in the winter of 1883–84. This partly explains Chamberlain's dogmatic stand in 1899: he claimed to have known Kruger, and the ways of the Boers, since the early 1880s, placing him in a unique position in the Salisbury Cabinet. It also provides a salutory reminder of the long-term

---

[1] *Hansard*, Chamberlain: 19 October 1899; *Collected Speeches*, II, 25–33.

nature of Anglo-Boer relations which culminated in the war of 1899, and is a useful antidote to schools of thought that would write of 'Milner's War'.[1]

The Derby negotiations, and the resultant Treaty, is thus central to the main theme of southern African history—why the imperial factor declined. Much the same might be said of the complex background to these vital negotiations. Derby, in mid-1883, was already well aware of what was soon to be the crux of the question of the future of British supremacy in southern Africa. 'It is the old story,' he wrote to Gladstone on 7 July, 'colonies always willing to help us and stand by us, provided we will find all the money and take all the risk.'[2]

This wry comment went to the very heart of the practical problem facing the Gladstone administration in South Africa: how to ensure stability without extending the frontiers of British control; how to dominate without administering. The obvious answer appeared to be a devolution of responsibility on to the most prosperous local ministry, in this case that of the Cape. The technique would provide the basis for Derby's 'middle course' policy; the *status quo* would be maintained at no extra cost, and the imperialists could drop the dilemma into the lap of the colonial ministers, and concentrate on the major African dilemma of 1883–84—Britain's involvement in Egypt.

Derby's thinking was not unreasonable. The Bechuanaland area was of no use to Britain, but it was of great use to the Cape; it was their trade-route to central Africa and beyond, a trade which in a good year could rise as high as a quarter of a million pounds. Further, as Britain was preparing to take Basutoland back into the imperial fold, and off the hands of the pressed Scanlen ministry, it was not too much to ask the Cape to rise to the occasion, and assume responsibility for the limited Keate Award area. Derby did not even demand that the Cape should sweep the territory clean of every freebooter, nor spend a great deal defending the Tswana tribes. He merely asked them to administer it as they wished, and stop the Transvaal 'drift' over the Convention frontiers, and across the road to the north, surely a matter in the Cape interest? Thus these eight months—

---

[1] G. H. L. Le May *British Supremacy in South Africa, 1899–1907*, chap. I: 'Sir Alfred Milner's War', pp. 1–37.

[2] Addit. MSS. 44141, f. 124. Derby to Gladstone, 7 July 1883, from C.O.

from mid 1883 to early 1884—were to be crucial for settling the working basis of Cape involvement in Bechuanaland; for attempting to get the Cape to work again in harness with the imperial factor; and also for providing a clear illustration of the extent to which central imperial policy had come to be governed by the wishes of the local colonial and republican ministries. These months were to witness the strange and bizarre sight of the imperial power having to consult Cape colonial politicians, who in turn found it necessary to refer the matter to the Boer leaders, before a British protectorate could be declared in the interests of the Tswana tribes, and against the interests of those same Boers.

Derby's position was also now suddenly complicated by the fact that other major crises developed during this period, and tended to overlap both in time and intensity with the Transvaal negotiations. Just as Kimberley's thinking had been biased by the Irish unrest, so Derby was now beset with the Egyptian crisis. If this crisis affected Derby differently from that of Kimberley and the Fenians, it did seriously weigh on his mind. At least he did not have the Radicals trying to work him out of the Cabinet; but it did mean that one major option for policy—a straight annexation and the creation of a Crown Colony—was ruled out. This was particularly so from the autumn onwards: in other words, just at that moment when the Transvaal delegates arrived. In October, Baring sent his dramatic despatch assessing the position in Egypt, and pointing out the complacency behind Dufferin's 'shallow thinking'. Instead of being able to withdraw at will, as Dufferin had hinted, Baring made it clear that Britain would have to reform the administration completely, put it on a new sound basis, before retrenchment could even be contemplated. This might take several years, but unless it was done Egypt would relapse into even worse chaos when Britain did leave.

If the Gladstonians' illusions about an easy way out of Egypt were not shattered by this report, the news of the following month completed the task. On 22 November—just when Derby was ready to have his first meeting with the Boers' delegates from the Transvaal—news was received that Hicks Pasha's entire force had been wiped out while advancing on the Mahdi. Baring spelt out what it meant: Tewfik was in great danger from the south, Khartoum could fall to the Mahdi at any moment, and if the Nile south of Wadi Halfa were lost, 'the political and military situation here will become one of great difficulty'.[1]

Such was the position in Cairo. In London the Cabinet was thrown into disarray, and began to take on the shape of two warring factions, groupings which were to co-exist and jar each other for the next twelve months in the Government. Hartington and Northbrook led the so-called 'forward group', demanding immediate and further involvement in Egypt, to hold the Sudan, and to put Tewfik's régime on a sounder footing; the Gladstonians, centred around the Premier and Granville, opposed this militaristic view. They did not so much have a policy themselves as merely took on the rôle of critics of the Hartington approach, trying to find the 'golden mean' between deeper involvement and immediate withdrawal. They were still trying to find it when the Gordon tragedy struck the Cabinet in February 1885.

Derby's involvement in all this was minimal; but it did mean that during a period of critical negotiations with the Boer deputies—November to January—he knew that the Cabinet would never acquiesce to a British colony in Bechuanaland, when they were trying to avoid having Egypt as a Crown Colony. This is a major consideration to bear in mind when examining Derby's handling of the London Convention negotiations. Historians have too glibly assumed that the option of annexation was open to Derby. It was not. Thus, he *had* to find a middle course, particularly as he had already committed Britain to retaking the vast Basuto territory. If policy consists of the margin of options available to a minister, then by late 1883 Derby must now be counted among the unfortunate. Not only did he have to take into account local opinion, and in particular the new-found links between the Cape Dutch and the Transvaal Boers, but he also had to consider the world-wide position of the imperial power in late 1883. Without accepting this constricting framework, within which he had to work, any judgment on Lord Derby's negotiations, which led to the London Convention settlement, is lopsided. To ignore British involvement in North Africa, and to see Derby as having a complete and full range of options,

[1] P.R.O. 30/29/161. Baring to Granville, 22 November 1883.

would be to place the Anglo-Boer negotiations in a vacuum.

It is easy to see Colonial Secretaries as being involved in colonial matters alone. It is easy, but misleading. Derby was a leading member of the Cabinet; and privy to all the inner Cabinets decisions and information. Thus, for example, in January 1884 he knew that the Chancellor, Childers, was very deeply worried over the increasing British responsibility in Egypt, and had warned Gladstone that further involvement must hit the British economy hard.[1] Was this the moment for Derby to talk about annexing the vast semi-desert Bechuana-land, and risking possible pan-Afrikaner unrest? Yet, this month of January 1884, was the very month in which Derby was forced to make a decision on the Boer demands for an extended frontier in Bechuanaland: and forced to grapple with the fact that the Cape Premier, Scanlen, then in London, was refusing to see why the Colony should help take part of the load off the imperial factor in southern Africa.

Derby was also unfortunate in that the latter part of the year which followed his appointment to the Colonial Office, 1883, was similar to that other very troublesome year for the Gladstone Cabinet. 1881. Thus some six months after Derby joined the Gladstone administration, he not only had to ride out dangerously high seas abroad, he also found that the ship of state was none too firm or stable; and that it was not unlikely that it would break-up. The Cabinet appeared to have a frivolous disregard for dangers, be they in North or South Africa, Afghanistan, or New Guinea, and to be using their energies for the sole purpose of disagreeing with each other. Harcourt still smarted at not being made Chancellor, and grumbled that Gladstone had not given him time in the parliamentary programme to put his London Government Bill before the House.[2] Childers, who had been given the office of Chancellor, complained that he was so overworked that his health might force him to resign, a threat he held over the Cabinet from April 1883.[3] Rosebery not only threatened but acted, and resigned

---

[1] Childers to Gladstone, 16 January 1884. Quoted in *Africa and the Victorians*, p. 137.

[2] Addit. MSS. 48633, f. 110 (Hamilton Diary). Entry for Thursday, 24 May 1883.

[3] Ibid., f. 114. Entry for Monday, 28 May 1883.

from the Government in the same month; he declined to remain a junior minister until he was in his declining years, as Gladstone seemed to propose.[1] The major split was over Egypt, with Hartington leading a 'Cabal' of malcontents against the Gladstonians. But other rifts were equally corrosive. Hartington was also 'at war' with Chamberlain, over the extent of the franchise in the coming 3rd Reform Bill.[2] Even Derby, as the newcomer, was immediately plunged into Cabinet wrangles. Granville rose to a surprising level of anger at Derby's public speeches about Madagascar;[3] and Hartington poured scorn on Derby's proposals concerning the Agricultural Holdings Bill.[4]

Nor could Derby turn to the Premier for assistance. Gladstone had his own private squabbles: with the Queen—over Transvaal policy, and over his autumn 'escapade' when Gladstone visited several Scandinavian countries without her 'permission';[5] with Hartington—over whether to advance or retreat in the Sudan; and with Chamberlain—on the latter's demands in regard to Reform Bill. Finally the Radicals prepared, throughout 1883, to walk out of the Cabinets at any moment if they did not get their way with Reform; and also because even Chamberlain and Dilke became weary of the perpetual tensions, animosities, delays and lack of achievement in the Government. Chamberlain best expressed the feeling in the Cabinet, in 1883, when he wrote to Morley:

I do not see my way very definitely out of the present difficulties. ... Our Foreign and Colonial Policy—on the whole a policy of

[1] Ibid., f. 121. Entry for Monday, 4 June 1883.
[2] Gwynne and Tuckwell, Dilke. II, 3. Hartington to Gladstone, 2 December 1883. Hartington complained that he was continually having 'to vote every day for things which he strongly approves, and this makes the position difficult'. (p. 8) Holland, Devonshire, p. 397.
[3] Addit. MSS. 43936, f. 271 (Dilke Memoir): 'On December 15th, 1882, there was a fresh trouble for Lord Granville was furious at a speech by Lord Derby, and, indeed I never knew him so cross. ... The difficulty was once more Madagascar.' Derby had in fact announced that Britain had no interest in the island and Granville was annoyed, for it allowed the French 'to look over his hand and see how bad the cards were'.
[4] Roy Jenkins, Dilke, pp. 166-7. 'He [Hartington] gave us to understand that Derby was a mere owner of Liverpool ground rents, who knew nothing about land.' (21 April 1883.)
[5] Letters of Queen Victoria, III, 439-40. Queen to Granville, 18 September 1883.

justice, of self abnegation and of peace—has not been so trium-
phantly successful. . . . Take the restoration of Cetewayo and the
surrender of the Transvaal for instance—virtue has found its own
reward, a very poor one in both cases. Then look at Ireland. . . .[1]

This opinion, and concern, was shared by many sober and
influential back-benchers, who sensed the malaise in the Cabinet without complete knowledge of the real divisions between
the ministers. On 9 May 1883 William Rathbone, a key Liberal
back-bencher, wrote confidentially to Gladstone of the discontent in the Liberal Parliamentary Party, and called for a more
definite leadership and a clear legislative programme.[2] It was to
no avail. The session of 1883 achieved nothing of worth, and the
most promising piece of legislation, Harcourt's London
Government Bill, never left the Cabinet. Hartington blamed it
on the lack of November planning Cabinets in 1882, and spoke
of 'our unprepared condition'.[3] Harcourt admitted, in February, that he was 'seriously uneasy at meeting Parliament without
any Cabinet consultations;'[4] an opinion which did not alter
with the passing of the months;[5] so that at the end of the
session, in December, he felt constrained to write to Granville:

> I am so uneasy at the present state of affairs that I cannot resist
> writing a line to you as I think if anyone can avert the disaster I
> see impending it is you. . . . Of course the main cause of the present
> situation is the manner in which the critical questions were
> shunted or evaded in the November Cabinets.[6]

The initial impetus given to Gladstone, by the great election
victory of 1880, was in fact spent; from the winter of 1883 the
administration lived on borrowed time.

The cumulative effect of these destructive and negative forces
on Derby's handling of colonial policy was twofold. It weakened
his position when it came to dealing with the Boer deputies, for
he could not be sure of finding Cabinet backing for anything
more than the most conservative of policies. To have presented

---

[1] Garvin, *Chamberlain*, I, p. 391. Chamberlain to Morley, 19 May 1883.
[2] Addit. MSS. 44480, f. 309. Rathbone to Gladstone, 9 May 1883.
[3] P.R.O. 30/29/27A. Hartington to Granville, 3 February 1883.
[4] Ibid., 2 February 1883.
[5] Addit. MSS. 48633, f. 61 (Hamilton Diary). Entry for Christmas Day, 1883.
[6] P.R.O. 30/29/29A. Harcourt to Granville, 16 December 1883.

a 'forward policy', involving annexing Bechuanaland, would merely have led to a split similar to that which already existed over Egypt. Secondly, it meant that few, if any ministers at all, were interested in his problems in southern Africa. Even Gladstone, who had taken such a close interest in Kimberley's policy over the Pretoria Convention, was now distracted by the rifts with Hartington, and also with the Radicals;[1] and ministers, like Chamberlain, who were knowledgeable on southern Africa were too deeply involved in their own personal crusades—in Chamberlain's case to secure the right Reform Bill—to give time to fight for the Pretoria Convention. A glance at Gladstone's Cabinet minutes reveals the low priority given to Derby's problems.[2] The Anglo-Transvaal wrangles over the Convention frontiers were not discussed at the Cabinet level from 23 June,[3]—the acceptance of the Transvaal deputation coming to London—to 10 November[4]—when the Cape attitude was revealed to the Cabinet. Derby was thus very much out on a limb: unable to annex, unable to threaten military action, unable to get the Cape to co-operate, and therefore unable to face the demands of the Boer delegates with anything like the firm front that Robinson, the Humanitarians, or Rhodes had hoped for.

Derby's position on southern Africa was yet further complicated by Granville's diplomatic relations with Bismarck, over the delicate British position in Egypt. By late 1883 he had a tacit, but unwritten undertaking from Bismarck, that Britain would have an unhampered approach to Egypt, and that Germany would not exploit the strained Anglo-French *entente*. It was equally understood that Bismarck was not to be excluded, by Britain, from a possible German settlement on the coasts of southern Africa.[5] It was not so much a bargain as a practical appreciation of their relative positions and aspirations; and, an agreement which Granville saw as working in Britain's favour, for he took Egypt as the real problem in Africa, not the troubles over the turbulent Bechuana/Transvaal frontier.

[1] Gwynne and Tuckwell; *Dilke*, I, 519.
[2] Addit. MSS. 44644, ff. 62–126 (Cabinet Papers).
[3] Ibid., f. 77.   [4] Ibid., f. 112.
[5] See *Africa and the Victorians*, pp. 202 ff., where this point is well made and amplified.

Granville's pleasure was Derby's displeasure. It worked against Derby's scheme of things in a particularly practical way. The Cape politicians had long looked to their own fishing settlements on the coast of South-West Africa as a Cape preserve. News that Bismarck was expressing interest in the area, as a result of the activities of certain German merchants, greatly upset the colonial ministry. Scanlen looked to Britain for a lead on the matter; and Merriman launched a vigorous campaign, which included endless letters to Derby and Robinson in London, calling for the declaration of a British 'Monroe Doctrine' over the coasts of southern Africa. As a result of Granville's diplomacy with Bismarck on Egypt, Derby was unable, and unwilling, to attempt such a declaration, though he knew in so doing he must offend the Cape, just at the moment when he earnestly required their collaboration, to take Bechuanaland in as an extension of the Colony.

It is yet another example of the manner in which Derby's position was now hedged about with difficulties. If his bargaining position was weak, because of other British commitments, his margin for initiative was even more restricted. This becomes even more apparent when it is remembered that quite apart from international complications and Cabinet rifts, the local position in southern Africa was hardening, and less open to 'informal' pressures. The situation now facing Derby was probably far less malleable than Carnarvon, or Hicks Beach, had attempted to shape; and as dangerous and difficult to work as when Kimberley had first opted for a conciliatory policy.

In Bechuanaland, the Freebooters' states—the 'Robber Republics', as Robinson called them—were fully established,[1] with the Stellaland flag flying from Vryburg, and the Goshen flag over Mafeking.[2] There was even talk of their uniting, to counter any possible combined Montshiwa–Mankurwane attack.[3] The 'republics' were extremely sure of themselves; Stellaland talked of levying 'fair' customs tariffs as their state

[1] C.O. 291/22. Kimberley to Derby, 22 January 1883, enclosing Rutherford's Report of 26 December 1882. See also *Parl. Pap.*, 1883, XLIX, C.3486, pp. 68 ff. Map of area on pp. 76–7.

[2] Ibid., pp. 16–17, Robinson to Derby, 12 February 1883.

[3] C.O. 291/22. Smyth to Derby, 6 November 1883, enclosed in Hudson to Smyth, 30 October 1883, with extracts from *Volksstem*. See also *Parl. Pap.*, 1884, LVII, C.3841, pp. 119–20.

371

was astride 'the main road to the interior';[1] and Goshen published its 'state proclamations' in the Transvaal Government's *Volksstem*.[2] Within Kruger's state the burghers were also in high spirits. The Mapoch tribe, which had defied the Transvaal authorities for some time, had been defeated: Mampoer, the chief was executed, and the tribe dispersed as indentured labourers.[3] All this was carried out in the face of protests from Hudson, and in defiance of the native's protection clauses in the Convention. A Colonial Office clerk was prompted to write of this: 'I should think we ought now—in our defence from a Parliamentary point of view—to write something strong to the Transvaal Deputation, respecting the gross breach of faith which has been practised by the Executive Council of the State'.[4]

The position in the Cape was no more comforting. Smyth, the acting-governor, reported with surprise the amount of anti-English feeling he found in the Colony. It was to be the traditional white colony complaint:

> The bitter memories which are left [by the Transvaal War] have been aggravated by the ill-considered and often unfounded statements made by well meaning and philanthropic persons in England . . . and has given rise to a feeling that the people of England desire to favour the interest of the black population even at the expense of the safety or welfare of Her Majesty's white subjects.[5]

Indeed, he detected, 'amongst all classes', a feeling 'of dislike to what is called "Imperial interference" '.[6]

His fears did not end there. He reported that the Afrikaner *Bond* had been expanded, and had increased its Cape Dutch support, by the absorption of the Farmers' Union. A new Constitution had been drawn up, and though it was like the *Bond*

[1] *Parl. Pap.*, 1883, XLIX, C.3686, pp. 16–17. Robinson to Derby, 12 February 1883, enclosed in Mankurwane to Robinson, 3 February 1883.

[2] *Parl. Pap.*, 1884, LVII, C.3841, p. 119. Hudson to Smyth, 30 October 1883.

[3] C.O. 291/23. Smyth to Derby, 23 July 1883, enclosed in Hudson to Smyth, 21 July 1883.

[4] Ibid., Minute by Hemming, 28 November 1883. See also Minutes by Herbert and Derby, same date.

[5] C.O. 48/507. Smyth to Derby, 20 July 1883, enclosed in Scanlen to Smyth 12 July 1883.

[6] Idem.

leader Hofmeyr himself, legalistic, conservative, and moderate, at the same time the movement was gaining great power in Cape politics. It was nurturing the anti-English feeling already in existence; and it was becoming a South Africa-wide phenomenon.[1] The Cape Premier, Scanlen, anxiously spoke to Smyth of the 'new departure in the history of what may be termed the Dutch question in South Africa'.[2] The fact that the *Bond* came out strongly in favour of the Transvaal demands for modifying the Convention gave substance to his concern.[3] After the Transvaal deputation had passed through Cape Town,[4] the *Bond* published this statement: they hoped Her Majesty's Government would 'favourably entertain the proposals which will be laid before them by the Deputation', for they appealed on behalf of 'many thousands of Your Majesty's faithful subjects, mostly of Dutch extraction, residing in the Colony of the Cape of Good Hope, who deeply sympathise with their compatriots of the Transvaal State'.[5]

Before the Colonial officials had even received this petition, or Smyth's comment upon its significance, they had already taken alarm at the growth of the *Bond*, and its meaning for the future. Herbert minuted, on the constitution of the *Bond*:

I see that, under Article I, I am an 'Africander', but nevertheless *I fear that this Bond is intended to become, if its promoters can effect it, as hostile and mischievious as Fenianism* or any other conspiracy against the established Government of a Country.[6]

[1] In May 1883—Richmond Congress of the Bond—the movement had the following branches:
Cape: 23 (plus 20 Farmers' Association branches)
O.F.S.: 10
Transvaal: 10 (at Utrecht, Walkerstroom, Standerton, Heidelberg, Potchefstroom, Makwassie, Rustenburg, Pretoria, Lydenburg, and Zoutbansberg).
T. R. Davenport, *Afrikaner Bond*. End-piece map.
[2] C.O. 48/506. Smyth to Derby, 10 October 1883. See also *Parl. Pap.*, 1884, LVII, C.3841, p. 79.
[3] Idem.
[4] The deputation sailed from Cape Town for England on 10 October 1883.
[5] Ibid., Smyth to Derby, 10 October 1883–enclosing Petition from Afrikaner *Bond*.
[6] C.O. 48/506. Minutes by Herbert and Derby, dated 30 June and 1 July 1883; on Smyth to Derby 4 June 1883, enclosing new Constitution of the Afrikaner *Bond*. (My italics.)

To which Derby added, below Herbert's comment: 'Yes, but the mischief will not come from the *Bond*, but from the existence of the feeling that has led to its being set on foot.'[1]

It was fears such as these, together with Derby's other complications, which combined to provide the long-term background to the approaching negotiations. However, during the six week period, from mid-September until the end of October —while the deputation bumped across the *veld*, and crossed the high seas—other factors came into play to produce a more immediate background to the winter discussions in the Colonial Office. These new factors which Derby had to consider were, in the main, the conflicting pressures created by the clash of personalities involved in the advocacy of particular policies.

Derby himself had long been contemplating this new phase of Anglo-Boer relations; and in his own mind was at least clear on the objects which he wished to achieve, though he had no real working concept of how he would bring these hopes to fruition. As he complained to Ponsonby, in a private letter: South African affairs were 'one degree worse in point of confusion and complication than those of Ireland'.[2] He saw no easy way out of his difficulties, bar a careful revision of the Convention to make it more acceptable to the Boers, and thus ease their insistent and flagrant breaches of the present treaty. He also hoped that it might be possible to get the Cape to take over a portion of Bechuananland—say that below the Molopo—and so negate the pressures from the Humanitarians for annexation. But these were hopes rather than plans; and it was on the working details that Derby was vulnerable, particularly as his own position was so delicate and hedged about by other complications.

If it is the duty of the permanent officials to suggest to the minister the available and practical courses open to him, the Colonial Office in 1883 singularly failed Derby. Fairfield declined to make any firm suggestion as there was 'an idea in the air of annexation to the Cape'.[3] Hemming could only write peevishly: 'I suppose because the Boers beat us at Laing's Nek

---

[1] Idem.
[2] *Letters of Queen Victoria*, III, 431–3. Derby to Ponsonby, 29 June 1883.
[3] C.O. 291/23. Memorandum, Fairfield to Bramston, 13 August 1883.

and Majuba, they think they are to be the arbiters of the destinies of S. Africa, and nothing is to be done there without consulting them.'[1] Herbert's only strong opinion was on whether
Mankurwane should be allowed to come to London and also
present his case. 'It is not easy to refuse it but I think it is best
to decline to deal with these savage kings and chiefs personally,
and especially in this country.'[2] His reasoning shows just how
far the Colonial Office itself feared offending the Boers: 'The
Transvaal Government would think, or pretend to think itself
insulted if we received the representatives of . . . petty black
chiefs together with their Transvaal delegates.'[3] Thus Mankurwane was stopped, literally at Cape Town docks, by Smyth.[4]
Montshiwa's similar protests met with an equal blank negative
from Herbert. In words which might be taken to be the essence
of the Colonial officials' approach, he minuted on Montshiwa's
plea for representation in London: 'I think I would only acknowledge. Anything more might be construed as undertaking
something.'[5]

In contrast to this refusal to be drawn into 'undertaking something', John Mackenzie on the other hand was even prepared to
make a clear stand for what he thought desirable in southern
Africa, namely more imperial rule. He had become the major
public spokesman on Bechuanaland, and the only determined
advocate, either in or out of the Cabinet, of a policy of annexation. During the summer he had rested in Scotland, and now
with the coming of autumn and the Transvaal deputation, he
returned to England to launch the second major phase of his
campaign.[6] Like the first it was to have minimal success; and
yet Mackenzie alone of all the participants in these events had a

[1] Ibid., Minute, Hemming to Bramston, 11 July 1883.
[2] Ibid., Minute by Herbert, 20 September 1883.
[3] Ibid., Derby's comment on the same minute paper is (as expected) 'I
entirely agree'.
[4] Parl. Pap., 1884, LVII, C.3841, p. 55. Smyth to Derby, 27 October; and
Derby to Smyth (Tel.), 5 October 1883.
[5] C.O. 291/23. Minute by Herbert, 25 September 1883, on Smyth to
Derby, 3 September 1883. It was decided eventually that John Mackenzie
'was to represent Mankaroane'[sic] interests'. Hemming, 7 November 1883.
[6] Mackenzie returned to London in September 1883, and had his first
major public meeting at the Mansion House on 27 November 1883. Life of
Mackenzie, p. 291.

sure grasp not only of the local southern African situation, but also of the broader issues at stake for the future. His letters of this period not only make sound sense, but they were later to take on a prophetic aura, as again and again Britain adopted the policy, and took the actions, which he had earlier suggested. His letters to Dr. Dale, of Birmingham, are particularly useful to the historian. To take but one particular example: his letter of 22 September, which might stand as the finest summary of the background to the coming negotiations:

> Now the Transvaal envoys are on their way to this country. What is the question which they come to decide?—Whether the Transvaal is or is not to be left without restraint, and if thus left, to become the paramount South African State.[1]

Thus Mackenzie, in 1883, already had his finger on the dilemma which created and made the Boer War inevitable:

> It is not a question of 'freedom' . . . much less is it a question of self-government. *It is a question of paramountcy.* Is it to be retained by England with and for the Cape Colony, and the more civilised South African communities, or is it to be handed to the Transvaal?[2]

A few weeks later he again took up this vital theme, in writing to W. T. Stead; and spelt it out in even plainer language:

> What they [the Boers] want is the supreme political position in South Africa, to be the empire State among its states, the highway to the interior, to have the native policy of the future etc. etc., all in their hands.[3]

Mackenzie's fears about Derby and the permanent officials were real; and he suspected that if the Cape did not make a gesture then Derby would simply give way to the Boer delegates. In a superb phrase he caught the Derby policy: 'the attitude of England is surely coldly supine'.[4] Mackenzie could take this stand for he was among the few observers who early recognised the broader significance of the Transvaal drift into Bechuanaland. On 7 November 1883 he wrote the leader article in the

[1] W. D. Mackenzie, *Life of Mackenzie*, pp. 285 ff. Mackenzie to Dr. Dale, 22 September 1883.
[2] Idem. (My italics.)
[3] Ibid., Mackenzie to W. T. Stead, (?) November 1883.
[4] Ibid., Mackenzie to Dale, 22 September 1883.

Pall Mall Gazette—'England and the Transvaal'—and sharply observed: 'Bechuanaland is the key to the interior and the key to political supremacy in southern Africa.'[1] The Colonial Office, and Lord Derby, were well aware of Mackenzie's opinion and analysis: the *Pall Mall Gazette* leader was cut out, and pasted into the official files.[2] But it had no apparent affect; and when the Liberal policy was questioned, in both Houses, an equally obdurate answer was given. In the Lords Salisbury had made a stinging attack on Derby's refusal to enforce the Convention.[3] Derby replied characteristically:

> If the object of the Convention is admitted to be the facilitation of order and good government, and of friendly relations between the Natives and the white population, that object cannot be accomplished over a country of immense extent, thinly populated and without a centralized Government, by any mere exercise of force. The only power we can employ to assist us is the co-operation of the people themselves.[4]

This is the key to Derby's 'middle course' approach; for, as he said to Salisbury, he could not 'conceive how anyone *could desire to establish another Ireland in South Africa.* But that is necessarily what would result,' should Britain go 'against the will of the inhabitants.'[5] Thus Derby was not ashamed to admit that he saw but two alternatives in dealing with the Boers—'either to take the people, and Government of the Transvaal as we find them, and establish a *modus vivendi* with them as best we can, or else accept that alternative . . . re-establish the state of things that existed after 1876'.[6]

In the Commons, Gladstone preached the same gospel. Forster had long battled to get the Premier to allow a full debate on the Convention,[7] but Gladstone had been decidedly uncooperative. Thus when the annual supply debate came round a motion was proposed to reduce the salary of Resident in the Transvaal, a useful indirect method of censuring Government

[1] *Pall Mall Gazette*, Wednesday, 7 November 1883. 'England and the Transvaal', by Rev. J. Mackenzie.
[2] C.O. 291/25 (M). No Minutes on it.
[3] *Hansard*, CCLXXX, cols. 668–84. (Lords, 15 June 1883.)
[4] Ibid., col. 669.   [5] Ibid., col. 675. (My italics.)   [6] Idem.
[7] Addit. MSS. 44160, f. 216. W. E. Forster to W. E. Gladstone, 30 June 1883.

policy.[1] Gorst attacked the apparent uselessness of the Resident in the face of Boer aggression;[2] and Forster reminded the House of the plight of the native chiefs both within the Transvaal— Mapoch in particular—and those without—Montshiwa and Mankurwane.[3] Hicks Beach made the best point of the debate by pointing out that, 'They might depend upon it that the Africander [sic] Party in South Africa were no more to be conciliated by action of this kind, or by concession, than was another Party [the Irish Fenians] who lived far nearer to Great Britain.'

Gladstone declined to see the logic behind such reasoning:

It was not primarily a question of money, but a question of blood. It was not only a question of blood; it was a question of dangers in South Africa lying in the rear of all those signs ... of stirring up animosities that would have pervaded the whole of the European communities, and the end of which it would have been difficult to foresee.[4]

As to the much abused Pretoria Convention—

Her Majesty's Government have certainly no vanity of authorship or affection of parentage in respect of the Convention. (Ironic cheers.) Those ironical cheers will not ... lead me into a statement of the reasons which led us to believe that the Convention was the best expedient remaining to us in a very difficult position.[5]

Gladstone ended with a point that must indeed have been effective: the Tory Party should not forget that South Africa was not exclusively a Liberal problem; rather it was a 'difficult and complicated problem which has now for more than a generation perplexed our statesmen'.[6] The Opposition had been silenced once again.

With such a determined approach it was unlikely that mere criticism would influence the Derby–Gladstone thinking. However, on the grounds of the practical methods of conducting the coming negotiations, they were far more vulnerable; particularly when that practical advice included a well thought-out

[1] *Hansard*, CCLXXXII, cols. 1659–1718. (Commons, 6 August 1883.)
[2] Ibid., cols. 1660–76. 'This Office of Resident and the expenses of the Office, are absolutely useless for the protection of British subjects, or for the protection of the Natives outside the Transvaal State, who we are bound to protect.'
[3] Ibid., cols. 1678–84.   [4] Ibid., col. 1715.
[5] Ibid., col. 1717.   [6] Ibid., col. 1718.

plan, which took into account South African opinion and imperial overlordship. Thus it was that the most important figure in the events which followed—apart from Derby and Kruger—was that of Sir Hercules Robinson. Where Mackenzie battled to influence policy from without, Robinson was able to bring pressure on Derby from within the Office. He was to play a crucial rôle in the negotiations; and for this reason a clear insight into his views is vital.

After his arrival in London, and his initial discussions with Derby, in May, Robinson had left for a vacation in Scotland. There, this eminently practical Victorian proconsul brooded on what could be a viable plan to have ready to meet the Boer demands. No idealist in the mould of either Mackenzie, or an 'imperialist' in the Milner–Curzon style, Robinson's mind worked on a lower level. His greatest gift as a colonial administrator was his sensitivity to colonial opinion, and his ability to work with colonial politicians. The summer of 1883 thus found him pondering on the nature of his two eventful years in southern Africa—on the Convention, the Boers, the Basuto settlement, the Cape Dutch, the rôle of the imperial factor—and putting his ideas on to paper, in letters to close friends. Significantly, most of these letters were written to Cape politicians, and the most frank and useful ones to Merriman. From these letters Robinson's whole philosophy, as regards the white colonies, can be discerned; and also the gradual emergence of his controversial views on the place of the imperial factor in South Africa. In so many ways this summer of 1883 saw his famous speech of 1889 taking on its embryonic shape.

The first necessity he recognised was the need to involve the Cape Dutch in Cape colonial politics; to see that their *Bond* and Farmers' Unions worked within the existing constitutional framework; and also to ease the birth of the first Dutch ministry. 'Until you can bring home to the Dutch party that they must be prepared to carry out in office the policy they advocate in Parliament there will be nothing but confusion and insincerity all round. I have long looked to the advent of a Dutch ministry. . . .'[1] Clearly Robinson wished to create such a thing as the loyal colonial Dutch, as against the independent repub-

[1] P. Laurence, *Life of John Xavier Merriman* (London, 1930). Hereafter cited as *Life of Merriman*. Quoted pp. 79–80.

lican Dutch. The search for collaborators and moderates—so much a theme of later colonial history—had begun.

The second reality which Robinson had to accept, and counter-balance, was the obvious 'weakness' of the Imperial Government—the reluctance to extend authority and administration, any further. He asked himself bluntly: 'Will the Imperial Government stand to its words and enforce the Convention? Certainly not . . .' This brought Robinson to the crux of what he saw as the dilemma—'it becomes then simply a question whether Mankaroane's [sic] country shall be annexed by the Colony or by the Transvaal, and bad as both courses are the former is least bad for the natives . . .'.[1]

The idea of persuading the Cape Colony to take on the area became Robinson's third conclusion, and his abiding wish. 'The more I think of the thing the more difficult do I find it to discover any way out of the mess which is free from objection and discredit, and so I am with reluctance coming round to the idea of Colonial Annexation as the least disadvantageous course now open to us.'[2]

He knew such an idea would not be popular with the very people who would have to undertake the annexation, the Cape ministry. But the alternative seemed so unfortunate that Robinson took courage. 'I suppose it will end in our having to recognize these ruffianly freebooters, or the equally bad purchasers of stolen property . . . but I confess such a course sticks in my gizzard. It will, I fear, be such a bad precedent and such an encouragement to freebooting which will become a recognized trade.'[3]

In preparation for the Cape objections to his idea, Robinson got ready his arguments, by writing to Merriman:

If we had only to deal with the Colony and the freebooters, and the natives, I should not hesitate to let things be, but how about the Transvaal? We may say you shall not extend your boundary, but they will do so in spite of your doing so, if we are not beforehand with them, and what then?[4]

A month later, having thought on the matter a deal more, and having come to the conclusion that it was highly unlikely

[1] Ibid., p. 82.   [2] Idem.   [3] Idem.
[4] Ibid., Robinson to Merriman (p. 82), (?) August 1883.

that the Cape would be persuaded to take on the area single-handed, Robinson turned back to his earlier idea. In September he wrote to Merriman: 'The more I think of it the more strongly I feel that the best solution . . . will be the maintenance of the existing Colonial and Transvaal boundaries, and a joint-protectorate by England, the Cape and the Transvaal, over the natives. I see great difficulties in the future from any other course.' The more Robinson pondered on the idea the more he warmed to the scheme. 'The Transvaal will, of course, object, but I think the thing could be managed; and if it can it will save the natives; save the Colonial trade; save honour all round; and dish the freebooters.'

It was now Merriman's turn to take on the unusual rôle of 'Cape imperialist'. To Robinson's surprise Merriman declined to accept the idea of a joint-protectorate, and instead spoke of a course of action which must necessarily be more expensive for the Colony: the result of such a plan would be the 'advent to power of a Hofmeyr–Upington–Sprigg administration pledged *inter alia* to a firm native policy, which means under a very flimsy disguise a partition of land on the Tembuland basis, and a cordial adoption of an Africander [*sic*] feeling looking to the Transvaal as the great exemplar of what the state of people should be'. Thus Merriman considered the crucial question which Robinson declined to admit—'Under such circumstances where would the Bechuana be? Very much I take it where the lamb was when the butcher and the wolf combined in a joint-protectorate.'[1]

In Merriman's terms the only answer would be for the Cape 'to make a bold stroke and annex Mankaroane [*sic*] and his country outright, for in that case our selfish interests would be bound up in seeing that the country was settled after Colonial and not after Transvaal ideas'. But was this a course likely to be adopted by the existing Cape ministry? This was Merriman's great doubt. 'I am sure that Mr. Scanlen's sound sense will have discounted the probabilities far better than I can pretend to forecast them. But I think that he is sometimes a little cautious in taking a course which he fancies the colony may not endorse.'[2]

Merriman's fears were not without foundation. On 25

[1] Ibid., Merriman to Robinson, (?) September 1883 (pp. 83–4).
[2] Idem.

October Scanlen wrote, from London, to Merriman at the Cape, pouring cold water on the idea of a Cape annexation of Bechuanaland: 'This would be the means of securing British interests . . . but *it would not prove of any immediate benefit to the colony.*'[1] This was a crucial admission from Scanlen, and goes far to explaining the difficulties experienced by Derby in getting the Cape to work with him to save the road to the north from falling to the Transvaal.[2]

At the Cape, Rhodes knew or suspected, what Scanlen's attitude would be to the area; and hence Rhodes began to preach his doctrine of Cape colonial 'imperialism'. On 16 August he had already stated succinctly his attitude to Bechuanaland, and also the guiding principle behind so much of his later thinking:

> I look upon this Bechuanaland territory as the Suez Canal of the trade of this country, the key of the road to the interior. . . . The question before us is this—whether this Colony is to be confined to its present borders, or whether it is to become the dominant state in South Africa.[3]

It is, ironically, Mackenzie's thinking with a white colonial twist. But it was the core of Rhodes' approach to all matters concerning the 'Imperial Factor'—a phrase he had recently coined in derision—and the key issue of Cape or Transvaal dominance of southern Africa.

Had Rhodes known though that this greatest 'enemy' was not Kruger's ambitions, but imperial intransigence, he might have changed his tactic from wiring urgently to Scanlen to pressing Lord Derby. But then he was an insignificant figure in 1883. He had only just gained his Oxford pass degree, and entered the Cape Assembly. It was Rhodes' good luck that Sir Hercules Robinson was in London. Had Robinson not played the vital rôle that he did, all Rhodes' plans for a push to the north would have collapsed at the level of ideas.

Leonard Courtney best captured the attitude of the official

[1] W. J. De Kock, '*Ekstra Territoriale Vraagstukke van die Kaapse Regering, 1872–1855*', *A.Y.B.* (1948), Part I. Quoted p. 131, Scanlen to Merriman, 25 October 1883. Hereafter cited as De Kock, *Ekstra Territoriale Vraagstukke.*

[2] See also Scanlen in Cape Assembly, 15 July 1884, *Cape Hansard*, p. 347.

[3] 'Vindex' *Speeches of Cecil John Rhodes* (London, 1910), p. 62 ff.

mind when he wrote to Gladstone, of Rhodes' 'Suez Canal' to the interior, 'I am for letting the Transvaal settle the matter themselves. Sir Hercules [Robinson] says this would be a fatal precedent as freebooters would raise difficulties on every side in turn; but my own view is that the only safeguard—an imperfect one—on this lies in fastening upon the Transvaal the responsibility of any extension'.[1] Courtney, like the permanent Colonial officials, declined to see in the matter the broader question of supremacy in southern Africa. Indeed he went so far as to state that he could see no real reason for Britain to exercise absolute control over the actions of the Boers, in a land-locked and ramshackle state:

> 'Are we to maintain an active and responsible control of the Transval or not? My answer would be, we are not.'[2]

Thus as autumn moved towards winter, and the two sides approached the negotiations, there were a multifarious number of arguments as to how the dilemma should be settled. Only the Boers knew what they wanted: a return, if possible, to the position at the time of the Sand River Convention. The British approach was less sure and more divided. There was Derby prepared to consider all the Boers had to say, and with no more constructive an argument in mind but that Britain was not going to annex a further portion of Africa. There was Robinson hoping to twist the arms of both Derby and Scanlen to produce a joint-protectorate. There was the attitude of the Colonial officials, that Bechuanaland was a Transvaal matter, and that the Boers should solve it in terms of the Convention. There were the Humanitarians, led by Mackenzie, vainly trying to save the chiefs by pointing out the strategic value of Bechuanaland to the imperial position in southern Africa. Lastly there was the attitude of Scanlen and the Cape ministry.

It was this last factor which was most important. So many of the other approaches hinged on the extent of responsibility which Scanlen's Cabinet were prepared to accept. In crude terms, it became evident that Derby's whole approach turned on whether the Cape would play collaborator and shoulder the burden of Bechuanaland with the imperial factor, or not. If

[1] Addit. MSS. 44476, f. 18. Courtney to Gladstone, 11 July 1883 (from Treasury, where he was now Parliamentary Under-Secretary).
[2] Idem.

Scanlen backed away, then Derby would very likely accede to the Boers. Derby saw no latent value in Bechuanaland; indeed he felt that if the area had any value at all it was in terms of the Cape's own trade. If the Cape was prepared to work in unison with the imperial power, then Derby was prepared to stand firm with Kruger's deputation. This is what the whole London Convention negotiations were about: whether the Cape would give that undertaking or not. By September Robinson had already isolated this as the key question—'But will she [the Cape] look at fresh native responsibilities of any kind? That is the point. . . .'[1] It was to take three months of tortuous arguments and wrangles before that crucial question was answered.

But, before those difficult negotiations began, the water was further muddied by a series of unfortunate personal frictions and incidents. The first concerned an argument between Robinson and Gladstone. The proconsul took grave exception to a speech of the Premier's, in the Commons, in which, Robinson claimed, Gladstone had seriously misrepresented his earlier idea of a police force to sweep the area clean of freebooters.[2] Gladstone took umbrage at Robinson's protests, and Evelyn Ashley had to appeal to the Liberal leader not to treat Robinson too sharply.[3] The unpleasant matter was dragged out, as Robinson was in Argyllshire, and Gladstone at Hawarden; they could hardly meet to settle the matter. It was finally dropped, but no apparent conciliation took place; to what degree it biased the British handling of the negotiations is still an open question.

Gladstone was also 'at war' on another front: his lingering controversy with the Queen had flared up yet again. This time the matter at dispute was the most innocent of Gladstonian pastimes: a sea voyage in one of Sir Donald Currie's large private yachts, in the company of Tennyson. Gladstone had set off to cruise in Scandinavian waters as a rest, in preparation for the coming Session. But, on the spur of the moment he had

[1] Laurence, *Life of Merriman*, p. 83. Robinson to Merriman, (?) September 1883.

[2] C.O. 291/25 (R). Robinson to Derby, 14 August 1883. See Minutes by Ashley, 17 August 1883.

[3] Addit. MSS. 44483, f. 57. Ashley to Gladstone, 18 August 1883, from C.O., enclosing Robinson's letter.

called at Denmark, where he was treated by the King as if he were visiting royalty. The news soon got back to Victoria. Why hadn't she been informed? Why had Gladstone not asked for permission? She wrote a characteristic letter to Granville: 'The Prime Minister—and especially one *not* gifted with prudence in speech—is not a person who can go about *where* he likes with impunity. . . . The Queen believes everyone is much astonished at this *escapade*. . . .'[1] Gladstone was deeply annoyed at having his holiday labelled an 'escapade'; he refused to take a conciliatory attitude about it.[2] This minor matter also dragged on for some weeks, and consumed much paper, and a great deal of Gladstone's time, at a crucial period in the Boer negotiations.

These two personal frictions were by no means the most important of the diversive forces at play. Far more serious than any other was the growing disenchantment in the Cabinet with colonial policy—and by implication with Derby's conduct of that policy.[3] This view was shared by many permanent officials. Gladstone's secretary was a close friend of Meade in the Colonial Office. He recorded, in his diary, on Saturday, 1 September:

> Meade, who came over this afternoon, was open-mouthed about the difficulty of transacting business with Lord Derby. Lord D., according to Meade, never can be got to make up his mind, [and] is for letting everything drift, is always trying to evade responsibility—and whenever he does give a decision it is merely an endorsement of what is put before him by the Colonial Office authorities.[4]

At the Cabinet level this disenchantment was expressed by several arguments at meetings in November–December 1883;[5] and, more explicitly, by a memorandum drawn up by Cham-

---

[1] *Letters of Queen Victoria*, 2nd ser., III, 439–40. Queen to Granville (from Balmoral), 18 September 1883.

[2] Addit. MSS. 48634, ff. 68–80 (Hamilton Diary). Entries for 9 and 27 September 1883.

[3] Derby Papers, Trunk X.24. Memorandum by Chamberlain, 21 September 1883.

[4] Addit. MSS. 48634, ff. 62–3 (Hamilton Diary). Entry for Saturday, 1 September 1883.

[5] Addit. MSS. 44644, ff. 112–26 (Cabinet Papers).

berlain.[1] This document displays two things: the considerable interest that Chamberlain already took in colonial matters; and also the fact that it was possible that a Radical group was forming to 'dish Derby', as they earlier attempted with Kimberley. But this time it looked all the more serious, as Derby's policy had hardly achieved any glories—he had only been Colonial Secretary for ten months—nor did it promise any great alleviation of imperial dilemmas.

The rumblings of this discontent reached Gladstone, while he was busy disagreeing with Robinson and the Queen. It took him by surprise, and it provoked him to new heights of indignation. He immediately turned to his close ally Granville, and complained:

> I do not see that D[erby] has been much behindhand in his practical recommendations since joining us, and as I understand the [Chamberlain] Mem. was not intended to convey any present deficiency. I am to visit him in October, and can then try to feel the ground. . . . Carnarvon and Beach, the two slashing critics, were the two men, the first since Lord Grey, who contrived to make it *burn*.[2]

In sum, it was these short-term frictions and wrangles, together with the long-term dilemmas and responsibilities, which formed the back-drop to the Gladstone government's preparations to deal with the Boer deputation. It would indeed seem that the historians who would see the negotiations in terms of two representative foes—Kruger and Derby—need to revise their interpretation. If it was a meeting of unequals then it was the Boers, and not the imperial power, who were likely to gain from the encounter; that it was Kruger who led a united front to face the Colonial Secretary; and that it was Derby, and not the Boer leader, who was most circumscribed in his actions, and who knew that unless he carried the Cape ministry with him, he must accede to the Transvaal demands. Gladstone well understood the position in which Derby was placed. As he admitted to Granville, Derby 'has not got the key to the S. African question: but who has?' With this in mind he watched

---

[1] Derby Papers, Trunk X.24. Memorandum by Chamberlain.

[2] P.R.O. 30/29/127. Gladstone to Granville (from Hawarden), 7 September 1883. (Ramm, II, 84.)

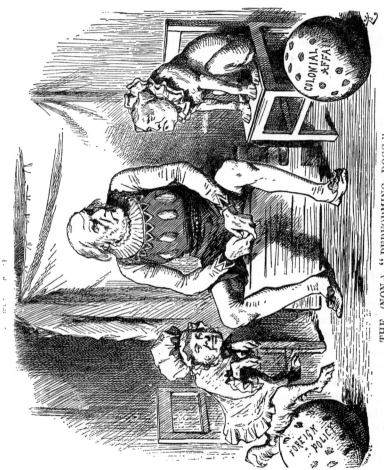

THE (NON-) "PERFORMING DOGS."

PROFESSOR (soliloquises—more in sorrow than in anger).—"ONE OF 'EM DOES IT ALL WRONG, AND T'OTHER DON'T DO IT AT ALL.—ENOUGH TO MAKE ONE CHUCK IT UP ALTOGETHER!!"

⁎ The lack of decision and want of success displayed by Earl Granville at the Foreign Office and Lord Derby at the Colonial Office tended, it was felt, to weaken and discredit the Gladstone Administration.

Derby lead out the British 'team' to face Kruger's militant burghers.

2. Robinson's finest hour: 14 November 1883–27 February 1884

'Rhodes did tell me a story once', Sir Hercules Robinson remarked in March 1895,[1] 'about his taking me up an exceeding high mountain and showing me all the wonders of the Northern Expansion; but the truth is, I saw the Northern Expansion before I ever saw Mr. Rhodes.' Robinson was equally emphatic about the rôle he had played in the London Convention negotiations 'The Northern Expansion could never have been if the road up to it had not been kept open. And the battle of opening the road was fought and won by me in London in the winter of 1883–4.'[2]

The records support his claim. The story of the creation, and the negotiations for the London Convention, is indeed the story of Robinson's endeavours to pull the Cape Premier into the orbit of British policy. Had he failed there is little doubt that Derby would have allowed the Transvaal frontier to straddle the Bechuana territory and the road to the interior. Never again was Robinson to wield such a power over a Colonial Secretary, or over a colonial policy; never again was he to have such a stature as a proconsul. It was to be the pinnacle of his career. From 1884 on he came increasingly under the corrosive, but all engrossing influence, of Cecil John Rhodes.

Robinson began the negotiations full of hope. He wrote to Merriman, on 8 November, that Derby was still open-minded about the Convention—Lord Derby has 'not made up his mind on any point and said he would not do so till he had the wishes of the [Boer] delegates on paper, and had gone through them with me'.[3] With this fact in mind Robinson felt he might well be able to save essentials in the Convention.[4]

The struggle for the Pretoria Convention was over; the

[1] Robinson interview with *Cape Times*, March 1895, printed as part of obituary in *Cape Times* (weekly edition), 3 November 1897.

[2] Idem.

[3] De Kock, '*Ekstra Territoriale Vraagstukke*', p. 131. Robinson to Merriman (from London), 8 November 1883. (Merriman MSS. 1883/224.)

[4] Ibid., pp. 130–31. Robinson to Merriman, 11 September 1883. (Merriman MSS. 1883/173.)

struggle for the London Convention was about to begin. 'They will soon be upon us,'[1] Herbert minuted anxiously on 8 October and the three-man Boer deputation duly arrived, at Plymouth, at the end of the month. To their surprise they found that there were no officials to meet them; and they had to make their own way to Paddington—where they arrived at 6 p.m. on 30 October 1883, and proceeded alone to move into the Albemarle Hotel,[2]—much to the amusement of the Colonial Office. An initial meeting was held between the Deputation and Derby on 7 November;[3] the first of five such meetings.[4] At this first discussion Derby suggested that the Deputation submit their demands to him in writing. This was agreed, and duly presented at the Colonial Office a week later.[5]

The weekly Saturday Cabinet—of 10 November—was thus largely concerned with the arrival of the Kruger Deputation, and the impending talks. Gladstone was anxious to carry the Cabinet with him on this matter, and to avoid the estrangement which Kimberley had undergone over the earlier Transvaal negotiations. 'I take it for granted', Gladstone prompted Derby on 7 November,[6] 'that on Saturday you will have something [to say] to us on the Transvaal, as well as *possibly* on Cetewayo.' Derby took the hint, and laid the question fully before the ministers,[7] the first time he had done so since 23 June.[8] Gladstone's Cabinet minutes record that Derby briefed the ministers on the central issue—the question of Cape co-operation.[9] This had become all the more pertinent an issue as Derby had found that the Boer deputation included the Rev. S. J. du Toit, now Director of Education in the Transvaal but who had been the

[1] C.O. 291/23. Minute by Herbert, 8 October 1883.

[2] C.O. 291/24. Minutes by Herbert and Fairfield, 30 October 1883, giving details of Transvaal Deputation's stay in London.

[3] Ibid., Minutes of 7 November 1883.

[4] Viz. 7 November 1883, 14 and 18 December 1883; and 8 and 18 February 1884.

[5] Ibid., Deputation to Derby (from Albemarle Hotel), 14 November 1883. Printed in *Parl. Pap.*, 1884, LVII, C.3947, pp. 2–4.

[6] Addit. MSS. 44546, f. 188 (L.B. copy). Gladstone to Derby, 7 November 1883.

[7] Addit. MSS. 44644, f. 112 (Cabinet Papers). Meeting of Saturday, 10 November 1883, at 2 p.m.

[8] Ibid., f. 77, for meeting of Saturday, 23 June 1883, at 2 p.m.

[9] Ibid., f. 112. Meeting of 10 November 1883.

founder of the Afrikaner *Bond* at the Cape. Never can the links between the Cape Dutch and the Transvaal Boers have been clearer to the Gladstone government than when Derby had personally met the Kruger Deputation, at the Colonial Office on 7 November,[1] and saw that it included the founder of the Afrikaner *Bond*.

The Cabinet discussed the Transvaal three times in the following week, 13, 14, and 17 November,[2] by which time the Kruger Deputation had presented their 'case' against the Pretoria Convention.[3] The document read like a calculated insult; it rests heavily on bravado, and righteous indignation. There was, in their eyes, nothing right about the Pretoria Convention. It was 'not the result of free negotiation but a unilateral document framed by a Royal Commission . . . we did not have the status of a contracting party'; in short, 'an arrangement imposed upon us against our will'. They had only accepted it as 'a temporary provision . . . invented for a period of transition'; and ratified in the *Volksraad* 'under compulsion to prevent further bloodshed'. But worse than even these factors, was the point that the Convention had not worked: the eastern boundary was in chaos; the suzerainty clause had complicated relations with friendly states; the provisions for the interests of the natives were cumbersome and did not make them law-abiding; and the financial settlement imposed an impossible financial strain on the young Boer state. The Boer deputies saw only one way of finally settling the difficult matters: they demanded that 'the Sand River Convention be again recognised as the historical basis of the new agreement'.[4]

The Colonial officials were staggered by the magnitude and ferocity of the Boer case; as was Lord Derby. He immediately forwarded the letter to Gladstone, who replied within 48 hours. Fortunately Gladstone had only recently been at Knowsley Hall, to stay with Derby—where they had discussed the coming

[1] C.O. 291/23. Minutes by Herbert, 7 November 1883. Unfortunately no record of the transaction at the meeting was kept. Nor of the other two meetings, of 18 December 1883, and 8 February 1884.

[2] Addit. MSS. 44644, ff. 115, 118, 120 (Cabinet Papers), for meetings of 13, 14, and 17 November 1883.

[3] C.O. 291/24. Transvaal Deputation to Derby (from Albemarle Hotel), 14 November 1883. Also printed in *Parl. Pap.*, 1884, LVII, C.3947, pp. 2–4.

[4] Idem.

Transvaal talks—so that the working bonds between the two men were exceptionally good at this stage, in contrast to their relations in late 1884. Hamilton could record in his Journal on Friday, 9 November 1883: 'Mr. G was much pleased with his recent visit to Knowsley and Lord Derby's return visit to Hawarden. He says Lord Derby's Liberalism is of the stoutest. . . . '[1]

After the Cabinet of 14 November, Gladstone drafted what he considered were the four basic questions to be answered, as a means of finding a working basis for the negotiations with the Boers.[2] (Derby's answers to Gladstone's queries are in italics.[3])

1. 'What is the exact juridicial relation of the Orange Free State to Great Britain?' *'Entire freedom. No control over internal or external relations.'*

2. 'What are the reasons against taking that relation for the basis of our relation to the Transvaal?' *'None if you do not object to sweeping away the Convention of two years ago.'*

3. 'Can the proposition be maintained that the Sand River Convention is utterly dead?' *'The Sand River Convention is utterly dead. If we return to any similar arrangement it should be an entirely new departure.'*

4. 'Has the deputation indicated in any way the nature of the connection with Great Britain . . . which they propose to maintain?' *'I know nothing as to this . . . beyond what is in this statement.'* [viz. page 6, section 8, subsection 2].

By the meeting of the full Cabinet the next day—17 November[4]—Gladstone already had Derby's reply to his questions; and thus the Cabinet got down to considering the Boer demands with an eye to the practical basis for a possible new treaty. According to Hamilton's Diary, 'The Cabinet today [17 November] were occupied with Transvaal matters (the Boer deputation having presented their case—it is somewhat exorbitant and likewise indefinite).'[5] The Cabinet briefed Derby to ascertain,

[1] Addit. MSS. 48634, f. 112 (Hamilton Diary). Entry for Friday, 9 November 1883.'

[2] Addit. MSS. 44644, f. 121 (Cabinet Memorandum). Gladstone to Derby, 16 November 1883. (Letters re-arranged.)

[3] Ibid., f. 122 (Cabinet Memorandum). Derby to Gladstone, 16 November 1883.

[4] Ibid., f. 120, 17 November 1883.

[5] Addit. MSS. 48634, ff. 126–7 (Hamilton Diary). Entry for Saturday, 17 November 1883.

and report back, the answers to three questions:

1. 'What connection is it that you [Derby] desire to uphold?'
2. 'What boundary do they ask for?'
3. 'What arrangements [do] they contemplate for on the frontiers?'[1]

It was agreed that Derby be given a free hand in conducting the negotiations,[2] and that 'It may be intimated, if need arise, that [the] Sand River Convention is dead and [the] idea of a new Convention not rejected.'[3] Derby was asked to obtain answers to these questions by the next Transvaal Cabinet, set for Tuesday, 20 November.[4]

These instructions to Derby are not without significance. Taken together, they suggest that the common mind of the Cabinet was for acceding to the Transvaal demands, and establishing a relationship very similar to that in existence with the Orange Free State. The possibility of annexation of Bechuanaland was not even raised as an alternative or option. This assessment of the mood of the Cabinet is further supported by Gladstone's minutes for the meeting of 20 November. Derby explained that it was too soon to receive a reply from the Deputation[5]—to the questions outlined on 17 November—but the Cabinet still discussed what they considered as the key question. In Gladstone's words, 'Shall we secure a veto over engagements they make with foreign countries? . . . Cabinet inclined to make this demand.'[6]

Here, in a nutshell, is the nucleus of the London Convention. The Cabinet cared little for the Tswana tribes; and even less for the Pretoria Convention frontiers. All that ministers wished Derby to secure was control of the foreign relations of the Transvaal, as a means of isolating the state in the interior. If the Cape wished to secure the trade-route to the interior that was their

[1] Addit. MSS. 44644, f. 120 (Cabinet Memorandum), 17 November 1883, at 12 p.m.
[2] Addit. MSS. 43937, f. 184 (Dilke Memoir); and Addit. MSS. 43925, f. 74 (Dilke Diary). Entry for 17 November 1883.
[3] Addit. MSS. 44644, f. 120 (Cabinet Papers), 17 November 1883.
[4] Idem.
[5] Ibid., f. 124. Meeting of 20 November 1883, at 2 p.m. Point 1: 'Transvaal. No answer yet recd.'
[6] Idem.

concern, not that of the British Cabinet, which saw no danger in allowing the Transvaal frontiersmen to spill into arid Bechuanaland over the western frontier. This of course was also Derby's view. When he was informed that certain Liberal M.P.s were calling for the establishment of a protectorate over Zululand, Derby replied with a crude remark which could equally well apply to the question of the Tswana tribes being included in the Empire—'I don't want more niggers.'[1]

The same day that he enunciated that considered opinion—20 November—he replied to the Transvaal letter of 14 November, and included the questions set him by the Cabinet of 17 November.[2] He asked the Transvaal Deputation for a factual and clear statement 'of the nature of the new agreement which you were proposing to take the place of the Convention of Pretoria'; for a definition of the proposed western frontier, as the Transvaal desired it; and he conceded that Britain might agree to a new Convention, but that this would not be a revived Sand River Treaty, for Her Majesty's Government considered that that Convention 'does not now in fact exist'.[3]

What this letter, and all the letters to the Deputation, does not in fact admit, was that Derby was in no real bargaining position at all. He could call on the Transvaal to state their demands, but he was in no position to deny them. It has been written of these negotiations that, 'At bottom, the position of the Deputation was strategically unsound. Whatever the practical success of the Joubert policy, [in Bechuanaland] the last word remained with the Secretary of State. . . .'[4] In fact, exactly the opposite is true; and Derby even admitted as much. At no time did he consider standing up to the Boers, he saw no advantage in doing so. Indeed, he saw every sign pointing against it. As to annexing the Tswana lands he was emphatic—'without the Cape it would be absurd of course'.[5] Derby was doing no more than pointing out his own weakness—he feared that an imperial annexation would rouse the South African

[1] Derby Papers, X.24. Memorandum by Antrobus (from C.O.) of 19 November 1883, with comment by Derby dated 20 November 1883.
[2] C.O. 291/24. Derby to Deputation, 20 November 1883. Printed in *Parl. Pap.*, 1884, LVII, C.3947, pp. 6–7.
[3] Idem. [4] Agar-Hamilton, *The Road to the North*, p. 261.
[5] C.O. 291/24 (Misc.) Minute by Derby, 21 November 1883, on British policy towards Bechuanaland.

Dutch; rouse the Gladstone Cabinet, now deeply involved in Egypt; and rouse the Commons, which had a pathological dislike for further expenditure abroad.

This attitude was supported, and made even more explicit, by the Cabinet of Thursday, 22 November 1883.[1] The meeting began at 2 p.m., but the Boer reply of that same day did not reach the Colonial Office until evening.[2] However, the Cabinet took two basic decisions in preparation for working a new treaty. First, ministers emphatically declared that the 'door [was] not shut against ratification of a new S.W. Frontier'; and, second, that the 'Cape must be consulted if it is altered'[3] in the Transvaal's favour.

Even so early in the negotiations the position of the Cape was already axial. The same day, 22 November, Derby had written to Scanlen (who was now in London) enquiring as to 'how far, and in what manner the Cape Government and Parliament is likely to be willing to assist in the settlement of these questions'.[4] Scanlen's reply arrived four days later, and left no doubt as to the Cape attitude to Bechuanaland and also towards the Transvaal[5]—'the Cape ministry are scarcely prepared to recommend to the Parliament ... any proposals for the annexation of Bechuanaland'. As to a Protectorate, 'the Cape Government would only be willing to assist *on the understanding that the Transvaal Government would be also ready to join*'.[6]

With this reply Derby found himself in the bizarre position of not only leaning heavily on the Cape, in dealing with the Transvaal Deputation, but in knowing that the Cape in turn was working hand in glove with those very same Transvaal deputies. In crude terms it meant that the imperial power was reduced to accepting the Transvaal veto before they could place any scheme before the Cape.

---

[1] Addit. MSS. 44644, f. 126 (Cabinet Papers). Meeting of Thursday, 22 November 1883, at 2 p.m.

[2] Ibid., 'Point 2 : No answer yet from Deputies.'

[3] Ibid., (Cabinet Memorandum), in Gladstone's hand, dated 22 November 1883.

[4] C.O. 291/24 (Misc.) Derby to Scanlen, 22 November 1883, based on Minute by Herbert.

[5] *Parl. Pap.*, 1884, LVII, C.3841, pp. 99–118. Scanlen to Derby, 26 November 1883.

[6] Idem.

The crucial question facing Derby was thus: how to secure an alliance with the Cape Premier which excluded the Transvaal? If and when this happened Derby's insecure position would overnight be revolutionised. In November, though, the chances looked very slight indeed. Scanlen refused to play collaborator and so be lured into the imperial camp. Privately he explained why to Merriman:

> I do not want to touch any further annexations if it can be possibly avoided . . . and just now our financial burden and diminishing revenue forbid the incurring of grave risks. If the Imperial Government would aid [us] something might be done. My belief is that they will not do much, if anything.[1]

In short, Scanlen feared that Britain was trying to place 'another Basutoland' on the hands of the Cape; and a more explosive Basutoland at that. The cost of administration would be equally heavy; the chances of frontier wars just as great; and, on top of this, there was the probability that such an annexation would anger the Transvaal—who wished to gain the area themselves—which in turn would rouse the Cape Dutch, who now held the balance in the Colony's politics.

Over and above this was another factor mentioned above, but rarely placed in conjunction with Scanlen's attitude. This was the question of Cape fishing and guano rights at Angra Pequena, on the South-West African coast. While the question had not yet been lifted to an international level, there was a private 'war' going on between the Cape and German merchant companies, for exclusive rights to the area. Both sets of merchants petitioned their respective Governments. The Cape had long seen the area as their natural prerogative, and Scanlen was far more concerned about this area than Bechuanaland. As he pointed out to Derby, the road to the north was not exclusively a Cape concern, for 'The Trade has been . . . almost exclusively in articles of British manufacture.'[2] In contrast Angra Pequena *was* an exclusive Cape concern. Scanlen wrote to Merriman: 'I have urged upon all influential men with whom I have come into contact that—from Cape Frio round to the Portuguese

---

[1] De Kock, '*Ekstra Territoriale Vraagstukke*', p. 186. Scanlen to Merriman, 15 November 1883.
[2] C.O. 291/24. Scanlen to Derby, 3 December 1883.

possessions at Delagoa Bay—the "Monroe Doctrine" should be applied and I think I told you Sir Robert Herbert concurred in this view. . . .'[1] Scanlen saw a 'Monroe Doctrine' as a cheap method of keeping the area as a Cape preserve. But if this failed, then it was possible that annexation to the Cape would be the only solution. Accordingly Scanlen wished to keep his hands free of commitments in Bechuanaland, for he might well have to act in the direction of South-West Africa. If Derby was restricted by Egypt, Scanlen was hampered by Angra Pequena.

In the week after the Cabinet of 22 November[2] the negotiations were taken a stage further by two letters from the Kruger Deputation. On 23 November they acknowledged Derby's letter of 20 November,[3] and put forward the dubious point that 'neither the *Volksraad* nor the people of South African Republic ever did acknowledge . . . that the Sand River Convention was ever brought to an end by the annexation of 1877'. On 26 November they submitted to the Colonial Office what they considered could be taken as the draft of a new Convention.[4] It is a lengthy document—taking up ten pages in the Blue Book[5]—but it in fact only made two determined claims: the Transvaal was to regain 'full independence', and the 'right to manage its own affairs'; and, secondly, there was to be a new western boundary, to include the *whole* of the road to the north. In fact they wished to return to the *status quo* of the Sand River period of the 1850s.

Reaction in official circles varied from 'astounding' (Hemming); 'cannot be accepted without severe rectification' (Bramston); 'the whole document is most insolent' (Ashley); to the more reasoned reactions of Sir Robert Herbert and Sir Hercules Robinson.[6] Herbert was inclined to blame Dr. Clarke's 'Transvaal Independence Committee' for encouraging the

[1] De Kock, '*Ekstra Territoriale Vraagstukke*', p. 186. Scanlen to Merriman, 15 November 1883.

[2] Addit. MSS. 44644, f. 126 (Cabinet Papers). Meeting of 22 November 1883.

[3] C.O. 291/24 (Misc.). Deputation to Derby, 23 November 1883.

[4] Ibid., Deputation to Derby, 26 November 1883.

[5] *Parl. Pap.*, 1884, LVV, C.3947, pp. 9–18.

[6] C.O. 291/24 (Misc.). Minutes of 27 November 1883, on Deputation to Derby, 26 November 1883.

Boers to ask for so much. None of these comments was for-warded to the Deputation as a reply, but rather Robinson's letter to Derby, of 23 November, in which he set out what he considered could be the working basis for a new Treaty.[1] Robinson refused to take the more extravagant demands of the Boer seriously; instead he suggested a *via media* to meet the de-mands of both sides. He thought the western boundary could be altered—but only to include the 'pro-Transvaal' chiefs, Moswete and Mosweu. The debt could be reduced slightly. The Transvaal could call itself the 'South African Republic'. And, they could control their own foreign affairs, so long as Britain was able to veto all relations with neighbouring tribes. A British Resident Commissioner would be stationed at Kuruman in Bechuanaland, and his salary, together with those of his police force, would be shared between the Transvaal, Cape, and Im-perial Governments.

Derby was so impressed with this document that he had it transcribed on to Colonial Office paper, and sent to the Kruger Deputation's hotel, over his own signature, as the official reply to the Deputation's letter of 26 November.[2] This was done on 29 November, by which time some very hard thinking had been done by the permanent officials and by the Gladstone Cabinet. The Transvaal's 'draft Convention' had shaken them severely. They, at last, grasped the realities of their position when faced with the determined Boer challenge. Herbert caught the imperial dilemma in a sentence:

> The Cape will not take in Mankaroane [*sic*] and Co; and the Transvaal will not consent to their country being independent; so it will practically rest with H.M. Govt. to decide whether it will defend the Bechuanas or leave them to do what they can for them-selves, with or without assistance and compensation.[3]

This is, of course, what Robinson and Mackenzie had been saying for the previous eighteen months; but then the Colonial Office was always a little behind events or realities. Herbert

[1] *Parl. Pap.*, 1884, LVII, C.3841, pp. 104–7. Robinson to Derby, 23 November 1883.

[2] C.O. 291/24 (Misc.). Derby to Deputation, 29 November 1883.

[3] C.O. 291/25 (Misc.). Minute by Herbert, 27 November 1883, on article by Mackenzie.

also, at last, tumbled to the significance of the Cape in the negotiations. He minuted sarcastically on a particularly negative
letter from Scanlen:

> This is quite unsatisfactory; and quite what we were bound to
> expect. The Cape Colony will not do anything to secure its trade
> road, or peace on its frontiers, *unless the Boers are graciously pleased
> to approve.*[1]

Derby was even more gloomy—if this were possible. He
forwarded the Transvaal's 'Draft Convention' to Gladstone, on
28 November, with these worried comments: 'It does not
promise well for our chances of being able to negotiate with
them. They ask everything and will concede nothing. They
claim all those parts of Bechuanaland to which [the] white freebooters have emigrated, the whole of Mankaroane's [*sic*] territory included.'[2] The only hope which Derby saw was to refuse
to discuss 'those questions on which we are prepared to give
way—the debt, the suzerainty, the control of internal relations'.
For Derby recognised his own weak position: 'They will not
like to go home *re infecta*, and this *is the only hold we have upon
them.*' His venom though was saved for the Cape, which he
rightly saw as the root of the majority of his difficulties: 'Scanlen, representing the Cape, will give no help. He is ready to
join in any arrangements about the Bechuanas which has received the assent of the Transvaal, but he will wait for them.'[3]
In fact Derby is already preparing his arguments for giving way
to the Transvaal, in Bechuanaland at least: 'If they [the Cape]
are indifferent—whose interests really are concerned—they can
scarcely expect us to do for them what they will not do for themselves.'[4] Here then is the crux of the Derby approach to Bechuanaland. He saw it as a Cape problem, and not a danger to
imperial supremacy in southern Africa. He was wrong, as he
soon found out in 1884, when the possibility of a Transvaal–
German alliance was broached, but the historian must record
the facts as he finds them. It is pointless to castigate Lord Derby.

[1] C.O. 291/26 (S.). Minute by Herbert, 27 November 1883, on Scanlen
to C.O. (My italics.)
[2] Addit. MSS. 44142, f. 10. Derby to Gladstone (Private), 28 November
1883, enclosing Deputation to Derby, 26 November 1883.
[3] Idem.   [4] Idem.

At this juncture in Anglo-Boer relations neither Derby, nor Granville, nor Gladstone, recognised the dangers of allowing the Transvaal frontier to drift out to the south-west.

Gladstone, however, was quick to grasp the fact that, of all the Deputation's demands, they put the extension of the western frontier above most others. Gladstone saw its usefulness as a bargaining counter against Kruger. Robinson had prepared a special map for Herbert, showing the Convention frontiers, and the extent of the Boer infiltration.[1] This was now forwarded to Gladstone, who studied it in conjunction with Derby's letter of 28 November. He was visiting Oxford at the time,[2] but he made it his business to reply promptly to Derby:

> I am sorry to share your impressions as to the Transvaal reply, but they correspond with my own. Indeed I assent to everything in your letter and especially to your suggestion, accordant with that of Robinson, that *we should make the S.W. boundary and the frontier policy in that direction the preliminary stage and first condition of the whole discussion.*[3]

This was good practical advice for the harassed Derby; and more came from John Mackenzie, who had a long interview with the Colonial Secretary on 27 November. This discussion is important, for Mackenzie made a very good impression on Derby, and this stood him in good stead when Robinson, two months later, suggested Mackenzie be appointed as the first Commissioner to Bechuanaland. Mackenzie left an excellent record of the meeting.[4] 'I found Lord Derby and Sir Evelyn Ashley, with Sir Robert Herbert . . . in the large room—I suppose Lord Derby's. They had just been glancing over my statement on behalf of Mankaroane [*sic*][5] Lord Derby came forward

[1] Addit. MSS. 44799, f. 93. Map of Transvaal, in Robinson to Herbert, 23 November 1883.

[2] Addit. MSS. 48634, ff. 134–5, and 48634, ff. 7–10 (Hamilton Diary). Entries for 23 November–3 December 1883. (Hamilton's date on f. 134 is incorrect.)

[3] Addit. MSS. 44547, f. 3 (L.B. copy). Gladstone to Derby, 29 November 1883, from Oxford. (My italics.)

[4] W. D. Mackenzie, *Life of Mackenzie*, John Mackenzie to his son Willie, 27 November 1883, pp. 292–4.

[5] See also C.O. 291/23. Mankurwane to C.O. (via C. J. Rhodes), 22 November 1883.

and very courteously met me.' They then studied the Robinson map of the area.[1]

> *Ashley:* 'But Mankaroane [*sic*] has not lost any of his good land, only his outlying *veldt* [*sic*]. At least, I said so in the House of Commons, and no one contradicted me.'
>
> *Mackenzie:* '. . . I'm afraid you could say a good many things about Bechuanaland and not be contradicted in the House of Commons.'
>
> *Derby:* '(Laughing) Very true. No doubt of that . . .'
>
> *Ashley:* 'Why don't all these people unite—they are so numerous— they could soon settle the matter . . .'
>
> *Mackenzie:* 'Well I should be glad of a settlement, but, to say [the] truth, I should not be glad to see people ranging themselves in an hostile attitude in South Africa—blacks, because they were blacks; and whites as whites.'
>
> *Derby:* 'Very true. I agree with you—it would be a bad thing. How would you do this?'[2]

Mackenzie then suggested three lines of action, most of them later to be incorporated in the settlement of Bechuanaland, if not actually in the new Convention itself. Mackenzie recommended increasing the Cape Border Police; clearing out the freebooters; and establishing European magistrates under a Resident Commissioner. Above all he wished to point out to Derby what he considered was 'the fallacy' of the Boer claims— 'that if they got more ground they would be more peaceful. . . .' Mackenzie very much doubted this. If anything an extension of the western border would only serve to encourage their land-hunger. Derby received his suggestions well: 'A policy, such as you have indicated, would doubtless, if firmly and judiciously carried out, avert many difficulties and dangers.'[3]

But this was still a long way from implementing such a policy. Mackenzie's ideas were only workable if the Cape were prepared to play its part; and this was still an open question in December 1883. Fairfield's comments on the 'Mackenzie scheme' captured the official reaction to any suggestions which involved imperial expenditure or added responsibility—'It would be a better plan to help the natives on particular occa-

---

[1] See Addit. MSS. 44799, f. 93. It was forwarded to Gladstone who apparently never returned it to the C.O.

[2] W. D. Mackenzie, *Life of Mackenzie*, pp. 292–4.   [3] Ibid., p. 289.

sions . . . or better still to proclaim that white adventurers would not be forbidden to help them. There are always plenty of Hicks Pashas about.'[1]

The negotiations had, though, reached a position approaching stalemate. On 29 November Derby had, on Robinson's advice, informed the Kruger Deputation that their 'draft Convention' was not acceptable 'neither in form nor in substance'; and had called for an assurance 'that you are ready to agree to such a definition of the western boundary of the Transvaal as will place outside the State those Native Chiefs and tribes who object to come within it'.[2] Gladstone began to grow impatient, and on 30 November wrote to Granville, the 'wheels drive very heavily in the Transvaal business.'[3] This pessimism was carried over to the Cabinet of the same day.[4] 'We talked of the Transvaal', Dilke recorded, 'which looks black.'[5]

Kruger's reply, to Derby's firm letter, did nothing to raise Gladstonian spirits. While Kruger was ready 'to agree to the regulation of the western boundary, on the basis laid down by your Lordship',[6] he declined to conduct any further negotiation until he had received a map, 'showing what extension of the present boundary of the Transvaal Her Majesty's Government can agree to. . . .'.[7] Clearly the Kruger Deputation must have felt they had Derby 'on the run', if he talked in terms of allowing them to expand their frontiers.

While Derby struggled to compose a suitable reply, a most unwelcome piece of news was broken to him: Robinson was thinking of resigning. On 3 December he sent Derby a curious letter.[8] He pointed out that the Governorship of the Cape was 'the most troublesome one' in the whole Empire; one which had proved 'fatal to so many reputations'; and that he was well equipped to judge, for he had served in 'nine Colonies in different

[1] C.O. 291/25 (R). Fairfield Minute, 24 November 1883.
[2] C.O. 291/24 (Misc.). Derby to Deputation, 29 November 1883.
[3] Addit. MSS. 44547, f. 3. Gladstone to Granville (L.B. copy), 29 November 1883. (Ramm, II, 118).
[4] Addit. MSS. 44644, f. 126 (Cabinet Papers).
[5] Addit. MSS. 43925, f. 76 (Dilke Diary), 30 November 1883. See also Addit. MSS. 43937, f. 202 (Dilke Memoir).
[6] C.O. 291/24 (Misc.). Deputation to Derby, 30 November 1883.
[7] Idem.
[8] C.O. 48/508. Robinson to Derby (Private), 3 December 1883.

parts of the world. . . .' But the excuse he gave for wanting to resign was strange indeed: that the salary was inadequate. In New Zealand he had received £7,500 p.a. with an 'easy job', while in South Africa he got a mere £6,000 p.a.—'my present position is unbearable, if to constant anxiety on public affairs must be added the daily worry and distraction of a salary insufficient for the proper maintenance of the position'.[1] Why Robinson chose this moment to put the matter forward can only be surmised. He could have mentioned it at any time in the previous two years; or when he saw Derby at the Colonial Office. It is possible he did it knowing that Derby was in a most difficult position, and therefore unlikely to want Robinson to resign on a mere money matter; or more likely that he hoped it would serve to warn Derby that his own views must be taken into account in drawing up the future Treaty. The matter soon passed over, for Derby quickly acceded to Robinson's request for a higher salary. But it remains a strange incident in the midst of these crucial negotiations.

The sense of inertia and stalemate was increased, in early December, by the arrival of a particularly negative letter from Scanlen, in which he not only declined to enter into a joint-protectorate without Transvaal agreement, but went so far as to point out to Derby that the road to the north was as much a British concern, if not more so, than that of the Cape.[2] The official reaction was, for once, rather astute and pointed. Bramston noted that what the Cape ministry was in fact doing was 'mildly folding its hands and saying, if the Boers like to close the road, and shut out British trade, our own is a secondary affair, we will not do anything to prevent them'.[3] Immediately below this Herbert pointed out the reasoning behind Scanlen's non-committal and non-co-operative attitude:

> Mr. Scanlen is clearly afraid of the Dutch party in the Cape, and his own party is very shy about accepting any further responsibilities for places and affairs beyond the frontier of the colony.[4]

Ashley added tartly: 'Mr. Scanlen is what the Yankees call "sitting on the fence".'[5]

[1] Idem. [2] C.O. 291/24 (Misc.). Scanlen to Derby, 3 December 1883.
[3] C.O. 291/25 (S). Minutes by Bramston, Herbert, Ashley, on Scanlen to Derby, of 3 December 1883.
[4] Idem. [5] Idem.

With this unpromising fact in mind Derby despatched his next letter to the Kruger Deputation, on 4 December 1883. It is indeed a remarkable document; and an abiding record of how weak he considered his own bargaining position to be. It is a long and complicated despatch,[1] but at the heart of it there are only two proposals. The Transvaal were offered the whole of the territory 'belonging to Basolong Chief Moshette [sic] and Koranna Chief Mossauw [sic]'—though the new boundary would 'keep to the eastward of the main road from Taungs to Kuruman'. On top of this Derby went further and offered the Transvaal a share in the control of the rest of Bechuanaland, which would become 'an independent native reserve under the joint-protection of Great Britain, the Transvaal and the Cape Colony'.

This extraordinarily generous offer was the most 'liberal' gesture that Derby ever made to the Transvaal. It so overwhelmed the Kruger Deputation—who had clearly not even hoped for such things—that they decided to decline it! Their reasoning was not so ill-advised as it later looked. If Derby had conceded this much so early in the negotiations, what might he further concede if they pressed him harder. Accordingly on 7 December the Boer leaders rejected his 'Joint Protectorate offer' (of 4 December),[2] and suggested a scheme whereby the local Tswana tribes should decide whether they wished to come under the Transvaal's 'protection' or not. This apparent selection would no doubt have been conducted by the Transvaal's agents, leaving little doubt as to what the outcome would be. Even Derby was aware of their aims: they now wanted the whole of Bechuanaland. The question thus became—could Derby give it to the Transvaal? He apparently himself had no objections to doing so; but was it politically expedient? Thus he could write to Gladstone, on 8 December, and talk in terms of nations—whether to annex them or not. The letter provides the key to his later attitude to Kruger, and must mark the first turning-point in the negotiations:

I am sorry to say that we have an unsatisfactory answer . . . from the Transvalers . . .

[1] Parl. Pap., 1884, LVII, C.3947, pp. 19–20. Derby to Deputation, 4 December 1883.

[2] C.O. 291/24 (Misc.). Deputation to Derby, 7 December 1883.

I must see them on Monday or Tuesday [10 and 11 December 1883], but we ought to consider whether we shall break off all [negotiations] rather than give them Bechuanaland, if they persist.[1]

The reasoning behind Derby's new attitude is highly significant, even if the tone is begrudging:

In that decision the feeling of the H. of Commons must be a main element. *I suppose we must stand by the Bechuanas and the 'trade route'?* Both seem to have got a strong hold on the public mind.[2]

Gladstone was inclined to agree; and the first major decision was now taken, to make a stand at the line of the trade road. As Gladstone put it, on 9 December.

We could not give up Bechuanaland against the inclination of the chiefs. Nor can any very new or important resolution, I think, be taken without a reference to the Cabinet.[3]

This, however, did not mean that Gladstone had either a deep concern for the chiefs, or a great desire to keep Bechuanaland out of Transvaal hands. Indeed, he favoured the Transvaal idea of 'drawing the frontier line according to the inclination of the Chiefs'; but he did wonder if this was workable, for 'the Dutchmen are obstinate'.

Privately Gladstone was more despondent. On 30 November he had observed that 'the Boer deputies are not very flexible';[4] now, ten days later, he remarked to his secretary, 'The Boer delegates appear to be in a very obstinate state: and to be inaccessible to admissible terms.'[5] Derby's next communication with the Transvaal delegates, of 11 December, was not sent with a great deal of hope.[6] In it Derby held out a new bait to the

[1] Addit. MSS. 44142, f. 19. Derby to Gladstone, 8 December 1883. In fact Derby did not meet the Deputation (for the second time) until Tuesday, 18 December 1883. (My italics).

[2] Idem.

[3] Addit. MSS. 44547, f. 11 (L.B. copy). Gladstone to Derby, 9 December 1883, from Hawarden. (My italics).

[4] Addit. MSS. 48634, f. 7 (Hamilton Diary). Entry for Friday, 30 November 1883.

[5] Ibid., f. 18. Entry for 12 December 1883.

[6] *Parl. Pap.*, 1884, LVII, C.3947, pp. 21–3. Derby to Deputation, 11 December 1883.

Boers: if the Deputation would accept his suggestions on the western frontier then the Imperial Government 'may be placed in a position to make liberal concessions in regard to foreign, the internal government, and the debt, of the Transvaal'.[1]

Kruger's reply was immediate, and cunning.[2] Not only did he question Derby's interpretation of the road to the north—in the Transvaal's eyes there were many routes, and many went through land occupied by chiefs wanting Transvaal protection—but, he also pin-pointed the basic weakness of the imperial position, the need to involve the Cape. Kruger wrote haughtily, and with great assurance: 'We are not aware that the Cape Government is prepared to enter into the proposed joint-protectorate.'[3] But, he was quick to point to the fact that the Transvaal Government had that very influence with the Cape which Britain did not. He made the most of this fact. 'We have good reason to suppose that the Cape Parliament will agree to such an arrangement as suggested by us, especially if such an arrangement would tend to the restoration and maintenance of peace and order.'[4] Whether this was true is debatable, but Kruger was certainly correct in supposing that the Cape would not help shoulder imperial burdens. That same day—12 December— Scanlen wrote to Merriman: 'It appears to be quite out of the question to think of assuming more territory and even if the [Cape] Cabinet were disposed to support the annexation of the territory, Parliament would not be inclined to agree to it.'[5]

On Friday, 14 December, Kruger led his Deputation to the Colonial Office, and left Derby in no doubt as to their determination to secure a favourable frontier line.[6] Derby's spirits sank to a new low. He wrote to Gladstone immediately after the meeting: '... had an interview with the Transvaal delegates today; not satisfactory. They seem disinclined to give way on any point, and we are no further advanced. I do not despair, but it is well to contemplate the probability of the negotiation

[1] Idem.
[2] C.O. 291/24 (Misc.). Deputation to Derby, 12 December 1883.
[3] Idem.   [4] Idem.
[5] De Kock, 'Ekstra Territoriale Vraagstukke', pp. 136–7. Scanlen to Merriman, 12 December 1883. (Merriman MSS. 1883/261.)
[6] See Addit. MSS. 44142, f. 23. Derby to Gladstone, 14 December 1883.

falling through.'[1] Once again Derby was forced back on his traditional lament—*if only* the Cape ministry would play its part as collaborators. 'The Cape Government would help us materially, if they would agree to take over Mankaroane's [*sic*] territory, as he wishes; but this they will not do, partly from fear of offending the Transvaal, partly from an unpleasant recollection of having wasted five millions in Basutoland, which makes them shy of incurring more native responsibilities.'[2]

Derby now wrote kindly, if despondently, to Mackenzie (on 14 December),[3] informing him that while his proposals 'for a combined and systematic administration of native affairs . . .' appeared to be 'well considered', it was not possible to put them into practice now, or in the future. The policy of Her Majesty's Government was 'for the Colonies and States of South Africa to agree upon and to administer' local affairs; and the Imperial Government 'do not propose in future to undertake fresh responsibilities in connexion with native affairs in South Africa beyond the British possessions. . . .'[4]

Gladstone, too, subscribed to the 'consolidation' approach. In his determination to avoid the acquistion of further territories he was prepared to bend over backwards to meet Kruger's demands. On Derby's despairing letter of 14 December he minuted: 'Their objections not wholly senseless. They should state fully what they [suggest] . . . for maintaining order beyond the frontier.'[5]

This urgent desire on Gladstone's part for a solution becomes all the more understandable when the Cabinet's other concerns are brought into focus. The month of December 1883 was long remembered by Gladstone—not because of the Transvaal negotiations, but because it nearly saw the break-up of the Gladstone administration and the Liberal Party. Hartington had for some time been uneasy about the exact scope of the coming 3rd Reform Bill; and in December these fears came to a head, in the form of a violent disagreement with Gladstone. Harcourt told

[1] Idem.   [2] Idem.
[3] *Parl. Pap.*, 1884, LVII, C.3841, p. 136. Derby to Mackenzie, 14 December 1883.
[4] Idem.
[5] Addit. 44142, f. 23. Derby to Gladstone, 14 December 1883. See note on back of letter by Gladstone. Undated, but probably 15–16 December 1883.

Hamilton that he feared the fall of the Government;[1] and Lord Granville definitely expected Hartington to resign, taking the Whigs with him.[2] There was a great deal of coming and going from Hawarden and Downing Street, as ministers and friends moved between the G.O.M. and the great Whig, trying to bridge the gulf that yawned between them. At the close of the month there was a series of confidential meetings between the two men, where they tried to reconcile their differences. But it was to little avail,[3] and the trouble drifted on into January, and the new year of 1884.

The Cabinet concerns did not end here. The position in Egypt was fraught with mischief yet to come. Northbrook grumbled: 'We have now been forced into the position of being the protectors of Egypt.'[4] Baring warned though that the Khedive could not just be abandoned. Little wonder that on 24 December the ministers broke up from a Cabinet 'greatly troubled'.[5] This problem too was not resolved, and thus dragged on into January when the fatal decision was to embark on a 'rescue and retire' policy in the Sudan, with General 'Chinese' Gordon at the head of local operations.

These two dilemmas,[6]—Hartington's threatened resignation and the latent dangers in Egypt—tended to 'obsess' the Cabinet just at the very moment when the Transvaal negotiations were at their most precarious. Derby prepared to break off the negotiations rather than have them drag on indefinitely, with the Boers steadily increasing their demands. He saw the Kruger Deputation again, on 18 December, and presented them with the equivalent of an ultimatum, unless they agreed to the proposed boundary, there could be no adjustment in the Pretoria

[1] Addit. MSS. 48634, ff. 134–5 (Hamilton Diary). Entry for 20 December 1883.

[2] Addit. MSS. 48635, f. 32. Entry for 20 December 1883.

[3] Ibid., f. 35. Entry for 22 December 1883.

[4] P.R.O. 30/29/139. Northbrook Cabinet Memorandum, 24 December, 1883.

[5] Ibid., Northbrook to Granville, 24 December 1883.

[6] There was also concern over two further matters: Ireland looked ready to burst into unrest again. See Addit. MSS. 48035, f. 44 (Hamilton Diary). And in Zululand a 'civil war' threatened to break out between factions of the tribe. See Addit. MSS. 44142, f. 25. Derby to Gladstone, 18 December 1883. See also f. 31, Derby to Gladstone, 19 December 1883, enclosed in Bulwer to Derby (Tel.), 16 December 1883, f. 29.

Convention. 'I still hope, however, that you may be able to make . . . that one concession which Her Majesty's Government has been compelled to press for as a preliminary to the concessions which it is ready to agree to.'[1]

To this the Deputation put forward a skilful reply, which was at once both conciliatory yet demanding: 'Let it be agreed that, for the present, we confine ourselves to the adoption of the principle that every Native Chief shall have the free choice . . . when re-survey and demarcation take place this principle shall be carried out with mutual forbearance.'[2] It was simply their old theme in a new guise; with the added proviso that if an agreement could not immediately be reached on the boundary dispute, then they suggested that a move be made on other points at question, such as 'the suzerainty'.

Derby was thus thrown back on his original strategy. He must either 'call their bluff', adopting an uncompromising line until they came round to his way of thinking, or he must bend to their pressures. The first course presented the possibility of destroying the negotiations; the second the probability of a howl of protest in Parliament for giving way so completely. Derby went away to Christmas at Knowsley with this crucial dilemma unresolved.

It was now that Robinson played his key rôle. In later years he considered it the moment when he had 'saved' the Bechuana territory from falling to the Boers, and so making possible Rhodes' great drive to the north in the late 1880s. Robinson spoke of this period, of late December 1883, with great pride:[3]

The question had arisen about the reversion of Montsioa [sic] and another chief [to the Transvaal]. Mr. Kruger was . . . trying to persuade the Colonial Office that there was no British interest in that bit of territory, except the interest of the thoroughfare. 'Look here,' he said. 'this is no use to you, and you have no concern with it, except to secure the road to your trade, and the rights of these chiefs. I will give what pledges you like about them and as for the thoroughfare we will neutralise a strip of road.'

[1] The terms offered are contained in *Parl. Pap.*, 1884, LVII, C.3947, p. 25. Derby to Deputation, 18 December 1883.
[2] C.O. 291/24 (Misc.). Deputation to Derby, 22 December 1883.
[3] *Cape Times*, 3 November 1897; Robinson obituary, including an interview of March 1895 with the *Cape Times* editor.

I think Lord Derby was inclined to listen to this notion, but as I was over there on leave the matter was referred to me, and I dealt with Mr. Kruger.

'Dealing with Mr. Kruger' took the form of a private letter to Lord Derby, of a 'do or die' nature. Robinson had seen the Transvaal Deputation's last letter of 22 December,[1] and he now —26 December—made it plain that he thought the cross-roads had been reached.[2]

In Robinson's eyes there were but four courses of action— allow the Transvaal a limited area of Bechuanaland including Mosweu and Moswete's territory, but keep them off the main trade-route, and 'a joint-protectorate established over the remainder of Bechuanaland; annex all of Bechuanaland outside the Pretoria Convention boundary line; give way to the Transvaal and allow them to absorb and overrun Montshiwa and Mankurwane'; or 'do nothing'. He considered these the four real options, and he favoured the first. Indeed he refused to consider any other option—'the only course that I can see free from very serious embarrassments for Her Majesty's Government is the first one. Should this fail [to be accepted] I do not see what is to be gained by negotiations with them.'[3] Robinson made out a very strong case for this firm stand, for as he argued: 'Why should Her Majesty's Government give up the debt, the suzerainty, the conduct of diplomatic intercourse ... if they [Kruger's Deputation] on their part are not willing to make any concession whatever, or any sacrifice in return?'[4]

This argument was doubly effective for reaching Derby just at the moment when he was not only feeling the agonies of indecision, but was inclined to give way to the Transvaal Deputation as the course of least resistance. For two weeks the matter hung in the balance. While Derby deliberated, or perhaps just put off the evil day, Robinson spent an anxious Christmas and New Year. On 3 January 1884, he wrote to Merriman: 'I have begged of the [British] Government not to enter upon any other point till the S.W. boundary is agreed to, and if Lord Derby will

---

[1] C.O. 291/24 (Misc.). Deputation to Derby, 22 December 1883.
[2] Ibid., Robinson to Derby (Private), 26 December 1884, Later printed as a C.O. Minute, in *Parl. Pap.*, 1884, LVII, C. 3841, pp. 144–6.
[3] Idem.   [4] Idem.

only be firm I feel sure that the [Transvaal] Delegates will give way. They are only playing a game of brag. . . .'[1]

Why then did Derby take over three weeks to reply to the Transvaal letter of 22 December 1883 ?[2] Two obvious reason are his own indecision, and the arrival of the festive season. But there was a third, and equally important factor, behind his behaviour. As already noted, in the last week of December 1883 there was a very strong chance that this Liberal administration would break up. Hartington's possible resignation over the terms of the coming 3rd Reform Bill had now moved to become 'a probability'. Gladstone had met the last of the great Whigs for several private discussions;[3] but the meetings had broken up with each 'side' as entrenched as before.[4] Derby was deeply involved in all this, as a close associate of Gladstone, and devoted a deal of time, at this crucial period in Anglo-Boer relations, in trying to bridge the gap between the Gladstonians and the Whigs. He was joined in this by Granville, but by no one else. He was very largely distracted from Colonial Office matters. On 30 December Gladstone had written him a long letter, headed 'secret', in which he revealed the extent and severity of the Cabinet crisis—'matters look ill with Hartington and the matter of Reform . . . '.[5] This was one of many such letters. Derby's replies were equally numerous. They were also well thought-out, and strongly influential in the Gladstone 'camp'. With a surprising degree of political acumen Derby put his finger on the very core of the trouble. He suggested, to Gladstone, that Hartington was only using the issue of Reform as a convenient moment to leave the ministry; for, as a result of Gladstone's own frequent talk of resignation and retirement, Hartington feared the day when he would be Liberal leader was growing near, and hence 'he dislikes the prospect of having to

[1] De Kock, '*Ekstra Territoriale Vraagstukke*', p. 132, footnote. (Merriman MSS. 18841/1.)

[2] Derby replied to the Deputation on 9 January 1884. See *Parl. Pap.*, 1884, LVII, C.3947, pp. 28–9.

[3] Addit. MSS. 48635, ff. 47–8 (Hamilton Diary). Entry for Sunday, 30 December 1883. Gladstone 'has made up his mind to come to Town tomorrow to have it out with Lord Hartington'.

[4] Ibid., f. 48: 'The net result was I fear "indifferent".' (Hamilton.)

[5] Addit. MSS. 44142, f. 33. Gladstone to Derby, (copy) 30 December 1883 (Secret).

lead, with the assistance of colleagues with whom he is not wholly in agreement, and is not sorry to find an excuse for getting out of the difficulty before he has to deal with it'.[1] This was an astute piece of diagnosis of the Whig malady. So equally was Derby's advice: Hartington might well be kept in the Gladstone Cabinet if only the Premier would give 'the assurance that you do not contemplate that early retirement at which you have so often hinted'.

Derby's close interest in the matter, and his sharp advice was not without success. By 3 January the crisis was largely over.[2] Gladstone had given Hartington the assurance suggested by Derby—that he would remain on as Liberal leader for some while yet—and had also given him 'a strong dose of Chamberlain'[3]: a 'lecture' on the effects of resigning from the party, and leaving it vulnerable to 'Joe' and his Radical allies.

The Cabinet of the afternoon of that day—3 January—was a deal happier and more constructive than had been anticipated.[4] Derby even got the ministers to discuss the Transvaal negotiations.[5] It was here that Derby proposed the offer of a limited extension of the western frontier, which was soon to be presented to the Boer Delegates.[6] This was, of course, no more or less than Robinson's suggestion (of 26 December) being taken up wholly by Derby,[7] such was his influence at this period. By the evening of 3 January the decision to stand firm, in the face of Kruger's demands, had been taken. But Derby was not acting on the basis of any new information; or from any fewer fears of the consequences of such a stand. Rather it constituted a bland act of faith in Robinson's determined assurances. What he was to do with the rest of Bechuanaland, and of how he was to halt further Boer encroachment over the proposed new line,

[1] Ibid., f. 35. Derby to Gladstone, 31 December 1883.

[2] Addit. MSS. 48635, f. 52 (Hamilton Diary). Entry for Thursday, 8 January 1884.

[3] Ibid., f. 49.

[4] Addit. MSS. 44645, f. 2 (Cabinet Papers). Meeting of Thursday, 3 January 1884, at 2 p.m.

[5] Ibid., Point 2: 'South Africa (a) Basutos . . .; (b) Zulus . . .; (c) Transvaal. Bechuanaland.'

[6] On 9 January 1884. See *Parl. Pap.*, 1884, LVII, C.3947, pp. 28–9.

[7] See C.O. 291/24 (R). Minute by Robinson, 26 December 1883 (in his own hand), on Deputation to Derby, of 26 December 1883.

he does not appear to have weighed at all. Nor could he have acted with the secure knowledge that the Cape would assume a fair share of a dual Anglo-Cape Protectorate over Bechuana-land, to keep the Transvaal out. For, on 22 December 1883, Scanlen had written a private letter to Robert Herbert, on the attitude of his ministry to the whole affair.[1] This letter, which Herbert showed to Derby—and indeed had placed in the Colonial Office files—left officials and ministers alike in no doubt as to the Cape policy of conciliating the Transvaal for fear of losing Cape Dutch support in the Colonial Assembly. In Scanlen's words:

> Having regard to our political position in the Colony, I have inti-mated in my official letters that it would be necessary that the Transvaal should be party to such an arrangement. . . . If the Transvaal Government enters into a treaty with you, acknow-ledging the Protectorate, and paying their share, I am willing to do the same.[2]

Scanlen also had a shrewd idea of the very great difficulties which Derby was likely to have in trying to get the Transvaal to agree to such an arrangement. A protectorate would be of no use to the Transvaal: indeed it would put an end to all their expansionist dreams and instincts. Scanlen doubted whether Derby could turn the poachers into game-keepers—

> I am, of course, aware that any restrictions of the kind will be dis-tasteful to the Transvaal Government, and can only be obtained in exchange for concessions which may more than counter-balance them. . . . But it is immaterial to me how that arrangement is arrived at.[3]

But even Merriman's pessimism could not encompass Derby's actual difficulties. Quite apart from the Deputation's inflexible demands, Derby experienced other misgivings about future Anglo-Boer relations. On 1 January he was informed by the Foreign Office that the Transvaal Government had awarded a contract to an American engineer, Edward McMurdo, to build the Republic a separate and independent rail-line to the east

[1] C.O. 417/2. Scanlen to Herbert (Private), 22 December 1883.
[2] Idem.
[3] Idem.

coast.[1] Derby was not to know that the railway would take a decade to build. At the time it appeared as yet another sign of the Transvaal's growing determination to be independent of imperial control or influence.[2]

He was also subject to other pressures and fears. John Mackenzie's campaign was again picking up momentum. He had just issued a long pamphlet describing his work in southern Africa and among the Tswana in particular.[3] Bramston was quick to minute on receipt of this pamphlet: 'His views are easily described—British protectorate, which has been rejected by Lord Kimberley, and not accepted by Sir M. Hicks Beach.'[4] Another unwelcome pressure came from the excutive committee of the 'International Arbitration and Peace Association', a body as dim and distant to historians as their title was pompous. Nevertheless they continually badgered Derby to allow them to hold a series of public meetings—to inform the 'average citizen' of the state of the Anglo-Boer negotiations.[5] Derby read nothing but mischief in their ideas; and he refused to aid them in any way.[6] As far as he was concerned the less public opinion was aroused the better.

This matter came to nil. But an even more worrying concern was the actual state of affairs in the Transvaal. Apart from the actual information that the frontier Boers were still encroaching over the boundary at every point, and with new energy into Zulu and Swazi lands, Derby heard disturbing rumours that Transvaal politics were not as dormant as Kruger made out. There was some substance for Derby's fears. On 5 January Merriman wrote from the Cape, to Forster, on the state of the Transvaal. 'The population is divided into factions, Kruger and Du Toit versus Joubert and Jorissen. In fact the situation immediately preceding the annexation [of 1877] is being rapidly

[1] C.O. 291/26 (Foreign). F.O. to C.O., 5 January 1884. The contract was for a line to the frontier of the Transvaal, at a cost of £296,000—or £4,270 per kilometre.

[2] Ibid., Minute by Herbert, 4 January 1884.

[3] C.O. 291/25 (Misc.). Mackenzie to C.O. 3 January 1884, enclosing his pamphlet: 'My unvarnished picture of Boer life.'

[4] Ibid., Minute by Bramston, 11 January 1884.

[5] C.O. 291/24 (Misc.). The Committee of International Arbitration and Peace Association to Lord Derby, 10 December 1883.

[6] Ibid., Derby to 'I.A.P.A.', 11 December 1883.

reproduced; a skilful diplomat could very soon bring about a peaceful revolution which would restore the country to the Empire. . . .'[1] Nothing could have been further from Derby's thoughts, but the situation had an eminently practical repercussion, which could not be ignored. Derby began to wonder if the Deputation did really represent Transvaal opinion; and whether the *Volksraad* would ratify any agreement concluded by Kruger's party. Ashley expressed it best when he reflected on 'how little unity of administration there is (in the Transvaal) and makes us doubt whether any agreement they may make with us here on other matters will be held binding by those left at home'.[2]

But there was little Derby could do, except worry and rely on Robinson. On 9 January he presented the Kruger Deputation with Britain's new terms for a settlement,[3] being an almost verbatim transcript of Robinson's memorandum of 26 December. Derby reasserted his determination that the new western boundary must be agreed upon before further negotiations could continue; and towards this end he offered the concession of the western boundary being extended. 'The territory which would be added to the Transvaal by this proposed alteration of the existing boundary may be described as a strip of country 130 miles long with an average breadth of about 20 miles. It comprises the whole of Massouw's [*sic*] territory and the greater part of Montsioa's [*sic*] country.'[4]

This was, in fact, to be Derby's final offer: and it is, ironically, less generous than his first vague general offer made to the Transvaal; but then Robinson had been at work since that early offer.[5] The climate of opinion was also beginning to veer round. An editorial in the *Pall Mall Gazette*, for 11 January, scented the wind of change that had blown through official policy.

When Mr. Scanlen . . . landed in England two or three months ago, the South African policy of England was vague and unde-

[1] De Kock, '*Ekstra Territoriale Vraagstukke*,' p. 134. (Merriman MSS.; L.B. copy, 1875–84.) Merriman to Forster, 5 January 1884.

[2] C.O. 291/23. Minute by Ashley, 28 December 1883.

[3] *Parl. Pap.*, 1884, LVII, C.3947, pp. 28–9. Derby to Deputation, 9 January 1884, enclosing a map of the new proposed boundary.

[4] Idem.

[5] See C.O. 291/26 (R.) Memorandum by Robinson of 23 December 1883, on question of extending the frontier.

cided, and ill defined. We stood at the parting of the ways, irresolute whether to adopt a policy of control or a policy of *laissez faire*. ... We in England are to do nothing, while the forces of natural selection were to be allowed full play, in order that we might arrive by the shortest cut at the survival of the fittest.[1]

However the changing situation in southern Africa, and most notably the new importance of retaining the loyalty of *all* the Cape citizens, had changed this: the road to the north was a Cape concern and need. 'We can no more entertain the proposal to allow the Boers to sit outside our trade route than we can allow France to annex the Isthmus of Suez.'[2]

Privately though the most important factor in the entire London Convention negotiations had taken place; and it too worked in favour of Derby taking a firm stand at this crucial moment. Scanlen had sailed for the Cape on 11 January,[3] but he had left behind a letter for Derby containing a final offer.[4] He stated that if Britain took over Bechuanaland as a protectorate the Cape would help share the cost. He made no mention of the Transvaal.

This was the offer for which Derby had long waited: a pledge of collaboration independent of the wishes and demands of the Kruger Deputation. Together with Robinson's advice this made the greatest impression on Derby's thinking.[5] It did not occur to him then that Scanlen might have no right or powers to give such an undertaking on the part of the Colonial ministry; and it can usefully be enquired as to why the Cape Premier changed his stand to make this pledge. There is no conclusive evidence either way, but an 'informed guess' would suggest that Robinson's influence was again at work. As the Cape Governor he had a useful working relationship with Scanlen, while at the same time he had all too clearly come to see the importance which Derby placed on gaining Cape participation in any Bechuanaland settlement, especially one which implied any form of administration. But whatever the explanation and background to Scanlen's undertaking, the fact remained that it was given; and given at just the moment when Derby urgently needed

---

[1] *Pall Mall Gazette*, 11 January 1884.   [2] Idem.
[3] See *Daily News*, 11 January 1884—interview with Scanlen.
[4] C.O. 291/26 (S). Scanlen to Herbert, 9 and 11 January 1884.
[5] Ibid, C.O. Minutes of 12 January 1884.

such an assurance, to help him face the Kruger reply to his strong line of 9 January.

Robinson made the most of the moment, and capitalised on the atmosphere created by Scanlen's offer. On 13 January he reported to the Colonial Office that he had heard it rumoured that Chiefs Lobengula and Khama were to present petitions to the imperial authorities, imploring Britain not to give way to the Deputation by giving the Transvaal effective control of the road to the north.[1] In his enthusiasm Robinson took up Mackenzie's tools of argument: it was important, he claimed, to preserve Khama from Transvaal control for the chief's needs were primarily 'Manchester, Birmingham, and Sheffield goods'; while to isolate Lobengula to the north, would be to surrender all possibilities of ever gaining his land for Britain—a land which 'has been described as probably one of the richest gold countries in the world . . .'. In short, 'it would be a serious injury to British commerce, and to the interest of the British communities in South Africa [i.e. the Cape], if the great highway from the Cape to the interior of the continent were given over to the Transvaal Government'.[2] In reading Robinson's conclusions, on the need to control this area of Bechuanaland, is to realise the unoriginality of Cecil Rhodes' dreams and strategy.

Three days later, on 17 January, Derby received the Kruger Deputation's reply to his letter of 9 January.[3] It is a curious document. Gone is a great deal of the pomp and bluff which padded out their earlier letters. In contrast this reply is reserved and amenable in tone. There was even a pretence at pleasure at the extent of Derby's offer of a modified Convention boundary. In fact, the document is so hedged with qualifying clauses, and requests for clarification on nearly every point, that its ultimate meaning or message is as elusive today as it was in 1884. The only clue to the real nature of the reply was the inclusion of a sketch map, on which Kruger had broadly outlined where the Transvaal would like the western boundary to be. The line he drew constituted a vast arc out into Tswana territory, and was very similar to the claims put forward by Pretorius a decade

[1] *Parl. Pap.*, 1884, LVII, C.3841, p. 152. Robinson to C.O., 13 January 1884.
[2] Idem.
[3] C.O. 291/26 (Misc.). Deputation to Derby, 17 January 1884.

before. To this extent the Deputation could be said to have returned a negative reply to the Derby (Robinson) proposals. Yet the letter does not state this emphatically.

Why this sudden ambivalence? Why the attempt suddenly to be servile yet demanding in the same breath? There can never be a final answer, but in fact Kruger knew he had been defeated—or rather, he had defeated his own ends and himself, to a large degree. At this point, mid-January 1884, Kruger had lost most of the advantages which had allowed him to take up such a formidable position but two months previously. He had calculated that Derby would steadily give ground to persistent pressure. In this he had been right, but only for a certain time. Robinson, a growing public concern with the fate of the Tswana chiefs, and Scanlen's promise, had given Derby new heart, and new reasons to advocate a stiffer approach to the Deputation. Kruger had been both outmanoeuvred, by unforeseen circumstances, and had damaged his own cause by not being more accommodating to the initial proposals put before him in November 1883—when Derby was, in fact, disposed to meet the Transvaal more than half way. It must have seemed to Kruger that having easily won the initial rounds, he would soon have Derby retreating, if not on the ropes. But just when it looked as though the Colonial Secretary was losing what fighting nerve he had, Derby had come out and put up a stiffer defence than in the opening stages of the 'conflict'. Kruger must indeed have kicked himself repeatedly in later life for not welcoming and accepting Derby's proposals of November 1883. The opportunity was lost, and not to be repeated. Kruger had gambled on two reasonable assumptions: that Derby wished to have the matter over at almost any price; and that the Cape Premier would make no attempt to help the Imperial Government without Boer assent. He had gambled and lost. Now all he could do was salvage as reasonable a new Convention as was possible, given Derby's unexpectedly commanding position.

Robinson has left the best contemporary report of how the balance swung from Kruger's dominance to his accommodating stance in the later stages of the negotiations:

> I said that whatever pledges were made by the Boer government it would not be able to make its subjects keep them; and as for the

neutralised road . . . [there] would be simply no thoroughfare as far as trade was concerned. Finally, I settled that we should take the Bechuanaland territory over. I said, 'I will undertake to run it for £10,000 [per annum] and I will get the Cape to bear £5,000 of that.' *Scanlen was over here at the time, and he agreed.* . . .[1]

Merriman, though, took a more sceptical view of the change. In his eyes Derby was merely obeying a 'natural law' of imperial politics and policy. 'The British statesman's chief occupation is throwing up straws in the daily Press to see how the wind of public opinion is veering, and then he promptly abandons himself to the favouring gale.'[2] This is an extreme view, but taken together with that of Robinson, a not unlikely picture can be gained of the later stages of the negotiations.

Derby's new rôle, as bearer of the flag and defender of the Empire, is all the more surprising if his 'conversion' to a more imperialistic solution is placed in the context of the prevailing Cabinet concerns of January 1884. The position in Egypt and the Sudan had now finally reached crisis proportions. The Cabinet met no less than six times in this month,[3] excluding the 'informal Cabinets'; and at each meeting the question of Britain's future rôle in North Africa was the central issue. South Africa was only discussed once, on 3 January,[4] and the decision to stand firm in the face of Kruger's demands appears to have been taken regardless of the Cabinet, which was obsessed with the Khedive, the situation on the southern Nile, and the state of the Egyptian economy. On 16 January Childers warned Gladstone that the crumbling position in Egypt could seriously affect Britain's own economy if the Cabinet declined to withdraw.[5] On the other hand, Baring painted an appallingly grim picture of what would happen if Britain did retire: the Khedive was already talking of abdication.

By 18 January a critical phase had been reached in North Africa. The 'Egyptian' Committee of the Cabinet—Hartington,

[1] *Cape Times*, 3 November 1897—interview with Robinson in March 1895, in London. (My italics.)

[2] De Kock, '*Ekstra Territoriale Vraagstukke*', p. 193. (Merriman MSS.; L.B. copy, 1883–84.)

[3] On 3, 4, 22, 24, 26, and 31 January 1884, See Addit. MSS. 44645, ff. 2–24 (Cabinet Papers).

[4] Ibid., ff. 2–4.

[5] This is admirably handled in *Africa and the Victorians*, pp. 138–41.

Granville, Northbrook and Dilke—decided on an immediate 'modus vivendi' policy, which would involve withdrawing from the Sudan, and consolidating the position to the north.[1] They also took the highly unusual step of appointing a man to supervise this 'rescue and retire' measure in the Sudan, without reference to the other members of the Cabinet. If this was unorthodox, so was the man they selected, General 'Chinese' Gordon. Why he was actually chosen is a story in itself:[2] suffice to add that the Cabinet Committee acted in defiance of all the known facts about Gordon. Even so moderate and reserved a man as Hamilton could write in his Diary of Gordon (on 23 January 1884): 'He seems to be a half-cracked fatalist and what can we expect from such a man?'[3] But Hamilton had to admit that the 'despatch of Chinese Gordon has been well received, and has for the moment satisfied public opinion'. *Punch* published a famous cartoon of Gordon carrying Gladstone through the dangers of the Nile's waters.[4]

The practical effects of this parallel dilemma on Derby, and colonial policy, was oblique but significant. While on the one hand it meant he was given a surprisingly free hand, for even Gladstone could spare him little time, it also meant as hinted above that Derby was not only distracted from the negotiations, but that a major option was closed to him. He knew that the Cabinet would now never accede to an outright British annexation of Bechuanaland. This fact in turn placed a great premium on Scanlen's offer; and on Robinson's work in assuring that colonial support. It forced Derby to rely even more heavily on the Cape Governor, and the Cape ministry, at a time when in theory he should have been able to manipulate the Kruger Deputation himself. It was yet another sign of the manner in which Africa, the Colonists and the Boers, were coming to dictate the pace and extent of local expansion, quite irrespective of the wishes of the Victorians.

For the moment if that initiative lay anywhere it lay with the

---

[1] See Holland, *Devonshire*, I, 415–16.

[2] A. Nutting, *Gordon: Martyr and Misfit*, (London, 1966), is best on Gordon.

[3] Addit. MSS. 48635, f. 68 (Hamilton Diary). Entry for Wednesday, 23 January 1884.

[4] See *Punch*, 2 February 1884—'Getting a lift! or the Grand Old Man of the (Red) Sea.'

Cape, and not the Transvaal. Kruger was now paying the price of having overstated his case, and of allowing Scanlen to fall to Robinson's influence. On 25 January he was to see the full extent of Derby's new-found confidence. Kruger was informed that the Imperial Government rejected his proposals of 17 January outright.[1] 'The boundary sketched by you appears to Her Majesty's Government to be such as they would be quite unable to entertain. It would place within the Transvaal about 90 miles of the direct trade road from the Cape to the interior of the continent.'[2] As to Kruger's other hopes—of a local commission to draw up the exact boundary—these too were dashed by Derby, on Robinson's advice. 'Her Majesty's Government proposes to place within the Transvaal *as much of the territory as can be given without including the road.* . . .'[3] This was merely a reiteration of the basis for negotiation offered by Derby of 9 January, and was to form the substance of his next despatch to the Deputation. Derby considered it the basis for an agreement and he now clung to it with a tenacity that must have unnerved Kruger.

The Transvaal's reply to this categorical statement was immediate and devious.[4] For the second time Kruger replied in a letter hedged with qualifications, and abounding with strange proposals. Some were clearly intended as a technique for clouding the issues—could the kraal of Machadi, at Rietfontein, 'be included in the South African Republic?'—while others were quite acceptable—Kruger assumed that the new Griqualand West frontier would be drawn up entirely by the Cape and Transvaal in discussion. As to the major issue at stake, the western boundary, Kruger only mentioned it in passing: Derby's suggestion was unacceptable, but he thought there appeared to be a chance of agreement on many other matters.

Derby's reaction to this bizarre letter was to forward it immediately to Robinson, on 28 January. The proconsul drafted a memorandum,[5] and Derby used it as the basis for his reply to Kruger of 4 February. It was a subtle letter, and adopted

[1] C.O. 291/26 (Misc.). Derby to Deputation, 25 January 1884. See also *Parl. Pap.*, 1884, LVII, C.3947, pp. 36–7.
[2] Idem.   [3] Idem. (My italics.)
[4] C.O. 291/26 (Misc.). Deputation to Derby, 28 January 1884.
[5] Ibid., Memorandum by Robinson, 28 January 1884.

Kruger's own techniques.[1] Derby suggested that as Kruger was now confining himself to details, such as Machadi's kraal, it was to be assumed that the Deputation had dropped their major objections to the proposed boundary line. 'I trust that I may conclude that the various questions of detail in connection with the western boundary of the Transvaal have been disposed of. ...'[2]

Kruger's reply took the expected style and form:[3] he accepted Derby's remarks about the frontier in a unique manner: he simply ignored them. Instead he pointed out that the Transvaal Deputation had been in London for three months, and called for a speeding-up of the negotiations. He also had the temerity to enquire whether 'provisions similar to some of the provisions of the Sand River Convention may not be adopted'[4] in the new Treaty.

This letter produced a series of wry and indignant comments in the Colonial Office.[5] Derby took it somewhat more seriously. It seemed to him that having just obtained Cape support, and having stood up to the Kruger Deputation, the whole negotiations were likely to break up with an inconclusive result. Derby took Robinson's view: if they could only get Kruger to agree on the British definition of the new western boundary they could easily agree on the other points at issue. Derby accordingly decided to take the initiative in two eminently practical ways. He invited Kruger and his Deputation to the Colonial Office, on the afternoon of Friday, 8 February;[6] and he had Robinson draw up a draft Convention to present to them,[7] incorporating a map of the western boundary, and the list of other concessions which the Imperial Government were prepared to make *if* Kruger accepted the limited expansion of the frontier.

[1] The letter was drafted by Herbert, on 30 January 1884, after receiving Robinson's Memorandum of 28 January.
[2] *Parl. Pap.*, 1884, LVII, C.3947, pp. 38–9. Derby to Deputation, 4 February 1884.
[3] C.O. 291/26 (Misc.). Deputation to Derby, 5 February 1884.   [4] Idem.
[5] Ibid., Minutes by Fairfield, Bramston, and Herbert, 7 February 1874.
[6] Kruger had suggested this in his letter of 5 February, but Derby was unenthusiastic till Robinson had suggested that it might be a useful way of presenting the Deputation with the draft Convention and getting their immediate reaction. It might save time in the long run.
[7] Ibid., Minute by Robinson, 5 February 1884, enclosing draft of new Convention.

This meeting of the two sides (on 8 February) was to be of major importance.[1] It was the fourth such meeting, but it was considerably more successful than the others. It went a long way to bridging the gap that then existed between the Transvaal Deputation and the Colonial Office. It proved to be a 'victory' for the Derby–Robinson approach. Kruger was made to understand that all further concessions, in regard to the debt, the suzerainty and the title of the Transvaal, were consequent upon his acceptance of the western frontier. At last Kruger saw that Derby was now not going to give way to any pressure from the Deputation. He must also have been made to feel that it was he who had everything to be gained by continuing the negotiation, and everything to lose if they were broken off, because of his obstinacy over the boundary line.

Kruger accepted the Derby–Robinson terms, but not as a submission or defeat. He saw it as a bargain. He would reduce his demands over the boundary question but Britain had to give ground on the other questions, particularly the debt, which he wanted drastically reduced, and the suzerainty, which he thought should be abolished.

Verbal agreement was reached to this effect,[2] though the precise details were left to be agreed on once Kruger had further studied Robinson's draft of the Convention. Derby must have left highly satisfied with his afternoon's work. At last Kruger had agreed in principle that the road to the north should not be included in the Transvaal, while the concessions on the debt and other matters, were no more than Derby had already been prepared to offer.

The omens looked good. Kruger's first letter after the meeting, written on 13 February, raised no objection[3]. He merely asked for a clarification on the debt. He accepted Derby's concession of £127,000, 'thus reducing the debt of the Republic to Her Majesty's Government to £254,000'. However, he won-

[1] Unfortunately there is no verbatim transcript of the meeting. However, Derby's letter to the Deputation, of 15 February, includes a statement of the matters agreed to. See *Parl. Pap.*, 1884, LVII, C.3947, pp. 43–44. Derby to Deputation, 15 February 1884. And the C.O. kept a private record of the meeting. See C.O. 291/26 (Misc.). Minute of 5 February 1884.

[2] Idem.

[3] Ibid., Deputation to Derby, 13 February 1884. See also *Parl. Pap.*, 1884, LVII, C.3947, pp. 41–3.

dered if it would be possible further to reduce the £137,000 set against the Transvaal for war damages in 1881. He ended in a most reasonable tone—'a liberal settlement of the whole financial question will conduce greatly to the future friendly relationship between the two Governments'.[1]

Matters were proceeding so well that Derby decided it was time to plan ahead for the time when the new 'London Convention' came into force. The matter of most immediate concern was the appointment of an official to 'administer', or rather represent Britain in the Bechuanaland area. He was to be given the rank of Deputy-Commissioner, and a limited police force. His powers were not defined, nor was the exact size of this proposed police force specified. Presumably such a man was mainly to control the frontier infiltration, and to keep law and order in the area beyond the Transvaal border. But what of the land grants, legal and otherwise, which had already taken place? Here there was a convenient lack of specification or instruction. Clearly a great deal was to depend on the nature and quality of the man appointed—not to mention the size of his police force.

As was natural Derby turned to Robinson for suggestions as to whom they should appoint. To Derby's surprise Robinson put forward Mackenzie's name; and, despite Derby's objections, he secured his appointment. Robinson's grounds for appointing Mackenzie are still open to debate. He claimed that he did so because Mackenzie was 'by far the best fitted for the post'. Yet a mere six months later he was working to get Mackenzie recalled. Did he do it knowing that Mackenzie must fail with such limited resources?—Robinson claimed he would not need more than 100 police, and in fact Mackenzie ended with only 10. In the interim Robinson would presumably work on the Cape ministry to take the area over. This is a plausible answer; but perhaps the truth is a lot more simple. Robinson had been impressed with Mackenzie's knowledge of Bechuanaland, and with the energy and fire which obviously backed his campaign to save the area from the Transvaal. He also liked Mackenzie, and was to befriend him in Cape Town even after Mackenzie had been forced to resign. But, most important of all, Robinson, in early 1884, had not fallen under the influence of Rhodes. He

[1] Idem.

still saw problems on their merits, and not through the eyes of that dominating and single-minded Cape imperialist.

Before Derby had even offered the post officially to Mackenzie—on 21 February—Robinson had exchanged a series of warm private letters with the indefatigable missionary, proposing that he take the post. As early as 8 February—the day Kruger met Derby at the Colonial Office and cleared the air—Mackenzie had written to Robinson saying how grateful he was for the offer.

> I beg to express my thanks and my willingness to do my best. . . .
> P.S. If Her Majesty's Government will only give this a fair chance, and gradually, cautiously, and intelligently develop the policy I refer to, I hope to live to see a practically united South Africa, and England relieved of the present irritating responsibilities in that part of the world.[1]

Mackenzie's delight, at the opportunity it seemed to offer him, is patently obvious: he must have felt it was a fitting climax to two arduous campaigns on behalf of the Tswana people. He could not know that Rhodes was already working for the day when Cape, and not imperial, authority should predominate in the area, and beyond. Mackenzie's initial optimism knew no bounds though, and with a sense of touching naïvety he looked forward to the day when he would take up his post in Bechu-analand. On 15 February he happened to see Kruger and du Toit in London, and he wrote to a friend, 'I had a good look at each in passing. I hope to be introduced one of these days, for the fighting is over, so far as I am concerned; and I am quite willing to shake hands.'[2]

The second manner in which Derby was preparing for the future settlement also concerned Robinson's assistance. He had Robinson draw up a final draft of the proposed Convention, and forward it to the Deputation over Derby's name. This reached Kruger on 15 February,[3] and Derby quite expected the rest of

[1] W. D. Mackenzie, *Life of Mackenzie*, pp. 301–2. Mackenzie to Robinson, 8 February 1884.
[2] W. D. Mackenzie, *Life of Mackenzie*, p. 303. Mackenzie to Oates, 15 February 1884.
[3] *Parl. Pap.*, 1884, LVII, C. 3947, pp. 43–4. Derby to Deputation, 15 February 1884.

the negotiations to be a mere matter of formalities, particularly as the draft Convention was based exclusively on the successful meeting of 8 February. The title 'South African Republic' was to replace 'Transvaal State'; the western boundary was to be according to the 'Robinson map'; the British Resident was to be withdrawn; the Republic was to have full internal self-government; and it could even conduct its own foreign affairs, subject to the requirement that 'any new treaty with a foreign state shall not have effect without the approval of the Queen'.[1] No mention was made of the 'suzerainty'. Presumably it had lapsed with the new grants of independence contained in the draft treaty.

Kruger should have now signified his assent; but he did not. Like the newly broken horse he suddenly shied away from taking the jump at the last moment. Derby received a curt message, on 16 February, to the effect that 'The Deputation regret to say that they cannot accept, without modification of some of the Articles of the proposed new Convention.'[2]

Derby's reaction is not recorded: certainly he must have been extremely annoyed. He had been led to presume by Kruger that all the outstanding differences had been surmounted. What could Kruger be objecting to this time? Derby looked to Robinson for a quick answer. Accordingly the proconsul had invited Kruger to his hotel for a private meeting.[3] We do not know exactly what transpired; but we do know that a further meeting with Derby, at the Colonial Office, was fixed for 2 p.m. on Monday, 18 February.[4]

The permanent officials prepared for yet another afternoon of Kruger-style debate: argument, pleading, and cajoling, which made up the old Boer's style of negotiation. Herbert minuted a trifle anxiously, 'it will be necessary for us to have our expert Sir H. Robinson to assist us in understanding the true meaning and effect of the suggestions which will be made for altering the draft Convention'.[5]

---

[1] Idem.

[2] C.O. 291/26 (Misc.). Deputation to Derby, 16 February 1884.

[3] W. D. Mackenzie, *Life of Mackenzie*, p. 303.

[4] C.O. 291/26 (Misc.). C.O. Minute, dated 16 February 1884.

[5] Ibid., Minute by Herbert, 16 February 1884, on Deputation to Derby, 16 February 1884.

What Kruger hoped to achieve by this last-minute piece of posturing is difficult to ascertain. He had already committed himself, certainly verbally, to the basic clauses of the treaty. Did he hope for some last-minute concession? Perhaps. Though why Derby should now give way, having stood firm ten days previously, is difficult to gauge. Certainly Kruger's own position had not improved markedly in any way in the intervening period. It was only when he returned to South Africa that he learnt that Scanlen had been repudiated by his own ministers, for giving Derby the assurance of Cape collaboration;[1] that the Cape Dutch were extremely restive at the idea of John Mackenzie being made Deputy-Commissioner, and had called on Derby to assure them that no Dutchman would be deprived of his land in Bechuanaland;[2] and even the English colonists in the Cape were furious with Britain for allowing Bismarck a free hand in South-West Africa.[3]

But all this was in the future—in March and April 1884. In mid-February Kruger could hardly have known this, and his refusal to sign the Convention can only be attributed to the fact that he felt he had struck a bad bargain; that after an excellent start the negotiations had gradually gone against him. The Americans might refer to his frame of mind as 'cussed'. However, the meeting with Derby and Robinson of 18 February—their fifth—was not without effect.[4] They made it clear that they had made their final offer. He could take it or leave it. Kruger was ever a realist, and so he begrudgingly accepted. Next time, perhaps—when he was destroying the London Convention hoping for yet another treaty, as he had killed off the Pretoria Convention[5]—he might obtain even better terms.

[1] This is well handled in De Kock, 'Ekstra Territoriale Vraagstukke', pp. 206–7.

[2] C.O. 291/26 (Tel.), Smyth to Derby, 26 February 1884. See Minutes by Herbert and Bramston on this despatch.

[3] See Merriman to Mills, 6 February 1884: 'It is not as if we were asking Great Britain to spend money . . . all we want is an assertion of sovereignty . . . leaving us to manage the mode and provide for the expense of carrying it out when desired'. (Merriman MSS., L.B. copy, 1883–84). Quoted in De Kock, 'Ekstra Territoriale Vraagstukke', p. 196.

[4] C.O. 291/26. Deputation to see Derby and Robinson, at 2 p.m., on 18 February 1884, at C.O.

[5] C.O. 879/18, no. 235, for Official Draft of Pretoria Convention.

Only the British Treasury now delayed the final agreement. It was not until 26 February that Derby persuaded them to see the 'wisdom' of reducing the Transvaal debt to £250,000; and the interest to be fixed at only 3 per cent.[1] Once he had received an affirmative memorandum from the Treasury he forwarded it immediately to the Deputation;[2] and he invited Kruger and his fellow burghers to sign the London Convention the following day at the Colonial Office. Kruger readily agreed. Accordingly on Wednesday, 27 February 1884, the Deputation arrived at the Old Colonial Office in Downing Street. Robinson signed the London Convention on the part of Britain; Kruger, du Toit and Smit for the new 'South African Republic'.[3]

At last it was all over; the seemingly endless negotiations had produced a working document. Derby looked upon the Convention with optimism, and even well-being. It is doubtful though whether he saw the significance of the date of that Wednesday, when he had invited the Deputation to sign the Treaty. It was hardly an auspicious beginning for the London Convention: the 27th of February was exactly the third anniversary of Majuba.

3. Dismantling Kimberley's Convention: 'What happened to the Suzerainty?'

The aim, and the effect, of the Convention were to be two vastly different matters. It was intended to provide a new and more constructive basis for Anglo-Boer relations; to remove those frictions created by the Transvaal War and the consequent Pretoria Convention; and to strike a *via media* between Boer demands and imperial needs. It achieved none of these high hopes, and indeed worked in the opposite direction. The London Convention was to provide one of the celebrated and debated 'causes' of the Boer War.[4]

Why did this well-intentioned document become the root of

[1] C.O. 291/26 (Misc.). Treasury to C.O., 23 February 1884, see also *Parl. Pap.*, 1884, LVII, C.3947, pp. 46–7.

[2] Ibid., Derby to Deputation, 26 February 1884.

[3] C.O. 879/21, no. 278A. Dual English/Dutch text of the Convention; signed 27 February 1884.

[4] See J. S. Marais, *The Fall of Kruger's Republic* (Oxford, 1962), pp. 195–200, 245–6, 313. Hereafter cited as *Marais*, to which I am much indebted.

so much discord and controversy? Part of the answer lies in the Convention itself. Several of its twenty clauses were badly drafted,[1] and allowed for ambiguity in interpretation. But the major reason was the set of tensions and ambitions in which the Convention was supposed to work. Kruger, for one, did not see any air of finality about the document. Presumably it too could be eroded, and replaced just as the Pretoria Convention had been undermined, and revised for a more liberal treaty agreement. In retrospect Chamberlain well caught the Republic's aims:

> *Kruger's policy is to nibble at the Convention*—to provoke us in small things without actually intiating a rupture, and to leave us to take the first open action in the way of hostilities. . . .[2]

Not that Kruger was the only one who erred. On the British side successive Secretaries of State and Chamberlain in particular, saw in the Convention what they wanted to see. Its legal ambiguities worked in their favour, so that Kruger's Republic could be both independent yet controlled by Britain; the Secretary of State had no power over Transvaal internal affairs, yet in the last resort could claim to hold all powers.

On paper, and isolated from its contemporary pressures, it is a workable enough looking document.[3] The Preamble, and the following twenty clauses, set out to define the ideal basis for Anglo-Boer relations. The boundaries of the Transvaal were extended and fixed (Clauses 1 and 2); the title of 'Transvaal State' was abolished and the old name 'South African Republic' reinstated (Preamble); the debt to Britain, and the interest on that debt, were considerably reduced (Clauses 5 and 6); the British Resident at Pretoria was recalled, and replaced by a 'lower emissary', a Consul (Clause 3); the Transvaal was to be fully independent—the only stricture being that no treaty could be 'concluded' with a foreign power without British approval (Clause 4); and the rights of citizenship, especially in regard to the native peoples, was defined (Clause 14 and 19). Minor

---

[1] C.O. 879/21, no. 278A, for official text of Convention, in English and Dutch.

[2] C.O. 537/133. Chamberlain to Greene, 13 March 1897, Quoted in *Marais*, p. 158. (My italics.)

[3] See Appendix 2; the Convention is also printed in Evbers *Select Constitutional Documents*, pp. 469–74.

clauses concerned rights of property of British subjects (Clause 7); the freedom of all religions (Clause 9); a guarantee against slavery (Clause 8); the upkeep of British War graves (Clause 10); the independence of the Swazi people (Clause 12); free trade for British goods in the Republic (Clause 13); an agreement on the extradition of criminals (Clause 16); and the promise that no British citizen could be called up for military duty (Clause 15).

The most important clauses were those which were either soonest disregarded, or which caused the greatest friction. In the first category were Clauses 1 and 2, which defined the frontiers, and bound the Transvaal to keep within the lines drawn. If Kruger had ever intended to keep to this promise, his frontier Boers did not. Nor did he make any real attempt to control their pastoral *treks* and wanderings. Within a few years a 'fifth' Boer republic was to exist in the Zulu lands, under the name of the 'New Republic'.

In the second category were Clauses 4 and 14. The latter clause, concerning the rights of citizenship, could be said to be the one over which Britain went to war in 1899, for it contained the essence of the *Uitlander* dispute with Kruger. The former clause, number 4—British powers over Transvaal foreign policy —was also the cause of a great verbal battle between the Republic and Chamberlain; the hair-line difference between the definition of when a treaty is 'concluded', and 'completed', allowed for a two year and steadily embittered argument from 1897 onwards.

But the most divisive of all matters was that vital point completely omitted from the Convention—the existence, or not, of the British 'suzerainty' over the Transvaal. This vague legal word had implied an underlined constitutional 'overlordship' over the Boers; and it had been the main pillar of the 1881 Convention. Now, in 1884, it was completely missing from the London Convention. Kruger accepted the fact at its face value:[1] it was one of the concessions which he understood Britain was extending to the Deputation, in return for their acceptance of

---

[1] C.O. 477/1 (1884–96), for the Transvaal's 'Green Book' giving the Boer side of the negotiations, entitled: '*Officielle Bescheiden Gewisseld met de Engelsche Regeering in Zake de Conventie van London*'. Details of Convention, pp. 85–100.

the British definition of the western frontier. And, more than this, he not unnaturally assumed that the suzerainty would be abolished with the grant of full independence to the Transvaal, and the return to its old status as the 'South African Republic'. It is true that Britain still had a final veto over foreign treaties, but not over any other government matter at all. To all intents and purposes Kruger believed the Transvaal to be fully self-governing by the terms of the new Convention. Nothing which Lord Derby or Sir Hercules Robinson said during the negotiations, at any time gave him grounds to think otherwise.

However, the ink was hardly dry on the London Convention when Derby was emphatically claiming that at no time had he relinquished the suzerainty; indeed, as far as the Imperial Government was concerned, it was as much in force as in 1881. In Derby's definition the suzerainty was implied in the fact that Britain still had a veto over the Republic's foreign affairs:

> The word Suzerainty is a very vague word, and I do not think that it is capable of any precise legal definition. Whatever we may understand by it, I think it is not very easy to define. But I apprehend, whether you call it a Protectorate or a Suzerainty, or the recognition of England as a Paramount Power, the fact is that a certain controlling power is retained when the State which exercises this Suzerainty has a right to veto any negotiation into which the dependent state may enter with Foreign Powers.[1]

This was a far cry from Derby's offer of liberal concessions to Kruger; and it would seem that he had learnt the way of the *veld* and had become *slim* as well. He was also learning from Gladstone how to phrase matters in the most obtuse, but emphatic manner. He could state firmly that 'whatever Suzerainty meant in the Convention of Pretoria, the condition of things which it implies remains'; yet when asked why he had not gone to the simple technique of including this fact in the Convention he could reply, 'We have abstained from using the word because it is not capable of legal definition, and because it seemed to be a word which was likely to lead to misconception and misunderstanding'.[2]

The G.O.M. could not have clouded the issue more expertly.

[1] *Hansard*, CCLXXXVI, cols. 7–8. Derby in Lords, 17 March 1884, in answer to a question from Lord Cadogan.
[2] Idem.

But two questions remain: if it was not capable of definition why was it used? And, if it was deemed good enough to be included in the Pretoria Convention, why was it suddenly left out of the London Convention? It would seem that Derby's explanation is no more than a piece of sophistry, an attempt via verbal and mental gymnastics to suggest something that was not true.

Why was Derby prepared to go to these lengths to confuse the issue? The answer seems clear. He had left the phrase out of the Convention to please Kruger and to get the Transvalers to sign the treaty. But then he made sure that nowhere in the Convention was the suzerainty expressly abolished. Thus Derby hoped for the best of both worlds. Kruger signed happily; and when critics in the House pointed to this apparent major concession to the Boers, Derby was able to stand and claim that no concession had been made. It was hardly good diplomacy, nor the best way to create the right atmosphere for Anglo-Boer relations under the new Treaty; but it was good politics.

The endless debates on the existence of the suzerainty thus began, and were soon bedevilling and contributing towards the worsening relationships with Kruger's Republic. Derby was to leave office, in June 1885, with the matter still smouldering. It continued, in this state, until the Jameson Raid, the '*Uitlander* Crisis', and the advent of Chamberlain at the Colonial Office, when it really began to burn. It was Chamberlain who took up the matter in an energetic fashion, and added new trimmings and supports to Derby's argument of old.[1] Speaking in October 1899, after the Anglo-Boer War had begun, Chamberlain added a new dimension to the complexity of the suzerainty debate, by claiming that 'although the particular word was never used after 1884 . . . it was never renounced'.[2] Indeed he was prepared to state emphatically that, 'no Secretary of State for the Colonies, from Lord Kimberley in 1881, down to myself . . . has ever stated, or, as I believe, has ever thought, that either the suzerainty was abolished or that the name of suzerainty had been abolished'.[3]

Chamberlain also produced a novel and even more oblique explanation as to why the suzerainty had not been included in the London Convention. It was, he explained, all due to the

[1] This is excellently expounded by *Marais*, pp. 195–200.
[2] Chamberlain, *Collected Speeches*, II, 30–35.   [3] Idem.

fact that the suzerainty had originally been included in the Preamble to the Pretoria Convention. In Chamberlain's eyes this Preamble to the earlier convention was not revoked by the later treaty: thus it still stood.

> The second Convention had nothing to do with the preamble; the second Convention substituted articles by which the suzerainty was limited. *The preamble remaining, it was not necessary to put that preamble once more in the Convention* . . . there is no reason for putting it in. It does not follow that because you did not put it in in 1884 that you therefore repealed it in 1884.[1]

This is extremely dubious reasoning. The logic is very strange—and under close examination, Chamberlain's (and Derby's) whole case, simply falls apart.

When the matter was raised just before the Jameson Raid, Lord Loch—Sir Hercules Robinson's successor—had put the 'Boer side' in a common-sense statement: '. . . the Government of the South African Republic were under the impression that the suzerainty had been abolished [by the London Convention], and that impression has been very generally held throughout South Africa.'[2] This view was substantiated by Milner, who had the pluck, or audacity, to write to Chamberlain in 1897: 'The Convention is *such a wretched instrument* that even an impartial Court would be likely to give such an interpretation to it as would render it perfectly worthless to us.'[3] Privately Chamberlain had to admit this was true. 'This is a useful letter', he minuted on Milner's despatch.[4] 'I agree with every word of it.'

Much the same attitude was taken by the law officers under W. H. Smith who, in 1894, had been asked to give an 'unofficial ruling' on the matter. They came to the obvious conclusion that the London Convention 'contains no express reservations of the Queen's right of suzerainty'.[5] They also looked into the question of how and why the phrase was omitted, and concluded with an air of finality that,

[1] *Hansard*, Commons, 19 October 1899.
[2] Loch to Ripon, 2 July 1894. Quoted in *Marais*, pp. 196–7.
[3] Ibid., Milner to Chamberlain, 11 May 1897. Quoted in *Marais*, p. 196.
[4] Idem.
[5] B. A. Imperial White Books, vol. 50. no. 470. Law Officers to C.O., 3 July 1894. Quoted in *Marais*, p. 197.

On the whole, having regard to the negotiations which preceded the London Convention of 1884, the construction of that document itself and the subsequent attitude of Her Majesty's Government towards the Republic, we are of opinion that the suzerainty has been abandoned.[1]

The crux of the matter is therefore whether the London Convention did indeed replace the Pretoria Convention—whether it was a 'new treaty' between the two contrasting parties, or whether it was merely amending the earlier agreement—and thus whether the vital Preamble in the first Convention could still be said to be in force. There is no need to go to a law officer's report for the answer to this vital question. The answer is to be found in the first few paragraphs of the London Convention itself.

On the question of the Preamble alone Chamberlain's argument will not wash, for the London Convention has its own Preamble. Further, it is this Preamble which states emphatically that this was a 'new Convention', and one which replaced the Pretoria Convention. Derby, it seems, was not quite adroit enough. Not only does the document demolish his and Chamberlain's claims, but so too do the Colonial Office files. The actual working document, on which Derby and permanent officials had prepared for the Deputation's demands, is still there to consult.[2] It consists of a printed copy of the Pretoria Convention, on which Derby, in his own hand, has scratched out, in thick black ink, those clauses which he was prepared to see abolished and excluded from the new Convention. And he has struck out the whole of the Preamble.

Clearly it was intended that a new Preamble would be written for the new Convention; which is exactly what did happen. The old Preamble, like the clauses about the Resident, the debt, the control of internal affairs, were all done away with by the London Convention. If Derby hoped to deceive he did not cover his tracks very well, for the document in the Colonial Office files can leave no doubt as to his intentions.

It is strange that this matter has so long remained one of the debatable historical controversies of South African and colonial

[1] Idem.

[2] C.O. 291/26 (Misc.). Printed copy of Pretoria Convention, with deletions by Derby.

433

history, for as long ago as 1903 John Morley, in his remarkable biography of Gladstone, had obviously seen this specific document, for he commented in a footnote:

> I do not desire to multiply points of controversy but the ill-starred raising of the ghost of suzerainty in 1897–99 calls for a twofold remark, that the preamble was struck out by Lord Derby's own hand, and that alike when Lord Knutsford and Lord Ripon were at the colonial office, answers were given in the House of Commons practically admitting that no claim of suzerainty could be put forward.[1]

There the matter is best left. All that remains to be asked is why Derby, and later Chamberlain, went to such lengths to give substance to so implausible an argument. Milner, in his clear prose, has left the best answer:

> I don't suppose the word [suzerainty] matters much to us, so long as we have got the substance, and that the President [Kruger] does not deny, inasmuch as he acknowledges more explicit than I expected, the restriction upon his treaty-making power. This is, since the unfortunate substitution of the 1884 for the 1881 Convention, the strongest hold we have upon the Transvaal, and inadequate as it is, there is no doubt of its importance. . . .'[2]

In the last resort it all devolves upon the fact that the London Convention was a major concession to the Boers. In Salisbury's words, 'a Treaty of concession by which we are to go back—and back apparently under considerable pressure—from stipulations which we have already attained'. Even Derby, its architect, and Kimberley, its defender, had to admit that it contained 'large concessions' to the Boers; but concessions which had of necessity to be granted, in order that further conflict in southern Africa should be avoided.

In short, the price of peace with the Boers, was going up, just as the imperial options in southern Africa were going down. If the pendulum had come to rest at a point of balance in 1881, it had now moved in the direction of Kruger's Republic. He had not gained everything he had asked for; but there was not much that was denied to him. In like fashion, the style of Anglo-Boer

[1] Morley, *Gladstone*, III, 45, footnote 1.
[2] C. Headlam, *The Milner Papers*, 2 vols. (1931–33), I, 88. Quoted in full in *Marais*, pp. 199–200.

relations for the next decade had been set. The existence and the recognition of the New Republic, the Boer drift into Swaziland, Kruger's drive for the sea with an independent rail-line, and the growing Transvaal–German friendship, all testified to the fact that Britain had not so much abandoned her hold over the Republic, as at Sand River, but that the Republic had steadily taken its independence, despite the aims and wishes of the imperial authorities.

If the Victorians increasingly found the world a harder place in which to live and to dominate, it was not merely because of imperial aspirations on the part of other 'Great Powers' of Europe, it was equally as a result of local events in Britain's own colonies and areas of interest. Southern Africa was one classic illustration of this new dilemma of the 1880s, just as Ireland was another in the same decade. Local national revolt had begun to work at the bonds of Empire.

A TERRIBLE THREAT!

MR. W. E. G.—"LOOK HERE, MY CHRISTIAN FRIEND. YOU'VE THREATENED TO HORSEWHIP OUR FORCES; YOU'VE VIOLATED OUR TREATY; YOU'VE MARCHED INTO STELLALAND; AND YOU'VE PULLED DOWN OUR FLAG. A LITTLE MORE,—AND—AND—YOU'LL ROUSE THE *BRITISH LION!!*"

. The Boers, in violation of the Transvaal Convention, sent lawless bands into Bechuanaland, which was under British protection, to harass the country, and openly defied the authority of Great Britain.

VIII

CHAMBERLAIN AND THE LIBERAL CABINET 'GO JINGO'?

Despatching an Imperial Expedition, 1885

IN essence the story was complete. Kruger had led his nation from rebellion to independent self-government; from being a British colony to regaining and rejoicing in its old title, if not exactly its old status, as the 'South African Republic'.

The major Gladstonian impact on Anglo-Afrikaner relations was over. For the remainder of this second Gladstone administration the prime British concern with southern Africa centred on a quite separate matter, the problem of accommodating Bismarck's nebulous desires at Angra Pequena. In this Kruger, and the Boers, played little or no part. German aspirations to the interior of South Africa resided in the minds and fears of the Victorians alone. Prussia had no desire to bring the troublesome Boers, and their millions of native subjects, under German administrative control. Equally Kruger made no real attempt to link up with the Germans, a factor which decisively influenced Bismarck's attitude to the Boer-dominated interior.

But there was one aspect of this period, February 1884 to June 1885, which did involve Gladstone and Kruger: the Warren expedition and the annexation of Bechuanaland. If it is a minor, and separate theme of that relationship, it remains an interesting thread of that story which cannot simply be left as a loose end.

Moreover, it provides an intriguing perspective on the London Convention. It illustrates, in a prophetic manner, the stresses which that treaty was later to undergo; and it demonstrates the nature of the frictions, and strained relations, that were finally to lead, in 1899, to the outbreak of full-scale war between Britain and the Boers.

1. Convention and consequences, 1884–85

The London Convention was born amid great hopes. It was to herald a new era in Anglo-Boer relations. In fact it was ultimately no more than a variation on a mid-Victorian theme: a belief that the best Boer was a Boer who was neither seen nor heard. Having tried both poles of the possible range of options, direct administrative rule of the Boers and abandonment of the self-willed republicans in the interior, the Victorians had come profoundly to prefer the latter course. Edward Fairfield captured a long-felt official opinion when he minuted: 'The policy embodied in the Sand River Convention gave us 25 years of peace and freedom. We abandoned it, and we have been ever since in a horrid mess. We shall no doubt revert to it again some day, and be once more at rest.'[1] But, like all 'good old days', they could neither be reproduced, nor could the analogy be taken completely into the 1880s. However, the London Convention formed a determined effort to return to those apparently halcyon days.

Perhaps here lay the rub; and the explanation for the swift and inglorious violation and disregard for the newly-signed Convention. The Gladstonians were now attempting to be mid-Victorians, to behave as if the options were still the same; to deceive themselves into believing that neither the local situation, nor the international scene, had altered since the days of Russell and Palmerston.

They might have succeeded had it not been for the impossible conditions created by the legacy of half a century of vacillating policy towards the already dissident Boers. The attempt to make independent, yet collaborating, allies of the republican Boers was almost certain to fail. The record of the previous administration's relations with the Afrikaners simply let the Gladstonians down. The Boers had been totally alienated by 1881, perhaps even by 1877.

A policy which based itself exclusively on the informal con-

[1] C.O. 417/6. Minute by Fairfield, 27 July 1885.

trol and the moral suasion of a High Commissioner at the Cape, was likely to be challenged, or at least exploited, by a nation which respected force alone. Now, since Majuba, even that aspect of the imperial presence in southern Africa no longer instilled fear or respect in Boer minds.

Clearly, the London Convention, for all its good intentions was in for a hazardous life.

The month of February 1884, when the Convention was signed, is therefore significant for more than merely that document. In the same manner as February 1881 had ushered in a new approach to the republican Boers, and to the Afrikaner in general, so now February 1884 came in retrospect to be seen as the point of departure for yet another 'South African Policy'.

Having placed their faith in a revised Convention approach, with the emphasis on conciliation and withdrawal, the Gladstonians found that local African events were cutting at the very basis of this approach, making withdrawal impossible and intervention highly dangerous.

The imperial power was to twist this way, then that, to avoid the dreaded possibility of being 'lured back into Africa'; but, in the end, they had to succumb to the realities of the African situation. The Warren expedition, of late 1884, was apparent admission that Gladstone's Convention policy had been suspended; that the Boers had taken 'informal control' to mean that 'informal violation' was permissible; and that the Gladstonians were forced to present a policy which did not exclude the possibility of challenging Kruger's frontiersmen with military force, with all the dangers which that implied.

Yet, the year 1884–85—which formed the remainder of the life of this Gladstone government—witnessed the steady erosion of British influence and standing in southern Africa among the predominant Afrikaners, mainly as a result of the interplay of local and imperial rivalries. In particular this meant two activities. First, Bismarck's move on South-West Africa, at Angra Pequena, in mid-1884; and second, 'Boer imperialism', which took the form of a renewed drive for agricultural and grazing lands on the borders of the 'South African Republic'.

Taken together these local challenges, to Britain's position in southern Africa, forced Gladstone to re-enter the region with a so-called 'expansionist policy'.

2. *Rescue and retire? Britain and the Tswana chiefs, February– October 1884*

Gloom had descended on No. 10 Downing Street. 'Events in S. Africa present a very disagreeable appearance,' Hamilton recorded in his Journal in the autumn of 1884.[1] 'The Boers are getting boorish beyond measure. Not content with making raids into Zululand, they are encroaching onto Bechuanaland . . . and it looks as though we shall be obliged to assert ourselves in that land.'

The background to this bleak position was as intriguing as the decisions which flowed from this period were to be vital to the imperial presence in southern Africa.

The summer of 1884 had seen several important, if isolated events, taking place deep in the interior of Africa which were markedly to effect the nature of policy in the autumn, when Derby, and the Cabinet, as a whole, were again forced to review the nature of the British approach to the Boers.[2] The most important of these local events had been the ignominious 'failure' on the part of the newly appointed Deputy-Commissioner to Bechuanaland, John Mackenzie, to implement the London Convention. Yet he can hardly be blamed for his failure. The ten policemen with whom he was provided were a laughable gesture in the face of the ferocity of the 'freebooter' forces, who now roamed the Tswana lands at will.[3] His failure had also been aided and abetted by a new and sinister 'Cabal' at the Cape, formed about Rhodes, and including Jan Hofmeyr and Sir Hercules Robinson.[4] Together they had undermined his posi-

---

[1] Addit. MSS. 48637, f. 92 (Hamilton Diary). Entry for 24 September 1884.

[2] The best account of these events is to be found in J. A. I. Agar-Hamilton, *The Road to the North*, pp. 278–362. The most recent study is by Aké Holmberg, *African tribes and European agencies* (Gothenburg, 1966), pp. 89–130.

[3] John Mackenzie has left his own account of his 'failure'; and it makes interesting, if poignant reading. *Austral Africa, Losing it or ruling it*, 2 vols. (London, 1887), I, 350 ff.

[4] Hofmeyr, pp. 250–57, for a not unfair account of Hofmeyr's thinking on Bechuanaland.

tion, until there was no honourable course left to Mackenzie beyond resignation.[1]

On Mackenzie's return to the Cape[2] Robinson had sent Rhodes, his new-found ally, up to the area. Rhodes, the sensible man, the man with the Afrikaner contacts, the man who could accomplish anything 'on the personal', the man who had advised Gordon to 'square the Mahdi' with gold, would succeed where the earnest missionary had failed. In fact, Rhodes' failure was even greater than was Mackenzie's.[3] Admittedly he secured an agreement, signed on 8 September, with the freebooter republic of Stellaland; but it was hardly a treaty.[4] It was closer to a large-scale concession, a 'sell-out'. Where Mackenzie was prepared to recognise land claims by white settlers, after a Land Commission had investigated all their claims, Rhodes simply recognised all and any claims to the lands.[5] No wonder he was so popular in Stellaland!

From Stellaland Rhodes headed north to Goshen. But here not even the promise of a similar, and liberal agreement, would entice the freebooters to acknowledge Cape overlordship. They still hoped for yet more land from yet more fleeing Tswana. The magic of Rhodes' sophistry could not win the Goshenites over, and he had to return to the Cape, his life literally in danger the longer he stayed in the area.[6]

Kruger watched these events with interest. Indeed, with the eye of the opportunist, he quickly detected a situation which could be exploited to his own advantage. The *Volksraad* had ratified the Convention after several hostile and begrudging speeches. The limited eastern frontier, the major feature of the Convention, had not met with the happiest of receptions; and the younger frontier Boers had already begun to erode that frontier.[7]

The question which now faced Kruger was this: dare he now

[1] C.O. 417/1. Mackenzie's resignation, enclosed in Robinson to Derby, 19 August, 1884.
[2] *Parl. Pap.*, 1884, LVII, C.4213, pp. 11–13. Robinson to Mackenzie, (Tel.), 25 July 1884.
[3] See Lockhart and Woodhouse, *Rhodes*, pp. 97–105.
[4] *Parl. Pap.*, 1884–85, LVIII, C.4213, p. 65. Robinson to Derby, 11 September 1884.
[5] Idem.   [6] Lockhart and Woodhouse, *Rhodes*, pp. 97–105.
[7] Agar-Hamilton, *The Road to the North*, pp. 300–62.

take the opportunity to acquire on the *veld* that which he had been denied in London? He would gain the long-desired land of the Hertz River valley for the Transvaal; and, more import-ant yet, he would surely thus lift his own esteem among the younger Boers by his open support of their marauding into Bechuanaland.[1]

Kruger was tempted to act. As he pondered on the advan-tages of swift action he was greatly influenced by the Rev. S. J. du Toit, the founder of the *Bond* at the Cape, now Kruger's Minister of Education, a close confidant and a member of the London Deputation. Where Kruger's patriotism extended no further than the Transvaal, du Toit's concepts of patriotism and nationalism extended considerably further than the 'South African Republic'. Indeed, du Toit's make-up consisted of two elements; a passionate anti-English feeling, and a belief in the need for a pan-Afrikaner nationalism for all South Africa.

It was du Toit who now urged Kruger to act; to defy the British authorities, the British boundaries, and the 'British Con-vention'. He was successful. On 16 September 1884 du Toit had Kruger issue a 'provisional proclamation', taking Goshen into the Transvaal's protection 'in the interests of humanity'.[2] This brought the Tswana chiefs Moswete and Montshiwa into the Transvaal, or as Kruger put it, placed them under 'the protection and control of the Government of the South African Republic',[3] an embrace calculated to protect them against everything but their enemies.

This was a flagrant breach of the Convention—'simply the annexation by the Transvaal of about one half of the British Protectorate',[4] as Robinson put it—and a defiant gesture seem-ingly aimed at tempting Britain to 'assert herself', as Hamilton had gloomily prophesied.

Gladstone, too, had been watching these events. His irrita-tion at the Boer behaviour was heightened by the fact that it coincided with a most awkward series of difficulties which pressed in on his administration from other areas of the Empire.

[1] D. W. Kruger, *Paul Kruger*, II, 66–7.
[2] C.O. 417/1. 'Provisional Proclamation' of 16 September 1884, enclosed in Robinson to Derby (Tel.), 17 September 1884.
[3] Ibid., see also *Parl. Pap.*, 1884–85, LVII, C.4213, pp. 83–4.
[4] Ibid., Robinson to Derby (Tel.), 17 September 1884.

It was as if 1881 was repeating itself; except that this time it was not so much Ireland and Afghanistan which plagued him, as Egypt and Germany, with Kruger's Boers added in each case for full measure. In Egypt Gladstone had not only committed his administration to becoming an 'Egyptian Government' but, far worse, he had as already noted despatched 'Chinese' Gordon, to the Sudan on a 'rescue and retire' mission. Now Gordon refused to 'retire', and would himself have to be 'rescued'. Clearly he could not be allowed to enjoy his martyrdom: a large expedition would have to be sent.

It was a most unwelcome complication, coming as it did just at the moment when the Gladstonian Cabinet was anxiously watching Bismarck's sporadic burst of imperial fervour on the west coast of Africa. This too indirectly made Gladstone's Egyptian dilemma that much deeper, for it drew in an extraneous factor in balancing the options to policy over the eastern Mediterranean. Bismarck noticed Gladstone's difficulties, and like the superb politician that he was, he exploited the position without mercy.

Within Britain Gladstone also had his troubles. The Reform Bill had run up against the apparently immovable weight of Lord Salisbury. After fourteen committee-stage sittings the Franchise Bill had gone to the Lords in late June. 'The great question now is "what will the Lords do?"'[1] Gladstone soon knew. 'The Franchise Bill is stopped by the Lords a second time, and a crisis arises', Hamilton jotted in his Diary on 25 September 1884.[2] 'Harcourt is for [the Government] resigning. . . . The idea of resignation rather takes Mr. G.; but not so that of a creation of Peers.' Gladstone seriously considered going to the country over the issue; and of forcing a head-on clash with the Lords. In the end a compromise was agreed upon, which took the form of a Redistribution Bill, largely created by Dilke and Chamberlain, which was immediately to follow upon the Reform Bill itself.[3]

This solved the immediate crisis; but it could not cure the general crisis of confidence in the Government that was arising. This was not the result of a single isolated event, or the actions

[1] Addit. MSS. 48636, f. 134 (Hamilton Diary). Remark by Gladstone to Hamilton, on 25 June 1884.
[2] Ibid., ff. 95–6.   [3] Ensor, *England 1870–1914*, pp. 87–90.

"WAIT TILL THE CLOUDS ROLL BY!"

*** Mr. Gladstone, burdened with complications at home and abroad, and troubled with ill-health, was resting and recruiting at Hawarden. The advice here tendered him was the title of a song popular at the time.

444

of a single foolish man. It was, rather, the cumulative effect of the series of crises and reverses which had struck this Cabinet since its earliest days: of Fenians, Irish parliamentary obstruction, Phoenix Park murders, ineffective Coercion Acts, and ailing Land Acts; of Egyptian involvement, Cairo riots, Hicks Pasha's disaster, Gordon's behaviour;[1] of Bismarck's successful diplomacy and imperial policy in North and South Africa;[2] of Colley's folly at Majuba, Boer breaches of the Convention, and now of Kruger's 'provisional proclamation'.

All these matters tended to lower the stock of the Government; and they tended to suggest that if Gladstone himself was not at fault, then his ministers certainly were. There had already been one major Cabinet reshuffle, in December 1882. In the autumn of 1884 Gladstone was coming round to the same idea again. He had, at last, seen that Rosebery could be of great use on matters where he not only knew most, but was needed most, foreign and colonial affairs. But, how to get him into the Cabinet? Clearly neither Derby nor Granville could be stood down. The answer seemed to lie in retiring the aged Lord Carlingford. But the old man refused to go: he failed to respond to hints, and then ignored open requests from Gladstone. The collective brains of Granville, Spencer, Harcourt and Childers, at a specially convened meeting, failed to find an answer.[3] As Hamilton jibed: Lord Carlingford's 'skin will be discovered by his biographer (if he has one) to be made of buffalo hide'.[4] Gladstone was less amused and more angry. 'Carlingford's behaviour is extraordinary,' he confided in Hamilton,[5] 'What the deuce shall I do?'

That exasperated remark, indeed, neatly captured the difficult Gladstonian position in September–October 1884. The immediate and long-standing problems were numerous; the immediate, and permanent, answers were few. Nothing was simple; everything was hedged about by imponderables. Problems interlocked and exacerbated each other, just as the answers

[1] *Africa and the Victorians*, pp. 122–60.
[2] Hamilton's Diary is very good on this. Addit. MSS. 48636, f. 134.
[3] Addit. MSS. 48636, ff. 116–17. Special meeting, in Gladstone's rooms at the Commons, on 7 October 1884.
[4] Ibid., f. 91. Entry for 24 September 1884.
[5] Ibid., f. 120. Entry for 8 October 1884.

to those troubles, expressed in official policy, were deeply scored by the fact that crises could not be handled in isolation. Difficulties in the colonial sphere are the best examples; and Derby's position *vis-à-vis* Bechuanaland, an excellent illustration, in detail, of this. His refusal to act over the Tswana chiefs, the sheer inertia of his approach was, and has been, heavily criticised. His behaviour is characterised as the classic example of indolence taken to the extreme position. 'Lord Derby is hopeless—he is dreadful',[1] a senior Colonial Office official cried in late 1884.

Consider Derby's position though by now. As a result of the Egyptian involvement it was clear that the Cabinet would not approve of an expensive 'forward policy' in South Africa, which would involve protecting the new London Convention by rescuing the Tswana chiefs from the Boers, most likely via the creation of a Bechuanaland colony. Derby was thus being asked to accomplish the impossible: to restore peace and order to the frontier regions of southern Africa and to defend the Convention without the resort to arms, or the despatch of flag-bearing proconsuls.

That was one aspect of the manner in which his options to policy were reduced. But there were also other strictures on his actions; in fact, both his hands were tied. As shown above since the Transvaal War of 1881, the ministry was most reluctant to move against the Boers, in case it should rouse the Cape and Free State Dutch, thus provoking the unwelcome spectacle of a highly expensive, and probably extended, southern Africa-wide war, against the Afrikaners.

It would seem that to see Derby in isolation, from the rest of the Cabinet, and from the other Gladstonian concerns, is to misjudge the position. This becomes all the more apparent if the months of September and October (1884) are considered. Once Bismarck and Kruger had launched their series of local annexations then Derby was on a sounder footing. He could, and did, take the matter to Cabinet level,[2] with a clearly defined policy, set out in a lengthy confidential memorandum.[3] Just what the

---

[1] Remark by Sir Robert Meade to Hamilton (in Hamilton Diary). Ibid., ff. 100–104. Entry for 30 September 1884.

[2] Addit. MSS. 44645, ff. 179–90 (Cabinet Papers).

[3] C.O. 879/22. no. 287. Confidential Prints. Dated 30 September 1884.

policy entailed, and how Derby came to advocate a more strident policy can be understood only by reference to the Cabinets of that October.

At the vital Cabinet of Monday, 6 October 1884,[1] it was decided, after some debate, to call Kruger's bluff, by forcing him to withdraw his 'provisional proclamation'; and also, to consider what steps should be taken to enforce the terms, and boundaries of the recently signed, much abused London Convention.

This was a crucial decision; a calculated move towards an apparently more 'forward policy'; and a clear indication that the Gladstonians had wearied of accepting Kruger's bombast.

How and why had this come about? Had the Gladstonians put aside their fears of rousing the Cape Dutch? Had they disregarded expense, and their other commitments, in taking up this strong stance?

At first sight it would appear to be so. Sir Hercules Robinson had, since mid-1884, been forwarding lucid, yet alarming despatches, reporting the extent of Boer violation of the Convention via infiltration and activity in the Bechuanaland protectorate.[2] These despatches, which were circulated to all Cabinet members, left a sharp impression. Apart from painting a vivid picture of a defied Convention and of anarchy in Bechuanaland, Robinson also assured Derby, and the Colonial Office, that the Cape politicians were coming to be tired of the Transvaal behaviour. The Cape Dutch, said Robinson, felt that Kruger had gone too far this time in annexing Goshen. The Cape–Transvaal links of sympathy were not only pulled taut with strain, in Robinson's eyes, but they were beginning to pull apart. Unrest in the interior also meant a fall in Cape trade, up the 'Road to the North', and this too cut at Cape feelings for the Boers of Kruger's Republic. In support of his claims, Robinson pointed to a series of public meetings at the Cape all calling for prompt imperial action against the Transvaal's 'freebooters'.[3]

---

[1] Addit. MSS. 44645, f. 179 (Cabinet Papers). Meeting of 6 October 1884.
[2] Derby Papers, Trunk X.24. Robinson to Derby; numerous private letters, September–October, 1884. See also C.O. 417/2, Robinson to Derby; letters and telegrams, 23 September–6 October 1884. Notably Robinson to Derby, 23 September 1884 (Tel.)
[3] Ibid., See also *Parl. Pap.*, 1884–85, LVII, C.4213, p. 78.

Robinson was taken seriously in Britain. There was no reason to disbelieve him. He was noted for his caution; his experience; his administrative ability; his knowledge of the South African Dutch. It is therefore not surprising that the information contained in his despatches came variously to move individual ministers and officials to action. The significant factor to note, though, is the point that previously, in early 1882, he had said much the same thing, but had not moved anyone to action. Why the change?

The answer is complex; the final reason is unclear. Three factors seem significant. The first is a point already referred to: the weak standing of the Government in the public eye. Kruger's latest and most flagrant breach of the Convention was hard to ignore without further risk to the administration's waning popularity. The second pointer concerns the herculean activities of a single man, John Mackenzie. He had returned to Britain and was conducting his most successful public tour. It may not have changed the minds of officialdom overnight; but more important, it had drawn attention to the plight of the Tswana chiefs, just when Gladstone least wanted such a harsh light focused on this region of acute embarrassment for the Government. Robinson's diligent, and full despatches, gave Mackenzie's campaign the stamp of sober truth, just as Mackenzie's actions placed the Tswana dilemma in the forefront of Government anxieties. The third, and perhaps major, element that must be considered concerns Bismarck's sudden and almost quixotic bid for colonies, not only in Africa, but also in the Pacific. While few if any of his acquisitions in mid-1884 can honestly be said to have threatened British security abroad,[1] it was the manner of his actions that rankled, just as it was the very uncertain nature of where he would 'strike' next, that produced fears in official circles out of all proportion to his actual aims.

Taken together these three factors made a single point: dare Gladstone continue to talk in terms of 'reform and retrench-

[1] For example, I decline to believe that by his taking the Cameroons, British trade in West Africa was dramatically undermined; or that by his taking Angra Pequena, the British hold over South Africa was immediately in grave danger. Gladstone knew what he was about, and he took the Bismarckian moves in his stride.

ment' when his Government—and when the Press and a vociferous 'public opinion' would rather have substituted the words 'British nation'—were having continually to eat humble pie, in the form of rebuffs and effronteries being handed out by traditionally powerful nations, such as Germany, and equally, traditionally weak nations, like Kruger's Republic.[1] In a sense, the Gladstonians were forced round to the opinion that 'something' had to be done. The real question was not 'whether' any action should be taken, but rather 'what' action, and 'where?'

In considering this salient point certain ministers were not slow to express themselves. Hartington had, for some time, been arguing for a more forceful Egyptian policy, which implied greater involvement and greater expenditure.[2] In this stance he was supported by the majority of the other Whigs in the Cabinet; and, by a rather unusual ally, Joseph Chamberlain.

This period is an intriguing one for the change that came about in 'Joe's' political philosophy, as regards the Empire. A year previously, in the Commons debates of spring 1883, he had found every reason possible for arguing against the extension of imperial rule in southern Africa.[3] Bismarck's actions changed all this. Chamberlain shared Hartington's concern for the fate of imperial security abroad; Bismarck's moves, especially in the Cameroons and Angra Pequena, left Chamberlain angry, and passionately in favour of a strong colonial policy in the face of the Prussian challenge.[4]

Thus it is not surprising to find that it was Chamberlain who wrote the most influential 'Memorandum'[5] concerning the despatch of an expedition to save the Tswana chiefs; to show Kruger that his actions would no longer be tolerated; and thus indirectly to boost Britain's standing, not only in Africa, but in Europe as well—not to mention the effect which it might have on an apathetic if not hostile Press and electorate.

In retrospect Chamberlain firmly claimed to have been the

[1] Addit. MSS. 48636, f. 104 (Hamilton Diary). Entry for 30 September 1884.

[2] *Africa and the Victorians*, pp. 122–60.

[3] *Hansard*, CCLXXVIII, cols. 232–47. (Commons, 13 April 1883.)

[4] J. C. Papers, 'A Political Memoir', including the Memorandum of 1 October 1884.

[5] Ibid. Printed in full in C. H. D. Howard's edited version of the 'Memoir', pp. 105–7.

sole instigator of the Warren expedition,[1] which duly expelled the Transvaal from Tswana lands in early 1885. Clearly this is true only up to a point. As has already been pointed out, without Robinson's factual reports Chamberlain could not have written his important 'Memorandum'; and without Mackenzie's labours the Tswana dilemma might have been pushed into the background in favour of more 'prestigious crises'.

Equally, it should be noted that Chamberlain was not alone in advocating imperial action in southern Africa. Indeed two other extremely important documents were placed before the Cabinet of 6 October. The Colonial Office submitted a lengthy 'Confidential Print',[2] drafted by Herbert at Derby's instigation, and which said much the same things as did Chamberlain's memorandum, although Chamberlain claimed to find it unsatisfactory.[3] To the modern reader they are remarkably alike, although admittedly, Chamberlain's product had a 'fire and verve' lacking in the official presentation. The important fact remains that Chamberlain was preaching to the converted. Consider those already in favour of 'some' action before the Cabinet met: Derby, and thus the Gladstonians, who formed the centre of the Cabinet; the Whigs, by the very definition of their stand on imperial affairs elsewhere; and, the majority of the senior Colonial Office personnel.

The originality of Chamberlain's argument begins to fade, just as his claims for his own rôle in the decision begin to fall open to question when those other documents are considered. This becomes even truer when it is found that a third and major document lay on the Cabinet table that day. This lucid and forceful piece of analysis came from the War Office[4]—then presided over by Hartington. It contained strong suggestions for action: immediate despatch of an expedition; immediate demand for Transvaal withdrawal and apologies for the 'Provisional Proclamation'; and even, if thought necessary, immediate suspension of the Cape Constitution![5]—so as to facilitate imperial initiatives against the Boers in the interior.

[1] Idem.
[2] C.O. 879/22, no. 287. Memorandum by Herbert, 29 September 1884.
[3] J. C. Papers, Memorandum of 1 October 1884.
[4] W.O. 33/42, no. 971, Confidential Prints. Dated 1 October 1884. (See Appendix III.)
[5] Ibid., pp. 1–3.

This War Office confidential print took the extreme position, and represented the extreme view, at the important Cabinet of 6 October.[1] It was markedly unsuccessful. What is striking about the other major documents concerned in the decision, and about the Cabinet decision itself, is the tone of moderation that pervaded ministerial thinking in respect of southern Africa. This, in particular, meant being true to their already established beliefs concerning the probable behaviour of the Cape and Free State Dutch in the events of a clash with Kruger's burghers.

How then did the Cabinet reconcile the decision to move against the freebooters, and still take due cognisance of their fears about a pan-Afrikaner front? In the simplest terms, they did so by making all direct imperial action in South Africa dependent upon Cape concurrence. This is an aspect of the Cabinet decision that has hitherto been neglected; yet, in essence, this was the most important aspect of the policy. Indeed the entire policy was made conditional on getting colonial agreement and, if possible, colonial collaboration and participation. The Cabinet made this quite plain in communicating their deliberations to the High Commissioner at the Cape: 'Derby to Robinson (Tel.) 7 October 1884. Her Majesty's Government desire you, *on receiving concurrence of [Cape] Ministers,* to call upon the Government of South African Republic to disallow the recent acts which the South African Republic has assumed jurisdiction over Montsioa, [*sic*] as a violation of the Convention of 1884'.[2]

All things flowed from this brief telegram, and the moment of its despatch. In London the 'Chamberlain group' now really became important: they pressed for the immediate organisation of an expedition, so that it might be sent the moment Robinson replied in the affirmative. They clearly had a complete belief in Robinson's despatches; and, in particular, that Cape opinion genuinely was in favour of such a move against the freebooters. Hartington took personal charge of organising the military side of the expedition;[3] the Cabinet of 31 October fixed the size and

---

[1] Addit. MSS. 44645, f. 179 (Cabinet Papers). Meeting of 6 October 1884.
[2] Addit. MSS. 44645, f. 180. Draft of telegram, Derby to Robinson, 7 October 1884. (My italics.)
[3] *Hansard*, CCXCIII, col. 1655; Commons statement by Hartington, 13 November 1884.

planned the operational extent of the expedition;[1] and, on 11 November, Gladstone and Childers[2] presented the Cabinet[3] with a plan by which the Warren mission, and the Gordon relief expedition, would both be included in the same supplementary estimate, and would thus be voted at the same moment.[4] Ultimately an extra penny was put on the income tax, to compensate for the £2½ million combined budget for the two expeditions.[5]

At the Cape, however, the best laid plans of men and ministers were about to go agley. Having made Cape concurrence the touchstone of the new southern African policy, the Cabinet were soon dismayed to learn, first, of reticence on the part of the Cape ministry symbolically or economically to support the expedition; and, second, growing Cape Dutch restiveness, as rumours of the planned expedition appeared in the colonial Press.[6]

Had Robinson grossly misjudged colonial opinion? Had he, perhaps, deliberately misled the Gladstone government? How severe was Cape Dutch unrest likely to be when the decision was announced? Worst of all, after carefully nurturing the Cape and Free State Dutch since the Majuba débâcle, was Britain finally facing the possibility of a pan-Afrikaner front in southern Africa?

These were the questions which bedevilled the 'official mind' as they awaited the Cape response to the Cabinet decision; and as the year 1884 drew to a close.

There was no immediate or easy answer to the question that worried the Gladstonians. Indeed the concerns of the Victorians only received a series of complex answers with the passing of the months.

On Tuesday, 14 October, Derby received the first of those answers.[7] Cape Dutch opinion had 'exploded' in angry demon-

---

[1] Addit. MSS. 44645, ff. 190–217 (Cabinet Papers).

[2] Addit. MSS. 44547, f. 135. Gladstone to Childers, 5 November 1884.

[3] Addit. MSS. 43938, f. 295 (Dilke Memoir). Only Harcourt disagreed.

[4] Derby Papers, Trunk X.14. Childers to Derby, 8 November 1884.

[5] Addit. MSS. 48638, f. 45 (Hamilton Diary). Entry for Tuesday, 11 November 1884.

[6] *Cape Argus*, 1 November 1884.

[7] Derby Papers, Trunk X.24. Herbert to Derby, 14 October 1884, with enclosures from Robinson.

strations on the Cabinet decision being made public. In London the Colonial Office gave vent to apprehensive feelings;[1] and, from the Cape, Robinson ruefully admitted that opinion had indeed changed since his influential despatches in September.[2]

What was Derby to do? His worst fears had been realised. The Cape Dutch, via Hofmeyr, controlled the Cape ministry, so that it seemed most unlikely that plans for the expedition could go forward. In truth there was very little Derby could do, except wait on the Cape ministry's official reply.

This duly arrived, on 13 October, and complicated the situation yet further.[3] The Cape ministers claimed that affairs in Bechuanaland were intimately connected with the 'welfare of Her Majesty's subjects residing in the [Cape] Colony';[4] and therefore the Cape, its ministers and assembly, should alone settle the question of Bechuana unrest. They proposed to do this, not through a large military expedition, but by sending a small deputation to the area.[5] What this deputation was to do, and how it was to settle the land disputes, and put down the marauding, was left suitably vague. Robinson was not happy with the idea: this was hardly what he had desired in calling for a 'firm stance' over the Convention.[6] But he advised Derby to go along with the Cape approach. Indeed there was little else he could advise.

Gladstone and Derby took a surprisingly moderate and positive approach to the Cape suggestion;[7] they seemed glad that the Cape had put forward an idea which involved a Cape initiative, and which did not involve the imperial power. Gladstone had a deep belief that colonial affairs were best dealt with by the colonists involved. He, and Derby, also always nurtured the hope that perhaps by some modern miracle they could devolve imperial responsibilities on to the Cape, in particular

[1] Ibid., Herbert to Derby (Private), 16 October 1884.
[2] Ibid., Robinson to Derby (Private), 15 October 1884.
[3] C.O. 417/3. Robinson to Derby, 13 October 1884 (Tel.), enclosed in Upington to Robinson, 13 October 1884. See also *Parl. Pap.*, 1884–85, LVII, C.4213, p. 139.
[4] Idem.
[5] The mission was to be led by Sir Thomas Upington, then Cape Premier.
[6] Derby Papers, Trunk X.24. Robinson to Derby (Private), 15 October 1884.
[7] Addit. MSS. 44142, f. 88. Derby to Gladstone, 21 October 1884.

those responsibilities towards the tribes which bordered the Cape.

The rest of the Cabinet were not as easily assured. Some, like Hartington, doubted the motives of the Cape mission in view of the fact that the Cape team was to include a leading member of the Afrikaner *Bond*;[1] but Hartington at least expressed pleasure at the possibility of avoiding heavy expenditure on the expedition, which he felt could perhaps be cancelled. Chamberlain, however, both shared Hartington's doubts and, for that very reason, felt that preparations should continue for the expedition.

The argument swayed to and fro in the Cabinet in the week which followed 13 October. By 21 October one decision had been forced on the Cabinet by Derby:[2] the Cape deputation's mission was to go ahead. The question of an imperial expedition was now heatedly debated; and a compromise solution was agreed upon. On 23 October Derby was able to inform the Lords of the Government decision: the Cape mission was welcomed; the Imperial Government would watch its progress; but, most important, the British Government reserved the right to reject or accept any or all agreements signed by the deputation with the freebooters. In short, the Gladstonians determined to 'remain judges, in the last resort, of what should be done'.[3] In accordance with this, preparations for an imperial expedition were not halted: Derby wanted to make it quite clear that Britain was in earnest. The decision as to whether it would go into action waited upon the activities of the Upington mission.

For the moment the Derby policy appeared to be a happy compromise. British opinion was satisfied; and the Cape also expressed satisfaction. The Upington team departed for Goshen on 4 November.[4] The omens looked good. Clearly the Cape were doing something off their own bat for the first time in a long while; they might even accept financial responsibility for the area. At the same time Kruger's government announced that it was withdrawing its provisional proclamation as a result of Derby's protests.

[1] A reference to J. S. Marais, a noted Cape *Bond* leader. See Davenport, *The Afrikaner Bond*, pp. 90–94.

[2] Addit. MSS. 44142, f. 88. Derby to Gladstone, 21 October 1884.

[3] *Hansard*, CCXCIII, col. 38. (Derby in Lords, 23 October 1884.)

[4] C.O. 417/2. Minute by Fairfield, 26 November 1884.

The signs were misleading. Upington was completely *Bond*-controlled, and was hardly likely to enforce a withdrawal of the Transvaal 'freebooters'.[1] Robinson did not 'anticipate any good from their mission';[2] and on 29 November his prophecy came true. Upington telegraphed the details of a five-point agreement which he had signed with the 'freebooters'.[3] The details are superfluous; the document said one thing alone: freebooter land claims were to be recognised without query. Montshiwa was simply to lose the majority of his land.

Upington had played right into the hands of the Chamberlain group, who demanded the immediate despatch of the imperial expedition before it was too late. Derby's hand was forced; he could not go back on his announcement to the Lords. Yet he held back, by instinct, from rushing General Warren[4], (the newly appointed leader of the expedition) out to the Cape for fear of the results among the Cape Dutch.

Robinson came to his rescue. He suggested that Derby accept certain minor aspects of the Upington agreement; and that the expedition be sent to the Cape, but *not* despatched to the interior.[5] Robinson still believed that the freebooters could be 'scared off' the area by the sheer threat of force. He did not think it would come to actual fighting.

Derby clutched at this straw of hope. He took the matter to Cabinet level,[6] for he was not going to be solely responsible for launching an expensive imperial venture that might result in

[1] Ibid., Minute by Bramston, 5 November 1884.

[2] Derby Papers, Trunk X.24. Robinson to Derby (Private), 25 November 1884.

[3] C.O. 417/2. Robinson to Derby (Tel.), 29 November 1884, enclosed in Upington to Robinson (Tel.) of the same day.

[4] WARREN, General Sir Charles (1840–1927). Sandhurst and Woolwich.
1857   Royal Engineers.
1876   To Cape as boundary Commissioner in Griqualand.
1880–84   England, Middle East.
1884–85   Expedition to Bechuanaland.
1886   Commissioner of London Police.
1899   Boer War—blamed for Spion Kop disaster.
1900   Retired to England.

[5] Derby Papers. Trunk X.24. Robinson to Derby (Private), 15 October 1884.

[6] Addit. MSS. 44645, f. 190 (Cabinet Papers), Friday, 31 October 1884, 2 p.m.

the even more expensive Imperial–Afrikaner War.[1] The Cabinet duly took the Robinson view; it appeared to be the only sensible thing to do.

The despatch of an expedition was thus agreed upon.[2] Warren was to get to the area post-haste. He was given his instructions:[3] he was to expel all freebooters from the area; to reinstate Tswana tribes who had been dispossessed of their land; he was to restore general law and order; and he was to hold the area until its final future had been decided upon.

Warren duly arrived in Cape Town in early December.[4] He spent a month organising the expedition; and then set off to face the 'freebooter republics'. As the expedition disappeared into the interior of Africa there can have been few members of the Gladstone government who felt either secure in the probable outcome of the mission, or entirely satisfied with the decision itself. Gladstone spoke for all when he called upon Derby to keep a 'steadfast eye' on the progress of Sir Charles Warren dangerously close to the Transvaal border.[5]

3. Failure: Extending the Empire (January–March, 1885)

Warren's first act in Cape Town foreshadowed the events to come. He committed a bizarre mistake. On the advice of those 'terrible-twins' of Cape politics—Rhodes and Robinson—he sent an immediate telegram[6] to van Niekerk in Stellaland, in which he pledged himself, in advance, to accept the Rhodes settlement of September 1883.[7] The enormity of the mistake was only to strike him when he enquired on reaching Stellaland

[1] P.R.O. 30/29/120. Derby to Granville, 16 December 1884.

[2] Derby Papers, Trunk X.24. Derby to Hartington, 25 October 1884.

[3] C.O. 417/3. C.O. to General Warren, 10 November 1884. See also *Parl. Pap.*, 1884–85, LV, C.4227, pp. 4–5.

[4] Derby Papers, Trunk X.24. Robinson to Derby (Private), 10 December 1884.

[5] Addit. MSS. 44547, f. 138. Gladstone to Derby (Private), 17 November 1884.

[6] *Parl. Pap.*, 1884–85, LVII, C.4275, pp. 70–71. Warren to Niekerk, 6 December 1884.

[7] C.O. 879/22. Derby to Robinson, 3 January 1885, approving Warren's telegram of 6 December 1884.

as to what the Rhodes settlement really implied. Then, of course, Warren could not find reasons enough to repudiate his original telegram—to the amusement of the freebooters, and to the very great annoyance of the Rhodes–Robinson team.

As the expedition began so it continued. There was a sense of unreality about it. In the Cape it was suitably dubbed 'a bloomin' Lord Mayor's show';[1] and not without reason. Over 5,000 heavily armed men rode about scarcely populated areas, in a huge dusty column, establishing fortified supply lines, setting up military bases, and digging deep and immaculately constructed water wells, some of which are still in use today. The 'enemy' were nowhere to be seen. The majority of the freebooters had simply withdrawn into the Transvaal, awaiting Warren's departure, when they determined to slip back to their lands. Yet more enterprising were those freebooters who, on hearing of the Warren expedition, immediately proceeded south to Kimberley, and hired themselves out, at huge profits, as transport contractors to the expedition.[2] There was a certain amount of wry humour expressed in the Transvaal when the news came from the frontier that the Warren expedition included many of the 'freebooters' themselves.

Warren's behaviour throughout was bizarre. The kindest thing to say would be that he got 'the jitters'. He became convinced that, (a) the Transvaal administration was attempting to have him assassinated; (b) that there was a pan-Afrikaner conspiracy to ambush and annihilate his entire expedition; and (c) that the Cape *Bond*, in the guise of the Cape ministry, was implicated in this conspiracy. At one stage he reported the gathering of a large body of 'commandos', in the Free State, preparing to attack him. The Free State President asked only that he be told exactly where these men were, and he would deal with them. Warren detected irony in the request and refused to reply.[3]

Yet more serious than his fears were his quarrels.[4] It did not

---

[1] The best account of the Warren expedition is to be found in J. A. I. Agar-Hamilton, *The Road to the North*, pp. 394 ff.

[2] De Kiewiet, *Imperial Factor*, pp. 324–8.

[3] *Parl. Pap.*, 1884–85, LVII, C.4432, pp. 52–3. Warren to Robinson and vice versa (Tel.), 20 February 1885.

[4] They even reached Cabinet ears. See Addit. MSS. 44142, f. 122.

take him long to alienate the Cape ministry;[1] and, in quick succession, he found reasons to fiercely disagree with Kruger, Rhodes, and Robinson.[2] He had but one ally, John Mackenzie, who replaced Rhodes as Warren's advisor, in March 1885;[3] and who hoped, via Warren, to secure British annexation and protection of theTswana tribes.

What the Colonial Office saw occurring, to their annoyance was this: the creation of two rival sets of alliances, which threatened to complicate matters yet further. On the one hand there was the Rhodes–Robinson alliance arguing for Cape involvement in any settlement of the area,[4] which implied an escape from imperial responsibilities in Bechuanaland—but which equally promised a bleak future for the Tswana chiefs, if Rhodes' previous settlement was anything to go by.

On the other hand, there was the new friendship and alliance of Warren and Mackenzie.[5] This promised to be kind to the chiefs and expensive to the Treasury. The Union Jacks were not there for nothing in Warren's baggage; equally, John Mackenzie, who had laboured so long and so relentlessly for the Tswana people, was determined not to let this opportunity slip through his hands.

Derby, the Cabinet, and the Colonial Office, were thus faced with a clear choice between Robinson and Warren, which now symbolically represented the clear choice in policy. In propounding their new policy the Gladstonians played true to form. Their natural instincts were to support Robinson, and the policy of Cape co-operation, which he represented. But the choice was complicated by the very logic which had led to the despatch of the Warren expedition.

A compromise solution was struck, in true Gladstonian style. There was to be annexation, as a gesture to the Tswana chiefs; but it was to be a limited annexation, up to the Molopo River alone. It was intended to be a short-term addition to the Empire; and which Derby earnestly hoped could be transferred to the Cape, at the earliest possible date.[6]

[1] Ibid., pp. 22–4. Warren to Cape Ministry (Tels.), February 1885.
[2] Ibid., p. 52.   [3] W. D. Mackenzie, *Life of Mackenzie*, p. 381.
[4] Addit. MSS. 44142, f. 122. Derby to Gladstone, 1 April 1885, setting out the two alternative policies.
[5] Idem.   [6] Addit. MSS. 44142, f. 122. Derby to Gladstone, 1 April 1885.

Warren and Mackenzie took this decision and action to be a striking victory for their approach. Warren indeed saw it as a vote of confidence in himself, and a firm support for his belligerent tones used against the freebooters in general, and Kruger in particular, at their '14 Streams' meeting in mid-January.[1]

In fact Warren was singularly wide of the truth. Derby felt he had gone as far as he could in satisfying the needs of the Tswana chiefs. His immediate and long-term aims were now to support Rhodes and Robinson, in getting the Cape to co-operate by taking the region into the colonial fold.[2] Derby's limited annexation policy committed the imperial power to the hands of the dubious politics of Rhodes and Robinson; and it committed Britain to the recall of Warren as soon as possible.[3] For as Fairfield put it, 'Sir Charles Warren is now the principal obstacle to [Cape] annexation.'[4]

4. Further failure: Cape reticence to carry imperial burdens, April–October 1885

The further settlement of the problem turned on one matter alone: 'The real question', Hamilton jotted in his Journal on 17th April,[5] 'is whether Imperial control or Colonial annexation is wanted.' Derby was in no doubt where his own preference lay. He informed Robinson that his prime concern was 'to ensure' Cape co-operation.[6] Any measure that would work against such a partnership over settling the Tswana problem he found 'very undesirable'.[7]

Policy thus acquired a two-point aim: Derby was to see to the recall of Warren, in such a manner as not to produce critical

[1] *Parl. Pap.*, 1884–85, LVII, C.4432, pp. 19 ff. Points of disagreement enumerated on pp. 26–33.

[2] Addit. MSS. 44545, f. 3 (L.B. copy). Gladstone to Derby, 17 April 1885.

[3] Derby Papers, Trunk X.24. Robinson to Derby (with Derby's notes thereon), 24 March 1885; and shown to Gladstone.

[4] C.O. 417/5. Minute by Fairfield, 24 June 1885.

[5] Addit. MSS. 48630, f. 13 (Hamilton Diary). Entry for 17 April 1885.

[6] *Parl. Pap.*, 1884–85, LVIII, C.4432, p. 57. Derby to Warren (Tel.), 21 March 1885.

[7] Ibid., (Tel.), Derby to Robinson, 21 March 1885.

remarks from the Press and the Opposition; Robinson was to work closely with Rhodes, and the Cape ministry, to gain their assistance.[1] Derby succeeded eminently well in his own task. On 16 May he secured Cabinet approval for the recall of Warren;[2] and a carefully worded statement was issued praising Sir Charles Warren's work, stating that this work was now complete, and calling on Warren to make preparations to wind-up the expedition.[3]

So far so good. Derby now looked to Robinson to accomplish his task in the Cape. The solution there was neither so quick nor the position so pliable. The handling of local ministries had never been an easy task in self-governing colonies. The Cape was no exception. Robinson began to prepare the Colonial Secretary for bad news. He suggested that there was 'no prospect' of the Cape taking the area over that year, 1885.[4] The Cape ministry, and assembly, had not forgotten the trials of administering large tribal areas, and were now well pleased to have eased Basutoland back into imperial trusteeship. Equally, they had not forgotten their treatment, at the hands of the British Colonial and Foreign Offices, in the recent débâcle over Angra Pequena, when their claim had been put aside, in favour of letting Bismarck and the German trading companies into the area.

Derby's hopes were not so much destroyed as simply ignored. The Cape ministry did not close the door on the idea; but they refused to be hustled into a hasty decision to please the British Government, now that Britain wished to ease herself out of a difficult situation. It seemed that 'collaborators' could be as difficult as enemies.

Derby left office in June 1885, when the Gladstone ministry fell; and it was the incoming Salisbury administration which had to continue the tentative and tantalising negotiations with

---

[1] *Parl. Pap.*, 1884–85, LVII, C.4423, p. 57. Derby to Robinson (Tel.), 21 March 1885.

[2] Addit. MSS. 44642, f. 131 (Cabinet Papers). Meeting of 16 May 1885.

[3] Addit. MSS. 44548, f. 19 (L.B. copy). Gladstone to Derby, 23 May 1885, and *Parl. Pap.*, 1884–85, LVII, C.4432, p. 203. Derby to Robinson, enclosed in Derby to Warren (Tel.), 28 May 1885.

[4] C.O. 417/6. Robinson to Stanley (Tel.), 1 July 1885.

the Cape. Colonel Stanley, the new Colonial Secretary, (and Lord Derby's brother) could see no alternative but to pursue the same tactic: to wait on a Cape response or initiative.

This duly arrived at the Colonial Office[1] soon after Stanley took up his new post. The Cape wished to have their cake and eat it. They would take over the area *if* Britain contributed the cost of its administration (£50,000 p.a.), and if Britain handed over all control of settlement and development in the region to the Cape. Not content with demanding this 'bargain', they added as a rider, that if Britain did not agree to these terms then perhaps the Cape might invite Germany to acquire the Kalahari, and the remainder of the Bechuanaland, up to the Transvaal border.[2]

Stanley was not impressed either with the veiled threat, or with the actual terms of the so-called 'offer'.[3] But it did mean that his options to policy had been reduced yet further. Cape assistance was now ruled out of his calculations. Britain would have to accept the idea of being trustee for Bechuanaland for some while to come. Having accepted this fact the next step was almost inevitable. Having taken the area up to the Molopo River under British sovereignty, it was pointless not to complete the task begun, and so bring all Bechuanaland under the British flag.

By late September 1885, it had been announced that the Salisbury government had created 'British Bechuanaland'[4] (i.e. up to the Molopo) a Crown Colony, and declared the rest a 'Protectorate' (up to 22° S. and across to 20° E.).[5] A full-time Deputy-Commissioner[6] was to be appointed; and a Land Commission[7] was to be established to attempt to unravel the tangle

[1] C.O. 417/6 on 8 July 1885.

[2] *Parl. Pap.*, 1884–85, LVII, C.4588, pp. 31–2. Robinson to Stanley (Tel.), 7 July 1885.

[3] C.O. 417/6. C.O. Minutes, 8 July 1885, on Robinson to Stanley, 7 July 1885.

[4] For the background to the decisions see *Parl. Pap.*, 1884–85, LVIII, C. 4588, p. 106. Robinson to Stanley, 17 July 1885; and pp. 118–19, Stanley to Robinson, 13 August 1885. The best general analysis of the decision is to be found in A. Sillery; *Founding a Protectorate* (1967), p. 58.

[5] See folder map.

[6] C.O. 417/7. Robinson to Stanley, 30 September 1885.

[7] C.O. 417/5. Minute of 20 July 1885.

of claims that abounded, particularly in the area immediately across from the Transvaal border.

The 'Bechuana problem' had ended for the moment; not joyously but inevitably. Britain had acquired the region not because she had 'scrambled' for it, but because no one else, least of all the Cape, was prepared to concern itself with the fate of the Tswana people. Even this analysis directs attention to the wrong motives. John Mackenzie could die a happy man, yet Bechuanaland was not brought into the British Empire for philanthropic and humanitarian reasons; nor really to spite Germany. Rather the motives for annexation are to be found in that complex period of politics, in the autumn of 1884, when the Gladstonians were casting about for techniques to restore confidence in the declining stock of a dying ministry.

It was an object lesson in the latent dangers of becoming involved in colonial issues for the sake of home politics; and it was a lesson which, if the Gladstonians were looking for comfort, was to be pressed on Bismarck with yet more far-reaching and consequential results.

5. Some reflections on the period 1884–85

A few concluding thoughts suggest themselves. The first concerns the fact that, yet again, the local situation, and the local politicians, had triumphed. The Cape Dutch by their restiveness in 1881 had forced the Gladstone government to an unpopular, and what the critics termed an untimely, peace after Majuba. Now, in 1885, the same Cape Dutch, by their very default of action, by their ungracious refusal to consider easing the imperial burden, had forced the Gladstonians to accept Bechuanaland as a British responsibility, contrary to all the G.O.M.'s instincts and principles.

British umbrage over the Cape's attitude was severe. Having pledged themselves to a policy of defending the Convention—by saving the chiefs and assuring Cape trade to the north—Britain had arrived at a situation in which the Cape declined to see the reciprocal nature of an unspoken loyalty and allegiance to the 'mother country'; and in which Britain was left facing a perpetual administrative bill for a country which she neither wanted, nor really cared about. The Cape, for whom the area was of some importance, pretended not to be concerned. The final irony was that, of all the interested parties—the Cape, the Transvaal, Germany and Britain—the one who wanted the region least was to have to administer it for over three-quarters of a century.

The taking of Bechuanaland was also at odds with the mainstream of British policy in southern Africa: an attempt, via various ingenious techniques, to *escape* from direct responsibility for the internal security and well-being of the colonies and republics. Ignoring for a moment the acquisition of Bechuanaland and the renewed responsibility for Basutoland, this is very largely what the Gladstone government had aimed for and accomplished. They had attempted to devolve the major responsibilities of local government on to local assemblies. The London Convention, with its stress on internal independence for the Transvaal, had been an integral part of this pattern. Federation, which had been pursued for a troubled decade by various British ministries, had offered as its great promise the possibilities of escaping from southern African responsibilities. South Africa had not been federated by the Gladstone ministry; but it was largely self-governing, and even the one colony which was not, Natal, was clearly destined for this status in the near future. Federation may not have come about, but to a large degree its basic aims had been fulfilled.

One crucial and unwelcome complication clouded the happy moment though. While Britain had wished to see southern Africa self-governing they had never envisaged handing over this vital region of the Empire to Afrikaner-dominated ministers. But this is what happened. From the *Bond* at the Cape, to the Boer republican administrations of the Orange Free State and the Transvaal, the Afrikaner held sway.

Britain accepted the position, but reluctantly, even anxiously. Gladstone had referred to these 'dirty Boers' whom one could not trust; the Colonial Office in Whitehall had found the Afrikaners 'sly'; while the Press continued to see the southern African Dutch in terms of the Irish situation, so that Hofmeyr could be greeted in London with cries of 'Fenian' and 'rebel'.

In southern Africa the Victorians had however at last found their collaborating ministries; ministries which would secure imperial strategic bases yet accept the financial responsibility for the peace of the interior. But, they were Afrikaner-dominated ministries. As with so much else connected with the Victorian imperial presence in southern Africa, everything was at odds. Even when they succeeded they found they had failed.

IX

CONCLUSION: GLADSTONIAN LIBERALISM AND AFRIKANER 'NATIONALISM'

I

THE second Gladstone government was dead. It had at last shaken itself to pieces. In June 1885 it went out, not so much with a bang as with a whimper: Hartington and Rosebery did not even bother to attend the last Cabinet—they went to the races to watch the Derby. It was a bizarre finale to the great administration. But then it had not been a 'normal' government. It was exceptional for the personalities that it encompassed: the last true Liberal–Gladstonian government before the Home Rule débâcle destroyed the Party, and certainly the last 'Whiggish' administration. Yet it was also more than that. It was exceptional for the range, complexity, and ferocity of the crises which it had to weather.

Ireland alone was enough to sink a competent team; yet the Gladstonian problems had hardly ended here. There were Boers as well as Fenians to countenance; there were Egyptian and Sudanese entanglements to be manipulated; there were Anglo-French and Anglo-Prussian rifts to be faced; there were struggles for India in Afghanistan, and struggles for the 'dark continent', both along the coasts and within the interior of Africa.

These multifarious difficulties were remarkable not only for their extent and ferocity, but most of all for their timing. They were not so much consecutive as parallel in their incidence. They tended to interlock, so that both in the autumn and winter of 1881–82 and 1883–84, Gladstone faced simultaneously rebellious Fenians and insurgent Boers. This interlocking

465

of crises—not merely Ireland with South Africa, but also ultimately Egypt with India, Bismarck with the Mahdi—came to shape not just the behaviour of the Cabinet, but the very nature of the policy which that Cabinet compounded.

2

Policy, in the crucial imperial area of southern Africa, was knocked off course by both these prevailing and destructive trends which had biased Cabinet decision—viz. by the insurgence of simultaneous nationalist revolt, and by the pressures of European rivalry, most notably in the form of the Bismarckian challenge to the Victorians.

In 1880 Gladstone could still look to federation as a viable option to solve the problem of maintaining British dominance in South Africa. By 1886 not only was federation merely a moribund concept, but South Africa itself had changed so radically in the minds of the Victorians as to make a new approach to the Boers and colonists absolutely imperative.

What had brought about this revolution in attitude in the 'official mind'? In the simplest terms it had been the Gladstonians reading of opinion and events in South Africa consequent upon the Transvaal War of 1880–81. They had come to accept, as Chamberlain put it, 'that at the time of the retrocession we were within a few weeks of a general uprising of the Dutch population'.[1] This war, the Gladstonians were convinced had reunited Cape Dutch and Republican *trekkers*—for the first time since the *trekker* exodus of the late 1830s.' Are you not aware', Gladstone asked the Commons in 1883, 'that a strong feeling of sympathy passes from one end of the South African settlement to the other, among the entire Dutch population?'[2] The G.O.M. was to express this yet more clearly and forcibly when he later reflected on the nature of his Government's troubled relations with South Africa:

It is essential to a sound policy in South Africa that you should weigh your relations to those people. If it were the fact that there was an outlying handful of those people . . . that would be one thing, but it is not so. If there is one thing [that] comes out more

[1] *Hansard*, CCLXXVIII, cols. 232–47. (Commons, 13 April 1883.)
[2] Ibid., CCLXXVII cols. 721–2.

than another in the history of recent years it is that *the Dutch popu-lation is, in the main, one in sentiment throughout South Africa, from the Cape to the northern border of the Transvaal;* and that in dealing with one portion of it you cannot exclude from view your relations to the whole.[1]

Here, then, was the essence of the Gladstonian approach: a recognition of the fact that Britain must squarely face the question of how to create firm Anglo-Afrikaner ties for the future; and acknowledging that unless by some miracle the English colonists completely swamped the Afrikaner numerically, it was with those Afrikaners that the Imperial Government would have to conduct relations. In Gladstone's words: 'We are not entitled to speak either with contempt or with disrespect of the Dutch portion, which is the majority of the South African popu-lation.'[2]

The steady growth of the Afrikaner *Bond* at the Cape, and indeed throughout South Africa in these crucial years 1880–85, merely confirmed the growing political consciousness of the Afrikaners as a people. Sir Hercules Robinson had already, in 1883, written of a time when the Cape would have its first Cape Dutch-dominated ministry. This had soon taken place—though Hofmeyr preferred to have puppets, like Upington, leading the administration, while he stood in the shadows pulling the strings. Thus it became abundantly clear to the Gladstonians that what was happening before them was the rise of the Afrikaner to political power. By late 1885 Afrikaner-dominated ministries were indeed in charge of affairs from Cape Town to the Limpopo.

In plain and practical terms this meant that it was no longer possible to 'divide and rule' in South Africa. It had been safe in the halcyon days of mid-century to cast the *trekkers* to the mercy of the wilds of the interior, in the knowledge that the Cape remained doggedly loyal; and that the English-speaking minority in the Cape continued to take a disdainful view of their republican counterparts to the north. If Britain should chal-lenge the Boers—as she did in 1843 by annexing Natal, in 1868 by annexing the diamond fields and Basutoland, and even more directly in 1877 by annexing the Transvaal itself—then Britain could do so secure in the knowledge that the imperial base at

[1] Ibid., cols. 729–30.   [2] Idem.

the Cape was in no danger. Indeed the colonists appeared to be more royalist than the monarch.

Now all that had changed. The vital Cape, and its loyalty, was more than suspect. Evelyn Ashley reflected gloomily that if it came to a showdown with the Boers in another war 'the Dutch at the Cape and in the Orange Free State should join those . . . who had sprung from the same race, and spoke the same tongue'.[1]

Even in the period before 1885 this factor came crucially to bias the nature of policy by drastically reducing the options open to the Victorians. To take but two clear examples. Kimberley was attacked in the Lords for not doing more for the native tribes faced by Boer aggression. His reply was very much to the point: 'The difficulty of this country was that in dealing with South Africa on a Native question, *we had not the sympathies of the white population*. This prevented Her Majesty's Government from carrying into effect the policy which they naturally desired.'[2] In Kimberley's terms the margins of initiative for policy had been sharply narrowed. Either Britain 'must hold down South Africa by force', and risk a general Anglo-Afrikaner war, 'or else we must acquiesce in a great many things being done in those colonies which the majority of the people in this country do not approve.'[3]

Lord Derby, who had not been in the Cabinet for the years 1880–82, came independently to the same conclusion during his own tenure at the Colonial Office, in the years 1883–85. He was accused of permitting the existence of the 'robber republics' of Goshen and Stellaland, by not moving against the Transvaal, from where most of the freebooters originated. Derby admitted that he had been inactive; but he also claimed that his hands were tied. He reminded Parliament that it was not only the Transvaal Boers who were involved, for the freebooters had the 'very general support of the Dutch population . . . not only in the Transvaal but throughout South Africa, where we know a considerable majority of the white population are of Dutch descent, and the sympathies of that population are, I am afraid, all in one direction'.[4]

[1] Ibid., col. 439.
[2] Ibid., col. 339. (Kimberley in Lords, 13 March 1883.) (My italics.)
[3] Idem.   [4] Ibid., cols. 325–6.

This was an opinion soon be taken by the British Press, and best editorialised by the *Pall Mall Gazette*, in a leading article in 1883, on the latent dangers of an Anglo-Boer confrontation:

> The influence of the Dutch race, as Mr. Gladstone says, has not diminished but is still the dominant influence in South Africa. English statesmen will be slow to commit themselves to a policy that will bring us into sharper and sharper antagonism with this race. . . .[1]

This refusal to face the challenge of the Afrikaner head-on became the touchstone of the new policy. Kimberley's initial loss of nerve during the Majuba campaign—his desire to make a swift if not inglorious peace—had expressed itself in a more conciliatory approach to the Afrikaner. And it was now this new approach which had become ever more attractive and acceptable in the eyes of the Victorians. A new-found faith in informal paramountcy—to maintain the overlordship in southern Africa—and a profound belief in the values of conciliation—to retain and nurture the loyalty of the Cape Afrikaners, if not of the republican Boers—these became the new supports for policy.

It was seen to be a pragmatic approach in every sense. Not only did it appear to be the only viable policy (viable, that is, apart from another resort to arms), in the face of what the Victorians took to be a growing national consciousness among the Afrikaners, but it was also a course of action suggested by the experience gained by the Gladstone government in handling that other intractable problem, Irish nationalism. It was not without significance, or consequence, that the Boer dilemma was faced concurrently with the Fenian outbreaks. In both cases the margin for initiative appeared to be reduced by the month, so that the Gladstonians were forced to ask: was coercion anything more than a short-term remedy for a long-term dilemma?

In each case the G.O.M. came to see in coercion nothing but greater mischief for the future; and in conciliation the only hope for that future. In his eyes a conciliatory policy towards the Boers was far more likely to 'solve' the South African problem than a resort to coercive measures administered by the military.

[1] *Pall Mall Gazette*, Saturday, 17 March 1883.

"HERE WE ARE AGAIN!!!"

. The Government, unexpectedly defeated on an amendment to the Address, bringing in the question of agricultural relief, resigned, and Mr. Gladstone was summoned to form a Ministry.

In short, before the technique was taken to the Irish, it had already by 1885 been decided to attempt to kill the problem of the Afrikaner by kindness. For as Lord Derby could remark, 'We do not want another Ireland in South Africa.'[1]

3

Kindness through strength? or through weakness? Surely the latter. The Gladstonian emphasis on conciliation was an expression not merely of the G.O.M.'s morality taken to imperial questions, but rather more of a symptom of the Victorian condition in the mid-1880s. The technique of 'Home Rule' was the Gladstonian answer.

Just as there had been challenges to imperial might within the Empire itself, from Irish and Afrikaner dissidents, so there were equally serious challenges to the Victorians from outside their Empire, challenges which they found difficult first to comprehend, then later to counterbalance. The most important concerned the rise of Bismarckian Germany—first in the 1870s to grasp the supremacy in Europe, then in the next decade to rival Britain's hitherto isolated dominance in Africa. This resurgence of Prussia, coupled with the Anglo-French rift over Egypt, the Russian infiltration of Afghanistan, and the vacuum of power in the Levant, all tended to make the world a harder place for the Victorians to dominate, or manipulate.

Suddenly it became necessary, in the African case, to embark on an unprecedented scramble for further colonial possessions—'to keep what we have', as Derby explained. In their desire to maintain the old prerogatives and suasion, the Victorians had had to adopt new, formal and expensive methods of Empire. Their gains in the African scramble reflected a desire to be 'over-insured' rather than 'under-insured' should there be further challenges to the British world position.

But, of course, it was insurance at a price; a very high price indeed. The scramble left the Victorians not so much unassailable as over-extended. This tended to have the most practical and salutary effect on policy: it magnified each and every dilemma of Empire. The threat of an Afrikaner insurrection became more than an isolated local challenge when placed

[1] *Hansard*, CCLXXVII, col. 330. (Derby in Lords, 13 March 1883.)

alongside the demands and dangers of the German, Russian, Indian and Irish situations. The extent of the Empire now meant weakness not strength. The insuperable problem of attempting coercive and military action on more than one front at the same time not only bedevilled policy, it haunted those whose job it was to formulate policy.

4

The second Gladstone administration was, in sum, the victim of two parallel 'revolutions'. First, a revolution in the nature of the Victorian standing in the world; and second, the corollary of this, the inevitable overthrow and discarding of policies formulated in an era when Britain was thought to rule the waves. The supposition, of unlimited strength to face unlimited problems, was dead. Coercive policies would have implied having to police the whole of this extended Empire. This was now no longer feasible, even if desirable.

Kruger's challenge could thus not have been better timed, coming as it did in conjunction with other multifarious imperial troubles. Nor could it have been better expressed, being presented in the form of a pan-Afrikaner threat, involving both Cape and Transvaal Dutch.

It is hardly surprising therefore that British policy swung on its axis, moving away from the more militant options to those involving attempts at finding and cementing new bonds of co-operation and collaboration, as the bulwarks for the new Empire. In the South African case this meant specifically nurturing the Cape in the hope of weaning it away from its new allegiances with the Boers; and of placing faith in local politicians who could embrace both the imperial and Cape colonial cause. In other words, working in unison with men like the young Rhodes, and his tentative Hofmeyr alliance, in the hope that such a policy, would provide a stable pivotal point for the imperial presence in southern Africa.

The whole Gladstonian approach is indeed a salutary warning to those historians who would claim that it was but with the coming of gold on the Witwatersrand, in 1886, that Britain was seriously challenged for the dominance of South Africa.

In fact, if there is one lesson made by this Gladstone government, it is that Britain had already by 1886 lost the initiative to influence local events at will in southern Africa, to the Afrikaner, to Kruger's republicans and Hofmeyr's 'Bondsmen'. The days when a High Commissioner could dismiss a Cape ministry at his own discretion were gone. Equally, gone were the days when Britain could simply annex the Transvaal at will, and fear no more than a few isolated protest meetings out on the *veld*. As Sir Hercules Robinson was to put it forcibly, when retiring after his extended tour of duty as Cape Governor and High Commissioner in 1889:

> There are three competing influences at work in South Africa. They are Colonialism, Republicanism and Imperialism. As to the last, it is a diminishing quantity, *there being no longer any permanent place in the future of South Africa for direct Imperial rule on any large scale* . . . all the Imperial Government can now do is, by means of spheres of influence, protectorates and Crown Colonies, to gradually prepare the way for handing territories over to the Cape and Natal, so soon as such transfers can be made with justice to the natives and advantage to all concerned.[1]

The war of ten years later, in 1899, was to involve the seminal issue of supremacy in South Africa. It was an issue left unresolved in the years 1880–86; and yet, in retrospect, it can be seen that 1899 was no more than a belated attempt to reassert an imperial supremacy that had been given what was later to prove to be its death-blow, by the series of local events in those early years, of the 1880s. That period when Mr. Gladstone and President Kruger had faced each other, via the battlefield and then the conference table, and when the concept of local 'Afrikaner nationalism' was first introduced as a crucial complicating factor in British policy-making.

5

The Gladstone ministry had resigned its initiative, and formal dominance in southern Africa, in favour of a more 'informal policy' for making friends and winning influence. They had done so as a direct result of their reading of events on the *veld*, and of the behaviour of the Afrikaner in particular. But, it should be asked, had they read the signs correctly?

[1] Annual Register, 1889; Robinson speech, at Cape Town, quoted pp. 407–8.

While it can with justice be claimed that in the years 1880–81 there did exist a common bond of sympathy between Cape Dutch and Republican Boers—which justified the use of the term 'the Afrikaner people', signifying a united language and ethnic group, with sympathetic political aspirations—it is doubtful in the extreme if this 'unity' was anything but temporary. Like a mirage it was produced by the heat of the hour (i.e. the Transvaal War of 1881), and alike a mirage it faded when the political scene moved on cooler levels.

South African historians have been quick to seize on the sudden growth of unity and political consciousness among the Afrikaners in the early 1880s; and they have tended to date modern 'Afrikaner Nationalist South Africa' from this moment. It is an attractive idea, and one which clearly also took hold of the British 'official mind' in the 1880s.

In fact, the record of the behaviour of the Afrikaner in the following decade, sadly lets down both the nationalist apologias, *and* the Victorian Colonial Office officials. The unity of 1881 belonged alone to 1881. The branches of the *Bond* in the Transvaal dwindled away, being tied too closely to Joubert and S. J. du Toit. Kruger also became suspicious of Jan Hofmeyr's ambitions; then, over the Swaziland Convention of the 1890s, openly hostile. In the Cape Hofmeyr continued his oblique approach to power. He dropped his tentative and emotive ties with Kruger and Joubert, and preferred instead to create that remarkable working-alliance with the 'regular beefsteak Englishman' of the Cape—Hofmeyr's description of Cecil Rhodes.

Another major factor must also be borne in mind in considering the break-up of the Cape–Transvaal 'alliance'. Bismarck's intervention in southern Africa, at Angra Pequena in 1884, and his attempted intervention at St. Lucia Bay, was ultimately radically to affect the British position in regard to the Afrikaner. At the Cape Hofmeyr spoke ardently of preferring British to German overlordship; and attended the Imperial Conference of 1887 as a super patriot. In Africa, the tenuous Kruger–Hofmeyr link was broken for all time. 'You are a traitor, a traitor to the Africander [*sic*] cause', Kruger thundered at Hofmeyr.[1] In Britain, Gladstone astutely saw how the German

[1] Quoted in J. H. Hofmeyr, *Life of Hofmeyr*, p. 406.

presence would aid the imperial presence in southern Africa.

> For my part I should be extremely glad to see the Germans become our neighbours in South Africa, or even the neighbour of the Transvaal. We have to remember Chatham's conquest of Canada . . . . which killed dead as mutton our best security for keeping the British Provinces.[1]

Gladstone, though, was alone in this assessment. Other ministers were not as sanguine about Bismarck's actions, or his future plans. Nor did they grasp the lever which this gave them to pressure the Cape Dutch to remain the ever-faithful 'imperial collaborators' in the southern African setting.

Indeed, by 1890, the British position south of the Limpopo was much improved: the Cape–Transvaal rift was as wide as ever, while the gold discoveries had stiffened Kruger's independent spirit, allowing him to swing the Republic away from the Cape's economic orbit, and build his own outlet at Delagoa Bay, with his own customs tariff. The Cape supremacy in southern Africa was over: the British connexion acquired a new meaning and value for Hofmeyr's colony. This became all the more true when Rhodes' great counterpoise to the Rand (Zambesia, or 'Rhodesia' as it came to be called) proved to be as empty of promise, as it was empty of gold.

The legacy of 1881–84, however, proved too potent to be ignored. Victorian policy-makers continued to believe in the dangers of a united Afrikaner people, and of a possible pan-Afrikaner front which could one day deprive the British of their presence in southern Africa. Hofmeyr continued to be treated like a suspect Parnell; while events such as the 'Drifts Crisis' of October 1895—a sad reflection on the transitory Afrikaner unity of 1881[2]—were not enough to allay British suspicions that another 'Majuba situation' could not be recreated.

That the Victorian policy-makers ultimately came to believe

---

[1] Addit. MSS. 44547, f. 151 (L.B. copy). Gladstone to Derby, 21 December 1884.

[2] It does not seem unjust, or fanciful, to suggest that what Professor van Jaarsveld has so admirably described, in his *Ontwaking van Nasionale Bewussyn*, and what Professor Gallagher and Dr. Robinson have taken as a major theme of their *Africa and the Victorians* (notably pp. 53–75, 160–253, 410–61), was no more than a momentary aberration in Afrikaner behaviour in the nineteenth century.

475

in the dangers of a 'pan-Afrikaner movement' there can be little doubt. That they failed to grasp the unique hold which they had over their collaborators, the Cape Dutch, is clear. And equally, that their fears were groundless, and that the Afrikaner unity movement was temporary, there can also be little question. But, of course, the policy-makers were moved as much by the nature of their fears as they were by their reading of the dangers which prompted those fears.

The historian is left with a supreme irony. The Victorians, in a series of calculated gestures, abdicated power to Kruger's Afrikaners in the South African Republic, and accepted an unequal rôle in a partnership of collaboration with Hofmeyr's *Bond* at the Cape, in the face of what was perhaps no more than a mirage, a shadow, a spectre.

BIOGRAPHICAL NOTES

These brief notes are intended to identify the main participants in the narrative, they are not full 'biographical entries'. The figure in brackets after each name refer to the age of the particular character when this narrative begins, in 1880.

ACTON, John Emerich Edward Dalberg (46), 1st Baron 1896; Lib. M.P. 1859–65; Reg. Prof. of Modern History, Cambridge, 1895; Lord Granville's stepson; died 1902.

AMPTHILL, *see* RUSSELL, Lord Odo.

ARABI, Ahmed Arabi el Hussein (41), Pasha; Col. in Egyptian Army; Minister of War 1882; leader of National Movement; defeated at Tel-el-Kebir; exiled to Ceylon until 1904; died 1911.

ARGYLL, George Douglas, (57), 8th Duke; L.P.S. 1880–81; Sec. for India 1868–74; died 1900.

ASHLEY, Anthony Evelyn Melbourne (44), Lib. M.P. 1874–85; Und. Sec. B. of T. 1880–82; Und. Sec. for Colonies 1882–85; died 1907. Very actively concerned at the C.O. with fate of the Zulu people.

BALFOUR, Arthur James (32), Private Sec. to uncle, Lord Salisbury, 1878–80; Pres. Local Govt. Bd. 1885–86; P.M. 1902–6; died 1930.

BARING, Sir Evelyn (39), 1st Viscount Cromer 1892; Baron 1899; Earl 1901; Agent and Con.-Gen., Cairo, 1883–1907, died 1917.

BEACH, Sir Michael Edward Hicks (43), Viscount 1905; Cons. M.P. 1864–1905; Chief Sec. for Ireland 1874–78, 1886–87; frequent critic of Gladstonian colonial policy 1880–85; died 1916.

BEACONSFIELD, (Benjamin Disraeli) (76), Cons. M.P. 1837–75; Chanc. of the Exchequer 1866–68; P.M. 1868, 1874–80; died 1881.

BISMARCK, Fürst Otto Edward Leopold von (65), Prussian minister; Pres. and Min. for Foreign Affairs 1862–71; Chancellor of the German Empire 1871–90; died 1898.

BISMARCK, Fürst Herbert von (31), eldest son of Chancellor; worked in German F.O. 1873–82, 1885–90; in German Embassy, London, 1882–84; special German negotiator with Granville over colonial scramble 1884–85; died 1904.

477

BOWER, Sir Graham John (32), Irish-born son of Admiral; R.N. 1861; Private Sec. to gov. of the Cape 1880; 'imperial sec.' to High Comm. in southern Africa; implicated in Jameson Raid conspiracy 1895; became willing scapegoat for Cape Gov., Sir Hercules Robinson, in Jameson Raid enquiry; 'banished' to Mauritius as Col. Sec. 1897; wrote unpublished 'memoirs' to justify his rôle in Raid affair; retired in 1910 to work for cause of world peace; died, still in some disgrace, 1933.

BRADLAUGH, Charles (47), republican, advocate of birth-control, 'free-thinker'; M.P. 1880–91; not admitted to the House until 1885, on issue of the Oath; destroyed Gladstone legislative plans for the first session of 1880—due to wrangle over the Oath; died 1891.

BRAMSTON, John (48), C.O. official; held various appointments in Queensland and Hong Kong; Asst. Und.-Sec. for Colonies 1876; C.B. 1886; K.C.M.G. 1897; responsible, able man; died 1921.

BRAND, Henry Bouverie William (66), 1st Visc. Hampden 1884; Lib. M.P. 1872–84; Speaker of the H. of C. 1872–84; partly responsible for the failure to avert the Bradlaugh and the Oath issue; died 1892.

BRAND, Sir Johannes Hendricus (57), Afrikaner statesman; born Cape, and educated S.A. College; admitted to British Bar 1849; returned to Cape to become M.P. for Clanwilliam; invited to be Pres. of O.F.S. 1863; lifted it from bankruptcy to 'model republic'; three times Pres.; knighted for 'good behaviour'; aided peace after Majuba 1881; died, much respected, 1888.

BRASSEY, Thomas (44), Baron 1886; Earl 1911; Lib. M.P. 1865–86; a Lord of the Admiralty 1880–84; Sec. to Admiralty 1884–85; died 1918.

BRETT, Reginald Baliol (28), 2nd Visc. Esher 1899; Private Sec. to Lord Hartington 1875–85; Lib. M.P. 1880–85; died 1930.

BRIGHT, John (69), Radical M.P. 1843–89; Pres. B. of T. 1868–70; Chanc. of Duchy of Lancaster 1873–74, 1880–82; broke with Gladstone over forward policy in Egypt; died 1889.

BULWER, Sir Henry Ernest Gascoyne (44), Gov. of Natal 1882–86; High Comm. for Cyprus 1886–92; died 1914. Highly excitable, sometimes alarmist official, disliked by Kimberley and Derby.

CARLINGFORD, Chichester Samuel (57), 1st Baron 1874; Lib. M.P. 1847–74; L.P.S. 1881–85; Lord President of the Council 1883–85; died 1898.

CARNARVON Henry Howard Molyneaux (49), 9th Earl; Col. Sec. 1866–67; 1874–78; strong and effective critic of Liberals on colonial issues 1880–85; died 1890.

CAVENDISH, Lord Frederick Charles (44), 2nd son of 7th Duke of Devonshire; Chief Sec. for Ireland 1882; assassinated in Phoenix Park with his secretary, Burke, by 'Invincibles', with surgical knives.

CETEWAYO, King of all the Zulus 1873–79; source of great anxiety to both British and Boer authorities; broken during Zulu War 1878–89; exiled to Cape; restored in 1883; failed to maintain his old rôle as Chief; involved in civil war 1883–84; died (poisoned?) 1884.

CHAMBERLAIN, Joseph (44), made fortune in business; retired to devote himself to politics 1874; Mayor of Birmingham 1873–76; Lib., later (1866) Lib. Unionist M.P. 1876–1906; Pres. B. of T. 1880–85; Pres. Local Govt. Bd. 1886; Col. Sec. 1895–1903; died 1914. Expert on S. Africa.

CHILDERS, Hugh Culling Eardley (53), Lib. M.P. 1859–92; Sec. for War 1880–82; Chanc. of the Exchequer 1882–85; Home Sec. 1886; died 1896. Politician whom Gladstone much overrated.

CHURCHILL, Lord Randolph Spencer (31), Cons. M.P. 1874–94; Sec. for India 1885–85; Chanc. of the Exchequer 1886; brilliant critic of Gladstone administration 1880–85; died 1895.

COLLEY, Sir George Pomeroy (45), Private Sec. to Lord Lytton 1879–80; Gov. of Natal and High Comm. for S.E. Africa 1880–81; responsible for blunder of Majuba; killed by the Boers in battle, 27 February 1881.

CURRIE, Sir Donald (55), ship-owner, financier; Lib. M.P. 1880–86; Lib. Unionist 1886; tried to persuade Gladstone to embark on large-scale annexation in S.E. Africa in 1883–85; died 1909.

DERBY, Edward Henry (54), 15th Earl of Derby; Cons. Col. Sec. 1858; Sec. for India 1858–59; For. Sec. 1866–68, 1874–78; crossed over to Libs. 1882; Col. Sec., December 1882–June 1885; died 1893. Cautious, inclined to inertia. Great influence with Gladstone; perhaps too harshly treated by historians.

DE VILLIERS, Lord, of Wynburg Cape (38), born Cape and educated S.A. College 1853–61; studied law, London and Germany; returned to Cape 1866; elected to Cape Assembly 1867; appointed himself Chief Justice of Cape while Att.-Gen. in Molteno ministry; Pretoria Convention Peace negotiation delegate 1881; chairman of National Convention 1908; 1st Chief Justice of S.A. 1910; died 1914.

DILKE, Sir Charles Wentworth (37), Lib. M.P. 1868–86; For. Und.-Sec. 1880–82; Pres. Local Govt. Bd. 1882–85; ruined by sensational divorce case 1886; died 1911.

DILLON, John (29), Irish Home Ruler; M.P. 1880–1918; arrested by Gladstone administration 1882; released under Kilmainham 'treaty'; died 1927.

DINIZULU, last Zulu king; son of Cetewayo; fought his brother, Usibebu, in civil war 1884; defeated Usibebu with the aid of white volunteers; banished to St. Helena by Britain when he rebelled in 1887; involved in Bambatta Rising after return from exile 1906; banished for life to Transvaal; died 1913.

DODSON, John George (55), 1st Baron Monk Bretton 1884; Lib. M.P. 1857–84; Pres. Local Govt. Bd. 1880–82; Chanc. of Duchy of Lancaster 1882–84; died 1897.

DUFFERIN, Frederick Temple (54), 1st Marquis; Ambassador to St. Petersburg 1879–81; Ambassador to Constantinople 1881–84; Viceroy of India 1884–88; died 1902.

DUNN, John (44) white chief of the Zulus; English born; became game hunter to Zululand in 1853; friend of Cetewayo; accepted by Zulus; given title of chief and many Zulu wives; area of his authority taken over as 'Zulu Reserve' by Britain 1881–84; wrote vivid memoirs; died 1895.

DU TOIT, Rev. S. J. (33), born Cape; ordained minister in Dutch Reformed Church 1874; founded 'Genootskap van Regte Afrikaaners' 1875; launched *Di Patrioot* (1st Afrikaans newspaper); helped to establish *Afrikaner Bond* 1879; Superintendent of Education in Transvaal 1882; accompanied the Transvaal delegation to London Convention 1883–84; returned to Cape and *Di Patrioot* 1889; died 1911.

ESCOTT, Thomas Hay Sweet (36), well-known Victorian journalist; Ed. of *Fortnightly Review* 1879–86; wrote extensively on English society; died 1924.

FAIRFIELD, Edward (32), C.O. official; joined the C.O. 1866; promoted to 2nd-class clerk 1872; 1st-class 1880; C.M.G. 1885; Asst. Und.-Sec. C.O. 1892; C.B. 1895; said to have died of overwork, 1897.

FORSTER, William Edward (62), Lib. M.P. 1861–86; Chief Sec. for Ireland 1880–82; fought Gladstone continually within Cabinet on Irish and Boer issues; died 1886.

FOWLER, Robert Nicholas (52), Cons. M.P. 1868–74, 1880–94; Lord Mayor of London 1883–84; involved with 'South Africa Committee' 1883; died 1891.

FRERE, Sir Henry Bartle Edward (65), Col. Gov.; Gov. of Bombay 1862–67; Comm. to negotiate slave-trade treaty *re* Zanzibar 1872; High Comm. for S.A. and Gov. of Cape 1877–80; launched Zulu War 1879; recalled in disgrace by Gladstone government in 1880; died 1884.

GLADSTONE, William Ewart (71), Jun. Lord of the Treasury,

December 1834; Und.-Sec. for Colonies January–June 1835;
Vice-Pres. B. of T. September 1831; Pres. of B. of T. April 1843;
Col. Sec., December 1845–July 1846; Chanc. of the Exchequer,
December 1852–February 1855, June 1859–June 1866; P.M.
December 1868–74, April 1880–June 1885, February 1886–
August 1886, and August 1892–March 1894; died 1898.
GLADSTONE, Catherine (68), wife to W. E. G.; died 1900.
GLADSTONE, Herbert John (26), Visc. 1910; 4th son of P.M.; Lib.
M.P. 1880–1910; a Lord of the Treasury 1881–85; Gov.-Gen.
of S.A. 1910–14; died 1930.
GODLEY, John Arthur (33), 1st Visc. Kilbracken; Private Sec. to
Gladstone 1872–74, 1880–82; Private Sec. to Granville 1874–80;
died 1932.
GORDON, Arthur (51), 1st Baron Stanmore; 2nd son of Earl of
Aberdeen; Gov. of New Zealand 1880–82; Gov. of Ceylon 1883–
90; died 1912.
GORDON, Charles George, 'Chinese' (47), Royal Engineer 1852;
duty in Crimea and China 1855–56, 1860–65; Sudan 1874–
78; Sec. to Lord Ripon in India 1880; Mauritius 1881–82; S.A.
1882; Palestine 1883; Khartoum 1883–84; died, defying Gladstone and the Mahdi, 1885.
GORST, Sir John Eldon (45), Cons. M.P. 1866–68, 1875–1906;
member of the 4th party 1880–84; died 1916.
GOSCHEN, George Joachim (49), 1st Visc. 1900; Lib., later Lib.-
Unionist M.P. 1863–1900; missions to Egypt (1875), and Constantinople (1880–81); died 1907.
GRANT DUFF, Sir Mountstuart Elphinstone (51), Lib. M.P. 1857–
81; Und.-Sec. for Colonies 1880–81; Gov. of Madras 1881–86;
died 1906.
GRANVILLE, Granville George (65), 2nd Earl; W. E. G.'s closest
friend, adviser, and confidant 1870–86; Col. Sec. in Gladstone's
1st ministry 1868—promoted to For. Sec. on death of Lord Claren-
don 1870; For. Sec. on Gladstone's 2nd ministry 1880–85; Col.
Sec. in 3rd ministry 1886; died 1891. Ill health removed him from
politics (1886).
HAMILTON, Sir Edward Walter (33), Private Sec. to Gladstone
1873–74, 1880–85; died 1908. Left chatty, fascinating diary,
particularly re Mr. Gladstone, whom he worshipped.
HARCOURT, Sir William G. G. Venables (53), Lib., later Ind. M.P.
1868–1904; Sol.-Gen. 1873–74; Home Sec. 1880–85 (wanted to
be Chanc. of the Exchequer); at last made Chanc. of Exchequer
1886 and 1892–95; hoped to lead Liberals on Gladstone's retirement, failed; Rosebery chosen; died 1904.
HARTINGTON, Spencer Compton (47), 8th Duke of Devonshire

1891; Lib. M.P. to 1885; Lib. Unionist M.P. to 1891; Sec. for War 1866, 1882–85 (pressed on Gladstone a stronger policy in Egypt); Sec. for India 1880–82; died 1908.

HEALY, Timothy Michael (25), Irish Home Ruler 1880–1918; Gov.-Gen. of Irish State 1922–28; died 1931.

HEMMING, Augustus William Lawson (39), C.O. official; joined the C.O. 1860; C.M.G. 1885; K.C.M.G. 1890; Gov. of British Guiana 1896; Gov. of Jamaica 1898; G.C.M.G. 1900; the 'imperialist of the Colonial Office'; died 1907.

HERBERT, Sir Robert George Wyndham (49), C.O. official; born England, moved to Australia; Col. Sec. of Queensland 1859; P.M. of Queensland 1860–65; returned to England, joined B. of T. 1868; Asst. Und.-Sec. for Colonies 1870; Und.-Sec. for Colonies 1871–92; died 1905. Cautious, genial man; full of both common sense and strong English patriotism; saw Empire in realistic if positive light.

HICKS, William (50), Pasha; Gen. in Egyptian Army; died 1883.

HILL, Frank Harrison (50), journalist; Lib. sympathies; asst., later Ed. of *Daily News* 1865–86, died 1910.

HOFMEYR, Jan Hendrik (35), 'Onze Jan'; Afrikaner patriot and statesman; born Cape Town and educated S.A. College; acquired unique standing as editor of *Zuid-Afrikaan*, later named *Ons Land*; championed Cape Dutch cause and founded *Farmers' Association* 1870s; united and took control of both *Farmers' Association* and du Toit's *Afrikaner Bond* 1880–82; collaborated closely with Rhodes until Jameson Raid of 1895; struggled to halt Anglo-Boer War, nearly succeeded; helped to draft S.A. Constitution; conveyed Constitution to England 1909, where he died. A noble man: not enough 'force', to achieve his ends.

JORISSEN, Edward Johann Pieter (51), born Holland, moved to Transvaal 1870s; State Att. in S.A.R. 1878; accompanied Kruger to London 1879; took part in peace negotiations after Majuba; judge in S.A.R. 1888–1900; died 1912. One of Kruger's famous Hollander advisers.

JOUBERT, General Petrus Jacobus (49); born Cape, moved to Transvaal and entered *Volksraad*; acting Pres. 1875; opposed British annexation 1877–80; C.-in-C. Boer Forces in Transvaal War 1880–81; signed Pretoria Convention as one of the Triumvirate 1881; very jealous of Kruger, who became Pres., to Joubert's fury in 1883; sponsored *Bond* in the Transvaal hoping to use it against Kruger; failed, but became Vice-Pres. in 1896; appointed C.-in-C. Boer Forces in Natal on outbreak of Boer War; died, March 1900.

KEATE, Robert William (36), barrister, Lincoln's Inn; Lt.-Govr. of

Natal 1867; award on boundary between O.F.S. and S.A.R. 'Keate Award' 1870; selected to arbitrate between S.A.R. and Griqua chiefs, Waterboer and others; made award against republic; retired 1872.

KIMBERLEY, John (54), 3rd Baron; 1st Earl; L.P.S. 1868–70, 1880–82; Col. Sec. 1870–74, 1880–82; Chanc. of Duchy of Lancaster 1882; Sec. for India 1882–85, 1886, 1892–94; Lord Pres. 1892–94; For. Sec. 1894–95. Excitable, garrulous man, who could be sharp and incisive on paper. Better than '3rd class' administrator, as some historians imply.

KOTZE, Sir John Gilbert (31), born Cape, and educated S.A. College and London Univeristy; Inner Temple 1874; went to Cape to practice law 1874; Judge, High Court, Transvaal, 1877; Chief Justice, Transvaal, 1881; fought with Kruger 1897; returned to Cape 1899; Att.-Gen. of Rhodesia 1900; took Silk 1902; puisne judge 1918; died 1940.

KRUGER, Stephanus Johannes (65), born Cape, walked on *trek* as a boy; settled on farm 'Waterkloof', near Rustenburg, Transvaal; became strong protagonist Dopper Sect; present at Sand River meeting 1852; participated in Native wars with great bravery 1850s; worked for union S.A.R. and O.F.S.; backed van Rensburg in 'civil war'; led opposition to British annexation; protest delegation to London 1878–79; leading member of Boer Triumvirate 1881–83; signed Pretoria Convention, and saw it ratified by *Volksraad*; elected Pres. of S.A.R. 1883; headed delegation to London 1883; signed London Convention, February 1884; failed to acquire outlet to the sea at St. Lucia Bay, due to British annexation; gold discoveries on Rand solved all Transvaal financial problems—created immense political problems which Kruger never solved; led nation to war in October 1899; sailed for Europe before Pretoria was captured; died in Switzerland, 10 July 1904.

LABOUCHERE, Henry Dupré (49), Rad. M.P. 1867–68, 1880–1905; Ed. of *Truth* 1876–1905; died 1912.

LANYON, Sir William Owen (38), C.O. official; born Ireland; joined British Army—posted West Indies; saw service in Jamaica Rebellion 1865; administrator of Transvaal 1879; failed to foresee Boer revolt of December 1880; served in Egyptian campaigns 1882, 1884–85;; died of cancer, New York 1887. Was said to have been 'dark skinned' and so immediately disliked by Boers; also imperious and excitable, which aided his alienation from Transvaal populace.

LEFEVRE, George John Shaw- (49), Baron 1906; Lib. M.P. 1865–95; Chief Comm. Bd. of Works 1880–83, 1892–94; P.M.G. 1883–85; died 1928.

BIOGRAPHICAL NOTES

LETSIE, I, Paramount Chief of the Basuto 1870; eldest son of Moshesh; weak leader; much overshadowed by his own son, Lerotholi; succeeded by son 1891.

LEYDS, Dr. Willem Johannes (21), one of Kruger's Hollander advisers; Dutch born in Java, and educated in Holland; met Kruger when deputation in Europe after London Convention negotiations, spring 1884; accepted invitation to become Att.-Gen. in S.A.R. 1888; Boer representative 1899–1902; retired to Holland after Boer War; wrote extensively and misleadingly of Anglo-Boer relations; died 1940.

LOCH, Sir Henry Brougham (53), Baron 1895; C.O. official; Gov. of Victoria 1884–89; Gov. of Cape and High Comm. for S.A. 1889–95; died 1900.

LUDERITZ, Adolf (46), German trader; son of tobacco merchant, carried on father's business; Luderitz to Angra Pequena, September 1883; to his delight Bismarck annexed areas as German colony 1884; Luderitz now tried to press Bismarck to take Pondoland, and St. Lucia Bay, on south-east coast, through the work of August Einwald; lost mysteriously at sea 1886.

M'CARTHY, Justin (50), journalist and popular historian; died 1912.

MACKENZIE, Rev. John (45), missionary and advocate of Tswana people; born Scotland; joined L.M.S. in 1854; went to Kuruman, S.A. 1858; visited Moselikatze on long *trek* in 1863; advocated annex of Bechuanaland; rewarded in 1884 with limited British annexation; fought against grant of land to B.S.A. Co. of Rhodes; red-haired, fiery man, of ability; died 1899.

MAHDI, Mahommed Ahmed ibn Seyyid Abdullah; Sudanese religious leader; surrounded and destroyed Gordon at Khartoum; died shortly after, in strange circumstances.

MALET, Sir Edwin Baldwin (43), diplomat; Sec. of Embassy, Paris, 1867–71; Con.-Gen., Egypt, 1879–83; Ambassador to Berlin 1884–95; died 1908.

MANKURWANE, Chief of Batlapin Tribe; came to prominence in October 1881 with attack of Korannas of David Mosweu; aided by freebooter allies; July 1882 forced to pay price of aid—block of 416 farms which were to be the nucleus of Republic of Stellaland,—taken under British Protection 1884; died 1892.

MEADE, Robert Henry (45), C.O. official; joined F.O. in 1859; Private Sec. to Lord Granville 1864–70; Asst. Und.-Sec. for Colonies 1871; C.B. 1885; Und.-Sec. for Colonies 1892; K.C.M.G. 1894; died 1898.

MERRIMAN, John Xavier (39), born England, moved to Cape 1849; entered politics 1869; in Moteno ministry 1875; Comm. for Crown Lands 1875–78, 1881—84; Treas.-Gen. of Cape 1889–93;

484

member of Cape Jameson Raid enquiry 1896; Cape P.M. 1908–10; member of National Convention 1908–10; became private member of S.A. Parl. 1910; outspoken, conservative-styled politician; died, much respected 1926.

MILNER, Lord Alfred (28), C.O. administrator; born Germany; studied at Tübingen, London and Oxford; journalism 1880s; service in Egypt 1890s; appointed Gov. of Cape 1897; Gov. of Transvaal and O.F.S. 1901, after Boer defeat; reconstruction in Transvaal following war; returned to Britain 1905; joined Lloyd George War Cabinet 1914–18; died 1925.

MOLTENO, Sir John Charles (66), Cape politician; born England, moved to Cape 1831 to work in S.A. library; trader in wool 1837 in Karroo; fought in 'war of the axe'; elected to Cape Parl. 1854; appointed P.M. 1872—strong advocate of responsible government for Cape; dismissed by Sir Bartle Frere 1878; Col. Sec. at Cape 1881–82; died 1886. Known as 'lion of Beaufort'.

MONTSHIWA, Chief of the Barolong; war against Matlabe and Moswete in May 1881 with white freebooter aid; beaten back to Mafeking in October 1882; ceded land to freebooters led by commandant J. P. Snyman—on which republic of Goshen founded, placed under British authority and protection, May 1884; died in Mafeking 1896.

MORIER, Sir Robert Burnett David (54), diplomat; Minister at Lisbon 1876–81, Madrid 1881–85; Ambassador to St. Petersburg 1885–93; died 1893.

MORLEY, John (42), Visc. 1908; journalist and politician; Ed. of *Fortnightly Review* 1876–82; of *Pall Mall Gazette* 1880–83; Radical M.P. 1883–95, 1896–1903; Chief Sec. for Ireland 1886, 1892–95; died 1916. Great biographer of Gladstone and Cobden.

MOSHESH, (?1790–1870), Chief and creator of the Basuto nation; outstanding leader and politician; born northern Basutoland in 1790s; organised refugees from other tribes into a unit at Thaba Bosigo; welcomed French missionaries 1833; fought O.F.S. Boers 1840s—managed to hold them at bay; beat off major attack on Thaba Bosigo 1865; died 1870.

MÜNSTER, George Herbert (60), German diplomat; Ambassador to London 1873–85 and to Paris 1885–1900; died 1902.

NORTHBROOK, Thomas George (53), 2nd Baron 1866; 1st Earl 1876; Lib. M.P. 1857–66; Viceroy of India 1872–76; 1st Lord of the Admiralty 1880–85; died 1904.

NORTHCOTE, Sir Stafford (62), Earl Iddesleigh 1885; Private Sec. to Gladstone 1842–45; Cons. M.P. 1855–85; Leader of the Opposition 1880–85; died 1887.

O'SHEA, Capt. William Henry (40), Irish M.P. 1880–86; inter-

BIOGRAPHICAL NOTES

mediary between Gladstone and Parnell; wife was Parnell's mistress; helped to ruin Parnell by bringing divorce case in 1890; died 1905.

PARNELL, Charles Stewart (34), Irish M.P. 1875–91; Leader of Irish M.P.s in Commons 1880–91; died 1891.

PAUNCEFOTE, Sir Julian (52), Baron 1899; joined C.O. 1874; moved to F.O. 1876; Und.-Sec. F.O. 1882–89; died 1902.

PONSONBY, Sir Henry Frederick (55), Private Sec. to Queen Victoria 1870–95; died of strain and overwork 1895.

POTTER, Thomas Bayley (63), Lib. M.P. 1865–95; died 1898. Well-known member of the Cobden Club.

PRETORIUS, Marthinus Wessel (61), Boer leader; born Cape, walked Great *Trek*; fought Zulus in Natal; became one of four commandant leaders in the Transvaal; elected 1st Pres. of S.A.R. 1857; also elected Pres. of O.F.S 1860; led attack against Moshesh 1865; made wide-sweeping land claims for SAR in Tswana country 1868; resigned as Pres. of S.A.R. 1871; joined Boer forces against Britain 1881; died 1901.

RATHBONE, William (61), Lib. M.P. 1868–95; noted philanthropist; died 1902.

REAY, Donald James (41), 11th Baron; Dutch born; British naturalised 1877; Gov. of Bombay 1885–90; Und.-Sec. for India 1894–95; suggested as British representative to go to S.A. in 1883–84 to negotiate with Boers; Reay not sent; died 1921.

RHODES, Cecil John (27), born Hertfordshire, England, son of a parson; moved to Natal 1870, due to ill health; went to Kimberley to dig for diamonds 1871; took Pass Degree at Oxford 1878; founded De Beers Co. 1880; elected to Cape Parl. for Barkley West 1880; went to Bechuanaland, to make settlement with Stellalanders 1882; treasurer in Cape Ministry 1884; established 'Goldfields Co.' 1887 on Rand; secured mineral rights in Matabeleland; B.S.A. Co. formed to exploit Rhodesia; P.M. of Cape 1890; Jameson Raid 1895; famous 'indaba' in Rhodesia 1896; worked for united S.A.; said there would be no Boer War; 1899–1902 Boer War, beseiged in Kimberley; died 26 March 1902, revered and reviled—still holds that position.

RIPON, George Frederick (53), Marquis 1871; Viceroy of India 1880–84; 1st Lord of the Admiralty 1886; L.P.S. 1905–8; died 1909.

ROBINSON, Sir Hercules George Robert (56), Baron Rosmead 1896; eminent colonial governor, began service in Ireland and West Indies; Gov. of Hong Kong 1859–65; of Ceylon 1865–72; New South Wales 1872–79; New Zealand 1879–80; of Cape, and High Comm. for S.A. 1880–89, 1895–97; died 1897.

486

ROSEBERY, Archibald Philip (33), 5th Earl; Home Und.-Sec. 1881–83; L.P.S. and Comm. for Works 1885; For. Sec. 1886, 1892–94; P.M. 1894–95; died 1929.

RUSSELL, Lord Odo (Lord Ampthill), (51), diplomat; Ambassador to Berlin 1874–84; died 1884.

SALISBURY, Robert (50), 3rd Marquis; For. Sec. 1878–80, 1885–86, 1887–92, 1895–1900; P.M. 1886–92, 1895–1902; died 1903.

SCANLEN, Sir Thomas Charles (46), Cape politician; Cape born; member of legislative council for Cradock 1870–96; P.M. of Cape 1881–84; legal adviser to Rhodes' B.S.A. Co. 1894; acting administrator of Rhodesia 1898, 1903–6; retired 1908; died 1912. Gave the controversial promise to Lord Derby in London in early 1884 respecting Cape annexation of Bechuanaland, which was not redeemed.

SEKUKUNI, Chief of the Bapedi 1861; rebelled and attacked Lydenburg in eastern Transvaal; Pres. Burgess fails to put down rebellion; Sekukuni finally defeated by British troops under Sir Garnet Wolseley; murdered by Mampoer 1882.

SELBORNE, Roundell Palmer (68); Earl 1882; Lib. M.P. 1847–57, 1861–72; Lord Chanc. 1872–74; 1880–85; died 1895. Author of several hymn-books.

SHEPSTONE, Sir Theophilus (63), born England moved to Cape 1820; Sec. for Native Affairs Pietermaritzburg 1856; undertook annexation of S.A.R. 1877; retired 1880; recalled to administer Zululand 1884; died 1893.

SOLOMON, Saul (63), born St. Helena; elected to Cape Assembly 1853; owner of *Cape Argus*; offered premiership—refused; retired to Scotland 1883; tiny, quixotic man—'Disraeli of Cape'—stood on a box when addressing Assembly; often spoke for Native interests.

SPENCER, John Poyntz (45), 5th Earl; Ld.-Lieut. of Ireland 1868–74; 1882–85; Lord Pres. 1880–83; died 1910. Close friend of Gladstone.

STEAD, William Thomas (31), most famous of Victorian journalists; Ed. of *Pall Mall Gazette* 1883; founded *Review of Reviews* 1890; took up cause of new imperialism of Rhodes; author of best personal study of Rhodes; died 1912.

TEWFIK, Pasha (28), Khedive of Egypt 1879–92; died 1892.

VAN NIEKERK, Gerrit Jacobus (40), Boer freebooter; born O.F.S.; joined in intertribal wars in Bechuanaland; supported Mosweu against Mankurwane; founded republic of Stellaland 1883; when Britain annexed area 1884 became Chief of Police in Pretoria; died 1896.

WARREN, General Sir Charles (40), Welsh born; joined Royal

487

Engineers 1857; went to Cape in 1876 on boundary dispute work; fought in putting down Griqualand West Rebellion 1878; returned to S.A. in 1884 to clear freebooters from Bechuanaland and to establish Bechuanaland Protectorate; became Comm. of Metropolitan Police; returned to duty for Boer War; blamed for Spion Kop; died 1927.

WOLFF, Sir Henry Drummond (50), to F.O. in 1849; Cons. M.P. 1874–85; settlement of Egypt 1885–87; died 1908.

WOLSELEY, Sir Garnet Joseph (47), Visc. 1885; Field-Marshal 1894; Red River Expedition 1870; Ashanti War 1872; in Egypt 1882; leader of relief expedition to Gordon in Khartoum 1884–85; C.-in-C. Ireland, 1890–95; C.-in-C. British Army 1895–1900; model for Gilbert and Sullivan's 'modern major general'; died 1913.

WOOD, Sir Henry Evelyn (42), entered R.N. 1852; joined Army 1855; in S.A. 1878–82 during Boer revolt and Zulu War; Sirdar of Egyptian Army 1882–85; died 1918. Sister became Mrs. O'Shea and later Parnell's mistress.

WORMS, Henry (40), Baron de, of Austrian Empire; Cons. M.P., Greenwich, 1880–85; died 1908. Often spoke on colonial matters.

ZOBEIR, Pasha (50), slave-trader; chosen Gov. of Sudan by Khedive; dismissed and banished to Gibraltar 1885–87; died 1913.

APPENDIX I
THE CONVENTION
OF PRETORIA
3 August 1881

CONVENTION FOR THE SETTLEMENT OF THE TRANSVAAL
TERRITORY

Her Majesty's Commissioners for the settlement of the Transvaal territory, duly appointed as such by a Commission passed under the Royal Sign Manual and Signet, bearing date the 5th of April 1881, do hereby undertake and guarantee, on behalf of Her Majesty, that from and after the 8th day of August 1881, complete self-government, subject to the suzerainty of Her Majesty, her heirs and successors, will be accorded to the inhabitants of the Transvaal territory, upon the following terms and conditions, and subject to the following reservations and limitations:

ARTICLE I. The said territory, to be hereinafter called the Transvaal State, will embrace the land lying between the following boundaries, to wit: [Boundaries given here. See folder map.]

II. Her Majesty reserves to herself, her heirs and successors, (*a*) the right from time to time to appoint a British Resident in and for the said State, with such duties and functions as are hereinafter defined; (*b*) the right to move troops through the said State in time of war, or in case of the apprehension of immediate war between the Suzerain Power and any foreign State, or Native tribe in South Africa; and (*c*) the control of the external relations of the said State, including the conclusion of treaties, and the conduct of diplomatic intercourse with foreign powers, such intercourse to be carried on through Her Majesty's diplomatic and consular officers abroad.

489

III. Until altered by the Volksraad or other competent authority, all laws, whether passed before or after the annexation of the Transvaal territory to Her Majesty's dominions, shall, except in so far as they are inconsistent with, or repugnant to, the provisions of this Convention, be and remain in force in the said State, in so far as they shall be applicable thereto: Provided that no future enactment specially affecting the interests of natives shall have any force or effect in the said State without the consent of Her Majesty, her heirs and successors, first had and obtained and signified to the Government of the said State through the British Resident: Provided further that in no case will the repeal or amendment of any laws which have been enacted since the annexation have a retrospective effect so as to invalidate any acts done or liabilities incurred by virtue of such laws.

IV. On the 8th day of August 1881, the Government of the said State, together with all rights and obligations thereto appertaining, and all State property taken over at the time of annexation, save and except munitions of war, will be handed over to Messrs.

Stephanus Johannes Paulus Kruger,
Martinus Wessel Pretorius, and
Petrus Jacobus Joubert,

or the survivor or survivors of them, who will forthwith cause a Volksraad to be elected and convened; and the Volksraad thus elected and convened will decide as to the further administration of the Government of the said State.

V. All sentences passed upon persons who may be convicted of offences contrary to the rules of civilised warfare, committed during the recent hostilities, will be duly carried out, and no alteration or mitigation of such sentences will be made or allowed by the Government of the Transvaal State without Her Majesty's consent, conveyed through the British Resident. In case there shall be any prisoners in any of the gaols of the Transvaal State, whose respective sentences of imprisonment have been remitted in part by Her Majesty's Administrator, or other officer administering the Government, such remission will be recognised and acted upon by the future Government of the said State.

VI. Her Majesty's Government will make due compensation for all losses or damage sustained by reason of such acts as are in the 8th Article hereinafter specified, which may have been committed by Her Majesty's forces during the recent hostilities, except for such losses or damage as may already have been compensated for, and the Government of the Transvaal State will make due compensation for all losses or damage sustained by reason of such acts as are in the 8th Article hereinafter specified, which may have been committed by the people who were in arms against Her Majesty during the recent hostilities, except for such losses or damage as may already have been compensated for.

VII. The decision of all claims for compensation, as in the last preceding article mentioned, will be referred to a Sub-Commission, consisting of the Honourable George Hudson, the Honourable Jacobus Petrus de Wet, and the Honourable John Gilbert Kotze.

In case one or more of such Sub-Commissioners shall be unable or unwilling to act, the remaining Sub-Commissioner or Sub-Commissioners will, after consultation with the Government of the Transvaal State, submit for the approval of Her Majesty's High Commissioner, the names of one or more persons to be appointed by him, to fill the place or places thus vacated.

The decision of the said Sub-Commissioners, or of a majority of of them, will be final.

The said Sub-Commissioners will enter upon and perform their duties with all convenient speed. They will, before taking evidence, or ordering evidence to be taken, in respect of any claim, decide whether such claim can be entertained at all under the rules laid down in the next succeeding article.

In regard to claims which can be so entertained, the Sub-Commissioners will, in the first instance, afford every facility for an amicable arrangement as to the amount payable in respect of any claim, and only in cases in which there is no reasonable ground for believing that an immediate amicable arrangement can be arrived at, will they take evidence, or order evidence to be taken.

For the purpose of taking evidence and reporting thereon, the Sub-Commissioners may appoint deputies, who will without delay submit records of the evidence and their reports to the Sub-Commissioners.

The Sub-Commissioners will arrange their sittings, and the sittings of their deputies, in such a manner as to afford the greatest convenience to the parties concerned and their witnesses. In no case will costs be allowed to either side, other than the actual and reasonable expenses of witnesses whose evidence is certified by the Sub-Commissioners to have been necessary. Interest will not run on the amount of any claim except as is hereinafter provided for.

The said Sub-Commissioners will forthwith, after deciding upon any claim, announce their decision to the Government against which the award is made, and to the claimant.

The amount of remuneration payable to the Sub-Commissioners

and their deputies will be determined by the High Commissioner after all the claims have been decided upon. The British Government and the Government of the Transvaal State will pay proportionate shares of the said remuneration, and of the expenses of the Sub-Commissioners and their deputies, according to the amounts awarded against them respectively.

VIII. For the purpose of distinguishing claims to be accepted from those to be rejected the Sub-Commissioners will be guided by the following rules, viz: Compensation will be allowed for losses or damage sustained by reason of the following acts committed during the recent hostilities, viz.: (a) commandeering, seizure, confiscation, or destruction of property, or damage done to property; (b) violence done or threats used by persons in arms.

In regard to acts under (a), compensation will be allowed for direct losses only.

In regard to acts falling under (b), compensation will be allowed for actual losses of property, or actual injury to the same, proved to have been caused by its enforced abandonment.

No claims for indirect losses, except such as are in this article specially provided for, will be entertained.

No claims which have been handed in to the Secretary of the Royal Commission after the 1st day of July 1881, will be entertained, unless the Sub-Commissioners shall be satisfied that the delay was reasonable.

When claims for loss of property are considered, the Sub-Commissioners will require distinct proof of the existence of the property, and that it neither has reverted, nor will revert to the claimant.

IX. The Government of the Transvaal State will pay and satisfy the amount of every claim awarded against it within one month after the Sub-Commissioners shall have notified their decision to the said Government, and in default of such payment the said Government will pay interest at the rate of six per cent. per annum from the date of such default; but Her Majesty's Government may, at any time before such payment, pay the amount, with interest, if any, to the claimant in satisfaction of his claim, and may add the sum thus paid to any debt which may be due by the Transvaal State to Her Majesty's Government, as hereinafter provided for.

X. The Transvaal State will be liable for the balance of the debts for which the South African Republic was liable at the date of annexation, to wit: the sum of £48,000, in respect of the Cape Commercial Bank Loan, and £85,667, in respect of the Railway Loan, together with the amount due on the 8th August, 1881, on account of the

Orphan Chamber debt, which now stands at £27,226. 15s., which debts will be a first charge upon the revenue of the State. The Transvaal State will moreover be liable for the lawful expenditure lawfully incurred for the necessary expenses of the Province since annexation, to wit, the sum of £265,000., which debt, together with such debts as may be incurred by virtue of the 9th Article, will be a second charge upon the revenues of the State.

xi. The debts due as aforesaid by the Transvaal State to Her Majesty's Government will bear interest at the rate of three and a half per cent., and any portion of such debt as may remain unpaid 8th August 1882, shall be repayable by a payment for interest and Sinking Fund of six pounds and ninepence per £100., shall be . . . payable half-yearly, in British currency, on the 8th February and 8th August in each year: Provided always that the Transvaal State shall pay, in reduction of the said debt, the sum of £100,000, before the 8th August 1882, and shall be at liberty at the close of any half-year to pay off the whole or any portion of the outstanding debt.

xii. All persons holding property in the said State on the 8th day of August 1881 will continue to enjoy the rights of property which they have enjoyed since the Annexation. No person who has remained loyal to Her Majesty during the recent hostilities shall suffer any molestation by reason of his loyalty; or be liable to any criminal prosecution or civil action for any part taken in connexion with such hostilities; and all such persons will have full liberty to reside in the country, with enjoyment of all civil rights, and protection for their persons and property.

xiii. Natives will be allowed to acquire land, but the grant or transfer of such land will in every case be made to, and registered in the name of, the Native Location Commission, hereinafter mentioned, in trust for such natives.

xiv. Natives will be allowed to move as freely within the country as may be consistent with the requirements of public order, and to leave it for the purpose of seeking employment elsewhere, or for other lawful purposes, subject always to the Pass Laws of the said State, as amended by the Legislature of the Province, or as may hereafter be enacted under the provisions of the 3rd Article of this Convention.

xv. The Provisions of the 4th Article of the Sand River Convention are hereby re-affirmed, and no slavery or apprenticeship partaking of slavery will be tolerated by the Government of the said State.

xvi. There will continue to be complete freedom of religion and protection from molestation for all denominations, provided the same be not inconsistent with morality and good order; and no disability shall attach to any person in regard to rights of property by reason of the religious opinions which he holds.

xvii. The British Resident will receive from the Government of the Transvaal State such assistance and support as can by law be given to him for the due discharge of his functions. He will also receive every assistance for the proper care and preservation of the graves of such of Her Majesty's Forces as have died in the Transvaal; and if need be, for the expropriation of land for the purpose.

xviii. The following will be the duties and functions of the British Resident:

(1) He will perform duties and functions analogous to those discharged by a Chargé d'Affaires and Consul-General.

(2) In regard to Natives within the Transvaal State he will, (a) report to the High Commissioner, as representative of the Suzerain, as to the working and observance of the provisions of this Convention; (b) report to the Transvaal authorities any cases of ill-treatment of Natives, or attempts to incite Natives to rebellion, that may come to his knowledge; (c) use his influence with the Natives in favour of law and order; and (d) generally perform such other duties as are by this Convention entrusted to him, and take such steps for the protection of the persons and property of Natives as are consistent with the laws of the land.

(3) In regard to Natives not residing in the Transvaal, (a) he will report to the High Commissioner and the Transvaal Government any encroachments reported to him as having been made by Transvaal residents upon the land of such Natives, and in case of disagreement between the Transvaal Government and the British Resident, as to whether an encroachment has been made, the decision of the Suzerain will be final. (b) The British Resident will be the medium of communication with Native Chiefs outside the Transvaal, and, subject to the approval of the High Commissioner, as representing the Suzerain, he will control the conclusion of treaties with them, and (c) he will arbitrate upon every dispute between Transvaal residents and Natives outside the Transvaal (as to acts committed beyond the boundaries of the Transvaal) which may be referred to him by the parties interested.

(4) In regard to communications with Foreign Powers, the Transvaal Government will correspond with Her Majesty's Government through the British Resident and the High Commissioner.

xix. (Frontier details.)

494

xx. All grants or titles issued at any time by the Transvaal Government in respect of land outside the boundary of the Transvaal State, as defined in Article I., shall be considered invalid and of no effect, except in so far as any such grant or title relates to land that falls within the boundary of the Transvaal State; and all persons holding any such grant so considered invalid and of no effect will receive from the Government of the Transvaal State such compensation, either in land or in money, as the Volksraad shall determine. In all cases in which any Native Chiefs or other authorities outside the said boundaries have received any adequate consideration from the Government of the former South African Republic for land excluded from the Transvaal by the first article of this Convention, or where permanent improvements have been made on the land, the British Resident will, subject to the approval of the High Commissioner, use his influence to recover from the native authorities fair compensation for the loss of the land thus excluded, or of the present improvements thereon.

xxi. Forthwith, after the taking effect of this Convention, a Native Location Commission will be constituted, consisting of the President (or in his absence the Vice-President) of the State, or someone deputed by him, the Resident, or someone deputed by him, and a third person to be agreed upon by the President (or the Vice-President, as the case may be) and the Resident; and such Commission will be a standing body for the performance of the duties hereinafter mentioned.

xxii. The Native Location Commission will reserve to the native tribes of the State such locations as they may be fairly and equitably entitled to, due regard being had to the actual occupation of such tribes. The Native Location Commission will clearly define the boundaries of such locations, and for that purpose will, in every instance, first of all ascertain the wishes of the parties interested in such land. In case land already granted in individual titles shall be required for the purpose of any location, the owners will receive such compensation, either in other land or in money, as the Volksraad shall determine. After the boundaries of any location have been fixed no fresh grant of land within such location will be made, nor will the boundaries be altered without the consent of the Location Commission. No fresh grants of land will be made in the districts of Waterber, Zoutpansberg, and Lijdenberg, until the locations in the said districts respectively shall have been defined by the said Commission.

xxiii. If not released before the taking effect of this Convention, Sikukuni, and those of his followers who have been imprisoned with him, will be forthwith released, and the boundaries of his location will be defined by the Native Location Commission in the manner indicated in the last preceding Article.

xxix. The independence of the Swazis, within the boundary line of Swaziland, as indicated in the first Article of this Convention, will be fully recognised.

xxv. No other or higher duties will be imposed on the importation into the Transvaal State of any article, the produce or manufacture of the dominions and possessions of Her Majesty, from whatever place arriving, than are or may be payable on the like article, the produce or manufacture of any other country, nor will any prohibition be maintained or imposed on the importation of any article, the produce or manufacture of the dominions and possessions of Her Majesty, which shall not equally extend to the importation of the like articles, being the produce or manufacture of any other country.

xxvi. All persons other than Natives conforming themselves to the laws of the Transvaal State (*a*) will have full liberty, with their families, to enter, travel, or reside in any part of the Transvaal State; (*b*) they will be entitled to hire or possess houses, manufactories, warehouses, shops and premises; (*c*) they may carry on their commerce either in person or by any agents whom they may think fit to employ; (*d*) they will not be subject in respect of their persons or property, or in respect of their commerce or industry, to any taxes, whether general or local, other than those which are or may be imposed upon Transvaal citizens.

xxvii. All inhabitants of the Transvaal shall have free access to the Courts of Justice for the prosecution and defence of their rights.

xxviii. All persons, other than natives, who established their domicile in the Transvaal between the 12th day of April 1877 and the date when this Convention comes into effect, and who shall, within twelve months after such last-mentioned date, have their names registered by the British Resident shall be exempt from all compulsory military service whatever. The Resident shall notify such registration to the Government of the Transvaal State.

xxix. Provision shall hereafter be made by a separate instrument for the mutual extradition of criminals, and also for the surrender of deserters from Her Majesty's Forces.

xxx. All debts contracted since the Annexation will be payable in the same currency in which they may have been contracted.

All uncancelled postage and other revenue stamps issued by the Government since the Annexation will remain valid, and will be accepted at their present value by the future Government of the State. All licences duly issued since the Annexation will remain in force during the period for which they may have been issued.

xxxi. No grants of land which may have been made, and no transfers or mortgages which may have been passed since the date of Annexation, will be invalidated by reason merely of their having been made or passed after such date.

All transfers to the British Secretary for Native Affairs in trust for Natives will remain in force, the Native Location Commission taking the place of such Secretary for Native Affairs.

xxxii. This Convention will be ratified by a newly elected Volksraad within the period of three months after its execution, and in default of such ratification this Convention shall be null and void.

xxxiii. Forthwith after the ratification of this Convention, as in the last preceding article mentioned, all British troops in Transvaal Territory will leave the same, and the mutual delivery of munitions of war will be carried out.

Signed at Pretoria, this 3rd day of August 1881.

(Signed) HERCULES ROBINSON
    President and High Commissioner

    EVELYN WOOD
     Major-General, Officer Administering the Government

    J. H. de VILLIERS

We, the undersigned ... representatives of the Transvaal Burghers, do hereby agree to all the above condition, reservations, and limitations, under which self-government has been restored to the inhabitants of the Transvaal Territory, subject to the suzerainty of Her Majesty, Her Heirs and Successors, and we agree to accept the Government of the said Territory, with all rights and obligations thereto appertaining, on the 8th day of August 1881, and we promise and undertake that this Convention shall be ratified by a newly-elected Volksraad of the Transvaal State within three months from this date.

Signed at Pretoria, this 3rd day of August 1881.

(Signed) S. J. P. KRUGER
    M. W. PRETORIUS
    P. J. JOUBERT

Parl. Papers, LXVII, C.2998; and Eybers, *Select Documents*, pp. 455–462.

APPENDIX II
THE LONDON CONVENTION
27 February 1884

Whereas the Government of the Transvaal State, through its delegates, consisting of Stephanus Johannes Paulus Kruger (President of the said State), and Stephanus Jacobus du Toit (Superintendent of Education), and Nicholas Jacobus Smit (a member of the Volksraad), have represented that the Convention signed at Pretoria on the 3rd day of August 1881, and ratified by the Volksraad of the said State on the 25th October 1881, contains certain provisions which are inconvenient, and imposes burdens and obligations from which the said State is desirous to be relieved, and that the south-western boundaries fixed by the said Convention should be amended, with a view to promote the peace and good order of the said State, and of the countries adjacent thereto; and whereas Her Majesty the Queen of the United Kingdom of Great Britain and Ireland has been pleased to take the said representations into consideration.

Now, therefore, Her Majesty has been pleased to direct, and it is hereby declared that the following articles of the new Convention, signed on behalf of Her Majesty by Her Majesty's High Commissioner in South Africa, the Right Honourable Sir Hercules George Robert Robinson, . . . Governor of the Colony of the Cape of Good Hope, and on behalf of the Transvaal State (which shall hereinafter be called the South African Republic) by the above-named delegates, . . . shall, when ratified by the Volksraad of the South African Republic, be substituted for the articles embodied in the Convention of 3rd August 1884, which latter, pending such ratification, shall continue in full force and effect.

ARTICLE 1. [Boundaries of the new South African Republic see map, p. 98].

II. The Government of the South African Republic will strictly adhere to the boundaries defined in the first article of the Convention, and will do its utmost to prevent any of its inhabitants from making any encroachments upon lands beyond the said boundaries. The Government of the South African Republic will appoint Commissioners upon the eastern and western borders whose duty it will be strictly to guard against irregularities and all trespassing over the boundaries. Her Majesty's Government will, if necessary, appoint Commissioners in the native territories outside the eastern and western borders of the South African Republic to maintain order and prevent encroachments.

Her Majesty's Government and the Government of the South African Republic will each appoint a person to proceed together to beacon off the amended south-west boundary as described in article *one* of this Convention; and the President of the Orange Free State shall be requested to appoint a referee to whom the said persons shall refer any questions in which they may disagree respecting the interpretation of the said article, and the decision of such referee thereon shall be final. The arrangement already made under the terms of article *nineteen* of the Convention of Pretoria of the 3rd August 1881, between the owners of the farms Grootfontein and Valleifontein on the one hand, and the Barolong authorities on the other, by which a fair share of the water supply of the said farms shall be allowed to flow undisturbed to the said Barolongs, shall continue in force.

III. If a British officer is appointed to reside at Pretoria or elsewhere within the South African Republic to discharge functions analogous to those of a Consular Officer he will receive the protection and assistance of the Republic.

IV. The South African Republic will conclude no treaty or engagement with any State or nation other than the Orange Free State, nor with any native tribe to the eastward or westward of the Republic until the same has been approved by Her Majesty the Queen.

Such approval shall be considered to have been granted if Her Majesty's Government shall not, within six months after receiving a copy of such treaty (which shall be delivered to them immediately upon its completion), have notified that the conclusion of such treaty is in conflict with the interest of Great Britain or of any of Her Majesty's possessions in South Africa.

V. The South African Republic will be liable for any balance which may still remain due of the debts for which it was liable at the date of annexation, to wit, the Cape Commercial Bank Loan, the Railway Loan, and the Orphan Chamber Debt, which debts will be a first charge upon the revenues of the Republic. The South African Republic will moreover be liable to Her Majesty's Government for £250,000, which will be a second charge upon the revenues of the Republic.

VI. The debt due as aforesaid by the South African Republic to Her Majesty's Government will bear interest at the rate of three and a half per cent., from the date of the ratification of this Convention, and shall be repayable by a payment for interest and sinking fund of six pounds and ninepence per £100 per annum, which will extinguish the debt in twenty-five years. The said payment of six pounds and ninepence per £100 shall be payable half-yearly, in British currency, at the close of each half-year from the date of such ratification; provided always that the South African Republic shall be at liberty at the close of any half-year to pay off the whole or any portion of the outstanding debt.

Interest at the rate of three and a half per cent. on the debt as standing under the Convention of Pretoria shall as heretofore be paid to the date of the ratification of this Convention.

VII. All persons who held property in the Transvaal on the 8th day of August 1881, and still hold the same, will continue to enjoy the rights of property which they have enjoyed since the 12th April 1877. No person who has remained loyal to Her Majesty during the late hostilities shall suffer any molestation by reason of his loyalty; or be liable to any criminal prosecution or civil action for any part taken in connection with such hostilities; and all such persons will have full liberty to reside in the country, with enjoyment of all civil rights and protection for their persons and property.

VIII. The South African Republic renews the declaration made in the Sand River Convention, and in the Convention of Pretoria, that no slavery or apprenticeship partaking of slavery will be tolerated by the Government of the said Republic.

IX. There will continue to be complete freedom of religion and protection from molestation for all denominations, provided the same be not inconsistent with morality and good order; and no disability shall attach to any person in regard to rights of property by reason of the religious opinions which he holds.

X. [British Residents and graves of British soldiers.]

XI. All grants or titles issued at any time by the Transvaal Government in respect of land outside the boundary of the South African Republic, as defined in article *one*, shall be considered invalid and of no effect, except in so far as any such grant or title relates to land that falls within the boundary of the South African Republic; and all persons holding any such grant so considered invalid and of no effect will receive from the Government of the South African Republic such compensation, either in land or in money, as the Volksraad shall determine. In all cases in which any native chiefs or other authorities outside the said boundaries have received any adequate consideration from the Government of the South African Republic for land excluded from the Transvaal by the first article of this Convention, or where permanent improvements have been made on the land, the High Commissioner will recover from the native authorities fair compensation for the loss of the land thus excluded, or of the permanent improvements thereon.

XII. The independence of the Swazies, within the boundary line of Zwaziland, as indicated in the first article of this Convention, will be fully recognised.

XIII. Except in pursuance of any treaty or engagement made as provided in article *four* of this Convention, no other or higher duties shall be imposed on the importation into the South African Republic of any article coming from any part of Her Majesty's dominions than are or may be imposed on the like article coming from any other place or country; nor will any prohibition be maintained or imposed on the importation into the South African Republic of any article coming from any part of Her Majesty's dominions which shall not equally extend to the like article coming from any other place or country. And in like manner the same treatment shall be given to any article coming to Great Britain from the South African Republic as to the like article coming from any other place or country.

These provisions do not preclude the consideration of special arrangements as to import duties and commercial relations between the South African Republic and any of Her Majesty's colonies or possessions.

XIV. All persons, other than natives, conforming themselves to the laws of the South African Republic (*a*) will have full liberty, with their families, to enter, travel or reside in any part of the South African Republic; (*b*) they will be entitled to hire or possess houses, manufactories, warehouses, shops, and premises; (*c*) they may carry on their commerce either in person or by any agents whom they may think fit to employ; (*d*) they will not be subject, in respect of their persons or property, or in respect of their commerce or industry, to any taxes, whether general or local, other than those which are or may be imposed upon citizens of the said Republic.

XV. All persons, other than natives, who established their domicile in the Transvaal between the 12th day of April 1877 and the 8th August 1881, and who within twelve months after such last-mentioned date have had their names registered by the British Resident, shall be exempt from all compulsory military service whatever.

xvi. Provision shall hereafter be made by a separate instrument for the mutual extradition of criminals, and also for the surrender of deserters from Her Majesty's Forces.

xvii. All debts contracted between the 12th April 1877 and the 8th August 1881 will be payable in the same currency in which they may have been contracted.

xviii. No grants of land which may have been made, and no transfers or mortgages which may have been passed, between the 12th April 1877 and the 8th August 1881 will be invalidated by reason merely of their having been made or passed between such dates.

All transfers to the British Secretary for Native Affairs in trust for natives will remain in force, an officer of the South African Republic taking the place of such Secretary for Native affairs.

xix. The Government of the South African Republic will engage faithfully to fulfil the assurances given, in accordance with the laws of the South African Republic, to the natives of the Pretoria Pitso by the Royal Commission in the presence of the Triumvirate and with their entire assent (1) as to the freedom of the natives to buy or otherwise acquire land under certain conditions; (2) as to the appointment of a commission to mark out native locations; (3) as to the access of the natives to the courts of law; and (4) as to their being allowed to move freely within the country or to leave it for any legal purpose under a pass system.

xx. This Convention will be ratified by a Volksraad of the South African Republic within the period of six months after its execution, and in default of such ratification this Convention shall be null and void.

Signed in duplicate in London this 27th day of February 1884.

(Signed) HERCULES ROBINSON
     S. J. P. KRUGER
     S. J. du TOIT
     N. J. SMIT

Parl. Papers, LVII, C.3914; and Eybers, *Select Documents*, pp. 469–74. (See also C.O. 879/21 (Confidential Prints) for dual English–Dutch version.)

APPENDIX III
POSITION OF AFFAIRS IN THE CAPE COLONIES AND THE TRANSVAAL (1884)

WAR OFFICE MEMORANDUM

The present position of affairs in the Cape Colonies and the Transvaal presents so many aspects that it is necessary, before attempting to lay down any definite line of action, to make certain initial assumptions.

It has been assumed, therefore:

1. That the complete abandonment of the Cape Colonies to the Africanders, or, as would probably result, to a German protectorate, is a policy which Her Majesty's Government could not possibly entertain.
2. That it is impossible, for obvious political reasons, to create a Gibraltar out of the Cape Town peninsula, and that the permanent retention of this peninsula—essential to what the Royal Commission on Colonial Defence has pronounced to be one of the most important of the Imperial coaling stations—is dependent upon the maintenance of British ascendancy in all South African Colonies.
3. That a temporary or permanent interference with the constitution at present existing in the Cape Colonies may even be necessary, and, if proved necessary, must be entertained by Her Majesty's Government.
4. That Her Majesty's Government is prepared to enforce—if necessary by arms—the terms of the Convention of 1884, or such

modification of that Convention as may prove desirable in the interests of the future.

5. That Her Majesty's Government would not shrink, if circumstances should compel military action, from raising and employing local forces for the rectification or defence of the frontier fixed by the Convention.

6. That the present state of affairs in the Cape Colonies is emergent, and that action of some kind is immediately necessary.

Having laid down the above premises, the main question may be divided into two heads:

(a) The measures necessary to enforce the existing Convention, to re-assure the well affected population now under great apprehension for the security of their property, and to restore the credit of the colony at present considerably affected, as evidenced by the recent fall of 5 per cent. in Cape securities.

(b) The larger measures required to produce a lasting security for the tranquillity and well-being of the South African Colonies; in a word, the re-establishment of those colonies on a sounder political basis.

It will be found at starting that the military and the political conditions are so intimately connected that it is impossible to divorce them. In order that military action on certain lines may be possible, political changes or re-organization may be necessary, and if necessary must be accepted as inevitable. Further, it may appear that the present state of affairs arises mainly from radically unsound political conditions, and can be remedied only by organic changes.

It is proposed to consider first the nature and scope of the military operations necessary to enforce the terms of the late Convention of 1884 with the Boers, to restore the violated frontiers and to ensure their future observance.

Military action positive, or merely demonstrative, can be directed from two principal bases, which will be separately considered, viz.:

1. Griqualand West.
2. Natal.

Before military action of any kind is taken, it is necessary for the Imperial Government to establish a more definite status west of the Transvaal and annex Bechuanaland up to the line of the Molopo by proclamation. The terms on which the territory should be handed over to the Cape Government would be the subject of subsequent arrangement. This territory might even be administered for a time by the Imperial Government, as was the case with Griqualand West.

APPENDIX III

I. GRIQUALAND WEST

In considering the question of the force requisite to enforce the terms of the Convention, the possibility of a general rising in the Transvaal in support of the cause of the freebooters cannot be left out of consideration, although it is highly improbable, if the legal aspects of the question are clearly put forward, and there is a firm declaration on the part of England to adhere to, and enforce the terms of the Convention.

Two cases, viz.:

1. It may be asserted that the Convention having been broken in certain of its clauses, with the concurrence of the Government of the Transvaal, the other clauses lapse, and, a *casus belli* being made out, the action of England is unimpeded by any considerations as to frontiers.
2. It may be considered that the violation of the frontier established by the Convention is the act of freebooters, which it was not within the power of the Transvaal Government effectually to restrain. In this case action would at first be confined to the dispossession, after due notice, of the violaters of the frontier, and the seizing of their property if not removed within the Transvaal.

Such action evidently is justified by the breach of Convention. By Article II. of the Convention of 1884, the Government of the Transvaal undertook to "do its utmost to prevent any of its inhabitants from making any encroachments upon lands beyond the said boundaries." The Government of the Transvaal having clearly failed to prevent such encroachments, it is the undoubted right of the Imperial Government to dispossess by force the freebooters who have broken its laws as well as those of the Transvaal. By Article XI., it is laid down that the Transvaal Government cannot claim to confer titles to land outside the boundaries established by the Convention. Land thus held is, therefore, an illegal possession with respect to the laws of the Imperial Government and those of the Government of the Transvaal alike.

The last hypothesis—that it is the undoubted right of the Imperial Government to dispossess the freebooters by force if necessary—is adopted, since it is obviously not the policy of Her Majesty's Government to make deliberate war upon the Boers of the Transvaal.

Action should be preceded by a declaration of the annexation by the Imperial Government, of Bechuanaland up to the line of the Molopo. This declaration should set forth, in the clearest language,

505

the illegal position, with respect to the Convention, occupied by the freebooters; and it should be definitely announced that all claims to land beyond the frontier of the Convention are null and void, and that, after a fixed date, it is the unalterable determination of Her Majesty's Government to re-establish the frontier by force of arms, and to confiscate the property of all persons illegally found on the Bechuanaland territory. The language in which this proclamation is couched should be carefully chosen, since it is of cardinal importance that the illegal position of the freebooters should be made apparent, not only to the people of the Transvaal, but also to the Boers of the Cape Colony and the Orange Free State. If this illegality is made sufficiently clear, the prospects of a general rising in the Transvaal, or among the Boers of the Cape Colony, or of interference of the Orange Free State on the behalf of the freebooters, will be reduced to a minimum.

Simultaneously with the issue of the Proclamation the following military action should be taken, it being premised that no Imperial forces, other than those now stationed in South Africa, are at present available.

One Infantry regiment 800 strong, with a proportion of Royal Engineers and Commissariat, and a certain number of special Officers for transport and other duties, should be sent by sea from Natal to Port Elizabeth, and forwarded by rail to the present terminus of the Kimberley railway near Hopetown. Thence they would march to a point near Phokwana, on the Hartz River, beyond the northern frontier of Griqualand West.

The object of this movement would be moral and political, proving that Her Majesty's Government in issuing the proclamation had entered upon a definite line of policy, and was prepared to enforce it. Further, these troops, entrenched in a good position, would afford protection to the Bechuanas and the loyal population of North Griqualand West; and at the same time provide an assured advanced base from which a corps of irregulars would freely operate.

The time required for this movement of troops would be, approximately:

Durban to Port Elizabeth	4 days.
Port Elizabeth to terminus of railway	2 days.
Railway terminus to Phokwana	14 days.
Total	20 days

In estimating the strength necessary for a corps of irregulars sufficient to dispossess the encroaching farmers and re-establish the frontier, it is to be considered that, according to numerous accounts, the Boers have been able to bring together as many as 300 men for comparatively unimportant raids. In August it was stated that they had 450 men in laager in Montsioa's territory, and proposed to increase this number to 1,000. It appears probable, therefore, that for defence of the farms and property on the hither side of the frontier as many as 1,000 to 1,500 men might be put into the field, brought from considerable distances in the Transvaal. It may be assumed that these men would fight desperately, since they have already shed their blood freely, and may be expected to do so again. Under these circumstance it would be necessary to employ a force of not less than 2,000 irregular troops, of whom 500 might be dismounted men.

In raising the required force the first step should be to communicate with the old commanders of regiments, and ascertain from them how many of the men who have previously served in these regiments would give their services.

The regiments in question are:

1. Diamond Fields Horse.
2. Diamond Contingent.
3. Du Toits Pan Hussars.
4. Kimberley Light Horse.
5. Barkly Rangers.
6. Hopetown Volunteers.
7. Griquatown Burghers.

It is probable that this call would produce from 1,000 to 1,500 men of good stamp. In addition 500 men should be raised in this country, care being taken to select good shots. The balance would be obtained in the Colony, or from the Cape Mounted Police.

The two 7-prs., M.L., and two 6-prs., B.L. employed in the previous operations, if not now at Kimberley, should be sent there at once, or better still, the material of a screw battery might be at once despatched to Cape Town for employment by a local corps.

To the force 3 Surgeons of the Army Medical Staff should be attached, as well at 3 Commissariat, 1 Ordnance Store Officer, and 2 Officers Army Pay Department. By this means considerable economy, combined with greater efficiency in these several departments, would be obtained.

The purchase of horses should be one of the first steps taken, and should be carried out through an agent in England who knows the country. The terms of purchase should include delivery at a stated place when required. Till that time, the horses would remain on the farms.

The equipment would be the same as that provided in 1877–8.

The force would rendezvous in the first instance at Barkly, but a standing camp would be formed at Kimberley.

The force should be constituted under an Order in Council, and and the same terms should be offered to the men as those previously given in the Crown Colony Griqualand West.

Owing to the peculiar circumstances of the case, it is necessary that while the Officer entrusted with the conduct of the operations on the Griqualand frontier should have perfect freedom of action and full responsibility, as on previous occasions in 1878–9, yet at the same time it is most desirable that the general course of action should have the concurrence of the General Officer Commanding in Chief, who should be instructed to give him his cordial co-operation and to render him every assistance in his power, both as to supply of men and material and moral support. With this understanding the General Officer will be enabled to place at the disposal of the Officer such British troops from time to time as circumstances demand. The Line regiment previously referred to should be placed at the disposal of this Officer. It is further necessary that the latter should hold a special commission from Her Majesty, and be invested with special authority.

The Cape Government must be given to understand that all their resources are to be placed at his disposal, and that he must be loyally supported in carrying out the difficult task assigned to him. He should also have powers of compulsory requisition on payment of fair prices throughout the Hopetown district and Griqualand West district.

The Imperial Government must provide at once a sum of £50,000 for the purchase of horses, arms, uniform, equipment, etc., and a monthly charge of £30,000, until the operations are ended.

It is evidently desirable that precedence in the allotment of farms under the Occupation Clause in the newly annexed territory should be promised to Volunteers who serve with credit during the operations. This will not only have the effect of calling out the best men, but will afford a strong guarantee for the future security of the frontier.

For this reason, as well as on the higher ground of ensuring fair treatment to the natives, it is essential that the whole settlement of the land newly annexed should be dealt with immediately after the clearing of the frontier by an Imperial Commissioner. And finally, it would be of great value that the Officer entrusted with this Expedition should be empowered to attach to his personal staff a barrister, conversant with the local laws, in whom he could place implicit confidence to advise him on the many legal difficulties inseparable from the condition of affairs in that country.

2. NATAL

Both the circumstances and the grounds of apprehension are some-what different on the Natal and Zululand frontiers. Here the danger is that the Zulus, if action is not immediately taken to re-establish and maintain the frontier of the Convention, will inevitably be pushed out by the encroaching Boers, and, passing into Natal in large numbers will constitute a serious danger to the Colony, swelling the locations and encroaching on the farms of white settlers. England has completely destroyed the military organization of the Zulus—the standing check on all Boer pretensions in this quarter—and then left the country practically at the mercy of the Boers without any species of protectorate or guarantee, except in so far as regards the Reserve. Thus, although there has been no specific promise of pro-tection to the Zulus as there has been to the dispossessed Bechu-anas, strong moral obligations have unquestionably been incurred by England.

The action of the Boers in this region, as in Bechuanaland, consti-tutes a clear breach of Article II. of the Convention of 1884; but there is nevertheless a difference between the two cases. In Zululand, the encroaching farmers have entered by arrangement with native chiefs. There have, however, been declarations in Parliament, with regard to the limitation of the responsibility of England to the Re-serve which might, in a sense, be held to justify the action of the Boers.

Somewhat different action might therefore be adopted with regard to the violation of the Zululand frontier. An Imperial Commissioner might be subsequently sent up to ascertain what has really taken place—the present information being incomplete—and to inquire into the means by which the land in question has been acquired. It would not therefore be at first advisable to include the violaters of the Zulu-land frontier in the proclamation announcing confiscation after a fixed date to the freebooters in Bechuanaland.

At the same time it is essential that military action should be taken on the Zululand side as likely to have a powerful moral effect, tend-ing to a peaceful solution of the difficulties in Bechuanaland, by executing a restraining influence on the Transvaal generally, and tending to minimize the probability of a rising in support of the property of the evicted Bechuanaland freebooters.

Thus, simultaneously with the issue of the proclamation before alluded to, and with the military movements on the western side, the troops now in Natal and the Reserve should be formed into a field force, 2,000 strong, including the Cavalry regiment; and should occupy Fort George and Fort Cambridge beyond the frontier of the

Reserve, and within about 35 miles of the frontier of the Transvaal. Such a movement, if begun at the moment of the issue of the proclamation, and promptly carried out, could not fail to have a powerful moral effect.

It would be advisable to supplement the Cavalry Regiment by a force of 500 irregulars, which could rapidly be raised in Natal.

No further line of action can be laid down for this force, as its operations would depend entirely upon events on the western side.

SUMMARY

Summing up, the recommendations as to the measures immediately necessary are as follows:

1. The acquisition of Bechuanaland up to the line of the Molopo either by concession from native chiefs or by direct annexation. This is necessary to give England a legal status and full power to effect such a subsequent settlement as may insure future tranquillity.

2. The issue of a clear declaration of policy by Her Majesty's Government, couched in language which cannot be misunderstood, and setting forth, in the plainest terms, the illegal position occupied by the freebooters with respect to the Convention of 1884.

3. The issue of a proclamation that all claims to land outside the western frontier of the Transvaal, as fixed by the Convention, are null and void; that the personal property of all persons who have seized land beyond this frontier will be confiscated after a fixed date, and that all resistance after annexation will be treated as rebellion. Finally, that on the eastern side a Commissioner will be appointed to inquire into the means by which land has been occupied beyond the frontier of Zululand, as laid down by the Convention; and that until this Commissioner has reported there will be no interference with the farmers provided that measures be taken to hinder the inroads of any more whites, and that no resistance is offered to any movements of troops in Zululand which her Majesty's Government may consider necessary.

4. Instant preparation to carry out the proclamation by an irregular force operating from Griqualand West, and supported by an Infantry regiment stationed on the Hartz River, beyond the northern portion of Griqualand. The whole operation to be entrusted to an Imperial officer of proved experience.

5. A concentration of troops in Zululand beyond the frontier of the Reserve, supplemented by a small force of irregular cavalry raised in Natal.

It is considered that the above measures will be sufficient to enforce the terms of the Convention to the extent indicated, and that if no general rising in the Transvaal takes place the operations will present no difficulty. For the maintenance of the frontier, however, and the future prevention of the recurrence of the present state of affairs, further measures are required which will be separately discussed.

1st October 1884.   A.C.
W.O. 33/42, No. 971.   CONFIDENTIAL

APPENDIX IV
VACILLATION IN POLICY
IN SOUTH AFRICA

COLONIAL OFFICE MEMORANDUM, 1885

Colonel Stanley has asked for some notes of instances in which there has been vacillation in the policy of this country towards South Africa. To tell the story in full would be to rewrite the history of the country. The evil has long been acknowledged and deplored. Writing on the 5th of February, 1836, Lord Glenelg spoke of "our inability (? instability) of purpose" and that "frequent change of policy by which our conduct towards the native tribes has been characterised;" and said that "our proceedings have assumed an appearance of caprice and of a confusion perfectly unintelligible to the natives, who in their turn have been led into a course of conduct uncertain and liable to sudden changes." Similar remarks have frequently been made by later authorities during the intervening half century, but the evil does not appear to abate. What the causes are, is a matter of opinion. There are two schools in South African frontier politics just as distinct as the two Indian schools. Sometimes the "forward school" (though it does not bear the name) has prevailed in the councils of the Home Government, and sometimes the school of inactivity. Moreover, once and again, at important junctures, either through blundering or masterfulness on the part of local agents the hand of the Home Government has been forced in a disastrous manner. Add to all this the consideration that the conditions of the problem are so strange and so difficult to master, that even where there has been neither fraud nor usurpation of authority on the part of our local agents, the Home Government has often been led into courses, apparently reasonable and prudent in themselves, from the consequences of which it has afterwards recoiled as soon as they began to be manifest. Every course of policy which can now be adopted in South Africa has its drawbacks, and while one particular policy is in course of execution, these come into prominence, and are made so much of by the people who have the opposite policy at heart, that the Government at home is often deterred from persevering in the path on which it has set out. When we lean to the policy of controlling all sections of the population, and regulating their mutual relations, we find that a huge bill has been run up. Then the advocates of retirement and retrenchment have their day, until it is perceived that retirement and retrenchment have involved the abandonment of some weak and friendly tribe to the mercy of the Africander, or the triumph of anarchy among the natives themselves. Then there is a cry for a resumption of responsibility, the change being often facilitated by assurances on the part of its advocates that if it is only sufficiently thorough, it will be the cheapest in the end. The usual *formula* of persuasion is that "nothing will be necessary but a very simple form of administration and a small mounted force, the expenses of which will be more than covered by a hut tax and licences." Sometimes steps are taken without authority which attract no notice for some time, but are afterwards explained to us as having irrevocably committed our honour to a course which we should not have sanctioned if consulted in the first instance. Thus it comes about that not only do one set of Ministers reverse the action of their predecessors, but that the same set of Ministers, after a time, reverse their own policy, and seem to go back from their own declarations.

The Cape Colony was of very small dimensions when we conquered it from the Dutch. It has since been continuously enlarged by conquests or treaties, generally against the inclinations of the Home Government, and after more or less resistance on its part. In one notable case, the Secretary of State (Lord Glenelg) took the strong step of formally re-ceding to the natives a large strip of country—that between the Keishamma and the Kei—which had been annexed by the Governor, and been for several months under British rule, and reinstating therein the conquered natives; but eleven years later the Whig Government, in whose name he had acted being again in power, reannexed the same country, and constituted it the province of British Kaffraria. The settlement of Zululand, effected by Lord Beaconsfield's Government after the Zulu War of 1879, has been regarded by South African politicians of the forward school as a proceeding of much the same nature, being characterised as a meaningless and wanton abandonment of fruits of conquest in the very hour of victory. But in that case the hand of the Government had been forced in making the war at all, and it was only reverting to its own declared principles in declining to assume direct responsibility for the government of Zululand. To the Zulus themselves the arrangement is known to have been unintelligible, and it did not work in practice. Her Majesty's late Government conceived that the only alternatives lay between assuming the responsibility of government or restoring Cetywayo, and they chose the latter course as an experiment, and not, it may be remarked, for the sentimental reasons to which the step has been generally attributed.

That experiment might possibly have succeeded, if Cetywayo had been left free to maintain order in his own former drastic fashion; but this was felt to be impossible. He was forbidden to re-establish his military system. He was put under the control of a resident, and a strip of territory, in which the chief strength and wealth of his adherents lay, was withheld from him. His enemy, Usibebu, was under no similar disabilities, and was therefore easily able to crush him. Thus not only did the late Government reverse by a very conspicuous proceeding the action of the preceding one, but it failed to back its own man, and allowed him to be so used by the Natal Government and his enemies as to give him no chance of success. His own criticism on the transaction was that the Government had thrown him down in the grass to be murdered by his enemies.

On one point, policy has run pretty steadily in one direction, namely, that where a native territory has been annexed, the Home Government has always desired to transfer, and has usually succeeded in transferring, the burden of its administration to the Cape Colony—as for example, in British Kaffraria, the Transkei, Griqualand West, and Basutoland. In the latter case alone has there been a reversal of the process. The circumstances were peculiar. Nothing could have been more satisfactory than the administration of Basuto affairs by the first responsible Cape Ministry. But in 1878 Sir B. Frere dismissed his Ministers, though undefeated, and from that time took upon himself *la haute direction* of native affairs in South Africa, acting, as far as the Cape and its dependencies were concerned, through his minority Ministers, who were in effect his creatures for the time being. It was through his influence that the Cape Ministry issued the Disarmament Proclamation, which brought on the Basuto war. That war cost the Cape £4,000,000, and the Colonists got nothing for it. They were not, however, left to settle the matter entirely in their own way. Lord Kimberley, strongly backed by public opinion, had insisted on the intervention of the High Commissioner as arbitrator. In taking the matter out of the hands of the Colonists, Lord Kimberley was acting in apparent disregard of a declaration of his own, made ten years before, in replying to an inquiry of the High Commissioner whether the affairs of Basutoland were to be administered unreservedly as the local Legislature might see fit; on that occasion his lordship had said. "If responsible Government is adopted in the Cape Colony, and Basutoland is annexed to it, the Central Colonial Administration would, of course, exercise the same control over it as over the rest of the Colony. . . ." (See C.459 —pp. 54 and 67. Lord Kimberley to Sir H. Barkly, 17 November, 1871.) If the Colonists had been left to settle the matter uncontrolled, they would probably have adopted a policy of booty and confiscation, which would have placed such forces at their command as would have insured success, at a far less cost than that of the abortive operations which they actually undertook. Looking to all these circumstances of hardship attending the case, Her Majesty's late Government agreed to an arrangement by which they were to take over Basutoland as an experiment, and govern it with such taxes as could be collected in addition to a subsidy of £20,000 a year from the Cape. The experiment has lasted nearly a year and a half and cannot be said to have broken down, or to be *certain* to break down, though it is not a brilliant or assured success. Such success as has been achieved is due to the excellent sense of the officer who was appointed Resident. Colonel Marshall Clarke, C.M.G. ('one-armed Clarke').

In the dealings with the Colonists there has been no more consistency than in dealing with the natives. Fifteen or twenty years ago, serious efforts were commenced with a view to throwing the burden of defence against the natives on the Colonists, and to reducing the garrison to the amount necessary for purely Imperial purposes. In pursuance of this policy, Lord Kimberley almost forced responsible Government on the Cape in 1872; and when Lord Carnarvon opened the question of Confederation in 1875, his proposals were such as necessarily involved the handing over of all South African affairs, including native affairs, to the South Africans. A special power of disallowing laws affecting natives, was, indeed, reserved to the Home Government by the South Africa Act of 1877, but, in dealing with natives, legislation has little importance compared to administration and had Confederation succeeded as a policy, it would have followed that the South African Europeans would, for the future, have controlled the administration of native affairs. Sir B. Frere, however, developed quite a different policy from that implied by the establishment of responsible Government, the reduction of the garrison, and, the mooting of Confederation. During the Cape War of 1877, he induced the Home Government to send out regiment after regiment to aid in the war, although not asked for by his Ministers, whom he dismissed for not placing their levies under Imperial control, and for showing an inclination to treat the whole affair more as one for the police than as a formal war. Then he made the Zulu War, and what more wars he would have made, it is impossible to say. In a despatch he happened casually to observe that the fighting in Zululand was only a preliminary to the operations that would have to follow in other places, mentioning *inter alia* Pondoland and Basutoland. Then the Government cut off half his High Commissionership and sent out Sir Garnet Wolseley, and little opportunity was left him of developing his ideas, beyond working for the disarmament measure in Basutoland, which led to the Basuto War.

Lastly, it remains to review our relations with the Boers, especially those who emigrated from the Colony about half a century ago. In the Cape Colony, before our time, the Boers had a system of self-defence and reprisal called the Commando system. It was confirmed by Lord Macartney in 1797, when we first held the Cape, and afterwards put in constant practice under English Governors, until 1833, when Governor Sir Lowry Cole passed an Ordinance to consolidate and amend the law on the subject. This Ordinance the late Lord Derby disallowed, and the whole system from that time fell into desuetude, the Government undertaking the task of protecting the farmers against the natives and the natives against the farmers. The new arrangement did not work well for either side, and the farmers on account of this and other griefs, trekked away to Natal and beyond the Orange River, and even beyond the Vaal. Natal was taken from them and made a colony with Lord Derby's sanction. The Orange River Territory was likewise declared British, and the Boers beyond the Vaal were more or less threatened with an interference which was never actually exercised. An Act of Parliament, of a somewhat one-sided character, was passed and held *in terrorem* over them (6 & 7, Will. IV. c. 57). It provided that they as British subjects were to be punished for crimes committed South of the 25th Parallel of South Latitude by the Cape Courts; but it did not subject the natives to punishment for crimes against them. Their leader also was outlawed and a price promised for his capture. The policy in the ascendant was one of following the Boers wherever they might go; but under the stress of the Kaffir War of 1851–2, that policy was found irksome, and a treaty of peace and friendship was made with the Boers beyond the Vaal, in which their right of self-government was recognised, all alliances with natives beyond the Vaal were disclaimed, and a promise made that munitions of war would be withheld from the natives but supplied on sale to them. This (the Sand River) Convention was ratified by Lord Derby's Government in 1852. It was the first step in the reversal of a policy, in which Lord Derby had borne his share, of controlling the relations between the Boers and the natives wherever they might come in contact. It was followed up by the Bloemfontein Convention of 1854, ratified by the Duke of Newcastle, abandoning the Orange River Territory, and containing similar provisions to those agreed to in the Sand River Convention. There was never any serious question of giving back Natal to the Boers, and the Dutch in South Africa were well contented that their relations with the Imperial Government should stand upon the basis of the Conventions of 1852 and 1854. South Africa was never in so satisfactory a state as during the 23 years which followed the second of them. On two occasions, indeed, Dutch opinion was excited, and in the second case seriously angered by what it deemed to be a violation of the Bloemfontein Convention; but in each case the excitement was allayed by the adoption of just and conciliatory measures. The two instances referred to are the taking over of the Basutos as British subjects in 1868, and the seizure of the Diamond Mines in 1871. The Basutos were taken over when on the point of being crushed by the Orange Free State at the end of a long war. The Free State sent a deputation to London to protest against the measure, but they were told that it could not be reversed, and the President, being a sensible man, accepted the situation and entered into a convention, known as the Convention of Aliwal North, with Sir Philip Wodehouse, by which he obtained a good strip of Basuto territory as a *solatium*, and also a formal renewal of the Bloemfontein Convention of 1854. This latter concession, however, only served to aggravate our offence in the eyes of the Dutch, when we seized the Diamond Fields two years afterwards. The Blomfontein Convention contained a disclaimer of all alliances with natives north of the Orange River, save and except one Adam Kok, a Griqua, and a promise not to enter into any fresh ones "injurious or prejudicial to the Orange River Government". Adam Kok and the Boers did not get on well, and in 1861 Sir George Grey removed that Chief to No-Man's-Land, leaving his territory to the Boers, who thus found themselves with another Griqua, named Waterboer, as their next neighbour. The old line between Waterboer and Adam Kok ran somewhere about where the diamonds were found. It depended on certain points, the exact location of which was in dispute. Sir Henry Barkly accepted a cession of his territory from Waterboer, and ran the line so as to cut the mines into the ceded territory. Whatever was the true line, the Orange Free State had for years been granting titles over the ground on which the diamonds were discovered, and for three years the Orange Free State officials had been keeping order, at the fields and administering Free State law. In Dutch eyes this was, indeed, a violation of the provision in the Bloemfontein Convention against forming alliances with the native Chiefs 'injurious or prejudicial to the Orange River Government.' After five years of protests and controversy, Lord Carnarvon settled the matter by a Convention with President Brand, by which, without acknowledging that we were in the wrong, he settled the matter by giving the Orange Free State £90,000 in satisfaction of its claim—an extraordinarily good bargain for us, seeing what the mines have since produced.

This act, coupled with Mr. Froude's mission, and certain friendly declarations of Lord Carnarvon in despatches and speeches, put the Dutch in thorough good-humour for the time; until Sir T. Shepstone annexed the Transvaal and thus tore up the Sand River Convention—a step, the consequences of which were aggravated by the confident assertions of pro-British partisans in South Africa that it was a mere preliminary to the absorption of the Orange Free State. Sir T. Shepstone's Commission was peculiarly worded, and the preamble and enacting parts were not consistent one with the other. The enacting parts only contemplated annexation under certain conditions, but the third clause of the preamble recited without qualification that it was expedient that the territories, or portions of them where war had recently been going on, should be administered in the Queen's name. There are no instructions extant explaining what was intended, and it is believed that Sir T. Shepstone read his commission as making it incumbent on him to annex in any case.

When we got into the Transvaal, our conduct and declarations appeared (to outsiders) totally at variance with those which had proceeded from us before. Lord Carnarvon had declared that he could see no justification for the Transvaal making war on Sikukuni. Sir H. Barkly had held up the Boers to execration for employing Swazis as allies. Sir T. Shepstone had declared that Sikukuni did not understand the peace which he had at length been forced to sign by the Boers. And yet we renewed the war with Sikukuni in order to enforce that peace to the letter, and we brought 15,000 Swazis into the field as allies.

In the old standing border dispute between the Transvaal and the Zulus, Sir T. Shepstone, who had always countenanced the Zulu claims, now took up the Transvaal claims as strongly; professing to have found records at Utrecht, which entirely altered his opinion. But this did not commit the Home Government very deeply, and the Natal Commission, which adjudicated in the case, gave it in favour of Cetywayo.

The measure of annexation, whatever might be thought of its wisdom, was not one which the Government of Lord Beaconsfield conceived it possible to reverse. This opinion was adopted (somewhat unexpectedly) by Mr. Gladstone's Government on coming into office in May 1880, and ten months after, even when the Boers were in full rebellion, they announced in the Queen's Speech, opening the Session of 1881, that military measures were being taken for the prompt vindication of Her Majesty's authority, and implied that this necessity postponed the possibility of granting to the Boers self-governing institutions.

With the object of vindicating Her Majesty's authority three or four actions were fought, in each of which our troops suffered reverse, the last being the Majuba disaster. After that the Government made peace. It is right to say, that the way in which Sir Evelyn Wood understood and carried out his instructions would have rendered it somewhat embarrassing for them to have adopted a different course. It is hardly possible to explain this. It can only be stated as a fact which was evident to those who were cognisant of the telegraphic correspondence as it passed from day to day; but at all events, the Government forewent the satisfaction of retrieving its military reverses, and concluded the Pretoria Convention of 1881. That Convention reserved certain large but not very workable powers to Her Majesty. In many respects it turned out a bad arrangement, and was replaced by the more satisfactory, if looser, Convention of London, concluded by the present Lord Derby in 1884.

The two Conventions taken together would have amounted to a return in spirit to the policy of the late Lord Derby's Government in ratifying the Sand River Convention, and was so regarded for a time; but we left behind us beyond the Vaal two Chiefs (Montsioa and Mankaroane) who were considered by the public to have claims on us, and whom it was felt that we could not abandon, although by their own rash efforts at asserting supremacy over their rivals they were greatly contributing to their own misfortunes. The late Government long resisted the necessity of taking these Chiefs formally under protection; and, as a solution of the difficulty, Lord Derby mooted a suggestion in the House of Lords, that locations should be purchased for them in some quarter where they would be out of harm's way. Moderate as was then the estimate of the cost of fighting their wrongs, his lordship pointed out that it was more than the fee-simple value of all Bechuanaland. The proposal was based to some extent on a measure actually put in force for two years by the Griqualand Government with Sir M. E. Hicks Beach's approval, by which a farm was temporarily rented for Montsioa at a time when he was being harassed by Boer neighbours; but Lord Derby's suggestion was received with public derision, and the matter ended by the Chiefs being taken under protection, at a cost of over £800,000 up to the present, one-tenth of which sum would have provided the Chiefs and their followers with everything they could want. The establishment of the protectorate might not have been a costly measure, had it not been for the reckless act of an English adventurer, Christopher Bethell, in burning down the town of Rooi-Grond, thus provoking a renewal of war, and . . . necessitating Sir Charles Warren's costly expedition. Since then the protectorate of Bechuanaland has been formally extended over Sechele and Khama. Viewing the story of Bechuanaland as bearing on the subject of vacillation, it may be mentioned that in 1874 Lord Carnarvon emphatically refused to back up Mankaroane and Montsioa in their claims to paramountcy over all Bechuana Chiefs, and rebuked Sir H. Barkly and Lt.-Governor Southey for proposing such a course. It may also be mentioned that during the administration of Lord Beaconsfield, Khama was told once or twice that he could not receive protection or aid. This up to the present completes the history of the Vacillations of Policy in South Africa.

Downing Street,   E. FAIRFIELD
4 August, 1885

C.O. 879/23.

APPENDIX V

THE FUTURE OF ZAMBESIA:
ROBINSON TO DERBY, 1885

This private letter, from Sir Hercules Robinson to Lord Derby, is of much interest: it shows that it was Robinson, not Rhodes, who first placed the question of the future of 'Zambesia' before the Colonial Office; and it was Robinson who advocated that it be kept open as a 'safety valve' for pent-up Transvaal expansionist spirit. This would divert the Boers from pressing towards the coast; and it would allow them to expand safely onto what he considered to be lands of no great strategic value.

Government House,
Cape Town
8 May 1885

Dear Lord Derby,

You will see from the despatch going home by this mail that the Transvaal Government are anxious for information as to whether a British Protectorate has been established on the northern frontier of their territory. Some maps place the 22° of South Latitude south of the northern border of the Transvaal. Juta's (?) map which is generally compiled from good sources places the parallel, as you will see from the copy I enclose, about 20 miles north of the Limpopo, thus including within the Protectorate a narrow belt of Matabele land, running along the northern border of the Transvaal until the Portuguese border is reached. As this delineation may involve important questions of policy I should be glad if you will let me know whether the incorporation of this strip within the new British Protectorate is intended.

If I remember correctly at one of the interviews with the Delegates [to the London Convention] you gave them to understand that they would not be shut in to the north. Lobengula was considered strong enough to be able to take care of himself, especially as the lower part

521

of his country bordering on the Transvaal is infested with tsetse fly. Besides we had incurred no obligations whatever to the natives to the north, and so the provisions in the London Convention for mutual maintenance of order on the Eastern and Western Boundaries, and the restrictions as regards making treaties with native tribes beyond those boundaries were advisedly omitted as regards the Northern Frontier.

Even if we were free to shut in the Transvaal to the north I am not sure that it would be wise to do so, as it would close the only safety valve now left to the restless spirits of that country.

I am afraid too that taking this 22° S.L. as the northern boundary of the Protectorate will give rise not only to Transvaal complaints but also to native difficulties, as it includes a strip of Matabele land but cuts the Bamangwato country in two.

Lobengula,—the Chief of the Matabele—and Khama,—Chief of the Bamangwato—have both been very friendly to the English. In my despatch printed at p. 152 of C.3841, you will find a short account of these two Chiefs, and of the resources of their respective countries.

Lobengula is probably the most powerful Chief in South Africa, and is said to be able to place an army of 15,000 Zulus in the field at a few days notice. Although very cruel in the government of his tribe, and his treatment of the tributary tribes in his neighbourhood, he has hitherto shown special favour towards the English. His country is said to be rich in gold, and he has hitherto restricted his mineral concessions to Englishmen, rejecting all applications from other Europeans.

Khama is a very intelligent man who has worked hard to civilise his tribe, and further their advancement. He too, as I have said, is very friendly to us.

For many years these two Chiefs have been at war with each other, the precise boundary line between them is, as usual, disputed; and there have been periodical cattle raids between the cattle outposts on each side.

Sir Charles Warren has now started off post-haste to Shoshong, in consequence of a rumour reaching him that the Matabele were about to invade the Protectorate, by attacking the Bamangwato. The report if not wholly untrue is probably exaggerated, and may mean no more than one of the frontier skirmishes which have for years constituted the normal conditions of things between the two tribes. Besides, the place which the Matabele are said to have attacked, namely Sirule, is outside the Protectorate—being north of the 22nd parallel South Latitude.

What I fear is that as part of Khama's country has been left outside the Protectorate, he will try to seek to involve us in trouble with the Matabele as regards that part, and try to utilize us generally in supporting him against his old enemy, Lobengula. It will be greatly to be regretted if Warren's presence at Shoshong as the friend and supporter of Khama should affect prejudicially our relations with Lobengula, who has hitherto been so friendly towards us. Lobengula is very much the stronger Chief of the two, and war with him would be a serious matter.

I am the more anxious about this because I know that the Mackenzie policy, which is being so insidiously and pertinaciously pursued, is to prevent Colonial annexation [i.e. to the Cape Colony], and to bring the whole of the interior up to the Zambesia under the control of the Imperial Government.

It is very unfortunate that the rumour as to the present Matabele raid should have arisen, and Warren's hurried visit to Shoshong taken place, just as Parliament is about to meet here, as these circumstances are affecting prejudicially the chances of annexation [to the Cape]. Many of the Dutch Members [of Parliament] who might have been disposed to vote for the annexation of the protectorate will be induced to set their faces against it, if they are led to think there is any chance of it involving the Colony in an expensive war with such a powerful tribe as the Matabele . . .

> Yours sincerely,
> (signed) HERCULES ROBINSON

Original (D.P.X.24, at Knowsley Hall, Lancs.)

BIBLIOGRAPHY

I. MANUSCRIPT SOURCES

(a) OFFICIAL PAPERS

(i) *Colonial Office Files* (in the Public Record Office)
Transvaal: C.O. 291 Original correspondence.
    C.O. 417. Correspondence and minutes.
      (These files include Boer activity in Bechuanaland and Zulu-
        land.)
Cape Colony: C.O. 48. Original correspondence.
    C.O. 49. Entry-books of correspondence.
    C.O. 336. Registers of correspondence.
Griqualand: C.O. 107. Original correspondence.
Natal (including St. Lucia Bay): C.O. 179. Correspondence.
    C.O. 357. Registers of correspondence.
Colonies (General): C.O. 537. Original correspondence.
    C.O. 854. Circular correspondence.

(ii) *Orange Free State Papers* (in the British Museum)
Addit. MSS. 36590.

(iii) *Foreign Office Files* (in the Public Record Office)
F.O. 566. Registers of correspondence.

(iv) *War Office Files* (in the Public Record Office)
W.O. 33. 'Confidential Prints'.

(b) PRIVATE PAPERS

(i) *In the British Museum*
Gladstone Papers. Correspondence, Cabinet Minutes, and Letter-
    books.
Dilke Papers. Correspondence, Diaries, and Memoir.
Hamilton Papers. Diaries, 1875–90.

(ii) *In the Public Record Office*
Granville Papers. Correspondence and Letterbooks.

(iii) *In the Bodleian Library, Oxford*
(All these papers are housed in the Rhodes House Library, except for the Froude Papers which are in the old Bodleian.)
Rhodes Papers. Correspondence—notably with Merriman.
Bower Papers. 'Memoir' (unpublished).
Misc. Cape Colony Letters (Afr. MSS. S.2).

(iv) *In Birmingham University Library*
Joseph Chamberlain Papers. Correspondence and 'Memoir'.

(v) *In Private Possession*

Derby Papers. Letters, Minutes, and Confidential Prints, in the possession of the Earl of Derby, at Knowsley Hall, Lancs.
Hartington Papers. Correspondence of Lord Hartington, in the possession of the Duke of Devonshire, at Chatsworth.

II. OFFICIAL PRINTED DOCUMENTS

(*a*) *Colonial Office Confidential Prints*

C.O. 812. Misc. Prints.
C.O. 879 (formerly C.O. 806). African Prints.

(*b*) *Parliamentary Papers, 1877–88*

1877, House of Lords, VI. South African Confederation Bill.
    LX, C.1732, Correspondence *re* Confederation; C.1748. Transvaal Native affairs; C.1776, C.1814, C.1883. Annexation of the Transvaal; C.1815. Shepstone Commission in Transvaal.

1878, LV, C.1961, C.2000, C.1980. South African correspondence.
    LVI, C.2079, C.2100, C.2144. C.2128. Transvaal and further confederation correspondence, notably vital letter from Kruger and Joubert, 10 July 1878.

1878–79, XLIII (68), (69). South African War vote of £1,500,000.
    LII, C.2220, C.2222, C.2242. South African correspondence, 1878–79.
    LIII, C.2252, C.2260, C.2269, C.2308. C.2316, C.2318, C.2367. Wolseley correspondence *re* South-East Africa.
    LIV. (257). Military correspondence and expenditure *re* South Africa, 1871–79.

LIV, C.2374, C.2454. Zulu War begins. Field reports.

1880, XLI (68), (105). Zulu War, supplementary estimates.
L, C.2482, C.2505. War correspondence.
LI, (148). Reports of administrative expenditure in South Africa.
LI, C.2584, C.2586, C.2655, C.2676, C.2695. General South African correspondence, 1879–80.
LI, C.2569. Basutoland.
LI, C.2601, C.2668. Frere appointed as High Commissioner; Instructions, reports, allowances, 1877–80.

1881, House of Lords, XII (45). Basuto War begins. Telegrams, including replies of new Secretary of State, Lord Kimberley.
LVIII (164), (165), (166). War votes of credit.
LVIII (412). Casualty and expenditure returns on South African Wars, 1875–80.
LVIII, C.2963. Return *re* troops stationed in Natal and Transvaal, 1881.
LXII (385). Transvaal estimates for 1881–82.
LXVI, C.2740, C.2783. C.2755, C.2821. South African correspondence including Basuto War.
LXVI, C.2754. Instructions to Sir Hercules Robinson, as High Commissioner and Governor of the Cape, 30 December 1880.
LXVI, C.2794. Transvaal War begins; British and Boer Proclamations.
LXVII, C.2837, C. 2838, C.2858, C.2866, C.2891. General South African correspondence, 1881.
LXVII, C.2892. Instructions to Royal Commissioners to negotiate Transvaal peace, 31 March 1881.
LXVII, C.2950, C.2959, C.2961, C.2962. Cape and Transvaal correspondence, 1880–81.
LXVII, C.2998. Convention of Pretoria, 3 August 1881.
LXXIV, C.2984. Reports on colonial assemblies.

1882, XXVIII, C.3114, C.3219. Report of the Royal Commission, 1881.
XXXVIII (114). South African War estimates, 1881–82.
XLVII, C.3098, C.3381, C.3419. Transvaal correspondence, 1881–82.
XLVII. C.3112, C.3113, C.3175. General South African correspondence, including Basutoland War, 1880–82.
XLVII, C.3174, C.3182. Natal and Zululand Correspondence, 1880–82, including Instructions to Sir Henry Bulwer.
LXXX, C.3410. Transvaal–Portuguese Treaty, 11 December 1875.

1883, XLIII (110). Transvaal estimates for 1883.

XLVIII, C.3493, C.3708. Basuto correspondence.

XLVIII, C.3796. Natal correspondence.

XLIX, C.3466, C.3616, C.3705. Correspondence *re* Zulu unrest.

XLIX, C.3486. Transvaal correspondence, 1882–83, notably on Boer infiltration of Bechuanaland.

XLIX, C.3635. Warren and Harrel reports on Bechuanaland.

XLIX, C.3654, C.3659, C.3686. Transvaal correspondence, including débâcle on Transvaal debt.

XLIX, C.3717. Cape and Basuto correspondence.

1884, LVI, C.3855. General South African correspondence.

LVI, C.4190. Angra Pequena correspondence, 1883–84.

LVII, C.3841. Transvaal correspondence, mainly concerned with Transvaal protests over frontiers.

LVII, C.3914. Convention of London, 27 February 1884.

LVII, C.3947. Correspondence leading to the Convention of London.

LVII, C.4036. Cape and Transvaal correspondence, May 1884.

LVII, C.4194. Transvaal correspondence, 1884 (now styled 'South African Republic').

LVIII, C.3864, C.4037, C.4191. Correspondence *re* Zululand, concerned mainly with Boer infiltration, 1883–84.

1884–85, C.4224. Correspondence leading to Warren Expedition, 1884.

LV, C.4227. Instructions to Warren, 10 November 1884.

LV, C.4414, C.4442. Anglo-Belgian Convention *re* Congo, signed at Berlin on 16 December 1884; and Anglo-German spheres of action, Berlin, 16 December 1884.

LVI, C.4214, C,4274, C.4587. Zulu affairs, notably the creation of the New Republic by Transvaal Boers. 1884–85.

LVI, C.4262, C.4265. Angra Pequena correspondence.

LVI, C.4263, C.4589, C.4590. Basuto and Pondo correspondence.

LVII, C.4213, C.4252, C.4275, C.4310, C.4432, C.4588. South African Republic correspondence; implementation of the London Convention.

1886, XLVII, C.4889. Report of Commissioners on land settlement in British Bechuanaland, 29 May 1886.

XLVIII, C.4643, C.4839, C.4890. General South African correspondence, 1885–86.

XLVIII, C.4645. New Republic and St. Lucia Bay correspondence.

XLVIII, Sess. 2 (52). Zululand expenditure.

1887, LIX, C.4956, C.5070, C.5237. Bechuanaland correspondence.
LXI, C.4913, C.4980. C.5143. New Republic and Zululand.
LXI, C.5022, C.5089. Pondo and Swazi correspondence, 1887.
LXI, C.5180. German South-West Africa claims, 1884–87.
LXI, C.5238. Clarke Report on Basutoland.

1888, LXXIV, C.5390. Cape Town Conference on Customs Union and Railways, 30 January 1888.
LXXIV, C.5432. St. Lucia Bay and Zulu Reserve.
LXXV, C.5331, C.5522, C.5363, C.5524. Boer republics, in Zulu and Tswana territory.

(c) *Hansard, 1877–86*

Hansard's Parliamentary Debates, 3rd series, vols. for 1877–86.

(d) *Colonial Office List, 1877–86*

While not an 'official' publication this invaluable annual volume was based on information supplied by the Colonial Office. It contains a complete list of C.O. officials, their length of service, and positions held.

III. UNOFFICIAL PRINTED DOCUMENTARY SOURCES

ARTHUR, SIR G. (Ed.), *The Letters of Lord and Lady Wolseley, 1870–1911* (London, 1922).

BELL, K. N. and MORRELL, W. P. (Eds.), *Select Documents on British Colonial Policy, 1830–60* (Oxford, 1928).

BENNETT, G. (Ed.), *The Concept of Empire: Burke to Attlee, 1774–1947* (London, 1953).

BUCKLE, G. E. (Ed.), *The Letters of Queen Victoria, a Selection from Her Majesty's Correspondence and Journal between the years 1862 and 1885*, 2nd ser., 3 vols. (London, 1926–28).

CHAMBERLAIN, JOSEPH, *Mr. Chamberlain's Speeches*, ed. by C. W. Boyd and introduced by Austen Chamberlain, 2 vols. (London, 1914).

DERBY, LORD EDWARD HENRY, 15th Earl, *Speeches and Addresses of Edward Henry, XVth Earl of Derby, K.G.*, ed. by T. H. Sanderson and E. S. Roscoe. Preface by W. E. H. Lecky, 2 vols. (London, 1894).

DRUS, ETHEL, (Ed.), 'A Journal of Events during the Gladstone Ministry, 1868–74,' *Camden Miscellany*, XXI, (London, 1958), ii.

EYBERS, G. W., (Ed.), *Select Constitutional Documents Illustrating South African History, 1795–1910* (London, 1918).

GLADSTONE, W. E., *Political Speeches in Scotland* (Midlothian campaign), rev. ed. (Edinburgh, 1880).

GUEDALLA, P., *The Queen and Mr. Gladstone*, 2 vols. (London, 1933).

KEITH, A. B., (Ed.), *Selected Speeches and Documents on British Colonial Policy, 1763–1917*, 2 vols. (Oxford, 1918).

RAMM, AGATHA (Ed.), *The Political Correspondence of Mr. Gladstone and Lord Granville, 1868–76*, 2 vols. *Camden 3rd Series*, vols. LXXXI, LXXXII (London, 1952).

RAMM, AGATHA (Ed.), *The Political Correspondence of Mr. Gladstone and Lord Granville, 1876–86* (Oxford, 1962).

ROBINSON, SIR HERCULES, *Speeches of Sir Hercules Robinson*, (as Governor of New South Wales). Privately published by subscription (Sydney, 1879).

'Vindex' (Rev. F. Verschoyle), (Ed.), *Cecil Rhodes, His Political Life and Speeches, 1881–1900* (London, 1900).

IV. CONTEMPORARY WRITINGS

(*a*) *Daily Newspapers* (consulted for the years 1877–86)

Cape:
  Cape Times.
  Cape Argus.
  Di Patriot.
  Die Volksstem.

British:
  The Times (London).
  Pall Mall Gazette.
  Daily Telegraph.
  Daily News.
  Standard.
  Observer.

(*b*) *Periodicals* (consulted for the years 1870–90)

Annual Register.
Blackwood's Edinburgh Magazine.
Contemporary Review.
Edinburgh Review.
Fraser's Magazine.
Nineteenth Century.
Punch
Quarterly Review.
Saturday Review.
Spectator.
Westminster Review.

(c) Contemporary Articles of Particular Interest

ADDERLEY, C. B., (Lord Norton), 'How Not to Retain the Colonies', *Nineteenth Century*, VI (July 1879), 170.

Blackwood's Edinburgh Magazine, 'The South African Question', CXXIV (July 1878), 97.

'The Zulu War', CXXV (March 1879), 376.

'Mr. Gladstone's Pilgrimage', CXXVII (January 1880), 124.

'The Boers at Home: Jottings from the Transvaal', CXXX (December 1881), 753.

BOWEN, SIR G. F., 'The Federation of the British Empire', *Proceedings of the Royal Colonial Institute*, XVII (15 June 1886).

BRAMSTON, J., 'The Colonial Office From Within', *Empire Review*, I, (April 1900), 279.

BUTLER, W. F., 'The Boers and the Transvaal', *Contemporary Review*, XXXIX (February 1881), 220.

CARNARVON, EARL OF, 'The Cape in 1888', *Fortnightly Review*, new ser., XLIII (June 1888), 862.

COX, REV. SIR G. W., 'The English Nation and the Zulu War', *Fraser's Magazine*, new ser., XXI (February 1880), 261.

CURRIE, D., 'Thoughts upon the Present and Future of South Africa, and Central and Eastern Africa', *Proceedings of the Royal Colonial Institute*, VIII (7 June 1877), 380.

DE BEAUFORT, W. H., 'Holland and the Transvaal', *Nineteenth Century*, IX (March 1881), 573.

Edinburgh Review, 'South Africa', CXLIX (April 1879), 534. 'The New Parliament', CLI (1880), 547.

FOWLER, W., 'The Basutos and Sir Bartle Frere', *Nineteenth Century*, IX (March 1881), 547.

Fraser's Magazine, 'The Annexation of the Transvaal', new ser., XVI (August 1877), 179.

FRERE, SIR BARTLE, 'Have we a Colonial Policy?' *National Review*, (1883–84), 1–22.

'The Transvaal', *Nineteenth Century* (February 1881), pp. 211–36.

'The Basutos and the Constitution of the Cape of Good Hope', *Nineteenth Century*, IX (January 1881), 177.

FROUDE, J. A., 'England and Her Colonies', *Fraser's Magazine*, new ser., I (January 1870), 1.

'English Policy in South Africa', *Quarterly Review*, 143 (January 1877), 105.

'South Africa Once More', *Fortnightly Review*, new ser., XXVI (October 1879), 449.

GLADSTONE, W. E., 'England's Mission', *Nineteenth Century*, IV (September 1878), 560.

531

GREY, EARL, 'Past and Future Policy in South Africa', *Nineteenth Century* (April 1879), 583.

'How Shall We Retain the Colonies?' ibid. (June 1879), p. 935.

'South Africa', ibid. (December 1880), p. 933.

HAMILTON, W. A. B., 'Forty Four Years at the Colonial Office', *Nineteenth Century*, LXV (April 1909), 599.

HOLUB, E., 'The Past, Present and Future Trade of the Cape Colonies with Central Africa', *Proceedings of the Royal Colonial Institute*, XI (16 December 1879), 55.

MORLEY, J., 'The Plain Story of the Zulu War', *Fortnightly Review*, new ser., XXV (March 1879), 329.

PINE, B. C. C., 'The Boers and the Zulus', *Contemporary Review*, XXXV (June 1879), 541.

Quarterly Review, 'The South African Problem', 147 (April 1879), 552.

'The Conservative Defeat', 149 (April 1880), 549.

ROGERS, F. (Lord Blachford), 'Native Policy in South Africa', *Edinburgh Review*, CXLV (April 1877), 447.

'South African Policy', ibid., VI (August 1879), 264.

SEEBOHM, F., 'Imperialism and Socialism', *Nineteenth Century*, VII (April 1880), 726.

SMITH, GOLDWIN, 'The Policy of Aggrandizement', *Fortnightly Review*, new ser., XXII (1 September 1877), 303.

STATHAM, F. R., 'A Story of Annexation in South Africa', *Fortnightly Review*, new ser., XXVIII (November 1880), 617.

'How to get out of the South African Difficulty', ibid., XXIX (March 1881), 285.

TROLLOPE, ANTHONY, 'Kafir Land', *Fortnightly Review*, XVI (February 1878), 701.

Westminster Review, 'South Africa', new ser., XXXV (April 1869), 307.

'Our South African Colonies', (April 1879), 386.

'India and Our Colonial Empire; South Africa', LVII (October 1880), 511.

WILSON, E. D., 'What is a Colonial Governor?' *Nineteenth Century*, (December 1878), 1053.

(d) Contemporary Books, Memoirs, and Pamphlets

AYLWARD, A., *The Transvaal Today* (Edinburgh, 1878).

BEZUIDENHOUT, C. P., *De Geschiedenis van het Afrikaansche Geslacht van 1688 tot 1882* (Bloemfontein, 1883.)

CACHET, F. L., *De Worstelstrijd der Transvaalers* (Amsterdam, 1882).

CARTER, T. F., *A Narrative of the Boer War* (London, 1883).

CHESSON, F. W., *The Dutch Republics of South Africa* (1871).

CLARK, G. B. (Secretary to 'Transvaal Independence Committee'), *British Policy towards the Boers—an Historical Sketch* (Pamphlet), (London, 1881).

Our Future Policy in the Transvaal; a Defence of the Boers (Pamphlet), (London, 1881).

COLLEY: *Life of Sir George Pomeroy Colley*, by Sir W. F. Butler (London, 1899).

DAVISON, C. F., *The Case of the Boers in Transvaal* (Pamphlet), (London, 1881).

DILKE, SIR CHARLES, *Greater Britain: a record of travel in English-speaking Countries*, 2 vols. (London, 1868).

Problems of Greater Britain (London, 1890).

DU TOIT, J. D., *Ds. S. J. du Toit in Weg en Werk* (Paarl, 1917).

DU TOIT, REV. S. J., *Die Geskiedenis van Ons land in die Taal van ons Volk* (Paarl, 1877).

Het Program van Beginselen van de Nationale Party, opgesteld, verklaard en toegelicht (Paarl, 1880).

Die Geskiedenis van die Afrikaanse Taal-beweging (Paarl, 1880).

ESCOTT, T. H. S. (Ed.), *Pillars of the Empire: Sketches of living Indian and Colonial Statesmen, Celebrities, and Officials* (London, 1879).

FAURE, D. P., *My Life and Times* (London, 1907). Faure was the official interpreter at the London Convention negotiations in 1883–84.

FORSTER, W. E., *Our Colonial Empire. An address delivered before the Philosophical Institution of Edinburgh* (Edinburgh, 1875).

FORSTER: *Life of Rt. Hon. William Edward Forster*, by T. Wemyss Reid, 2 vols. (London, 1888).

FOUCHÉ, LEO, *Die Evolutie van die Trekboer* (Pretoria, 1909).

FRERE, SIR BARTLE: *The Life and Correspondence of Sir Bartle Frere*, by J. Martineau, 2 vols. (London, 1895).

The Union of the Various Portions of British South Africa (Pamphlet), (London, 1881).

FROUDE, J. A., *Oceana, or England and her Colonies* (London, 1886).

GRESWELL, W. H. P., *Our South African Empire*, 2 vols. (London, 1885).

HAGGARD, RIDER, *The Last Boer War* [i.e. of 1881] (London, 1899).

HOBSON, J. A., *Imperialism: A Study*, 4th imp. (London, 1948).

HOFMEYR: *The Life of Jan Hendrik Hofmeyr, Onze Jan*, by J. H. Hofmeyr and F. W. Reitz (Cape Town, 1913).

HOFSTEDE, H. J., *Geschiedenis van den Oranje Vrij-Staat* (The Hague, 1876).

JEPPPE, CARL, *The Kaleidoscopic Transvaal* (London, 1906).

JORISSEN, E. J. P., *Transvaalsche Herinneringen* (Amsterdam 1897).

KRUGER: *Paul Kruger en die Opkomst van den Zuid-Afrikaansche Republiek*, by J. F. van Oordt (Amsterdam, 1898).

The Memoirs of Paul Kruger, 2 vols. (London, 1902).

LAKEMAN, SIR S., *What I saw in Kaffir-Land* (Edinburgh, 1880).

LEYDS, W. J., *The Transvaal Surrounded* (London, 1919).

First Annexation of the Transvaal (London, 1906).

LUCAS, T. J., *The Zulus and the British Frontiers* (London, 1879).

LUCY, HENRY W., *A Diary of Two Parliaments; The Gladstone Parliament, 1880–85* (London, 1886).

MACKENZIE, REV. JOHN, *Bechuanaland, the Transvaal and England. A Statement and a Plea, prepared for the Directors and Friends of the London Missionary Society* (London, 1883).

Bechuanaland, and our Progress Northward (Cape Town, 1884).

Bechuanaland: Its lessons for the Cape Colony (Cape Town 1884).

The High Commissionership as Connected with the Progress and Prosperity of South Africa (London, 1886).

Austral Africa, Ruling it or Losing it, 2 vols. (London, 1887).

MACKENZIE: *John Mackenzie, South African Missionary and Statesman*, by W. Douglas Mackenzie (his son), (London, 1902).

MCCARTHY, JUSTIN, *Reminiscences* (London, 1899), pp. 140–49 very good on Sir Hercules Robinson, whom he knew from the 1840s.

MERIVALE, H., *Lectures on Colonization and Civilization* (London, 1861).

MOLESWORTH, W., *Materials for a Speech in Defence of the Policy of Abandoning the Orange River Territory* (London, 1854), republished by Kruger, 1878.

MOLTENO: *Life and Times of Molteno*, by P. A. Molteno, 2 vols. (London, 1900).

MOODIE, G. P., *Annexation of the Transvaal* (London, 1881).

MORLEY, JOHN (Viscount), *Recollections*, 2 vols. (1917).

NEWNHAM-DAVIES, N., *The Transvaal under the Queen* (London, 1900).

NIXON, J., *The Complete Story of the Transvaal* (London, 1885).

ORPEN, J. M., *Bechuanaland* (London, 1885).

Reminiscences (Durban, 1908).

PAULING, GEORGE, *The Chronicles of a Contractor* (Ed. by D. Buchan) (London, 1926). Best first-hand account of Warren expedition, particularly the reaction of Goshenites, p. 55.

RHODES: *The Rt. Hon. Cecil John Rhodes, A Monograph and Reminiscence*, by Sir Thomas Fuller, K.C.M.G. (London, 1910). Though a close friend of Rhodes, Fuller gives a remarkably good picture of Cape politics in the 1880s.

Cecil Rhodes, His Private Life by his Private Secretary, Philip Jourdan (London, 1910), which just proves he had no such thing as a private life.

Life and Times of Cecil John Rhodes, by Lewis Michell, 2 vols. (London, 1910). Too close a friend.

Cecil Rhodes, a personal record, by Vere Stent, Introduction by Sir Percy Fitzpatrick (Cape Town, 1924). Good on the famous 'Indaba'.

ROSE-INNES, JAMES, *Autobiography* (Oxford, 1949). Good, sound, and sharp.

SCHREINER, T. L., *The Afrikaner Bond, and other Causes of the War* (London, 1901).

SCOBLE, J. and ABERCROMBIE, H. R., *The Rise and Fall of Krugerism. A personal record of 40 years in South Africa* (London, 1900).

SEELEY, PROF. J., *Expansion of England* (London, 1883).

SELBORNE, EARL OF, *Memorials,* 4 vols., Part I, (London, 1896); including several most interesting letters from Kimberley, a close friend.

SELLAR, A. C., *The Transvaal 1877–81* (Pamphlet), Edinburgh, 1881). Printed by the Liberal Party.

SLATER, J., *The Birth of the Bond* (London, 1900).

SMUTS, J. C., *A Century of Wrong,* Preface by W. T. Stead (published anonymously), (London, 1900).

Society in London, by a 'Foreign Resident' (Leipzig, 1885).

SOUTH AFRICAN VIGILANCE COMMITTEE, *The Anti-British Crusade in South Africa* (Cape Town, 1900).

STEAD, W. T., *The Last Will and Testament of Cecil John Rhodes* (London, 1902). Without any doubt the best and most sensitive contemporary analysis of Rhodes and his ideals.

THEAL, GEORGE MCCALL, *The History of South Africa from 1873–1884,* 2 vols. (London, 1884).

TODD, A., *Parliamentary Government in the British Colonies* (London, 1880).

TROLLOPE, A., *South Africa,* 2 vols., 2nd ed. (London, 1878).

VERNEY, E.H., *Four Years of Protest in the Transvaal* (Pamphlet), (London, 1881). Verney was a leading member of the 'Transvaal Independence Committee' in London.

WEILBACH, J. D. and DU PLESSIS, C. N. J., *Geschiedenis van den Emigranten-Boeren en van den Vryheidsoorlog* (Cape Town, 1882).

WHEELER, J., *The War Office, Past and Present* (London, 1914).

WILLIAMS, RALPH, *The British Lion in Bechuanaland* (London, 1885).

WILMOT, A., *History of the Zulu War* (London, 1880).

WOOD, SIR EVELYN, *Winnowed Memories* (London, 1918).

V. LATER WORKS

(*a*) *Bibliographies and Guides*

FORD, P. and FORD, G., *A Guide to Parliamentary Papers* (Oxford, 1958).

HEWITT, A. R., *Guide to the Resources for Commonwealth Studies in London, Oxford, and Cambridge* (London, 1957).

INSTITUTE OF HISTORICAL RESEARCH. *Theses Supplements to the Bulletin of the Institute of Historical Research*, nos. 1–21 (1933–65).

LIBRARY ASSOCIATION, *The Subject Index to Periodicals* (London, 1915–60).

VARLEY, D. H. (Ed.), *Bibliography of African Bibliographies South of the Sahara*, Grey Bibliographies, no. 6, compiled by A. M. Lewin Robinson, 3rd rev. ed. (Cape Town, 1955).

(*b*) *Learned Articles*

ADAMS, M., 'The British Attitude to German Colonisation, 1880–85', *Bulletin of the Institute of Historical Research*, XV (London 1937–38), 190–93.

BIXLER, R. W., 'Anglo-Portuguese Rivalry for Delagoa Bay', *Journal of Modern History*, VI (1934), 425–40.

BLAINEY, G., 'Lost Cause of the Jameson Raid', *Economic History Review*, 2nd ser., XVIII (August 1965), 350–67.

CREIGHTON, D. G., 'The Victorians and the Empire', *Canadian Historical Review*, XIX (1938), 138–53.

CURTIN, P. D., 'The British Empire and Commonwealth in Recent Historiography', *American Historical Review*, LXV (1959–60), 72–91.

DAVENPORT, T. R. H., 'The Responsible Government Issue in Natal, 1880–82', *Butterworth's South African Law Review* (1957), 84–133.

DE KOCK, W. J., 'Die Rol van J. A. Froude in Suid-Afrika', *Historiese Studies*, Jaargang 1 (1939–40), 35–45.

ENSOR, SIR R. C. K., 'Some Political and Economic Interactions in Later Victorian England', *Transactions of the Royal Historical Society* (1949).

FIELDHOUSE, DAVID, ' "Imperialism"—an Historiographical Review', *Economic History Review*, 2nd ser., XIV (1961–62), 187–209.

FRASER, P., 'The Liberal Unionist Alliance: Chamberlain, Hartington and the Conservatives, 1886–1904', *English Historical Review* (1962).

GALBRAITH, J. S., 'The "Turbulent Frontier" as a Factor in British Expansion', *Comparative Studies in Society and History*, II (1959–60), 150–68.

GALLAGHER, J. and ROBINSON, R. E., 'The Imperialism of Free Trade', *Economic History Review*, 2nd ser., VI (1953–54), 1–15.

GOODMAN, G., 'Liberal Unionism: The Revolt of the Whigs', *Victorian Studies* (1959).

HARLOW, V., 'The Historiography of the British Empire and Commonwealth since 1945', *International Committee of Historical Sciences—XI Congress of Historical Sciences* (Stockholm, 21–8, August 1960).

HATTERSLEY, A. F., 'The Annexation of the Transvaal, 1877', *History*, XXI (1936–37), 41–7.

HOWARD, C. H. D., 'Joseph Chamberlain and the Unauthorised Programme', *English Historical Review* (1950).
'Lord Randolph Churchill', *History* (1940).

HURST, M. C., 'Joseph Chamberlain, the Conservatives and the Succession to John Bright, 1886–9', *Historical Journal* (1964).

INGLIS, B., 'The Influence of *The Times*', *Historical Studies*, III (1961), 32–44. (4th Irish Conference of Historians.)

KOEBNER, R., 'The Concept of Economic Imperialism', *Economic History Review*, 2nd ser., II (1949–50), 1–29.
'The emergence of the concept of Imperialism', *Cambridge Journal*, V (1952), 726–41.

LEWSON, P., 'The First Crisis of Responsible Government in the Cape Colony', *A.Y.B.*, Part II (1942), 205–65.

MACDONAGH, O., 'The Anti-Imperialism of Free Trade', *Economic History Review*, 2nd ser., XIV (1961–62), 489–501.

MCCRACKEN, J. L., 'The Members of the Cape Parliament, 1814–1910', *Historical Studies*, II (1959), 79–88. (3rd Irish Conference of Historians.)

NEWBURY, COLIN, 'The Partition of Africa, II; Victorians, Republicans and the Partition of West Africa', *Journal of African History*, III (1962), 493–501.

NOWELL, C., 'Portugal and the Partition of Africa', *Journal of Modern History*, XIX (1947), 1–17.

OTTO, J. C., 'Oorsake en Gebeurtenisse wat indirek en regstreeks aanleiding gegee het tot die Veldtog teen Sekockoenie, 1876', *Historiese Studies*, Jaargang 7 (1946), 148–63.

PENNER, C. D., 'Germany and the Transvaal before 1896', *Journal of Modern History*, XII (1940), 31–58.

PYRAH, G. B., 'Reflections on Responsible Government', *History*, XLI (1956), 158–75.

ROACH, J., 'Liberalism and the Victorian Intelligentsia', *Cambridge Historical Journal*, XIII (1957), 58–81.

ROBINSON, R. E., 'The Official Mind of Imperialism', *Historians in Tropical Africa* (Salisbury, 1962), pp. 197–208. (Leverhulme History Conference, Salisbury, 1960.)

STENGERS, JEAN, 'The Partition of Africa, I; L'Imperialisme Colonial de la Fin du XIXᵉ Siecle; Mythe ou Realite', *Journal of African History*, III (1962), 469–91.

THOMPSON, A. F., 'Gladstone's Whips and the General Election of 1868', *English Historical Review* (1948).

THOMPSON, L. M., 'Constitutionalism in the South African Republics', *Butterworth's South African Law Review* (1954), 49–72.

THOMPSON, P., 'Liberals, Radicals and Labour in London, 1800–1900', *Past and Present* (1964).

THORNLEY, D., 'The Irish Home Rule Party and Parliamentary Obstruction, 1874–87', *Irish Historical Studies*, XII (1960).

VAN JAARSVELD, F. A., 'Die Vrystaat-Transvaalse Vriendskapverdrag van 1872', *Historia*, Jaargang 2 (1957), 148–62.

WALKER, E. A., 'The Franchise in South Africa', *Cambridge Historical Journal*, XI (1953), 93–113.

(c) Modern Biographies

BALFOUR: *Arthur James Balfour*, by B. E. C. Dugdale, 2 vols. (London, 1936).

BRADLAUGH: *The Bradlaugh Case*, by W. L. Arnstein (Oxford, 1965).

BRAND: *De Levensgeschiedenis van President J. H. Brand*, by J. F. van Oordt (Amsterdam, 1914).

President Johannes Henricus Brand, 1823–1888, by G. D. Scholtz (Johannesburg, 1957).

BRYCE: *The Life of James Bryce, O.M.*, by H. A. L. Fisher (London, 1927 (2 vols.)

BRYCE, J., *Studies in Contemporary Biography* (London, 1903).

BURGERS: *Thomas Francois Burgers; 'n Lewenskets*, by T. F. Burgers and S. P. Engelbrecht (Pretoria, 1937).

CAMBRIDGE: *The Royal George; The Life of the Duke of Cambridge*, by Giles St. Aubyn (London, 1963).

CARNARVON: *The Life of the 4th Earl of Carnarvon*, by Sir Arthur Hardinge, 2 vols. (Oxford, 1925).

CETYWAYO: *The Last Zulu King. The Life and Death of Cetywayo*, by C. T. Binns (London, 1963).

CHAMBERLAIN: *The Life of Chamberlain*, by J. L. Garvin and J. Amery, 4 vols. (London, 1935–51).

Joseph Chamberlain: Radicalism and Empire, 1868–1914, by Peter Fraser (London, 1966).

CHILDERS: *The Life and Correspondence of Hugh C. E. Childers, 1827–1896*, by Lt.-Col. Spencer Childers (his son), 2 vols. (London, 1906).

CHURCHILL: *Lord Randolph Churchill*, by (Sir) W. S. Churchill, 2 vols. (London, 1906).

DALE: *The Life of R. W. Dale of Birmingham*, by A. W. W. Dale (his son), 2nd ed. (London, 1899).

DEACON, R., *The Private Life of Mr. Gladstone* (London, 1965).

DE VILLIERS: *Lord De Villiers and His Times*, by E. A. Walker (London, 1925).

DILKE: *The Life of the Rt. Hon. Charles Dilke*, begun by S. Gwynn, completed by G. Tuckwell, 2 vols. (London, 1917).

Dilke: A Victorian Tragedy, by the Rt. Hon. Roy Jenkins (London, 1958).

DISRAELI: *The Life of Benjamin Disraeli, Earl of Beaconsfield*, by W. F. Monypenny and G. E. Buckle, 6 vols. (London, 1910–20).

Disraeli, by Robert Blake (London, 1967).

(Also useful: Morison, J. L., 'The Imperial Ideas of Benjamin Disraeli', *Canadian Historical Review*, I (1920), 267.

FRERE: *Sir Bartle Frere*, by Basil Worsfold (London, 1923).

GATHORNE HARDY (Lord Cranbrook): *A Memoir of Gathorne Hardy, First Earl of Cranbrook*, by A. E. Gathorne Hardy, 2 vols. (London, 1910).

GLADSTONE: *The Life of Gladstone*, by John Morley, 3 vols. (London, 1903).

Gladstone, A Biography, by Philip Magnus (London, 1960).

The Story of Gladstone's Life, by J. McCarthy (London, 1907).

Gladstone and the Bulgarian Agitation, 1876, by R. T. Shannon (London, 1963).

Gladstone and the Irish Nation, by J. L. Hammond (London, 1938).

Mr. Gladstone, by W. Bagehot (London, 1860).

Life of W. E. Gladstone, by H. W. Paul (London, 1901).

Mr Gladstone at Oxford, by C. R. L. Fletcher (London, 1908).

Correspondence on Church and Religion of W. E. Gladstone, by D. C. Lathbury (Ed.), 2 vols. (1910).

Gladstone's Speeches, by Tilney Basset (Ed.) (London, 1916).

Gladstone as Financier and Economist, by F. W. Hirst (London, 1931).

Gladstone, by Frances Birrell (London, 1933).

Gladstone at the Board of Trade, by F. E. Hyde (London, 1934).

The Rise of Mr. Gladstone, 1859–68, by F. E. Williams (Cambridge, 1934).

BIBLIOGRAPHY

Disraeli, Gladstone and the Eastern Question, by R. W. Seton-Watson (London, 1935).

Gladstone and Liberalism, by J. L. Hammond and M. R. D. Foot (London, 1952).

Gladstone and Britain's Imperial Policy, by P. Knaplund (1927).

GLADSTONE: *After Thirty Years*, by the Rt. Hon. Viscount Gladstone (London, 1928).

GOSCHEN: *The Life of George Joachim Goschen, 1st Earl, 1831–1907*, by the Hon. Arthur D. Elliot, 2 vols. (London, 1911).

GRANVILLE: *The Life of George Leveson Gower, 2nd Earl of Granville, K.G. 1815–91*, by Lord Edmund Fitzmaurice, 2 vols. (London, 1905).

GREY: *Sir George Grey, K.C.B., 1812–1898*, by J. Rutherford (London 1961).

HARCOURT: *The Life of Sir William Harcourt*, by A. G. Gardiner, 2 vols. (London, 1923).

HARTINGTON: *Life of Spencer Compton, 8th Duke of Devonshire*, by Bernard Holland, 2 vols. (London, 1911).

HERBERT, SIR R. G. W., *The Times*, Obituary (8 May 1905).

HICKS BEACH: *Life of Sir Michael Hicks Beach*, by Lady Victoria Hicks Beach, 2 vols. (London, 1932).

JAMESON: *The Life of Jameson*, by Ian Colvin, 2 vols. (London, 1922).

KRUGER: *Paul Kruger: His Life and Times*, by Manfred Nathan, 4th ed., (Durban, May 1944).

Paul Kruger, by D. W. Kruger, 2 vols. (in Afrikaans), (Johannesburg, 1963).

The Pace of the Ox. The Life of Paul Kruger, by Marjorie Juta (London, 1937).

LABOUCHERE: *The Life of Henry Labouchere*, by A. L. Thorold (London, 1913).

MERRIMAN: *The Life of John Xavier Merriman*, by P. M. Laurence (London, 1930).

MILNER: *Alfred Lord Milner; the man of no illusions, 1854–1925*, by John Evelyn Wrench (London, 1958).

MOUTON, J. A., 'General Joubert in die Geskiedenis van Transvaal', *A.Y.B.* (Pretoria, 1957).

NORTHCOTE (Lord Iddesleigh): *Sir Stafford Northcote, 1st Earl of Iddesleigh*, by A. Lang, 2 vols. (London, 1890).

PONSONBY: *Henry Ponsonby, His Life from His Letters*, by Arthur Ponsonby (London, 1942).

POPE-HENNESSY, J., *Verandah; Some Episodes in the Crown Colonies, 1867–1889* (London, 1964).

540

RHODES: *Cecil Rhodes*, by Basil Williams (London, 1921).
Cecil Rhodes, by W. Plomer (London, 1933).
Rhodes: a life, by J. G. McDonald (London, 1928).
Rhodes, by Sarah Gertrude Millin (London, 1933).
Rhodes of Africa, by Felix Gross (London, 1956).
Rhodes, by J. G. Lockhart and the Hon. C. M. Woodhouse (London, 1963).
ROSEBERY: *Rosebery*, by Robert Rhodes James (London, 1963).
SALISBURY: *The Life of Robert, Marquis of Salisbury*, by Lady Gwendolen Cecil, 4 vols. (London, 1921).
Lord Salisbury, 1830–1903; Portrait of a Statesman, by A. L. Kennedy (London, 1953).
SHAKA: *Shaka Zulu: The Rise of the Zulu Empire*, by E. A. Ritter (London, 1955).
SOLOMON: *Saul Solomon, the Member for Cape Town*, by W. E. G. Solomon (Cape Town, 1948).
STANMORE: *Life of Lord Stanmore*, (Arthur Gordon), by J. K. Chapman (Toronto, 1965).
STEAD: *The Life of W. T. Stead*, by F. White, 2 vols. (1925).
WARREN: *Life of General Sir Charles Warren*, by W. W. Williams (his grandson), (Oxford, 1941).
WOLSELEY: *All Sir Garnet. A Life of Field-Marshal Lord Wolseley, 1833–1913*, by J. Lehman (London, 1964).

(*d*) *General Works: Books dealing with British Politics, the Empire and Africa as a whole*

ASHWORTH, W., *An Economic History of England, 1870–1939* (London, 1960).
ANSTEY, R., *Britain and the Congo in the 19th Century* (London, 1962).
AUSUBEL, H., *The Late Victorians* (New York, 1955).
AYDELOTTE, W. O., *Bismarck and British Colonial Policy* (Philadelphia, 1937).
BLUNT, W. S., *The Land War in Ireland* (London, 1932).
BODELSEN, C. A., *Studies in Mid-Victorian Imperialism* (1924) (Reprinted London, 1960).
BROWN, B. H., *The Tariff Reform Movement in Great Britain, 1881–95* (New York, 1943).
BUSCH, M., *Bismarck, Some Secret Pages from His History* (London, 1898).
CAIRNCROSS, A. K., *Home and Foreign Investment, 1870–1913. Studies in Capital Accumulation* (Cambridge, 1953).
CAMBRIDGE: *The Cambridge History of the British Empire*.
Vol. II: 'The Growth of the New Empire, 1783–1870' (1940).

Vol.   III: 'The Empire–Commonwealth, 1870–1919' (1959).

Vol.   VI: 'Canada and Newfoundland'.

Vol. VIII: 'Southern Africa', 2nd ed. (1962).

The New Cambridge Modern History.

Vol.   X: 'The Zenith of European Power, 1830–70' (1960).

Vol.   XI: 'Material Progress and World-wide Problems, 1870–98' (1962).

COLLINGS, J., *Land Reform* (London, 1906).

COUPLAND, R., *The Exploitation of East Africa, 1856–90; the Slave Trade and the Scramble* (London, 1939).

CROWE, S. E., *The Berlin West African Conference, 1884–5* (London, 1942).

CURTIS, L. P., *Coercion and Conciliation in Ireland, 1880–92. A Study in Conservative Unionism* (London, 1963).

DICEY, A., *England's Case Against Home Rule* (London, 1886).

DILKE, SIR CHARLES, *The Present Position of European Politics* (London, 1887).

DUFFY, J., *Portuguese Africa* (London, 1959).

ENSOR, R. C. K., *England, 1870–1914* (Oxford, 1936).

EYCK, E., *Bismarck and the German Empire* (London, 1950).

FARR, D., *The Colonial Office and Canada, 1867–1887* (Toronto, 1955).

FRANKEL, S. H., *Capital Investment in Africa* (London, 1938).

GRETTON R. H., *Imperialism and Mr. Gladstone, 1876–87* (London, 1923).

HALLBERG, C. W., *The Suez Canal, its History and Diplomatic Importance* (New York, 1931).

HAMILTON, SIR IAN, *Listening for the Drums* (London, 1944).

HANHAM, H. J., *Elections and Party Management: Politics in the Time of Disraeli and Gladstone* (London, 1959).

HARDIE, F., *The Political Influence of Queen Victoria, 1861–1901* 2nd ed. (London, 1938).

HODGE, A. L., *Angra Pequena* (Edinburgh, 1936).

HURST, M. C., *Joseph Chamberlain and West Midland Politics, 1886–95* (Oxford, 1962).

Joseph Chamberlain and Liberal Reunion (London, 1967).

KOEBNER, R. and SCHMIDT, H. D., *Imperialism: The Story and Significance of a Political Word, 1840–1960* (Cambridge, 1960).

LANGER, W. L., *European Alliances and Alignments* (New York, 1950).

LEWIN, EVANS, *The Germans and Africa* (London, 1939).

LOWE, C. J., *Salisbury and the Mediterranean, 1886–96* (London, 1964).

LYONS, F. S. L., *The Fall of Parnell* (London, 1960).

MARDER, A. J., *British Naval Policy, 1880–95* (London, 1940).

MCDOWELL, R. B., *The Irish Administration, 1801–1914* (London, 1964).

O'BRIEN, CONOR CRUISE, *Parnell and His Party, 1880–90* (Oxford, 1957).

RAPHAEL, L. A. C., *The Cape to Cairo Dream* (New York, 1936).

ROBINSON, R., GALLAGHER, J. with DENNY, A., *Africa and the Victorians, The Official Mind of Imperialism* (London, 1963).

SAUL, S. B., *Studies in British Overseas Trade, 1870–1914* (Liverpool, 1960).

SCHLOTE, W., *British Overseas Trade from 1700–1930* (English trans.), (Oxford, 1952. First published, Jena, 1938).

SCHUMPETER, J. A., *The Sociology of Imperialism*, 2nd ed. (New York, 1955).

SCHUYLER, R. L., *The Fall of the Old Colonial System; a Study in British Free Trade, 1770–1870* (London and New York, 1945).

SEMMEL, *Imperialism and Social Reform* (London, 1960).

SOUTHGATE, D., *The Passing of the Whigs, 1832–86* (London, 1962).

STANSKY, P., *Ambitions and Strategies: The Struggle for the Leadership of the Liberal Party in the 1890's* (London, 1964).

STRAUSS, E., *Irish Nationalism and British Democracy* (London, 1951).

STRAUSS, W. L., *Joseph Chamberlain and the Theory of Imperialism* (Washington, 1942).

TAYLOR, A. J. P., *Germany's First Bid for Colonies, 1884–1885* (London, 1938).

The Struggle for Mastery in Europe (Oxford, 1954).

THOMPSON, F. M. L., *English Landed Society in the 19th Century* (London, 1963).

THORNTON, A. P., *The Imperial Idea and Its Enemies* (London, 1959).

The Habit of Authority: Paternalism in British History (London, 1966).

TOWNSEND, MARY, *The Origins of Modern German Colonialism* (New York, 1921).

The Rise and Fall of Germany's Colonial Empire, 1884–1919 (New York, 1930).

TREVOR-ROPER, H., *Essays in British History* (London, 1965).

TYLER, J. E., *The Struggle for Imperial Unity* (London, 1938).

VINCENT, J., *The Formation of the Liberal Party, 1857–68* (London, 1966).

Pollbooks; How the Victorians Voted (Cambridge, 1967).

WALKER, E. A., *The British Empire; Its Structure and Spirit* (London, 1943).

WIGHT, M., *The Development of the Legislative Council, 1606–1945* (London, 1946).

BIBLIOGRAPHY

WILLIAMSON, J. A., *A Short History of British Expansion* (London, 1961).
WRIGHT, H. M. (Ed.), *The 'New Imperialism'* (Boston, 1961).
YOUNG, G. M., *Victorian England; Portrait of an Age* (London, 1953).

(e) Books on Southern Africa

(This list is not exhaustive. Only those works I found especially useful are listed.)
AGAR-HAMILTON, J. A. I., *The Road to the North, South Africa 1852–86* (London, 1937).
AMPHLETT, G. T., *History of the Standard Bank of South Africa Ltd. 1862–1913* (Glasgow, 1914).
ARNDT, E., *Banking and Currency Development in South Africa, 1652–1927* (Cape Town, 1928).
ASHTON, E. H., *The Basuto* (Cape Town 1951).
BACKEBERG, H. E., 'Die Betrekkinge tussen die Suid-Afrikaanse Republiek en Duitsland, tot na die Jameson-Inval, 1852–1896, *A.Y.B.*, Part I (1949).
BIXLER, R. W., *Anglo-German Imperialism in South Africa, 1880–1900* (Baltimore, 1932).
BOESEKEN, A. J., *Geskiedenis-Atlas vir Suid-Afrika* (Cape Town, 1959).
BOTHA, P. R., *Die Staatkundige Ontwikkeling van die Suid-Afrikaanse Republiek onder Kruger en Leyds* (Amsterdam, 1926).
BREYTENBACH, J. H., *Die Tweede Vryheidsoorlog* (Cape Town, 1948).
BROOKES, E. H., *The History of Native Policy in South Africa from 1830 to the Present Day*, 2nd ed. (Pretoria, 1927).
CAMPBELL, W. B., 'The South African Frontier, 1865–85. A Study in Expansion', *A.Y.B.*, Part I (1959).
COETZEE, J. A., *Politieke Groepering in die Wording van die Afrikanernasie* (Johannesburg, 1941).
COETZEE, J. C., *S. J. du Toit en die Onderwys* (Johannesburg, 1946).
CORY, SIR G. C., *The Rise of South Africa*, 5 vols. (Cape Town, 1910–30).
DAVENPORT, T. R. H., *The Afrikaner Bond* (Cape Town, 1966).
DAVEY, A. M., 'The Siege of Pretoria, 1880–81', *A.Y.B.* Part I(c), (1956).
DE KIEWIET, C. W., *The Imperial Factor in South Africa* (Cambridge, 1937).
A History of South Africa, Social and Economic (Oxford, 1941).
DE KOCK, M. H., *Selected Subjects in the Economic History of South Africa* (Cape Town, 1924).

544

DE KOCK, W. J., 'Ekstra Territoriale Vraagstukke van die Kaapse Regering, 1872–85', *A.T.B.* Part I (1948).

ENGELBRECHT, S. P., *Geskiedenis van die Nederduits Hervormde Kerk van Afrika* (Pretoria, 1936).

GALBRAITH, J. S., *Reluctant Empire: British Policy on the South African Frontier, 1834–54* (California, 1963).

GARSON, N. G., 'The Swaziland Question and the Road to the Sea, 1887–95', *A.T.B.*, Part II, (1957).

GOODFELLOW, D. M., *A Modern Economic History of South Africa* (London, 1931).

HINTRAGER, O., *Geschichte von Südafrika* (Munich, 1952).

HOBART HOUGHTON, D., *The South African Economy* (Cape Town, 1964).

KILPIN, R., *The Parliament of the Cape* (London, 1938).

KRUGER, D. W., 'Die Weg na die See', *A.T.B.*, Part I (1938).

LE MAY, G. H. L. *British Supremacy in South Africa, 1899–1907* (Oxford, 1965).

LOVELL, R. I., *The Struggle for South Africa, 1875–99* (New York, 1934).

LUGTENBERG, A. H., *Geskiedenis van die Onderwys in die Suid-Afrikaanse Republiek* (Pretoria, 1925).

MALCOLM, D. O., *The British South Africa Company, 1889–1939* (London, 1939).

MARAIS, J. S., *The Fall of Kruger's Republic* (Oxford, 1961).

MCCRACKEN, J. L., *The Cape Parliament* (Oxford, 1967).

MOLTENO, J. T., *The Dominion of Afrikanerdom* (London, 1923).

NEUMARK, S. D., *Economic Influences on the South African Frontier, 1652–1836* (Stanford, 1956).

NIENABER, G. S. and P. J., *Die Geskiedenis van die Afrikaanse Beweging* (Pretoria, 1941).

OBERHOLSTER, J. A. S., *Die Gereformeerde Kerke onder die Kruis in Suid-Afrika* (Cape Town, 1956).

PAKENHAM, E., *Jameson's Raid* (London, 1960).

PATTERSON, S., *The Last Trek; a study of the Boer people and the Afrikaner Nation* (London, 1957).

PELZER, A. N., *Die Geskiedenis van die Suid-Afrikaanse Republiek*, Deel I, Wordingsjare (Cape Town, 1950).

PIETERSE, D. J., 'Transvaal en Britse Susereinteit, 1881–84', *A.T.B.*, Part I (1940).

PYRAH, G. B., *Imperial Policy and South Africa, 1902–10* (Oxford, 1955).

SARON, G. and HOTZ, L. (Eds.), *The Jews in South Africa* (Cape Town, 1955).

545

SCHOLTZ, G. D., *Suid-Afrika en die Wêreldpolitiek* (Johannesburg, 1954).

SCHOLTZ, J. DU P., *Die Afrikaner en sy Taal* (Cape Town, 1939).

SCHUMANN, C. G. W., *Structural Changes and Business Cycles in South Africa, 1886–1936* (London, 1938).

SILLERY, A., *The Bechuanaland Protectorate* (Oxford, 1952).
Founding of a Protectorate: Bechuanaland 1885–95 (The Hague, 1966).

THEAL, G. M., *History of South Africa from 1873 to 1884*, 2 vols. (London, 1919).

THOMPSON, L. M., *The Unification of South Africa, 1902–10* (Oxford, 1960).

UYS, C. J., *In the Era of Shepstone* (London, 1933).

VAN DER HEEVER, C. M. and PIENAAR, P., *Die Kultuur-geskiedenis van die Afrikaner*, 3 vols. (Cape Town, 1945–50).

VAN DER MERWE, P. J., *Die Noordwaartse Beweging van die Boere voor die Groot Trek* (The Hague, 1937).
Dir Trekboer in die Geskiedenis van die Kaapkolonie (Cape Town, 1938).
Trek (Cape Town, 1945).

VAN DER POEL, J., *Railway and Customs Policies in South Africa, 1885–1910* (London, 1933).
The Jameson Road (Cape Town, 1951).

VAN DER WALT, A. J. H., WIID, J. A., and GEYER, A. L. (Eds.), *Die Geskiedenis van Suid-Afrika*, 2 vols. (Cape Town, 1915).

VAN DER WALT, H. R., 'Die Suid-Afrikaanse Republiek in die Britse Buitelandse Koloniale Beleid, 1881–99', *A.Y.B.*, Part I (1963).

VAN JAARSVELD, F. A., *Die Eenheidstrewe van die Republikeinse Afrikaaners* (Johannesburg, 1951).
Die Ontwaking van die Afrikaanse Nasionale Bewussyn, 1868–81 (Johannesburg, 1959).

VAN NIEKERK, L., *Die Eerste Afrikaanse Taalbeweging* (Amsterdam, 1916).

VAN ROOYEN T. S., 'Die Verhouding tussen die Boere, Engelse en Naturelle in die Geskiedenis van die Oos-Transvaal tot 1882', *A.Y.B.* (1951).

VAN WINTER, P. J., *Onder Kruger's Hollanders*, 2 vols. (Amsterdam, 1937).

WALKER, E. A., *A History of Southern Africa*, 3rd ed. (London, 1957).
An Historical Atlas of South Africa (Oxford, 1922).

WARHURST, P. R., *Anglo-Portuguese Relations in South-Central Africa, 1890–1900* (London, 1962).

INDEX

Aberdeen, Earl of, 40
Aborigines Protection Society, 72,
  317, 344
Acton, 1st Baron, 159
Aden, 297
Afghanistan, 53, 310, 367, 443, 465;
  Russia and, 471
'Africa for the Africanders', (Kruger
  slogan), 126, 128, 211, 299
Africans, of South Africa; *see*
  Basuto, Swazi, Tswana, Zulu
Afrikaner, definition of, 3; beliefs of,
  19–21
Afrikaner Bond, 30, 83, 258; Robinson
  analysis (1882), 298–99; in Tvl.,
  300, 372–3, 390, 454, 457, 463,
  474; failure in Tvl., 474, 476
Alexandria, bombarded (1882), 287
Alsace-Lorraine, 44
Anglo-Boer War (1899–1902), 13,
  29; causes, 363, 427
Arabi, 229, 287–8
Argyll, 8th Duke, 37, 79, 100, 103,
  123, 143, 178, 186–7, 207
Army Estimates (1881), 223
Ashley, E. and Tswana, 283–5;
  317–19; and *Bond*, 299; on Cape
  Dutch, 330; and Bech. 396, 399,
  402; and Boers, 468; also, 358,
  384
Australia, investment in (1878),
  11–12; tariffs, 48–50

Balfour, A. J., 82, 286
Balliol College, 217
Baring, 1st Visc., 365, 407
Barkly, Sir H., 282
Barolong tribe, 338

Basuto tribe, 90, 320, 337–42; and
  'gun war' (1880–1), 73, 83, 95,
  100, 107, 113; and annexation,
  13, 24, 256, 292, 316, 339–44,
  358; Cape fear of, 395–6; return
  to British trusteeship, 460, 467
Batlapin tribe, 266
Beaconsfield, *see* Disraeli
Bechuanaland, 13, 203, 214, 290;
  to be Crown Col.?, 293, 294; and
  Tvl. expan. (1882), 297–8, 300–2;
  frontier war, 319; and Tory pol.
  (1883), 323; and Tvl. (1883), 345
  passim; and London Convention,
  394 *passim*; and joint-protectorate,
  407–10; and Tvl. demands, 412–
  14, 416, 419; and Brit, annex up
  to Molopo, 458; 'Brit. Bech.'
  (1885), 461; *see also* Monstshiwa,
  Mankurwane, and Tswana
Bellairs, Col., 85
Bentham, J., 48
Berlin, 257
Bermuda, troops from, 139
Bethel, C., 263
Bezuidenhout 'wagon affair', 88
Bismarck, Prince O. von, 4–5, 230,
  256, 291, 370–1, 437, 445, 448–9,
  471
Bloemfontein Convention (1854), 22
Blyth, P. J., 107
Board of Trade, 56, 82
Boere Beschermings Vereeniging, 27, 112
Boers, *see* Tvl., Kruger, *Bond*, Cape
  Dutch, South Africa
Bok, E., 84, 140, 265, 346
Bokenhoutfontein, 216
Bomvanaland, 74

547

INDEX

Derby—*continued*
407–12; on need for Cape collaboration in S.A., 411–17; faces Kruger, 417; and Scanlen pledge, 418–20; firmer policy, 421; and suzerainty, 430–3; new S.A. policy, 446–8, 450, 454; recalls Warren; résumé of policy, 468 *passim*

Dilke, Sir C., 10, 13, 15, 65, 68–71, 91, 111, 122; 'plot' *vs* Kimberley, 136; Tvl. pol. of, 140, 170, 214, 252; and Egypt, 291; to Loc. Govt. Bd., 306; and French Tr., 307; and new Tvl. pol. (1883–4), 323, 324, 335, 356, 368, 419; and redistribution bill, 443–4; resigns, 460

Dillon, J. 186, 207
Dingaan's Day (16 December), 88, 258

Disraeli, B. (Ld. Beaconsfield), 1, 2, 6, 37–9, 40, 42, 43, 52, 53, 54, 56; death, 188; memory invoked, 291; on Stanley family, 308

Dodson, 1st Baron, 79, 306
Drakensberg Mts., 175
Dublin, 73, 286
Dufferin, 1st Marquis, 365
Dutch Reformed Church, 75; and Tvl. freedom, 127

Du Toit, S. J., 28, 111, 112, 361, 389; in Tvl. (1884), 413, 424, 427; and influence over Kruger, 442–4, 474

East India Co., 8
'Eastern Question', 232

Egypt, crisis (1882), 4, 53, 82, 100, 142, 207, 228; and Anglo-French *entente*, 230, 246, 256; and Anglo-French *detente*, 283, 286, 287–90; concurrent with Irish crisis, 291; Hartington on, 323; Sudan crisis (1883–4), 407, 418–20, 443; *see also* 343, 364, 370, 471

Empire Loyalists (Cape), 170

Fairfield, E., 16–17, 22, 61, 68, 113, 123, 166, 276, 287, 341, 400, 421, 459

Fenianism, 1, 2, 5, 32, 177, 211, 227, 232, 234, 247, 292, 310, 445, 463, 465

Field Cornets, of Tvl., 262
Foreign Office (British), 109, 194, 251, 412, 460

Forster, W. E., 72–3, 97, 99, 103, 136, 178, 186, 207, 214, 229, 246, 282, 286, 331, 332; and Bech. (1884), 413

France, 167, 212
'Freebooters', in Bech. (1882), 260, 293; (1883), 318 *passim*; republics of, 371; (1884–5), 455, 468

Frere, Sir B., 60, 62, 66, 68, 78, 88, 127; dismissal, 66–72, 78–80, 162

Galekaland, 74
Genootskap van Regte Afrikaners, 27, 112
George Town, protest of (1881), 126

Germany, 167; in Africa, 369–71; and S.W.A., 395–6; and Boers, 449, 461, 463, 475

Gibraltar, 18

Gladstone, W. E., col. pol. of, 45–52; for. pol. of, 41–5, 52–4; and Liberalism, 31–2; 1st admin., 39; 2nd admin., 4–6, 31, 121, 128, 136, 138, 230, 286; and Cab. rifts, 290–1; reshuffles Cab., 306; and 'England's Mission', 37, 213; (ii) Midlothian campaign, 37–9, 52–6, 66, 81, 91; election (1880), 55; (iii) promises to Boers, 89–92, 96; and Tvl. pol. (1880), 29, 60–89, 95; Tvl. pol. (1881), 140 *passim*; and Boer revolt, 94–6; on peace, 150–6; and Pretoria Convention, 205, 217 *passim*; concern over renewed rebellion, 229–39; on 'dirty Boers', 232, 236, 248–50; and ratification of Convention, 250–3; on 'Robinson plan' (1882), 274; and

550

Derby's Tvl. pol. (1883), 306 *passim*; weary of Boer problem, 319; justifies inactivity in S.A., 331–4; on *Bond*, 333; and Convention violations, 354 *passim*; concern over Cape Dutch, 361; defends Derby pol., 386–88, 391; and London Convention, (1883–4), 397 *passim*; despairs of Boer demands, 404–5; concerned over Convention (1884), 420–56; on Afrikaner's and S.A. dilemma, 466–77; accepts German expansion in S.A., 475; (iv) on 'unsolvable' nature of Boer problem, 15, 16, 63; and Britain in Africa, 41; and dislike of imperialism, 313, 318; and faith in *laissez faire*, 41; (v) and 'Eastern Question', 42, 55, 81, 232; (vi) *vs* Harcourt, 286; *vs* Whigs, 136, 256; *vs* Radicals, 138; *vs* Queen Victoria, 142, 368–9; (vii) as 'People's William', 39; as G.O.M., 39, 81, 92, 179, 207, 231, 244, 287, 407, 430, 462, 469, 471; as Christian statesman, 41, 45, 53, 101; (viii) and desire for retirement, 254, 306; *see also* Kruger, South Africa, Transvaal, Pretoria and London Conventions, 'Home Rule'
Gladstone, Mrs W. E., 256
Gladstone, Herbert (son of W. E. G.), 135
Gordon, Gen. 'Chinese', 231; and Basutoland, 294; at Khartoum, 295, 407, 419, 443, 445
Gorst, Sir J., 211, 323, 329
Goshen Republic, 267, 277, 371; annexed by Tvl., 447, 468; *see also* Transvaal
Graaf Reinet, petition of (1881), 125
Grahamstown, 76
Granville, 2nd Earl, 39, 42, 49, 100, 101, 120, 123, 148, 177, 192, 195, 206, 207, 229, 231, 235, 244, 246, 252, 291–2, 310, 369, 370, 399, 401, 407–8, 410–11, 419, 445

Great Trek (1835–8), 128, 165, 258, 259
Grey, Sir G., 23
Grey, Ld., 282, 386
Griqualand West, 24
Guizot, F., 50

Haggard, Rider, 169
Hamilton, A.D.C. to Colley, 139
Hamilton, Sir E., 79, 101, 110, 135, 156, 158, 211, 212, 231, 254, 255, 289, 324, 359, 361, 391, 404, 410, 419, 440
Harcourt, Sir W., 56, 70, 82, 103, 123, 137, 176, 209, 214, 286, 310, 323, 356, 367, 369, 445
Hartington, 8th Duke of Devonshire, 31, 42, 43, 55, 80, 91, 100, 102, 123, 152, 178, 186–7, 207, 214, 229, 231, 241, 255; and Egypt, 291–2; *vs* Granville policy, 310, 323, 324–5, 366, 369, 370, 406; to resign?, 407–8, 410–12; *see also* 449, 451, 454, 465
Heidelberg, besieged in Tvl. war (1881), 89, 140, 143, 144–5, 299
Hemming, Sir A., 106, 123, 258, 266, 319, 350, 362, 396
Herbert, Sir R., and S.A. pol., 9, 26, 61, 67, 74, 83, 85, 89, 92, 93, 96, 104, 105, 112, 113, 123–4, 250, 263, 267, 302, 313, 353, 373, 397, 412, 425
Het Volksblad, 110
Hicks Beach, Sir M., 27, 31, 190, 201, 210, 334–5, 354, 371, 386, 413
Hicks Pasha, 310, 319, 365, 401
Hofmeyr, J., 28, 30, 33, 75, 77, 83, 112, 147, 223, 300, 335, 361, 373, 453, 467, 472, 473, 475, 476
Holland (Netherlands), 167
Home Office (British), 82
Homer, Gladstone and, 40
'Home Rule', 2, 3, 31, 39, 46, 75, 83, 178, 180–1, 363, 465, 471; *see also* Ireland

INDEX

Palmerston, Ld. (3rd Viscount), 38, 40, 43, 438
'Pan-Afrikaner danger', 164–6, 180–1, 191, 222–3, 238, 304, 310, 328, 332, 336, 367, 452, 472–4
Parliamentary debates and questions on S. Africa (1881), 110–11, 129, 149, 161–9, 191, 200, 202, 207, 208 *passim*, 214, 218, 233; (1882), 282; (1883), 323–37, 377–8, 384
Parliamentary Reform, '3rd Reform Bill', 255, 368, 370, 406, 410–11, 443
Parnell, C., 5, 82, 119, 121, 178–80, 207, 228, 232, 233–4, 243; arrest of (1882), 244–8, 255–6, 283; and Kilmainham Tr., 285–7; attacks Land Act, 290–1
Peel, Sir R., 38, 42, 307
Phoenix Park, murders, 286
Ponsonby, Sir H., 102, 124, 142, 157, 355
Port Elizabeth, 76
Portsmouth, 296
Portugal, and Tvl. revolt, 109, 167, 183; Treaty with (1881), 192; and cols., 395
Potchefstroom, 88, 116, 183–6, 190, 202, 205
Pretoria Convention (August 1881), text of, 490–8; 96, 166, 173, 181–94; object of, 203, 222; negotiation of, 204 *passim*; finalised, 209–11; signed, 215, 245; 'Native Locations Commission', 209, 270, 271; rejected by *Volksraad*, 217, 287; ratified, 249; hopes for, 256; Kruger and, 259; Robinson on (1882), 297; to be abandoned?, 303, 315–16; frontiers abandoned, 304; 20th Article abandoned, 318; Tvl. defies, 320; modification of, 351 *passim*; demise of, 363, 370, 388, 390; finally 'dead', 426, 430
Pretoria, siege of (1881), 67, 86, 122, 197; Commission in, 202 *passim*, 215, 240, 314, 346

Pretorius, M. (Pres.), 23, 416
Pretorius, M. W., 64, 152, 154, 197, 215
Punch, 36, 53, 57, 131, 288, 419, 436, 444, 470

Queen Victoria, *see* Victoria Regina
Queen's Speech (1880), 102; (1881), 210
Queen's Town, petition on Tvl. (1881), 125

Rathbone, W., 369
Reay, 1st Baron, 356, 358, 359, 361
Resident, (British) in Tvl. (1880–4), 148, 151, 155, 158, 166, 170, 180–2, 195, 202, 209, 218, 240, 271, 346, 350; to be abolished, 352 *passim*; abolished, 428
Reuter's Agency, 319
Rhodes, C. J., 30, 181, 227, 357, 358, 370, 383, 398, 416, 424, 440; as Dep. Commr. in Bech., 441–2, 456, 458; and annex of Bech., 459, 475
Rhodesia, B.S.A. Co. in, 12
Ripon, 1st Marquis, 434
Roberts, Sir F., 159
Robinson, Sir H. (1st Baron Rosmead), 79, 80; 'Instructions' to (Dec. 1880), 83–8; and Boer revolt, 91, 93–6, 105, 109, 125–7, 162; and Cape unrest, 127, 129; and Tvl. peace negotiations, 144 *passim*; and Pretoria Convention, 173 *passim*; and ratification of Convention, 241 *passim*; and S.A. problems (1881–2), 272; 'Robinson plan' for Bech. (1882), 273–6; failure of, 275–8; and Goshen–Stellaland Republics, 277–9; and Tvl. debt (1882), 280; abandons Tswana, 281–95; on Cape Dutch (1882), 297–8; on *Bond*, 298–9; on anti-Tvl. feeling in Cape (1883), 311; renews Bech. campaign, 314; defending Pretoria Convention, 316–19; 'clean up

555

Date Due

BJJJ